MICROPOLITICS
Individual
and Group Level
Concepts

JOHN H. KESSEL
ALLEGHENY COLLEGE

GEORGE F. COLE
UNIVERSITY OF CONNECTICUT

ROBERT G. SEDDIG
ALLEGHENY COLLEGE

HOLT, RINEHART AND WINSTON, INC.
New York Chicago San Francisco Atlanta
Dallas Montreal Toronto London Sydney

PREFACE

Just as the nature of political science has changed, so has the character of an appropriate introduction to it. For decades, students had their first encounter with politics in an American government course. This hardy perennial was gradually replaced or supplemented with "something different," a discussion of great issues, a hint of comparative government, or an introduction to the discipline with each and every sub-field being given equal time and attention. Recently, as political scientists have become more concerned with data analysis and empirical theory, a number of newer courses have been introduced dealing explicitly with political systems. Many of these have been influenced by the theoretical interests of Gabriel Almond, David Easton, Robert Dahl, Karl Deutsch, or William Mitchell.

We have no wish to deny the importance of system level concepts, but we think a strong case can be made for the complementary importance of concepts at the individual and group level—the study of which we call "micropolitics." Recent years have seen the introduction of many microconcepts into political science. The raw materials are now available for these to be knit together into impressive political theories. If students are to understand what has happened in political science, as well as what may occur in the not too distant future, a thorough grasp of microconcepts is vital.

The intellectual excitement of new ideas should not be confined to professors while their students are spoon-fed notions that appeared in the journals many years ago. If these concepts are as important in our discipline as we believe, then students should be introduced to them as soon as possible. There are several reasons for this. First, a professor is most likely to be enthusiastic about work he regards as interesting. His interest is likely to make his classes more exciting. Second, there is too much substantive work now being done in this field to cover any significant portion of it in a single course. But if students learn to apply concepts to a variety of political situations, they can interpret whatever happens to catch their fancy. Third, teaching concepts at the introductory level has an effect on the type of students who become interested in political science. Brighter students enjoy the intellectual challenge, and those who have been initially attracted by the concepts are less likely to be put off by the same concepts when they are examined in greater depth in advanced courses. Fourth, if one delays "real" political science too long, the teacher finds he encounters substantial student resistance when he does try to present it. If the student already has invested considerable time and effort mastering some simpler interpretation, it is natural for him to believe that this is all he *really* needs to know.

We can state confidently that this kind of an introduction is effective in the classroom based on our four years' experience with this approach at Allegheny College. A liberal arts college with a lively, intelligent student body is an ideal setting for educational innovation. We have found that our suspicion that beginning students could master material heretofore presented to advanced undergraduates and graduate students has been borne out.

The book itself originated as a pure and simple response to a pedagogical need. Most of the available teaching materials for introductory courses were pitched at a lower level, and most of the articles using more sophisticated approaches were concerned with presenting technical evidence to a professional audience. Our great need was for articles that were good examples of microanalysis, and were at the same time intelligible to students who were not yet professionals. The criteria we used in making our selections, in descending order of importance, were:

1. The selection should clearly illustrate the use of the concept in question, or should illuminate some important theoretical point, or both.

2. The article should be understandable to a student who is encountering these concepts for the first time. We did not exclude articles that were rich in analytical detail, but we did assume that the student would not have any training in methodology. This meant that we opted for articles which would give the student a "feel" for the concepts, rather than those articles which are concerned with the measurement of phenomena or marshalling evidence.

3. The selections should be explicitly political in character. Students often have difficulty in transferring concepts based on psychological experiments with, say, college sophomores to the National Security Council or the Supreme Court.

4. The illustrations of the concepts should be at the level of individual or group behavior. Therefore, analyses of political systems and complex organizations are excluded except for the final article in each section.

5. Where possible, we tried to include some pieces on topics, such as civil rights and Vietnam, which are of particular interest to the current generation of college students.

6. We tried to avoid "over-anthologized" articles so as to minimize duplication between this reader and those which might be used in other courses.

7. In order to introduce the students to as wide a range of the current work as possible, we did not use more than one article by any one author. Obviously there were some—Robert A. Dahl, for example—who have written a number of pieces we otherwise might have used.

We would not want to claim that every one of the thirty-four articles here in

Micropolitics meets every one of these criteria, but we are satisfied that our more important standards have been met. And because it turned out that most of the articles were written by political scientists (though we did not limit ourselves to articles by political scientists), this collection is one that affords a fair introduction to the discipline. There are important men, and important areas, we have omitted. We do not have any work by Gabriel Almond, Karl Deutsch or David Easton because most of their work has been at the system level. We do not have any articles by Hayward Alker, Donald Stokes, William Riker or Michael Leiserson because their most important work has come in the emerging field of mathematical political analysis, and this is an area which lies beyond the reach of most beginning students.

The ultimate value of microanalysis in political science, obviously, will depend in an important way on the success of these related endeavors. Micropolitics and macropolitics are both necessary for an understanding of politics, and if we are to knit microconcepts and macroconcepts together the polimetricians among us are going to have to solve some theoretical and operational problems. But while we recognize that these are important omissions, we are not troubled by them. It was never our intent to provide a comprehensive introduction to all of political science. Our goal was to assemble an introduction to micropolitics.

J.H.K.
G.F.C.
R.G.S.

Quigley Hall
Allegheny College
August, 1969

ACKNOWLEDGMENTS

First, we should like to thank those who generously responded to our requests for ideas and suggestions at the time that our course in Micropolitics first began to evolve. There were many who agreed that the common corpus of political science, sociology, psychology, and anthropology had developed to a point where it would make sense to offer some of the central findings in a single introductory course. We were, of course, grateful for their good wishes. We are particularly grateful for the suggestions of two men, Professors George Homans and Harold Guetzkow, whose own thinking on this topic was sufficiently advanced for them to make concrete suggestions. They were most helpful, and it is a pleasure to acknowledge their contributions—even though they may not be visible to others in the present organization of the course.

In our course at Allegheny College we use *Social Psychology* by Theodore M. Newcomb, Ralph H. Turner, and Philip E. Converse (New York: Holt, Rinehart and Winston, 1965). When our thoughts turned to the need for an accompanying book of readings to satisfy the quest for political examples and applications, they encouraged us by granting permission to use their terminology and conceptual framework wherever appropriate. We appreciate this encouragement and the authorization to use their concepts.

For their contributions which fit our purposes nicely, we wish to thank our authors: James David Barber, Raymond A. Bauer, Jerome S. Bruner, Philip E. Converse, Robert A. Dahl, David J. Danelski, Anthony Downs, Leon D. Epstein, Heinz Eulau, Richard F. Fenno, Jr., Edmund S. Glenn, Fred I. Greenstein, Harold Guetzkow, Ole R. Holsti, Herbert Hyman, Herbert Kaufman, Allan Kornberg, Robert E. Lane, Kurt D. and Gladys E. Lang, Harold D. Lasswell, Donald R. Matthews, William C. Mitchell, Richard E. Neustadt, Samuel C. Patterson, James W. Prothro, Wallace S. Sayre, Wilbur Schramm, Lester G. Seligman, Paul B. Sheatsley, Herbert A. Simon, J. David Singer, M. Brewster Smith, Donald W. Smithburg, Victor A. Thompson, David B. Truman, John C. Wahlke, Warren Weaver, Ralph K. White, Robert M. White, Myron Wiener, and James S. Young. We also appreciate the permission granted by their publishers allowing us to use their articles.

Professor Fred I. Greenstein reviewed the manuscript at two stages, and offered suggestions which we believe resulted in significant improvements. In addition, Herbert J. Addison and Gloria C. Oden, our editors at Holt, Rinehart and Winston, offered many constructive suggestions. To them we are most grateful.

A grant from Allegheny College enabled us to mimeograph portions of *Micropolitics* for experimental use in our course; in this way we were able to gauge the usefulness of certain articles. Another grant aided in the preparation of the manuscript. We wish to thank the College for both of these. To the many students who have taken the course at Allegheny College, we wish to express our appreciation for criticism, comments, and suggestions. For help in preparing the manuscript, we wish to thank our students William H. Penniman and Sherry Ransford. We are especially grateful to Suzanne Sekerak who devoted many hours to checking some editorial details for us. And, finally, to Mrs. Pauline Mooney, an impeccable typist and effective social leader, we owe many thanks.

CONTENTS

A Real-World Application

IV. ATTITUDE

The Basic Concepts

Perception

Cognition

Attitude Systems

Attitude Change

A Real-World Application

V. COMMUNICATION

The Basic Concepts

Technical Problem

Semantic Problem

INTRODUCTION

*Micro*politics is an approach to political analysis using individual and group level concepts to study political phenomena. *Macro*politics, in contrast, focuses on the aggregate characteristics of political systems. Since the two concentrate on different analytical levels, microconcepts, macroconcepts, or both may be used to study the same subject matter. Elections may be investigated with a microlevel model of individual voting behavior or through a macrolevel analysis of aggregate election statistics. Legislatures may be thought about in terms of the norms of a group of legislators or the mechanics of interest aggregation. International politics may be interpreted on the microlevel in light of the cognitive structuring of an important diplomat or on the macrolevel as related to equilibrium in an international system. Micropolitics and macropolitics are complementary approaches, and one may choose to work at microlevel, macrolevel, or explore the linkages between the two.

Our dominant concern is with micropolitics. There are three principal uses for this approach. The first is direct application of these concepts to the many important political activities involving relatively few people. The second is the reduction of complex system level questions into answerable microlevel questions. The third is the construction of empirical political theory by linking microlevel concepts to one another.

Political scientists have only recently begun to use the word micropolitics,[1] but the distinction between microanalysis, which deals with small components, and macroanalysis, which focuses on larger entities, is familiar in other sciences. The physicist's interests range from elementary particles to entire galaxies. The chemist has long distinguished between molecular and molar solutions. Biologists have found the study of microbiology can provide some answers that eluded them when they were preoccupied with the taxonomy of plant and animal kingdoms. Economists use the term microeconomics to refer to price and wage relationships in particular markets, and employ the word macroeconomics to speak of such aggregative phenomena as national income and employment levels.

Micropolitics does not have an entirely stable meaning. The microlevel is defined by its relation to the macrolevel rather than by intrinsic characteristics. The problem is akin to that faced by Alice when she had to decide whether Humpty Dumpty was wearing a tie or a belt.

---

[1] Stephen K. Bailey, in a discussion at the 1961 American Political Science Association Meetings, was the first person we heard using the word. Stein Rokkan presented a fine analysis of micropolitics in a paper at an International Political Science Association round table at the University of Michigan in September, 1960. See "The Comparative Study of Political Participation" in Austin Ranny (Ed.), *Essays on the Behavioral Study of Politics* (Urbana, Ill.: University of Illinois Press, 1962), pp. 47–90.

"What a beautiful belt you've got on!" Alice suddenly remarked. "At least," she corrected herself on second thoughts, "a beautiful cravat, I should have said—no, a belt, I mean—I beg your pardon!" she added in dismay, for Humpty Dumpty looked thoroughly offended, and she began to wish she hadn't chosen that subject. "If only I knew," she thought to herself, "which was neck and which was waist!"

Evidently Humpty Dumpty was very angry, though he said nothing for a minute or two. When he *did* speak again, it was in a deep growl.

"It is a—*most—provoking*—thing," he said at last, "when a person doesn't know a cravat from a belt!"

"I know it's very ignorant of me," Alice said, in so humble a voice that Humpty Dumpty relented.

"It's a cravat, child, and a beautiful one, as you say. It's a present from the White King and Queen. There now!"

"Is it really?" said Alice, quite pleased to find that she *had* chosen a good subject, after all.[2]

Alice's quandary, of course, was that Humpty Dumpty's middle could be regarded as both his neck and his waist. Neck because it was directly below his head, and waist because it was at the top of his trousers. Alice was puzzled by a relational concept.

The most important factor in determining what is micropolitics is the analytical universe being employed at that particular time. *Once having decided on the universal set $\mathcal{U}$ for a particular discussion, all other sets in that same discussion become subsets of $\mathcal{U}$.*[3] A nation is often taken as an analytical universe. Questions are raised about the integration of the social, economic, and political systems, about the relationships between executive, legislative, and judicial subsystems, and so forth. But students of world politics have reason to consider an international system as their analytical universe, in which case entire nations conceivably could be considered as microlevel actors. At the opposite extreme, a small group of legislators may be considered a system that is itself intensively studied. Richard Fenno has done this with the House Appropriations Committee. Consequently, his microanalysis concerns the interaction of individual legislators, the socialization of new members into Committee norms, and the like. In this book, we use the word micropolitics to refer to activity on the individual and group level. It should be clear, however, that others may use the word differently, and that they have legitimate grounds for doing so.

The distinction between analytical levels has been present in political theory for some time, but political scientists are just beginning to deal with the difficult questions raised by their many relationships to each other. For approximately two hundred years, Western political theorists focused on the proper relationship between man and the state. Here the distinction between individual and collectivity was so clear that it did not have to be discussed. But once some consensus developed as to the rights and liberties of individuals (at least in Western democracies), political thinkers began to turn to detailed empirical analyses of govern-

---

[2] Lewis Carroll, *Through the Looking-Glass* (New York: Macmillan, 1928), pp. 120–121.

[3] Samuel Goldberg, *Probability: An Introduction* (Englewood Cliffs, N.J.: Prentice-Hall, 1960), p. 16.

mental institutions. Nineteenth century classics such as John Stuart Mill's *Representative Government*, Walter Bagehot's *The English Constitution*, and Woodrow Wilson's *Congressional Government* are leading examples of such scholarship.[4] The twentieth century has seen attempts to capture more of the political dynamics on the governmental level, and recent decades have brought a more sophisticated understanding of the role of the citizen on the individual level. Indeed, it could be argued that the development of political theory in recent decades could be summarized as "the withering away of the state." This has not meant the fruition of utopian hopes of nineteenth century socialists, but rather the disappearance of the state as such as the central concept in political thought. What was earlier seen as a simple dichotomy between man and the state has dissolved into a rich variety of possibilities for political participation on the microlevel, and a complex set of political institutions on the macrolevel. And as this change has taken place, the problem of how these levels of analysis may be knit together has been emerging as a most important methodological question.

THE USES OF MICROPOLITICS

A major thesis of this book is that no one set of concepts is preeminent in political science. There are many in use, and the analyst picks and chooses among them according to the nature of the problem at hand. We do not wish to imply in any way that the concepts we have included are the only microconcepts, that the only logical relations between these concepts are those suggested by the order in which we have arranged them, or that the articles could appear only as exemplars of the concepts under which they are listed. It would be more appropriate to think of each set of concepts as a set of lenses through which one views the political world, with each set of lenses bringing some aspects into sharper focus while obscuring certain other facets. To use another metaphor, each set of concepts provides a different language one can use to talk about politics. If one wishes to master these concepts, he should try translating something formulated in terms of one set of concepts into the language of another set of concepts. He also might try analyzing a single political situation using different theoretical perspectives in turn—role, group, attitudinal, communication, and power. Each of these ways of thinking yields somewhat different insights, and a facility in moving from one set of concepts to another increases his mastery of them all.

A political scientist's decision to use role theory or group theory or communication theory or some other approach is not entirely a matter of whim. He is constrained by the "fit" between the requirements of a particular theory and the data at hand, as well as by his own experience and skill in working with the approach in question. But there are elements of artistic preference in the decision mix, and one should not think a given phenomenon *must* be studied in a specific way just because someone else has done so.

What is true of the choice between concepts on one analytical level also applies to the choice between micro- and macroconcepts. One is not always prefera-

---

[4] Avery Leiserson, *Parties and Politics: An Institutional and Behavioral Approach* (New York: Knopf, 1958), p. 31.

ble to the other. "There is really no opposition between micro- and macroeconomics," writes Paul Samuelson. "Both are vital. You are less than half-educated if you understand the one while being ignorant of the other." [5] Precisely the same argument can be made with respect to microanalysis and macroanalysis in political science. There are, however, certain possibilities which microanalysis opens up. An understanding of these potentialities is of value in deciding when microconcepts can be used to greatest advantage.

Direct Application

First of all, many important political activities involve small numbers of individuals. The Supreme Court consists of nine justices, and no other person is present at their conferences. Congressional subcommittees often meet with only one or two members present, and half a dozen decide the fate of legislation. An even dozen, including President John F. Kennedy, sat together in the White House to choose the course of action of the United States in the Cuban missile crisis in the fall of 1962. The actual bargaining on such matters of international consequence as the nuclear test ban treaty and the Vietnam peace negotiations is carried on by small teams of diplomats. Clearly some of our most vital political processes involve relatively few persons. Here microlevel concepts have direct application. In such cases it is most illuminating to know what role behavior is exhibited by the various actors, what the group structure is, how the actors perceive each other, and who is exercising the most influence over whom.

Another class amenable to this type of analysis is formed by those activities which reflect individual decisions. Even though an entire population may be involved, microanalysis is entirely proper if each person must decide for himself whether he is going to engage in the activity.[6] There are a variety of ways in which one may engage in politics: he may or may not write to elected officials, he may or may not join a political organization, he may or may not discuss politics with his neighbors. Differences in the levels of these activities distinguish between a population that is politically involved and one that is politically apathetic. Individuals form their own personal opinions about the desirability of certain public policies. Individual changes may cancel each other out. Person A may decide that welfare policies are desirable at the same time Person B is coming to the opposite view. But a preponderance of individual shifts in the same direction may produce a change in the level of public support for a particular policy. Shifts in public opinion on civil rights and the wisdom of American involvement in Vietnam are notable recent examples of this. Individual attitudes also set the norms of a political culture. The rights of minorities, freedom of speech, belief in stipulated legal procedures and the like are constitutionally protected in the United States, but the ultimate support for these "rules of the game" lies in the belief of most Americans that they represent the right way to do things. Recent urban riots have illus-

---

[5] *Economics: An Introductory Analysis,* 7th ed. (New York: McGraw-Hill, 1967), p. 362.

[6] Robert M. MacIver distinguishes between distributive and conjunctural phenomena. Distributive phenomena are individual activities carried out separately but resulting in some characteristic of the population, as individual decisions about marriage and divorce result in marriage and divorce rates. Conjunctural phenomena also reflect individual decisions, but the act is carried out in some institutionally prescribed way, as votes which are cast on the same day. Both classes of phenomena require individual level analysis. See *Social Causation* (New York: Ginn, 1942).

trated the destructive capacity of even small numbers of persons who opt for force and violence in lieu of normal political procedures. And, of course, the politician's appeal for individual votes is much more than lip service. Each person makes up his own mind how he will cast his ballot.

J. David Singer, who has paid a great deal of attention to the level of analysis problem, has recently suggested some societal level counterparts for individual level characteristics. On the individual level, he distinguishes between *personality, attitude,* and *opinion.* Among other things, he points out that one's personality is lasting while one's opinions may shift. Having made these distinctions, he suggests that we "treat *personality* as the basis for national *character, attitude* as the basis for *ideology,* and *opinion* as the basis for *climate of opinion.* That is, when we have ascertained which individuals score where on one or more personality, attitude or opinion scales, we have the basis for descriptive statements about the culture (or portions thereof) of the entity which they constitute." [7] Here is another domain of macrolevel behavior which can be explained through the direct application of microlevel concepts.

Analytic Reduction

"How does one observe whole systems?" asks Heinz Eulau. "Well, I would say that, at the present time, it is impossible to observe whole systems. I think that one can make statements about whole systems, large systems, but that one cannot observe them." [8] In making this argument, Eulau points to another set of reasons for microlevel analysis. Many system level questions presently beyond our grasp for either theoretical or methodological reasons can be broken down into answerable micropolitical questions.

One of the problems hampering the study of the presidency is that only five men—Truman, Eisenhower, Kennedy, Johnson, and Nixon—have held the office while America has been one of the nuclear superpowers. General statements made on the basis of five examples are always suspect. We know that the Nixon presidency differs from the Johnson presidency in particular ways, but another chief executive, say Nelson Rockefeller or Eugene McCarthy, might have organized things still differently. Donald Stokes has suggested handling this problem by developing a theory of presidential decision-making using known principles of communication among small human groups. "It would indeed be possible to formulate Richard Neustadt's insistence that competing sources of information be built into the organization of the Executive Office in terms of much more general theories of communication." [9] An understanding of presidential decisions in terms of information flow and cognitive functioning would do several things for us. It would give us a sufficiently large number of cases to make generalizations. It would enable us to test our findings against other knowledge about human communication. And it would give us a sufficiently detailed under-

[7] "Man and World Politics: The Psycho–Cultural Interface," *Journal of Social Issues,* July, 1968, p. 138.

[8] James C. Charlesworth, (Ed.), *A Design for Political Science: Scope, Objectives and Method* (Philadelphia: American Academy of Political and Social Science, 1966), p. 207.

[9] "Analytic Reduction in the Study of Institutions," a paper prepared for delivery at the 1966 Annual Meeting of the American Political Science Association, Statler-Hilton Hotel, New York City, September 7–10, 1966, p. 5. Many of the examples given in this section on analytic reduction have been drawn from Professor Stokes' paper.

standing to be able to explain cases which did not fit our general principles.

Important questions about legislative institutions, whether the 435 member U.S. House of Representatives or the 630 member British House of Commons, can often be answered by reducing them to microanalytical terms. Take a query about the kinds of issues that will produce party line votes in representative bodies. This can be related to the ways individual members are recruited. In the United States, men on their own volition tend to join parties with which they share common beliefs. The implication is that issues dividing congressional Republicans and Democrats are apt to be those with long histories; issues, in other words, that were salient at the time the bulk of the membership entered the system. In Britain, on the other hand, legislative leaders have somewhat more to say about who is selected. In extreme instances, a sitting M.P. who has stepped out of line can be dropped at the next election. The leaders' ability to exercise greater discipline gives British legislative parties the potential of responding to a wider range of issues. Response to issues can be related equally well to the role the legislator chooses to play. For example, in the United States Senate, Ralph Huitt has pointed to the difference between the Inner Club Member who works with the Senate hierarchy to shape public policy, the maverick Outsider who is likely to attack these proposals, and the Errand Boy "who eschews controversy but renders himself unbeatable by causing his beneficence to fall like gentle rain on all his constituents." [10]

Micropolitics has improved our general understanding of political parties a great deal. Institutional explanations based on apparent system level characteristics had been passed on from one academic generation to another without serious challenge. The century-old American two-party system, for example, was said to be "the direct consequence of the American election system." Individual level concepts give us quite a different idea. The concept of party identification, the subjective belief of an individual that he belonged to one party or another, suggests that the loyalty of the "members" had as much to do with the survival of the parties as did the formal election system or the tactics of the party leaders. Thinking in these terms gives us a reason for the "outer bounds" of partisan strength in the electorate, limits beyond which the vote for one party does not rise and the vote for the other party does not fall. Fluctuations in the proportions of persons who regard themselves as Republicans, Independents, and Democrats also enable us to make predictions about the behavior of the total party system. During the 1950's, these levels were quite stable. The politics of the period was rather tranquil. Between 1960 and 1968, however, the proportion of independents who do not think of themselves as close to either major party has risen from 8 percent to 17 percent.[11] This dramatic shift on the microlevel makes it easier to understand why we are witnessing more volatile politics on the macrolevel.

A final example of the power of analytic reduction comes from the work of Gabriel Almond and Sidney Verba. These scholars compared five different nations by studying the attitudes of individuals. By asking such questions as how aware individuals were of political life, how much psychological distance there

[10] "The Outsider in the Senate: An Alternative Role," *American Political Science Review*, September, 1961, pp. 573–574.

[11] Richard A. Brody, "Vietnam and the 1968 Elections: A Preview," *Trans–Action*, October, 1968, Table 1.

was between rival political parties, how much obligation persons felt to take part in political life, and how much trust existed between individuals, they were able to document significant differences between political cultures. In Italy they found "unrelieved political alienation and social isolation and distrust." Mexico, they said, was marked by a combination of low evaluations of the present level of governmental performance and a pride in their political institutions. Germans, despite a high level of technology and education, were found to be passive and detached from political life. And "the British political culture, like the American, approximates the balanced civic culture; but the balance is weighted somewhat differently from that in the United States. In the latter country there tends to be too much weight placed on the participant role, in Britain the deferential subject role is more strongly developed and widespread." [12]

Theory Building

It can also be argued that it is *possible* to construct a more powerful theory on the basis of microconcepts than with macroconcepts. The word possible is italicized for two reasons. One is that very little has been realized to date from the theoretical possibilities of microanalysis. The other is to accent the existence of the possibility. There are methodological reasons which place real limits on the ultimate explanatory power of system level analysis. These reasons do not limit the potential of microanalysis.

The lack of accomplishment in theory building is easy to document. For every effort to knit concepts together, there are several laments about how little has been done. Gabriel Almond and Sidney Verba summarize the present situation when they point out that much of the literature "fails to make the connection between the psychological tendencies of individuals and groups, and political structure and process. [T]he currency of political psychology, though of undoubted value, is not made exchangeable in terms of political process and performance." [13] For the most part, the importance of micropolitical concepts has been asserted rather than demonstrated. Our research, as James Prothro and Marian Irish remind us, "has dealt primarily with mass attitudes or with elite activities. The difficult and complex task of tracing the connective thread between mass opinions and the attitudes and performance of government officials has barely begun." [14] Conceptual problems are likely to be evident for some little while before someone ingenious enough to solve them comes along. "To acknowledge the interdependence of national and international systems," as James Rosenau has written, "is not necessarily to make conceptual allowance for it." Awareness of the problem of links between systems is not the same thing as research that focuses on that particular question. At the present time, "virtually all of the findings and insights bearing on linkage phenomena are derivative of other concerns and thus their common content has never been probed and compared." [15]

Three reasons may be cited for this lack of progress in relating microconcepts

[12] *The Civic Culture* (Boston: Little, Brown, 1965), chapter 12.

[13] *Civic Culture*, p. 31.

[14] *The Politics of American Democracy*, 4th ed. (Englewood Cliffs, N.J.: Prentice-Hall, 1967), p. 215.

[15] *Linkage Politics* (New York: The Free Press of Glencoe, 1969), p. 8.

to each other. First, we are still in the very early days of microanalysis. Most microlevel concepts have been known to political scientists for only a decade or so. Second, many political scientists have not had the level of analysis problem in the forefront of their consciousness. The result, in the words of Joseph LaPalombara, is that "so many of our generalizations about the political process move with apparent randomness from the micro- to the macro-analytic levels that it is difficult to know when, for example, a study of legislative roles is designed to test psychological theories about individual or group behavior or sociological theories about the institution of the legislature itself." [16] Third, as James Rosenau has discerned, the typical units of analysis differ from specialty to specialty within political science.

> Where students of comparative politics are accustomed to analyzing the behavior of thousands and millions of actors (voters, party officials, interest groups, elites), their counterparts in the international field are used to only a few hundred or so (nations, foreign secretaries, diplomatic representatives, decision-makers); where specialists in national systems are interested in what large groups of people (the citizenry) do either to each other or to the few (officialdom), international specialists concentrate on what the few (nations) do either to each other or to the many (foreign publics).[17]

Since most political scientists are busy enough within their own special areas of competence, a realization that conceptual linkage was a methodological problem in many areas of the discipline has not been quickly understood.

Not surprisingly, initial awareness of the importance of knitting concepts together has come within those subfields having a special concern with conceptual levels. In public administration, with its concern for organizational levels, Herbert Simon was writing in 1952:

> Complexity in any body of phenomena has generally led to the construction of specialized theories, each dealing with the phenomena at a particular 'level.' Levels are defined by specifying certain units as the objects of study and by stating the propositions of theory in terms of intra-unit behavior and inter-unit behavior. (Cf. the sequence of elementary particle–atom–molecule in physics and the sequence: gene–chromosome–nucleus–cell–tissue–organ-organism in biology.) . . . the phenomena of organization constitute an important level of theory—a level that is encompassed neither by the usual conceptualizations of small group processes nor by those of the more macroscopic analyses of cultures and institutions.[18]

In domestic politics, a somewhat parallel notion enunciated by Gabriel Almond in 1950 divided the opinion-policy process into four levels: a general public, an attentive public, policy and opinion elites, and the official policy

[16] "Macro-Theories and Micro-Applications in Comparative Politics: A Widening Chasm" in *Comparative Politics*, October, 1968, p. 72.

[17] *Linkage Politics*, pp. 9–10.

[18] "Comments on the Theory of Organizations," *American Political Science Review*, December, 1952, pp. 1030, 1031, 1039.

makers.[19] By the end of the decade, the late V. O. Key, Jr., was devoting an entire section of his *Public Opinion and American Democracy* [20] to an attempt to detail some of the linkage between attitudes of the general public and actions taken by the government. Stein Rokkan provided a most sophisticated discussion of macro–micro interdependencies in a comparative context. He wrote that the existing literature could be divided into four classes.

(1) "micro–micro" studies focusing on relationships between individual background characteristics, roles, cognitions, and motivations on the one hand and political dispositions and decisions on the other;

(2) "macro–micro" studies exploring the effects of variations and changes in structural contexts on the rates of given political decisions and on the strength and direction of "micro–micro" relationships;

(3) "micro–macro" studies concerned with the effects of attitudes and decisions of the general citizenry on the policies, strategies, and tactics of the parties and on the operation of established systems of structural restraints on decision-making; and finally

(4) "macro–macro" studies concerned with the functions of given structural restraints in the maintenance, legitimation, and stabilization of the overall system.[21]

And in 1961, J. David Singer published a paper explicitly discussing the international system and the national state as separate levels of analysis in international relations.[22] More specific discussions of the problems of knitting conceptual levels together have followed these pioneering efforts.

If we are still so close to the beginning of theory building using microconcepts, then how can it be claimed that "the sub-systemic or actor orientation is considerably more fruitful" [23] for explanation? Here we are led back to the point that there are methodological reasons which inhibit the explanatory power of system level analysis. As Philip Converse points out, "there are questions deftly answered by [microlevel] survey information that aggregated data comment upon only after a frightening series of inferential leaps, or leave as a nest of complete indeterminacy." [24] Information about the characteristics of the total system permits only *inferences* about the characteristics of individuals within that system. A

[19] *The American People and Foreign Policy* (New York: Harcourt Brace, 1950), chapter 7.

[20] (New York: Knopf, 1961).

[21] "Comparative Study of Political Participation," p. 57.

[22] "The Level of Analysis Problem in International Relations," *World Politics*, October, 1961, pp. 77–92.

[23] "Level of Analysis Problem," pp. 89–90.

[24] "Survey Research and the Decoding of Patterns in Ecological Data," a paper prepared for delivery at the Symposium on Quantitative Ecological Analysis in the Social Sciences, Evian, France, September 12–16, 1966, p. 1. In order to avoid distorting Professor Converse's position, attention should also be called to his succeeding sentences: ". . . the two types of data [aggregate and survey] open up to us an extent of ground that neither taken alone would permit us to cover. A far larger and more fascinating domain of problems, however, lies at the intersection of the two data bases: classes of inquiry that can best be pursued with joint or complementary use of aggregate and survey materials."

macrolevel statement, "That is a Republican legislature," tells us little about whether any individual legislator is a Republican or a Democrat. Since the statement implies a Republican majority, we may infer that the probability that a legislator will be a Republican is greater than that he will be a Democrat, but we cannot make a confident statement about any individual case. It may also be that the Republicans in our hypothetical legislature are split into two rival factions, that these factions vote against one another, and that effective control over policy decisions lies with the Democrats. This again is something we could not know if we were limited to information about the characteristics of the total legislature. If, on the other hand, we began on the individual level and worked up to the system level, we would know whether each member was a Republican or a Democrat, how the Republicans and Democrats are organized, and, ultimately, that the legislature had a Republican majority. It is possible to begin with microlevel information and ultimately put together macrolevel conclusions. If one begins with macrolevel data (and has no way of getting information about smaller components), one can only guess why the system operates as it does.

There are many instances of microlevel studies which have shown that inferences drawn from macrolevel data were unwarranted. For some time, it has been believed that children belonged to the same political party as their parents. Early studies of political socialization (the processes through which persons learn appropriate forms of political behavior) seemed to bear this out. A 1952 study of the presidential preferences of high school students predicted the outcome of the popular vote for Eisenhower and Stevenson with less than one-half of one percent error. This led the author to say: "While . . . we made no study in the 1952 pre-election poll of the direct relationship between voting intentions of parents and children, the accuracy in predicting the Eisenhower vote mentioned above is highly persuasive with reference to the inference that this relationship must be very high." [25] But was it? A recent microlevel study of the party identification of high school seniors and their parents shows that some 41 percent of the students think of themselves as having a different party identification than their parents. These results clearly indicate, Kent Jennings and Richard Niemi tell us, "the eighteen-year old is no simple carbon copy of his parents." [26] The similarity in the overall distribution in party loyalty from generation to generation does not mean that everyone tends to adopt his parents' political habits, but rather that inter-generational shifts in opposite directions tend to cancel each other out.

A related, though slightly more technical point, is that statistical estimates made on the basis of aggregate data cannot be used as indicators of individual behavior. A well-known paper published in 1950 pointed out that ecological correlations (measures of association based on macrolevel data) are almost never the same as individual correlations, and that ecological correlations usually exaggerate the extent of association between phenomena. As an example, W. S. Robinson used the relationship between illiteracy and race. If one checked to

[25] H. H. Remmers, "Early Socialization of Attitudes," in Eugene Burdick and Arthur J. Brodbeck, (Eds.), *American Voting Behavior* (Glencoe, Ill.: The Free Press, 1959), p. 57.

[26] "The Transmission of Political Values from Parent to Child," *American Political Science Review*, March, 1968, pp. 169–184. Children of Republicans or Democrats who considered themselves to be independents made up the largest group of those who had shifted away from their parents' party identification.

see which region of the country had the highest proportion of blacks, and then asked whether that region also had a high proportion of illiterates, he would conclude that if he knew a person's race, his prediction about whether or not they were literate would be correct nine times out of ten. But if he checks the characteristics of individuals, he would learn that an attempt to predict whether or not a person is literate on the basis of knowing only whether he is white or black will be right only four times out of a hundred. The reason the ecological correlation is so much higher than is justified by the true relationship between race and literacy is that the sections of the country having the highest proportion of illiterates (in the South) also *happen to be* the sections having the highest proportion of blacks.[27] Since Professor Robinson called this "ecological fallacy" to the attention of behavioral scientists, investigators have been much more cautious about drawing inferences from macrolevel data. Having noted these real limits on the explanatory power of system level analysis, it should now be hastily added that microdata do not, in and of themselves, permit an understanding of larger aggregates. Hayward Alker has pointed out that there is an "individualistic fallacy" that is the opposite of the ecological fallacy.[28] If individuals in a population have particular attitudes or habits, it does not *necessarily* follow that these attitudes or habits will determine the behavior of the larger social units into which they are organized. To cite a simple example, American nomination politics is organized in such a way that the views of active partisans have greater weight than the views of independents in the selection of the presidential nominee. Hence one would commit the individualistic fallacy if he predicted the identity of the nominee on the basis of individual attitudes among the general population without giving due weight to the particular persons who are likely to be convention delegates. When constructing theories using microconcepts, the theories must be validated on all levels up to and including the largest social aggregate being considered.

Still it is possible to construct powerful theories using microconcepts. It is not likely that we shall easily or quickly realize the explanatory potential which is inherent in these concepts. There are enough problems involved in operationalizing the concepts, obtaining good real world data, relating the concepts to one another, and validating the resulting theories to absorb the energies of at least an academic generation. But enough work is underway to be optimistic about the eventual result.

It might be well to close this discussion of theory building in micropolitics by briefly calling attention to a couple of examples of work that has already been done. The first draws entirely upon role theory. In *The Legislative System*,[29] four political scientists report on the purposive, representational, areal, pressure-group, and partisan roles in four state legislatures. (Articles selected from this

[27] "Ecological Correlations and the Behavior of Individuals," *American Sociological Review*, June, 1950, pp. 351–357. The ecological correlation between race and literacy based on 1930 Census data for nine geographic regions was .946. The individual correlation based on data from the same Census was .203.

[28] *Mathematics and Politics* (New York: Macmillan, 1965), p. 103. See also, Hayward R. Alker, "A Typology of Ecological Fallacies: Problems of Spurious Associations in Cross-level Inferences," a paper presented at the Symposium on Quantitative Ecological Analysis in the Social Sciences, Evian, France, September 12–16, 1966.

[29] John C. Wahlke, Heinz Eulau, William Buchanan, and Leroy C. Ferguson, (New York: Wiley, 1962).

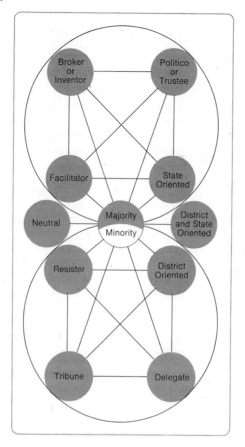

Figure 1.   Ideal-type network of roles

important study begin the section on role theory.) They then present an ideal-type network of legislators' roles based upon their findings about the interpenetration of pairs of legislative roles. This is diagrammed in Figure 1. Any roles which are usually associated with each other are connected with lines. The result is that two essentially reciprocal clusters of roles can be discerned. Role behavior often exhibited by members of the majority party is in the upper half of the diagram; role behavior characteristic of minority members is in the lower half.

Professors Wahlke, Eulau, Buchanan, and Ferguson next use their ideal-type model as a base of comparison for the four state legislatures. The actual role structures they found in the lower houses of Ohio, New Jersey, California, and Tennessee are shown in Figure 2. In both Ohio and New Jersey, the majority roles are dominant, but there is enough difference that they characterize the Ohio House as "broker–majoritarian" and the New Jersey chamber as "tribune–majoritarian." In California, where party roles were not as salient at the time of this study, they found a "populist–bipartisan" role structure. And in the Tennessee House behavior corresponding to that of minority parties in a multi-party system showed up in a "populist–minoritarian" role system. It is worth noting here that by beginning on the microlevel, the four political scientists were able to knit concepts together so as to arrive at a quite distinctive understanding of the legislative system. They found that the legislatures, although quite similar in their formal structures and processes, differed significantly in their behavior pattern. Thus the "roles taken by legislators in different political contexts (such as the degree of competition between parties or factions, or the relative strength of majority and minority) constitute a role structure of consequence for the performance of legislative tasks, especially the resolution of conflicts, and for the achievement of democratic integration." [30]

Our second example unites findings from group theory, communication

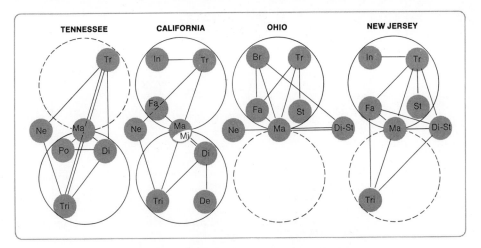

Figure 2.   Role structure of four lower houses

theory, and attitudinal research. It is a computer simulation model of community referenda developed by Robert P. Abelson and Alex Bernstein.[31] Although designed specifically to study fluoridation decisions, the model may be applied to any type of community controversy. Further, if the concept of "community" is broadly interpreted, the scope of the model need not be limited to city decisions. By bringing together many microconcepts, Abelson and Bernstein have built a theory of very considerable explanatory power.

This model functions in such a way as to affect three characteristics of each individual in the population. (Another way of saying the same thing is that there are three dependent variables in this model.) These are the individual's position on fluoridation (Would he vote for or against it?), his level of interest in the issue, and his acceptance of assertions made by proponents or opponents. The simulation is begun by assuming that assertions have been made by supporters of fluoridation (e.g., it is necessary to reduce cavities) or by opponents. These assertions are then transmitted through communication channels and may or may not come to the attention of individuals according to propositions such as: *The probability that an individual will be exposed to a source in any channel is a direct function of that individual's attraction toward that channel;* and *Exposure probability to each source in any channel is also a direct function of the individual's interest in*

[30] *Legislative System,* p. 431.

[31] "A Computer Simulation Model of Community Referendum Controversies," *Public Opinion Quarterly,* Spring, 1963, pp. 93–122.

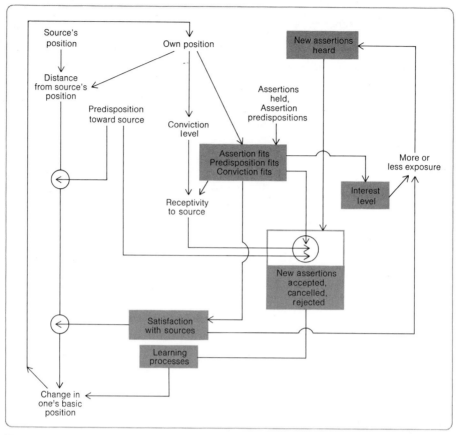

Figure 3. Some consequences of exposure to a single channel in the Abelson–Bernstein Referendum Simulation

the issue. If an individual's characteristics are such that he receives the message he may then accept or reject it according to the rules of another set of propositions. For instance, using cognitive balance theory the authors posit that: *An assertion is less apt to be accepted by an individual if it is inconsistent with his position on the issue.*

In Figure 3, Hayward Alker has summarized all the relationships governing the effects of media exposure in the Abelson–Bernstein simulation. Direct effects of media exposure are shown with single arrows. A change in one's basic position, as indicated in the lower left of Figure 3, for example, depends directly on one's learning processes. More complicated relationships, such as effects being multiplied together, are indicated by circled arrowheads. Two examples of complex decision rules appear in the line above "change in one's basic position." These govern changes resulting from one's predisposition toward, or satisfaction with, a source of assertions. Finally, if an effect is determined by passing through several different steps, a box is drawn to indicate a separate subroutine. Examples of this are at the bottom, referring to satisfaction with sources, learning processes, or when new assertions are accepted, cancelled, or rejected.

Another process (not shown in Figure 3) follows before each cycle is completed. A series of simulated conversations takes place. Each person is matched with likely conversational partners, and each may thereby be exposed to still more assertions. Professor Alker's diagram of the media exposure process, however, is sufficient to give us a sense of the richness and power of theories of this type.[32] In each cycle, complex changes may take place. If changes do take place in any individual's position, interest level, or the assertions he accepts, this alters the way that person will participate in the next cycle. The Abelson–Bernstein model allows up to five hundred persons to be affected in this way by assertions coming from fifty sources over fifteen different channels.

The explanatory power of such theories lies in the number of different things which may be tested. If one is interested in the extent of individual-level attitudinal change, he can simply check to see how many individuals change their positions under what kinds of conditions. If one is interested in group processes, such as cohesion among conversational partners, several runs may be made with the assertions held constant, observing what happens to the group processes. Mass communication may be studied by passing identical assertions through high-salience media and low-salience media. And if one is interested only in system level effects, then he can create populations having different mixes of partisanship, interest in the issue, and so forth, and see which of the resulting "communities" accept or reject fluoridation. In short, we see here both the complexity and the explanatory power of the microtheory we may expect to develop. Building such theories will take a great deal of effort, and they may be so complex that computers will be required to store all of the relevant information. But such theories would permit simultaneous investigation on the microlevel, the macrolevel, or any analytical level in between, and this would be no small accomplishment.[33]

[32] "Computer Simulations, Conceptual Frameworks, and Coalition Behavior" in Sven Groennings, E. W. Kelley, and Michael Leiserson (Eds.), *The Study of Coalition Behavior* (New York: Holt, Rinehart and Winston, 1969), chapter 20. This article should be consulted for a more elegant argument for the desirability of individually tailored, nonrational, multi-level, process-specific theories.

[33] Unfortunately, Hugh Douglas Price's thoughtful discussion of many of these points did not come to our attention until this book was in galley proof. For his insights, see "Micro- and Macro-politics: Notes on Research Strategy" in Oliver Garceau (Ed.), *Political Research and Political Theory* (Cambridge: Harvard University Press, 1968), especially pp. 124–140.

PART ONE:
LEADERSHIP

The need for concepts is clear. For one thing, we have passed the time when one could comprehend the corpus of substantive information. Estimates that human knowledge is doubling every decade or so are commonplace. One might ask who counts all the facts, but there is little doubt that there is much scholarly activity. There is certainly a great deal of research in political science. Scholars read over 130 research papers at the most recent meeting of the American Political Science Association, and journal articles have been appearing at the rate of 1,500 a year. Since the volume of information now makes it impossible to be acquainted with much of it, concepts are necessary to enable one to organize the particular domains of inquiry of interest to him.

A focus on concepts is also appropriate in view of the present state of development of political science. As we noted in the Introduction, while microconcepts have come into wide use in recent years less progress has been made with the job of theory building. It is much more accurate to speak of emerging analytical frameworks than it is to suggest there are validated general theories. We do not know yet which concepts will prove to be the most important components of the emerging theories. It is safe to say, though, that some microconcepts will at least be used as the building blocks of theory. Consequently, paying attention to concepts gives us a way to understand the current interests of political science, and perhaps provides some basis for comprehension of political theories yet to be developed.

Now what is it that we want concepts to do for us? What tasks would we like each to perform before we judge it as ideal? There are nearly as many lists as there are philosophers of science who have considered this question, but the major functions may be grouped under three general headings. These are the theoretical, observational, and heuristic requirements.

In order to develop theories, we want to create concepts that can be linked to other concepts. To do this requires several things. First, our definitions should be disjoint and exhaustive. If we wish to divide partisans (Republicans and Democrats) into two categories reflecting the strength of their identification with their party, this requirement means there should not be any partisan who falls exactly on the borderline between weak and strong, and that we should be able to divide the *entire* population of partisans in this way. Second, there should be uniformity of application. There should not be one way to define a strong partisan when we think of Republicans and another way when we think of Democrats. Nor should there be one way to define a strong partisan to relate this concept to voting behavior, and another way when relating partisan strength to interest in politics. Third, our concepts should be framed in such a way that we can work with them. In the present example, partisan strength should obey logical laws (We should not, for instance, find that strong partisans were less likely to vote for their party's candidate than weak partisans.), and we should be able to apply appropriate statistical techniques to measure the degree of association between partisan strength and other concepts. Finally, we ought to be able to relate each concept to several other concepts. If the concept of partisan strength is to be of real theoretical use, we do not want to relate it just to voting behavior. It also should be related to interest in politics, political involvement, perception of political events and many other concepts. The more concepts it can be related to, the greater its theoretical value.

The observational requirements concern our ability to apply our concepts to real-world data. Concepts may be linked to several other concepts to form an elegant theoretical structure, but unless we can observe the presence or absence of the properties implied by the concepts we have no way of verifying the theory. Consequently we need operational definitions for our concepts. Let us say that we are interested in consensus, and that we wish to determine whether the existence of consensus among members of a legislative committee speeds their consideration of bills or has any other consequences. This means we must be able to measure "consensus." We must decide how many of the committee members' attitudes should be included, whether our definition will permit dissent by any committee members, whether we want to measure the intensity of the committee members' views or content ourselves with just knowing whether they favor or oppose certain activities, whether the committee members must be aware of the views of their colleagues, and so forth. At the minimum, provisional decisions on such definitional questions must be made before we can gather any data on the presence or absence of "consensus."

A weakness in many descriptions of observational requirements is the suggestion of a one-way relation between the concept and its measure. One first decides what one means by a concept, then gathers real-world data. In fact, as Robert K. Merton has emphasized, the conduct of the research itself often leads to the clarification of concepts. Naturally, the researcher must know how to begin. "If he is not to be blocked at the outset, he must devise indices which are observable, fairly precise and meticulously clear. The entire movement of thought which was christened 'operationalism' is only one conspicuous case of the researcher demanding that concepts be defined clearly enough for him to go to work." But in addition, "the very requirements of empirical research have been instrumental in clarifying received concepts. The process of empirical inquiry raises conceptual issues which may long go undetected in theoretic inquiry." [1] Let us say that we had been undecided as to whether we should include a requirement that the legislative committee members be aware of their colleagues' attitudes in our definition of consensus, and that we had elected, therefore, to collect data on this and make a later decision. The results of experimental work in this area show that "a measure of consensus does not indicate the extent of sharing, since members' perceptions of consensus may not be accurate. For this reason an index of sharing must be devised that measures the percentage of accurate estimates among members of the group. This index has proven a useful tool for studying sharing and the factors associated with it." [2] So in this case, experimental work would not only have

---

[1] *Social Theory and Social Structure*, rev. ed. (New York: The Free Press of Glencoe, 1957), pp. 115, 117.

[2] Theodore M. Newcomb, Ralph H. Turner, and Philip E. Converse, *Social Psychology: The Study of Human Interaction* (New York: Holt, Rinehart and Winston, 1965), p. 380.

clarified the nature of the concept of consensus, but would have suggested another concept, sharing, which is equally important in developing a theory of group behavior. Hence it is important to remember there is a dual relationship between concepts and real world measures of them. Hunches about concepts permit real-world data to be gathered; analysis of the real-world data clarifies the concepts somewhat; the improved concepts then suggest additional data which should be collected and analyzed. Viable operational definitions emerge over time as a result of continued interaction between conceptualization and research.

The meaning of the word heuristic—serving to indicate or point out; stimulating interest as a means of furthering investigation—tells us much about what heuristic qualities a concept should have. First, a concept should suggest additional questions one might ask. In communication theory, the concept of noise [3] is useful because it leads us to think of other messages as competitors for the attention of a person to whom a message has been dispatched. This concept of noise also suggests a canvass of sources of noise, and attention to time periods when the noise level might be high or low in a particular channel.

Second, a concept should have extensibility, the capacity to apply the concept to other substantive domains. As Henry Margenau has observed, "scientists judge the quality, and ultimately the correctness, of a given theory by its range of application, taking the generality of a system as a measure not only of its usefulness but of its credibility." [4] In this sense, noise and the other concepts in communication theory are useful because the "communication" to which they refer may take place in settings as divergent as a computer circuit, the nerves of a human brain, a symphony hall, or the comic pages.

Third, concepts ought to call attention to the most significant features of a complex subject matter. This is obviously more important in a complex political situation than it would be with a simple mechanical system. The press often devotes a good deal of attention to the size of the crowd that hears a speech delivered by a presidential candidate. The concept of noise, however, suggests that the number of other news events taking place on the day the candidate happened to make an important speech may be more important. In the absence of other dramatic events, the candidate's speech may be the lead item on television that evening, and thus come to the attention of a very large television audience. But if the deciding game of the World Series has been played, or if an air crash has killed scores of people, or if important foreign events have occurred, the candidate's speech may get only a passing reference at the end of the newscast. Such matters are far more important than crowd size, and communication theory does lead our thoughts in this direction.

Fourth, the concepts should be related to the subject matter of interest to the analyst. If an analyst's interest happens to lie in the congruence between personality and the demands of a particular role, or if he wants to know the details of a

---

[3] In communication theory, noise means any addition to the signal which was not intended by the original source of the message. In the event that a letter arrived in the mail together with five other letters, for example, the additional letters would be considered noise. The addressee would be less likely to absorb the information contained in the first letter as quickly because his attention would be to some degree distracted by the news contained in the other letters.

[4] *The Nature of Physical Reality* (New York: McGraw-Hill, 1950), p. 90. Many of the conceptual requirements mentioned above have been drawn from chapter 5 of Professor Margenau's book.

formal legal structure, the most elegant communication theory is not going to suggest any questions he might want to ask.

Finally, we must recognize that there is an important personal element in the heuristic value of concepts. One person thinks more easily in terms of a set of simultaneous equations; another finds poetic imagery far more suggestive. One person finds abstractions easy to handle; another finds that process-specific theories have more subjective meaning for him. Consequently we always need to ask about the fit between the logical requirements of a particular set of concepts and the cognitive style with which an individual is most comfortable. Questions of this nature, of course, allow only personal answers.

Having listed these theoretical, observational, and heuristic requirements, one should add at once that many concepts do not meet all these tests. The thoughtful reader will have noticed already that some of these requirements are at war with others. There is possible opposition between theory-building and experimental work. Motivation, for example, can be linked to many other concepts, but it is most difficult to observe. There is possible opposition between operational definitions and extension of the work to other domains of inquiry. Indexes of consensus developed for a legislative committee are often difficult to apply, let us say, to the electorate voting in New York or California. There is possible opposition between theoretical and heuristic requirements. Political scientists now have a reasonably stable definition of party identification, but this concept suggests relatively few questions about how candidates are likely to discuss foreign policy. So we ought to acknowledge that our list consists of ideal criteria, and admit that one must set priorities among the requirements according to his interests at any given time.

Our concerns often depend on the maturity of the science with which we are working. It is possible to visualize two rather different conceptual networks. Figure I-1 suggests what the relationships might be in an established theory.[5] The single lines signify links between individual concepts; the double lines stand for operational definitions which have been used to measure the existence of some of the concepts. In the diagram certain concepts, C_1 through C_5, are connected both to other concepts and to observable data. Another set of concepts, C_6 through C_{10}, do not have any operational definitions. Their interpretation depends solely on theoretical linkages. The conceptual network as a whole, however, does meet the theoretical and observational criteria we have set forth. Each concept has multiple links to other concepts, and each can be interpreted, either directly or indirectly, in terms of observable data.

Figure I-2, on the other hand, represents a developing conceptual network. Here the symbols have the same meaning, except that the dashed lines indicate suggested operational definitions and theoretical linkages which have not yet been fully accepted. Of the concepts in this diagram, only C_1, C_3 and C_8 meet our requirements. Operational definitions have yet to be worked out for C_2 and C_5. C_4

---

[5] This figure is based on those in chapter 5 of Henry Margenau's *The Nature of Physical Reality*. Similar adaptations may be found in Warren S. Torgerson, *Theory and Methods of Scaling* (New York: Wiley, 1958), p. 3; Fred N. Kerlinger, *Foundations of Behavioral Research* (New York: Holt, 1964), pp. 36–37; and Hubert M. Blalock, Jr., "Measurement and Conceptualization" in H. M. Blalock and A. B. Blalock, (Eds.), *Methodology in Social Research* (New York: McGraw-Hill, 1968), p. 25.

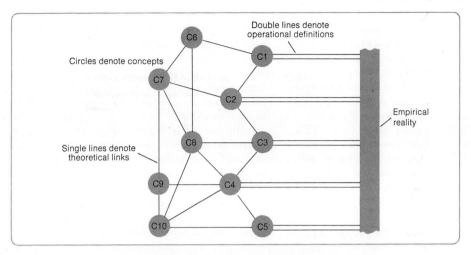

Figure I-1. An established conceptual network

has a real world interpretation, but no theoretical links to other concepts. C_7 can be interpreted only in terms of C_8; C_9 can be interpreted only in terms of C_5. C_6 and C_{10} are still isolated concepts. Neither an operational definition nor any theoretical linkages have been suggested for them. Since we are assuming that work is going on in this area we might guess that some of the suggested relationships will be validated but it is always risky to predict just which concepts will ultimately meet enough of the theoretical and observational tests to provide a scientifically useful theory. If all of the suggested relationships in Figure I-2 should work out,

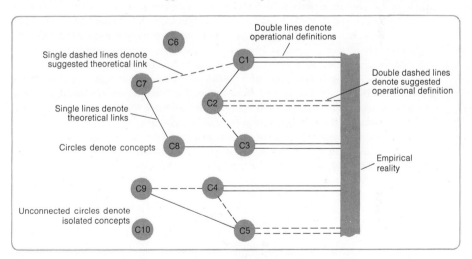

Figure I-2. A developing conceptual network

then further developments might link C_6 to C_1 and C_7, and C_{10} to C_5 and C_9. This would lead to two partial theories, neither fully satisfactory, but both explaining some aspects of the subject matter. Such partial theories are familiar, especially in those areas of science that lack an established paradigm.[6]

The selections on leadership provide an example of the development of two partial theories. In fact, this section is included because of what it tells us about the difficulty of developing suitable concepts, and the brain-sweat required before they can be linked together to form a theory and tested with real-world data. Sometimes subjects that are "obvious" candidates for investigation prove to be intractable or yield such meager results that researchers do not persist. In the past half century two major attempts have been made to gain some intellectual purchase on leadership. Two partial theories, a trait theory and a situation theory, have resulted. Both explain some things about leadership, but if the concepts employed are measured against the theoretical, observational, and heuristic criteria we have been discussing, then neither theory is satisfactory.

Charles E. Merriam, the author of our first article, was among the foremost of those pioneers who urged a scientific study of political behavior. In his presidential address to The American Political Science Association in 1925, he declared:

> Some day we may take another approach than the formal, as other sciences tend to do, and begin to look at political behavior as one of the essential objects of inquiry. Government, after all, is not made up merely of documents containing laws and rules, or of structures of a particular form, but is fundamentally based upon patterns of action in types of situations.

For many years, Merriam was Chairman of the Department of Political Science at the University of Chicago; there he trained political scientists who were one day to reshape the discipline along the lines he suggested. The article in this collection, based also on a book of the mid-twenties, shows some of the qualities that made Merriam such a great influence on the development of political science. He had enthusiasm for his subject matter, an ability to convey the essential facts, an appreciation of the vast effort necessary to gain the understanding he thought necessary, and optimism that all this work could be done successfully. The list of attributes he suggests as typical of a political leader is incomplete, but, as Merriam himself says, it was intended to be only a "temporary scaffolding." This piece was an initial attempt to develop some concepts, and an invitation to students to continue the work. It should be read in this light.

One of Merriam's most prolific and original students was Harold D. Lasswell. A citation given him on the awarding of a $10,000 prize by the American Council of Learned Societies testifies to the range of his interests:

---

[6] Thomas S. Kuhn has used the concept of a paradigm to interpret scientific history. "The study of paradigms . . . is what mainly prepares the student for membership in the particular scientific community with which he will later practice. Because he there joins men who learned the bases of their field from the same concrete models, his subsequent practice will seldom evoke overt disagreement over fundamentals. Men whose research is based on shared paradigms are committed to the same rules and standards for scientific practice. The commitment and the apparent consensus it produces are prerequisites for normal science, i.e., for the genesis and continuation of a particular research tradition." [*The Structure of Scientific Revolutions* (Chicago: University of Chicago Press, 1962), pp. 10–11.] In this sense, Figure I-1 may be interpreted as suggesting a field in which there is an established paradigm. Figure I-2 suggests either a field which is passing from a pre-scientific stage to its first paradigm, or a field in which an incompletely developed paradigm is replacing one that has been abandoned.

> . . . master of all the social sciences and pioneer in each; rambunc-
> tiously devoted to breaking down the man-made barriers between the social
> studies, and so acquainting each with the rest; filler-in of the interdisciplin-
> ary spaces between political science, psychology, philosophy, and sociol-
> ogy. . . .

Lasswell's training in both psychoanalysis and political science gave him the skills necessary to pursue the study of the traits of political leaders in a sophisticated way. He took as his point of departure a concept advanced by C. E. G. Catlin, a "political man" who would always seek to increase his power in the way that "economic man" presumably always sought to increase his wealth. In his early work, published in *Psychopathology and Politics* in 1930, Lasswell argued that there are three political types, a political agitator, a political administrator, and a political theorist. By the time *Power and Politics* was published in 1948, Lasswell's earlier typology had been broadened into a discussion of a dramatizing character, a compulsive character, and a third he is less willing to categorize rigidly, but who was more detached. Examples of these three character types are presented in the second selection as Judge Z, Judge X, and Judge Y.

This trait approach did not, however, result in concepts that could be knit together into a fully satisfactory theory of leadership. For one thing, the focus was as much on the personal needs of the leaders themselves as it was on the study of leadership. As Lasswell himself put it: "To describe a personality system at any cross-section in time is to discover the pattern of value demands (and specifications) of the person, and to describe the mechanisms chiefly relied on by the person in seeking to maintain internal order within the changing configuration of external environments."[7] A second limit on the development of these concepts has been the small number of political scientists—Robert E. Lane, Arnold A. Rogow, Alexander George, Lewis Edinger, Fred Greenstein, and James D. Barber—who have the professional qualifications to seek out the links between personality and politics. And an obvious theoretical limit appears when we consider our desire to have disjoint and exhaustive definitions. There are few politicians who can be regarded as purely compulsive, or purely dramatic, or purely detached, and there are few persons who do not occasionally exhibit some compulsive or dramatic behavior. For several reasons the study of leadership began to shift away from a search for leadership traits. Lester G. Seligman's "The Study of Political Leadership," published in 1950, marks a conscious shift away from the trait approach. "Traits are not to be ignored or dismissed," he argued, "but recent literature has refined our perception of the functional interdependence of leadership traits and situational factors." In his discussion of leadership situations, Professor Seligman noted a number of aspects in need of further research, and, as a matter of fact, he has since devoted much of his research time to one of these, the study of leadership recruitment.

The succeeding years have brought many fine analyses of leadership situations, and we have gained a good deal of insight into how men exercise influence within particular sets of constraints. Our fourth selection provides an example of just this. James S. Young had extensive training in anthropology as well as in political science, and he put these skills to good use in *The Washington Community*

---

[7] Harold D. Lasswell, *Psychopathology and Politics,* new ed. (New York: Viking, 1960), p. 277.

1800–1828 for which he won a Bancroft Prize in 1966. In the early sections of his book, Young sets forth a detailed analysis of the environment in which the early Presidents had to operate. He found that the relationship between the executive and legislative branches of government, a matter on which the Constitution was virtually silent, was made more distant by the attitudes of our early leaders and by the physical separation between Capitol Hill and the White House. The Jeffersonians' outlook was marked by a suspicion of each other and a hostility toward their community.

> "I do not know how it is, but I cannot get into these men," wrote a Senator of his colleagues; "there is a kind of guarded distance on their parts that seems to preclude sociability. I believe I had best be guarded too." . . .
> "Figure to yourself," wrote a Congressman in 1807 after having fallen from his horse midway between the White House and the Capitol, "a man almost bruised to death, on a dark, cold night, in the heart of the capital of the United States, out of sight or hearing of human habitation, and you will have a tolerably exact idea of my situation." [8]

The exercise of leadership in this situation required great interpersonal skill, and it is to this subject that Professor Young gives his attention in "The Statecraft of President Jefferson."

Our final selection is not limited to leadership per se. Rather Fred I. Greenstein, currently one of the leading scholars in political psychology, takes a wide-ranging look at the whole field of personality and politics. Naturally he deals with political leadership, pointing out, for example, that leadership positions are typically free from fixed content, and personality variations between leaders are therefore likely to manifest themselves. But Professor Greenstein's real concern is with a wider topic. Given the evident need for a political psychology, he asks, why is it that it has been so slow to develop? Part of his answer concerns the state of development in the two disciplines of political science and psychology. Part of the answer is that objections have been raised to the quality of work done thus far in the field of political psychology. Greenstein suggests that it would make more sense to reformulate these objections heuristically. Rather than debating the proposition that "personality is not an important determinant of political behavior" it would be more profitable to ask under what circumstances actors do vary in their behavior and under what circumstances their behavior is uniform. By such reformulations, Professor Greenstein indicates the subjects on which he thinks research should now be focused.

The question of why political psychology has been so slow to develop is, of course, a fundamental one. It is, after all, nearly half a century since Charles Merriam urged political scientists to develop a theory of political leadership. A great deal of effort by some very talented people has resulted in two partially satisfactory sets of concepts, one relating to leadership traits and the other concerning leadership situations, but neither one of which satisfies the criteria we reviewed earlier. Why is this? One rejoinder is to ask why one should expect any more rapid progress. This brief review of the development of leadership concepts

[8] James S. Young, *The Washington Community 1800–1828* (New York: Columbia University Press, 1966), pp. 53, 75.

illustrates an axiom of intellectual history. *The development of concepts and the validation of theory—in any field—are intellectual tasks which cannot be rushed.* One must have a creative mind to think of the concepts in the first place. Once they are proposed, some time will elapse in communicating them to one's colleagues. Then operational measures must be developed and validated for the concepts, and finally possible theoretical relationships must be investigated. In this last phase, empirical work often disconfirms what seem to be plausible relationships. And even if all this happens and new theories are validated, studies have shown that scientists tend to resist new ideas. Acceptance of a new theory, to say nothing of a new paradigm for a discipline, usually has to wait for a new generation whose members do not have psychological and intellectual investments in the established interpretation. Intellectual progress is slow, and in this perspective half a century is not a very long time.

It may also be that scholars will conclude that while leadership is an appropriate subject for study, it is not a very good point of departure for theory building. We do know that we do not have a crisp, clear concept of a leader, much less a leadership theory. Furthermore, the concepts presented in the other sections of the book all provide ways of thinking about aspects of leadership. Role theory calls our attention to possible conflicts between the subjective needs of the leader and the expectations of others with whom he has necessary relationships. Group theory distinguishes between social leadership and task leadership. The study of attitudes suggests questions about how much difference there can be in the cognitive complexity of a leader and those he would persuade. Communication theory invites attention to the importance of a central position in a communication network. And investigations of power have raised quite directly questions about how one measures influence. None of these approaches tells us all about leadership. Nor is there any guarantee that these concepts will continue to be employed by future researchers. James G. March's comment about organizations—"Since they tend to be highly personal exercises in wishful fantasy, forecasts of future developments in a field of research such as organizations have dubious intellectual validity. I do not know where the study of organizations is going." [9]—is appropriate for any developing intellectual endeavor. But for the moment all of these approaches represent investments made by some of our finest scholars. All of them offer some insights into political phenomena. And any or all of them may continue to be important in the emerging field of micropolitics. It is on this basis that we commend them to your attention.

[9] "Introduction" in James G. March (Ed.), *Handbook of Organizations* (Chicago: Rand McNally, 1965), p. xiv.

A PLEA FOR THE STUDY OF POLITICAL LEADERSHIP
CHARLES MERRIAM

Leadership is one of the basic factors in the organization of life, and its implications are everywhere of profound significance. Wherever we look, whether among plants, animals or humans, we find dominant centers emerging and the relations of dominance and subordination developing. This is universally true, whether we are dealing with the simplest and most elementary types of existence or the most complex forms of social and political organization. In the plant and animal worlds these functions have been studied intimately by many careful and persistent workers; but in the higher forms of social and political life much less careful attention has been given to the analysis of the nature and effects of these relations.[1]

Perhaps there is much of kin in the general, the cardinal, the magnate and the political leader or boss. The development of psychology is likely to throw much light upon this subject in the next few years, and, of course, the

CREDIT: Reprinted from Charles Merriam, *Four American Party Leaders* (New York: Macmillan, 1926), pp. vii, xi–xii, 85–100, xii–xiv. The editors wish to thank Robert C. Merriam for permission to reprint this section.

[1] See C. M. Child, *Physiological Foundations of Behavior*, Chapter X; C. J. Herrick, *Neurological Foundations of Animal Behavior*, Chapter XVIII; W. M. Wheeler, *Social Life Among Insects*.

literature of political leadership will be correspondingly enriched. But the special study of the political types of leadership will always remain an object of inquiry by the political scientists.

In my volume on the *American Party System*, I traced the common qualities of political leaders, and outlined some of the outstanding traits that seemed significant. That analysis was not designed, however, to be an exhaustive examination of the topic, but suggestive of the possibilities of more minute research in this field. In addition to the possession of certain other basic qualities I suggested the following as a working list of the common attributes of the political leader.

1. Unusual sensitiveness to the strength and direction of social and industrial tendencies with reference to their party and political bearings.
2. Acute and quick perception of possible courses of community conduct with prompt action accordingly.
3. Facility in group combination and compromise—political diplomacy in ideas, policies and spoils.
4. Facility in personal contacts with widely varying types of men.
5. Facility in dramatic expression of the sentiment or interest of large groups of voters, usually with voice or pen—fusing a logical formula, an economic interest

and a social habit or predisposition in a personality.

6. Courage not unlike that of the military commander whose best laid plans require a dash of luck for their successful completion.

This was intended, however, only as a temporary scaffolding, and has been so used by others and me. It will be necessary to accumulate more individual studies before much substantial progress can be made. A study of four leaders is only a small step, but a rough analysis of the qualities of Woodrow Wilson, Abraham Lincoln, William Jennings Bryan, and Theodore Roosevelt may be made, and perhaps this may be useful in further study of other leaders, or of the same characters on the basis of more adequate methods and material.

All of these men were endowed with great physical vigor, except Wilson. Lincoln and Bryan from childhood, and Roosevelt by training were extraordinary in their physical capacity. We do not have accurate measures of their strength to show the salient facts, but the universal testimony as to their strength and endurance is adequate for this purpose.

All were gifted with great intellectual capacity. Two were highly trained, Roosevelt and Wilson, and two, less highly schooled, Lincoln and Bryan. It is difficult to compare their intellectual characteristics, for they were in many respects different types. Two of these leaders were legally minded or used the legal analogy and style, Lincoln and Bryan. One used the literary style, while Roosevelt employed a combination of all of them ranging from one analogy to another, and seeking his illustrations every-where from the Scriptures to the prizering. Lincoln was a profound thinker with rare capacity for analysis and statement. Bryan was far less profound but in parliamentary and dialectical situations rose to great heights. Wilson was not primarily profound, but was extraordinarily gifted with hypnotic power of expression. Roosevelt would have made a good scholar or a good scientist, if he had not entered a political career.

The most evenly balanced temperament was that of Bryan. Lincoln was brooding and at times melancholy, a trait offset by his marvelously compensatory capacity for humor. Roosevelt was impetuous to the verge of rashness, although his facility in personal control saved him from disaster. Wilson was aloof and more inclined to be independent than to coöperate. Bryan was a medium type, undisturbed by all the vicissitudes of fortune, the bitterness of malignant foes, and the applause of his devoted worshipers. He had a balanced and sunny temperament, which served as a significant base for his generation of strenuous activity.

In all instances they seemed born to politics, or at least to have achieved a burning interest in government at a very early age. But Bryan was the only one who came from what would be termed a political family. Lincoln, Bryan and Roosevelt were actively interested in practical political affairs from their earliest days, passing from one phase of public life to another. Wilson was interested in the theory of politics in his early life, studied and taught it, but singularly abstained from participation until the autumn of his life.

All these persons were richly endowed with a sense of humor, a safety valve against over-assertiveness and self-importance, a useful means of attracting friends, and also of avoiding awkward breaks or crises in personal relations. This quality was most conspicuous in Lincoln, whose humor became a characteristic familiar to the whole nation, and was sometimes charged against his seriousness of purpose. Yet Roosevelt, Wilson and Bryan were likewise noted for their responsiveness to humorous situations, and for the facility with which they employed this dangerous faculty in their personal relations. Bryan's wit was a weapon formidable to his opponents, while the humor of Roosevelt and Wilson was less a platform tool and more a medium of personal interchange. Had Wilson been able to talk to the public as he talked to his circle of intimate friends, his political profile would have been notably changed.

Two were gifted with a highly developed mimetic faculty, but in fact the power to mimic was possessed by all of them. Lincoln in particular possessed a remarkable facility in vivid narration which reproduced interesting situations. But the others were not far behind in this characteristic accomplishment. Bryan was perhaps less strictly mimetic, but was gifted with histrionic ability of a very high order, and would probably have achieved notable success upon the stage.

In these leaders may be observed the transition from the earlier type of qualities, often associated with the leader of the *ancien régime*. The voice and manner of command are not sharply developed in them, while there is little haughtiness of demeanor in evidence. In Roosevelt and Wilson there is evident a high sense of personal dignity, but in Lincoln and Bryan there was an informality of a notable kind. Lincoln in particular did not rely upon the externalia of authority, but preferred the untrammeled simplicity of the Jeffersonian days. Bryan was equally remote from formality of manner or conduct. There were many men in America and some in political life whose voice, manner, air, more nearly corresponded to the traditional kingly style, but the nation followed the lead of more unassuming figures.

It is equally notable on the other hand that these figures were not typical of the exaggerated form of the democratic courtier, not infrequently found in popular systems and in America. None of them was boisterously genial, of the back-slapping, hand-shaking style, breezing through the community, radiating noisy goodwill. Roosevelt was the most effusive of this group, but even his "delighted," though often used, was not sycophantic. The highly exaggerated personal emphasis was lacking in the manner of the group as a whole. In all of them there was a certain reserve beyond which it was not easy to penetrate, and in the case of Lincoln this approached a form of inscrutability.

In fact only one of the group, and he the least successful politically, corresponded to the traditional stereotype of a statesman. Lincoln's features and figure, now idealized in martyrdom, were ready material for the cartoonist, who saw in him only the "Illinois ape." His sadness covered the sternness that guided him through seas of blood, and his humor covered his inner practical shrewdness. Roosevelt's physical equipment never seemed to me to fit him, but gave quite another picture, for a wholly different Roosevelt is found under his physical set up—a personality in no sense bellicose, bustling, squeaky or tangential, but cool, keen, calculating, decisive, purposeful. Wilson seemed somewhat boyish, aloof, with a certain *je ne sais quoi* of the non-social or non-political, and some lack of ponderousness often associated with weighty men of affairs. Bryan corresponded more closely to the composite figure of the traditional statesman, genial, rotund, impressive, in form and feature reflecting the earlier but passing type.

In sensitiveness to currents of political opinion around them, all of these leaders were masters, of almost equal ability. All were gifted with keen social and political insight and possessed high ability as interpreters of social movements. All failed from time to time to sense the actual situation, but in general were able to observe with unusual clearness the powerful tendencies of the times, gauging their strength, speed and direction. Usually, this political "feel" or sense came as a result of many human contacts, but in the case of Wilson the interpretation seems to have been reached much more independently. Many voices seem to confuse rather than clarify his thinking, and he preferred his own counsel upon numerous occasions.

In inventiveness Lincoln and Wilson rank high, especially in the development of widely accepted formulas. Roosevelt was swift in the discovery of expedients in a short time period. Bryan was fertile in devices, but did not always hit upon ways of advance that were generally adopted and followed. All were, however, of the type which, when the way is lost, finds a new trail that men will follow; or who contrive and construct useful political devices. Sometimes they failed, as in the case of Lincoln's plan for compensation to owners of slaves, Roosevelt's recall of judicial decisions, Bryan's free silver, and Wilson's League of Nations; but on many notable occasions they were able to invent formulas or types of action that were eminently adapted to the situations.

In group diplomacy I should rank Roosevelt first and Bryan last. The New York statesman understood the art of bringing diverse elements together and holding them together better than any other with the possible exception of Wilson. He was able in many instances to organize the unorganizable, reconciling for the time incongruous and even unfriendly elements, recruited from business, labor and the middle class. Wilson was notable in his successful dealing with the Democratic party organization which he was able to hold as a group in remarkable fashion. In 1912, and during the war he rallied to his support a vari-colored array of supporters; but during the 1916 campaign he was not able to hold the support of the business and Eastern group in the community. Lincoln was unable to hold together the various sections, North and South, but cemented the northern group in masterly fashion during the war. Bryan's combination of farmer, labor and church support was more notable than his analysts have usually observed. All of these leaders possessed in preeminent degree the power of combining discordant groups into a political unity. Just what factors enter into this kind of ability, we do not know, but presumably further analysis will more fully disclose its constituent characteristics. Apparently insight, sympathy, constructive intelligence all play their rôle in producing the formula that fuses the incompatible elements into temporary solidarity.

In personal contacts Lincoln undoubtedly would rank first and Wilson last. Lincoln was not "magnetic" in the sense in which the term is sometimes employed, but drew men to him in far more subtle ways. He gathered men around him by an amazingly diverse combination of joy and grief, by an appeal through humor and an unspoken appeal through profound sadness, in which there was a touch of tragedy. At one moment he was irresistibly amusing, at another overwhelmingly melancholy, at another impressively shrewd and cunning in some swift stroke. These three overtones constitute a matchless combination with a many-sided appeal. Bryan was impressively human, with a sunny disposition, and a fundamentally serious attitude. But his humor was not so marked as that of Lincoln, and his seriousness was not so tragic. His is a pattern in some ways similar to that of Lincoln, but characterized by narrower limits, right and left, and by greater balance, but with less keen intelligence. Roosevelt's range and variety of human contacts was very great, unsurpassed perhaps by any modern leader, and in these contacts he was impressive. Vigor, intelligence, friendliness radiated from him, and gave him a wide circle of personal followers, many of whom relied upon his compe-

tence regardless of the particular policy he might advocate at a given time. To many of his friends he seemed greater than his cause;—a source of weakness, this, as well as of strength. Wilson was a charming and attractive person to those who came within the circle of his intimacy, but the many who followed him did not know the man. They admired his scintillating intelligence, or perhaps revered him as a prophet in certain moods. The Wilsonians unlike the Rooseveltians were likely to be devoted to the cause rather than the man. The contrast between their types of leadership was as marked as the personal incompatibility between them.

In power of dramatic expression all were masters;—Lincoln and Bryan and Roosevelt as orators, and Wilson weakest here, but greatest with the pen. All understood also the art of dramatizing their attitudes and policies, although this was more marked in Roosevelt and Wilson than in Lincoln and Bryan, both of whom seemed less concerned with spectacular behavior. Lincoln and Wilson, under the stress of supreme military struggles, reached great heights of expressive statement. The Gettysburg Address has become a part of world literature and some of the passages in Wilson's war messages are likely to survive in the history of human aspiration. If the more poetical faculty was lacking in the words of Roosevelt and Bryan, they were, nevertheless remarkable for the facility with which they interpreted policies in terms of pungent phrase and telling epithet.

As an orator, Bryan was unmatched. He must be given a plus rating in this particular quality, a factor in his equipment without which he could not have survived throughout a generation. None of the others was notably gifted with the physical qualities ordinarily possessed by the platform orator, but all were impressive oral expounders of principles and creeds. Lincoln and Bryan, both lawyers, were masters of argumentation, while Roosevelt and Wilson were less inclined to this form of political persuasion.

The dramatics of political behavior were most highly developed in Roosevelt, whose modes of expression were very vivid. The cowboy costume, the Rough Rider uniform, the hunt for big game, the personal intensity of manner, were characteristic of a general course of conduct. Politics was not drab or gray to him, but colorful and intense,—melodramatic even. He was well adapted to a newspaper and movie world. The others were comparatively modest in methods, although none was devoid of the dramatic in conduct and career. They did not make vivid changes of costume, or eagerly pursue dangerous beasts. They were neither hunters nor fishers, but wore black and walked sedately. Yet in a larger way they were fully aware of the political effect of striking political strokes, and not infrequently employed them.

In courage all were beyond reproach, although none reached the extreme of foolhardiness. A certain prudence in compromise was a factor in the career of all of them. If any be given the palm in courage I should award it to Bryan, but in so stout a group of souls it is almost impossible to discriminate. All but Bryan had the dash of luck that goes with the final touch of victory. Lincoln and Wilson won the presidency through the division of the opposition in 1860 and again in 1912, while Roosevelt rose through the death of President McKinley. Fate did not so favor the Nebraskan. Indeed the Great War interrupted the climax of his career as a pacifier of the world.

In a period of widespread corruption in politics, all of these leaders were marked for their absolute integrity and for their lack of a patronage-made machine as an original basis of power. Their prestige brought them patronage which they used, but it was not the organization and the patronage that gave them their chief power, however advantageous these devices may have been at times. No shadow of the graft system that darkened the career of so many of their contemporaries fell upon them at any time. Honest Abe was unassailable. The others survived the bitterest assault of the most vindictive enemies without any successful intimation of their association with the kingdom of graft. It is a notable fact that in a time of widespread and shameless corruption, all of these leaders rose above the system of which they were a part. They were in charge of bosses and bosslets, but leaders still.

Their careers give the lie to the cynical conclusion that only graft and greed and narrow vision win political recognition in public affairs. Their success is proof of the survival of fundamental confidence in integrity and high ideals, at the high points in American public life, whatever may be the case on lower levels.

Summarizing, all of these leaders possessed a keen and permanent political interest, evidenced in early youth and sustained at a high level through life. How they came by this is an important question which we cannot now answer. With one exception all were gifted with extraordinary strength and vigor, which animated their lives with color and action. All had intelligence of a high order, in most cases of an unusual kind. However, this intelligence was not critically scientific as much as it was parliamentary, poetical, prophetic in nature. Lincoln had law as a basic interest, Roosevelt had administration and war, Wilson was inclined to literature and Bryan leaned toward theology; but all of them subordinated these interests and inclinations to the major task of politics in which all were absorbed. All possessed a keen sense of humor, which in Lincoln rose to the quality of a notable characteristic.

All were highly sensitive to the strength and direction of significant social and political tendencies, and seldom mistook the eddy for the main current. Bryan was less skillful in this divination, but was none the less notable for a high degree of intuition. All were adept in the art of group combination and diplomacy upon which organized strength so often is founded. All were skilled in personal contacts, marked by what is called magnetism, although Wilson was less highly rated here. All were gifted with dramatic power of expression with both voice and pen—an attribute without which it is difficult to see how they could have functioned as leaders. But the greatest orator was not the most successful leader. All of them were equipped with political inventiveness as to policies and situations. They were fertile in expedients, resourceful in devising

ways of advance, either when confronted with policies or with men. Keen political eyesight and quickly organizing political brains enabled them to divide and destroy the enemy of many battlefields. All were fundamentally courageous, risking their political lives upon many significant occasions where more timid men would have fled the field. Yet their courage was not that of the suicidal impulse, but the dash of the commander who risks all his reserves in the reasonable hope of turning the tide.

Once embarked upon their careers, all developed the attribute of prestige, and thus compounded the interest on their original capital. Thus Bryan captured his audience with his initial smile reminiscent of past events; Roosevelt with one glimpse of his flashing teeth, the emblem of war; Wilson with his mesmeric phrases recalling earlier hypnotisms; Lincoln at the sight of his singular countenance. And whatever they said or did was multiplied by the factor of what they had done.

It would be interesting to compare these leaders with figures such as that of Gompers in the labor field, or Morgan in the financial, or Eliot in the educational, or Grant in the military, or Gibbons in the ecclesiastical, but time will not permit of so important an inquiry. It would also be valuable to study the attributes and characteristics of the non-leader, or of the average man, with a view of observing the differential that might appear upon thoroughgoing analysis of the essential traits involved. But such an inquiry will not be possible upon this occasion. In any case a far greater amount of basic data of a biological and psychological nature would be necessary before scientifically satisfactory conclusions could be reached.

In view of the fundamental importance of leadership in any community, and especially in modern democracy, it is of the greatest consequence that studies of the qualities of political leadership be energetically and intelligently prosecuted. And I venture to express the hope that the necessary interest and enterprise for this purpose may be forthcoming in the not distant future.

A series of careful studies would make possible much more minute analysis than has hitherto been possible and would pave the way for more careful comparison. It would be desirable to study the background of the leader, the type of community in which he developed and in which he was active politically. It would be necessary to examine the special social, economic and political features of the particular situation in question. It would be important to scrutinize the beginnings of the leader, his ancestral origins, his parents, his early companions, and surroundings, his early life and his education, recreations, interests, dominant reveries. It would be useful to review his achievements, his training, the history of his career, noting the special forms of success and failure, of attainment and celebrity.

We should find it advantageous to obtain all possible data regarding the physical characteristics of the leader, including the fullest medical history and all possible biological and psychoanalytical data. We should want to know about his size, strength, endurance, health, voice, energy, manner, special tonicities, and a variety of other facts bearing upon the physical foundation of his leadership.

We should inquire into his intellectual and temperamental traits, using all the devices of modern psychology, psychiatry and common sense. We should look for self-assertiveness, strength of conviction, tact, geniality, patience, decisiveness, judiciousness, sense of humor, reputation for goodness of heart, and all other pertinent elements in his constitution. We should in short make every effort, leaving no stone unturned in the attempt to solve the secret of personality still in the main a riddle defying science. We should not be unmindful of the fact that the qualities of leaders can be determined only when we know also the qualities of non-leaders or followers from whom they are being differentiated. And finally we should want to know more about the problem of leadership as it is found not only in the political field, but also in the broader field of social relations of all sorts and descriptions.

THREE JUDGES
HAROLD D. LASSWELL

Within the broad stream of personal development that culminates in the political type, many variations occur. An inner tie is evolved not only with power in general but with particular manifestations of political life. Agitators and administrators, for example, may be distinguished from one another.[1] When the emphasis is upon arousing and sustaining widespread emotional response, the role is agitational, and the agitator seeks to acquire the appropriate oratorical and literary skills. If the role is specialized toward carrying on activities within an officially prescribed frame, the task is administration, which may be sought and prepared for, producing an administrative type.

Political specialization may emphasize certain perspectives toward change. Obviously demands for innovation can be basic or restricted in scope, and radical or moderate in method. The basic changes are revolutionary, and restricted changes are reforms. The most extreme positions in the spectrum advocate or pursue revolution by radical methods. Revolution can be directed toward introducing a new order or toward restoring a past system (counterrevolution).

It is a matter of common knowledge that political demands are affected by the hopes and fears that people entertain about what the future has in store for them. Will effort be rewarded? Will things turn out well even without effort, thanks to the nature of history or Divine Plan? Such expectations about the factual structure of the universe as it affects the value position of the self may exert a fundamental influence upon programs to support or resist change.

In many ways the most uncompromising denial that change can improve man's lot is de Maistre's: "It does not belong to man to change institutions for the better. . . . Hence the automatic aversion of all good men for innovations. The word reform, in itself and before any investigation, will always be suspect to wisdom, and the experience of the ages justifies this instinct."[2] Saint-Simon would have been justified in citing this as an example of his "stationary" type of opinion (the other two being "retrograde" and "liberal").[3]

A. Lawrence Lowell made a more comprehensive typology of political perspectives by combining two kinds of expectations (estimates of the self in the present and in the future).[4] First, he separated people into the contented

CREDIT: Reprinted from *Power and Personality* by Harold Dwight Lasswell, pp. 59–88. By permission of W. W. Norton & Company, Inc. Copyright 1948 by W. W. Norton & Company, Inc.

[1] See Chapters 6, 7 and 8 in H. D. Lasswell, *Psychopathology and Politics*.

[2] Joseph de Maistre, *Essai sur le Principe Générateur des Constitutions Politiques*.

[3] Developed in vol. XIX of the collected works of Saint-Simon.

[4] A. Lawrence Lowell, *Public Opinion in War and Peace*, ch. 7.

with their current lot and the discontented. Next, he separated those who are sanguine about the future (including human efforts at improvement) and those who are not sanguine. On this basis he came out with the following simple and workable scheme:

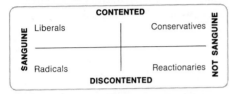

Fruitful lines of inquiry are opened if we take this system of classification as a series of hypotheses. Lowell's formulation is that expectations affect demands, but he says nothing about demands influencing expectations. There is certainly substantial ground for asserting that those who *want* often adjust their statements of fact to fit the want. Very likely we deal with interaction rather than a one-way determinative relationship between expectations and demands.

It is not within the scope of our present undertaking to pass in review all of the political typologies that have been presented for serious consideration. Our aim is to link the study of political types somewhat more closely with the work that is being done on basic forms of personality development by scientists from several fields of medicine, psychiatry, psychology and social psychology.

CHARACTER TYPES

Temperament types, however, after the manner of Kretschmer [5] or Shel-

don,[6] are not as close to our present concern as what are often called character types.[7] A character type is formed when a particular dynamism or set of dynamisms is relied upon to cope with the anxieties that occur during conflicts of development. How do basic character patterns operate in power situations; or, more generally, how is the accentuation of the power possibilities of a situation affected by the type of character? The temperament undoubtedly has a selective effect on character; but the correspondence appears to be far from perfect.

Varieties of political development are affected by two character types which are to be discussed at some length. (Brief observations will be made about other types later.)

Of special utility in accounting for specializations of political type is the *compulsive* character, which is distinguished by the degree to which it relies upon rigid, obsessive ways of handling human relations.[8] Another type is what we call the *dramatizing* character. This term is not in general use but refers to several well-understood phenomena whose unifying feature is the demand for immediate affective response in others. The dramatizing character may resort to traces of exhibitionism, flirtatiousness,

[6] W. H. Sheldon, S. S. Stevens, W. B. Tucker, *The Varieties of Human Physique;* W. H. Sheldon and S. S. Stevens, *The Varieties of Temperament.*

[7] Beginning with Freud, psychoanalytic characterology was advanced by Karl Abraham and Sandor Ferenczi; and more recently by Wilhelm Reich, Franz Alexander, Theodore Reik and Karen Horney.

[8] See especially, Karl Abraham, *Selected Papers,* Anna Freud, *The Ego and the Mechanisms of Defense,* Sigmund Freud, *The Problem of Anxiety.*

[5] E. Kretschmer, *Physique and Character.*

provocativeness, indignation; but in any case all devices are pivoted around the task of "getting a rise out of" the other person.

From what we have learned of compulsiveness, we expect it to exercise a significant effect upon the public targets and justifications which are substituted for the figures in the primary circle of the developing political personality. The compulsive character will select less varied objects for displacement and rationalization than the dramatizer. The compulsive inclines toward carefully defined limits and the well-worked-out ordering of parts; the dramatizer excels in scope and abundance of loosely classified detail. The hallmark of the former is the imposition of uniformity, while the latter tolerates diversity and excels in nuance. The compulsive desubjectivizes a situation, while the dramatizer remains sensitized to psychological dimensions; the one denies novelty, while the other welcomes it; one squeezes and compresses the dimensions of the human situation which the other complies with and allows to spread. The compulsive monotonizes the presentation of the self to the other, while the latter multiplies the faces and façades which can be presented to other persons.

What is involved can be made most apparent by reviewing three histories. The information herein summarized was obtained in the usual way by several procedures of investigation, ranging from psychiatric (or partially psychiatric) interviews, to the testimony of colleagues and intimates, and participant observation in ordinary life situations. (The customary precautions are taken to protect the memory of the subjects. Minor details have been altered, but the basic profile has not been retouched.) The three men ended their careers playing comparable political roles, since all became judges. But there are notable variations in political type. One is unmistakably an agitator, while another is basically an administrator. The third is a less specialized political leader. The administrator owes the peculiarities of his development in part to the compulsive character which he acquired comparatively early, while the agitator was undoubtedly a dramatizing character. The third judge had a less distinctive character type, although he was more closely related to the dramatizer than to the compulsive.

These men will exemplify one of the subtle dynamic processes by which established institutions are subject to change. There is a continual interplay between office and personality. At any given moment a complicated pattern of expectation and demand may be attached to an "office." To some extent perspectives may be spelled out in the authoritative language of a statute book. In some degree the office is defined by the perspectives of those who have the most direct working relationship to it, as superiors, opposite numbers or subordinates. Besides, there are expectations and demands made by those who have more remote or occasional contact, such as reporters, editors, group leaders, group publics or the general public. Hence the act of entering an "office" is to appear at the focus of attention of those who are predisposed to expect and demand rather definite modes of conduct from the office holder. In addition to demands and expectations, the office may be a focal point of loyal identifications on the part of many persons and groups.

The office holder acts selectively on the basis of the predispositions with which he enters in the new situation. If he is an agitational type, he tends to respond to agitational opportunities. If, on the contrary, he is an administrative type, he goes in the other direction. In either case the office changes, and the perspectives entertained about it are modified. Both Roosevelts developed the agitational possibilities of the presidential office, while Herbert Hoover underlined its administrative potentialities. A given trend may be reversed, as when William Howard Taft de-emphasized the impetus given to presidential leadership by Theodore Roosevelt, and Woodrow Wilson, in his turn, rejected the comparative inactivity of his predecessor and resumed the march toward expanding the office.[9]

Our interest in the following case fragments is, therefore, many-sided. Space constrains us to be overschematic and overbrief in alluding to many political figures. I hope that these fragments will provide a reminder of the fullness with which personality probes need to be made, since these extracts are the most extended case reports that it will be feasible to introduce in this book. Sufficient detail is offered to give an inkling of what is involved in looking into the developmental links between character type, political type and political role.

The procedure in presenting each

history is to outline the consensus about the judge's official conduct among brethren of the bench and bar. Then follows a sketch of what an observer saw who watched the judge's behavior in the courtroom situation. After this comes some indication of the roles played off the bench in public or private political life. The next step is to examine the intimate life of the subject, including private evaluations and ambitions. Finally, the sequence of development is indicated, providing some clue as to how the person was seen by others and by himself. In general, the aim is to occupy observational standpoints of varying degrees of intensity (intensiveness-extensiveness) throughout the entire career line.[10] One standpoint is that of the *stranger* who describes the public image of the subject; a second standpoint is that of the *acquaintance-friend;* a third is that of the *intimate friend;* and a fourth is that of the *intimate scientist* (whether psychologist or psychiatrist). Without following the sequence too pedantically, the aim is to allow the political role to dissolve into the political type, and then into the character type.

Judge X

Judge X had an impeccable reputation for integrity. He was also regarded as exceedingly severe with offenders, and given to imposing higher fines and longer prison terms than his colleagues. In general, he was reputed to be a "government judge," meaning that he was strongly disposed to uphold the government in tax cases, as well as in cases involving narcotics,

[9] One of the neglected fields of political research is the interplay of office and personality.

[10] On observational standpoints see H. D. Lasswell, *World Politics and Personal Insecurity,* ch. 1.

white slavery, kidnaping and the like. The exception was antitrust cases. The judge appeared very reluctant to "unscramble" big businesses or to hold businessmen criminally responsible for violations. On labor matters the judge was popularly tagged as "anti-union" on the basis of a small number of well-publicized situations in which injunctions were issued. Where civil liberties were plainly at stake, Judge X followed the "liberal" line more often than not. In a word, the judge was believed by the bar to be upright, severe in ordinary criminal matters, friendly to big business and quite respectful of the Bill of Rights. On the basis of detailed knowledge of Judge X's life on and off the bench, I believe his general reputation was well founded. For instance, his integrity was often tested in connection with bankruptcy cases, where the appointment of a receiver is an important factor and where existing managements often try to perpetuate themselves by court appointment.

In the judgment of the bar the written opinions of Judge X were competent, though overcondensed as a rule and colorless. Occasionally the opinion would labor a point exhaustively and (in the general view) pointlessly. This was characteristic of what often went on in the courtroom when a case was being argued. Although a man of high intelligence, Judge X would often get exceedingly concerned about some point that failed to impress anybody else as especially germane. A stickler for niceties, he would permit the proceedings to get bogged down in the game of piling technicality on technicality. Attorneys complained privately that the judge wore them out with his overinsistent and rather nagging style.

The courtroom picture presented by Judge X was one of great austerity. A little short, rather thin and sallow, the prevailing mood ran from sternness to controlled irritation. A strict disciplinarian, exceedingly sensitive to noise or disorder, the judge was given to admonishing spectators and counsel at the drop of a pin. His forehead was characteristically knit into a frown, and one of his brows twitched with such a regularity that it was doubtless a tic. The lips were tightly closed, and the lip line was straight. Mounting irritation was expressed by frowning and by slight motions of the jaw that bespoke the grinding of the teeth. The voice was rather high pitched, and the *s* consonants were often spoken with great sibilance, and the explosive possibilities of the *t* and the *p* were not overlooked. Many observers got the impression that the judge was chronically alert, tense and full of suppressed annoyance. And this impression was strengthened by his occasional outbursts of irritable moralizing, and by the vitriol sometimes packed in his speeches when passing sentence.

Despite the hushed, sober and tense atmosphere of the courtroom, Judge X was not notably efficient in getting through the calendar. On the contrary, he was usually in arrears. It was obvious to those who worked with him closely that the judge worked hard on his opinions and read widely and well. But there was a great sense of strain continually present, an all-pervading sense of being driven and overworked. Humor and wit were almost entirely absent from courtroom or chambers.

The reputation of the judge went beyond the bar to the general public, chiefly because of the role played early in life during a reform administration when the newly appointed judge presided over sensational cases in which public officials were successfully prosecuted for bribery and other abuses of office. The judge was a clear if somewhat dull and pompous speaker, greatly in demand on civic and professional occasions. From time to time he lent the weight of his name to worthy nonpartisan campaigns, and was recurrently mentioned for elevation to the highest court in the land, or for a senatorship from his state. Behind the scenes his voice was listened to in party as well as in civic and professional circles.

Although he never disclosed his ambition directly, Judge X hoped to maneuver himself into a situation where he would be an "inevitable" and preferably bipartisan choice for a major elective office. (The truth about his ambitions came out in intimate interviews to be referred to later). From an early time the judge fantasied himself turned to unanimously by his fellow countrymen as the man of the hour, the leader of unimpeachable integrity who would bring honesty, efficiency and justice into public life. In this purpose he was not entirely successful, but he was several times on the verge of an uncontested nomination. Often the judge would draw up elaborate instructions to himself, imagining that he was governor, senator or president. These were full of imposing ethical and legal slogans. Needless to say, these documents were destroyed without being shared with anyone else.

The home life of the judge was exceedingly formal, and although the more intimate facts were concealed even from friends, the emotional atmosphere was full of tension. For it was at home that the judge allowed himself much freedom in expressing his hostilities and in domineering over others. His wife was a colorless, though socially suitable, person. The judge regarded her as an incapable person and interfered in every detail of the household and in the rearing of the children. Opposed to disorder and a convinced apostle of discipline, he constantly criticized her alleged carelessness and overindulgence of the children. The youngsters grew up to be "disappointing," often failing at school and getting into disciplinary difficulties that were covered up out of respect for the judge.

From an early age the judge worried about his health and devoted himself to elaborate rituals in the interest of warding off the many bodily illnesses of which he stood in terror. His medicine cabinet was a well-equipped drugstore, and he experimented clandestinely with nearly every health fad from chewing his food until all meals were dragged out to unconscionable lengths to stuffing and scratching his interior with "roughage" to aid elimination. Beset by minor gastro-intestinal troubles, he finally sought medical assistance for a rather serious gall-bladder condition, in the course of which he was willing to talk freely about himself, partly from a growing sense of dissatisfaction with himself and his life. This was accentuated at the time by the physical and mental decline of his long-suffering wife and by the obvious shiftlessness of his children.

The development of X's personality is clarified somewhat when we learn that he was born into a wealthy and highly respected family in which the father was stern, melancholy and aloof, while the mother was religious, prudish, overtense and overprotective. At the mother's instigation—and this was established from direct testimony—the nurse tried to force the pace of cleanliness training, and imposed a severe regimen on the infant and child. Owing to the father's sensitivity, every effort was made to reduce noise around the home. As a lad Judge X had been subject to frequent illnesses (stomach upsets and headaches in particular).

In the course of a brief series of interviews Judge X recognized fully for the first time how much of his own career was related to his younger brother, whose arrival had aroused his jealousy and whom he sought to excel and to discredit in the eyes of mother and father. From an early time X was excellent in his studies and devoted himself to impressing adults with his brilliance and trustworthiness. He became a rather withdrawn, hostile, cold and somewhat embittered youth with little spontaneity and with a great sense of being goaded by forces outside himself that kept him on the move. As a child his rare outbursts of rage had been punished physically; but he was especially sensitive when shamed by his parents or subjected to withdrawals of affection and privileges. As X learned self-control, he disciplined himself in order to retain and enlarge his privileges, frequently by putting his brother in the wrong.

An excellent though not a popular student, X went through first-class educational institutions, and partly through family influence soon became a partner in a highly influential law firm. It was at this point that crises of conscience began to interfere with his work to a point that made it troublesome to complete any assignment. He resented the advocate's job of preparing a brief for one side only and declared with much indignation that it was against his principles to twist and turn in the preparation of a case for the sole purpose of "blinding the eyes of justice" for the benefits of one side. The senior members of the firm were disturbed by this and finally hit upon a way out. They used political influence to obtain a judicial nomination for this young and overscrupulous partner. At the moment there was a local reform wave in which civic associations were passionately rising against the "scourge of lawlessness and corruption" with which their city had been cursed. With his well-known name and impeccable connections, X was an ideal candidate, won easily, and consolidated his public reputation as presiding judge in the prosecutions that soon began.

Looking at X from the standpoint of our basic conception of political personality, it is rather clear that his displacements from the intimate circle (and the accompanying rationalizations) were highly overcompensatory. Exposed to an early environment with notably indulgent and deprivational features, X was constantly struggling against aggressive tendencies provoked by frustration. Since it was impossible to express these tendencies directly without being overpowered and deprived of indulgences, aggressiveness was internalized in the form of compulsive strictness, busy-ness, rigidity (and light somatic conversions). But in some degree these drives were externalized in the form of burning ambition to excel by destroying the unworthy. Human relations became unspontaneous and calculated. Energy went into the making of plans for success in public life and for acquiring and applying the techniques that appeared to be the most instrumental. Relying upon compulsive mechanisms to hold his own aggressions in check, Judge X was attracted to the well-systematized authority of the bench, where he was given to excessive concern with legal technicality at the expense of the rapid administration of justice. Appealing solely to the conscience of the community, and having little warmth of personality, X's public career, distinguished though it was, fell short of his ambition. With the exception of his auspicious start in public life, he never came to grips with a crisis situation in which the conscience values (the mores) were uppermost, where he might well have been the rallying symbol. Actually, his range of ready identification with people was narrow, and neither imagination, training nor experience supplied him with much knowledge of the total impact of the decision-making process upon the life of society. He was unmistakably conservative in outlook, reflecting the standards of judgment prevailing in the upper-class circles in which he moved. (The protection of civil liberty, by the way, was a feature of this tradition.) His excellent talents were spent on drawing distinctions that made little impression on legal doctrine or on the public.

Clearly, the compulsive features of X's adjustment led him to select certain opportunities offered on the bench and to neglect others. He showed the capacity of the compulsive character to become preoccupied with detail and to allow the whole context to elude him. The atmosphere of the courtroom stressed the stern and fussy aspects of the judicial office. It was plain that the judge used the opportunities of his position to dehumanize the people who came in contact with him, especially on official business; and that beneath his propriety lurked a destructive contempt for himself and for others which betrayed itself in a chronic state of irritable tension. A compulsive character made an administrator in fact who daydreamed of becoming a versatile and commanding public leader, a dream that never came off, partly from the lack of effective capacity to project human warmth into casual and official relations.

Judge Y

In several particulars Judge Y presents a contrast to the colleague we have been considering. He was appointed to the bench late in his political career. People at large thought of him as a successful boss, and there were many protests against his elevation. But the opinion of the public and the bar turned more and more in his favor, and at the time of his death there was no judge with a higher reputation for integrity and fairness. Perhaps the clearest contrast with Judge X was in the imposition of sentences. Where X was ruthless, Y was benevolent. However, Y was not "soft," and he was not thought of as unduly sympathetic with the parties who were defending themselves against the government's prosecutor. On questions of taxation and business regulation, Y was far less "legalistic" than X and sought constantly for light on the actual economic and social consequences of the various practices upon which he was called to pass judgment. Partly because of his business experience (to say nothing of his political life) Judge Y was treated with special consideration by his colleagues of the bench and bar and was frequently credited with having "cut through the arguments" to the core issues. In litigation involving labor and management, he took a "middle way" and was looked upon by both sides as open minded. At first the bar had imagined that Y had long since "forgotten his law." But they were soon disabused of this notion and agreed that his opinions were cogently if not gracefully put together.

The atmosphere of Y's courtroom was in striking contrast with that of Judge X. Judge Y was ruddy, round-faced, bald and big. His voice was casual though distinct and musical. He made a minimum number of movements and displayed no tenseness. The impression was one of quiet mastery.

Courtroom habitués felt that the judge was particularly careful to reassure timid young lawyers or halting witnesses, especially if they were poor and Catholic. But they did not insinuate that the judge was antagonistic to the rich or the Protestants or the Jews. Many times he would take the direct interrogation of witnesses out of the hands of a lawyer who seemed to be asking clumsy questions or in any way confusing the witness. He was especially thoughtful of the foreign born, or of anyone who spoke with a foreign or an unacademic accent.

Actually the political career of Judge Y is a success story of no inconsiderable magnitude. He came up the hard, tough, rough way. He was reared in the working-class district of a big city and had been the leader of his neighborhood gang. The gang was predatory but not notably vicious or cruel. That is, the gang stole food and loose articles and fought with rival gangs, but became entangled in no systematic looting and had little trouble with the police or the community at large. Judge Y became a proficient boxer at the athletic club run by one of the political parties, and he and his gang were frequently used in election fights. Occasionally there was intimidation of voters or ballot-box stealing, but all this was taken as part of the game.

An older politician took a liking to Y, advised him to study law, and got him a soft job on the police force until he passed the bar. Then Y was "cut in" on a number of businesses that depended on political patronage, such as insurance, trucking and street-paving. By using advance information about utility extensions, he was able to invest successfully in real-estate developments. But he scrupulously kept out of "smelly" operations. For instance, he did not use squads of window smashers to demonstrate to the store owner that insurance was needed. He did not use his political influence to pass complicated building codes which could be used for extorting protection money from property owners. He did not take bribes, either to intercede with "political" judges or other administrative officials or to put through special legislation. Also, he did not profit directly from gambling, prostitution or dope peddling, although he often closed his eyes to what members of his political machine did.

It was not until well along in middle life, long after he had been a powerful boss, that Y began to dream of stepping from unofficial power to responsible public leadership. The change came largely at the instigation of his wife who had become socially ambitious and felt the stigma of being "Mrs. Boss." Under her prodding, Y began quietly to use his money to increase the prestige of his name. He used the usual channels, either directly or through his wife, contributing to hospitals which were the pet charities of the local dowagers (presently getting elected to various boards), contributing to the expansion of the medical school of an eminent local university, contributing to the symphony orchestra and the theater. In addition, there were well-placed donations to the activities of his church and fraternal orders. After these preparations, he put himself on the ballot and got elected judge. Judge Y had always been a fluent speaker, although not a major orator, and his public appearances were dignified.

Looking further back into Y's career, we find that he was subject to loving but earnest prodding by his mother. His parents were evidently happy and affectionate. The father was a skilled mechanic who was easygoing and outgoing and the mother, with a somewhat better education, determined that her sons should "amount to something" in the world and was continually strict and watchful.

It appears that Y incorporated much of his mother's ambitious, energetic, optimistic and friendly outlook and approached the world outside the family with confidence. He assumed family responsibilities when young, marrying a neighbor girl who was a great favorite of the community. She had much the same balance of ambitiousness and warmth that characterized his mother.

The accentuation of politics in the personality development of Y was less on the basis of overcompensation against low estimates of the self than in the case of many other leaders of whom we have knowledge. His environment provided indulgences for him as he went up the ladder, and it is quite possible that Y could have been thrown out of his job as boss or judge without "taking it too much to heart." He was, of course, exceedingly quick in recognizing where power lay, and although it was not possible to apply any measuring instrument, the trained observer could not fail to be impressed by the high level of intelligence he displayed in dealing with political problems. Part of the impression of ambitionlessness created by Y came from the great speed with which he foresaw political contingencies and prepared for them. Hence he usually maneuvered himself into a winning position before making a final move. (Deeper psychological analysis of Y was precluded by the fact that the only time available for talking intimately about his past was when he was laid up with an accident.)

The personality of Y was quite

free of compulsiveness. Obviously he belongs to the dramatizing group we mentioned above, in the sense of responding sensitively to other human beings and of cultivating skills adapted to sustaining an emotionally significant contact. We find, for instance, that his range of emotional responsiveness in dealing with people easily passed through the entire gamut. He was reserved and friendly, deferential, humorous, witty, angry, reproachful, sympathetic, earnest. Y's affects flowed spontaneously in ways that knit people to him from all walks of life.

Judge Y's conduct on the bench was in keeping with the selective processes anticipated from such a developmental type. This was reflected not only in his benevolence, in the tendency to assist and take responsibility for the young or the handicapped, but in the alert and self-possessed way in which he explored the possible consequences of his decisions. He was not rigidly bound to cloud his eyes with technical arguments before he had a clear picture of the factual situation to which they were supposed to apply. Manifestly, the judge found it unnecessary to retire behind a pedestal or a technicality to protect himself from human or physical facts.

Judge Z

A more striking example of the dramatizing type may indicate some of the dangerous possibilities inherent in such a development. It was generally agreed that Judge Z had a keen intellect and was quite capable of following the most involved argument. As one man put it: "He's not like Judge Blank; Blank is lost after the first verb. Judge Z is usually ahead of you." At the same time the consensus among the older members of the bar was that Z was erratic in his judgment, often appearing to be wholly uninterested in the legal aspects of the case.

A common remark about Z was that he would "do anything for a laugh," or that he was a "publicity hound." He was invariably genial, though reserved, with the press, and the impression that he played to the gallery came from a few cases in which he did something popular and sensational. In each instance he had dug up some ancient statute and applied it literally—and with astonishing results. In these cases the ideas had been brought to his notice by a bright law secretary, or had been thought up by himself. He took great delight in showing up the "imbecilities of the law," as he called them in private. At the same time, in so far as he personified the majesty of the law, he was obviously impressed by the mantle and permitted no liberties to be taken with his authority. Significant, however, is the contradiction between this attitude and the occasional breaches of decorum in the courtroom and the private expressions of contempt for the law. The truth is that the judge would give an ear to any argument if it seemed to point toward startling consequences.

However, there is no evidence that Z thought consistently of the law as part of the social process, seeking to extend and maintain the values of the community. Although his opinions have been studied with care, few straight lines emerge. Actually the opinions present a highly varied patchwork. They were written in a rather florid style, studded with "color" adverbs and adjectives. The legal points were not systematically, but discursively, handled. As remarked before, his sole contribution to legal doctrine appears to have come as an incident of some startling application of a sleeping statute.

Taken in conjunction with the parties involved, however, the role of Judge Z in the administration of the law is somewhat clarified. In criminal cases he was "soft" with young offenders, "tough" with men in middle life, and exceedingly "soft" with the old. This comes out in the relative severity of the sentences imposed, and is confirmed by his conduct toward the parties in the courtroom (especially his tendency to dismiss cases).

Further inquiry into Judge Z's conduct in criminal cases reveals additional traits. His sympathies were, by all accounts, genuinely enlisted by calm, suffering victims; but he was equally impressed by self-possessed defendants. He was exceptionally "anti-government" whenever the prosecution failed to "personalize" the victim, especially when the latter was young, physically attractive, or notably self-possessed, even defiant. He was promptly repelled—and visibly over-reacted—at any sign of hysteria among women; and he was touched by unaggressive old people, especially if they were poor and suffering.

In civil cases Judge Z showed no well-thought-out attitude toward industrial concentration or government control of business. There were evidences of bias against bigness—against the giant corporation—but he had no confidence in regulation or socialization. However, toward the end of his career, there was an unmistakable drift toward favoring both strong and expanded government. Trips abroad impressed him with what nationalistic and totalitarian regimes were capable of accomplishing. Also, as the years went by and Russia seemed to consolidate, he began to admire collectivization and to speculate about what was later called "the wave of the future." In private talk he began to say that the corruption of American politics and business was so complete that only a rebirth, a reawakening led by young men, could save the country.

Judge Z was not noticeably tall, but he conveyed an impression of being above average height on account of the thinness of his skull and the creases that lined his face. His hair was parted differently than was common in his part of the country and slicked down. The most conspicuous feature of the countenance were luminous eyes, which he used with dramatic effect when he fixed counsel, witness or juror with his gaze. There was a frequent play of expression around the corners of his eyes, and the lids were often lowered or raised to convey what could be variously construed as interest, boredom, disbelief, certainty, doubt, amusement or repugnance. The lashes were long and the brows jutted over rather receding sockets. One mannerism was the raising and lowering of the eyebrows. His mouth was not firmly closed and the lower lip was full and red. Occasionally he would purse or lick his lips, and sometimes pass a hand over his mouth and chin in a light, caressing movement. Usually he was overdeliberate. He seemed to initiate any expressive act as though it were worthy of being carried through with dignity. This was especially noticeable in the use of his long, tapering fingers. Many of his wrist gestures were graceful; he often allowed his hands to hang limp from the wrist. A musical, flowing voice added to the total expressiveness. But there were jerky interruptions in voice and gesture which signified to a trained observer that some impulses not in harmony with the deliberateness were not far below the surface.

So far as clothes were concerned, Judge Z was conspicuous. He wore colors usually associated with actors and other less drab professions than the law. Often the hue of his shirts was arresting; and the lapel flower might be, too. The cut of his suits and the style of his shoes, to say nothing of his snappy hats, were even foppish. There was a faint aroma of hair tonic—he was freshly barbered daily—and of perfume.

To a close observer of Judge Z's behavior in the courtroom it was apparent that he was given to playing favorites among counsel, parties and witnesses; and that he used his supple features and hands to convey his attitudes to the jury. His favors would sometimes pass suddenly from one counsel to the other; and he would flit from calm to flashes of vexation. Witnesses, too, were subjected to mercurial treatment—sometimes being reassured by the sympathetic voice, sometimes rasped by intonations of distrust. There were many examples of sudden reversals of favor toward a counsel who had received especially deferential treatment through several trials. Most of these instances involved young lawyers. The judge, in dealing with elderly men, was very indulgent,

particularly if they were down at the heel and were neither aggressive nor querulous. Often he selected Masters in Chancery from this group of broken-down lawyers, commenting to his secretary that law was a risky profession and even the humble, if honest, deserved a break. But the counsel who tried to browbeat the Court, or the distinguished practitioners who adopted a strong and condescending tone, these he blocked at every turn. He usually maintained great decorum in the courtroom, but permitted himself irony, sarcasm and contemptuous wisecracks when confronted by the behavior of the type mentioned. At such times he would grow pallid and press his lips in a straight line, digging the nails of his fingers into the palms of his hands.

Clues to the personality of Judge Z can be gleaned by examining the role he played off the bench on public occasions. He was a favorite orator at party gatherings and patriotic celebrations. On the platform he was decidedly theatrical in style, fond of deliberate movements and dramatic pauses, such as the ancient trick of reaching for a glass of water. His mellifluous voice was pleading, commanding, exhorting, expounding, chiding—it was capable of expressing every nuance of emotion. The vocabulary was flowery, full of emotive language about morality, justice, love of home and country. He broke into poetry without effort and told stories with enormous gusto and mimetic skill. His perorations at Fourth of July celebrations were famous, and he was very effective at pathos. He could denounce or defy. But he was actually more effective as a glorifier than as a prosecutor.

Often in his speeches Judge Z referred to his contacts with great names, and he did go abroad enough to be received by the heads of foreign states and to be decorated. (There were large blocs of voters of European origin in his constituency.)

Although the judge evaded any direct avowal even to his intimates of specific political ambition, it was obvious that he was a popular leader who might step from the bench to the Senate at any time. He was absorbed by the problem of political power and read the lives of famous men, analyzing the technique that enabled them to "shape history." As he grew older the ordinary ladder of politics in this country failed to arouse his imagination. Stimulated by developments abroad he speculated privately on the possibility of organizing a young men's movement in the United States, with himself at the head, beginning first as a secret order. He welcomed speaking engagements around the country that would bring him in contact with young people, and kept on the lookout for promising lieutenants. In particular he considered the possibility of launching the secret society with the support of industrialists in mining and in the capital-goods industries, who he believed were particularly afraid of bolshevism. Many owners and executives were, he believed, in the reserve corps of the army, and he hoped to gain the informal support of the military for his movement. He kept physically fit, and even in later middle life was always sun-tanned and athletic, especially in an individualistic sport like tennis. He sun-bathed a great deal and paid strict attention to weight and diet.

In his own home the judge did a great deal of formal entertaining. His wife was older by a decade, but he kept a certain fondness for the motherly, if somewhat limited, woman. He found her, as he once phrased it to intimates, as restful as an old-fashioned hammock. At the same time her slow mind, limited outlook and slightly depressive temperament bored him. All during his married years he maintained a very discreet though active sexual life outside the home. The women were usually beautiful, exuberant and sophisticated. He enjoyed the thrill of pursuing a new woman, especially if he knew that another man was after her. He was inclined to grow indifferent as quickly as a woman grew "demanding," as he put it. He gave lavish gifts and was alienated by any sign of deep or lasting affection ("possessiveness"). Because of his own charm, this occasionally led to difficult situations, from which he was able to extricate himself by ingenuity and ruthlessness. His more abiding attachments were with youths to whom he turned, as he sentimentally put it, feeling like an old Greek hero.

The information about Z thus far summarized enables us to form a working model of a dramatizing personality. First of all, his intense craving for deference is evident. In court he managed to keep in the center of attention by the use of many subtle devices, such as permitting many shades of expression to cross his countenance, playing off one counsel against another, and abruptly shifting his favors. His dress and demeanor were bids to look and like; and this demand went far beyond the courtroom or his home. He keenly craved deference in the form of power, respect and affection; he perfected many skills and sought opportunities to get what he wanted.

To the trained eye Z's public appearance showed a great many exhibitionistic and homosexual trends. Although quite aware of his sexual interests, Z was not aware of the degree to which they influenced his judgment in a great many situations which he did not think of as specifically sexual.

For instance, he displayed many signs of overreaction against submissive tendencies, notably in the form of sudden hates, especially of assertive personalities, particularly when he began by feeling amiably disposed. Furthermore, it is apparent that he made use of his polished manner to keep people at a distance and to reduce the emotional stresses of friendship among equals. His intimacies were with women and youths, not age mates.

Physical virility was an exceptionally strong interest throughout Z's life, including athleticism and sexuality. There is ample evidence of soaring ambition, especially revealed in the partial planning of a national movement to seize power. When drunk— as he occasionally was among intimates—he regularly bragged of his virility, of his superiority to other men, and of his ultimate destiny of ruling America and the world.

In this connection it is worth taking note of his double attitude toward playing an authoritative role. On the one hand was the ambition to play the judge to perfection and to rise to yet more authoritative positions; on the other hand was his hostility toward authority, revealed by his occasional tendency to make the court ridiculous with outbursts of levity, by his joy in ridiculing statutes and precedents, and by his persisting unawareness of his own social values. Although married, he refused, in the beginning, to have children, despite the hopes of his wife, and by the time he reluctantly agreed, his wife was too old. In short, he did not assume all the responsibilities conventionally attached to the marriage institution. Also, he was dependent upon his wife's money, and spent freely. Occasionally he would fantasy about resigning from the bench and "cleaning up" in private practice. He had no doubt he could do this, because most of the lawyers who appeared before him struck him as "dopes." Judge Z was able to indulge his cravings to be supported and admired (with comparatively little effort on his part) when the indulgence was coming from a devoted woman or from someone to whom he felt superior on grounds of age, sex or intellect.

His driving ambition and extreme deference cravings, can be interpreted as means of overcoming certain deep doubts about the self, doubts about being fully masculine.

The earlier history of Z throws further light on the genesis of his pattern of personality. His mother was a schoolteacher who had rather "come down in the world," as she believed, by marrying a laborer. Actually her husband was a highly skilled mechanic, but he was not the banker, doctor or lawyer whom the community thought she would marry. This middle-class woman, then, flouted the conventions. But she had no intention of being the wife of a "dirty-fingered mechanic." Partly with the help of her savings, and most certainly as a result of her pressure, Z's father left his trade and became a salesman, thus joining the white-collar, if not the professional, class. Actually the husband seems to have been an easygoing person who did not greatly resent having a strong executive in the house. He did, however, show signs of strain occasionally by getting drunk and abusive, or by staying away longer than necessary on trips and, as neighborhood gossip put it, "running around with other women." The mother, meanwhile, was intent upon the future career of her only son and pushed him hard to do well in school, which he obligingly did. He was praised and encouraged continually for any bright thing he said or did and from an early time acquired many ways of making himself acceptable to older people. He could recite, sing and be generally charming from the earliest years. He became very skillful in playing his parents off against each other, so that they were rivals for his affection. During early school years he became conscious of some contemptuous attitudes in the community toward his father, but these were modified by respect for his great physical prowess and by appreciation of his joviality and gifts. At the same time the father's absences sometimes gave him the sense of being rejected and unloved; and the occasional outbursts of drunken rage both terrorized him and confirmed his doubts about being loved. Although strict, the mother was free with praise, and looked after Z's physical needs and tastes with constant pride. She appears to have been prudish and to have supervised the boy's play contacts very closely. Apparently Z had little opportunity to gang up with other children for fear he would acquire what were vaguely called "bad habits."

From these data it appears that Z was given every opportunity to be loved and admired, even though this was made conditional upon striking achievement. At the same time the boy acquired some doubts about himself and definitely ambivalent attitudes toward authority. It is significant that he never fought back when cuffed by his father but inhibited any expression of rage, feeling merely shocked and helpless even when his father attacked his mother. The mother, too, was careful to insist that he must under no circumstances "flare up" against his father "who didn't really mean it." Z learned to rely on such techniques as patience, followed by sulking withdrawal of affection, succeeded by a gradual giving in to being wooed with renewed expressions of love—and new gifts. In adolescence came a series of circumstances which gave him a precocious start on his political career. As a boy orator he was much in demand and made the acquaintance of a powerful political boss who took him up as a protégé (including sexual intimacy). In the boss there was a powerful hero of the sort Z longed to depend upon, and from him came an unceasing stream of indulgences, which eventually included elevation to the bench.

The history of Z clearly shows the ways in which the agitator bends the opportunities open to him in official and unofficial positions according to the special dynamism of his personality. The bench is to some extent a stage; and it was Z, not Y or X, who magnified the potentialities of the bench for publicity. In any official position, there is an opportunity to play the role of a strong and benevolent authority, or to interpret authority as despotic, erratic, pedantic, inefficient and querulous. It was Y who incorporated within his own personality the conception of himself as a strong, yet benign, authority, who most fully realized these possibilities during his years on the bench. Judge X, on the other hand, thanks to his compulsiveness, emphasized certain despotic, pedantic, inefficient and querulous possibilities. It was Judge Z who most directly and flagrantly tended to cast the whole institution into contempt by his search for notoriety and by a form of erratic conduct different from that of X.

THE STUDY OF POLITICAL LEADERSHIP
LESTER G. SELIGMAN

It is a lesser question for the partisans of democracy to find means of governing the people than to get the people to choose the men most capable of governing.

ALEXIS DE TOCQUEVILLE, in a letter to John Stuart Mill.

Politics by leadership is one of the distinguishing features of the twentieth century. If the eighteenth century enunciated popular sovereignty and direct democracy as a major theme in democratic thought and the nineteenth century was concerned with the challenge of stratification and group conflict, then twentieth century trends have made us sensitive to the role of leadership. The search for the values of security and equality have led to changes in the character of politics. If one were to delineate this newer pattern of a *politics by leadership,* it would include the following: (1) the shift in the center of conflict resolution and initiative from parliamentary bodies and economic institutions to executive leadership; [1] (2) the proliferation of the immediate office of the chief executive from its cabinet-restricted status to a collectivity of co-adjuting instrumentalities; (3) the tendency toward increased centralization of political parties, with the subordination of the victorious parties as instruments for the chief executive; (4) the calculated manipulation of irrationalities by political leadership through the vast power-potential of mass communications; (5) the displacement of the amateur by the professional politician and civil servant; (6) the growth of bureaucracy as a source and technique of executive power but also as a fulcrum which all contestants for power attempt to employ; (7) the growth of interest groups in size, number and influence, with the tendency toward bureaucratization of their internal structure; (8) the changing role of the public that finds its effective voice in a direct and an interactive relation with the chief executive.

What are the social sources of this new pattern of politics? The centralizing tendencies [2] of the modern democratic state need no elaborate recapitu-

CREDIT: Reprinted by permission of author and publisher from *American Political Science Review,* December, 1950, pp. 904–915.

[1] Otto Kirchheimer, "Changes in the Structure of Political Compromise," *Studies in Philosophy and Social Science,* Vol. 9, pp. 264–89 (1941).

[2] On the leadership political trends, see Herman Finer, *The Future of Government* (London, 1946), Ch. 1; Ernest Barker, *Reflections on Government* (London, 1942), pp. 123 ff.; W. Ivor Jennings, *Cabinet Government* (London, 1942); Max Weber, "Politics as a Vocation" in H. H. Gerth and C. Wright Mills (eds.), *From Max Weber: Essays in Sociology* (New York, 1946), pp. 77–128; E. Pendleton Herring, *Presidential Leadership* (New York, 1940); Carl J. Friedrich, *Constitutional Government and Democracy* (New York, 1946), Ch. 18.

lation. The pressing needs arising from economic instability, war, technological change and urbanization have caused new tasks and functions to be entrusted to executive leadership.[3] The new commitments to a sustained full employment policy and national defense augment these tendencies by calling for increased direction and decision by government, while underlying all of the tendencies toward increased executive direction there lies the basic technical factor that in the large state, characterized by universal suffrage, political action presupposes large organization that tends to thrust initiative to the top.[4]

What bears more iteration is the record of failures of leadership as part of the history of our times. The failure to recognize the importance of concentration of responsibility is a principal factor in the defeats of the Weimar Republic, Republican Spain, Austrian Social Democracy, the French *Front Populaire*, America in the 1920's and 1930's, and England during its Baldwin and Chamberlain regimes.[5] Although these failures of leadership arose in part from constitutional limitations and political practices,[6] including the restraint imposed by political traditions, the inadequacies in the caliber of prevailing leadership must be reckoned with. Nor were the failures in leadership confined to organs of the state alone. They also involved such voluntary associations and functional groups as labor, business and church organizations; for democracy rests upon a plurality of capable leadership rather than upon the selection of the single leader. The question may thus be seriously raised as to whether the democracies have been defective by impeding the free and continuous rise of adequate leadership.[7]

However, if the periods of defeat prevailed when crises and men were not congruent, there has also been another source of politics by leadership in the trend of political personalism of dynamic leaders—the two Roosevelts, Wilson, Lloyd George, Clemenceau, Churchill, Poincaré—who have expanded the meaning of executive leadership. By their acts and ideas, these decisive leaders carved new sources and methods of power which have proved indispensable for democratic survival. Each, paradoxically, while

[3] For the growing literature on "constitutional dictatorship," see Frederick M. Watkins' essay, "The Problem of Constitutional Dictatorship," in C. J. Friedrich and Edward S. Mason (eds.), *Public Policy* (Cambridge, 1940), pp. 324–79; Lindsay Rogers, *Crisis Government* (New York, 1934); Clinton L. Rossiter, *Constitutional Dictatorship* (Princeton, 1948).

[4] Studies of large-scale organizations indicate that formal centralization may in fact result in the devolution of authority to elements that are away from the center; thus formal centralization may well result in decentralization in terms of effective influence. This decentralization to other elements of leadership in the structure does not do violence to a conception of politics by leadership, but is quite consistent with it.

[5] On England, see Hamilton Fyfe, "Democracy and Leadership," *Nineteenth Century and After,* Vol. 129, pp. 465–76 (May, 1941); on France during the Popular Front regime, see Lindsay Rogers, "Personal Power and Popular Government," *Southern Review,* Vol. 3, pp. 225–42 (1937–38).

[6] See Arnold Brecht, "Constitutions and Leadership," *Social Research,* Vol. 1, pp. 265–86 (May, 1934). F. A. Hermens stresses the role of P. R. as a major deterrent to leadership in *Democracy or Anarchy* (Notre Dame, 1941).

[7] On this general theme see the stimulating essay by Albert Salomon, "Leadership and Democracy," in Max Ascoli and Fritz Lehmann (eds.), *Political and Economic Democracy* (New York, 1937), pp. 243–54.

resisting institutional restraints contributed to the further institutionalization of executive leadership. Today, with more "built-in" provisions for executive leadership, we have possibly become less dependent upon the dynamic individual figure.[8]

In the larger sphere of social relations, the laying bare of the stresses of urbanization, economic insecurity, large-scale organization and the decline of community has tended to confirm the Hobbesian diagnosis that under certain conditions widespread insecurity seeks resolution in submission to leadership.[9] The bureaucratization process in both the occupational and the non-occupational aspects of living is consonant with impersonality in social relations, creating a vacuum that may be filled by the "solicitude" of a "sincere" leader.[10] As control becomes concentrated at the apex of the pyramid in the large-scale organization, the participant citizen tends to become a dissipated entity. Many observers, searching for the strategic factor to rekindle participation and involvement, have contended that it lies within the discovery and train-

[8] We may note the resurgence of demands for "cabinet government" in America as an expression of this desire to institutionalize executive leadership. (Institutionalization may result in generating the "myth" of the leader although the capacities of the man are not in accord with the myth.)

[9] Karl Mannheim, *Man and Society in an Age of Reconstruction* (London, 1940); Erich Fromm, *Escape from Freedom* (New York, 1941).

[10] See the interesting study by Robert K. Merton, *Mass Persuasion* (New York, 1947). On bureaucratization and leadership generally, see Robert Michels, *Political Parties: A Sociological Study of the Oligarchical Tendencies of Modern Democracy* (Eden and Cedar Paul trans.; Glencoe, 1949), together with the writings of Gaetano Mosca and Max Weber.

ing of a liberating, democratic leadership. Attesting to this is the growing literature in education, industrial management, voluntary associations and public administration, which is devoted to the study of the recruitment and training of such leadership.

Such are the roots of the new concern with political leadership in democracy. One of the tasks that confronts us is defining the concept of democratic leadership. The empirical face of the new politics requires new democratic self-assessments in terms of its value consequences and implications. It is patent that democratic leadership must not mean the surrender of any of the values of free expression, public sharing in policy, the consideration of men as men and not things, and the procedural processes of discussion and compromise. Yet the pattern of politics associated with leadership and centralization which brings indispensable democratic virtues of more widespread social welfare and equalization of opportunity cannot but challenge other democratic values.

We might therefore suggest that the concept of leadership for democracy should include in its formulation an attempt to answer the following questions: How can a democracy set up leaders, from whom it desires direction, without paying submission as its price? Can democracy furnish leadership that will provide for change with responsibility and for power that is scrupulously used? There are also subproblems of leadership for democracy: Can democracy provide for the orderly continuity and succession of leadership? Is the recruitment of leadership representative and not restricted? Does the path of ascent enhance or weaken the capacity of potential leaders to cope with the problematic situation confronting leadership today?[11] Does the institutionalization of the executive tend to screen leaders from accurate perception of public needs?[12] These are problems of institutional adjustment but also problems for democratic values. Democratic thought has not yet adequately wrestled with the problems of the implications of leadership.[13] Motivated perhaps by its opposition to authority,[14] it has regrettably left to the proponents of authoritarian and aristocratic-conservative politics the elaboration of a political theory of leadership.[15] Yet leadership concern is but the new aspect of the age-old problem of representation in politics, a question that has always been a root one for democratic theory.

These remarks are but introductory to the consideration of the status of political leadership study today. If the subject is indeed of considerable importance, what is being done towards its exploration?

I. RECENT STUDIES OF LEADERSHIP

A. Leadership as a Social Status-Position. The study of leadership is sometimes focussed upon the conception of leadership as a status index and position.[16] Such studies attempt to answer the following types of questions: Whom is the social and political struc-

---

[11] A question asked by Brooks Adams in *The Law of Civilization and Decay* (New York, 1943).

[12] The writer is engaged in preliminary research on the men of the "inner circle" of presidential leadership, in which this question, among others, is explored.

[13] Joseph A. Schumpeter addresses himself to this question of reformulation of the conception of democratic politics in *Capitalism, Socialism, and Democracy* (2d ed.; New York, 1947), Chs. 21–23. Schumpeter stretches his "theory of competitive leadership" too far in relegating the public to a mass-passivity status, and he does not go far enough in considering extra-governmental group factors in politics.

[14] Locke's chapter "Of Prerogative" in his *Second Treatise of Civil Government* showed appreciation of the necessity of executive leadership in the democratic state.

[15] See Carl Schmitt, *Staat, Bewegung, Volk* (Hamburg, 1935); Ernst Rudolf Huber, *Verfassung* (Hamburg, 1937), pp. 90 ff; René de Visme Williamson, "The Fascist Concept of Representation," *Journal of Politics*, Vol. 3, pp. 29–41 (Feb., 1941); Émile Faguet, *The Cult of Incompetence* (Beatrice Barstow trans.; New York, 1911), among others.

[16] Illustrative are the following: Harold J. Laski, "The Personnel of the English Cabinet, 1801–1924," *American Political Science Review*, Vol. 22, pp. 12–31 (Feb., 1928); John G. Heinberg, "The Personnel Structure of French Cabinets," *American Political Science Review*, Vol. 33, pp. 267–78 (April, 1939); Pitirim A. Sorokin, "Leaders of Labor and Radical Movements in the United States and Foreign Countries," *American Journal of Sociology*, Vol. 33, pp. 382–411 (Nov., 1927); (for a summary of many such studies, Pitirim A. Sorokin, *Social Mobility* [New York, 1927]); John Brown Mason, "Lawyers in the 71st to 75th Congress," *Rocky Mountain Law Review*, Vol. 10, pp. 43–52 (Dec., 1937); Madge M. McKinney, "The Personnel of the Seventy-seventh Congress," *American Political Science Review*, Vol. 36, pp. 67–75 (Feb., 1942); J. F. S. Ross, *Parliamentary Representation* (London, 1948); Marion Brockway, *A Study of the Geographical, Occupational, and Political Characteristics of Congressmen* (M.A. thesis, University of Kansas, 1934); Frank P. Bourgin, *Personnel of the American Senate* (M.A. thesis, Claremont College, 1933). Consult especially Bruce Lannes Smith, Harold D. Lasswell, and Ralph D. Casey, *Propaganda, Communication and Public Opinion* (Princeton, 1946), for references to many studies on the social recruitment of political leadership.

ture elevating to eminence? From what strata of society are leaders recruited? What occupational skills do they possess? What are the channels of their ascent to power? Generally, the broad significance of such studies is their attempt to answer to what extent there is circulation and representativeness in the composition of political leadership. All too frequently, however, this type of research results in little else than statistical tabulation of collectivities of leaders. It fails to answer completely why particular individuals rose to the top. From this standpoint, such collectivity studies would be enriched by including more intensive case studies of one or more representatives of the sample. Moreover, the negative implications of such studies are sometimes more significant than the positive reports. Thus one question that ought always to be asked is to what extent there are blocks, and what is the nature of the blocks, to the free recruitment of leadership in our society. How do changes in leadership recruitment occur as related to (1) political changes (such as the direct election of Senators); (2) economic changes (such as inflation-depression periods); (3) war, etc. We are indeed in need of systematic and historical trend studies of ascent and recruitment aspects of politics as a career line, which arrive at generalizations in answer to the questions posed above.

B. *Leadership in Types of Social Structures.* Owing principally to the stimulating work of the late Kurt Lewin, there has been much interest and research in the subject of small primary-group leadership. Lewin and his students conducted several ingenious experiments involving the change of leadership in small groups, and obtained results which pointed out the decisive role of leadership in the formation and maintenance of group morale.[17] The experiment conducted with three "atmospheres" (democratic, authoritarian and laissez-faire) attempted to prove that democratic leadership is the most constructive and creative type of leadership,[18] although it did not prove that democratic leadership is best under all situations. This experiment does not justify leaping from a small, relatively simple situation in order to argue its homologies with the larger, more complex political milieu.[19] The democratic atmosphere of an experimental group is not the microcosm of a democratic society. Political life occurs for the most part in large, institutional types of organizations, in which contacts are secondary and of which rules and forms are more characteristic than

[17] See Ronald Lippit, "Field Theory and Experiment in Social Psychology: Autocratic and Democratic Atmospheres," *American Journal of Sociology*, Vol. 45, pp. 26–49 (July, 1939); and also Alex Bavelas and Kurt Lewin, "Training in Democratic Leadership," *Journal of Abnormal and Social Psychology*, Vol. 37, pp. 115–19 (Jan., 1942). For other studies in small group leadership, see Paul Pigors, *Leadership or Domination* (Boston, 1935); Thomas N. Whitehead, *Leadership in a Free Society* (Cambridge, 1936); Fritz Redl, "Group Emotion and Leadership," *Psychiatry*, Vol. 5, pp. 573–96 (Nov., 1942); Ferenc Merei, Group Leadership and Institutionalization," *Human Relations*, Vol. 2, pp. 23–40 (no. 4, 1949).

[18] Lippit, *loc. cit.*

[19] Lewin never committed this error. See "The Special Case of Germany," in his posthumous *Resolving Social Conflicts* (New York, 1948) and note its kinship to Mary P. Follett's emphasis upon primary groups as the base of a dynamic citizenry. (Her collected papers appear as *Dynamic Administration* [New York, 1942].) See also Alexander Dunlop Lindsay's *The Essentials of Democracy* (Philadelphia, 1929).

they are of face-to-face groups. Moreover, leadership in politics is associated with emergent features of leadership to a greater extent than would be true in an experimentally-imposed one. Political leadership is likewise associated with office-holding, which provides an increment of legal power to the office-occupant, and which in turn contributes to leadership acceptance.

However, the study of leadership in small groups does have several potential uses for the study of politics. Among them are the following: (1) In understanding the internal workings of large political parties, we would profit from the study of informal group leadership. (2) In studying the use of mass communications by political leaders, we could learn much from the function of small-group leaders as transmission belts or resistances in the communication process. (3) In the study of chief executives in their inner circles, "kitchen cabinets," etc., we would again find application for this type of study. (4) Much work remains to be done on small-group leadership in public administration agencies, in interest groups, etc. And there are doubtlessly many more possible applications of the facts governing small-group leadership to the study of political relations.[20]

C. *Leadership as Organizational Function and Institutional Position.* In recent years there has been a burgeoning of the literature on leadership in formal industrial organizations.[21] Owing largely to the work of Elton Mayo and the group whose center is the Harvard Business School, there has appeared a series of studies addressed to the problem of the malaise of morale in such organizations.[22] These excellent studies have laid bare the informal structure that underlies any formal organization. The studies have indicated that the problems of morale, coordination and efficiency in large-scale organizations have been erroneously conceived to be those of technical arrangements. In the task of integrating the web of informal relationship to the goals of the association, lies the crucial problem. And toward the solution of this problem, leadership plays a vital role. Leadership, to use Chester I. Barnard's phrase, is the "strategic factor" in establishing the kind of communication which resolves the tensions arising from the task of coordination. Much of the writing of

[20] Political scientists, in developing our comparatively rich literature on urban political machines, long ago recognized the influence of primary contact relationships. See, for example, Sonya Forthal, *Cogwheels of Democracy* (New York, 1946); J. T. Salter, *Boss Rule* (New York, 1935); Roy V. Peel, *The Political Clubs of New York City* (New York, 1936).

[21] The literature of this group is abundant and is largely summarized in Elton Mayo, *The Social Problems of an Industrial Civilization* (Boston, 1945). The most significant work for a theoretical treatment of leadership is Chester I. Barnard, *The Functions of the Executive* (Cambridge, 1946).

[22] Political scientists should find much of relevance to their interests when the study of personal ascendancy in economic development, viz., business entrepreneurship, is advanced. See the following three papers, which were presented at the annual meeting of the Economic History Association, 1946, and which may be found in Supplement VI of the *Journal of Economic History*, entitled *The Tasks of Economic History* (1946): Arthur H. Cole, "An Approach to the Study of Entrepreneurship," pp. 1–15; Robert A. East, "The Business Entrepreneur in a Changing Colonial Economy, 1763–1795," pp. 16–27; Chester McArthur Destler, "Entrepreneurial Leadership among the 'Robber Barons': A Trial Balance," pp. 28–49.

this school is, therefore, devoted to the problem of the selection and training of able administrative leadership that will effectively organize cooperation.

As outstanding as has been the research by this school, its relevance to the study of political leadership is subject to some limitations. The first lies in the fact that politics occurs within a consensual framework of more conflicting purposes than the dominant purposes that characterize industrial organizations. Second, it is not the primary function of the political leader to *administer conflicts* or devise structural devices for their mitigation (although this is one of his available methods). Third, the analysis offered by this group ignores the factor of power. The term *communication* is used positively as the lubricant of coordination, so as to suggest that upon effective communication solely hinges proper coordination. That the hierarchical structure in industrial organization may represent power and value divisions between those who have more and those who have less, is virtually ignored. Contrast the type of analysis of executive function in the writings of this group with the analysis of leadership as organizational power in political machines in Harold F. Gosnell's *Machine Politics*. Fourth, the explicit goal of administered social harmony generates a somewhat antipolitical bias.[23] Fifth, since a large area of political relations is concerned with competition and conflict between hierarchies, the analysis of a formal organization cannot adequately explain such relations. It is true, of course, that leadership relationships within formal organizations have much to do with their external political behavior; that is to say, other factors than political ones must bear analysis for explanations of this external behavior.

D. Leadership as a Personality Type. The attempt to elucidate political behavior by personality types dates back to the work of Ernst Kretschmer[24] and Edward Spranger.[25] The individual most influential in recent times in formulating such a typology in terms of the newer dynamic psychology is Harold D. Lasswell. In his *Psychopathology and Politics*[26] he employed psychoanalytic insights to lay down the basic premise that political motivations had their roots in subconscious sources framed during the early periods of human development. From this developed the basic formulation that the "political personality" displaced private motives onto public objects and rationalized them in terms of the public good.

More recently, Lasswell has gone beyond his earlier formulations by using the recently advanced concept of "character structure" as the basis for a typology of political functional types, such as the agitator, theorist, bureaucrat, etc. The concept of political type is defined as embracing individuals

[24] *Physique and Character* (W. J. H. Sprott trans., from the 2d rev. ed.; New York, 1931).

[25] *Lebensformen* (Halle, 1924).

[26] (Chicago, 1930). One of the significant virtues of Lasswell's work is that he has consistently viewed the leadership phenomenon in terms of its power and policy implications and in terms of a broad context of an empirical political theory.

[23] See the penetrating treatment by Chester I. Barnard, *The Dilemmas of Leadership in the Democratic Process* (Princeton, 1939). One is tempted to ask whether these dilemmas are "abnormal" or whether they are not virtues of democracy.

who are "power seekers, searching out the power institutions of the society into which they are born and devoting themselves to the capture and use of government." [27] The political type is thus a "developmental type who passes through a distinctive career line in which power opportunities of each situation are selected in preference to other opportunities." [28] The character-type delineation would stress that leadership is both a function of a structural personality type, and in dynamic interaction with larger social situations that select individuals of particular types for leadership.

The question has been asked, however, whether the concept of character types adequately permits us to assess not only developmental factors but situational factors as well. There is a tendency on the part of some students employing this approach to make "character structure" an all-inclusive "sack" in terms of which all behavior of political figures is explained, disregarding the influence of the immediate situations and institutional factors as determinants.

The concept of character structure is a notable advance since it attempts to catch social determinants in behavior. With this tool, much work remains to be done. Those who anticipate the complete synthesis of psychological and social factors in political behavior must await developments in social psychological research. A good full-length treatment of particular political leaders that will attempt to cast psychological factors in their social contextual mold is needed. In the meantime, those employing character structure concepts are doing some of the most vibrant and stimulating work in the analysis of political leadership.[29]

E. Political Biography. In America political biography never achieved the vogue characteristic in other countries. However, there has of late been a renaissance in such writing after a long decline. The late nineteenth century gave us the "conservationist" biographies, such as Nicolay and Hay's *Abraham Lincoln.* The twentieth presented us with Albert J. Beveridge's *The Life of John Marshall,* a somewhat unbalanced study that was nevertheless a stride toward analysis beyond mere recording. Henry F. Pringle's *Theodore Roosevelt* must rank high because its author attempted to discover a meaningful pattern in a most complex political figure, although it suffers from Pringle's limited data and sardonic dislike of his subject. Compare Pringle's study, however, with Claude Bowers' study of the challenging figure of Albert Beveridge, wherein the author meanders gracefully with no apparent attempt at interpretation and analysis. In more recent days we have had some examples that elevated the quality of this craft. Harry Barnard's study of John Altgeld was more than historical revelation in its keen, detached grasp of the man and his political context. C. Vann Woodward has drawn an excellent delineation of both the man and his setting in his biography of the Populist demagogue, Tom Watson. The work of Allan Nevins and Arthur Schle-

[27] *Power and Personality* (New York, 1948), p. 20.

[28] *Ibid.,* p. 21.

[29] See David Riesman, *The Lonely Crowd—A Study of The Changing American Character* (New Haven, 1950).

singer, Jr., has likewise represented advances. Dixon Wecter's *The Hero in America,* a series of essays, caught the key factor of the representational character of leadership and gave adequate attention to the function of public acceptance.

In general, political biography abounds in rich insights but suffers from its lack of criteria and conceptualization. Either no questions are asked or there is confusion as to the types of questions which a full-length treatment of the political leader might answer. It is somewhat paradoxical that, despite the marked stress given in American historiography to the role of the political personality, the analytical literature in political biography is as sparse as it is. One consequently awaits the application of theoretical insights of social science to the study of political biography. (It is encouraging to note that some historians, notably Roy Nichols, T. Cochran and Walter Johnson, are proclaiming the necessity for a more adequately delineated history of politics.)

II. THE MEANING OF LEADERSHIP —TRAITS OR REPRESENTATION?

The preoccupation with the "essence" of leadership has long beset the conception of leadership. It may be, as Professor Carl J. Friedrich has indicated, a reflection of democratic thinking that we have become disenchanted with a conception of leadership posited upon the existence of a peculiar substance possessed only by some. In the literature alluded to in the previous pages, the conception of leadership as relational, that is, dependent upon acceptance within particular contexts, is universally acknowledged. Thus the long search for leadership traits has apparently come to the trough of its promise, where it may well rest for some time.[30] R. M. Stogdill concludes, after his long and exhaustive analysis of the experimental literature, that "leadership is not a matter of passive status, or of the mere possession of some combination of traits. It appears rather to be a working relationship among members of a group, in which the leader acquires status through active participation and demonstration of his capacity for carrying cooperative tasks through to completion." [31] With regard to traits, he adds, "Significant aspects of this capacity for organizing and expediting cooperative effort appear to be intelligence, alertness to the needs and motives of others, and insight into situations, further reinforced by such habits as responsibility, initiative, persistence, and self-confidence." It is noteworthy that the lists of traits that are distilled from the literature usually result in some tautologies, since they refer to conduct by the leader in a particular situation. Traits are not to be ignored nor dismissed, but recent literature has refined our perception of the functional interdependence of leadership traits and situational factors.

[30] The relational concept of leadership was elaborated some time ago by sociologists, notably Max Weber, Robert Michels, Georg Simmel and C. H. Cooley. See Irving Knickerbocker, "Leadership: A Conception and Some Implications," *Journal of Social Issues,* Vol. 4, pp. 23–40 (Summer, 1948).

[31] Ralph M. Stogdill, "Personal Factors Associated with Leadership: A Survey of the Literature," *Journal of Psychology,* Vol. 25, p. 66 (Jan., 1948).

The characteristic of active participation as a leadership trait calls for comment. Active participation follows from the conventional conceptions of leadership as "dynamic." This overt dynamic quality may be a presumption about leadership not applicable in all instances. Thus it is conceivable that leadership may be exercised without the leader's awareness or conscious striving to be a leader. For situations of this type the concept of a "central person" might be useful.[32] The term might well be used to describe a person who represents a new trend in conduct or ideas without being conscious of leading or directing, a person who even is subject to imitation without *attempting* to influence.

More recent literature has stressed two central factors in the analysis of leadership. First, emphasis has been placed on the hypothesis that *leadership is a function of acceptance by followers*. A leader is not a leader unless he is accepted by followers; leadership is a representational role. Over a generation ago, Charles Horton Cooley expressed this point in the following manner: "All leadership takes place through the communication of ideas to the minds of others, and unless the ideas are so presented as to be congenial to those other minds, they will evidently be rejected." [33]

Secondly, the point has been stressed that *who is chosen as a leader is related to the tensions and values of a particular situation*. This point has been made repeatedly in the literature, but perhaps most cogently in the experimental work of Helen Hall Jennings.[34] Employing the sociometric methods of J. L. Moreno, she arrived at the following conclusion: "Both leadership and isolation appear as phenomena which arise out of the individual differences in interpersonal capacity for participation and as phenomena which are indigenous to the specific social milieu in which they are produced. Individuals who in this community appear as leaders may or may not be found to be leaders in another community of which they later become a part; likewise, individuals who in this community appear as isolates may or may not be found in another community later to remain isolated." [35] The same point was made in the conclusion of the experimental work performed in selecting leaders for OSS during the war by Dr. H. A. Murray and his associates.[36]

In sum, the recent literature on leadership has given us a synthetic

---

[32] The term is used by Redl, *loc. cit.*

[33] *Human Nature and the Social Order* (New York, 1902), p. 294. Chester I. Barnard, in addition to his contributions in other works cited, carefully analyzes this relational aspect of leadership in his chapter on "The Nature of Leadership," in *Organization and Management* (Cambridge, 1948).

[34] See her *Leadership and Isolation* (New York, 1943) and her "Leadership—A Dynamic Redefinition," *Journal of Educational Sociology*, Vol. 17, pp. 431–33 (Mar., 1944). For an interesting application of these methods to discover "political leadership," see the note by Charles P. Loomis, Douglas Ensminger and Jane Woolley, "Neighborhoods and Communities in County Planning," *Rural Sociology*, Vol. 6, pp. 339–41 (Dec., 1941); also Albert J. Murphy, "A Study of the Leadership Process," *American Sociological Review*, Vol. 6, pp. 674–87 (Oct., 1941).

[35] Jennings, *Leadership and Isolation*, p. 204. See also Pigors, *op. cit.*, p. 16.

[36] U.S. Office of Strategic Services, *Assessment of Men; Selection of Personnel for the Office of Strategic Services* (New York, 1948).

view of both traits and functional relationship to group and situation. The more organic view of leadership should permit a convergence of points of view that should make leadership no less complex, but clearer in its basic conception.

III. SOME SUGGESTIONS FOR THE AGENDA

A paper that attempts a survey of the literature must consider the various approaches to the study of leadership. It is apparent that present methods are widely varied. In the consideration of each approach, suggestions were offered as to potential lines of inquiry. In the present stage of development of the social sciences we cannot suggest one single approach as *the* method, and we must necessarily lean upon a fruitful eclecticism. But perhaps we can help solve the problem of approach by delimiting a frame of reference within which the study of political leadership may be pursued.

As political scientists, we are concerned with the conflict, power and policy implications of leadership. Our present literature is largely concerned with understanding leadership within types of social structure and in terms of defining political roles. It thus focusses largely upon leader-led relationships within the confines of group structures. For political scientists this is but one aspect of the study of leadership, to wit, its representative and technique dimensions within groups. We are not interested exclusively in these relationships, nor in the phenomenon of leadership per se. We are instead concerned with a politics by leadership, that is, a conception of politics that finds power factors in society best approachable through the understanding of leader-led and leader-leader relations.[37]

A politics by leadership conception would concern itself with generalizations concerning four types of relations: (1) the relations of leaders to led within particular political structures, (2) the relationship between leaders of political structures, (3) the relationship between leaders of one structure and the followers of another, and (4) the relationship between leaders and the "unorganized" or non-affiliated.[38] *Within such a matrix the study of leadership may be actively pursued.*

For the formulation of such a conception it is necessary that we elaborate concepts of (1) types of relationship between leaders and led, that is, a characterization of kinds of representative relationships we may find, (2) the classification of leaders by functional types, and (3) types of relationships between leaders in the formation of public policy. The problem of developing such categories as these is made difficult by the plurality of approaches which may be used. In other words, if we say that we are interested in types of relationship between leaders and led, shall we characterize the relationship in terms of the rank and file, in terms

---

[37] It should be emphasized that such a conception of politics entails no value presuppositions as to the inferiority of the public. It is not elitism. On the contrary, such an approach recognizes the vital and sustained role of the public in political direction.

[38] It may be somewhat paradoxical to our notions that political influence is directly correlated with the degree of organization of interests, but if the relatively isolated are identified with the "white collar" floating vote, their isolation makes them most influential politically.

of the leader's inner circle, or in terms of the hierarchy of sub-leaders among his following? It would appear that the type of relationship would vary in each instance. In a similar vein, the classification of leaders by functional types can be made in terms of their skill function, their institutional position, the character of the group they lead, or the function they perform in the policy process.

The approach which we would find most useful is the one that centers always on the power and policy context of leadership behavior. Thus leader-led relationships ought to be considered in terms of the distribution of power and influence between leader and led. Leadership types ought to be cast in terms of the role they play in influencing policy. From this standpoint, leadership might be characterized in terms of the scope of the leaders' activities and in terms of the techniques they employ.

One final question must be raised. If leadership research must see the leader in terms of his intra-group relationships as a basis for relating this to his inter-group relationships, to what extent should the power contestants be categorized as groups? For example, if one lumps together the full galaxy of pressure groups, lobbies and functional groups as "groups," the differences in cohesiveness and articulation of structure are so great as to stretch

the meaning of "group" beyond the limits of its elasticity. Leader-led relations do exist in these groups, but case studies are necessary to indicate what type of relationships exist within such groups as part and parcel of the study of leadership between these groups.

We may sum up by stating that the areas for profitable leadership research may be denoted as (1) recruitment or developmental studies, i.e., studies concerned with social origins and career-lines of political leaders; (2) studies of the representative dimension of leadership—the character of acceptance by followers; (3) studies of political leadership techniques; (4) specific case studies of leadership functions in typologically expressed political situations.

This paper has touched on some research questions and avenues for research. Its general purpose has been, in short, (1) to indicate the problems that make the study of political leadership of importance from both the empirical and the value standpoint, (2) to point out the nature of some recent research on leadership and its relevance for political science, (3) to urge the importance of theoretical formulations that will build a conception of politics by leadership, within which particular problems for research would assume significance, and (4) to suggest some specific areas for research.

THE STATECRAFT OF PRESIDENT JEFFERSON
JAMES S. YOUNG

To assert that the constitutional framers intended to prevent the President from exercising influence over men and policies on Capitol Hill would be an overstatement. But it seems beyond argument that the Constitution provided a wholly inadequate vehicle for presidential leadership of Congress. That the framers made the Chief Executive independent of the representative body was no inconsiderable accomplishment in a nation whose colonial experience gave every reason for mistrusting executive power. Nothing would have been more out of keeping with the post-Revolutionary political mood nor out of character with the organizing principles of the Constitution than for the framers to have admitted into it the concept of presidential leadership of the legislative branch.

As ratified, the Constitution indeed opened fewer and less promising avenues for legislative influence to the head of government than it did to ordinary citizens outside government. If the constitution gave the President the authority to propose action and rec-

ommend measures to Congress, it gave not only this but more to the citizenry: upon citizens but not upon the President it conferred the right to petition Congress—in modern usage, to mount "pressure" campaigns—and an all but unlimited freedom to organize as need dictates for the pursuit of legislative objectives. If the President was given a potentially important source of influence in the conditional veto over measures passed, the ultimate sanction against unwanted legislation was given to the voters, not to the President. None of the framers' objectives was more explicit than to deny the head of government any influence over the selection, tenure, or career advancement of legislators. If the Constitution gave the President authority to summon Congress in extraordinary session, nothing in the Constitution ensured a hearing for the President's views. Upon citizens and states, but not upon the President, the Constitution conferred the opportunity and the right to have spokesmen on Capitol Hill. Far from providing legislative representation for the President's interest, the framers took special pains to avoid it. The ingenuity of their devices for ensuring disharmony or at least divergence of viewpoint between Congress and President—devices ranging

CREDIT: Reprinted by permission of author and publisher from *The Washington Community, 1800–1828* by James S. Young, pp. 157–178. Copyright 1966 © Columbia University Press. [*Footnotes renumbered.*]

from staggered elections to different constituencies for the two—was matched only by the elaborateness of their schemes to ensure frustration of action when different viewpoints proved irreconcilable. There remained, as a potential instrument of leadership, the President's appointive power; but this was shared with the Senate for all those executive positions which were, at Congress' option, made subject to confirmation.

Of legal authority for presidential leadership of Congress, then, the Constitution was nearly as bare as Mother Hubbard's cupboard.

No more promising avenues to presidential leadership were opened by the social structure of the governmental community. If the Constitution preferred constituents over the President for access to the legislative branch, the retreat of legislators into a separate and exclusive community of their own, and their deployment inside their community into boardinghouse fraternities, ensured priority to the influence of their associates over the influence of the White House across the swamp. The Constitution and the structure of the Washington community together thus tended to relegate the President to third place in the hierarchy of influence over the legislative branch, after constituents and colleagues. And, just as the Constitution legally defined the President's position as an outsider to Capitol Hill, the structure and values of the governmental community defined the President socially as an outsider. Tacit rules reinforcing social segregation were especially stringent in the case of the President, and community custom, more explicitly than anything in the Constitution, kept the presidential tiger from the gates of Capitol Hill. Etiquette forbade the Chief Executive to set foot inside the legislative compound for any purposes but inauguration, attendance at a few other ceremonial functions, and to sign bills on the last day of the session, the last being an accommodation to Congress and one which must have gone far toward neutralizing the political feasibility of the pocket veto.[1] Early-rising legislators might glimpse President Adams trotting around the Capitol on his dawn constitutionals, and President Jefferson might be seen on rare occasions at the Sunday sermon in the Hall of Representatives; but confinement in the White House was a rule never broken by any Jeffersonian President for missions of persuasion, political negotiation, or leadership to Capitol Hill.

The morass of the Tiber swamp intervening between the Capitol and the executive mansion, and the rutted causeway pretending to bridge it, were fitting symbols for what the community arrangements of the governing group offered the President by way of access to power on the Hill.

What, then, was left to the President for providing that "rallying point" which his party, and that stabilizing force which the Congress, so sorely needed? There remained precisely what presidential power in Congress has always largely, though not exclusively, depended upon: the exercise of political skill, of statecraft, by the occupant of the White House. The

---

[1] John Quincy Adams, *Memoirs*, ed. Charles F. Adams (Philadelphia: J. B. Lippincott, 1874–1875), IV, 80–81; V, 118–119.

means and tools of leadership which the Constitution and the community culture all but denied to him the President had to improvise out of wit and ingenuity, as his political talents, circumstance, statutes, and good fortune permitted. Possibly the framers of the Constitution intended it this way—intended that leadership be politically achieved rather than legally ascribed. Probably they did not intend leadership at all. Probably they believed they had invented a system of government that would make leader-follower relationships unnecessary within the ruling establishment. More likely they never comprehended the risks of government by "separate and rival interests," never foresaw a Congress unable to control conflict within itself, and never foresaw that the Presidency would have to supply the unifying influence needed to secure the Congress and the fragments of the nation it represented against disintegration. For it would tax the imagination to believe that the framers intended so much to depend so largely on the chance of having a skilled politician for a President.

It is, therefore, statecraft more than institutions one must study in dealing with presidential-congressional relations during the Jeffersonian era. The task of analysis is infinitely the more difficult because of it: difficult because American political literature has yielded, to guide analysis, but one published work on the principal subject of statecraft; [2] diffi-

cult because the historical distance of the Jeffersonian era makes it impossible to recapture the subtleties involved in this most subtle of political relationships; difficult because of the inherent elusiveness of a relationship in which matters of personality and individual style are so pervasively involved and so vitally important; difficult, finally, because the relationship had to be in large measure arcane, and one can never be sure that all its most important aspects have found their way into the written record of early Washington.

Yet the historical record is not barren. It provides, indeed, somewhat more evidence of presidential efforts at leadership on Capitol Hill than of efforts made by legislators themselves. [We] . . . will attempt to answer, on the basis of this record, four principal questions. First, were there in the Jeffersonian era any circumstantial aids to the winning of presidential influence on the Hill? Second, what were the means devised and used by Presidents for this purpose? Third, were the means sufficient? Did they allow Presidents to perform from a distance and as outsiders the task of political management that legislators themselves would not regularly perform? Fourth, what explanations does a community study of the governing group suggest for the success or failure of presidential leadership in the period 1801–28?

As to circumstantial aids, four aspects of the political environment in Jeffersonian times would appear, on the surface at least, to have facilitated presidential influence on Capitol Hill.

There was, first, the predominance of foreign affairs over the domestic work of the governmental com-

---

[2] No nation has been so dependent upon statecraft for the effective management of its conflicts and produced so little literature on the subject. Richard Neustadt's *Presidential Power* stands alone.

munity. Except for the admission of new states and the administration of territories, the attention of the Washington community during the period 1801–28 was principally absorbed in that area of activity which has traditionally given large scope to presidential initiative, namely, foreign affairs: the war against the Barbary pirates; the acquisition of Louisiana from France; the tortuous negotiations with Spain for the acquisition of West Florida; the Seminole War; the working out of a policy toward the emerging nations of Latin America and the formulation of the Monroe Doctrine; the readjustment of relationships with France in the aftermath of her revolution, during a period which saw Napoleon's rise and fall; and the prosecution of the second war against the colonial parent of the young nation, the War of 1812. Predominance of foreign policy issues by no means assures a President of influence in Congress. But the tendency of such predominance, recognized generally by students of American politics, is to increase the political risks of opposition to the President, to elicit whatever forces there be for unity, and to heighten that dependence of legislators upon the President (in this case, for policy initiative and information) which is the keystone of presidential influence on the Hill.

Second, Presidents of the Jeffersonian era faced only negligible competition from organized citizen groups for access to, and influence among, legislators. The negligibility of organized citizen demands upon Congress was, to be sure, a mixed blessing. For if it tended to reduce the President's competition and saved Congress from what

might well have been, in the Jeffersonian era, divisive influences the community could not have begun to cope with, it also denied the President the important supplementary source of support for his legislative objectives that lobbyists may provide. Nonetheless, the virtual absence of organized "pressure-group" representatives at the seat of government heightened the chances for the President to dominate the communication channels to Congress. It saved the voice of the White House from being lost in a general noise of lobbying.

Third, the method of presidential nomination by congressional caucus (and of presidential election by the House of Representatives when, as in 1801 and 1824, no candidate received an electoral majority) assured Jeffersonian Presidents of some degree of personal support on Capitol Hill at the time of their accession to office. This was not necessarily majority support, as discussion of the nominating caucus . . . indicates. Nor was the caucus without its liabilities to the President. For if it assured incoming Presidents a circle of partisans on the Hill, it also must have brought them into office with a passel of political debts to legislators, not so easily discharged without compromising the independence of their office as indebtedness to the politicians outside government who now manage presidential nominations. Nevertheless, the fact that congressional approval was virtually a precondition to attaining the headship of government gave Jeffersonian Presidents stature, at the time of their accession, as the men with the largest demonstrated support inside the governmental community, as well as a potential sphere of influence on Capitol Hill.

Last, all Presidents of the Jeffersonian era had service experience in Congress prior to entering the White House. Jefferson served four years as presiding officer of the Senate, moving directly from one of the largest boardinghouse groups on Capitol Hill to the executive mansion. Madison was a Republican leader in the House for a considerable period before moving to the Secretaryship of State and thence to the Presidency. Monroe had served four years, and John Quincy Adams five, in the Senate. All Jeffersonian Presidents were members of the governmental community at Washington when they were elected to the Presidency, and none came into the office without having had the opportunity to learn at firsthand the facts of political life on Capitol Hill.[3]

With these more or less favorable auguries, among the several unfavorable ones mentioned earlier, how did Presidents go about the work of preserving and enlarging that sphere of influence with which they came into

---

[3] Previous service in Congress was not a peculiar attribute of Jeffersonian Presidents. Except for Zachary Taylor, all Chief Magistrates through Abraham Lincoln had seen previous service in Congress, if the Presidency of the Senate is counted as congressional service. In the four-year span of Monroe's second administration (1821–25) seven of the next ten Presidents were office-holders at Washington, all but one of the seven, Secretary Adams (a former Senator), being legislators. The common belief that Andrew Jackson was a "rank outsider," as Elmer E. Schattschneider calls him, is erroneous. [See his *Party Government* (New York: Farrar and Rinehart, 1942), p. 152.] He had served in both houses of Congress, resigning from the Senate in 1825, presidential ambitions thwarted, to return triumphant from Tennessee three years later, dressed conspicuously in the political garb of an "outsider."

office? The record indicates four presidentially improvised practices directly or indirectly related to the acquisition of influence in Congress: the selection of confidential agents among legislators themselves; the deputizing of cabinet members for political liaison with Congress; "social lobbying" of legislators at the executive mansion; and the use of a presidential newspaper. A dubious fifth may have been the political use of the President's appointive power. Of the Presidents holding office from 1801 to 1828, the first was the only one to employ all the techniques mentioned above and the only one, it seems, to pursue with vigor the task of leading Congress. Any exploration of presidential leadership of Congress must therefore have to do principally with Thomas Jefferson's eight years in the White House.

Jefferson's enlistment of legislators to act as his agents on the Hill has been noted. The practice was to single out individual legislators for "confidential" communication who, privy to the President's wishes and presumably acting under his guidance, would steer desired bills through the legislative process. What Jefferson had to gain by this innovation in presidential-congressional relations is obvious enough to require no elaboration. So long as enough legislators— and the right legislators—could be persuaded to undertake the job, the President acquired not merely that legislative representation of his interest which the Constitution denied but also an indirect participation in internal legislative processes where direct participation was constitutionally proscribed. Equally important must have been the advantages to the President of having confidential sources of political intelligence from the Hill. Jefferson's apparently impressive record of legislative successes, which is widely believed to have resulted from "drilling" the membership in party caucuses, may well have been due instead to his foreknowledge of congressional sentiment afforded in part by these confidential agents, and the resulting opportunity to adjust the timing, language, and content of his legislative proposals accordingly.

What limits there were to the effectiveness of this technique, and the reasons why it ceased to have prominence when its innovator went out of office, will be assayed after the other presidential techniques have been described. At this point, however, it is necessary to take issue in part with the leading interpretation that congressional "leadership was neither the prerogative of seniority nor a privilege conferred by the House; it was distinctly the gift of the president." [4]

As previously noted, it is questionable whether the term "leaders" accurately denotes the relationship of these men to their fellow party members on the Hill. "Spokesmen" for the President would appear better to describe the legislative role of men whose position was not legitimated by seniority or by election of their colleagues, as leadership in the modern Congress is; of men who, on the evidence of the written record, enjoyed no opportunities for influence over legislative procedure that were not available to any other legislator; and whose only distinguishing characteristic indicated by the historical record was their special relationship to Jefferson.

Also questionable is the view implicit in the interpretation that the absence of party organization and of legitimated party leaders on the Hill worked wholly to the President's advantage. Recent understanding of the historical and functional relationship between the Presidency and the congressional party runs counter to this view, and would indicate rather that Presidents are more the beneficiaries than the victims of organized congressional parties with self-selected leaders.[5] That it was an advantage for the President to be able to choose the individuals with whom he would deal in Congress seems likely. But the circumstance which gave him this choice— namely, the failure of the congressional party to organize and select its own leaders—seems just as likely to have canceled out this advantage. The fact that his congressional agents were not legitimated as leaders meant, for one thing, that they could not speak authoritatively to President Jefferson for the party membership. Nor could they, on the President's behalf, approach the party's membership with the authority and the bargaining leverage that accrue to the elected leadership positions of organized congressional parties. Far more significant, the fact that these agents were not legitimated as leaders by their own colleagues must have heightened, to the

---

[4] Ralph V. Harlow, *The History of Legislative Methods in the Period before 1825* (New Haven: Yale University Press, 1917), p. 177.

[5] See David B. Truman, *The Congressional Party* (New York and London: John Wiley and Sons, 1959), chap. 8, and "The Presidency and Congressional Leadership: Some Notes on Our Changing Constitution," *Proceedings of the American Philosophical Society*, CIII, (October, 1959), 687–92.

President's great disadvantage, the conflicts inherent in a role which required loyalty to the White House in a community where independence of the White House tended to be a measure of a man's personal integrity. Lack of an elective base or other recognition of their legitimacy must, in other words, have made Jefferson's spokesmen far more sensitive to intralegislative pressures and sentiments adverse to the President than to party leadership in the modern Congress, which combines spokesmanship for the President with a demonstrated base of support within the congressional community. Circumstances can of course be imagined when spokesmanship for the President conferred some degree of status on Capitol Hill. But there can be little doubt that, given a congressional atmosphere resistive to the President, to be marked as a man under the influence of the Chief Executive was more a liability than an asset on the Hill; and that to be involved in a collusive relationship with the White House in any circumstances was to run a continuous risk of social stigmatization for sycophancy as one of the "toads that live upon the vapor of the palace." [6]

The record affords a vivid glimpse of these values being asserted against one legislator who had consented to act as administration spokesman. He was, in the words of a cabinet officer,

subjected to such sneering hints and innuendoes . . . as if he were a dependent tool of the Executive [that] he has suffered himself to be goaded . . . not only into disavowals of any subserviency to the views of the Executive, and to declarations in the face of the House that he did not care a fig for the Administration or any member of it, but into the humor of proposing measures which the President utterly disapproves. From mere horror of being thought the tool of the Executive he has made himself the tool of . . . [the] opposition.[7]

Almost certainly, the stressful nature of the role had much to do with the defection of Jefferson's most prominent congressional spokesman, John Randolph, in 1805–6. The overriding influence of legislative over presidential loyalties is suggested by Randolph's subsequent explanation of his conduct:

I came here prepared to cooperate with the Government in all its measures. . . . [But I soon] found that I might cooperate or be an honest man. I have therefore opposed and will oppose them. Is there an honest man disposed to be the go-between and to carry down secret messages to this House? No. It is because men of character cannot be found to do this business that agents must be got to carry things into effect which men of uncompromitted character will not soil their fingers or sully their characters with.[8]

The troublesome problem of divided loyalty was not so apparent, at least, in the case of cabinet members, and this may have been one of the reasons why all Jeffersonian Presidents used them for political liaison with Capitol Hill. Not only because they were members of the President's own executive community and formally subordinate to him, but also because

[6] Edmund Quincy, *Life of Josiah Quincy* (Boston: Ticknor and Fields, 1868), p. 287.

[7] John Quincy Adams, *Memoirs*, IV, 65–66.

[8] United States Congress, *Annals of the Congress of the United States* (Washington, D.C.: Gales and Seaton, 1832–61), XV (9th Congress, 1st sess.), 984.

the President had no staff of his own to dispatch on political missions to the Hill,[9] department heads figured prominently as intermediaries between President and Congress in every administration. Secretary of the Treasury Albert Gallatin was President Jefferson's principal executive agent for congressional relations, and he is the only high-level executive officer known to have resided permanently on Capitol Hill.[10] Henry Adams has written of this arrangement:

[The] close neighborhood [of his residence] to the Houses of Congress brought Mr. Gallatin into intimate social relations with the members. The principal adherents of the Administration in Congress were always on terms of intimacy in Mr. Gallatin's house, and much of the confidential communication between Mr. Jefferson and his party in the Legislature passed through this channel. . . . But the communication was almost entirely oral, and hardly a trace of it has been preserved either in the writings of Mr. Gallatin or in those of his contemporaries.[11]

President Madison regularly instructed his department heads to take advice concerning legislation to Congress and to discuss policy matters with congressmen, commenting as follows:

I remarked that where the intention was honest and the object useful, the convenience of facilitating business in that way was so obvious that it had been practiced under every past administration, and would so under every future one.[12]

Although President Monroe privately objected to official communications from Congress directly to department heads and bypassing the President,[13] he and his successor in office encouraged direct communication from department heads to legislators, extending their instructions to include political liaison with congressional committees:

It has always been considered as a practical rule [wrote Secretary of State Adams] that the Committee of Foreign Relations should be the confidential medium of communication between the Administration and Congress. . . . The Chairman . . . has always been considered as a member in the confidence of the Executive . . . [and] the President has . . . directed me to communicate freely to him.[14]

To the extent that Presidents utilized cabinet members from choice rather than because they had no personal staff, the practice conceivably had some advantages over direct presidential liaison with legislators. The use of "front men" allowed Presidents to maintain, for what it was worth, the

---

[9] Only one individual besides the President comprised the President's office. This was his personal secretary, often a member of the President's family, paid out of general funds for the maintenance of the executive mansion. So far as can be told from the written record, the position was of no political significance.

[10] Jefferson used other cabinet members also, though never so frequently or confidentially as Gallatin, it would appear. See Leonard D. White, *The Jeffersonians* (New York: The Macmillan Company, 1951), p. 51.

[11] Careless reading of this passage in Henry Adams' *The Life of Albert Gallatin* [(New York: Peter Smith, 1943), pp. 302–3] appears to be responsible for the widely held belief that Jefferson attended or presided over secret party meetings on the Hill.

[12] Quoted in Irving Brant, *James Madison, the President, 1809–1812* (Indianapolis: Bobbs-Merrill, 1956), p. 298.

[13] John Quincy Adams, *Memoirs*, IV, 217.

[14] *Ibid.*, p. 65, and V, 474.

outward appearance of conformity to community norms which decreed social distance between the President and Congress. It also gave them a medium of influence perhaps more palatable to lawmakers than direct confrontation with the President himself, since cabinet members had inferior social status to elected persons; and it gave Presidents particularly good access to the congressional committees with which department heads had, then as now, much business. The use of executive agents also permitted what neither public messages to Congress nor personal transactions between the President and legislators did: a means for presenting and pressing upon Congress legislation in which the President did not want or could not afford to be directly implicated. Just such an instance occurred in 1805–6. Clearly intended for diplomatic ears, public messages threatening invasion of Spanish Florida were being sent to Congress by President Jefferson while his agents, ostensibly without White House authorization, were presenting a draft bill appropriating funds to purchase West Florida from Spain.[15]

And in theory department heads, as members of the President's official family, were more nearly subject to presidential direction and closer to the President's interests than intermediaries who belonged to the legislative branch. Theory and reality may have jibed for Jefferson, blessed with a Secretary of the Treasury who apparently kept his departmental interests subordinate to his obligations as presidential agent. For Jefferson's successors, the gap between theory and reality would become abundantly clear. Pending later discussion, the question might also be kept in mind of how likely the use of department heads for congressional liaison was to exert a unifying influence upon the President's party on the Hill.

A third power technique was the wining and dining of legislators at the executive mansion. If etiquette restrained the President from crossing the Tiber to make the acquaintance of congressmen, he could lure them across to the White House. Like the enlistment of congressional spokesmen for the President, legislative dinners were Jefferson's innovation and a device conspicuously employed by him alone among Presidents. Before and after his two terms in office, the President's after-hours social life was restricted almost exclusively to obligatory dinners and state functions, a once or twice weekly White House levee, and holiday receptions. Jefferson abolished the levee immediately upon assuming office and substituted small dinners held almost nightly when Congress was in session, with legislators predominating among the guests. The dinners were the talk of Washington. In the judgment of observant diplomats from abroad, for whom food and wine were standard accessories of political persuasion, they were the secret of Jefferson's influence.

Political purpose pervaded the conception and execution of Jefferson's legislative dinners, and if no one but foreign emissaries seemed to perceive the fact, that was but testimony

---

[15] It was this "double-dealing" that provided the occasion for John Randolph's breach with Jefferson. See William C. Bruce, *John Randolph of Roanoke* (New York: G. P. Putnam's Sons, 1922), I, 222 ff.

to their political success.[16] Rarely more than a manageable dozen guests were invited at the same time, and each evening's dinner group was selected "not . . . promiscuously, or as has been done [by Jefferson's successors], alphabetically, but . . . in reference to their tastes, habits and suitability in all respects, which attention had a wonderful effect in making his parties more agreeable, than dinner parties usually are." [17] Guests received invitations penned in the President's own hand, often with a personal note; hundreds of mementos sent over the Tiber in those eight years later found cherished places in family albums. All legislators were invited, most more than once during the course of a session. Jefferson apparently made more of a distinction between Federalists and Republicans than did the legislators themselves in their own community. While Federalists received their share of invitations, the President seems never to have invited them at the same time with legislators of his own party, save for a maverick like Senator Adams, whom he regularly surrounded with Republicans at the dinner table, and who subsequently defected to the Republican fold. "He ought to invite them without regard to their political sentiments," a Federalist Senator grumbled; "the more men of good hearts associate, the better they think of each other." [18] But nothing would have been more out of keeping with Jefferson's desire to cultivate a sense of comity among his partisans on the Hill. Not only did he avoid mixing Federalists with Republicans, but fragmentary evidence suggests that Jefferson made it a practice to bring Republicans from different boarding-houses together around his dinner table, while Federalists were invited by boardinghouse bloc. Nor did Jefferson ordinarily mix cabinet members with his congressional guests. The field was reserved for the Chief Executive and legislators.

The dinners could not have been better staged. A round table was used, thus avoiding a place of precedence for the President and putting him among peers, at the same time that it prevented separate, private conversations. The risk of distraction and eavesdropping by waiting servants was averted by Jefferson's installation of a dumbwaiter situated near his elbow, bringing up victuals and potables from belowstairs to be served by the President himself: "You see we are alone," he announced, "and *our walls have no ears.*" [19] A French chef was "his best ally

[16] Numerous firsthand accounts of these dinners are available. Descriptive material presented in the paragraphs following is drawn from these principal sources, *passim:* John Quincy Adams, *Memoirs*, Vol. I; William Plumer, Jr., *Life of William Plumer* (Boston: Phillips, Sampson, and Company, 1857); Margaret B. Smith, *The First Forty Years of Washington Society* (New York: Charles Scribner's Sons, 1906); Anne C. Morris (ed.), *The Diary and Letters of Gouverneur Morris* (New York: Charles Scribner's Sons, 1888); Anne H. Wharton, *Salons Colonial and Republican* (Philadelphia: J. B. Lippincott, 1900); William P. Cutler and Julia Perkins, *Life, Journals and Correspondence of Rev. Manasseh Cutler* (Cincinnati: Robert Clarke, 1888), Vol. II; Samuel L. Mitchill, "Letters from Washington," *Harper's New Monthly Magazine*, LVII, (April 1879), 740–55. Claude G. Bowers gives an excellent description of the dinners in his *Jefferson in Power* (Boston: Houghton Mifflin Company, 1936), pp. 46–49.

[17] Margaret B. Smith, *First Forty Years*, pp. 388–89.

[18] Plumer, *Life*, pp. 245–46.

[19] Margaret B. Smith, *First Forty Years*, p. 388.

in conciliating political opponents" and the finest of imported wines put "all their tongues . . . in motion." [20] "You drink as you please and converse at your ease," a bedazzled Senator wrote home.[21] The President's uniform for the occasion was nondescript, marking his for a humble station: slippers down at the heel, faded velveteen breeches, hairy (not quite threadbare) waistcoat. Politics seemed somehow the one subject never discussed, talked around but not about, with the conversation adroitly steered away from shoptalk: enough of that in the boardinghouses from which the guests had now escaped. An Adams might, however, come away with an idea of what the President's views were on a question of national boundaries; [22] another congressman on a prospective presidential appointee.[23] Dominating the situation but never the conversation, Jefferson "took the lead and gave the tone, with a *tact* so true and discriminating that he seldom missed his aim; which was to draw forth the talents and information of each and all of his guests and to place every one in an advantageous light and by being pleased with themselves, be enabled to please others. Did he perceive any individual silent and unattended to, he would make him the object of his peculiar attention and in a manner apparently the most undesigning would draw him into notice and make him a participator." [24] To farmers he talked of agriculture; to classicists, of philosophy; to geographers, of Humboldt; to lawyers, of Blackstone; for naturalists he brought out his elegantly illustrated bird books from Europe. Raconteur extraordinary, he played the buffoon with zest, and improved upon the Baron Münchhausen himself. "You can never be an hour in this man's company without something of the marvellous. . . . His genius is of the old French school." [25]

It was a virtuoso performance, and the foreign diplomats rightly saw method in it all. But they quite misjudged the first Virginian President in thinking that his manner was "put on." Jefferson in politics was Br'er Rabbit thrown in the briar patch.

Why Jefferson's three successors in office failed to continue the tradition can only be speculated upon. Perhaps the usefulness of the dinners lay in their novelty, and maybe there was little political mileage left in them by the time of Jefferson's retirement.[26] Perhaps their usefulness derived from the lack of competition elsewhere in the executive community; for in the administrations of Jefferson's successors, as will later be shown, congressmen did not want for a multitude of eager hosts and hostesses along execu-

---

[20] Bowers, *Jefferson in Power*, p. 46; Cutler and Perkins, *Life*, II, 132–33.

[21] Mitchill, "Letters from Washington," *Harper's New Monthly Magazine*, LVIII (April, 1879), 744.

[22] John Quincy Adams, *The Diary of John Quincy Adams*, ed. Allan Nevins (New York: Longman, Green and Company, 1928), pp. 37–38.

[23] White, *The Jeffersonians*, p. 33.

[24] Margaret B. Smith, *First Forty Years*, p. 389.

[25] John Quincy Adams, *Diary*, pp. 25–26, 28.

[26] The dinners may well have outlived their usefulness even to Jefferson. His Washington wine expenditures declined as follows:

1801	$2,622.38	1805	546.41
1802	1,975.72	1806	659.38
1803	1,253.57	1807	553.97
1804	2,668.94	1808	75.58

See Esther Singleton, *The Story of the White House* (New York: S. S. McClure, 1907), I, 42.

tives' row. Perhaps the ever-swelling ranks of Congress, with reapportionment and the admission of new states, made small dinners impractical and dictated large receptions for congressmen (as in Jackson's time), invited in alphabetical segments according to the first letter of their last names. Perhaps none of Jefferson's successors had the inclination or the stamina to spend long hours nightly listening to congressmen after a hard day's work. Perhaps none saw the political opportunities in it.

In any case, none of the three Presidents following Jefferson had any opportunities remotely comparable to the legislative dinners for meeting informally with legislators. Madison reinstituted the levee, much to the delight of the diplomatic corps, who could once more parade in state attire, as well as of the townspeople, from bank president to musky stableboy, for the levee, announced weekly in the local newspaper, was open to all without invitation.[27] In Madison's time, the inimitable Dolley kept dignity uppermost at these affairs, and managed with the aid of a tall turban topped with "towering feathers" to preside over the throng.[28] She had the finesse but, alas, none of the objectives of the politician, and her very brilliance reduced her husband to an insignificant presence, sometimes unrecognized by her own guests.[29] "Being so

low of stature, he was in imminent danger of being confounded with the plebian crowds; and was pushed and jostled about like a common citizen." [30]

How utterly useless this institution was for purposes of confidential communication with legislators is indicated by the fact that the Chief of Staff's pocket was picked at one of the levees;[31] and at another manpower had to be summoned to subdue a raucous domestic from one of the legations who had come to hobnob with society.[32] Hack drivers, after depositing their fares, did not scruple to hitch their nags to the White House post and drop in for a toddy themselves. "It is a mere matter of form," wrote a congressman; "you make your bow . . . eat and drink what you can catch . . . and if you can luckily find your hat and stick, then take French leave; and that's going to the 'levee.' " [33]

Madison's successor spent a small fortune in France and Belgium to refurbish the White House after the British had finished with it. But if Monroe gave congressional guests an acquaintance with elegance, what he got in return was a congressional investigation into his vouchers.[34] He had the misfortune, too, of an English wife given to stiff stately dinners, migraines, and prolonged periods of withdrawal from what had then be-

---

[27] President Monroe regretted he had ever decided to continue the practice, and proposed to restrict the guests to invitees. He was, however, dissuaded by his Secretary of State. See John Quincy Adams, *Memoirs,* IV, 493–94.

[28] Singleton, *White House,* I, 71.

[29] Helen Nicolay, *Our Capital on the Potomac* (New York: Century Co., 1924), p. 135.

[30] Quoted in Singleton, *White House,* I, 71.

[31] Margaret B. Smith, *First Forty Years,* p. 183.

[32] John Quincy Adams, *Memoirs,* IV, 493–94.

[33] Fletcher Webster (ed.), *The Private Correspondence of Daniel Webster* (Boston: Little, Brown, 1957), I, 234.

[34] It seems that the Commissioner of Public Buildings had absconded with some of the appropriated funds. John Quincy Adams, *Memoirs,* VI, 287–88.

come a viciously competitive social life.[35]

In daring and in sheer lavishness of output the second family of Adamses to occupy the White House outdid all their predecessors. They threw open the great east hall and had a ball where Adams' mother had hung out the laundry, even though the chamber was still partially unplastered during the son's regime. Dinner parties and dances became the order of the day, and while Adams enjoyed not a minute of it he surprised everyone by coming out "in a brilliant masquerade dress of social, gay, frank, cordial manners." [36] But Adams buried his puritan conscience only to have it rise upon him, like a phoenix, from Capitol Hill. Coming on top of the Monroes' elegance, the importation of continental entertainment styles brought forth chastisements from across the swamp, by legislators always predisposed to view White House social life as "the resort of the idle, and the encourager of spies and traitors." [37] Adams' particular reward for his efforts was a shower of rebuke for installing a billiard parlor in the White House at public expense.

Note in contrast, then, the virtues of Jefferson's social technique. The dinners allowed him to make the personal acquaintance of each legislator in a community whose membership was in constant flux, to appraise the strengths, prejudices, and foibles of the men he wished to lead, and to spot the potential troublemakers and the potential spokesmen for himself. They allowed the President to accomplish, under his personal supervision, what no institution on Capitol Hill existed to accomplish: to bring legislators belonging to different boardinghouse fraternities together in circumstances conducive to amicability and free from contention, and in such a way as to stimulate a sense of common party membership among them. They gave him an opportunity to build general good will in Congress which would give his agents a more favorable atmosphere in which to do their work and which would at the same time react favorably upon his efforts to preserve their loyalty by minimizing the risk to them of acting as presidential agents on the Hill. The personal acquaintances made through the dinners also afforded Jefferson knowledge about his party members independently of his agents, an independent source of political intelligence about congressional mood and opinion against which to evaluate the reports of his agents, and a means of assessing the performance and standing of his agents vis-à-vis other legislators. The dinners gave the President a chance to encourage a sense of personal obligation and indebtedness to him among the lawmakers: a chance to please, to flatter, and to make them feel important. Last, but by no means least important—community attitudes toward power and politicians being what they were—he was able to display himself as a plain human before the men he wished to lead. He gained the opportunity to disarm men mistrustful of power and authority, and to convince them that the fellow in the White House was an exception to the stereotype they and the country har-

[35] Singleton, *White House*, I, chapter 8.

[36] Margaret B. Smith, *First Forty Years*, p. 248.

[37] Singleton, *White House*, I, xxii, 78.

bored of politicians and power-seekers.

None but Jefferson with his shabby dress, irresistible humor, and ingratiating manner could have carried it off. Well might he have said, with Shakespeare's King Henry,

I stole all courtesy from heaven
And drest myself in such humility
That I did pluck allegiance from men's
    hearts.

Presidential newspapers deserve brief mention as a means of influence, though they were at best of secondary importance, and not so specifically directed as the other techniques to the persuasion of legislators. Here again the innovation seems to have been Jefferson's. Before the transfer of the government to its Potomac locale, he persuaded a Philadelphia editor and friend to transport his printing press to Washington, and Samuel Harrison Smith began publication of the *National Intelligencer* there on October 1, 1800.[38] Precisely what the relationship was between Jefferson and Smith cannot be told from the community record, other than their common partisanship in the Republican cause, and apart from the fact that Smith was also selected as official reporter for the congressional debates, receiving sundry public printing contracts as well. The *Intelligencer* was, however, universally acknowledged inside the governmental community to be, and was spoken of as, the "official" or "administration organ." It remained so until 1824, the last of the Jeffersonian Presidents using instead the *National Journal,* also published in Washing-

ton, as his principal publicity medium.[39]

Nor can the specific political uses to which Presidents put these newspapers be defined without a separate, comprehensive study of their content; and even then the difficulty of identifying the presidentially inspired items would be vexing, for the *Intelligencer* was not merely a partisan sheet but a legitimate newspaper in its own right, and one of high quality. It seems reasonable to suppose, nevertheless, that Presidents availed themselves of newspapers for much the same reasons as the leadership in any organization employs organs of propaganda: to make and select "news" which will reinforce attitudes favorable to the leadership and its objectives, and to counter other media communicating unfavorable attitudes toward the leadership. Since the *Intelligencer* and the *Journal* had only local circulation, they may be considered principally as organs of internal propaganda, rather than a presidential device for reaching the larger public outside Washington, although items appearing in the *Intelligencer* were occasionally reproduced in the partisan press of other localities.[40]

A special virtue for Presidents lay, presumably, in the semi-anonymity of communication that newspapers afforded them. Without attribution of source, views might be expressed, awareness of events might be revealed,

[38] Wilhemus B. Bryan, *A History of the National Capital* (New York: The Macmillan Company, 1914, 1916), I, 365–66.

[39] Fred A. Emery, "Washington Newspapers," Columbia Historical Society *Records,* XXXVII–XXXVIII, 48–50.

[40] *Ibid.* A cursory scanning of the *Intelligencer* indicates that Presidents did not dictate or control its content. There was that important difference with internal propaganda media utilized by the leadership in most organizations.

rumors might be scotched or created, of which Presidents could not take official cognizance. For purposes of self-defense or counterattack, opportunity was offered them to participate pseudonymously or covertly in the exceedingly vicious political warfare of their day, where overt participation would have lowered the dignity of their office.[41] In addition to providing cover, use of newspapers by Presidents may well have been an effort to recoup some of the opportunities lost by their exclusion from the busy network of extraofficial communication that was social life outside the White House walls.[42]

Until 1816 the presidential newspaper appears to have dominated, though it did not monopolize, the "mass" media inside the governmental community. It lost that preeminence in Monroe's administration, and by the 1820s the President shared the local propaganda field with at least four factional newspapers. They were under the paronage, respectively, of the Secretary of the Treasury, the Secretary of War, the Secretary of State, and Andrew Jackson.[43]

As to patronage, the definitive work on early public administration states unequivocally that "the institution of bartering patronage for legislation . . . did not exist." Leonard White has found that before Jackson "no President . . . undertook to buy leadership with patronage. . . . The practice of using patronage to get votes in either House was rare and would have been thought corrupt."[44] As White implies, then, community attitudes and values tended to foreclose the use of patronage as an instrument of pressure upon Congress. More than this, they did not offer any but the most equivocal sanction for the partisan use of the President's removal and appointive power. No President before Jackson either subscribed to or practiced on more than a small scale the principle that vacancies ought to be created to make way for partisan appointments. Such a practice would, as Jefferson saw it, "revolt our new converts, and give a body to leaders who now stand alone."[45] "There is a Scylla as well as a Charybdis," John Quincy Adams commented on the question of

---

[41] Witness the familiar charges against Jefferson for illicit liaison with a Negro servant, against Adams for white slavery, against Jackson for adultery—all widely circulated in the public press. Pseudonyms were characteristically used for such partisan accusations in the battle of the presses during Jeffersonian times.

[42] Under a precedent established in George Washington's administration, Presidents did not appear at any social function outside the executive mansion, nor did they pay visits at any residence. The rule was breached only thrice during the Jeffersonian era, on the evidence at hand, if we exclude presidential appearances at church. One occasion was Monroe's attendance at a banquet in honor of General Lafayette and another was a series of visits he paid to Mrs. John Calhoun when the Secretary of War's child was mortally ill. W. P. Cresson, *James Monroe* (Chapel Hill: University of North Carolina Press. 1946), pp. 365, 460. The third was Monroe's attendance at a private party after Congress had adjourned in 1820. John P. Kennedy, *Memoirs of the Life of William Wirt, Attorney General of the United States* (Philadelphia: Lea and Blanchard, 1849), II, 107.

[43] Emery, "Washington Newspapers," Columbia Historical Society *Records*, XXXVII–XXXVIII, 49–50; John Quincy Adams, *Memoirs*, VI, 49, 56, 59; John S. Bassett, *The Life of Andrew Jackson* (Garden City: Doubleday, Page and Company, 1911), II, 378.

[44] White, *The Jeffersonians*, p. 43. See Chapter 24 of White's work for as excellent account and analysis of staffing and personnel administration in the Republican era.

[45] Quoted *ibid.*, p. 351.

partisan appointments to maintain favor with the party or nonpartisan appointments to maintain general good will.[46] Jeffersonian Presidents steered the middle course, thus helping to neutralize what has long since been recognized as one of the most potent weapons of presidential leadership.

It is "probable," as White also points out, that no President "failed on occasion to smooth the path of legislative accommodation by a suitable appointment."[47] But even where community values did not restrict partisan use of the President's appointive power, it is certain that availability of positions did—and not alone because "the number of vacancies was relatively small."[48] Another reason was that the principal responsibility for staffing the appointive offices did not rest with the President. Precisely how many of the appointive positions were the President's to dispose is not known.[49] Jefferson stated that six hundred of the roughly twenty-seven hundred civil appointive positions were "named by the President" when he came into office;[50] it is not clear from his choice of phrase whether he was referring to the number of positions *de facto* falling under the President's disposition, or the number he was authorized by law to appoint. In the postal service alone more than this number were put by law under the ap-

pointive jurisdiction of the Postmaster General. The entire service throughout the Jeffersonian era—a very large proportion of the government's personnel complement—was appointed by the service chief, and "it was unusual for the Postmaster General to consult the President, or to be called in by him to receive executive advice" on appointments.[51] It seems that most of the revenue collectors were appointed by the Secretary of the Treasury; in Jefferson's administration Gallatin cleared his choices for these important jobs with the President. Treasury officers subordinate to the collectors were, in turn, appointed by the collectors themselves, subject to approval by the Secretary of the Treasury. As to the civil staff at Washington, "department heads . . . [made] their own selections of clerks and subordinates without reference to the President."[52]

What principally remained to the President seems to have been therefore the relatively small number of district attorneys and marshals (only 24 each in 1801), territorial governorships, diplomatic and cabinet posts, and judgeships.[53] It was presumably in this limited area that the main opportunities were offered to "smooth the path of legislative accommodation by a suitable appointment."

But here the President's choice was by no means free, for all these positions required Senate confirmation. This fact, considered together with the

---

[46] Quoted *ibid.,* p. 367.

[47] *Ibid.,* p. 43.

[48] *Ibid.,* p. 129.

[49] This information is not given by White in his definitive work in the subject cited above.

[50] Thomas Jefferson, *The Works of Thomas Jefferson,* ed. Paul Leicester Ford (fed. ed.; New York: G. P. Putnam's Sons, 1905), X, 393–94.

[51] White, *The Jeffersonians,* p. 322.

[52] *Ibid.,* pp. 151–52, 355.

[53] Excluded here are appointments of uniformed officers. These were apportioned among the states in so far as practicable and candidates were required to pass written examinations. See *ibid.,* pp. 360–64.

President's implicit or explicit political obligations to legislators deriving from the mode of presidential nomination by congressional caucus, makes it not at all surprising that legislators figured very prominently among the presidential appointees to high-level executive positions. Diplomatic posts went ordinarily to legislators:

[The President] said he did not approve the principle of appointing members of Congress to foreign missions, but as it had been established in practice from the first organization of the present Government, and as the members of Congress would not be satisfied with the opposite principle, he did not think proper to make . . . a [different] rule for himself.[54]

As to cabinet posts, two of every three appointees from the administration of John Adams through Jackson's second administration had seen previous service on Capitol Hill, and well over half of the 49 cabinet appointees during this period (28, or 57 percent) were initially brought into the executive branch from a last preceding government service in Congress.[55] Not all of these went immediately to cabinet posts; ten of the 49 appointees were elevated to cabinet rank after first serving in other executive posts, most of them diplomatic. Of the remaining 39 who were appointed directly to the cabinet from outside the executive branch, 23 (59 percent) were appointed from a last preceding government service in Congress, 20 being members of the congressional community at the time of their appointment; 14 (36 percent) were appointed from a last preceding service in state government; and only two (5 percent) were appointed directly from private life without recorded previous government service.[56]

The practice of appointing legislators to high executive places, considered together with a presidential nominating procedure which put incoming Presidents under obligation to legislators for having won the Chief Magistracy, would seem to indicate

---

[54] John Quincy Adams, *Memoirs*, IV, 72. The President was Monroe, and the year 1818.

[55] Service careers of cabinet members were reconstructed from the available biographical sources, principally the *Dictionary of American Biography*. The base figure of 49 confirmed cabinet appointees excludes chief clerks and others serving *ad interim* as department heads, and one confirmed appointee for whom sufficient biographical information is not available. The positions included are the Secretaries of State, Treasury, War, and Navy, and the Attorney General. The Postmaster General was not of cabinet rank, nor was the Post Office separated from the Treasury Department, until Jackson's administration. The administrations of Jackson and John Adams have been included to gain a more significant number of cases for analysis, and because these Presidents utilized the same principal source of recruitment for cabinet positions as the four Jeffersonian Presidents, Jackson drawing somewhat more heavily than they on members of the congressional community.

[56] The average elapsed time from termination of congressional service to cabinet appointment was three years; from termination of service in state government to cabinet appointment, six and one-half years. The numerical incidence of cabinet members appointed from a last preceding service in state government may exaggerate the real importance of this secondary source of recruitment. Some of such appointees (James Madison and Martin Van Buren, for example) had achieved their most conspicuous service as legislators in the governmental community, and the state government posts from which they were appointed to the cabinet were but brief interludes between their congressional and their cabinet service. Unwillingness of some legislators to accept a cabinet post may have induced Presidents to turn to state officers as second choice; Jefferson, particularly, experienced difficulty in finding men to accept the less prestigious portfolios of War and Navy. See White, *The Jeffersonians*, p. 83.

that the prestige patronage available to Jeffersonian Presidents was employed more to repay their own pre-inaugural political debts on Capitol Hill than to create congressional indebtednesses for purposes of winning influence on the Hill.

Indeed, the choice of legislators personally as beneficiaries of this patronage may have hindered more than it facilitated presidential leadership of the legislative branch. Consider the dilemmas posed for the President in thus bringing about the transfer of important men in Congress from one to the other side of the Tiber. If executive appointments were given to repay political services pre-inaugurally rendered, who would be left behind on Capitol Hill to render party services to the President after inauguration? How helpful was it to Presidents in mobilizing party majorities and winning friends on the Hill to have removed from the congressional community, by executive appointment, the very men who had helped organize the congressional backing that had given them the Presidency? No wonder Jefferson was constantly on the search for men to replace his congressional spokesmen, and resorted to letter-writing campaigns imploring trusted friends to run for Congress where they might act on his behalf.[57]

If, on the other hand, executive appointments were used to co-opt rivals, pacify factional leaders, and woo potential opposition, which of the two courses of action would have made less trouble for the President: to leave potential adversaries on the Hill, disaffected, there to become marplots; or to bring them into his own executive family and confer upon them the organizational apparatus of an executive department or the prestige and responsibility of a diplomatic post? "Why, good God!" Jefferson replied when President Monroe asked his advice about dispatching Andrew Jackson to the diplomatic post farthest from American shores, as minister to St. Petersburg; "he would breed you a quarrel before he had been there a month!"[58] And whose was the hostage thus brought across the Tiber to the executive reservation? The President's, the better to bargain with the Hill? Or the Hill's, the better to bargain with the President? Who would call the tune for the legislator-become-department-head—his old friends in Congress, or the President? President Jefferson's much-quoted comment is suggestive: every executive post filled, he wrote, "me donne un ingrat, et cent ennemis."[59] His words might be kept in mind pending inquiry . . . into President-cabinet relationships.

Not only, therefore, was the constitutional authority to remove and appoint public officers largely unexploited by Jeffersonian Presidents for the purpose of winning influence on Capitol Hill. It would seem that the manner and the restrictive circumstances of its exercise in Jeffersonian times entailed large liabilities to the power interests of the President.

These, then, comprised the known inventory of presidentially improvised tools for achieving influence on Capitol Hill from 1801 to 1828: enlistment of individual members to

---

[57] See, for example, Jefferson, *Works*, X, 370–71.

[58] John Quincy Adams, *Memoirs*, IV, 76.

[59] Jefferson, *Works*, X, 342.

work confidentially for the President from positions inside the congressional community; enlistment of cabinet officers to work as presidential agents from positions outside the congressional community; personal contact with legislators through entertaining them at the executive mansion; employment of intracommunity public propaganda media; and appointment of legislators to executive offices.

Did they suffice for the purpose employed, and enable the President to supply that unifying influence which a representative legislature needed if it was to govern effectively? For Thomas Jefferson they apparently did, but not for his successors in the Presidency.

PERSONALITY AND POLITICS: PROBLEMS OF EVIDENCE, INFERENCE, AND CONCEPTUALIZATION
FRED I. GREENSTEIN

I. THE NEED FOR SYSTEMATIC STUDY OF POLITICAL PSYCHOLOGY [1]

Fifty-some years ago, Walter Lippmann observed that "to talk about politics without reference to human beings . . . is just the deepest error in our political thinking." [2] That it would be unfortunate to attempt political explanation without attention to the personal psychology of political actors seems on the face of it an unassailable, even a platitudinous, assertion. It is an assertion which seems to hold no matter which of the two standard approaches to defining politics we use. We can treat as "political" all of the activities that go on within the formal structures of government, plus the informal extragovernmental activities impinging upon government, such as political parties, interest groups, political socialization, and political communication. Or we can, in Lasswell's term, define politics "functionally" [3] to refer to some distinctive pattern of behavior that may manifest itself in any of the conventionally designated institutional settings (ranging from families and other face-to-face groups to international interaction). This pattern of behavior might, for example, be the exercise of power and influence, or it might be the processes of negotiation, accommodation, and bargaining that accompany conflict resolution, or it might be "the authoritative allocation of values."

"Politics," by both of these definitional tacks, is a matter of human behavior, and behavior—in the familiar formulation of Lewin and others—

CREDIT: Reprinted by permission of the author from Fred I. Greenstein, "Personality and Politics: Problems of Evidence, Inference, and Conceptualization," pp. 5–9. Panel paper delivered before The American Political Science Association in Chicago, September, 1967, and by permission of author and publisher from Fred I. Greenstein, "The Impact of Personality on Politics," *American Political Science Review*, September, 1967, pp. 630–631, 633–635, 636–641. [*Footnotes renumbered.*]

[1] Substantial portions of Sections I–III draw on my "The Need for Systematic Inquiry into Personality and Politics: Introduction and Overview," *Journal of Social Issues*, 24 (July, 1968), pp. 1–13.

[2] Walter Lippmann, *Preface to Politics* (New York: Mitchell Kennerly, 1913), p. 2.

[3] Harold D. Lasswell seems first to have introduced the distinction between functional and conventional definitions of politics in *Psychopathology and Politics* (Chicago: University of Chicago Press, 1930), chapter 4.

is a function of both the environmental situations in which actors find themselves and the personal psychological predispositions they bring to those situations. As Lazarus puts it:

The sources of man's behavior (his observable action) and his subjective experience (such as thoughts, feelings, and wishes) are twofold: the external stimuli that impinge on him and the internal dispositions that result from the interaction between inherited physiological characteristics and experience with the world. When we focus on the former, we note that a person acts in such-and-such a way because of certain qualities in a situation. For example, he attacks a friend because the friend insulted him, or he loses interest in a lecture because the teacher is dull or uninformed, or he fails in his program of study because the necessity of supporting himself through school leaves insufficient time for studying. It is evident that a man's behavior varies greatly from moment to moment, from circumstance to circumstance, changing with the changing conditions to which he is exposed.

Still, even as we recognize the dependency of behavior on outside stimuli, we are also aware that it cannot be accounted for on the basis of the external situation alone, but that in fact it must arise partly from personal characteristics.[4]

It would not be difficult to proliferate examples of political events that were critically dependent upon the personal characteristics of key actors, or of actors in the aggregate. Take Republican politics in 1964. An account of the main determinants of the Republican nomination that year, and of the nature of the subsequent election campaign, would have to include

much more than descriptions of the personal characteristics of the party leaders and members. But any account would be incomplete that did not acknowledge the impact of such factors as the willingness of one of the strongest contenders for the nomination to divorce his wife and marry a divorced woman; the indecision of one of the party's elder statesmen; a politically damaging outburst of temper in a news conference (two years earlier) by the man who had been the party's 1960 presidential candidate; the self-defeating political style of the man who received the 1964 nomination (his unwillingness to placate his opponents within the party, his propensity to remind voters of the issues on which he was most vulnerable). Not to mention aggregate psychological phenomena bearing, for example, on the behavior of voters in the Republican primaries of that year and the actions of delegates to the national conventions.

Attempts to explain the outcomes of adversary relationships often place in particularly clear relief the need for psychological data. For example, the overwhelming defeat in 1967 of numerically superior, better equipped Arab armies by Israel quite obviously was a function of gross discrepancies between the levels of skill and motivation of the two sides, both among leaders and subordinates. A further example, which lays out with a rather grim clarity the possible life-or-death policy relevance of reliable knowledge of the inner tendencies of political actors, is provided by the 1962 Cuban Missile Crisis.

Clearly each phase of the Kennedy Administration's (and the Soviet Union's) strategic decision-making

---

[4] Richard S. Lazarus, *Personality and Adjustment* (Englewood Cliffs, N.J.: Prentice-Hall, 1963), pp. 27–28.

during that confrontation was intimately dependent upon assumptions about the psychological dispositions of the adversary, as can be seen from an exchange of correspondence by several scholars in the New York *Times* shortly after the initial success of Kennedy's blockade in reversing the Soviet missile-bearing ships, but before the withdrawal of the additional missiles that had already been installed in Cuba.[5] One group of correspondents argued that it was of the utmost importance for the Administration not to assert its demands on the Soviet Union in aggressively uncompromising terms. The Russians, their letter suggested, must be provided with face-saving means of acceding to American demands, lest they conclude that they had no recourse but to fight. In reply, another writer (Bernard Brodie, a RAND Corporation strategic theorist) drew on the special theory of the psychology of Communist leadership developed by Nathan Leites in his controversial *Theory of Bolshevism*. For the Communist leader, Leites suggests, it is an imperative that any sign of capitalist weakness be exploited for maximum advantage. But if the Communist advance meets determined resistance by an opponent capable of inflicting serious damage, retreat is not only possible but *necessary*. And to allow oneself to be influenced by considerations of prestige and provocativeness would be the worst kind of sentimentality. Thus the second correspondent, drawing upon diametrically opposed assumptions about the psychology of Soviet leadership, contended that an uncompromising

[5] New York *Times*, Oct. 28 and Nov. 13, 1962.

American stance would make it *easier* rather than more difficult for the Russians to give in, and would decrease rather than increase the likelihood that miscalculations would lead to war.[6]

My concern at the moment, of course, is not to offer substantive hypotheses about the psychological questions raised by the foregoing examples, but rather to point out that there is a pressing need for what we presently have very little of: systematic attention to questions that lie in the overlapping territories of psychology and political science. And the last of my examples should suggest why this need exists in the arena of politics as well as in the literatures of the social sciences.

II. WHY HAS POLITICAL PSYCHOLOGY BEEN SLOW TO DEVELOP?

An answer to why political psychology is not a well-developed field, but rather is in questionable repute, may be found partly in the sociology of inquiry and partly in its vicissitudes. A

[6] Nathan Leites, *The Operational Code of the Politburo* (New York: McGraw-Hill, 1951) and *Theory of Bolshevism* (Glencoe, Ill.: Free Press, 1953). For a later formulation by Leites, taking account of the missile crisis, see his "Kremlin Thoughts: Yielding, Rebuffing, Provoking, Retreating," RAND Corporation Memorandum RM-31618-ISA, May, 1963. These alternative theories of the psychological assumptions underlying policy options in the missile crisis are presented for illustrative purposes, and do not purport to deal adequately with the psychological and strategic issues raised by that sequence of events. Cf. Alexander L. George, "Presidential Control of Force: The Korean War and the Cuban Missile Crisis," paper presented at the 1967 Annual Meeting of the American Sociological Association.

full account would draw upon the following points:

1. Systematic empirical study of politics has had a rather brief history.

2. For much of this history, political analysis has seemed to proceed in a quite acceptable fashion without making its psychological assumptions explicit. If one is studying "normal" actors in a familiar culture, it is often convenient simply to look at variations in the setting of politics, or merely to deal with the portion of the actor's psychological characteristics that relate to his social position (socioeconomic status, age, and sex, for example).

3. Implicit, common-sense psychological assumptions become less satisfactory when one attempts to explain (a) actors in one's own culture whose behavior deviates from expectations, or (b) actors from a different culture. (An example of the first is Woodrow Wilson's determined unwillingness, under certain circumstances, to follow the American politician's practice of compromising with one's adversaries, as described by George and George[7]; an example of the second is the possible applicability of Leites' theory of Bolshevik leadership to the Cuban Missile Crisis.) But when the political scientist does sense the importance of making explicit his assumptions about psychological aspects of politics, he is put off by the state of psychology. Rather than finding *a* psychological science on which to draw for insight, he finds a congeries of more or less competing models and frames of

reference, with imperfect agreement on the nature of man's inner dispositions, the appropriate terms for characterizing them, and the methodologies for observation.

4. If the political scientist persists in his determination to make systematic use of psychology, he is likely to experience further discouragement. Much of the research and theory he encounters will seem singularly irrelevant to explaining the kind of complex behavior which interests him. And where psychological writers do address themselves to his subject matter, their political observations often seem naive and uninformed. Psychologists' insights seem irrelevant to political scientists, for the good reason that many psychologists do not conceive of their science as one which *should* attempt to explain concrete instances of social behavior, but rather as a means of understanding general principles underlying that behavior. A deliberate attempt is made, as one psychologist puts it, to treat psychology as "socially indifferent"—to strip away the elements that are specific, say, to behavior on a congressional committee, or at a political party convention.

When colleagues in other disciplines (mainly sociology, anthropology, political science, and economics) turn to psychology for help they are disappointed, and, indeed, often aggrieved. What they begin to read with enthusiasm they put down with depression. What seemed promising turns out to be sterile, palpably trivial, or false and, in any case, a waste of time. . . . Psychologists do study and must study things and activities possessing social content. There is no other way. . . . It is only that psychology has been a science that abstracts out of all these content-

[7] Alexander L. and Juliette L. George, *Woodrow Wilson and Colonel House: A Personality Study* (New York: John Day, 1956), pp. 290–291.

characterized behaviors the concepts which form the jargons of its subdisciplines. . . .

The writer goes on to suggest why it is that when psychologists *do* pronounce on problems of politics and society, their observations so often strike politically knowledgeable readers as dubious.

I am impressed with how naive and conventional my colleagues [in psychology] and I are when confronted with most social phenomena. We are ignorant of the historical dimensions of most social activity, we do not see the complex interweaving of institutions and arrangements . . . In general, psychologists tend to be like laymen when they confront social phenomena, particularly those that involve large scale patterns. And the reason for all of this is that the main areas of social activity are only the *place* where psychologists study interesting sorts of things, rather than being the *focus of inquiry*.[8]

5. A final, and perhaps the most important, determent to a systematic political psychology has paradoxically been that a literature already existed —namely, the mare's-nest of research, theory, and controversy on "personality and politics." Objections have been raised to this literature on empirical, on methodological, and on what might be called formal grounds.

The more intellectually challenging of the various objections asserting that *in principle* personality and politics research is not promising (even if one avoids the methodological pitfalls) seem to fall under five headings. In each case the objection is one that can be generalized to the study of how

personality relates to any social phenomenon. Listed rather elliptically the five objections are that:

1. Personality characteristics tend to be randomly distributed in institutional roles. Personality therefore "cancels out" and can be ignored by analysts of political and other social phenomena.

2. Personality characteristics of individuals are less important than their social characteristics in influencing behavior. This makes it unpromising to concentrate research energies on studying the impact of personality.

3. Personality is not of interest to political and other social analysts, because individual actors (personalities) are severely limited in the impact they can have on events.

4. Personality is not an important determinant of behavior because individuals with varying personal characteristics will tend to behave similarly when placed in common situations. And it is not useful to study personal variation, if the ways in which people vary do not affect their behavior.

5. Finally, there is a class of objections deprecating the relevance of personality to political analysis in which "personality" is equated with particular aspects of individual psychological functioning. We shall be concerned with one of the objections falling under this heading—*viz.*, the assertion that so-called "deep" psychological needs (of the sort that sometimes are summarized by the term "ego-defensive") do not have an important impact on behavior, and that therefore "personality" in this sense of the term need not be studied by the student of politics.

The first two objections seem to be

8 Richard A. Littman, "Psychology: The Socially Indifferent Science," *American Psychologist*, 16 (1961), pp. 232–236.

based on fundamental misconceptions. Nevertheless they do point to interesting problems for the student of political psychology. The final three objections are partially well taken. These are the objections that need to be rephrased in conditional form as "Under what circumstances?" questions. Let me now expand upon these assertions.

Two erroneous objections

The thesis that personality "cancels out"

The assumption underlying the first objection seems, as Alex Inkeles points out, to be that "in 'real' groups and situations, the accidents of life history and factors other than personality which are responsible for recruitment [into institutional roles] will 'randomize' personality distribution in the major social statuses sufficiently so that taking systematic account of the influence of personality composition is unnecessary." But, as Inkeles easily shows, this assumption is false on two grounds.

First, "even if the personality composition of any group is randomly determined, random assortment would not in fact guarantee the *same* personality composition in the membership of all institutions of a given type. On the contrary, the very fact of randomness implies that the outcome would approximate a normal distribution. Consequently, some of the groups would by chance have a personality composition profoundly different from others, with possibly marked effects on the functioning of the institutions involved." Secondly,

there is no convincing evidence that randomness does consistently describe the assignment of personality types to major social statuses. On the contrary, there is a great deal of evidence to indicate that particular statuses often attract, or recruit preponderantly for, one or another personality characteristic and that fact has a substantial effect on individual adjustment to roles and the general quality of institutional functioning.[9]

The objection turns out therefore to be based on unwarranted empirical assumptions. It proves not to be an obstacle to research, but rather—once it is examined—an opening gambit for identifying a crucial topic of investigation for the political psychologist: How are personality types distributed in social roles and with what consequences?

The thesis that social characteristics are more important than personality characteristics

The second objection—asserting that individuals' social characteristics are "more important" than their personality characteristics—seems to result from a conceptual rather than empirical error. It appears to be an objection posing a pseudo-problem that needs to be dissolved conceptually rather than resolved empirically.

Let us consider what the referents are of "social characteristic" and "personality characteristic." By the latter we refer to some inner predisposition of the individual. The term "characteristic" applies to a state of

[9] Alex Inkeles, "Sociology and Psychology," in Sigmund Koch (ed.), *Psychology: A Study of a Science*, VI (New York: McGraw-Hill, 1963), p. 354.

the organism. And, using the familiar paradigm of "stimulus→organism→response," or "environment→predispositions→response," we operate on the assumption that the environmental stimuli (or "situations") that elicit behavior are mediated through the individual's psychological predispositions.[10]

But we also, of course, presume that the individual's psychological predispositions are themselves to a considerable extent environmentally determined, largely by his prior social experiences. And it is these prior environmental states (which may occur at any stage of the life cycle and which may or may not persist into the present) that we commonly refer to when we speak of "social characteristics." Social "characteristics," then, are not states of the organism, but of its environment. (This is made particularly clear by the common usage *"objective social characteristics."*)

It follows that social and psychological characteristics are in no way mutually exclusive. They do not compete as candidates for explanation of social behavior, but rather are complementary. Social "characteristics" can cause psychological "characteristics"; they are not substitutes for psychological characteristics. The erroneous assumption that social characteristics could even in principle be more important than psychological characteristics probably arises in part

from the misleading impression of identity fostered by the usage of "characteristics" in the two expressions.[11]

Three partially correct objections

The three remaining objections bear on (a) the question of how much impact individual actors can have on political outcomes, (b) the question of whether the situations political actors find themselves in impose uniform behavior on individuals of varying personal characteristics, making it unprofitable for the political analyst to study variations in the actors' personal characteristics, and (c) the numerous questions that can be raised about the impact on behavior of particular classes of personal characteristics—including the class of characteristics I shall be discussing, the so-called "ego-defensive" personality dispositions. In the remainder of this essay, I shall expand upon each of these three questions, rephrase them in conditional form, and lay out a number of general propositions stating the circumstances under which the objection is or is not likely to hold. As will be evident, the propositions are not hypotheses stated with sufficient precision to be testable. Rather, they are quite general indica-

---

[10] It is a matter of convenience whether the terms "personality" and "psychological" are treated as synonymous (as in the present passage), or whether the first is defined as some subset of the second (as in my discussion of the fifth objection). Given the diversity of uses to which all of the terms in this area are put, the best one can do is to be clear about one's usage in specific contexts.

[11] My criticism of the second objection would of course not stand in any instance where some acquired inner characteristic (such as a sense of class consciousness) was being defined as a social characteristic, and it was being argued that this "social" characteristic was "more important" than a "personality" characteristic. In terms of my usage this would imply an empirical assertion about the relative influence of two types of psychological, or "personality" variables. My remarks in the text on the meaning of terms are simply short-hand approaches to clarifying the underlying issue. They are not canonical efforts to establish "correct" usage.

tions of the circumstances under which political analysts are and are not likely to find it desirable to study "personality" in the several senses of the term implicit in the objections.

When do individual actors affect events ("action dispensability")?

The objection to studies of personality and politics that emphasizes the limited capacity of single actors to shape events does not differ in its essentials from the nineteenth and early twentieth century debates over social determinism—that is, over the role of individual actors (Great Men or otherwise) in history. In statements of this objection emphasis is placed on the need for the times to be ripe in order for the historical actor to make his contribution. Questions are asked such as, "What impact could Napoleon have had on history if he had been born in the Middle Ages?" Possibly because of the parlor game aura of the issues that arise in connection with it, the problem of the impact of individuals on events has not had as much disciplined attention in recent decades as the two remaining issues I shall be dealing with. Nevertheless, at one time or another this question has received the attention of Tolstoy, Carlyle, Spencer, William James, Plekhanov, and Trotsky (in his *History of the Russian Revolution*). The main attempt at a balanced general discussion seems to be Sidney Hook's vigorous, but unsystematic, 1943 essay *The Hero in History*.[12]

[12] Sidney Hook, *The Hero in History* (Boston: Beacon Press, 1943).

Since the degree to which actions are likely to have significant impacts is clearly variable, I would propose to begin clarification by asking: *What are the circumstances under which the actions of single individuals are likely to have a greater or lesser effect on the course of events?* For shorthand purposes this might be called the question of *action dispensability*. We can conceive of arranging the actions performed in the political arena along a continuum, ranging from those which are indispensable for outcomes that concern us through those which are utterly dispensable. And we can make certain general observations about the circumstances which are likely to surround dispensable and indispensable action. In so reconstructing this particular objection to personality explanations of politics we make it clear that what is at stake is not a psychological issue, but rather one bearing on social processes—on decision-making. The question is about the impact of action, not about its determinants.

It is difficult to be precise in stipulating circumstances under which an individual's actions are likely to be a link in further events, since a great deal depends upon the interests of the investigator and the specific context of investigation (the kinds of actions being studied; the kinds of effects that are of interest). Therefore, the following three propositions are necessarily quite abstract.

The impact of an individual's actions varies with (1) the degree to which the actions take place in an environment which admits of restructuring, (2) the location of the actor in that environment, and (3) the actor's peculiar strengths or weaknesses.

1. *The likelihood of personal impact increases to the degree that the environment admits of restructuring.* Technically speaking we might describe situations or sequences of events in which modest interventions can produce disproportionately large results as "unstable." They are in a precarious equilibrium. The physical analogies are massive rock formations at the side of a mountain which can be dislodged by the motion of a single keystone, or highly explosive compounds such as nitro glycerine. Instability in this sense is by no means synonymous with what is loosely known as political instability, the phrase we typically employ to refer to a variety of "fluid" phenomena—political systems in which governments rise and fall with some frequency, systems in which violence is common, etc. Many of the situations commonly referred to as unstable do not at all admit of restructuring. In the politics of many of the "unstable" Latin American nations, for example, most conceivable substitutions of actors and actions would lead to little change in outcomes (or at least in "larger" outcomes). Thus, to continue the physical analogy, an avalanche in motion down a mountainside is for the moment in stable equilibrium, since it cannot be influenced by modest interventions.

The situation (or chain of events) which does not admit readily of restructuring usually is one in which a variety of factors conspire to produce the same outcome.[13] Hook, in *The Hero in History,* offers the outbreak of World War I and of the February Revolution as instances of historical sequences which, if not "inevitable," probably could not have been averted by the actions of any single individual. In the first case the vast admixture of multiple conflicting interests and intertwined alliances and in the second the powerful groundswell of discontent were such as to make us feel that no intervention by any single individual (excluding the more far-fetched hypothetical instances that invariably can be imagined) would have averted the outcome. On the other hand, Hook attempts to show in detail that without the specific actions of Lenin the October Revolution might well not have occurred. By implication he suggests that Lenin was operating in an especially manipulable environment. A similar conclusion might be argued about the manipulability of the political environment of Europe prior to the outbreak of World War II, on the basis of the various accounts at our disposal of the sequence of events that culminated with the invasion of Poland in 1939.[14]

2. *The likelihood of personal impact varies with the actor's location in the environment.* To shape events, an action must be performed not only in an unstable environment, but also by an actor who is strategically placed in

---

[13] Compare Wassily Leontief's interesting essay "When Should History be Written Backwards?" *The Economic History Review,* 16, (1963), pp. 1–8.

[14] For an account of European politics in the 1930's that is consistent with this assertion see Alan Bullock, *Hitler: A Study in Tyranny* (New York: Harper, rev. ed., 1962). Needless to say, any attempt to seek operational indicators of environments that "admit of restructuring" in order to restate the present proposition in testable form could not take the circular route of simply showing that the environment *had* been manipulated by a single actor.

that environment. It is, for example, a common place that actors in the middle and lower ranks of many bureaucracies are unable to accomplish much singly, since they are restrained or inhibited by other actors. Robert C. Tucker points out what may almost be a limiting case on the other end of the continuum in an essay on the lack of restraint on Russian policy-makers, both under the Czars and since the Revolution. He quotes with approval Nikolai Turgenev's mid-nineteenth century statement that "In all countries ruled by an unlimited power there has always been and is some class, estate, some traditional institutions which in certain instances compel the sovereign to act in a certain way and set limits to his caprice; nothing of the sort exists in Russia." [15] Elsewhere, Tucker points to the tendency in totalitarian states for the political machinery to become "a conduit of the dictatoral psychology" [16]—that is for there to be a relatively unimpeded conversion of whims of the dictator into governmental action as a consequence of his authoritarian control of the bureaucratic apparatus.

3. *The likelihood of personal impact varies with the personal strengths or weaknesses of the actor.* My two previous observations can be recapitulated with an analogy from the poolroom. In the game of pocket billiards the aim of the player is to clear as many balls as possible from the table. The initial distribution of balls parallels my first observation about the manipulability of the environment. With some arrays a good many shots are possible; perhaps the table can even be cleared. With other arrays no successful shots are likely. The analogy to point two—the strategic location of the actor—is, of course, the location of the cue ball. As a final point, we may note the political actor's peculiar strengths or weaknesses. In the poolroom these are paralleled by the player's skill or lack of skill. The greater the actor's skill, the less his initial need for a favorable position or a manipulable environment, and the greater the likelihood that he will himself subsequently contribute to making his position favorable and his environment manipulable.[17]

The variable of skill is emphasized in Hook's detailed examination of Lenin's contribution to the events leading up to the October Revolution. Hook concludes that Lenin's vigorous, persistent, imaginative participation in that sequence was a necessary (though certainly not sufficient) condition for the outcome. Hook's interest, of course, is in lending precision to the notion of the Great Man. Therefore he is concerned with the individual who, because of especially great talents, is able to alter the course of

[15] Robert C. Tucker, *The Soviet Political Mind* (New York: Praeger, 1963), pp. 145–165; quotation from Turgenev, at p. 147.

[16] Robert C. Tucker, "The Dictator and Totalitarianism," *World Politics*, 17 (1965), p. 583.

[17] In other words, the skill of the actor may feed back into the environment, contributing to its instability or stability. To the degree that we take environmental conditions as given (i.e., considering them statically at a single point in time), we underestimate the impact of individuals on politics. For examples of political actors shaping their own roles and environments see Hans Gerth and C. Wright Mills, *Character and Social Structure* (London: Routledge and Kegan Paul, 1953), Chapter 14.

events. But for our purposes, the Great Failure is equally significant: an actor's capabilities may be relevant to an outcome in a negative as well as a positive sense.

When does personal variability affect behavior ("actor dispensability")?

Often it may be acknowledged that a particular action of an individual is a crucial node in a process of decision-making, but it may be argued that this action is one that might have been performed by any actor placed in a comparable situation, or by anyone filling a comparable role. If actors with differing personal characteristics perform identically when exposed to common stimuli, we quite clearly can dispense with study of the actors' personal differences, since a variable cannot explain a uniformity. This objection to personality explanations of political behavior—and here "personality" means personal variability—is illustrated by Easton with the example of political party leaders who differ in their personality characteristics and who are "confronted with the existence of powerful groups making demands upon their parties." Their "decisions and actions," he suggests, will tend "to converge." [18]

The task of rephrasing this objection conditionally and advancing propositions about the circumstances under which it obtains is not overly burdensome, since the objection is rarely stated categorically. Exponents of the view that situational pressures

eliminate or sharply reduce the effects of personality usually acknowledge that this is not always the case. Similarly, proponents of the view that personality *is* an important determinant of political behavior also often qualify their position and note circumstances that dampen the effects of personal variability. These qualifications point to an obvious reconstruction of the question. *Under what circumstances,* we may ask, *do different actors (placed in common situations) vary in their behavior and under what circumstances is behavior uniform?* We might call this the question of *actor dispensability.* [19]

1. *There is greater room for personal variability in the "peripheral" aspects of actions than in their "central" aspects.* Examples of "peripheral" aspects of action include evidences of the personal *style* of an actor (for example, his mannerisms), the *zealousness* of his performance, and the *imagery* that accompanies his behavior at the preparatory and consummatory phases of action (for example, fantasies about alternative courses of action).

By "central" I refer to the gross aspects of the action—for example,

---

[18] David Easton, *The Political System* (New York: Knopf, 1953), p. 196.

[19] Strictly speaking, it is not the actor who is dispensable in this formulation, but rather his personal characteristics. In an earlier draft I referred to "actor substitutability," but the antonym, "non-substitutability," is less successful than "indispensability" as a way of indicating the circumstances under which an explanation of action demands an account of the actor. On the other hand, "substitutability" is a very handy criterion for rough and ready reasoning about the degree to which the contribution of any historical actor is uniquely personal, since one may easily perform the mental exercise of imagining how other available actors would have performed under comparable circumstances.

the very fact that an individual votes, writes a letter to a Congressman, etc.

Lane suggests that "the idiosyncratic features of personality" are likely to be revealed in the "images" political actors hold "of other participants." There also is "scope for the expressions of personal differences," Lane points out, in "the grounds" one selects "for rationalizing a political act," and in one's style "of personal interaction in a political group." [20]

Shils, after arguing that "persons of quite different dispositions" often "will behave in a more or less uniform manner," then adds: "Naturally not all of them will be equally zealous or enthusiastic. . ." [21]

Riesman and Glazer point out that although "different kinds of character" can "be used for the same kind of work within an institution," a "price" is paid by "the character types that [fit] badly, as against the release of energy provided by the congruence of character and task." [22]

2. *The more demanding the political act—the more it is not merely a conventionally expected performance—the greater the likelihood that it will vary with the personal characteristics of the actor.* Lane suggests that there is little personal var-

iation in "the more conventional items, such as voting, expressing patriotic opinions and accepting election results as final." On the other hand, his list of actions which "reveal . . . personality" includes "selecting types of political behavior over and above voting," [23] writing public officials, volunteering to work for a political party, seeking nomination for public office, etc.

3. *Variations in personal characteristics are more likely to be exhibited to the degree that behavior is spontaneous—that is, to the degree that it proceeds from personal impulse, without effort or premeditation.* Goldhamer refers to "a person's . . . casual ruminations while walking along the street, sudden but perhaps transient convictions inspired by some immediate experience, speculations while reading the newspaper or listening to a broadcast, remarks struck off in the course of an argument. . . . If we have any theoretical reason for supposing that a person's opinions are influenced by his personality structure, it is surely in these forms of spontaneous behavior that we should expect to find the evidence of this relationship." [24]

We may now consider two propositions about actor dispensability that relate to the environment in which actions take place.

4. *Ambiguous situations leave room for personal variability to mani-*

[20] Robert E. Lane, *Political Life* (Glencoe: The Free Press, 1959), p. 100.

[21] Edward A. Shils, "Authoritarianism: 'Right' and 'Left'," in Richard Christie and Marie Jahoda (eds.), *Studies in the Scope and Method of "The Authoritarian Personality"* (Glencoe: The Free Press, 1954), p. 43.

[22] David Riesman and Nathan Glazer, "The Lonely Crowd: A Reconsideration in 1960," in Seymour M. Lipset and Leo Lowenthal (eds.), *Culture and Social Character* (New York: The Free Press, 1961), pp. 438–439.

[23] Lane, *op. cit.*, p. 100.

[24] Herbert Goldhamer, "Public Opinion and Personality," *American Journal of Sociology*, 55 (1950), p. 349.

fest itself. As Sherif puts it, "the contribution of internal factors increases as the external-stimulus situation becomes more unstructured." [25] (A classically unstructured environmental stimulus, leaving almost infinite room for personal variation in response, is the Rorschach ink blot.)

Budner [26] distinguishes three types of ambiguous situations. Each relates to instances which have been given by various writers of actor dispensability or indispensability. Budner's three types of situations include: (a) a *"completely new situation in which there are no familiar cues."*

Shils comments that in new situations "no framework of action [has been] set for the newcomer by the expectations of those on the scene. A new political party, a newly formed religious sect will thus be more amenable to the expressive behavior of the personalities of those who make them up than an ongoing government or private business office or university department with its traditions of scientific work." [27]

Goldhamer argues that the public opinion process moves from unstructured conditions admitting of great personal variability to more structured conditions that restrain individual differences. Immediate reactions to public events, he argues, reflect personal idiosyncrasies. But gradually the individual is constrained by his awareness that the event has become a matter of public discussion. "There is reason to believe that, as the individual becomes aware of the range and intensity of group preoccupation with the object, his orientation to it becomes less individualized, less intimately bound to an individual perception and judgment of the object . . . [H]e is drawn imperceptibly to view this object anew, no longer now as an individual percipient, but as one who selects (unconsciously, perhaps) an 'appropriate' position in an imagined range of public reactions . . . a limitation is thus placed on the degree to which the full uniqueness of the individual may be expected to influence his perceptions and opinions." [28]

The second type of ambiguity referred to by Budner is (b) *"a complex situation in which there are a great number of cues to take into account."* Levinson suggests that the availability of "a wide range of . . . socially provided . . . alternatives" increases "the importance of intrapersonal determinants" of political participation. "The greater the number of opportunities for participation, the more the person can choose on the basis of personal congeniality. Or, in more general terms, the greater the richness and complexity of the stimulus field, the more will internal organizing forces determine individual adaptation. This condition obtains in a relatively unstructured social field, and, as well, in a pluralistic society that provides numerous structured alternatives." [29]

---

[25] Muzafer Sherif, "The Concept of Reference Groups in Human Relations," in Muzafer Sherif and M. O. Wilson (eds.), *Group Relations at the Crossroads* (New York: Harper, 1953), p. 30.

[26] Stanley Budner, "Intolerance of Ambiguity as a Personality Variable," *Journal of Personality*, 30 (1960), p. 30.

[27] Shils, *op. cit.*, pp. 44–45.

[28] Goldhamer, *op. cit.*, pp. 346–347.

[29] Daniel J. Levinson, "The Relevance of Personality for Political Participation," *Public Opinion Quarterly*, 22 (1958), p. 9.

Finally, Budner refers to (c) *"a contradictory situation in which different elements suggest different structures."* Several of Lane's examples fall under this heading: "Situations where reference groups have politically conflicting points of view . . . Situations at the focus of conflicting propaganda. . . . Current situations which for an individual are in conflict with previous experience." [30]

5. *The impact of personal differences on behavior is increased to the degree that sanctions are not attached to certain of the alternative possible courses of behavior.* "The option of refusing to sign a loyalty oath," Levinson comments, "is in a sense 'available' to any member of an institution that requires such an oath, but the sanctions operating are usually so strong that non-signing is an almost 'unavailable' option to many who would otherwise choose it." [31]

The foregoing environmental determinants of actor dispensability suggest several aspects of actors' predispositions which will affect the likelihood that any of the ways in which they differ from each other will manifest themselves in behavior.

6. *The opportunities for personal variation are increased to the degree that political actors lack mental sets which might lead them to structure their perceptions and resolve ambiguities.* The sets they may use to help reduce ambiguity include cognitive capacities (intelligence, information) that provide a basis of organiz-ing perceptions, and pre-conceptions that foster stereotyping.

Verba, in an essay on "Assumptions of Rationality and Non-Rationality in Models of the International System," comments that "the more information an individual has about international affairs, the less likely it is that his behavior will be based upon non-logical influences. In the absence of information about an event, decisions have to be made on the basis of other criteria. A rich informational content, on the other hand, focuses attention on the international event itself. . ." [32]

Wildavsky, in an account of adversary groups in the Dixon-Yates controversy, points to ways in which the preconceptions of members of factions lead them to respond in predictable fashions that are likely to be quite independent of their personal differences. "The public versus private power issue . . . has been fought out hundreds of times at the city, state, county, and national levels of our politics in the past sixty years. A fifty year old private or public power executive, or a political figure who has become identified with one or another position, may well be able to look back to twenty-five years of personal involvement in this controversy. . . . The participants on each side have long since developed a fairly complete set of attitudes on this issue which have crystallized through years of dispute. . . . They have in reserve a number of

[30] Lane, *op. cit.*, p. 99.

[31] Levinson, *op. cit.*, p. 10.

[32] Sidney Verba, "Assumptions of Rationality and Non-Rationality in Models of the International System," *World Politics*, 14 (1961), p. 100. By "non-logical" Verba means influences resulting from ego-defensive personality needs, but his point applies generally to personal variability.

prepared responses ready to be activated in the direction indicated by their set of attitudes whenever the occasion demands. . ." [33]

7. *If the degree to which certain of the alternative courses of action are sanctioned reduces the likelihood that personal characteristics will produce variation in behavior, then any intense dispositions on the part of actors in a contrary direction to the sanctions increase that likelihood.* "Personality structure . . . will be more determinant of political activity when the impulses and the defenses of the actors are extremely intense"—for example, "when the compulsive elements are powerful and rigid or when the aggressiveness is very strong." [34]

8. *If, however, the disposition that is strong is to take one's cues from others, the effects of personal variation on behavior will be reduced.* Personality may dispose some individuals to adopt uncritically the political views in their environment, but as a result, Goldhamer comments, the view adopted will "have a somewhat fortuitous character in relation to the personality and be dependent largely on attendant situational factors." [35] (Dispositions toward conformity are, of course, a key variable for students of political psychology. The point here is merely that these dispositions reduce the impact of the individual's other psychological characteristics on his behavior.)

9. *A situational factor working with individual tendencies to adopt the views of others to reduce personal variation is the degree to which the individual is placed in a group context in which "the individual's decision or attitude is visible to others."* [36] Another predispositional determinant:

10. *The more emotionally involved a person is in politics, the greater the likelihood that his personal characteristics will affect his political behavior.* Goldhamer comments that "the bearing of personality on political opinion is conditioned and limited by the fact that for large masses of persons the objects of political life are insulated from the deeper concerns of the personality." [But, he adds in a footnote], "this should not be interpreted to mean that personality characteristics are irrelevant to an understanding of the opinions and acts of political personages. In such cases political roles are so central to the entire life organization that a close connection between personality structure and political action is to be expected." [37]

Levinson argues that " [t]he more politics 'matters,' the more likely it is that political behavior will express enduring inner values and dispositions. Conversely, the less salient the issues involved, the more likely is one to respond on the basis of immediate external pressures. When a personally congenial mode of participation is not readily available, and the person cannot create one for himself, he may nominally accept an uncongenial role

[33] Aaron Wildavsky, "The Analysis of Issue-Contexts in the Study of Decision-Making," *Journal of Politics*, 24 (1962), pp. 717–732.

[34] Shils, *op. cit.*, p. 45.

[35] Goldhamer, *op. cit.*, p. 535.

[36] Verba, *op. cit.*, p. 103.

[37] Goldhamer, *op. cit.*, p. 349.

but without strong commitment or involvement. In this case, however, the person is likely . . . to have a strong potential for change toward a new and psychologically more functional role." [38]

The final proposition has reference to political roles and does not fit neatly into any of the three elements of the Environment→Predispositions→Response formula.

11. *Personality variations will be more evident to the degree that the individual occupies a position "free from elaborate expectations of fixed content."* [39] Typically these are leadership positions. We have already seen that such positions figure in the conditions of action indispensability; their importance for the student of personality and politics is evident a fortiori when we note that the leader's characteristics also are likely to be reflected in his behavior, thus meeting the requirement of actor indispensability.

The military leader, it has been said, may have an especially great impact. "Even those who view history as fashioned by vast impersonal forces must recognize that in war personality plays a particularly crucial part. Substitute Gates for Washington, and what would have happened to the American cause? Substitute Marl-

borough or Wellington for Howe or Clinton, and what would have happened? These are perhaps idle questions, but they illustrate the fact that the course of a war can depend as much upon the strengths and failings of a commander-in-chief as upon the interaction of geography and economics and social system." [40]

Under what circumstances are ego-defensive needs likely to manifest themselves in political behavior?

The final objection to explanations of politics in terms of personality is one in which the term "personality" denotes not the impact of individuals on social processes (action dispensability), or the mere fact of individual variability (actor dispensability), but rather the specific ways in which "personalities" vary. Once we have found it necessary to explain political behavior by referring to the ways in which political actors vary, objections can be made to whatever specific personality variables we choose to employ. (Objections falling into this final category might be summarized under the heading "actor characteristics.")

Some choices of variables are particularly controversial, especially the variables based on "depth" psychology that have so commonly been drawn upon in such works as Lasswell's *Psychopathology and Politics*, Fromm's *Escape from Freedom*, and *The Authoritarian Personality*.[41] It is the

[38] Levinson, *op. cit.*, p. 10.

[39] Shils, *op. cit.*, p. 45. The term "role" is commonly used so as to have both an environmental referent (the prevailing expectations about his duties in a role incumbent's environment) and a predispositional referent (the incumbent's own expectations). For a valuable discussion see Daniel Levinson, "Role, Personality, and Social Structure in the Organizational Setting," *Journal of Abnormal and Social Psychology*, 58 (1959), pp. 170–180.

[40] Henry Wilcox, *Portrait of a General* (New York: Knopf, 1964), pp. ix–x.

[41] Harold D. Lasswell, *Psychopathology and Politics*, originally published in 1930, reprinted in *The Political Writings of Harold D. Lasswell*

deep motivational variables that many commentators have in mind when they argue that "personality" does not have an important impact on politics. It is sometimes said, for example, that such personality factors do not have much bearing on politics, because the psychic forces evident in the pathological behavior of disturbed individuals do not come into play in the daily behavior of normal people. Rephrasing this assertion conditionally, then, we arrive at the question: *Under what circumstances are ego-defensive* [42] *needs likely to manifest themselves in behavior?* It should be emphasized that my selection of this particular question about actor characteristics carries no implication that "personality" should be conceived of in psychodynamic terms, or that it should be equated with the unconscious, the irrational, and the emotional. It simply is convenient to consider this class of personality characteristics, because psychoanalytic notions have guided so much of the personality and politics literature and have antagonized so many of the literature's critics.

(Glencoe, Ill.: The Free Press, 1951); Erich Fromm, *Escape From Freedom* (New York: Rinehart, 1941); T. W. Adorno, et al., *The Authoritarian Personality* (New York: Harper, 1950).

[42] For the present purposes a detailed conceptual side-trip into the meaning of "ego-defensive needs" will not be necessary. In general, I am referring to the kind of seemingly inexplicable, "pathological" behavior that classical, pre-ego psychology psychoanalysis was preoccupied with. A rough synonym would be needs resulting from "internally induced anxieties," a phrase that appears in Daniel Katz's remarks on ego-defense. "The Functional Approach to the Study of Attitudes," *Public Opinion Quarterly* 24 (1960), pp. 163–204. Also see Fred I. Greenstein, "Personality and Political Socialization: The Theories of Authoritarian and Democratic Character," *Annals* 361 (1965), pp. 81–95.

Much of what I have said about actor dispensability also applies to the present question. Wherever the circumstances of political behavior leave room for individuality, the possibility exists for ego-defensive aspects of personality to assert themselves. These circumstances include "unstructured" political situations; settings in which sanctions are weak or conflicting, so that individuals of diverse inclinations are not coerced into acting uniformly; and the various other considerations discussed under the previous heading. These circumstances make it *possible* for ego-defensive personality needs to come to the fore. They do not, of course, make it necessary—or even highly likely—that behavior will have a significant basis in ego defense.

Given the foregoing circumstances, which make ego-defensive behavior possible, what, then, makes it likely (or at least adds to the likelihood) that deeper psychodynamic processes will be at work? We may briefly note these three classes of factors, locating them conveniently in terms of environment, predispositions, and response.

1. *Certain types of environmental stimuli undoubtedly have a greater "resonance" with the deeper layers of the personality than do others.* These are the stimuli which evoke "disproportionately" emotional responses—people seem to be "over-sensitive" to them. They are stimuli which politicians learn to be wary of—for example, such issues as capital punishment, cruelty to animals, and, in recent years, fluoridation of drinking water. Often their stimulus value may be to only a rather small segment of the electorate,

but their capacity to arouse fervid response may be such that a Congressman would prefer to confront his constituents on such knotty matters as revision of the tariff affecting the district's principal industry than on, in the phrase of the authors of *Voting,* a "style issue" [43] such as humane slaughtering.

One element in these sensitive issues, Lane and Sears suggest, is that they touch upon "topics dealing with material commonly repressed by individuals . . . Obvious examples are war or criminal punishment (both dealing with aggression) and birth control or obscenity legislation (both dealing with sexuality). Socially 'dangerous' topics, such as communism and religion, also draw a host of irrational defensive maneuvers. The social 'dangers' that they represent frequently parallel unconscious intra-psychic 'dangers.' For example, an individual with a strong unconscious hatred for all authority may see in Soviet communism a system which threatens intrusion of authoritarian demands into every area of his life. His anti-communism may thus stem more from a residual hatred for his father than for any rational assessment of its likely effects on his life."

Lane and Sears also suggest that, "Opinions dealing with people (such as political candidates) or social groups (such as 'bureaucrats,' 'blue bloods,' or the various ethnic groups) are more likely to invite irrational thought than opinions dealing with most domestic economic issues. Few people can give as clear an account of why they like a man as why they like an economic policy; the 'warm'— 'cold' dimension seems crucial in many 'person perception' studies, but the grounds for 'warm' or 'cold' feelings are usually obscure. Studies of ethnic prejudice and social distance reveal the inaccessibility of many such opinions to new evidence; they are often compartmentalized, and usually rationalized; that is, covered by plausible explanation which an impartial student of the opinion is inclined to discount." [44]

2. *The likelihood that ego-defensive needs will affect political behavior also is related to the degree to which actors "have" ego-defensive needs.* This assertion is not quite the truism it appears to be. We still have very little satisfactory evidence of various patterns of psychopathology in society [45] and even less evidence about the degree to which emotional disturbance tends to become channelled into political action.

Although it is not a truism, the proposition *is* excessively general. It

---

[43] Bernard Berelson, et al., *Voting* (Chicago: University of Chicago Press, 1954), p. 184.

[44] The quotations are from Robert E. Lane and David O. Sears, *Public Opinion* (Englewood Cliffs, New Jersey: Prentice-Hall, 1964), p. 76. Also see Heinz Hartmann, "The Application of Psychoanalytic Concepts to Social Science," in his *Essays on Ego Psychology* (New York: International Universities Press, 1964), p. 90 f. Lane and Sears also suggest that "irrational" opinion formation is fostered where the "referents of an opinion" are "vague," where the issue is "remote" and it is "difficult to assess its action consequences," and where the "terms of debate" are "abstract." These are points which, in terms of the present discussion, apply generally to the possibility that personal variability will affect behavior (actor dispensability), as well as more specifically to the possibility that ego-defense will come to the fore.

[45] But see Leo Srole *et al., Mental Health in the Metropolis* (New York: McGraw-Hill, 1962).

needs to be expanded upon and elaborated into a series of more specific hypotheses about types of ego-defensive needs and their corresponding adaptations as they relate to political behavior. For example, one of the more convincing findings of the prejudice studies of a decade ago was an observation made not in the well-known *The Authoritarian Personality* but rather in the somewhat neglected *Anti-Semitism and Emotional Disorder* by Ackerman and Jahoda.[46] Personality disorders which manifested themselves in depressive behavior, it was noted, were not accompanied by anti-semitism. But anti-semitism was likely if the individual's typical means of protecting himself from intra-psychic conflict was extra-punitive— that is, if he was disposed to reduce internal tension by such mechanisms as projection. There is no reason to believe that this hypothesis is relevant only to the restricted sphere of anti-semitism.

3. *Finally, certain types of response undoubtedly provide greater occasion for deep personality needs to find outlet than do others*—for example, such responses as affirmations of loyalty in connection with the rallying activities of mass movements led by charismatic leaders and the various other types of response deliberately designed to channel affect into politics. Both in politics and in other spheres of life it should be possible to rank the various classes of typical action in terms of the degree to which the participants take it as a norm that affective expression is appropriate.

[46] Nathan W. Ackerman and Marie Jahoda, *Anti-Semitism and Emotional Disorder* (New York: Harper, 1950).

SUMMARY AND CONCLUSIONS

My purpose has been to reconsider a topic that too often has been dealt with in a rather off-hand (and sometimes polemical) fashion: "Is personality important as a determinant of political behavior?" Five of the more intellectually challenging assertions about the lack of relevance of "personality" to the endeavors of the student of politics have been considered. Two of these seem to be based on misconceptions, albeit interesting ones. The three additional objections can be rephrased so that they no longer are objections, but rather provide the occasion for advancing propositions about how and under what circumstances "personality" affects political behavior.

In rephrasing these objections we see three of the many ways in which the term "personality" has been used in statements about politics: to refer to the impact of individual political actions, to designate the fact that individual actors vary in their personal characteristics, and to indicate the specific content of individual variation (and, particularly, "deeper," ego-defensive, psychological processes). It therefore becomes clear that the general question "How important is personality?" is not susceptible to a general answer. It must be broken down into the variety of sub-questions implied in it, and these—when pursued —lead not to simple answers but rather to an extensive examination of the terrain of politics in terms of the diverse ways in which "the human element" comes into play.

FOR FURTHER READING

BARBER, James D., *The Lawmakers* (New Haven: Yale University Press, 1965).

BARBER, James D. (Ed.), *Political Leadership in American Government* (Boston: Little, Brown, 1964).

DAVIES, James O., *Human Nature in Politics: The Dynamics of Political Behavior* (New York: Wiley, 1963).

EDINGER, Lewis, *Kurt Schumacher: A Study in Personality and Political Behavior* (Stanford: Stanford University Press, 1965).

GEORGE, Alexander L. and JULIETTE, L., *Woodrow Wilson and Colonel House: A Personality Study* (New York: John Day, 1956).

GOTTFRIED, Alex, *Boss Cermak of Chicago: A Study of Political Leadership* (Seattle: University of Washington Press, 1962).

JANOWITZ, Morris, *The Professional Soldier* (Glencoe: Free Press, 1960).

LASSWELL, Harold D., *Power and Personality* (New York: Norton, 1948).

LASSWELL, Harold D., *Psychopathology and Politics* (New York: Viking, 1960).

MATTHEWS, Donald R., *The Social Backgrounds of Political Decision Makers* (Garden City: Doubleday, 1954).

NEUSTADT, Richard, *Presidential Power* (New York: Wiley, 1960).

ROGOW, Arnold, *James Forrestal: A Study of Personality, Politics and Policy* (New York: Macmillan, 1963).

SCHLESINGER, Joseph A., *Ambition and Politics: Political Careers in the United States* (Chicago: Rand McNally, 1966).

SELZNICK, Philip, *Leadership in Administration* (Evanston: Row, Peterson, 1957).

WOLFENSTEIN, E. Victor, *The Revolutionary Personality: Lenin, Trotsky, Gandhi* (Princeton: Princeton University Press, 1967).

PART TWO: ROLE

The first of the microconcepts useful for the analysis of leadership and other political phenomena is role. Unlike those concepts drawn from individual psychology in which a single personality is taken as the domain of inquiry, role analysis is
appropriate when one is interested in the interaction of several actors. It takes
into account the personal needs of the individual who is the focus of analysis at
any point in time, but it also includes the expectations others have about his
behavior. You will probably find that, because role theory is concerned with
interpersonal behavior, your understanding of it will be improved after you have
studied groups and attitudes as well. Then you will be in a position to appreciate
how these succeeding sets of concepts support and enlarge role theory.

The notion of role is ancient, yet the concept of role has a relatively brief
history. Since the time of Aeschylus, in the sixth century B.C., playwrights have
been prescribing the words to be spoken by actors.[1] But it was not until the 1930's
that the term was given a scientific meaning. The first writers who used the word
in a precise theoretical way were George Herbert Mead and Ralph Linton.

Mead and Linton used the word in slightly different ways. Professor Mead, a
social psychologist whose ideas were published posthumously in *Mind, Self, and
Society* [2] was interested in the ability of one person to take the view of another
person, or what we would now call *psychological substitutability*.

> The principle which I have suggested as basic to human social organization
> is that of communication involving participation in the other. This requires
> the appearance of the other in the self, the identification of the other with the
> self, the reaching of self-consciousness through the other. . . . This taking
> the role of the other, an expression I have so often used, is not simply of
> passing importance. . . . The immediate effect of such role-taking lies in
> the control which the individual is able to exercise over his own response.
> The control of the action of the individual in a co-operative process can take
> place in the conduct of the individual himself if he can take the role of the
> other.[3]

---

[1] There is heuristic value in simply reflecting on the theatrical connotations of the word *role*.
Roles as played by various actors have common elements, yet each actor plays the role in his
own way. The common elements in roles suggest the concept of *role expectations;* the actor's
way of playing the role points to *role behavior*.

[2] George Herbert Mead (Chicago: University of Chicago Press, 1934).

[3] Mead, *Mind, Self, and Society*, pp. 253–254.

Professor Linton, an anthropologist whose seminal *The Study of Man* [4] was published in 1936, was concerned with somewhat broader questions of culture and social structure. In Linton's view

> . . . the functioning of society depends on the presence of patterns for reciprocal behavior between individuals or groups of individuals. The polar positions in such patterns of reciprocal behavior are technically known as *statuses*. . . . The relation between any individual and any status he holds is somewhat like that between a driver of an automobile and the driver's place in the machine. The driver's seat with its steering wheel, accelerator, and other controls is a constant with ever-present possibilities for action and control, while the driver may be any member of the family and may exercise these potentialities very well or very badly. A *role* represents the dynamic aspect of a status. . . . When (an individual) puts the rights and duties which constitute the status into effect, he is performing a role.[5]

Although Mead's interest in interaction is still a most important component in role theory, Linton's conceptualization was the more influential. His definitions of status and role provided the basic mold from which much later work has developed. Within a decade and a half, role theory had emerged as a most important technique for describing and understanding complex human behavior.[6] Within that time new concepts had been suggested, and role theory occupied a prominent place in textbooks in anthropology, sociology, and social psychology. Theodore Sarbin had suggested the concept of role enactment, Robert Bales had distinguished between task roles and social roles, and Robert K. Merton had presented the idea of a status-set and a role-set. Kingsley Davis's *Human Society* was published in 1949, Theodore Newcomb's *Social Psychology* in 1950, and S. F. Nadel's *The Foundations of Social Anthropology* in 1951.

Political scientists began to make explicit use of role theory about this time. In *The Governmental Process*, published in 1951, David B. Truman wrote, "When a man enters a legislative position he takes on a new role that is prescribed for him by society. His success as a legislator depends in large part on how well he performs that role. . . . (Legislative norms) require some behaviors and forbid others; still others are a matter of the officeholder's direction." [7] Ralph K. Huitt extended this analysis of legislative roles in a paper published in 1954.[8] Relying upon the work of Ralph Linton, Huitt analyzed the roles played by the members of the Senate Committee on Banking and Currency during hearings

---

[4] Ralph Linton (New York: D. Appleton-Century Co., 1936).

[5] Linton, *The Study of Man*, pp. 113–114.

[6] Edwin J. Thomas and Bruce J. Biddle use the phrase "complex human behavior" to describe the domain of this approach in *Role Theory: Concepts and Research* (New York: Wiley, 1966). The editors of this very useful compendium argue that the use of the term "role theory" is premature. "This implies that there is actually more theory than is in fact the case. The role field exhibits much speculation, and there are certainly hypotheses and theories about particular aspects of the subject, but there is no one grand 'theory.' " See *Role Theory*, p. 14.

[7] David B. Truman, *The Government Process* (New York: Knopf, 1951), p. 347.

[8] "The Congressional Committee: A Case Study," *American Political Science Review*, June, 1954, pp. 340–65.

concerning the continuation of the 1942 price control program. Professor Huitt found that the role of representative was variously interpreted by the Senators to mean spokesman for interest groups, sectional needs, political parties, or the administration. Clinton Rossiter's prizewinning *The American Presidency*, published in 1956, analyzed that office in terms of ten roles—Chief of State, Chief Diplomat, Chief Legislator, Chief of Party, and so on—each President must play. Rossiter did not, however, consciously draw upon the role concepts developed in other behavioral sciences.

The most thoroughgoing use of role theory in political science thus far has been a comparative study of four state legislatures undertaken in the late 1950's by John C. Wahlke, Heinz Eulau, William Buchanan, and LeRoy Ferguson. Our first selection, "American Legislative Roles" by John C. Wahlke, is drawn from one of the working papers for that project. Professor Wahlke first makes the case that there is a need for some more adequate model of human behavior than the rational man and other simplistic models which have animated preceding political theories. Then, in typically careful and exact language, he presents the basic concepts of role. Each person perceives himself in a series of roles, which he defines to himself in terms of actions and attitudes toward other persons and things. It follows that interpersonal behavior can be conceived as a series of role-relationships. In each such relationship, one actor engages in certain actions because he has been cued to do so by his observations of the behavior of another actor or set of actors.[9]

Our next selection, Heinz Eulau's "The Legislature as Decision-Maker: Purposive Roles" presents some of the fruits of that study. Here Eulau is concerned with the broadest set of legislative roles, the institutionally derived legislative role orientations. Professor Eulau notes that there are four general postures one may take toward the actions that should be associated with a legislative position, and he terms these roles Ritualist, Tribune, Inventor, and Broker. He is able to show that there are historical roots for each of these roles, as well as contemporary legislators whose descriptions document the reasons for the continued existence of these four roles. While this selection illustrates the use of the basic concepts, the explanatory power of this approach is better hinted at by Figures 1 and 2 in the Introduction. Here we find support for Professor Wahlke's claim that "we can conceive *any* sub-system of the social system as a system of roles." The ideal construct of *The Legislative System,* and the role systems actually found in the four states, show that the purposive roles are related to more specific representational, interest-group and partisan roles.

The next four articles deal with some aspect of role theory on which a good deal of work has been done. James D. Barber's "The Spectator" concerns the fit between the needs of the self and the actions prescribed for a particular role. The *self* and *role prescriptions* are separate concepts. Self refers to the cognitive organization of qualities about the individual, a cognitive structure which develops as

[9] One of the unfortunate aspects of role theory is that while a number of concepts are basic to the field, no consensus exists on the words that should be used to refer to the concept. Many scholars have been working in this developing specialty, and not a few have used words on their own special way. What one calls role behavior is role enactment for another. One writer uses the phrase role demands while another refers to role expectations. In this book we follow the usage of Newcomb, Turner, and Converse's *Social Psychology,* but it is well to note how each author uses his words in reading about role theory.

the individual matures and as he interacts with others. "Role prescriptions are normative descriptions of ways of carrying out the functions for which positions exist—ways that are generally agreed upon within whatever group recognizes the particular position." [10] It follows that the *role behavior*, the actual behavior an individual displays when he occupies a position depends both on the actions he sees as consistent with his self-concept and the actions stipulated by the role prescription. Studies suggest that role behavior "is more convincing, proper, and appropriate under conditions of self-role congruence, and less convincing, proper, and appropriate under conditions of incongruence." [11]

Professor Barber, one of the small number of political scientists who has shown real skill in handling psychological materials, is particularly interested in how the self affects the role behavior of politicians. In *The Lawmakers,* he depicts four behavior patterns exhibited by Connecticut legislators which he calls the Spectator, the Reluctant, the Advertiser, and the Lawmaker. In each case, he examines the ego needs of the individuals, and then shows how their strategies of adjustment permit them to fill the position of legislator in a way consistent with their self needs. The Spectator, Barber tells us, has an impoverished ego. He is likely to be an observer rather than a vital participant in the legislative process, but is rewarded for faithful followership by expressions of esteem and affection which serve his need for approval from others.

To an important degree, role behavior is learned behavior. The individual brings his own concept of self to the position, but he must learn the expectations of others about appropriate behavior. This may be a difficult process. An adult does not have to go through the complex process of socialization by which a child gains the ability to play the basic roles in society. An adult is likely to have a strong motivation to master the new roles, and he may already occupy roles whose behavior is quite similar to that required by the new role. In this case role acquisition becomes a process of discrimination in which the actor has to learn only the specific behaviors he has not already mastered. But there are still difficulties in his adult role acquisition. These come from ambiguity in cues about what he regards as proper behavior, his possible lack of the necessary personal skills, and the psychological costs of his having to go through a period in which it is obvious to his peers that he is not quite sure of what to do.

"The Initiation Rites of the House Appropriations Committee" is a fragment from Richard F. Fenno's monumental *The Power of the Purse,* a richly detailed study of the entire appropriation process. As illustrated by the case of Fred Santangelo, a Congressman from New York City, a role is learned through a series of interactions with the significant others in the relationship. Representative Santangelo was displeased by his initial assignment to the Appropriations Subcommittee on Agriculture, an area which he believed would not result in meaningful service to his East Harlem constituency. But despite this improbable beginning, Mr. Santangelo went through the normal period of apprenticeship. As

---

[10] Theodore M. Newcomb, Ralph H. Turner, and Philip E. Converse, *Social Psychology: The Study of Human Interaction* (New York: Holt, Rinehart and Winston, 1965). *Position* in their vocabulary has the same meaning as Linton's original term, *status.*

[11] Theodore R. Sarbin and Vernon L. Allen, "Role Theory" in Gardner Lindzey and Elliott Aronson (Eds.), *The Handbook of Social Psychology,* 2nd ed. (Reading, Mass.: Addison-Wesley, 1968), vol. 1, p. 527.

he became more involved in the committee's work, he learned there were activities of the subcommittee of direct concern to his urban voters. By the end of his third year on the subcommittee, Congressman Santangelo had become fully socialized to the norms of the group and had become an advocate of appropriations for agricultural programs.

"Actual role behavior," Newcomb, Turner, and Converse remind us, "may vary from forms that are almost totally determined by personal factors to those that are almost totally determined by positional prescriptions." [12] One can think of a continuum at one end of which almost all of the actions associated with a role would be permitted. At the other end, all the behaviors would be prescribed or prohibited. In the former case, an actor would have a great deal of personal discretion. In the latter, he would find that he was completely constrained by the demands of the position he held. The role prescriptions associated with most positions are made up, of course, of some prohibited, some permitted, and some prescribed actions. But it is still possible to speak of relatively specific [13] and relatively flexible role expectations, and it is important to keep this distinction in mind.

Raymond A. Bauer, a psychologist who has concerned himself with the Soviet Union, took up the challenge of a colleague to weave what he knew into fictional accounts of "typical" Russian citizens. In "The Soviet Party Secretary," we have a fascinating account of A. T. Teplov, First Secretary of the Baltinsk Raion Committee. The role expectations associated with this position gave Teplov some discretion, but there were certain activities in which he had to engage, and other behaviors he had to avoid at all cost. Professor Bauer's description of the flux in leadership positions, the insecurity of the political situation, and the competition for support make for a dramatic account which also lends itself to an analysis of the rigidity of the roles played by Teplov and his associates.

William C. Mitchell is a political theorist who has made important contributions on the macrolevel using two different intellectual approaches. His *The American Polity* [14] is the closest we have in political science to a full-blown functional analysis, and *Introduction to Political Science,*[15] which he wrote in collaboration with his wife Joyce, draws on the quite different tradition of political economy. In "Occupational Role Strains: The American Public Official," he deals on the microlevel with several sources of the pressure and insecurity to which we subject our politicians. Role strain, as Mitchell uses the term, is a broad concept which includes both role conflict and characteristics of the position which cause difficulty for the officeholder.

Role conflict is a concept which has occasioned more research than any other component of role theory. Essentially role conflict arises when the actor is faced

[12] Newcomb, Turner and Converse, *Social Psychology* p. 331.

[13] By reviewing theories of the structure of organizations, D. J. Hickson argues that they reduce to a single aspect of role expectations: the degree of specificity (or precision) of role prescriptions. This contrast between roles with higher and lower specificity corresponds to the terminologies used by Weber (bureaucratic-charismatic), Simon (programmed-nonprogrammed), and Presthus (structured perceptual field-unstructured) in their theories of organization. See, "A Convergence in Organization Theory," *Administrative Science Quarterly*, September, 1966, pp. 224–237.

[14] (New York: The Free Press of Glencoe, 1962).

[15] (Chicago: Rand McNally, 1969).

with contradictory expectations. A number of sources of role conflict have been identified. Role conflict may result from simultaneous occupancy of positions having incompatible role expectations, and from contradictory expectations about the behavior of an actor in a particular role. Professor Mitchell's analysis of conflict between public and private roles illustrates conflict between positions, and his discussion of the problems of occupants of executive positions points to particular roles which have contradictory demands. A number of factors have also been noted which mitigate the effects of role conflict. The most general of these is Ralph Linton's [16] distinction between active and latent roles. Many potential role conflicts do not need to be considered because an individual does not exercise all his roles simultaneously. Other techniques for the reduction of role conflict include support from others who recognize that an actor is subject to role conflict, some formal segregation of the roles, and that familiar aspect of the political world, compromise.

Myron Weiner's "Traditional Role Performance and the Development of Modern Political Parties: The Indian Case" [17] employs microconcepts to analyze a subject—political development—usually dealt with on the system level. "In the age-old attempt to balance stable authority and competitive politics," Weiner tells us, "some countries such as Ghana and Guinea have moved toward stable authority without competitive politics, or, as in the Congo, competitive politics without stable authority. Relatively few countries—Nigeria, India, Malaysia, and the Philippines come to mind—have been able to provide both." An important factor in the Indian case was the Congress Party's success in changing from a mass-based nationalistic movement concerned primarily with breaking the tie with Britain to a political party capable of governing a new nation.

Professor Weiner has studied this transition in terms of role behavior in the Congress Party, and has found that certain traditional roles in Indian society were adapted to the new requirements. In the Belgaum district, the new party role of Expeditor was related to a similar role which served as a link between the citizens and the local administrator during the period of British rule. The party role of Constructive Worker, a person working for the government to extend social services, corresponds to a traditional philanthropic role. The Mediator role, essential to the maintenance of internal party cohesion, is close to the activities of a traditional specialist in dispute settlement. All of these modern party roles could be filled by those with traditional skills, and Weiner finds that these roles are effectively played in the Congress Party. However, there was no traditional counterpart for the modern role of Party Organizer, and this is a task at which Congress Party members have been less successful. Professor Weiner closes his analysis by turning again to macrolevel considerations. "So long as the party's leadership is based largely on those who wield local power and their modes of operation are derived largely from the past, it is unlikely that the Congress Party

---

[16] Ralph Linton, *The Cultural Background of Personality* (New York: Appleton-Century-Crofts, 1945), p. 78. This distinction has since been criticized on the ground that Linton's formulation permits only one role to be active at one time, and subsequent work has shown that an actor can occupy more than one role at once. While granting that the limitation of an actor to a single role is too stringent, the general distinction between active and latent roles is still useful in discussing the avoidance of role conflict.

[17] *Journal of Politics*, November, 1964, p. 830.

in Belgaum district could become revolutionary. But then it is wise to recall that
the changes which often occur under the leadership of those linked with the past
may be no less revolutionary than those which occur under the banner of self-
acclaimed revolutionaries." [18]

[18] "Traditional Role Performance and the Development of Modern Political Parties: The Indian
Case," p. 849.

AMERICAN LEGISLATIVE ROLES
JOHN C. WAHLKE

THE PROBLEM OF A LEGISLATIVE MODEL

If there were a satisfactory general theory of politics, it would include hypotheses about the determinants of legislators' and other political actors' behavior. One difficulty with most available theories of political behavior —individualistic, group, class, and other theories—is their too-great generality: we are interested primarily in the peculiar and unique contributions of legislative actions to the process of governance. But the available theories usually discuss supposedly universal determinants of behavior which affect legislators and other actors alike. Each of these theories would require considerable modification and extension before it could help answer the kinds of questions we think legislative research should answer, questions which concern the functioning of a political system. This is not to say that we may not find significant hypotheses and major propositions in any or all of these theories, but that, on purely logical grounds, we can expect any of them to be inadequate for our purposes.

CREDIT: Reprinted by permission of the author from John C. Wahlke, "The Theory of Legislatures: A Summary of Working Papers and Reflections from the State Legislative Research Project," pp. 8–16.

a. Rationality, perception and behavior: the question of a model political man

Any conception of a legislature pictures it to begin with as a collection of individuals engaging in various actions. No theory or explanation of why a legislature does what it does, therefore, can altogether dispense with a conception of why individuals do what they do. Some theory or model of individual behavior must underlie every model or theory of legislative behavior.

In the ideal-type scientific situation, the behaviorist political scientist would have merely to adopt the substantially validated theory of psychologists concerning human behavior and apply it to his political curiosities. Unfortunately there is not a substantiated theory of behavior; there are fragments of theory, bound up in two loose bundles known respectively as "individual" and "social psychology," not to mention the fact of competing theories within these bundles. Nevertheless, there are certain basic concepts and broad base-line propositions reasonably widespread throughout all the fragments and competing theories of psychology and sociology which can be used in constructing a crude but serviceable model of the political actor as a human being.

Perhaps the weakest point of political theories to date has been their frequent acceptance of an unserviceable model of the political actor which has been called the *rational-man model*. The coldly calculating Benthamite robot, painstakingly guiding each physical jerk by the mental arithmetic of pain and pleasure has been sufficiently belabored to dismiss him from discussion summarily. But it should be recognized that the political actors of Plato, Aquinas, Aristotle and other long-dead theorists, as well as the actors of Rousseau and many later theorists are basically as rationalistic as that of Bentham and other disciples of Hobbes. In every case mentioned, the political actor is pictured as a man who somehow or other (writers disagree on how) is apprised of an end and takes action as a means to that end. Even though there may be the utmost disagreement about proper ends for actors to pursue, there is remarkably little disagreement that action will be motivated by pursuit of the perceived end. Whether the action will in fact produce the desired result is irrelevant to this discussion; the important thing is that action is seen as motivated by the perception of ends and the selection of means (actions) to attain them.

The model of Hume and Burke, which envisions a man engaging in many actions through sheer force of habit, without rational consideration of the ends–means relationship, is in many respects more realistic; but the psychological-theory details of the mechanism of habit is so incomplete as to require considerable supplementing for any analytical use. Besides, for certain crucial purposes, the rational man

was allowed to maintain his sway even in these conservative theories.

Following the suggestive remarks of Wallas and Merriam, some theorists, notably those of the school of Harold Lasswell, sought consciously to adapt the *psychoanalytical* model first made familiar by Freud. More common, if less substantial in the long run, are adaptations of the notions of Jung and other non-Freudians which often resembled or amounted to substantially the same thing as the ancient rational-man model, with something called "power" postulated as an end consciously pursued by political actors.

The models previously mentioned concern themselves primarily with the *motivational* aspects of the individuals' actions, and constitute, in fact, so many competing theories of individual motivation. A more useful focus would seem to be what might be called the *perceptual* aspects. The guiding ideas of such an approach are essentially those suggested by George Herbert Mead and utilized for political analysis first and most notably by Walter Lippmann. Borrowing from the rationalistic conception, we picture any actor acting politically only in a certain *situation,* which, from the actor's standpoint, is an objective set of things and persons influenced by his actions and acting with effects on him. Borrowing from the phenomenological viewpoint in psychology, and explicitly modifying the rationalistic conception, we postulate that the actor's view of this situation is a construct and not an exact picture or replica of the "real" situation. Whether we have in mind the actor's view of something called the total situation or his view of some "object" constituting a component part of this situation, his perception presents two distinct aspects—a cognitive aspect, which has to do with his recognition of the object, person, or situation, and an affective aspect, which has to do with his emotional posture or preferences toward it. Without pursuing further the psychological theory of the interaction between these two aspects, it can be stated that we accept as one of our base-line propositions that what the situation "is" for any actor is his perceptions comprising these elements. Where the situation is one involving a number of actors (as any political situation is, by definition), it must be assumed that however similar they may be in some respects, the various actors' perceptions of the situation differ in many other respects. But the more important theoretical assumption is that action will always be related to these perceptions, and not to what is sometimes thought of as the "real" or "objective" situation. (It should be obvious, of course, that this "real" or "objective" situation is nothing more than a perception by the theorist or commentator ascribing objectivity to it).

Perception thus becomes (at least for purposes of political analysis) an intervening variable between motivation in the general sense (instinct, drive, purpose) and action. The significant feature of such a concept (again for purposes of political analysis) is that it spans all the models of the individual actor previously described. Whether he is motivated by rational pursuit of an end, subconscious, sublimated, displaced, or projected drives and instincts, or other-

wise, insofar as his actions impinge on other persons or objects in a situation, these actions will be in some discoverable relationship to the actor's perception of the objects, persons, and events making up the situation for him. By fastening upon the intervening variable of perception, the political scientist is able to avoid needless commitment to a particular psychological school—"needless" being any commitment which limits his range of choice more narrowly still than his original philosophical and behavioral assumptions. Such generality and freedom of choice is justified by the fact that the aim of legislative research is not to explain the idiosyncratic behavior of any individual legislator or to contribute directly to theories of individual behavior in general. It is rather to explain the constellations of individual actions which constitute legislative behavior and to explain their relation to the political system. Our legislative researcher is assumed to be a political scientist, not a psychologist or sociologist, however much he can profit by intellectual collaboration with sociologists and psychologists.

b. The concept of role

An important corollary of the perceptual outlook leads us, at last, to a notion which can serve us better than any other as an organizing concept. This corollary asserts that an important part of the perceptual apparatus of any actor is his perception of himself, his *self-concept,* which comprises the same cognitive and affective aspects as any other perception. To a large degree, the person sees himself not as a mere isolated and unique "thing" in a universe of unique things, but as standing in certain relationships to other things and persons. The word which refers to his perceptions of his relationships to the things and persons in the universe around him is *"role."* A person in any situation perceives not merely himself and an "objective" situation; he perceives himself in a series of roles, which he defines to himself in terms of actions and attitudes toward other persons and things. To put it another way, the situation "is," to any actor, largely the roles he thinks himself and others do or should play.

The concept of role is a concept relating to social rather than individual psychology. It refers not to the actions, even regular and uniform actions, of a single individual but to the actions of an individual with reference to others. It refers, that is, to *relationships* among people. It is a normative concept in that it refers not to unique, particular actions of individuals but to uniformities and regularities of an individual's actions (behavior) over time. It is a normative concept also in that it refers to expected and preferred actions, to imperatives of behavior, as well as to description of observed statistical regularities.[1]

The behavior of any individual—A, B, C, . . . or N—comprises a finite but almost infinite sum of actions—a, b, c . . . n. A social (interpersonal) situation consists of acting individuals, which we can represent (taking the simple case of two persons) as follows:

[1] The conceptual framework which follows is adapted largely from S. F. Nadel, as set forth principally in his *Theory of Social Structure.*

$$A(a, b, c, \ldots n) : B(d, e, f, \ldots o)$$

The concept of role predicates that significant actions of an individual in such a situation will be "cued" by the observed actions of other individuals. Thus, whenever A sees B, he may engage in actions b, c, e, g (along with many other actions occurring uniquely at the time of each encounter). If these four actions always accompany A's sight of B, we can suspect we are dealing with a role of A. Likewise, if B, upon seeing A do actions b, c, e, g, always responds with actions h, l, m, q, we can be pretty sure we are dealing with a role of B. Putting the two together, we have a role-relationship between A and B:

$$A(b, c, e, g)—R—B(h, l, m, q)$$

Two facets of this relationship deserve special notice. First, from the fact that certain cues always produce certain actions by each individual, we can postulate that there is some notion of propriety or legitimacy surrounding the perceptions of each actor by the other. However unconsciously or subconsciously, A can be presumed to feel that he *ought* to do actions b, c, e, g, under certain circumstances, just as B can be presumed to feel obligated in some fashion to actions h, l, m, q. Second, we can postulate further that each has certain expectations with respect to the actions of the other. In the simplest case, A can perform actions b, c, e, g, *expecting* B to respond with actions h, l, m, q, or *vice versa*. It follows that the role relationship comprises not only the manifest actions and not only the perceptions or feelings of legitimacy concerning those actions on the part of each actor for himself, but also the expectations of each toward the other.

There arise from this conception of the role-relationship three possible situations which differ from the generic role-relationship previously described. In two of them, a given actor has conflicting notions of the actions appropriate for him in a given situation (i.e., in response to given cues). He may be uncertain about the responses appropriate for him to a clear and unambiguous cue, by virtue of entertaining two (or more) conceptions of appropriate actions. Symbolically, he cannot choose between the alternatives represented:

$$(1) \quad B(x) \longrightarrow A(b, c, e, g)$$

$$OR$$

$$B(x) \longrightarrow A(b, c, e, h)$$

Another possibility is that simultaneous cues suggest to A closely related but yet not identical sets of appropriate responses:

$$(2) \quad B(x) \longrightarrow A(b, c, e, g)$$
$$\quad\quad B(y) \longrightarrow A(b, c, e, h)$$

$$BUT$$

$$B(x, y) \longrightarrow A(b, c, e, ?)$$

$$OR$$

$$B(x) \longrightarrow A(b, c, e, g)$$
$$C(y) \longrightarrow A(b, c, e, h)$$

$$BUT$$

$$\left.\begin{array}{l} B(x) \\ C(y) \end{array}\right\} \longrightarrow A(b, c, e, ?)$$

In either of these two cases A experiences role-conflict. It makes little difference at this point whether we choose to look upon this as conflict about how one particular role should be played or as conflict about which of two roles he should play in the given situation. Which interpretation should be preferred depends upon the system actually being investigated and its actual, i.e. empirically demonstrable, character. There is no theoretical reason to think that one of the other type of conflict is more important in controlling the behavior of the system.

The third case to be considered is one where there is no role-conflict for any of the actors of the two sorts just described. But its importance for system-analysis is equally great. This is the case where the occupants of a role-relationship have clear but incompatible or at least different conceptions of their respective roles. Divergent conceptions of a given role may be entertained by two persons linked in a given role-relationship or they may be entertained by two persons with respect to a common role they play toward a third person:

$$(3) \quad \text{It appears to A that } B(x)$$
$$\longrightarrow A(b, c, e, g)$$
$$\text{It appears to B that } B(x)$$
$$\longrightarrow A(b, c, e, h)$$

$$OR$$

$$\text{It appears to } A_1 \text{ that } B(x)$$
$$\longrightarrow A(b, c, e, g)$$
$$\text{It appears to } A_2 \text{ that } B(x)$$
$$\longrightarrow A(b, c, e, h)$$

In general it can be postulated that a system can subsist only if there is a minimum occurrence of all three of the above types of role-conflict. Role-theory further postulates (though we need not pursue the matter further here) that there are mechanisms operating in any system to bring all role-concepts (self's concept of self and others' concepts of him, self's concepts of others and others, concepts of themselves) into congruence and to maintain them in congruence. It is sufficient here to point out that explication of any role-system must include all such instances of incongruence found or suspected.

The character of the role-relationship is significant at this point in demonstrating the connection between that behavioral approach which concentrates exclusively on uniformities of observed, concrete behavior (actions) and that which incorporates a perceptual focus. For one thing, if roles are the normative sort of thing we have suggested, we can elicit (by questionnaire, e.g.) from any actor his perceptions of the actions he considers appropriate toward any given person in any given situation. We thus elicit action (verbal responses) of the kind the strict behaviorist demands. For another thing, we now have a logical (theoretical) framework which enables us to establish theoretical relationships, working through perceptions, among two or more observed uniformities. We have also a concept so defined that we can always establish empirically, for any desired case, the correspondence between a role-relationship defined by the perceptions of the role-takers and the same relationship defined by an outside observer. In other words, we can dispense with one troublesome theoretical and methodological problem which has at times plagued behavioral researchers. We can be "loose constructionists" with respect to the types of admissible data for empirical research without sacrificing the empirical rigor demanded by strict behaviorists.

There remains but one more comment concerning the general role-concept. We have so far talked as if role-relationships exist only between particular individuals, as if they were particularized for innumerable face-to-face sets of persons. This restriction is by no means necessary. It is, in fact, undesirable. Social psychologists have long talked about the "generalized other," just as political scientists have long talked about "the public." There is good grounds for assuming that an individual will see certain actions as appropriate for himself in the light of what he perceives as "public" expectations. So long as we can specify the cues which lead A to think it proper for him to undertake actions b, c, e, g, even if there is no particular person B toward whom he sees himself acting, we can define his role-concept exactly as if we were dealing with a two-person, A to B, relationship. No new theoretical problems are raised.

c. Role theory and political theory

The word "model" has been used during the preceding discussion deliberately to point up the degree of theoretical commitment involved in acceptance of role theory as a guide to legislative research. In taking it for a guide we are doing no more than accepting a model of individual behavior in terms of which we can describe and classify the political behavior of legislators. We acquire, by assuming role theory as a basis, a primitive organizing concept and a limited number of categories for organizing data, but we acquire no hypotheses about relationships among the data. In short, we take on an explicit conceptual framework but not yet a theory. The enormous theoretical power of the concept of role for political analysis stems from the fact that it entails no commitment to or rejection of any existing body of political theory but enables us to incorporate significant contributions from all of them, by interpreting these theories themselves (class, group, etc.) in role terms and thereby relating them to each other.

For example, the concept of role is particularly fruitful for incorporating insights from so-called "group-approaches" to the study of political behavior and institutions. It is compatible with the basic premise of group-based theories: that institutionalized governmental groups (e.g. Congress, the Supreme Court, the Democratic National Committee, etc.) are generically comparable and commensurate with all other groups of persons. It goes beyond this, however, to suggest that what differentiates one from the other type of group is to be found in the role-concepts of the various group-members and the role-concepts of others in their relationships with group-members. A given citizen plays a role as Chamber-of-Commerce member; he plays a role too as member-of-the-political-community. For him, legislative decisions constitute a significant class of cue-giving actions; for him, the legislature is a "generalized other" toward whom he must play roles. Comparison of his role-concepts respecting legislatures with his role-concepts respecting the Chamber of Commerce and of his with others' role-concepts will go far toward explaining for us the character and functions of the political system in society.

An important concept in the literature of groups and institutions is that of "organization." It should by now be fairly obvious how organization-theory can be translated into role-theory terms. Indeed, the very concept of role began with the attempt to describe and explain something called social "structure." Briefly, organization approached in this way becomes an abstracted system of roles which can be described independently of the particular persons playing those roles at any particular time. An organization can be described in terms of the roles which *any* person occupying certain *statuses* empirically found to constitute the organization will play if they assume those statuses. This brings us back to the conception of institutional groups as sets of *offices* which specify roles for all incumbents of those offices.

In short, we can conceive *any* sub-system of the social system as a system of roles. We can describe the principal roles (or statuses, if they are fully abstracted) which make up the subsystem. We can do the same thing for more than one sub-system. We can therefore explore the linkages (through relevant role-relationships) between sub-systems. The concept of role is therefore strategically located whether we wish to move from legislative decisions forward towards explaining "end-variables" of political inquiry or move backward towards explaining why a given system of roles exists in some political sub-system or why individuals occupying certain statuses in that system hold the kinds of role-concepts which produce the role-system we find.

Finally, use of the role concept helps to eliminate some spurious argumentation between "institution-alists" and "behaviorists." The concept of institutions is meaningless if divorced from the behavior of people. The usual way of defining institutions is to call them regularized ways of doing things, which immediately says that institutions are visible only as uniform classes of activity by people. Whatever else they are, institutions are uniformities of behavior. This alone, even without the notion of roles, suggests the futility of dichotomizing behavioral and institutional study into mutually exclusive approaches. This implication is frequently overlooked because many "institutional" studies concentrate upon the functional or what-is-accomplished aspect of the behavioral uniformities called institutions. Use of the role-concept to conceptualize behavior does not require abandoning all concern with functional questions of this sort; on the contrary, we arrived at this organizing concept because we started with just such a concern.

THE LEGISLATOR AS DECISION MAKER: PURPOSIVE ROLES

HEINZ EULAU

As a structure of power, the legislature is functionally interdependent with other structures of power in the political system—the executive establishment, the political parties, the gamut of interest groups, and the aggregate of constituencies, to name only the most significant. Of course, these relations are subject to numerous constitutional requirements and limitations, but within the parameters of the formal institutional context they are forever subject to changing conditions. If the executive branch of the government is dominant, the legislature may primarily function as an agency ratifying executive decisions or attempting to check executive usurpation of power. If the political parties are effective instruments of policy making, the legislature may chiefly function as a disciplined organization of partisans following and supporting the majority or minority leaderships. If the constituencies effectively assert themselves, the legislature may function mainly as a body carrying out the popular mandate. If pressure groups permeate the political system and project their in-terests into the public sphere, the legislature may be more of an institution compromising between and integrating conflicting group demands.

In a system as complex as the political, comparative institutional analysis is difficult. For the institutional variables are gross, and their isolation for the purpose of analysis is not easy. Moreover, the power situation in the political system is never as clear-cut as ideal-type constructions of the relationships among institutions suggest. Empirically, mixed situations are more likely to occur than not. Constituencies may vie with interest groups for the attention of the legislature. The parties may be effective fronts for special interests. The executive may be the voice of grassroots opinion. For these reasons gross institutional analysis may not permit the degree of refinement necessary to identify those legislative functions which are correlates of the power situation, and to relate them to observable legislative behavior.

POLITICAL POWER STRUCTURE AND LEGISLATIVE ROLE ORIENTATIONS

Analysis of legislative role orientations is therefore one way of studying the power position and the functions of

CREDIT: Reprinted by permission of author and publisher from Heinz Eulau, "The Legislator as Decision Maker: Purposive Roles," in John C. Wahlke, Heinz Eulau, William Buchanan, and Leroy C. Ferguson, *The Legislative System*, pp. 245–258. Copyright © 1962 by John Wiley & Sons, Inc. [*Some footnotes renumbered.*]

the legislature in different political systems. Role orientations are legislators' own expectations of the kind of behavior they ought to exhibit in the performance of their duties. They may be considered as providing the premises in terms of which legislators make decisions.[1]

Since "lawmaking" is accepted as the central function of American state legislatures, participation in the making of decisions is not only expected of the legislator but is authorized and legitimized by his occupancy of the official position. But "participation in lawmaking or decision making" is hardly a satisfactory characterization of the role of legislator. Rather it is role orientations which are the specifications of the legislative role, without which the central concept of "legislator" does not, and probably cannot, have much analytical meaning.

His role orientations are probably not unrelated to the legislator's perception of the power pattern of a political system and the kinds of functions which the legislature is called on to perform. For instance, in a party-disciplined legislature the individual legislator is unlikely to find much room for independence or inventiveness; the purely routine aspects of his job probably loom large in his legislative role orientations. In a legislature particularly exposed to the pulls and pressures of interest groups, role orientations are likely to derive from the need to arbitrate, compromise, and integrate group conflicts. In a legisla-

ture subservient to the whims and wishes of the electorate, the spokesman function is likely to be accentuated in legislative role orientations. In a legislature which enjoys relatively great independence from the executive, legislative role orientations may stress the creative, policy-making aspects of the job. Moreover, legislative role orientations need not occur in pristine singularity. Two and three, or even more, orientations may be held by a legislator.

The complexity of institutionally-derived legislative role orientations becomes even more apparent if we place them in a historical perspective. They may be, and probably are, patterned by past as well as current configurations in the power structure of the political system. For as institutions, legislatures are phenomena in time, with memories of their own going beyond the limitations of time. These memories are transmitted by legislators themselves from generation to generation, consciously or unconsciously shaping the perceptions of the present. The past may thus continue to serve as a model for contemporary role orientations.

A legislature is the product of a long and slow growth over centuries, with a veritable maze of rules, procedures, privileges, duties, etiquettes, rituals, informal understandings and arrangements. Every phase of the lawmaking process—from the introduction of bills through their deliberation in committee and debate on the floor to the final vote—has gradually become circumscribed by appropriate strategies and tactics. The legislator was always expected to master the rules of parliamentary procedure and

[1] For an interpretation of role as setting "premises" in decision making, see Herbert A. Simon, *Models of Man* (New York: John Wiley and Sons, 1957), p. 201.

be familiar with available strategies. Hence the legislator could traditionally orient himself to the job of lawmaking in terms of the parliamentary rules and routines, rather than in terms of legislative functions as they may be shaped by the power situation in the political system. Parliamentary ritual rather than parliamentary goals would absorb his attention. One may call this orientation to the legislative role that of the *Ritualist*.

A second orientation is particularly deeply rooted in American political history. It was probably generated by the conflict between the British Crown, acting through the agency of the appointed governor, and the colonial legislatures. In the course of this conflict the legislature came to be viewed as the instrument through which colonial interests could be defended against what were perceived as royal encroachments on colonial rights. It does not matter, in this connection, that the colonists differed among themselves with regard to the proper object of legislative activity— whether the defense of property rights or the natural rights of man were the goals of colonial claims. The crucial point is that the legislature and legislators were expected to be advocates or defenders of popular demands. Wilfred E. Binkley has aptly described the role orientation of the colonial legislator—what we shall call the role orientation of *Tribune:* "The assemblyman, chosen by popular election as a representative of his neighborhood . . . set forth to the provincial capital, commissioned, as he believed, to fight the people's battle against the governor." [2]

[2] Wilfred E. Binkley, *President and Congress* (New York: Alfred A. Knopf, 1947), p. 4.

A third major orientation seems to have originated at a later stage of colonial-executive relations, the stage when the legislature asserted itself as an institution capable of performing independent, policy-making functions. As Alfred De Grazia has summarized this later development, "The Colonial legislatures already conceived of themselves as possessed of a positive legislative capacity removed from the ancient English idea of Parliament as an agency for wresting concessions from the Crown. They had learned well the lessons of the seventeenth century revolutions as well as those to be obtained from the Bill of Rights. Legislatures, they had come to realize, could govern." [3] Once the colonial legislature was expected to be an instrument of governance, rather than an instrument of obstruction, a role orientation more appropriate to the legislature's new function was likely to emerge. We shall call this the orientation of *Inventor*. The legislator was now expected to be sensitive to public issues, discover potential solutions and explore alternatives, both with regard to means as well as ends. The problems of government were deemed soluble by way of rational deliberation and cogent argument in debate, partly because the issues were relatively simple, not requiring technical, expert knowledge; partly because the range of governmental activity was seen as very limited.

Just as the role orientation of inventor derived from the conception of the legislature as a creative, policymaking institution, a fourth orientation—we shall call it that of *Broker*

[3] Alfred De Grazia, *Public and Republic, Political Representation in America* (New York: Alfred A. Knopf, 1951), p. 70.

—developed in response to the rise of interest groups and the increasing number of demands made on legislatures by pressure groups. The legislature became, in the course of the nineteenth century, a major integrating force in the pluralism of American political, social, and economic life. This development had been foreshadowed by the struggle of interests in the Constitutional Convention, in early Congresses and state legislatures, and had suggested to the authors of *The Federalist* the balancing function of legislative bodies. The role orientation of broker was probably implicit in Hamilton's notion of the disinterested representative,[4] and though everyday politics seemed to confirm this conception of the legislator's role as a working principle, it was not articulated in political theory until fairly recently.

This review of legislative role orientations, whether theoretically derived from the legislature's place in the power structure of the political system or historically reconstructed, has suggested four major types—ritualist, tribune, inventor, and broker. There may be others. For example, journalistic accounts suggest many legislators have an orientation which might be called *opportunist*—the legislator who holds the office without really "taking" the associated role, who accepts the bare minimum of expectations, such as voting on roll calls and attending committee meetings or sessions as a passive participant, but who mainly uses the legislative office, or "plays *at*" the legislative role while concealing that he is really playing other, essentially non-legislative roles.[5]

CONTEMPORARY PERCEPTIONS OF THE PURPOSIVE ROLE

Our primary concern here is with how legislators themselves might formulate or define the legislative role as it relates to the lawmaking function in the contemporary setting. We therefore asked our respondents an open-ended question:

How would you describe the job of being a legislator—what are the most important things you should do here?

It was found, in analyzing the interview protocols, that responses to the succeeding question also contained a good deal of the respondents' relevant perceptions:

Are there any important *differences* between what *you* think this job is and the way *your constituents* see it? (What are they?)

Responses to these questions yielded the typology of purposive role orientations, as well as others to be discussed later. . . . At this point we must explicate in greater detail the various purposive role orientations which have been theoretically and historically suggested.

Ritualist. So numerous and complex are the formal rules and procedures of the legislative process that their mastery may appear as the essence of the legislator's role. In the knowledge of parliamentary rules,

---

[4] *The Federalist*, No. XXXV.

[5] Our data do not permit any analysis of such a role orientation (opportunist). It might, however, be profitably investigated by future research.

Finer has pointed out, the legislator "will find all the permissions and prohibitions affecting his right to intervene in discussion. He will discover weapons to defeat his rivals and opportunities to advance his own cause. . . . By adroit use of these rules he may exact concessions by threatening to obstruct his opponents' path with amendments. . . . He will also be able to obtain concessions by the intrinsic merits of his argument, his rhetoric." [6]

Although the rules and procedures of the legislative process are designed to regulate conflict about goals, so overwhelming may be the routine of the process, so consuming its daily impact, that the member's preoccupation with and involvement in legislative maneuvering can become an end in itself rather than remain a means to an end. The legislator then relates himself to the task of lawmaking in terms of the parliamentary routine alone, and he may fail to rationalize his actions by any purpose or goal other than performance of the legislative routine. He is content to list for himself the various tasks which he feels he is expected to perform as a cog in the legislative wheel. In the role orientation of ritualist, therefore, the legislator is particularly sensitive to the flow of legislative business, the intricacies of the legislative maze and the bureaucratic organization of the legislature. The following response is more explicit than most, but its very fullness illustrates the ritualist orientation:

[6] Herman Finer, *The Theory and Practice of Modern Government* (New York: Holt, Rinehart and Winston, 1949), p. 383.

The majority of work is done in committees and then tested by vote on the floor. A legislator should be interested in all legislation. The Speaker has tremendous responsibility as does every committee chairman to determine arbitrarily from a procedural standpoint which bills get precedence and which ones lag. The reference committee and the rules committee in the House determine when a bill moves and to what committee. We're supposed to give out every bill, but that's never enforced as there isn't enough time. Obviously important bills go first and minor ones subsequently. Personal bills of no general interest to those outside of a specific locale get precedence or they are lost in the shuffle. Less than one in twenty bills is partisan. While there are some major conflicts in political philosophy, everyone wants to improve the law, to amend and clarify and repeal the unworkable.

Apparently the minimum expectation of the ritualist is that "the legislature in the last analysis involves voting." Voting is seen as crucial because "you must understand that some of your colleagues and friends may disagree, and this can be cannon fodder for present and future opponents." Through voting, another ritualist suggested, "you can 'backstop the catcher'—stop bills that hurt your county or the state." Indeed, as a ritualist the legislator may really be opposed to lawmaking. As one respondent reported, "an old gentleman once suggested to me that all we should do is pass the budget and go home. He didn't like laws. I agree with him in some respects." The ritualist does not see the budget process as a creative series of acts full of policy implications, but as part of the minimum routine. In this routine the "killing" of bills is seen as more appropriate behavior than enacting needed legislation. At most, lawmaking is seen as a patching-up job if it cannot be helped. The ritualist does not stick his neck out:

Of course, we must review situations, and old situations must be corrected. For old laws have bugs in them. But this way we never get into too much trouble, though we may make mistakes. But then we meet again in two years.

However, the routines of legislative work may be seen as helpful in the performance of some other role, like that of representative:

Primarily, I should acquaint myself with parliamentary procedures and rules and regulations, and finding out where I may avail myself of the necessary information to enable myself to represent my constituency to the highest degree.

But this functional linkage of the ritualist role and another role is rarely articulated. The ritualist emphasizes some particular aspect of parliamentary procedure without concern for consequences beyond those of the lawmaking process as such. One may feel that "the work itself is 90 percent research—determining the facts." Another may say that it is important to attend sessions faithfully and analyze bills before voting. Watching bills may be a passion:

The most important thing, which isn't done enough, is to watch the type of bills that pass and to watch the language of bills. A legislator will serve the highest purpose if he watches every bill to be passed. For when it comes to the floor, this is the last opportunity there is to scrutinize the bill before it will become the law. Too many members will look at a bill but not see certain features that should not be included. I can't stress how important I think it is for every legislator to read and understand every bill before he votes on it.

The concern here is not with the policy content of a bill, but with its technical perfection.

Committee work looms large in the ritualist's orientation. If the legislator cannot hope to understand all the bills, as the perfectionist would have him, he is at least expected to know the bills that come to the committees of which he is a member. The ritualist is impressed by the committee, for it is here that much important work is done. "Voting on the floor is far less important than anything else," a ritualist pointed out; "I guess I would say that committee work is maybe the most important thing. You ought to know the bills that come before your committee." Committee work is central, another respondent said, because "it's in committee that bills are won. You can't understand a bill from floor discussion. It's work on committees and subcommittees I follow religiously."

Knowing one's way around the legislature and various state departments is another facet of the ritualist's orientation: "If you get requests for information, you can't stumble around. I have seen people with experience of four terms not knowing, old-timers not knowing departments." Finally, the ritualist seems to be particularly sensitive to the need of maintaining good relations with his colleagues:

People don't realize that one of the most important jobs here in the legislature is that of making friends—especially on the other side of the aisle. You really have to be friendly and cultivate friends in the legislature, because the more friends you have, the easier it is to get your bills passed.

The ritualist, then, tends to stress the mechanisms of the legislative process and the mechanics of the legislator's job. As an orientation it appears, of course, quite frequently with some other orientation. But it may also appear alone. As a role, the ritualist orientation is highly functional to the maintenance of the legislature as a system and its internal cohesion. But a legislature composed only of ritualists would not be a viable system. In combination with other role orientations, the ritualist's definition of the legislator's job brings a good deal of rationality into the legislative process.

Tribune. In approaching his lawmaking tasks, the legislator may primarily perceive himself as the discoverer, reflector, advocate, or defender of popular needs and wants. It is not relevant, in this connection, whether he sees himself as being guided in his decisions by a mandate from the people he feels he represents, or by his own principles and judgment of what the legislative situation requires him to do.[7] Initially the role orientation of the tribune may have been negative—in the sense that the legislator's primary task was to prevent executive encroachment on what he

deemed to be the people's rights. But the contemporary orientation of tribune includes neutral and positive aspects as well. The tribune may express one or more of three conceptions of his role. He may perceive himself as the discoverer or connoisseur of popular needs, as the defender of popular interests, or as the advocate of popular demands. Different as these conceptions undoubtedly are, their generic focus of attention is invariably the popular environment within which the legislator relates himself to his lawmaking task.

At the very minimum, therefore, the tribune considers it an essential part of his legislative role to discover or know the feelings of the people, their needs, hopes, and desires. He sees it as part of his role to stay close to popular problems, to make himself available to people, to sound out and understand public opinions, if not on each issue, at least on major issues. This does not mean that the tribune must commit himself to popular views, though he may do so. If commitment is thought necessary, it may be counter to the legislator's conviction, as appears in this plaintive note:

It's the same old story of any public official. Once he was expected to furnish leadership, now he's expected to find out what the masses want and go along with them. Legislators now must feel out public opinion and commit themselves to it.

The process implicit in this attitudinally neutral interpretation of the tribune role may be quite conscious:

Well, most important is to keep in close touch with your constituents and find out what they want. That's your primary job. I'm right where they can get hold of me.

---

[7] What, from the standpoint of the legislator as a *lawmaker,* appears as the orientation of tribune, may become, from another standpoint, his orientation towards the area he thinks he represents. This "areal" orientation may, of course, be independently analyzed in terms of different conceptions as well.

That's why I come back—because I offer myself to the people. Other guys were farmers and you could never find them, or they were retired and spent most of their time in Florida.

But the process of knowing people's problems may be unconscious, resulting, it is alleged, from the basic similarity in the experiences of the legislator and his people:

Basically, you represent the thinking of people who have gone through what you have gone through, and who are what you are. You vote according to that. In other words, if you come from a suburb, you reflect the thinking of people in the suburbs; if you are of depressed people, you reflect that. You represent the sum total of your background.

This neutral conception of the tribune may be elaborated in terms of a negative view of the legislative process. The tribune then sees himself not only as a mirror of popular experiences, but he thinks of himself as the guardian and defender of people's interests, either as they are communicated to him, or as he senses them. He considers himself a watchdog of the people's welfare, their liberties and rights:

A legislator has an obligation to protect people's rights; every time you pass a law you take some away from them. The main job is to take away as few as possible. The legislature is a poor man's court, especially the House. Here you can protect him against banks, corporations, insurance companies, and so on.

With me the only reason is to improve things for the ordinary man and the underdog. Big business and rich people have attorneys, accountants and loopholes in the laws, but damn few people are interested in the underdog and minorities.

This negative conception of the legislative process expresses the strongly populist component of the legislator's role which has been traditionally at the core of the tribune orientation. But the tribune may have a positive conception which also derives from the populist tradition. He will indicate not only sensitivity to the people's concerns and interests, but also responsiveness to popular demands and commitment to act on behalf of the people. The tribune appears then, not as a defender, but as a spokesman and advocate. He "must do the most good for the most people to benefit the people"; he must be "an agent of the people's will"; or he "must represent the welfare of the community as he sees it." Here the populist conception is reinforced by a strong dose of utilitarian ideology.

The tribune orientation is one having considerable functional significance in a democratic political system. Although one may take a cynical view of this role, tribunes may be major communication links between the legislature and a more or less clearly differentiated popular environment. From the point of view of democratic politics, tribunes are the "consciences," so to speak, of the legislature. In so far as their commitment to the role is genuine, they serve an important function in the legislative process.

Inventor. Once the technological development of society has reached a scale where expert knowledge rather than lay enlightenment has become a condition of effective government, where the scope of governmental activities has increased so enormously that general understanding is not sufficient as a source of decision making, the formulation of public policy tends to be either a function of the executive, with its corps of expert civil servants, or the product of policy suggestions from well-informed, interested groups outside the formal governmental apparatus. Under these conditions, the individual legislator tends to become less the creator and more the register of public policy. Finer has pointed out that "in modern legislatures everywhere, the large majority of members does little more than vote, . . . only a few discuss, and . . . only a very small minority thinks effectively." [8] Sophisticated state legislators are aware of this. As one of them put it:

We're the policy-making body for the state government, and basically we should give leadership necessary to meet the problems the state faces. In practice it comes from the executive branch.

In spite of the transformation in the distribution of power between executive and legislature, contemporary legislators may continue to perceive themselves as initiators of policy. The

[8] Finer, *Modern Government*, p. 379. In a study of the origin of bills introduced in the Ohio Senate in 1929 and 1939, Harvey Walker found that only about one-fourth of the bills were "member bills," while the remainder were "lobby bills" or "public bills." Of the bills enacted into law, only 8 per cent in 1929 and 16 per cent in 1939 were member bills. Fifty–two per cent of the bills passed in 1929 were "public bills," as were 45 per cent in 1939. See Harvey Walker, "Well Springs of Our Laws," *National Municipal Review* 28 (1939), pp. 689–693. The type of legislator Garceau and Silverman have called "policy oriented" bears interesting resemblances to our "inventors." Similarly, their "Non-generalizers" resemble in some ways our "ritualists." See Oliver Garceau and Corinne Silverman, "A Pressure Group and the Pressured: A Case Report," *American Political Science Review* 48 (1954), pp. 672–691.

type we shall call inventor still sees as his primary task the formulation of the general welfare or of particular policies. He directs his attention to what he considers to be the creative aspects of the legislative job. As one inventor said, the legislator "should try to work for something, rather than just work against things. Also, he should try and seek out problems and use some imagination to solve them." The inventor is interested in solving the current problems of his state—public welfare, education, highway construction, the rehabilitation of the mentally ill, and so on. His self-image is that of the thoughtful and far-sighted legislator, a man of "vision, fortitude, and imagination." The analogy may be made with the role of the doctor:

One has to have certain qualities to be a good legislator. Like a doctor, his job is to cure ills. This state has many economic and social problems, and a legislator with lots of background can grasp these problems and introduce legislation to better them. He can cure just like a doctor can.

But amelioration is not enough. As another inventor put it, the legislator "should be in front of things." Fair employment practices, increased workman's compensation, unemployment insurance and minimum wages, regulatory and tax problems were mentioned as the kind of legislation in which inventive effort is called for. That creative endeavor along these lines is still considered possible, despite the severe limitations under which the legislature must work as a result of the concentration of expertness in the administrative service and executive dominance in policy making, appears in this response:

My primary interest is in legislation as such. I'm amazed and delighted with the freedom I have as an individual to present my own views in terms of what I believe is to the public good.

Is the inventor orientation wholly outdated and unrealistic in view of contemporary requirements for expertise and executive power in policy making? It may well be, and we shall return to this question later on. But it may be that, precisely because modern society depends so much on governmental action, because its technical problems are so perplexing and the pressure of a great variety of special group interests is so urgent, a legislature's effective performance will depend on the presence of members whose orientation to their legislative role is in terms of social inventiveness. These, it seems, are the legislators who, by virtue of a broad view of the lawmaking task, can give meaning to the whole legislative business.

Broker. The idea that the legislature referees the struggle of interest groups, constituencies, and executive agencies, and that in this struggle the legislator plays the role of broker, is probably the dominant theme in studies of the legislative process.[9] But the legislature's function in the context of group pressures and conflicts

involves more than the simple notion of brokerage might suggest. As Latham has pointed out:

. . . in these adjustments of group interests, the legislature does not play the inert part of a cash register, ringing up the additions and withdrawals of strength, a mindless balance pointing and marking the weight and distribution of power among the contending groups. For legislatures are groups also and show a sense of identity and consciousness of kind that unofficial groups must regard if they are to represent their members effectively.[10]

It would seem, therefore, that because of this feeling of identity the broker role is not only to compromise and arbitrate, but also to coordinate and integrate conflicting interests and demands.[11]

The broker may define his role as a legislator in a variety of ways. He may, perhaps naively, interpret it as involving a rather automatic operation which requires him to maintain, within the context of opposing pressures, an "overall picture," best gained by "looking at all sides of a question." The broker may say that "you must not give undue consideration to one group over another"; or, "you must solve the state's problems without being unduly influenced by the feelings of persons who are committed and paid"; or, "you should not make up your mind until you hear both sides, keep an open mind, listen to both sides

[9] The conception of the legislative process as a struggle among groups in conflict is the dominant assumption in such works as David B. Truman, *The Governmental Process* (New York: Alfred A. Knopf, 1951); Stephen K. Bailey, *Congress Makes a Law* (New York: Columbia University Press, 1950); or Bertram M. Gross, *The Legislative Struggle* (New York: The McGraw-Hill Book Company, 1953). But these works are primarily interested in the group character of political conflict rather than its impact on legislators' roles or behavior.

[10] Earl Latham, *The Group Basis of Politics* (Ithaca, N.Y.: Cornell University Press, 1952), p. 37.

[11] The broker role focus is internal, directed towards integration and coordination *within* the legislature, rather than towards the outside, towards compromise among pressure groups.

of any issue, draw your conclusion, and vote accordingly."

The balancing function may be seen largely in terms of personal attributes—"you should be unbiased and tolerant, see both sides, be broadminded"; or:

Most important is to be honest, not only in your dealings, but also intellectually. That's a prime requisite for a politician or statesman. "Politician" has a bad connotation. It's important to see the other man's point of view. Even if you feel that what you want is the absolute best, give a bit and get the next best thing.

Some legislators interpret the broker role in judicial terms:

My job is quasi-judicial. I try to solve differences of opinion within the county to bring out in advance a solution in the best interests of the constituency.

The job is similar to that of a judge. One is faced with a problem. In order to solve this problem, he must have the various facts involved. He must weigh these facts, and make a fair decision.

In this conception of the broker role not only is the fiction perpetuated that all sides must be heard, but the assumption is made that all sides are of equal importance and must be given equal weight. The public interest is expected to emerge from the judicious weighing of all sides, and the decision is assumed to be "just" because it has been judiciously weighed. This elaboration of the broker role reflects a rather undifferentiated view of the structure of the group struggle in politics.

The more sophisticated broker does not see his clienteles as undifferentiated, but is sensitive to the fact that he is exposed to the conflict of group interests whose reconciliation and integration does not simply require impartiality on his part, but an appraisal of opposed claims and demands in terms of their moral worth, the power potential of the groups in combat, and the political consequences for his own position. The following comments illustrate these considerations:

There are always some groups who see things differently and don't agree with the way you vote. Union people want us to vote one way and get mad if we don't. The doctors and insurance people act as a group and want you to vote certain ways, and they all want favors from you.

It's important to watch out that pressure isn't exerted on you from a very vocal minority group where it's against the general public interest. The majority of mail is almost all by special interest groups, while those who support you you don't hear from. Take this dog bill. You hear from all those damn humane groups, but the doctors, whom the bill would benefit, don't even vote. You've to get used to getting somebody mad at you. The more times you are right, the more enemies you'll make.

It's difficult to use the term "constituents" to give a complete picture. Generally speaking I feel I have to find out what's best for the whole county, but particular groups have particular interests that sometimes interfere with the common good. Most constituents feel I'm *their* representative rather than a common representative, and, as a result, I must weigh the conflicting desires of various groups to determine what will benefit the most people in my district.

Others holding the broker orientation differentiate between competing demands in terms of the geographical units with which they may more or less identify themselves. The dichotomy of local district and the state is a major focus of attention associated with the broker role, and it is seen as a source of continuing conflict:

It is my duty and job to introduce laws of interest to my constituents which, of course, are not detrimental to the state. Then I have to make decisions on prospective laws on the basis of how they affect my constituents and the state as well as the nation.

Every legislator is faced with two facts. First, he should be interested in legislation as it affects his district. Sometimes, and I have had it happen, I have had interests at home which were more or less selfish, and there were conflicts. The legislator must look towards problems facing the state and his district and should be introducing and supporting measures for the welfare of both.

These comments suggest that the broker legislator, in Friedrich's words, "is a specialist in diagnosing group opinion in his constituency, and knows just how far to go in order to strike a balance between the pressure from various special groups and the resistance (passive pressure) from the group as a whole." [12]

[12] Carl J. Friedrich, *Constitutional Government and Democracy* (rev. ed.; Boston: Ginn and Company, 1946), p. 319.

THE SPECTATOR
JAMES D. BARBER

REACTIONS: THE SEARCH FOR APPROVAL

In order to understand the personal needs that underlie the Spectator's political style, we must examine his reactions to his political experiences. What pleasures does he derive from political life? What causes him personal discomfort or pain? The Spectator "learns while he's there" in the legislature—learns how to be the kind of politician he eventually becomes. But his learning depends not on what lessons are directed to him but only on those he perceives and incorporates into his own behavior. This process in turn is shaped by the special sensitivities which he bears with him from the past. In the freedom of a long, exploratory interview, these sensitivities crop up repeatedly.

We have seen already in the general characterization of the Spectator a tendency to look to other people for reward; he is entertained, even fascinated, by others. But the interviews indicate that he wants more than a good show from his fellows: his main pleasures in politics seem to come from being appreciated, approved, loved, and respected by others. And his complaints center around situations in which he is left out, rejected, or

CREDIT: Reprinted from *The Lawmakers* by James David Barber, pp. 30–54, with the permission of the author and Yale University Press. Copyright © 1965 by Yale University. [*Footnotes renumbered.*]

abused. A closer look at the three Spectators interviewed illustrates this need for approval.

Sam Thompson: "A warm handshake"

The high point of Sam Thompson's day comes when someone appreciates him. Back in his home community, a small industrial town, he occasionally got the satisfaction of a friendly greeting: "And it makes you feel good when you walk through town and somebody comes up to you and says, 'Hiya, Sam, gee whiz, thanks for that favor.' It does make you feel good." But usually, back home, a legislator is "just an ordinary guy": "You get back home and a representative is not appreciated. A representative is just a person, well a $400 a year man. I've noticed it on several occasions—not that I expect a heck of a lot. I don't."

As an example, Sam cites his experience at the Victory Picnic in honor of the winning candidates. He had to buy his own meal. His picture was left out of the paper. "There, again," he says, "that's a little blow to your ego." What he missed were not free food and pictures but the approval due a winner from his party: "There could have been an apology or something." Similarly, he feels that the salary of the legislators should be raised in order "to give the person that certain lift—not just in money matters, but in personal esteem." When he misses out on minor patronage, when the party in the legislature does not hold caucuses, the significant thing for Sam is, as he says, "I feel left out." Material rewards are important as signs of approval.

In contrast to his home-town experience, the legislature provides for Sam "a good feeling," "a warm feeling." "No matter how small it is," he says, "you are still a part" of it. He feels "the same as anybody else" there. "Everybody has a good morning—a friendly good morning, and people will go out of their way to be nice to you. At least that's the way I find it. I look forward to being here. It gives me that certain buildup." Perhaps the clearest example of Sam's reward from legislative service is found in his story of the Governor's Tea. A euphoric tone runs through his account of this event, only to be followed by a sort of ego-crash:

We were very impressed. I mean you couldn't help but be impressed. It's a beautiful home. The Governor and his wife met us graciously and gave us the full roam of the house—"Go ahead, look at anything you want. Make yourself at home. We'll see you later on." And we wandered around. It's a beautiful home. Everything in it is beautiful. And, ah, then tea was served—so we had coffee (laughs). So we were sitting around, or standing there, and the Governor came by and he talked to everybody, and his wife talked with everybody. So—before that, we drove up in front of the house and a state trooper, there, he opened the car door. The passengers got out. I got out. The state trooper took the car, parked it for me. And, ah . . . so we had tea, and the Governor talked with us. His wife talked with us. And when it came time to leave, we departed. And again, why—a warm handshake. None of this fishy handshake, but a warm handshake. And, ah,

they thanked us for coming—whereas normally we should have thanked them for being invited. They thanked us for coming. And we got out there, the state trooper, he opened the car door. And off we go.

Well, as I say, we had a wonderful afternoon there. As I say, we were only there an hour, hour-and-a-half. It was very impressive. You couldn't help but be impressed. And, ah, got back to town, tell different people about it and they got that—"Yeah? That was nice." No comment, you know? I mean your ego is built up so high, you're impressed here one moment. Then in the [time] it takes to get home, you're right back down on street level again.

This incident was apparently the high point of Sam's legislative experience. The doors opened for him, the gracious greetings and the carefully evaluated handshake, the unexpected "thanks for coming"—perfunctory as they may have been—all strike Sam as signs of approval. Others will go out of their way to show their affection. The callous indifference of his small-town neighbors stands in marked contrast to the warm social environment Sam finds in the legislature.

Sam's few complaints about his life in the legislature are heavily veiled behind the general aura of acceptance and warmth. Jokingly he says that back home, "If they want to call you a so-and-so, they'll call you that, whereas up here they can insult you and do it politely." And in the course of watching others—"how they react to different people"—he notices that "They'll be so friendly to them one time and then another time, maybe a day or so later, they'll walk by and ignore that person. Probably didn't make out too well."

Sam may have had such experiences himself. On the surface, though, he feels personally rewarded by even the most trivial of attentions: being spoken to, being allowed to watch. After the interview, he told the researcher, "What I want to know is your impression of me."

Tom Minora: "Everybody can be a gentleman"

Tom Minora is a quiet, tall, personable fellow from another small town. He is obviously somewhat less dependent on the approval of others than Sam is. In fact, he feels some sense of personal accomplishment as a legislator and takes some pride in having done a legislative job well. But several strands of the same seeking-for-approval pattern run through his conversation and receive special emphasis. Like Sam, he resents the slights he has received in his home town, especially from leaders of the dominant party. "If you're not [an other-party member] there, you're *nothing*," Tom says. "While they're nice, they're not as friendly as they could be."

The legislature is a different world for Tom. In the Assembly "everyone you meet is friendly, no matter who it is—whether it's the Governor or the Secretary of State or all the way down the line, through the legislators, senators and all of them. Very, very nice people." Simply by being a member of the legislature, Tom feels a warm fellowship with the other members. "Once you're a member there," he says, "you're just a part of everybody." On inauguration day he found the most impressive thing "being so close to the Governor, having the Governor speak to you—

almost privately, you know?" He derives a glow of approval from such situations, despite the obvious fact that he was one of a vast audience for the Governor's speech and one of a long line of handshakers.

In contrast to the disdainful attitude of the dominant party at home toward him and his party, the legislators treat him with respect. "I have yet to meet anybody that was other than a gentleman there," he says. "Very, very —I don't know if I should call it the best behavior, but . . . I think probably they're there with, and they know they're there with gentlemen and they behave as such. I think everybody can be a gentleman if they want to." Tom can thus feel accepted into a company that was, by and large, closed to him at home.

Personally, Tom is gentlemanly in the extreme—polite, considerate, cooperative. He seeks in the legislature the approval of other gentlemen, as a sort of confirmation of his status. In part this relates to his own estimate of his background, as revealed in the following passage describing his family's reactions to his nomination:

Tom: Well, they liked it very much —my family [he lists them]—they thought I should do it.

Interviewer: Well, why was that?

Tom (small laugh): Well, I don't know what their thinking was but they thought I—there was no one in our family that ever went into politics too much. Maybe . . . (long pause) . . . maybe it's because we have lived in the same town [for a long time] and . . . we weren't wealthy by any means. We had to work hard. . . . Well, ah . . . we never owed anybody any money. We weren't the best dressed in the world, and so on and so forth. We lived on what we made, in other words, you know? And didn't . . . and had come up it the hard way. And ah, maybe it's because we, ah, I thought that the family would be recognized more than we would have if we didn't have it. You know? There's a certain amount of prestige goes with the job anyway. And like I said, none of my family had ever been part or taken part in politics. Thought maybe this would be the break to get someone interested in it, you know?

To be accepted in the gentlemanly world of the legislature, where prestigeful persons treat him as a fellow gentleman, is a pleasant thing for Tom.

May Perkins: "We should speak to everybody"

May Perkins is a plump, well-dressed, highly voluble person, one of the many small-town lady legislators in the Connecticut House. During the interview it was hard to keep her on the subject. She chatted on and on, describing incident after incident in great detail. Almost all the tales have a common theme: they concern her adventures in conversation, her constant social round of speaking to others and being spoken to in return. It is in the course of this continual social interaction that May Perkins seeks the signs of approval that appear to mean so much to her.

Before she came to the legislature, May says, she had "always held it in awe, as something real nice, very— quite an honor to be in and all." But she quickly gets on to her main interest in the legislature: "In fact, I've met a lot of people—I feel, when we're in there, we're all in there for the same reason, we're all in the House or the Senate or something, so we should

speak to everybody." She was "real upset" when a member failed to greet her, even after repeated introductions. "He didn't even speak!" she exclaims. "What a snob. What's the matter with him?" Generally, however, she finds the legislature a place where "I don't find any of them now that actually *will not speak*. I haven't noticed anybody that I wanted to speak to. In fact, some of them are more than friendly, you know, make a point of speaking and finding out your name and everything." In a situation she describes as "wonderful," "just so nice," she was spoken to from all directions: "One man called me up to come up and talk to him and another man flagged me before I could leave—'Come over here and see me.' And there were a couple of others I spoke to. So it's real nice."

May is enthusiastic about the "many nice social affairs" connected with the legislature, especially the formal dinners ("fabulous!") and the regular get-togethers with the other female members. Before and after House sessions, she visits continually with those in neighboring seats, pausing to say hello and pass a few words with legislators as they find or leave their seats. May Perkins' happiness is increased when she is surrounded by acquaintances who reward her with attention, recognition, and approval.

May is little interested in the questions the interviewer asks. She has her own tales to tell, stories which almost always point out how others approve her. When others "appreciate anything you do and they recognize— they know you"; when she is told she is "no detriment to society"; when another "listens very carefully now, because maybe my name will be mentioned" on television; when she is told that her group will be honored when others know she is a member—when these things happen, May feels a sense of well-being and, at the same time, demonstrates in the telling of the stories her need for the interviewer's approval.

These three Spectators thus appear to derive considerable personal satisfaction from the approval of others, and to feel hurt or at least uncomfortable when others reject them. This search for approval is perhaps best indicated by Sam's final plea to the interviewer: "What I want to know is your impression of me." The answer he wants is evident: that he is all right, that the other person feels positively toward him. In the legislature he finds, by and large, just the sort of warm, accepting social environment he is looking for.

The spectator's rewards

The rewards the Spectator experiences are of three kinds, each stressed by one of our three Spectators.

In the first place, there is the reward of *admission,* of being allowed to become part of the group. All three Spectators show a positive reaction to this aspect of legislative life. They "become a part of everybody" simply by becoming members of the legislative body. For Sam especially, being admitted—having doors opened to him, being allowed the "roam" of the Governor's mansion, being invited to attend the political show—are signs that he is valued by others. Thus the new member becomes an insider, with all the joys of belongingness at his disposal. He has passed through the elec-

toral initiation ceremonies, and is now a full-fledged member of the fraternity. Simply being with others, close to them, seems to show that they value him. For otherwise, would they not send him away? His tendency is to blur over the fact that he holds his seat by right, that he cannot be excluded, and to feel his membership as a privilege accorded to him personally by his fellow members, thus proving that they like him and want him there.

In a second way, illustrated especially in Tom's case, the *prestige* of membership gives pleasure to the Spectator. The others who accept him are worthy as well as friendly. Tom grew up amid hard times in a community where people of his political persuasion were "nothing." Now he is in the company of gentlemen and feels that he can be a gentleman too, if he tries. To have the approval of one's peers is pleasant; to be accepted by one's betters is more so. The person who comes to the legislature from a generally lower status position may be particularly impressed by the fact that he is thrown together with governors and secretaries and chairmen.[1]

Prestige is, of course, a relative thing. The step into the legislature is upward, downward, or horizontal, depending on where one begins.[2] Certain-

[1] In their questionnaires, Spectators are the members most likely, after the session, to choose "Generally, the public looks up to a state legislator with respect" rather than "Generally, the public is overly critical of state legislators." Spectators 89% (N = 27), other new member respondents 71% (N = 56).

[2] This is nicely illustrated by contrasting observations on the same session of Congress, as quoted by George W. Galloway, *History of the House of Representatives* (New York: Crowell, 1961), p. 35 Cf. Charles L. Clapp, *The Congressman* (Washington: Brookings Institution, 1963) pp. 17–20.

ly many a prosperous, highly educated legislator does not feel particularly flattered by his status as a representative. But neither does every lower-status person. Status-mindedness, here in the form of a desire to be approved by those one considers his betters, is in part a personal sensitivity, an inclination to perceive and attend to gradations in rank. The Spectator increases the quantity of affection he receives by thinking of himself as being liked by everybody, by all those other legislators. He increases the quality of the affection he receives by thinking of the others as worthy. To have the admiration of the admirable multiplies the joys of belonging.

Finally, the Spectator is rewarded by approval *expressed directly* to him. In his imagination Tom is able to feel that the Governor's address is aimed at him personally, "almost privately." It would have been even more rewarding if the Governor had paid his respects directly, face-to-face, so that there could be no doubt that they were meant for him. May Perkins, more than either of the other Spectators, is concerned with this problem. She must be spoken *to* in an approving way, and it is very important that her name be mentioned. In her continual participation in ceremonial greetings and small talk she gathers in tokens of affection that have a higher value for being paid in person. Sam's emotional apex ("your ego is built up so high") comes when the Governor greets him personally, and with a "warm handshake" grants him approval from on high.

Expressed most abstractly, then, the Spectator's rewards of approval can be seen in three stages: first, he is allowed near the other; second, the other is worthy; and third, the other expresses approval to him.

SELF: THE IMPOVERISHED EGO

When we find members of the legislature continually turning to others for expressions of esteem and affection, showing marked sensitivity to the opinions and evaluations others express to them, we suspect the presence of some underlying need for this kind of behavior. Undeniably, all of us stand in need of affection from our fellow men. But the Spectator appears to demand this kind of reassurance from his social environment to an unusual degree. Why this continual reaching out for approval?

Apathy?

"Whenever we see glamour in the object of attention," writes David Riesman, "we must suspect a basic apathy in the spectator."[3] Our Spectators, as we have seen, place a good deal of emphasis on the glamorous aspects of the legislative show. And indeed, a close look at their interviews does reveal a basic apathy, a lack of deep feeling about themselves and their world. In a number of passages this emotional impoverishment shows through:

I hadn't really any complete desire.
I had no feelings one way or another.
If I win, I win; if I lose, I lose.
As far as any special plans or dreams, I
   have none.
. . . And to me it didn't make a damn bit
   of difference whether I voted for or
   against it.
I don't care if I get it or not.

[3] *The Lonely Crowd—A Study of the Changing American Character* (New Haven: Yale University Press, 1950), p. 214.

Furthermore, the pleasures he does experience seem peculiarly superficial and temporary—

I get a big charge out of that.
It's such a nice new experience and we're all getting such a kick out of it.
It gives a person that certain lift.

—or vague and clichéd: "wonderful," "interesting," "new," "nice." The Spectator as an individual, a person with his own special ideas, interests, and wants, does not emerge strongly in the interviews. Even in May Perkins' continual chatter there is a strain of the "weariness, anxiety and diffuse malaise" Riesman found among his "other-directed" subjects. Indeed, Tom Minora illustrates the other-directed type precisely, in this passage: "It's like the old story—when you're in Rome, do as the Romans do, you know? If you're a legislator, act as a legislator. And when you're outside, you act to . . . the environment, I guess." He appears to lack internal guidelines of his own, basing his behavior on a sensitive perception of the demands of the environment.

For such a person, the glamor and occasional excitement of legislative activities lend a much-needed spice to life. Lacking passion, he seeks amusement. So long as he can get a "charge," a "kick," a "lift" out of life, he can perhaps forego the deeper satisfactions. And his own temporary excitement helps to reassure him that he is capable of feeling.[4]

But in the light of psychological research, we must be suspicious of this characterization as well. Surface placidity or indifference may well conceal intense inner turmoil.[5] Riesman's formula can be extended as follows: "Whenever we see a basic apathy, we must suspect conflict within the personality."

Furthermore, "apathy" does not go very far to explain the Spectator's need for approval. Why should the person without feelings of his own ask affection of others? We need to take a careful look at the few occasions on which the Spectator talks about himself and describes the kind of person he is.

Self-doubt

Sam Thompson gives us an indication when he tries to answer the question, "How would you rate your own performance as a legislator so far?" Sam, hesitating, is encouraged with "That's a hard question."

No, not necessarily. I think I've done fairly well, to the extent that [long pause] well, gosh, that *is* a hard question. I think I've done fairly well to the extent that . . . I've a feeling of self-consciousness.

[4] Glamour "is not only a veneer for apathy but also a sign that people crave a political leadership that, by dispelling their apathy, would allow them to become excited, committed, and related to politics. That is, glamour has an ambivalent effect: it reinforces apathy by invoking consumership motivations, while at the same time people look to glamour as a way of altering their motivations" (ibid., p. 215).

[5] For detailed analysis of conflicts underlying placidity, cf. Anna Freud, *The Ego and the Mechanisms of Defense* (New York: International Universities Press, 1946), chap. 8; Harry Stack Sullivan, *The Interpersonal Theory of Psychiatry* (New York: Norton, 1953), pp. 55–57; Otto Fenichel, *The Psychoanalytic Theory of Neurosis* (New York: Norton, 1945), pp. 185–86; Ralph Greenson, "The Psychology of Apathy," *Psychoanalytic Quarterly*, 18 (1949), 290–302; Nathan Leites, "Trends in Affectlessness," in Clyde Kluckhohn and Henry A. Murray, (eds.), *Personality in Nature, Society and Culture* (New York: Knopf, 1956), chap. 40.

And since I've come here to Hartford, I don't feel self-conscious any more. I feel as if I can mingle right in with them, and, ah—I first had a fear that, well, all that run for representatives are probably retired people, well-to-do people, people with financial means, so they could take the time off from their occupations and spend the day—and that all went through my mind between the time I was elected and the time I should go. But as the sessions went on, I feel I'm just as qualified to present myself to the Assembly as [another legislator]. Sounding a little like an egotist. [laughs] . . . And for that reason, I feel good. I mean I've overcome—yeah, over . . . came some of this self-consciousness. Or whether it's self-consciousness, or, ah—doubt.

Sam classes himself with the "ordinary people" on a legislative committee, in contrast to the witnesses who come before it—people who, with "their vocabulary, their wordage," are "educated—they know what they're talking about." He feels he failed as a salesman: "Well, I'm not aggressive enough."

Similarly, Tom Minora sees himself as "the type of person that's—I, ah—self-conscious, shall we say?" He would have preferred another committee than the one he is assigned to, "if I could have handled it." He feels "like a plain dope" in conversation about politics. "If I'm anything," Tom says, "I'm too much on the conservative side," by which he means too unassertive, in contrast to people who "force themselves on you." And May Perkins had doubts about accepting the nomination: "I was a little bit scared at the idea of, maybe, what if I couldn't do it satisfactorily?"

When he rates himself, the Spectator points to "self-consciousness," lack of aggressiveness, fear of performing unsatisfactorily. These self-characterizations are consistent with the idea that the Spectator is lacking in self-confidence. In fact, however, he seldom rates himself directly. His main evaluations come in the course of watching others watch him.

What others think

Sam makes a particularly revealing comment in this regard when he is explaining why he finds the legislative experience "wonderful." "You get back home, you're just an ordinary guy. You get up here, it's 'Mister' and 'Sir'—*nobody knows who you are,* your bank account, the mortgage on your house. And so it's like a tonic to get up here."

Later he repeats this thought: "You're treated with respect because nobody knows who you are." The implication is clear: if the others "knew who he was," they would not respect him. Who would then call him "Mister" and "Sir"? The real Sam Thompson, he seems to be saying, is not worthy of respect.

In Sam's search for approval a great deal depends on maintaining a protective external façade, behind which his supposed inadequacies can be safely hidden. When the front begins to break down, he expects disapproval: "I've seen different members of the committee—not that I'm knocking them personally, but this is just a broad statement—they got holes in their shoes. Their heels are run down. Their ties got spots on them."

When high-class witnesses appear, Sam says, "Sometimes I have my doubts. Sometimes I feel as if there might be some scorn in their eyes or something." His need to keep his inner nature hidden is evident: "I've countered some of my nervousness, so that a person looking at me might have some doubt that I'm nervous. I mean, I know myself that I'm nervous, but the person watching might have some doubts."

Sam can take care of his physical front by dressing neatly and guarding against the outward betrayal of his nervousness. It is when he has to speak to others that the danger of revealing his inadequacies is greatest. No wonder, then, that Sam feels threatened when he anticipates having to address the legislature: "Yeah, when you're in the session there and you have the mike in front of you and the button [for voting] there, that thing can scare you, you know? You have to pick it up and you have to speak into it and there is a tenseness."

Even in informal conversation, he feels a necessity for avoiding the revelation of his own personal preferences: "For myself, I like to play games with people. I like to confuse them. I get a little—I'll say one thing to them, and then in the course of conversation I'll twist my feelings around to the complete opposite. And, ah, I'll look at the people and they'll look at me and wonder what's going on. Words—it's only words."

The outlines of Sam's adaptation to the legislature become clearer in these passages. He judges himself harshly; he has doubts about his worth as a person. For this reason, he avidly seeks the approval of others, the reassurance of their affection. But sensing his own unlovableness, he fears that others will reject him if they find out what kind of person he is. Therefore he hides behind a conventional front, remains silent, and, when he must interact with others, avoids revealing his feelings to them. He thus cuts himself off from the deeper, more abiding affection that comes with mutual understanding. He must make do with the meager rewards of being called "Mister," of perfunctory handshakes and greetings. This is not much but is better than nothing at all. And the alternative—discovery and rejection—is considerably worse.

There is a similar theme in Tom Minora's makeup. One reason he would like to return to the House, he says, is that there he can remain "not too much in the limelight." He avoids political discussions in which he thinks he would perform badly. He tells of an innocent social mistake at the beginning of the session in which he wondered why he was "getting these kind of funny looks, you know?" and concludes, "That was stupid." Tom feels "a little bit squeamish" about speaking and was "very nervous" when he had to once. His retiring habits— "unaggressiveness"—very likely serve protective functions.[6]

In turning to others for self-evaluation, Tom finds a general reac-

[6] For the approval-seeking person, Horney writes: "The timidity serves as a defense against exposing one's self to rebuff. The conviction of being unlovable is used as the same kind of defense. It is as if persons of this type said to themselves, 'People do not like me anyhow, so I had better stay in the corner, and thereby protect myself against any possible rejection.'" Horney, *The Neurotic Personality*, p. 137. This protective device decreases the person's chances for gaining affection, because the need remains concealed. For further evidence of the relation of concealment and low self-esteem, see Leonard I. Pearlin, "The Appeals of Anonymity in Questionnaire Response," *Public Opinion Quarterly*, 25 (1961), 644.

tion of friendliness in the House. But on several occasions he expresses doubt that others mean what they say when they praise him. When a town party official asked him to run, he said he thought Tom would be a good man. Reporting this, Tom immediately adds: "You know how they spread it on." His friends congratulated him— but, Tom says, "Of course there's no way of knowing whether they really mean it or not." He finds that witnesses before his committee are "very respectful," but implies that this is only because they are forced to act that way:

TOM: Very respectful.
INTERVIEWER: They look up to the committee members?
TOM: They know we're their judges —they've got to. If they don't know that then they shouldn't be there.

Thus Tom seems to feel it is implausible that others really respect and admire him, freely and willingly. When he is praised, he doubts the sincerity of the praise. Like Sam, Tom also seems to take a somewhat condemnatory view of himself, and to seek approval and reassurance in order to help assuage doubts about his worth. But he cannot quite bring himself to believe in the affection he receives. This suspicion hampers the confident acceptance of direct expressions of approval, and Tom settles for the lesser, indirect rewards of membership, vicarious participation, and withdrawal from the center of attention.

May Perkins appears in the interview as a lady who protests too much. She relates no fewer than eighteen incidents to show that others approve her. If she were confident of her worth,

would she go to such lengths to demonstrate it to the interviewer? Why the repeated effort to show that she really is appreciated, to prove in specific detail that others have responded favorably to her? It is a safe conclusion that she herself has doubts about her value and is trying to assuage these feelings by gathering compliments.

May, as we have seen, is excessively sensitive to the impressions that she gives to others and others give to her. Yet there is little in her interview to indicate insight into others' characters or individual variations at any level below the superficial outward aspect. She moves in a world of social surfaces. Her praise is reserved for those who put themselves over by the manipulation of their impressions.

Thus May is enthusiastic about a person who "is so *nice*" as a speaker. "He's got a nice face, to begin with," she says, and "he's so pleasant." "He always speaks and he always passes the time of day." "I guess I just like the Irish," May concludes. "There's something awfully nice—personable about them." The important thing is to give an impression of sincerity, not to be too "cocky" or "aloof," not too "stuck-up" to speak to people. "Did you hear Amos Walker speak?" she asks. "Wasn't he wonderful? He is so good, and he is so darn sincere. And everybody knows that he has nothing to gain by anything he talks on. . . . He's very sincere about it." "The only thing I've found in true experience," May continues, is that "everybody's sincere in his thinking." She then goes on to relate an experience when she was let down by someone who did not fit this rule—who tricked her into a situation in which *she* had to appear insincere. She felt considerable anxiety in this situation because her image was almost compromised.

In another context, May evaluates a party leader: "I think he is trying sincerely to remember everybody. And he's very friendly—he just speaks every time he sees anybody. Maybe he doesn't know who we are from Adam, but at least he speaks, and he acts like he's seen you before." Here the importance of maintaining an impression is most fully revealed: the other is appreciated because he *acts* as though he knows her. A sincere front is the important thing. The reality may be too much to ask.

The differences between May and Sam and Tom in this respect are thus not as wide as casual observation might indicate. May is a talker; Sam and Tom are quieter types. But all three are excessively concerned with presenting a social exterior which they feel will bring them the rewards of approval and protect them from disapproval. The clear implication is that, from the Spectator's point of view, this protective exterior is necessary for approval, because the person behind the mask is unlovable.

The Spectator's need for approval from others, then, appears to spring from his doubts about his own worth. When he appraises himself, he reaches a discomfiting conclusion: he feels inadequate and inferior. Political participation offers opportunities to palliate these feelings. To gain a sense of personal worth by gaining from others signs of approval.[7]

But from the Spectator's own viewpoint, this dependence on others has a threatening aspect, too. The approval he receives is fundamentally spurious; others appreciate him only because they do not know him. His primary problem is a strategic one: he must manipulate his social environment in ways that maximize approval of him and minimize disapproval.

What techniques does the Spectator employ for these purposes?

STRATEGIES: FOLLOWERSHIP AND ITS ALTERNATIVES

When a person confronts the gap between what he is and what he wishes he were, he experiences feelings of tension, feelings that may range from minor dissatisfaction to despair. Certain familiar social strategies are used to cope with such feelings. Without going into the genesis of these strategies,[8] we can summarize them briefly as follows. First, the person may react aggressively. He lashes out at others (either actually or within his own mind) and thereby displaces a good deal of the aggression he feels toward himself. This scapegoating behavior is familiar from studies of intergroup relations. Secondly, he may withdraw

---

[7] On anxiety and company-seeking, cf. Stanley Schacter, *The Psychology of Affiliation: Experimental Studies of the Sources of Gregariousness* (Stanford: Stanford University Press, 1959).

[8] Cf. Alexander L. George, "Some Uses of Dynamic Psychology in Political Biography," p. 14: "The usefulness of the technical literature to the biographer will be enhanced if the distinction is kept in mind between the question of the *origins* of compulsiveness and compulsive traits, about which there are various views, and the *dynamics* of such behavior, about which there is less disagreement." Cf. Erik H. Erikson on "originology," *Young Man Luther* (New York: Norton, 1958), pp. 18–19.

into himself. Especially if his inferiority feelings are based on a sense of failure to meet the norms of the groups he is in, he may fall back on internal norms of his own that he *can* satisfy. The superficially self-satisfied person who seems oblivious to his inadequacies is an example. A third technique for assuaging such feelings is achievement. The person recognizes his shortcomings and sets out to do something about them, to achieve self-respect by accomplishing valued ends. Finally, the self-doubting person may react by adopting a follower role. In effect, he seeks to satisfy and placate the demands of those who would reject him by giving in to them. He thus buys a certain amount of self-approval, at the cost of a certain amount of subservience.[9]

Over the course of a lifetime such strategies of adjustment tend to become habitual.[10] It is as if the person makes a decision, adopts one main method of adjustment, and then sticks to it. For each of these patterns pays off with some sort of reward: when the aggressive person finds that he feels better after having hurt someone else; when the withdrawn experiences a comfort in his own mind that he could not obtain from without; when the achiever knows the satisfaction of accomplishment; when the submissive person feels that others approve him for his service—these comforting feelings, if repeated often enough, tend to solidify into a fixed style of adjustment. The person has found a "solution" to his main adjustment problem.[11]

The more severe the internal problems an individual experiences, the more rigid this pattern becomes. At the extreme the psychotic person develops a fixed pattern, which ordinary experience simply cannot alter.

[9] Cf. Karen Horney on "moving toward people," and "moving away from people," in *Our Inner Conflicts* (New York: Norton, 1945).

[10] This is not to say, of course, that no significant changes take place after one reaches adulthood, or that personality becomes permanently fixed in the early years, though evidence of the latter appears inconclusive. See Ian Stevenson, "Is the Human Personality More Plastic in Infancy and Childhood?," *American Journal of Psychiatry*, 114 (1957), 152–61. On adult consistency, E. Lowell Kelly found considerable stability in some variables (e.g. attitudes toward marriage, rearing children) among 446 subjects after twenty years of adult life: "Consistency of the Adult Personality," *American Psychologist*, 10 (1955), 659–81. D. P. Morris, E. Soroker, and G. Buruss, "Follow-Up Studies of Shy, Withdrawn Children. I. Evaluation of Later Adjustment," *American Journal of Orthopsychiatry*, 24 (1954), 743–54. Cf. G. W. Allport, J. S. Bruner, and E. M. Jandorf, "Personality under Social Catastrophe: Ninety Life-Histories of the Nazi Revolution," in Clyde Kluckhohn and Henry Murray, eds., *Personality in Nature, Society and Culture*, p. 443: "Very rarely does catastrophic social change produce catastrophic alterations in personality. . . . On the contrary, perhaps the most vivid impression gained by our analysts from this case-history material is of the extraordinary continuity and sameness in the individual personality." For evidence that ability to dispense with minor habits is strongly related to childhood experience, see Charles McArthur, Helen Waldron, and John Dickinson, "The Psychology of Smoking," *Journal of Abnormal and Social Psychology*, 56 (1958), 267–75. On the meaning of "habit" or "habit potential" as "the probability of evocation of the response," rather than a fixation, compulsion, or obsession of some kind, see John W. M. Whiting and Irving L. Child, *Child Training and Personality* (New Haven: Yale University Press, 1953), pp. 18 ff.

[11] Cf. Horney, *Neurosis and Human Growth*, pp. 185–86. Newcomb notes that "threat-oriented behaviors are commonly rewarding, and hence persistent, because they are perceived as defending the ego—perhaps imperfectly, but nonetheless in the best way in which the person knows how." *Social Psychology*, p. 462.

Even when his behavior results in disastrous disruptions of his life, he still cleaves rigidly to a pattern that has brought him some reward or relief in the past. Reality no longer has any relevance to his happiness.

As we move from the psychotic extreme toward the "normal" person,[12] the interplay of internal problem and external environment alters. The individual is more and more in touch with reality, more and more able to alter his course according to the rewards and punishments he receives. The fixity of his pattern of adjustment depends, on the one hand, on the intensity of his need for a particular kind of reward, and on the other, on the availability of reward from the environment for the pattern he has adopted. If he feels only an occasional mild twinge of self-doubt, for example, he will probably be able to handle this problem with an occasional mild burst of aggression, withdrawal, achievement, or submission. He need not invest all his efforts in one reward-gaining pattern.

Even if his need for reward is great, however, the fixity of his pattern of adjustment will depend also on the availability in the environment of the particular kind of reward he seeks. The pattern will tend to break down under the impact of repeated punishments for attempts to maintain it—again, assuming that the individual is in touch with reality. The shy, withdrawn person, for example, who finds himself in a group where every member is required to perform publicly and receive criticism of the performance, tends either to leave the group or to change his pattern, perhaps by engaging in some tentative experiments in self-assertion. When the need is great and the environment offers reinforcing rewards, the pattern will tend toward rigidity and permanence. When the need is mild and the environment offers pattern-contradicting rewards and punishments, the pattern will tend toward flexibility and change.

We proceed now to examine the Spectator from this viewpoint. Which set of strategies does he tend to pursue? Given his particular needs, what is involved for him in changing this pattern? Given the legislative environment, what reinforcements does this pattern receive from without? And, therefore, how likely is it that the Spectator will continue to pursue this set of strategies?

Submitting

According to Sam Thompson, the proper role of the freshman legislator can be summed up in a simple for-

[12] This is probably as good a place as any to assert categorically that I do not consider the subjects of this study "psychotic," "neurotic," or even especially troubled in comparison with the theoretically normal population. Such terms represent overlapping categories. The use of clinical language implies only that certain concepts have an applicability to the generally well-adjusted as well as to those under treatment. For evidence of such continuities see, for example, Gerald Gurin, Joseph Veroff, and Sheila Feld, *Americans View Their Mental Health* (New York, Basic Books, 1960), especially chap. 11; Raymond B. Cattell, *Personality* (New York, McGraw-Hill, 1950), especially chap. 1 and 17; William Schofield and Lucy Balian, "A Comparative Study of the Personal Histories of Schizophrenic and Nonpsychiatric Patients," *Journal of Abnormal and Social Psychology*, 59 (1959), 216–25. For a good introductory discussion of such matters, see Fenichel, *The Psychoanalytic Theory of Neurosis*, or Newcomb, *Social Psychology*, pp. 392 ff.

mula: "The main function, far as I can see, in my position—I'm a freshman. The main functions of a legislator here are to keep your ears open, your mouth shut, and follow your party leaders." His main complaint against the leadership is that they have not taken a stronger hand:

SAM: I feel left out. I feel that leadership is doing a poor job.

INTERVIEWER: How's that?

SAM: Well, it's a known fact that—I believe there is about 100 new members of the legislature who have to be told what to do and what not to do. Otherwise, I—getting back into known fact—leave a [party group] alone and they'll fight. Right or wrong, they'll fight. And I think they have to be led, have to be steered. . . . The leadership has been too busy or they've taken the attitude that, well, the fellows can operate on their own. And I don't think that's right.

Similarly, Sam takes a "serving" stance toward his constituents. One of the things that has helped him as a legislator, he says, is

the desire to show the townspeople that they didn't make a mistake, that I can get up there and work for them. Of course, in my campaign I told the people there that my—the limits with which I could work for them would be limited. Because I'm unfamiliar. I wouldn't know the patterns or the channels that certain things had to go through. Might be limited, but I'd certainly try. And for that reason I feel good.

These passages seem to indicate a searching for opportunities to submit to others, a searching for masters to serve.

Tom Minora agrees with Sam that "freshmen aren't supposed to open their mouths." He says that the party leaders should have done more by way of instruction at the first of the session, "so that you'd know which foot to step on first." "The senior legislators," he says, "don't take you by the hand—at least in my estimation—the way they should, and say, 'Now, look, this is the way you should do it.' " Tom resents the fact that his party has not held many caucuses to familiarize the new members with procedures and the leadership's wishes, "the party thinking." Personally, he does not like to bother the leadership with his problems, but he thinks they could have "done a much better job than they did" in instructing the membership. He seems to welcome the leaders' suggestions, particularly when he has no convictions of his own in regard to a bill.

May Perkins' attitude is somewhat different. She says that some feel her party has "passive leadership" in the House. On an important bill, she wondered "just how to go along" when pulled in one direction by a few of her constituents and in another by the party leadership. Finally she decided she "was safe in going along" with the people in her town. She explains that on "such big issues as that you just wonder if you're doing the right thing, but now I find that I did, because everybody in town has spoken since and they're very glad that I voted as I did. At least I feel that I'm not a party to it if it doesn't materialize properly."

May has a large collection of acquaintances to whom she turns for advice, especially among the older, experienced legislators. And although she says that "I still have to think for myself," her conception of the proper role of the legislator is strongly centered in the representative function: "The main thing is to be voting for the good of the people. We're supposed to be doing things for the people that they cannot do for themselves. We're representing the whole group of the people who couldn't come in here to do it. And we're supposed to think of them at all times, not ourselves personally." Others "know that I'm going to have to go along" with the views of the home-town party. May is in something of a dilemma about whom to go along with, but she, like Sam and Tom, is looking for guidance from others.

The taboo on personal aggression

Expressions of aggression in the Spectator interviews are extremely rare. May is friendly to everybody. "It's all hearts and roses for a while," she says. "You know how—throwing bouquets back and forth. And then we have our first big fight against the sides. He said, 'Well, the honeymoon is over.' [laughs] But on both sides, everyone's very congenial and, ah, nice. Nice harmony throughout." Sam realizes that he is "not the type to go in there and bang people over the head and say you've got to have this for your own good." He is careful to qualify his complaints about others: "not that I'm knocking them personally," "not that I expect a heck of a lot." Tom knows he is "a little reluctant to push myself on to someone —which isn't good, either."

Only two occasions appear in the interviews in which Spectators show fairly open hostility to others. The first is May's reaction to being snubbed. She "just got fed up" with being neglected by another member, and told

him directly that she was "sick and tired" of his impoliteness. It is significant that this outburst resulted from a social snub. May can take a good deal from others, but being addressed is too important to her to be allowed to pass. In this case, repeated introductions had failed to gain friendly greetings from the other member. As a last resort, May strikes out at him. "So he doesn't forget me now," she says. The aggression has thus served to force the other to act as if he approved her, whether he does or not. This behavior, then, is entirely consistent with May's approval-seeking behavior.

The second appearance of marked hostility in the interviews comes from Tom. He starts to report the "general opinion" that the lawyers in the House are resented. " 'They have another profession,' members say; 'they shouldn't even be in there.' " Tom then takes a personal stand: "And that is my point, too. I'm quoting myself and I'm thinking that those people that resent them concur with my feelings. I don't believe the lawyers should be allowed in the House." Tom feels the lawyers "tend to make laws to suit themselves," selfishly using the legislature for their own benefit. He seems unusually irritated on this point.

But he immediately pulls back from this aggressive stance. He amends his original statement: "Probably, I shouldn't say that there shouldn't be *any* of them there," he says. He explains that he does not express this feeling in public: "That's my own personal feeling—I haven't discussed this with anybody." And he concludes by reminding the interviewer that his irritation is shared by others: "I have heard several others make the remark about too damn many lawyers being up there." Thus Tom's attack is quickly blunted and hidden among his fellow legislators.

Such aggression as the Spectator feels is far more likely to be expressed indirectly, in the form of complaints about being abused by others. Sam complains that people back home do not appreciate him. Tom tells of a relative who was treated unfairly by opposition-party politicians. May feels she was taken advantage of by a constituent. But none of them goes on to say, "Therefore I am mad at that person" or to show an intention of taking aggressive action toward those who have abused them. The abused feeling remains.[13] The tension is not relieved by attack.

Avoiding loneliness

Nor do the Spectators appear to choose withdrawal as a pattern of adjustment. On the contrary, they place considerable emphasis on feeling related to others. It is important to Sam, for example, that he finds others in the legislature who are as lowly as he feels he is. At first, he says, "I supposed I might be faced with all these individuals who were financially responsible," but "since I've come up here I've found out I'm not alone." And, he explains, "That helped to build up my ego and helped me to like coming up here, to know that you're not alone in a certain

group." May dislikes loneliness: "I couldn't just sit home and do nothing. It isn't my nature. I'm always either doing something for my relatives, baby-sitting, or for my neighbors, or doing something. I—I don't feel it's taxing me too much." Tom is more of a homebody than the other Spectators, but he, too, gains satisfaction from feeling "like any other businessman" and from knowing that he "fits into the middle group" on an issue.

Spectators are not much given to musing about themselves—adding up the past and planning for the future. Rather, they seem to avoid introspection, to restrict their attention to events in the passing environment. Part of the reason the legislature is a grand place is, as Sam says, that "everything is new. You come up here, you don't know what to expect. You don't know what to find on your desk." May sums up her legislative experience by calling it "such a nice, new venture." Her attention seems to be focused on the surfaces that surround her, perhaps *because* this is an alternative to introspection. In the midst of all the "nice social affairs" she has little time for thinking about herself. The "diversion" she finds in such affairs is evident in her description of a party for members of the House:

MAY: On both sides of the ballroom—you know how long the ballroom is?

INTERVIEWER: Yes.

MAY: They had tables set up the full length of both sides, loaded with food. And on one side was a great big basket of flowers—real flowers. A great big floral display. On the other side was an ice-basket, one of those molded ice-baskets? And that had real flowers in it, too. And

---

[13] "In a typically self-effacing person, feeling abused is an almost constant undercurrent in his whole attitude toward life. If we wanted to characterize him crudely and glibly in a few words, we would say that he is a person who craves affection and feels abused most of the time." Horney, *Neurosis and Human Growth*, p. 230.

they had a spotlight on it. Different colors? And it was just a beautiful sight. And then the food was arranged—the turkey and the ham were cut real pretty and laid on trays with pansies and parsley and all kinds of decorations on it. There were molded salads, potato salad and just everything imaginable to eat. And the place was just elegant—and French pastry for dessert—usually you don't get much for dessert at an affair like that.

None of the three Spectators thought long or deeply about accepting the nomination. None has given his political future a thorough personal assessment. Immersed in a world of other people, the Spectator seems to focus little of his concentrated attention on himself. In fact, he apparently needs interesting externalities as a distraction from introspection.

In a sense, the Spectator does withdraw from his environment: he keeps his social relationships superficial, avoids investing his emotions in others, builds a protective shield around his supposedly unlovable qualities. But he does not withdraw *into himself.* His retreat from others stops short of isolated, conscious self-examination. He pauses permanently at the self-other border, with his attention always turned outward.

The dangers of success

The fourth pattern of adjustive strategies, personal achievement, is also largely missing in the Spectator's behavior. There are scattered references to legislative success in the Spectator interviews. Sam feels that he "controlled" one executive session of his committee—although his control seems to have consisted of making the first motion to approve a series of bills

he knew the committee majority favored. Still, this experience gave him "a shot in the arm." Tom is pleased that he and another member got one bill through—although he feels it was an "insignificant" bill. May says she is "satisfied with what I have done" and that she has "voted very fairly on everything." She, too, has joined in sponsoring a bill, but she says "I don't think it will do any good" because the bill is bound to be defeated. Thus the Spectators see their achievements as minor. They tend to rationalize their lack of participation by claiming that it results from their high standards: "I'm the type of person that I'd never want to speak unless I'm fairly positive about what I'm talking about. And being unfamiliar, I'll keep quiet and listen." Or from the impossibly difficult nature of legislative work: "By being a freshman there and being unfamiliar with all these bills—God, there's over three thousand bills— and I don't think that any individual should be expected to remember all those bills." Nevertheless, the satisfactions of personal achievement are not entirely missing.

When we look at other incidents in which the Spectator might be expected to take pleasure in personal achievement, however, we see what appears to be a strong tendency in the other direction—toward feelings of discomfort and anxiety at personal success. This is especially marked in his report of the election night. For the approval-seeking person, we might suppose that an election victory would bring a glow of satisfaction. He might feel that hundreds or thousands of people had thought enough of him to go to the polls and cast a ballot in his favor. Here is approval on a massive scale.

The Spectator does not react that way. Sam says that while being a candidate "didn't bother me that much," the "big shock" came when he was told, "You're elected." He had worried about arranging the time off from his job: "All the while there was uncertainty—How would I work? My job? Coming up here?" "Oh, well," he thought, "you probably won't get elected anyhow" and "you keep throwing it out of your mind, you know? Back and forth." His feeling when the results were in was one of "responsibility":

I've got beaten in other elections so it doesn't bother me. And the actual feeling of winning the election—I don't think that would have been such a surprise. Just the feeling of responsibility. Of course, I may have been subconsciously evading the issue beforehand, but the results were in—you can't evade it any longer. That's it.

Sam gives no indication here of personal pleasure at his success. Rather, he feels anxious about the responsibility he has attained almost inadvertently. He has won a victory, but his mind is occupied with thoughts of burdens he can no longer escape. Why does he pass up this chance to pat himself on the back? One gets the impression that he would have felt more comfortable as a loser.

Furthermore, Sam appears to want to excuse himself for any success he might attain. He explains that his nomination was almost accidental: "I'm inclined to believe that it was on the spur of the moment." The town chairman "just happened to see me" at the nominating meeting. If Sam had

not attended, someone else would probably have been chosen. Similarly, his election was due not to his efforts or his popularity but to the pulling strength of others on the ballot. "Sam Thompson didn't win the election" in his town; the Governor won the election, and "Sam Thompson was on his ticket."

Sam may be giving a fairly objective report of circumstances in these passages. That he chooses, however, to dwell on the self-deprecating aspects of the situation and neglects to express any self-satisfaction at his election is inconsistent with the pattern of pleasure in personal achievement.

Tom Minora's reaction to his election victory was extreme tension accompanied by sudden illness. "I was very happy I won," he says, "but unfortunately . . . I was deadly sick that night," so sick that he felt he would "rather be dead than alive." He attributes this trouble to "the pressure that apparently had built up inside of me, nervous tension and so on." Asked how he accounts for this tension, Tom says, "Well, you couldn't prove it by me that I was nervous. I didn't know that I was nervous myself. It was just subconsciously, you know?" We cannot, of course, be sure that the election victory brought on this illness, but Tom tells us directly of the extreme pressure, the nervous tension, he felt on that occasion. He does not indicate that the tension was assuaged by news of victory. Whatever the psychosomatic connection, Tom's reaction does not fit the picture of the happy winner.

May Perkins reports that she felt no gratification over her election. "In fact," she says, "I went home that night after election and I wasn't elated one little bit. I felt kind of bad because I didn't win by a terrific margin. . . . I was a little disappointed." May was chagrined that some others thought she had not worked hard enough. "So I just went home after we tallied the votes and that was it, that was the end of my celebration." No pride in success, no glow of approval, no self-congratulation. May, too, conveys a mood of dejection when she talks about her election victory.

Spectators show a consistent tendency to assert themselves or to seek success only in conjunction with others. Sam says that, in his campaigning, "I honestly don't think I've been talking for myself so much as talking for victory. And I consider myself not what you call a real candidate, but talking for the party's victory in the town." Party success, success which can be shared, is legitimate; personal success is questionable as a goal. Tom Minora feels that his success in the legislature "is not earned by myself . . . only in my efforts. The success of us being up here is dependent on so many other people up here who are willing to cooperate." Tom thinks that ambition for any political position above that of representative "would probably be selfish interest," "seeking for prestige." He doesn't have "the desire to be a big politician." May Perkins feels "it would be nice sometime" to hold a higher political office, but she appears to have no well-developed plans on this score. Her actions regarding legislation consist mainly of trying to figure out which side she is "safe in going along with."

Descriptions of political issues in the Spectator interviews tend to be in "we" rather than "I" terms. Furthermore, the Spectators expect initiative to come from others. All three, for example, want to take a receptive stance toward their constituents. Sam dislikes house-to-house campaigning because he sees it as "pleading, begging the people for their vote." He should not have to do that—the others should come to him: "If these people don't have the civic pride or the desire to get out to a town meeting or a caucus or any of these speaking occasions we have, then their interest is pretty small." "I'm sure that there's a lot of legislation that would benefit my town in particular," Tom says, "but yet we are never requested to do this, to put a bill in for it, you know? And I don't feel that we should go in on our own and introduce a bill. As representatives of the people it's O.K. for us to do it, but they should come to us and ask us to do it." May has let her constituents know that she welcomes their phone calls, so that she can "get their general ideas." And the Spectators take a similar attitude toward the party leaders: they should undertake to advise the newcomers.

The Spectator's inability to take pleasure in personal success, his tendency to submerge his achievements in those of the group, and his turning to others for initiatives indicate that the achievement pattern does not play an important role in his legislative adjustment.

The dynamics of followership

We are now in a position to attempt an explanation of the Spectator's choice of the follower pattern and his rejection of the other three patterns. We begin with the fundamental psychological problem he experiences: the nagging doubts about his worth as a person. In order to assuage these doubts he seeks signs of approval from others. But this turning to others involves the risk of rejection as well. If the others were to discover what he suspects about himself—that he is unworthy—they would disapprove of him. Therefore he develops a pattern of adjustment that maximizes his chances of gaining approval and minimizes the risk of exposure and rejection. Part of his pattern consists of a set of perceptual habits by which he can interpret events in his environment as indicating approval with minimal risk of exposure: he makes of his *membership* in a prestigeful body a sign of approval. He overinterprets perfunctory greetings as signs of approval. He participates vicariously in the course of watching others perform. He is able to reap these rewards without taking any legislative action whatever except the effort necessary to attend the session.

Beyond this passive reception of impressions, the Spectator attempts to convey impressions to others that will bring approving signs from them. He maintains a front of pleasant, moderate, polite conventionality, to which others are likely to respond with similarly superficial pleasantries. At the same time, the formalism of this front prevents others from penetrating below the surface, leaving his secret self-doubts undisclosed. Conversation is kept on the plane of conventional pleasantries.

On occasions when the Spectator is expected to take some positive position—as, for example, when he must vote on a bill—he seeks to gain approval by submitting to the appropriate authority. His own preferences are generally weak, diffuse, and not very interesting to him. Submitting to the preferences of others (e.g. the party leaders, experienced legislators, constituents, general opinions of the legislature, etc.) fulfills the requirement that he take a position, frees him from lone responsibility (being "in the limelight") for that position, and gives him a sense of belonging with others.[14]

The Spectator's adaptive strategy, then, consists primarily of three techniques: vicarious participation, superficial socializing, and submission to others.[15]

---

[14] For links between conforming behavior and personality variables, see Richard S. Crutchfield, "Conformity and Character," *American Psychologist, 10* (1955), 191–98; James E. Dittes and Harold H. Kelley, "Effects of Different Conditions of Acceptance upon Conformity to Group Norms," *Journal of Abnormal and Social Psychology, 53* (1956), 100–07; Hans L. Zetterberg, "Compliant Actions," *Acta Sociologica, 2* (1957), 179–201; John W. Thibaut and Lloyd H. Strickland, "Psychological Set and Social Conformity," *Journal of Personality, 25* (1956), 115–29.

[15] Some Spectator questionnaire replies reflect these themes. They are most likely to answer that "social affairs connected with the legislature were very enjoyable" (Spectators 37%, others 15%). They "made a special effort to memorize the names and faces of other members" at the start of the session (Spectators 80%, others 65%). With a stranger, the Spectator would "reserve my trust until I know him better" rather than "trust him until he lets me down" (Spectators 63%, others 36%). N's = 30, 66. Before the session Spectators answered "the new legislator will very frequently have to rely on the advice of others with more experience or ability" rather than "the new legislator ought to figure most things out for himself, to the best of his ability" (Spectators 74%, others 57%). N's = 27, 56.

THE INITIATION RITES OF THE HOUSE APPROPRIATIONS COMMITTEE
RICHARD F. FENNO, JR.

SUBCOMMITTEE MEMBER: ROLE AND ROLE BEHAVIOR

The norms which define the role of Committee member are virtually coterminous with those which define the role of subcommittee member. Both are roles shared by every member of the Committee. And since the key work units are the subcommittees, the most general Committee role discussed will be the role of subcommittee member. This refers to the cluster of norms which all members of all subcommittees are expected to follow. Insofar as these norms are observed, they will describe the configuration of Committee decision-making—first of all within each subcommittee and secondly, among the various subcommittees.

For all members the overarching norm is that of *hard work*. As recognized by both the House and the Committee, the norm of hard work gives to the Committee its distinctive political style. No matter what phase of Com-

CREDIT: From *The Power of the Purse: Appropriations Politics in Congress* by Richard F. Fenno, Jr., pp. 160–167, 209–219. Copyright © 1966, by Little, Brown and Company (Inc.). Reprinted by permission of the author and publisher. [*Footnotes renumbered.*]

mittee work is involved, members are expected to conform to the highest standards of diligence. Enough has already been said on this point. All that needs to be added is that an individual member's influence in the subcommittees, like the Committee's influence in the House, depends on his working hard and acquiring the reputation for working hard. Hard work brings information, and the two together constitute a necessary condition of internal Committee influence.

An important norm of the House of Representatives is that of *specialization*. The fact of subcommittee autonomy gives the norm an intensified application on the Committee. Each member is expected to play the role of specialist in the activity of one subcommittee. He will sit on from one to four subcommittees, but he is expected to specialize in the work of only one. If he is a subcommittee chairman or ranking minority subcommittee member, he will specialize in the work of that group. If one of his subcommittees represents a constituency interest or a personal interest, he may choose to specialize in that. Or, if all of his subcommittees are areas about which he knows little, he may choose on some other basis—his seniority, the attitude of his subcommittee chairman, etc. Within one subcommittee he may specialize by concentrating on the work of one agency or one program. This kind of specialization twice over occurs in such subcommittees as Agriculture, Interior, and Defense.

"We all have a tendency in our subcommittee to specialize along some line or other," said a member of the agriculture group in 1962.[1] A man whose father was the first county agent in Minnesota specialized in the work of the Extension Service and the Farmers Home Administration. A man from Washington specialized in the Forest Service. The two senior men specialized in soil conservation. And the New York City member worked on the school lunch and meat inspection programs. On the Interior Subcommittee, in 1962, a man from a constituency with badly eroded soil specialized in soil and moisture conservation programs. A Pennsylvania congressman whose father was a coal mine inspector and who was himself an M.D., specialized in the work of the Bureau of Mines and Indian health programs. In earlier years, a man from Oklahoma specialized in the Bureau of Indian Affairs, and a man from Idaho specialized in the activities of the Bureau of Land Management. On the Defense Subcommittee men became known from their prior service on subcommittee panels, as experts in the Army, Navy, Air Force, or the Marines. And, said a minority member of the State-Justice-Commerce Departments Subcommittee, "Some of those agencies I don't bother with at all. On some I do

a lot of digging. I get assignments to take care of—and the same with the others."

Committee members believe that specialization is especially appropriate to the task of guarding the Treasury. Only by specializing can they unearth the volume of information necessary for the intelligent, critical screening of budget requests. Only by developing their own expertise can Committee members successfully counter the battery of experts sent down by each executive agency to defend its budget. Since expertise is based on facts and since the facts can only be acquired through industriousness, he who is a specialist will, perforce, adopt the Committee's style of hard work. Thus the goal of budget-cutting, the norm of hard work, and the norm of specialization are interlinked and mutually supporting.

A Committee member who cherishes a dream of ranging widely throughout the area covered by the Appropriations Committee and who expects to wield influence in that broad arena, will find himself operating in the least congenial system imaginable. If, on the other hand, he curbs the scope of his activity, works hard, and becomes an acknowledged expert within a restricted area, he will win respect, deference, and, hence, influence in Committee decision-making. Within his own subcommittee, specialization can become the source of considerable influence for an individual member. Thus it may be said of a subcommittee specialist,

We on the subcommittee feel that we have in the gentleman from Washington a specialist in research and a specialist in prob-

[1] 98 *Congressional Record*, p. 4585.

lems relating to the great forest industry in America. We look to him when details relative to those general problems come up.[2]

During the six years he had been on the subcommittee we have turned over the job of looking after the health of Indians to him and he has really done a job. We never question his position when it comes to the health of the Indians, because we know he has looked into it thoroughly. The committee has also turned over the job of looking after the Bureau of Mines to the gentleman from Pennsylvania. He spends a lot of time on that.[3]

If it is to guide Committee decision-making, the norm of specialization must be supplemented by the norm of *reciprocity*. According to this norm subcommittee members are expected to act on the basis of mutual respect for one another's work. They are expected to acknowledge each other's specialized information and expertise and defer to it. Said one member, "After you have been here for a while, you become sort of a semispecialist with respect to legislation which interests you. And you say of the rest, 'I trust you to see that nothing wrong is done.' " [4] Within and between subcommittees, trust is expected to be reciprocal. It is expected that reciprocity should be observed within subcommittees and among subcommittees. Insofar as it is observed within subcommittees, it shores up the influence of individual members. Insofar as it is

observed among subcommittees, it becomes a basis for preserving subcommittee autonomy.

Members of each subcommittee are expected to observe reciprocity with respect to the recommendation of every other subcommittee. When a subcommittee brings its appropriation recommendations to the full Committee—that is to say, to the other subcommittees—for approval and legitimation, the full Committee could choose to reargue the recommendations *de novo*. But it is not expected to do so. In accordance with the norm of reciprocity, it is expected to defer to the subcommittee which has specialized in the area, has worked hard, and has "the facts." "It's a matter of you respect my work and I'll respect yours." "You don't go barging into another man's field unless something is patently wrong." "It's frowned upon if you offer an amendment in the full Committee if you are on the subcommittee. It's considered presumptuous to pose as an expert if you aren't on the subcommittee." Thus articulated, the norm of reciprocity shores up the autonomy and the influence of each subcommittee. "Trust," "confidence," "respect," and "faith" are the lubricants of full Committee activity.

It is impossible to know for certain the degree to which reciprocity is observed—that is, how often the full Committee accepts the recommendations of its subcommittees. No public records exist and private records, if such there be, are not systematically kept. Fortunately, however, the offhand estimates of Committee members do not vary much. Subcommittee recommendations, they agree are "very rarely changed," "almost always ap-

---

[2] *Ibid.*

[3] 98 *Congressional Record,* p. 2941. See also *ibid.,* p. 3070.

[4] Joint Committee on the Organization of Congress, *Hearings on the Organization of Congress,* 79th Congress, 1st Session (Washington: U.S. Government Printing Office, 1945), p. 340.

proved," "changed one time in fifty," "very seldom changed," "usually go through," "go smiling through," etc. A man with over ten years of service as a subcommittee chairman said, "I don't believe I've ever had a change made in full Committee in my bills." The optimum conditions for changing a subcommittee recommendation would seem to be present when the fight is led by a dissident member of that subcommittee—by a member, that is, who can draw on the norm of specialization and its concomitants of information and hard work. But insofar as it is observed, the norm of reciprocity is a foundation stone of subcommittee autonomy and influence.

Since no subcommittee is likely to command deference of the full Committee unless its recommendations have widespread support among its own members, a third norm—that of *subcommittee unity*—is expected to be observed by all subcommittee members. Unity refers to a willingness to support (or not to oppose) the recommendations of one's own subcommittee. Reciprocity and unity are closely dependent upon one another. Reciprocity would be difficult to maintain if subcommittees were badly divided, and subcommittee unity would have little appeal unless intersubcommittee reciprocity was likely to be observed. The norm of reciprocity functions to minimize intersubcommittee conflict; the norm of unity functions to minimize intra-subcommittee conflict. Committee members believe that both must be observed if subcommittee influence in decision-making is to be maintained.

In a positive way, members believe subcommittee unity should be achieved by applying the basic House norm of *compromise* to subcommittee action. In making their decisions, subcommittee members are expected to be flexible and to give and take in order to produce recommendations which all subcommittee members can support. Again, it is not possible to know for certain how frequently this norm is observed. But the high rate of acceptance of subcommittee recommendations by the full Committee is prima facie evidence to that effect. Subcommittee members also describe their markup sessions—which are the key points of subcommittee decision-making—as governed by efforts to achieve unity through compromise. A subcommittee chairman asserted,

Sometimes there are different ideas. We kick it around and we give a little, take a little. I've worked on the subcommittee with some pretty sharp people and we always like to have what we call a "round book." They do it at the race tracks and we do it here.

A ranking subcommittee member described his subcommittee markup sessions:

If there's agreement, we go right along. If there's a controversy, we put the item aside and go on. Then after a day or two, we may have a list of ten controversial items. We give and take and pound them down until we get agreement.

A Committee newcomer observed, with regard to still another set of markup sessions,

If there's any way to bring out a unanimous report, they'll do it. They'll sit there long hours. They'll backscratch and give and take and compromise.

In a negative way, Committee members believe that subcommittee unity can only be achieved by minimizing the most divisive force in legislative politics—partisanship. Every subcommittee is expected, therefore, to observe the norm of *minimal partisanship*. That is, under most conditions, Committee members are expected to minimize their party-oriented behavior. Nothing would be more dysfunctional for the observance of reciprocity, subcommittee unity, or compromise than bitter and extended partisan controversy. On the evidence, the norm seems to be widely observed. Nearly every respondent emphasized, with approval, that "very little" or "not much" or "amazingly little" partisanship prevailed on the Committee. Many newcomers find that this feature of Committee life provides the sharpest contrast with their previous committee:

Usually we come to an agreement and compromise things out. Most subcommittee reports are unanimous reports. I never saw a unanimous report on anything in my last committee. I guess you could say there's a lot less partisanship on Appropriations.

"Well," concurred a subcommittee chairman, "partisanship naturally enters in, but the surprising thing is how little there actually is." And a ranking minority subcommittee member said, "You might think that we Republicans would defend the budget of the [Eisenhower] administration; but we don't." We have already observed that the roles of Chairman and ranking minority member place far less emphasis on partisan leadership than they do on consultation across party lines. No committee operating within a party-organized system like the House is immune from the temperature of party conflict. But Committee members believe that their boiling point should be kept high. Minimal partisanship is believed to be a necessary condition of subcommittee unity and, hence, tightly intertwined with all of the other norms thus far elaborated.

Once subcommittee unity has been achieved, Committee members believe that they should stand behind their internal bargain. "There is a strong feeling that the subcommittee should stick together." "Sometimes," said one ranking minority member, "we compromise in committee on the understanding that we will stick together come hell or high water." The payoffs, they believe, are these: Only by presenting the full Committee with a united front can they win acceptance of their recommendations; only by winning acceptance can they preserve their influence on decision-making. Whatever behavior increases subcommittee influence will, in turn, preserve for each member that degree of influence which led him to seek Committee membership in the first place. Since his personal satisfactions depend upon the degree of subcommittee unity, subcommittee members will be constrained to play the role expected of them.

The norms of hard work, specialization, reciprocity, subcommittee unity, compromise, and minimal partisanship help define the role of every Committee member. They constitute an interdependent set of norms which, insofar as they are observed, help explain the sources of individual influence and the dominance of subcommittee influence in Appropriations Committee decision-making. They prescribe an overall decision-making configuration. They do not prescribe particular decision-making roles. And they do not, therefore, reveal much about who makes decisions within the subcommittees themselves. Every sub-committee member does not exercise equal influence on decision-making. Therefore, the Committee's role structure must be further elaborated.

COMMITTEE NEWCOMER: ROLE

The differentiation of roles between senior and junior Committee members provides one basic definition of who is expected and who is not expected to influence subcommittee decisions. Here, as in the case of specialization, the Committee's system of norms is strengthened because it follows that of the parent chamber. Seniority rules are among the most hallowed of congressional norms. So, too, on the Appropriations Committee. Of a junior member, it will be said, "Oh, he doesn't count—what I mean is, he hasn't been on the Committee long enough." He is not expected to play an active part in decision-making. A Committee newcomer—a man of one or two terms of Committee service—is expected to play the role of apprentice.

In answer to a question, "What advice would you give to a new member if he came to you and asked how he should behave on the Committee?" three subcommittee chairmen agreed:

Follow the Chairman until you get your bearings. For the first two years, follow the Chairman. He knows. He's been around a long time. Then take more of a part yourself.

Work hard; get to know what you're doing as quickly as you can. Be a good member of the Committee. Get along with the other members, and the rest comes easy. Don't be what we call a rabble rouser.

Work hard, keep quiet, and attend the Committee sessions. We don't want to listen to some new person coming in here. But after a while when you know what you're doing, we'll listen to you.

These norms define the role of apprentice. The newcomer is expected to work hard, to amass information, to learn the business of his subcommittee, to listen to the senior men, and to follow them. He is expected to devote himself whole-heartedly to the routine proceedings of the subcommittee. And, except in the case of pressing constituency needs, he is not expected to wield or to attempt to wield influence.

For their part, the Committee's veterans extol the virtues of the seniority rule which links influence to Committee experience:

On this Committee, it takes a long time to learn. They ridicule the seniority rule. God have pity if we didn't have it. It's like anything else, this business, your business, or anything, there's no substitute for experience. I'd hate to get in a plane and have the pilot tell me that this was his first solo flight.

Newcomers do not know the ways of the Committee, and they do not have enough information to merit the attention of others. Apropos of subcommittee hearings, a powerful subcommittee chairman asserted,

Newcomers look every bit as wise as the older members. But they don't know what the score is and they don't have enough information to ask intelligent questions.

And another exclaimed, with respect to markup proceedings,

When we get a compromise, nobody's going to break that up. If someone tries, we sit on him fast. We don't want young people who throw bricks or try to slow things down.

As far as floor action is concerned, the newcomer is expected to get out on the floor (if he has time) to observe. But he is not expected to speak out (except in the case, again, of constituency needs) until he stands on a foundation of hard work and information which only subcommittee experience can provide. A subcommittee chairman put it this way,

When I came down here . . . I was full of pep. So I asked Mr. Rayburn how long a congressman had to be here before he went on the floor and made a speech. He said to me that you should attend Committee meetings and learn about your subject. Then, when you bring a bill out onto the floor, you will know more about it than anyone else except the members of the subcommittee. Then people will listen to you.

As the Rayburn advice indicates, the apprentice role is common to all new members of the House. But it is wrong to assume that each committee will give it the same emphasis. Some House committees pay it scant heed. The Appropriations Committee makes it a cornerstone of its decision-making structure.

Socialization: learning norms and perceptions

New members do not come to the Committee equipped with the full complement of expectations, perceptions, and attitudes held by the in-cumbent members of the group. They must be taught and they must learn—and the process of teaching and learning Committee perceptions and Committee norms is called the process of socialization. Not all newcomers will have to be taught the same things. For the liberal Democrat the goal of budget-cutting may have to be learned; for the economy-minded Republican, the Committee's integrative norms may be little understood. The point is that Committee selection produces no fully socialized members. Committee-makers, indeed, stress responsiveness to the chamber and *not* responsiveness to Appropriations Committee norms as their main criterion. But the selection process does produce a group of Committee newcomers who are legislatively oriented and, hence, have a built-in responsiveness to the socialization processes of any legislative group of which they are members. Furthermore, since most Committee newcomers are strongly attracted to the Committee, they are more susceptible than otherwise to in-Committee training. In terms of aptitude for learning and of motivation for learning, therefore, the selection process produces excellent raw material.

The function of the apprentice role assigned to the newcomer is that it provides time during which socialization can proceed. It helps ensure continuities in Committee behavior by denying influence to those members who remain untutored in its ways. For the member who performs his apprentice role creditably and learns his lessons well, the passage of time holds the promise of Committee influence. But for his first term or two, he is viewed by his elders as a man with relatively little to contribute to the proceedings. His socialization begins by acquainting him with the role of apprentice and impressing upon him—as one newcomer put it—that whatever his previous House accomplishments, "You are a freshman all over again."

The prime technique of socialization on the Committee is that of learning by doing. Senior Committee members teach by the "do as I do" not the "do as I say" method. When asked to put apprenticeship norms into words, they advise "Keep quiet," "Follow the chairman," and "Learn the business of the Committee." Experienced members who had, within memory, sloughed off their apprenticeship role typically answered the question "How did you learn the ropes?": "You pick it up by ear" or "It's like anything else in the House—you learn it by yourself." Two others agreed that they were not taught by the lecture method:

Nobody tells you. You just go to subcommittee meetings and gradually assimilate the routine. The new members are made to feel welcome, but you know that you have a lot of rope learning to do before you carry much weight.

Nobody tells you anything around here. You find out for yourself by living with it. It's like any other experience—you live with it, that's all. There's a lot to be said for experience.

Two experienced members asserted that they did not have to learn any ropes. But the rest felt that they had something to learn, that apprenticeship was beneficial to them—and, most importantly, they were now prepared to enforce it on the current crop of newcomers.

Newcomers themselves are not as universally well disposed toward the role they are called upon to play. Most of them do what is expected of them; a few rebel. But all of them watch, listen, and imitate the older members. They speak freely about their learning experience, and, however painful a process it may be, they begin early to accept for themselves most salient aspects of the Committee's political culture.

For example, most of them become quickly aware of their own relative ignorance. Said one, "Sometimes I go home sick at night. When they start talking about these missiles and things, they just leave me. But I'm getting an education, and I study four or five hours a day." Said another, "If I became ranking minority member now, I'd be scared to death. I don't know my stuff yet." As the newcomers experience their first set of subcommittee hearings, they typically find themselves in a losing scramble to keep up with the detailed lines of questioning being advanced by senior members. One complained that in his first year his subcommittee "went along so fast I never did have time to get a grasp of things." Thus they come to learn early the need for information. One freshman declared, "I attended all the hearings and studied and collected information that I can use next year. I'm just marking time now." They discover, too, the value of hard work which one newcomer related in a perverse sort of way:

There are some old war horses on the Committee, some pretty dull-witted guys. They plug and plug and plug. And they get more than the smart fellow, because they're there all the time working at it.

If it is their first set of hearings that impresses upon them the need for specialized information, it is their first markup session that makes them conscious of the impulse ·toward unity. Several reported feeling "the great pressure to conform." Another observed that "Many times the older men stuck together on votes. They had things under control. Some of them have been on the subcommittee for 15 or 20 years." "These fellows want to report a bill they can all agree on," another recounted. "They don't want any minority reports. About all you can do is say, 'I reserve on that point, Mr. Chairman.'"

Since the Committee's norms are so largely informal and traditional, they cannot be internalized overnight. Rather they are absorbed after frequent and extended exposure. One very sensitive first-year man expressed his feeling that

The Appropriations Committee is a club. As one of the younger members of the club, there are a lot of things you don't understand. You don't understand them but you sure can feel their presence— like cosmic rays.

Another commented simply, "It's strange and mysterious." Slowly, however, the newcomer imbibes the important elements of the Committee's political culture. And as he does he comes to feeling increasingly like a member rather than an observer of "the club." A second-year man discussed his newly acquired sense of group identification:

It's like anything else in Congress. You have to sit in the back seat and then edge up little by little. I've made a lot of friends on the Committee and I feel like a member of the Committee now. In the be-

ginning you have a lot of trouble keeping up with the complications and intricacies of appropriations.

A man who feels like a member of the Committee will begin to act like one. His first public opportunity to demonstrate his allegiance comes when his subcommittee first brings its bills to the House floor. A newcomer who, before his service on the Committee, resented their rite of self-congratulation, may have acquired a new appreciation of its integrative function:

As a new member of this Committee who has been sitting here for the last four years, I have noticed that every time one of these committees came in here with a bill they started handing out orchids to the Chairman and other members of the Committee; and it made me a little shaky. It rather got under my skin. But I have had an education. I really want to add my word to this hard-working Committee and our Chairman, to the members on the minority side . . . if you worked mornings and afternoons and nights trying to keep up with them, then you will see that you have a job.[5]

Evidence that their socialization is progressing satisfactorily can be gleaned from comments such as these by Committee members making their maiden speeches as Committee men:

Mr. Chairman, during the past three months I have had my initiation as a member of the Committee on Appropriations, and as a member of the subcommittee that handled the bill under consideration at this time. It has been a pleasant revelation to me to see the vigor and the ability and the high purpose that the . . . members of the Committee displayed in examining the witnesses and really pursu-

[5] 93 *Congressional Record*, p. 1883.

ing questions to the point where we had just about all the information that it was possible to bring out from them. I feel that the older members of the Committee, who have had a great deal of experience have done just an excellent job, and I appreciate the opportunity of having been a member of this Committee and working with them.[6]

Mr. Chairman, in view of the fact that I only joined this subcommittee this present year, I have not sought to take part in general debate on the bill here today. I rise only for the purpose of publicly expressing the high esteem and appreciation I have developed for my colleagues on that subcommittee and for the fine conscientious job that I know they have done in bringing this bill here today. I also want to take this occasion to say that I have followed this bill and the leadership of my colleagues on the Committee as closely as I know how and that I am here supporting the bill as it was reported by the Committee.[7]

These men have accepted the role of apprentice and have begun to internalize norms of hard work, specialization, and unity. They have begun to develop positive affect toward their fellow members and have expressed it publicly. The consequences of these attitudes and actions are highly integrative for the Committee.

Socialization is in part a training in perception. Before members of a group can be expected to observe its norms, they must see and interpret the world around them with reasonably similar results. This kind of learning proceeds, too, during the apprenticeship period. The newcomers' perceptions are brought sufficiently into line

[6] 98 *Congressional Record,* p. 3412.

[7] 103 *Congressional Record,* p. 2268.

with those of the older members to serve as a basis for integration. Radically different perceptions of political reality could promote different sets of expectations and attitudes with seriously disruptive consequences for the group. Most important, perhaps, is the training of Committee newcomers to perceive their environment in terms that lead them to accept the Committee's definition of its goals. Their elders, for example, already perceive that all executive agencies ask for more money than they need. And this perception buttresses their goal of budget-cutting. A subcommittee chairman explained,

When you have sat on the Committee, you see that these bureaus are always asking for more money—always up, never down. They want to build up their organization. You reach the point—I have—where it sickens you, where you rebel against it. Year after year, they want more money. They say, "Only $50 thousand this year"; but you know the pattern. Next year they'll be back for $100 thousand, then $200 thousand. The younger members haven't been on the Committee long enough, haven't had the experience to know this.

The Committee's young must be trained to see things in this same way.

The Committee's self-starting, economy-minded Republicans and its conservative Southern Democrats are predisposed to accept such goals as Treasury guardianship and its supporting perceptions. But one-half of the Committee's Democratic members are Northerners and Westerners (primarily from urban constituencies) who come to the Committee favorably inclined toward domestic social welfare programs and the high level of federal spending necessary to support them. Their voting records are as "liberal" on behalf of such programs as non-Committee Democrats from like constituencies. For some of them, the Committee had no initial attraction; and they had to be coopted by their party's committee-makers. It is crucial to Committee integration that these men learn to temper their potentially disruptive welfare state ideology with a conservative concern for saving money. They must change their perceptions and attitudes sufficiently so that they view the Committee's goals in nearly the same terms as their Southern Democratic and Republican colleagues.

The Committee's liberal Democrats were not selected because of their economy-mindedness, but because of their political flexibility. And, though this is hardly their intention, Democratic Committee-makers send to the Committee precisely those individuals who are most easily socialized through Committee experience. In the early months of one "liberal's" service on the Committee, he received a call from the White House asking for his support (given in the past) on the administration's plan to continue financing the Export-Import Bank by direct Treasury borrowing. When the fledgling Committee member hesitated, saying "Well, I don't know," the White House liaison man shot back, "Do you have some deep philosophical objection or something?" The Committee member replied, "You're damn right I have." And, a few weeks later he explained, "I had some doubts about it before. But since I've been on the Committee, they have been re-enforced. What else have we got in

Congress but the power over spending." Clearly, he had already adopted the Committee's broadest goal—protecting the power of the purse—and his socialization was well under way.

Within one or two terms, Democratic liberals are differentiating between themselves and the "wild-eyed spenders" or the "free spenders" in the House. "Some of these guys would spend you through the roof," exclaimed one experienced liberal. And another newcomer explained, "I'm a liberal. But I can see myself getting more conservative." Repeated exposure to Committee work and to fellow members has altered their perceptions and their attitudes on money matters. Half a dozen new or experienced Northern Democrats agreed with two of their members who said,

Yes, it's true. I can see it myself. I suppose I came here a flaming liberal; but as the years go by I get more conservative. You just hate like hell to spend all this money. It's an awful lot of money. I used to look more at the program, but now I look at it in terms of money . . . you come to the point where you just say "by God, this is enough jobs."

Yes, I think you do [get more conservative on the Committee]. You get to sympathize more with the taxpayer. You get insight into where the money comes from and where it goes. You want to save as much as you can. You get to feel it. It's like a wage earner. He knows where the money comes from and how hard it is to get it, and he's careful in spending it. There's an inherent desire to economize in the members of the Committee.

These men remain more inclined toward spending than their Committee colleagues; but their perceptions and attitudes have been brought close enough to the others to support a consensus on goals. They are responsive, now, to appeals for budget-cutting that would not have registered earlier and which remain meaningless to liberals outside the Committee. In those cases, therefore, where Committee selection does not and cannot produce individuals predisposed toward guarding the Treasury, an equivalent result is achieved by socialization.

For the more conservatively inclined newcomer, Committee socialization has the effect of reenforcement. Committee elders state as a rule applicable to all members that, "The longer you are on the Committee the more conservative you become." And a senior staff member highlighted the extent of the learning process within the Committee in describing his own experience:

The more I stay around this branch the more conservative I get, the more mossback I get. Necessarily, we have to be negative, necessarily we have to be unpopular, and necessarily we have to develop a philosophy. You observe the growth of bureaucracy and you can't help developing a conservative philosophy. I've noticed that the congressmen can't escape this.

Another important perception which newcomers must learn involves the degree to which the internal influence of Committee leaders depends upon their adherence to Committee norms. As we have seen, the Chairman and the subcommittee chairmen (and their opposite numbers) have impressive formal authority. But they win the respect and deference of other members just as much because of their obedience to group norms of style. Newcomers do not immediately perceive this. The Democratic freshmen of 1963, for example, tended to exaggerate Clarence Cannon's influence and the importance of its formal sources.

Cannon exercises a constant surveillance. Nothing escapes him. He abolishes subcommittees and decapitates subcommittee chairmen. All the Committee's actions have the stamp of the Chairman on them.

The Republican newcomers of 1959 seemed to convert their own sense of powerlessness (felt the more strongly, perhaps, because of their minority status) into the perception that their subcommittee chairmen possess "inconceivable," "absolute," and "inordinate" influence. "If you're a subcommittee chairman, it's your committee." "The chairman runs the show. He decides what he wants and he gets it through." "He's the boss. He gets about what he wants." "Nine times out of ten what he says goes." "Some chairmen act like God Almighty." When the newcomer lists the resources of the subcommittee chairmen he tends to find them either in his formal prerogatives or in some deus ex machina such as the staff member.

Experienced members see through a different set of lenses. They perceive internal influence much more in terms of a contingent and revocable grant by which the deference of the members is tendered for so long as the leader meets their expectations. They do not see arbitrary or awesome power. Regarding Cannon: "Of course the Committee wouldn't follow him if it didn't want to. He has a great deal of respect. He's an able man, a hardworking man." Regarding subcommittee chairmen: "Occasionally one comes along that is too cocky: then one of the members of the Committee cuts him down to size and trims his whiskers a little." Newcomers must come to share these perceptions about internal Committee influence before they can understand and fit easily into Committee activity.

The socialization of Fred Santangelo

Newcomers get trained, for the most part, by the subcommittee members with whom they work. And special perceptions may have to be taught to particular subcommittee newcomers. The man, for instance, who has been appointed to a subcommittee partly because of his lack of interest in the subject matter under its jurisdiction and in the hopes that he will further reduce budgets presents a special problem. If his perceptions are not brought within tolerable limits, he may disrupt a well-established pattern of subcommittee behavior. An interesting case of this sort (i.e., subcommittee socialization in the direction of interest and generosity) was the education of Representative Fred Santangelo.

Congressman Santangelo, a New York City Democrat representing an east Harlem constituency, came to the Committee in 1958. He was immediately assigned to the Subcommittee on Agriculture. The appointment seems to have been designed to countervail a marked interest-sympathy-leniency syndrome operating within the subcommittee. (The relative liberality of the Agriculture Subcommittee is shown in Chapter Eight.) The rhetoric of the appointment was that of "balancing things up" and "representing the consumer interest." A very influen-

tial subcommittee member protested the appointment to Cannon. "I told him I didn't like it." Committee wags talked about the cross section now represented on the subcommittee— "You've got corn, cotton, tobacco, wheat, and the marijuana farmer from New York." And Santangelo himself was bitterly disappointed. In an early full Committee meeting he spoke openly, pointedly, and sarcastically against Mr. Cannon's decision:

I stated at that time to the Chairman that I appreciated the significance of this appointment and I knew that the farmers in my area, with their tremendous plantations and farm land in the rear of a tenement house, amounting to 18 feet by 12 feet, and with their truck gardens on the fire escapes and the window sills, would also appreciate the significance and importance of this assignment.[8]

The subcommittee wanted a newcomer with a similar interest in and perceptions about agriculture as they; the man they got admitted believing that REA was a foreign-made automobile. The liberal Democratic newcomer wanted an assignment from which he could help his urban constituency; the Subcommittee on Agriculture seemed to him the most remotely related one of all.

During his first year, Santangelo kept quiet and listened. In so doing, he discovered that his subcommittee did, indeed, have jurisdiction over some things of direct interest to his constituents—particularly the school lunch program. He also found an area of special personal interest—given the fact that his father had been a butcher—

[8] *Congressional Record,* Daily Edition, February 15, 1961, p. A916.

the meat inspection program. With these as a foundation, he gradually learned to perceive the overall interests of farm and city as intertwined rather than separate from one another. And he came to value his subcommittee associations. When the subcommittee brought its bill to the floor, the chairman singled out Santangelo for praise, saying "He has rendered excellent service [and] has shown great interest in the operation of the Department." [9] Translated, it meant that a proper apprenticeship was being observed. Santangelo was given five minutes to speak, during which time he praised the chairman for his "brilliant cross-examination of many witnesses which elicited . . . a wealth of information," praised his other colleagues, and spoke in support of the school lunch program. In his words of appreciation to his subcommittee colleagues, he revealed the extent of his socialization:

I want to take this opportunity of thanking the . . . members of the subcommittee . . . for giving me the benefit of their views, and for the courtesy, comfort, and encouragement which they have given to me as a neophyte member of the subcommittee, a person coming from the city dealing with matters which seem not to be germane to city life. Because of their cooperation and because of their help I have found work on this subcommittee to be very inspiring and it made me realize very clearly that the welfare of the farmer is intimately connected with the welfare and the dignity of the laborer in the city. . . .[10]

With his perceptions altered and the attractiveness of his role increased,

Santangelo was well on the way to being fully integrated into the work of the subcommittee.

During his second year on the subcommittee, he was asked to specialize in the school lunch program. When the chairman was invited to address a convention of school lunch administrators, he passed the opportunity to Santangelo. Soon, the New York City congressman was the acknowledged authority on the subject. Later, he added meat and poultry inspection to his list of specialities. And he, in turn, acknowledged and deferred to the expertise of the other members in forestry, agricultural research, soil conservation, production payments, or in dealing with specific crops. By the end of the second year, the man who had originally protested Santangelo's appointment was delighted with the outcome. "My fears were needless," he said. "He's a hell of a fine fellow and a good friend of mine. I didn't know him so well before, but he's cooperated and gone along and everything's worked out fine." In 1960, Santangelo's horizons were broadened by his being included on a trip with two subcommittee members—to western United States and Asia. When the Agriculture Appropriation Bill of that year came to the floor, Santangelo praised the chairman for helping "to educate a city member of the committee." And he thanked especially his two companions on the trip "who have taken a city boy in tow in the rural electrification program, in the rice paddies of Asia, and in the pens among the hogs and the pigs and the cattle in Nebraska and Illinois." And, once again, he reaffirmed his new perception:

---

[9] 104 *Congressional Record*, p. 5961.

[10] *Ibid.*, p. 5985.

I am no farmer. I have no farmers in my district nor do I have any farm in my district except rock gardens and small backyard plots. I do not even represent those crabgrass weekend farmers of suburbia, but I do know and am firmly convinced that in America there is an economic unity between the man who toils on the farm and the worker who labors in industry.[11]

The subcommittee chairman, representing a rural Mississippi district, reciprocated:

. . . . The gentleman from New York, and I mean downtown New York . . . is a splendid lawyer and a tireless worker who is interested in the subject. He works untiringly not only in the Committee but out in the field. He has more energy than most members . . . he has brought essential balance to this subcommittee which is a tribute to the arrangement which put him on this subcommittee. The gentleman from New York has done a great service on this Committee, a great service; and I am glad to say so.[12]

For two more years, a well-established role reciprocity inside the Committee and a harmony in perceptions were displayed in an ever more lavish exchange of gratitude and felicitation. A thoroughly socialized Santangelo became a distinct asset to the subcommittee. By 1961, the man who once thought REA was a car had extended his area of competence to include rural electrification. And he was invited to speak to the National Rural Electric Cooperative Association convention on the unity of farm and city. Saying that he had become "particularly in-terested in REA," he admitted that "it has not always been thus."

Before I came to Congress I had not been aware of REA. . . . As a member of the Appropriations Subcommittee on Agriculture, I have sat through hearings, listened, read, and inquired. I have been compelled to think about our soil, the trees, our streams, our electric power. . . . I've come to realize that they affect my way of life, my constituency, and my nation.[13]

More importantly, he worked to win urban allies for the farm appropriations in a time of declining political strength for agriculture. On the floor he spoke as an urban representative to urban Members: "I would like to direct my attention to those of my colleagues who come from the cities and urban areas."[14] And he was assigned to handle the criticisms from such Members. Consider this floor exchange:

CONGRESSMAN: I have almost no farmers in my congressional district. There are literally no farmers in my district. I represent a great urban district which pays $355 million in federal taxes. After reading this report, may I ask if the Committee is urging someone like me to vote for this appropriation? . . . Should I vote "Aye" when my name is called on this bill? The report would seem to indicate we have been pouring money down a rat hole here.

SANTANGELO: I believe I have the same type of district as the gentleman. . . . I believe you have some school children who are sharing in the school lunch program; is that not correct?

CONGRESSMAN: That is correct.

[11] *Congressional Record,* Daily Edition, May 10, 1960, p. 9171.

[12] *Ibid.,* pp. 9171–9172. See also a similar exchange in *Congressional Record,* Daily Edition, June 6, 1961, pp. 8925–8927.

[13] *Congressional Record,* Daily Edition, February 15, 1961, p. A916.

[14] *Congressional Record,* Daily Edition, July 24, 1962, p. 13604.

SANTANGELO: And your people are also sharing in the special milk program; is that not correct?

CONGRESSMAN: That is correct.

SANTANGELO: People in the gentleman's district are sharing in food donations for needy people. Therefore, to a large extent the people from the city districts are sharing in this abundance that the farmers are producing.[15]

Santangelo's behavior obviously met with the approval of Chairman Cannon. In 1959, Santangelo was given a second (relatively unimportant —but still a second) subcommittee assignment on the District of Columbia Subcommittee. And late in 1962, he was given a "midnight" appointment to the important Labor-HEW Subcommittee. This latter appointment seemed to be designed to help him during his re-election campaign. But Santangelo had been redistricted out of any realistic chance for re-election, and he was defeated. Chairman Cannon gave his place on the Agriculture Committee to the Committee's newcomer from New York City—Representative Joseph Addabo from Queens. With the successful education of Fred Santangelo as precedent, the Subcommittee was unruffled. The Subcommittee chairman rose, when his bill reached the floor in 1963, and said,

The only new member on our Subcommittee this year is the gentleman from New York, Congressman Addabo. I say candidly that some years ago when the first member from the city of New York, Fred Santangelo, was put on the committee, who was my personal friend and a fine person, the question arose in the minds of some as to why a man from the city of New York would be interested or why he would be chosen to serve on a committee dealing strictly with farm appropriation bills. But . . . I do not think there is anything more fitting than to have a representative . . . from the consuming areas of our nation on the Agriculture Appropriations Subcommittee . . . we are proud to have our new colleague, the gentleman from New York [Mr. Addabo] on the Committee because the gentleman does understand the consumer aspects of these matters.[16]

And the socialization process began anew.

[15] *Congressional Record*, Daily Edition, May 11, 1960, p. 9319.

[16] *Congressional Record*, Daily Edition, June 6, 1963, p. 9788.

THE SOVIET PARTY SECRETARY
RAYMOND A. BAUER

Teplov rubbed his eyes to keep awake. It was midnight and he wanted to go home to bed, but years of service in the Party apparatus had taught him the necessity of careful paper work. He was preparing an agenda for the meeting of the Executive Committee of the Raion Party Committee in the morning, and this was no time to make mistakes. It was one of those periods in which any action could have the profoundest political ramifications. Teplov was a technician first, and a politician second, but in a time of crisis politics inevitably saturated all of life.

Stalin's picture still hanging on the wall symbolized the instability of Teplov's world, which would not be peaceful until another picture hung in its place. But whose picture would it be? And when would it happen? It was risky to take sides, and it was risky not to take sides.

Kornetsky, the sardonic Second Secretary, had chanced into the office one day as Teplov was putting a picture of Malenkov in his desk drawer. "We must be prepared for any eventuality, eh, Antip Trofimovitch? One must also be careful that he does not

CREDIT: Reprinted from *Nine Soviet Portraits*, pp. 60–75, by Raymond A. Bauer by permission of The M.I.T. Press, Cambridge, Massachusetts. Copyright © 1955, Massachusetts Institute of Technology Press.

put in the same drawer the picture of two incompatible persons. This might prove to be a very serious business," Kornetsky had commented.

Teplov had looked up, angered. But he did not know how to respond to Kornetsky. He searched the Second Secretary's face for some trace of expression that would give him a clue as to what was on his mind. Kornetsky's teeth were fastened firmly on the huge pipe which he seldom smoked, but which was as fixed a feature of his face as his nose and ears. It gave his face a rigid, graven appearance that betrayed no feeling. Teplov muttered and slammed the drawer shut in embarrassment. If things turned out wrong, Kornetsky could use even so small an incident against him.

Many times in the course of the day, he looked at the door of the office and his name in reverse through the glass "A. T. Teplov, First Secretary, Baltinsk Raion Committee." When he did, the same unspoken question came to his mind that came when he looked at Stalin's picture. The sign painters weren't very skillful, but it took very little effort to scrape a name off the door and replace it with another—no harder than changing Stalin's picture on the wall.

But worrying about such things was a luxury a busy man could not afford. The life of the Raion was dependent on Teplov, and Teplov was dependent on the life of the Raion. If the Raion did not develop, flourish, and produce, he would have failed, and his career would be over. There was little he could do about the fight that was raging among the big shots, but his responsibilities to the Raion were many and immediate. He returned to his task, and was working furiously when he heard a tap at his door.

"Yes?" he called out, wondering who would be calling on him at this hour.

It was Shvartz, the Third Secretary, young, thin-faced, bookish-looking . . . probably, Teplov thought, because of his pince-nez, an incongruous affectation for a Party worker. Teplov thought Shvartz looked like Trotsky with a shave. He was a good fellow, though, and a hard worker.

"Well, Antip Trofimovitch," Shvartz said, "I see you're still working."

Teplov gestured silently, drawing his hands across the pile of work on his desk with a single sweeping motion. "How about you?" he asked.

Shvartz grimaced. "I had a class for the four new Party candidates. I'm leading them patiently by the hand through the Short History of the Communist Party. A lazy bunch—I thought they'd go to sleep."

"Well, keep them at it," Teplov answered, and returned to the work on his desk.

Shvartz seemed unperturbed by being cut off so shortly by his chief. He said, "Good night. I'll see you in the morning," closed the door behind him and turned to leave the building. On the way out he noticed a small light bulb burning in one of the offices— and right in the middle of the campaign to save electricity, he groaned as he stepped inside for a moment to turn it off.

"A funny chap, the old man," Shvartz mused as he left the building. "You'd think he'd be more interested in the job I'm doing. Political education is an important part of the Party's work."

Teplov in turn was reciprocating Shvartz's compliment. He smiled slightly as Shvartz closed the door behind him. "A funny chap," he thought, "like one of the enthusiasts from the early thirties or even the twenties."

Teplov was interested in political education, but not in the way that Shvartz was. Teplov wanted the Party and Komsomol members in the Raion to be sufficiently literate in the political classics and sufficiently up-to-date on the Party line so that they would not commit embarrassing errors. And he wanted Shvartz to keep the general populace at a sufficient level of apparent enthusiasm so that there should be no unfavorable reports going into the Center about morale in the Raion.

The Soviet state was built on deeds, not on words, but even a practical man had to have a proper respect for the role of persuasion. It took years of experience and a long process of ripening to appreciate the delicate balance to be maintained between persuasion and coercion. Many young men and women tended to regard persuasion as a façade. The young Party worker who read in the papers the endless telegrams from "workers committees" pledging production goals and contributions often became cynical.

He had been assigned the task of securing such "voluntary" actions. He would be told in advance by the Party what action should be taken. Then he would announce at the appropriate point in the meeting, "The adoption of such and such a program recommends itself to this meeting." Everyone understood "it recommends itself" meant "the Party wants." Nevertheless it was possible for the Party, in this manner, to direct affairs while retaining the façade of "democratic" action.

But some young Party workers never realized how this balance of coercion and persuasion worked. On Teplov's desk lay a note which read simply, "New Partorg for shoe factory." If Shvartz tended slightly to overestimate the importance of words, the former Partorg at the shoe factory had underestimated it badly. He was assigned the task of securing a ten percent voluntary contribution to the state loan from the workers of the plant. With guileless naïveté he had posted an announcement that ten percent would be deducted from their pay envelopes . . . without an agitation program in the shop to explain the need of the State for the funds . . . without calling a factory meeting at which the activists among the workers could pledge the required amount. He was so gauche as to assume that everybody knew this was a formality and that it served no purpose. His action caused a furor in the Raion Committee. At Teplov's direction the head of the industrial section called the young man in, gave him a good dressing down, and returned him full-time to his job of running a stitching machine in the factory. Now they would have to select a new Partorg—one with a greater sense of delicacy and of proper form.

Teplov's raw material for preparing tomorrow's agenda was the pile of crumpled slips of paper lying before him. It was difficult to keep in a supply of note pads. But for Teplov this was an item of utmost priority, and he used his connections in Moscow to make certain that two or three times a year a small package of these pads would be sent to him. It seemed like a small item, but without them he was convinced that he would never be able to keep the affairs of the Raion straight. There was no telling when and where some matter of urgency would be called to his attention. He would scribble an elliptical note, understandable only to himself in most instances, tear off the slip of paper, and "file" it in his jacket pocket. In the course of days these slips would migrate from pocket to pocket, and through the various sections of his desk as he took action on these bits of business.

There was one slip in the pile before him which bore the legend, "Chairman, Broad Meadows Kolkhoz." It had started out in his breast pocket, where he kept the note pad, two days before in the morning. He was on his way out of the building when he met the head of the agriculture sector, Nikitin. Nikitin was upset and agitated. He was running his hand around the back of his neck, inside his open collar—a gesture Teplov had long ago identified as meaning that there was trouble, and trouble for which Nikitin was afraid he himself might be held responsible.

"Antip Trofimovitch," Nikitin began, "you'll just have to call the

Oblast office again about the chairman at Broad Meadow. They're two weeks behind in sowing, the buildings are in terrible shape, and half the chickens are sick. I can't do a thing with them. Always he gives me nothing but excuses. He should be replaced. We told them that last year."

Teplov nodded slightly, and pulled out his inevitable pad on which he made this brief notation. It was true that they had recommended replacing this chairman. Broad Meadows had been a problem for several years. The chairman was a former brigadier who had gone into service and had a good war record. He joined the Party during the war, and when he returned home the Raion Committee had recommended him for chairman of the kolkhoz. This was before Teplov's time, and he had since suggested tactfully to the Ministry of Agriculture that the chairman should be replaced. Well, this time he would be more firm.

But he couldn't let Nikitin get off that easily. He might get the idea that he could blame everything that went wrong in the agricultural sector on the kolkhoz chairmen. Anyway, he looked like he expected a bawling out. So Teplov gave him a thorough tongue lashing, ". . . passing the buck . . . don't expect me to bail you out of all your problems . . . should have worked more closely with him . . . making excuses is not planting grain." Nikitin grew red-faced, as several people passing by slowed their step to hear the dressing-down he was getting. At first he tried to stem the flow of Teplov's abuse with protestations of "*but,* Antip Trofimovitch." Teplov greeted each "but" with a fresh onslaught. It wasn't until Nikitin gave in

and answered repeatedly "*Yes,* Antip Trofimovitch" that Teplov finally let him off.

The slip moved to the top of his desk that afternoon. He placed it there so that he would not forget to call the Ministry. The Ministry agreed to replace the chairman, and the slip moved to the top drawer of the desk with a number of other personnel problems that he had to take up with the head of the cadres section.

After that he called the head of the cadres section to his office and presented him with a list of positions which had to be filled in organizations under their jurisdiction. He instructed the head of the cadres division to prepare a list of recommendations from the card file, and then shoved the slip, along with the other notations on personnel matters, into his right-hand pocket.

Now, after its long migration it was back out on the desk top where he had emptied his pockets and desk drawers in an effort to restore some order to his records. He made an entry on the agenda, under "Personnel," "Chairman, Broad Meadows." Above it, the list read: "Principal, School # 3, Director of Cooperative Store, Z. village, and Partorg, Shoe Factory." Then the slip and its companions were crumpled in one broad gesture and thrown into the waste basket.

He worked his way patiently through the pile of notes. There were a few production problems in several of the small factories in the Raion, but thank God, not many. Nikitin, as head of the agricultural sector, would have to give them a report on the progress of the crops. Also a general propaganda and agitation program would have to be worked out in connection with the recent arrest of Beria. The editor of the Raion newspaper had taken his cue quickly, and of course printed the editorial that had been broadcast from Moscow. But the entire resources of the Raion would have to be mobilized.

Finally, about one-thirty, he finished. It was a warm July evening. Teplov wore a light coat as he walked home. His house was less than a quarter-mile from the office. Baltinsk, after which the Raion took its name, was a small provincial settlement. The streets were unpaved. There was a crude telephone connection with the nearest city. Electricity had been introduced only in the years after the war. As Teplov strolled along under the night sky, he was surveying his capital, for indeed this rural town was the center of the area over which he held sway.

But, now that he was no longer working, his feeling of uneasiness returned. The decision to seek a career in the Party apparatus was a risky one, although it hadn't seemed so to Teplov at the time. He was an engineering student, son of a foreman in a textile plant. His mother was a peasant who had come to the city to work in the same factory in which she met his father. It has seemed quite natural for him to enter the Komsomol, and quite natural for him to accept the assignments which were given him. Before he realized it, shortly after graduation he was no longer an engineer, but an "apparatchik," a member of the Party apparatus. First he was Party Secretary of the plant in which he had shortly before been a junior engineer; then head of the industrial sector in a Raion Committee; an interruption for the war, when he served as a political officer to a regiment and was wounded; and then he returned to be second, and, finally, first secretary of the Baltinsk Raion. Teplov had not been a very distinguished youth. He was a little more energetic than average, a little above average in intelligence, and below average in imagination, but that was more an asset than a liability. He was very little concerned with politics, but quite intent on making a career for himself, and was entirely content to do what was asked of him in order to attain that goal. He was a technician-bureaucrat in a world of politics. As much as possible he tried to stay apart from factional struggles within the Party, and by a considerable adroitness at evading issues he managed to survive a full dozen years in the Party without becoming identified as anybody's man.

But tonight he was worried. It was comforting that he was not involved in any of the contending factions in the Party. He could be sure that he would not automatically be liquidated if the wrong faction won. But, at the same time, he could not be sure of the support of any of the factions either . . . and even though he had no one group of enemies, he did have individual enemies. Particularly he knew that he had enemies in some of the agencies in Moscow, and in some of the central Party offices.

Relations with the Center were always difficult for anyone with a responsible position in the provinces. Not only was the Center forever putting unreasonable demands on you, but they had completely fantastic notions of how to do a job best. Teplov was primarily concerned with his own self-interest and with compiling a record which would in the long run reflect to his credit. But he was strongly identified with his own Raion, and was convinced that neither he nor the country would prosper if the Raion were not in good running order.

Perhaps his worst enemy was V. N. Rashevsky, now a fairly high official in the Kremlin. Rashevsky had been head of the Oblast industrial sector when Teplov was appointed to head the Raion industrial sector. They had a number of arguments—an act of rare audacity on Teplov's part since he was little given to open displays of resistance.

While Teplov was away at war he heard that Rashevsky had been appointed First Secretary for the Oblast. Fortunately for Teplov, Rashevsky moved on to Moscow before he returned. There was little doubt that if Rashevsky had been Oblast Secretary at the time of Teplov's appointment, it would not have gone through.

Teplov rose in the Raion on the basis of his energetic work. But he continued to have his brushes with Rashevsky, who was now in the agricultural sector of the Central Committee.

On one occasion a division of troops was moved into Teplov's Raion. They were authorized to draw on Raion food resources for subsistence. It was quickly clear that the Raion's resources were inadequate. And they had to make the regular grain deliveries in addition! There would have been rebellion on all the kolkhozes, and the workers in the towns would have been short of food. Teplov carried the fight to the Oblast Committee, insisting that the regular deliveries be reduced accordingly, and the new Oblast Secretary took the matter up to Moscow. It was only later, after the matter had been settled in his favor, that Teplov heard that his old antagonist, Rashevsky, had been behind the original order. Incidents like these preyed on his mind.

Still in an uneasy reverie, he arrived at his house, a small, four-room structure, with two bedrooms, a kitchen, and a living room. His wife was sleeping in one bedroom and his two boys in the other. It was typical that he should return home after the family was asleep. He occasionally lamented how little he saw his family. But, except for being deprived of his company, they were well provided for. They were well dressed, housed, and fed. You could tell them by their more prosperous appearance if you saw them in any gathering. His boys, together with the children of the few highly placed officials in the town's two factories, were regarded with deference by their schoolmates. They were growing up with the self-assuredness and cockiness of the kids of well-off parents. Their mother indulged them, and the militia in the town were afraid to discipline them. Teplov paid little attention to them except on infrequent vacations, or when their behavior precipitated some special "scandal" in the town. Then he would lecture them severely. But they sensed that his concern was for the difficulties that their misdemeanors caused him personally, and they became only more skillful in having their way without having their escapades come to their father's attention.

Teplov slipped into bed, and dropped off to sleep. He did this so quickly and quietly that his wife, Elena, was not disturbed. He slept well. In fact he always slept well. He drained so much of his energy into his job that he had no trouble falling asleep even when he was worried.

Teplov knew nothing from the time he hit the bed until his wife shook him awake at eight o'clock in the morning. The children were already eating breakfast. He drew his clothes on mechanically and shuffled to the table. A glass of hot tea and a piece of rye bread sat before him. He gulped on the tea and chewed the bread, and by his own exertions came awake gradually. As he passed from sleep to wakefulness, the voices of the boys advanced out of the background of his consciousness. They were engrossed in the model airplane that Sasha, the older boy, was building. But before Teplov could enter into the conversation, they were busily wiping their mouths on their sleeves, and hurrying off to school.

Elena had already left the table. She cleared a space in the sink, and poured hot water from the tea kettle into a shallow pan that stood beneath a small mirror. Elena placed his razor beside the pan, and went to straighten out the bedroom while he shaved. She came through the kitchen several times while he was shaving, and commented on various household problems, but she seemed to address him only at such disadvantageous moments that he could only grunt through his clenched lips. He slipped into his jacket, said good-bye, and started for the office.

His driver was waiting outside the house sitting in the car and reading the copy of the Raion newspaper which he picked up regularly for Teplov every morning. They exchanged good-mornings, and Teplov got into the back seat. The driver handed Teplov the newspaper.

Teplov was doubly interested in the paper. On one hand he was responsible for it, just as he was responsible for virtually everything that happened in the Raion. Therefore, he was anxious to see that it carried out policy properly. On the other hand, it told him of what was happening in the world outside the Raion. Of special interest were the items which Moscow sent out by radio to be printed verbatim. Occasionally when he had an evening to himself he would sit at home and listen to news stories and editorials being dictated at slow speed over the radio. Particularly in recent months the ponderous voice of the announcer would frequently intone statements reflecting the tremendous changes which were taking place: ". . . comma who has repeatedly committed anti-state activities comma has been taken into custody period" . . . "the doctrine of one-man rule comma which is completely contrary to the principles of the Party comma must be replaced by collegial decisions" . . . "a series of benefits colon lowered food prices semicolon an ever increasing standard of living semicolon . . ." These dispatches were like the acts of some unknown being who would suddenly and violently intervene in Teplov's life, sometimes doing good and sometimes doing evil. *"Deus ex machina,"* Shvartz had commented to Teplov on one occasion when the arm of the secret police had opportunely removed a member of a ministry who was causing them great difficulty. Teplov listened attentively to Shvartz's explanation, and for once was not bored with the Third Secretary's bookish references. He agreed with Shvartz that such events were very much like the timely appearance of the gods in a Greek play—but one never knew in these days on whose side the gods would intervene. He scanned the paper with mixed feelings of anticipation and anxiety, but there was little of interest.

As the car pulled up in front of the Raion headquarters, Teplov noticed an automobile sitting in front of the building. He recognized one of the chauffeurs from the shoe factory waiting in the car. For a brief moment he was puzzled, then he remembered that an inspector from the Chief Administration was expected. The factory had sent the car to the nearest railroad station to meet him. It was covered with dust from the hundred kilometers of dirt road that connected the town of Baltinsk with the railroad.

The inspector, Boris Aleksandrovitch Davidenkov, was waiting in Teplov's office. A round-faced, stocky man, his clothes marked him for a member of the Moscow bureaucracy, but their disheveled condition also showed the effects of his trip. He jumped up smiling, and pumped Teplov's arm warmly. "Just came in to see how the plastic soles are working out on the shoes, Antip Trefimovitch!" he said. "Needn't get scared. No charges of sabotage or anti-state activity." He guffawed loudly at his own joke.

Teplov grimaced and barely succeeded in looking amused. The inspector was a good fellow who caused no difficulty for the Raion, but his macabre jokes provoked little laughter from Teplov. However, his overactive sense of humor was coupled with a general talkativeness, and he brought Teplov many juicy bits of gossip from Moscow. For this Teplov was grateful. The bits of information he picked up from people like Davidenkov who traveled from place to place and brought the news that circulated by word of mouth in the big cities helped Teplov fill in the missing pieces in the pattern which he was constantly trying to put together from newspapers and radio.

"Good morning, Boris Mikhailevitch, I'm delighted to see you," Teplov replied. "I understand things are going fairly well with the plastic soles out at the shoe factory. They had a little trouble with the stitching machines at first, but I think that's pretty well in hand now. . . . But you can see for yourself when you visit the plant. Tell me, how are things in the Ministry?"

"So-so. Too many changes for comfort. But it looks pretty good. Looks like they're going to ease up on the pressure for once. At least you don't hear people going around screaming about raising the production quotas like they were before. Maybe we'll get a little peace."

"What's happening to my old friend Rashevsky?" Teplov asked.

"Oh, is he an old friend of yours?" —Davidenkov had missed the irony in Teplov's tone.—"Well, I guess you're in luck. The rumor is he's going to be head of the cadres division of the Central Committee. It looks like you're in for a promotion. Rashevsky's in with the right people now."

Teplov's head swam. There was no worse place to have an enemy . . .

unless it was in the secret police itself, and even they were under attack these days. There was no worse place.

But his face and voice showed little of his feelings. The more you revealed about yourself and your weakness, the more weapons you put into the hands of your enemies. He rose and shook hands with Davidenkov: "I suppose you're in a hurry to get out to the factory. I hope you will drop in here afterward and let me know what you think of how things are going here. I hate to rush you out, but you'll miss the director if you don't hurry. He's due here for a meeting of the executive committee at ten o'clock."

Davidenkov shook hands, and left. Teplov took care of several bits of routine business, but the threat of Rashevsky lay in the back of his mind, and as time for the meeting came closer he found himself ever less able to concentrate on the problems immediately before him. Under ordinary circumstances the worst an enemy in the cadres division could do would be to get one demoted or, in extreme cases, removed from the Party apparatus entirely. But there were always jobs outside the apparatus, and it was rare to have the displeasure of even a powerful person follow one that far unless there was some political charge he could pin on you. But in a time of crisis everything was political. The mere fact that he was not strongly aligned with the dominant faction at the moment could be used to make it appear that he was unreliable; then anything could happen.

Shvartz arrived about five minutes early for the meeting. He was followed quickly by several other members of the executive committee. By the time the clock on the office wall struck ten all the members of the Committee were present except three: Kornetsky, the Second Secretary, Voronsky, director of the shoe factory, and Blonsky, the editor of the Raion newspaper.

Teplov gave an impatient glance at his watch. As he did so, his secretary opened the door and said: "Comrade Blonsky's secretary just called and said Comrade Blonsky will be here in a few minutes." That left just Voronsky and Kornetsky to be accounted for. Voronsky, he supposed, had been delayed by the inspector. "Does anyone know where Kornetsky is?" he asked of no one in particular. No one knew. It gave Teplov a particular feeling of uneasiness that Kornetsky should be absent. There were rumors that Kornetsky was a strong supporter of Rashevsky. He had been transferred to this Raion while Rashevsky was Oblast Secretary, and Teplov knew that there had been suspicious leaks of information. . . .

At five minutes after ten Kornetsky and Voronsky arrived together. Teplov's hand trembled slightly as he shook hands with Kornetsky.

"Sorry to delay things, Antip Trofimovitch," Voronsky said. "But Davidenkov got to my office at twenty to ten, and I couldn't get away sooner. Comrade Kornetsky was with me at the time and we were both held up. That Davidenkov is too damned talkative. We couldn't get away from him. He had to give us all the Moscow gossip before he would let us leave."

Teplov picked up a pencil and quickly began to make a series of notes. He had the impression that Kornetsky was watching him closely, and he was afraid that the tremor in his hand would betray his emotion. Writing kept his hand steady.

Kornetsky's flat voice came from between clenched teeth. "Yes, he told us the news about your old friend, Rashevsky. Big things are happening."

Teplov heard the tip of his pencil snap. For a moment he had no feeling. There could be no doubt but that Kornetsky's use of the phrase "old friend" was deliberate irony. Had Kornetsky heard the pencil break? It sounded to Teplov as loud as a rifle shot. He slipped it into his pocket. He glanced up at Kornetsky, but again the Second Secretary's face was a mask, with the huge pipe sticking out from his mouth. Damn it, muttered Teplov to himself, I wish at least he'd put some tobacco in that goddamned furnace.

"Yes," Teplov answered, "Rashevsky is a very excellent man. He will do a very good job. However, I believe we had better get on with the meeting, since Comrade Blonsky will be delayed for a few minutes."

Teplov turned to the chief of the cadres section. He was not a member of the committee and ordinarily would not be attending the meeting, but since there were so many personnel decisions to be made, he was sitting in. Teplov asked him to present his recommendations. He began with the job of the Partorg in the shoe factory. He suggested a young foreman who had been a member of the Party for about three years. He had a good Party record, was an excellent worker, and seemed to be ambitious to move ahead in the Party.

Kornetsky objected: "He is a valuable worker. The shoe factory is one of the pilot plants developing the use of synthetic soles for the entire country. It cannot spare the services of so valuable a workman."

Teplov was dumbfounded. What was behind Kornetsky's protest? The job of Partorg in the shoe factory was not sufficiently important to take the man off his regular job more than part time. If it were a big factory with hundreds of Party members, Kornetsky's objection might make sense. Then there might be a full-time Party Secretary and he would have to be pulled off production. What, Teplov wondered, can Kornetsky be up to. Ordinarily he would have given Kornetsky a thorough dressing-down for such stupidity. But maybe this time there was more behind his protest than met the eye. Teplov turned his eyes questioningly toward Voronsky, the factory director.

Voronsky was flustered. He stammered and could not answer immediately.

Kornetsky cut in, and continued: "We must be extremely careful with our personnel decisions. At the present time even such an appointment as this may be reviewed by the cadres division of the Central Committee. But, of course, I defer to the judgment of Antip Trofimovitch."

Teplov began to perspire. So this is the game, he said to himself, he's going to make enough of a protest to get himself on the record, let me push the appointment through, and then use this as a lever to get me out by going to Rashevsky with it. Teplov fumbled for words, but before any could come to his lips, there was a noise in the hall, the door flew open, and Blonsky, the editor of the paper, bustled in. Blonsky was a short, round man, who waddled somewhat when he walked. This, coupled with the abnormal energy with which he propelled himself forward, gave him the appearance of an agitated duck. He was flourishing a sheaf of papers. "Sorry, sorry, gentlemen," he said. "Big news from Moscow. I had to wait around to make sure the stenographers got it off the radio correctly. Here it is, Antip Trofimovitch." He tossed the papers down on Teplov's desk.

Teplov glanced at the dispatch. This time there was no mistaking the fact that his hand shook. The men in the room watched him, waiting for some comment.

Teplov read the dispatch aloud:

"A group of enemies of the Soviet state have been arrested for a plot to capture key positions in the Central Committee of the Party itself. These scoundrels, supporters of Lavrenty Beria in his anti-state activities, had wormed their way into influential posts in the Party apparatus. They planned to effect their dominance over the Party by securing positions from which they could influence the appointments of personnel. A major step in this plan was to promote to the position of chief of the cadres section . . ." Teplov paused and stole a glance at Kornetsky. Kornetsky's pipe was not in its accustomed position. He had it in his hand and was stuffing it energetically with tobacco. Teplov continued: ". . . V. N. Rashevsky. Rashevsky, knowing that he could not escape from

Soviet socialist justice, took his own life yesterday evening. All other members of this bandit clique are in custody."

Teplov put the dispatch down. "The rest," he said, "just gives some details. Well"—he paused—"I suppose we had better get on."

He turned back to the chief of the cadres section. "I think we can take that man as Partorg. Now, how about the rest of the list?"

The man continued his report, but Teplov found himself not listening to the words. How much politics were beyond one's control! How arbitrary, unpredictable, uncontrollable, unexpected were such events. How powerless one felt when the gods quarreled among themselves. What, he asked himself, was that expression Shvartz used. . . . Oh, yes, *Deus ex machina* . . . like a god coming out of a machine, to lift the threat of politics from him and let him get back to the business of running the Raion.

He glanced again at Kornetsky. Kornetsky was sitting erect, as though listening attentively to the report. Clouds of smoke were billowing from his pipe, and his cheek worked spastically as he puffed furiously on the stem. Teplov reached into the top drawer of the desk, where he found a small knife. He retrieved his pencil from his pocket and began to sharpen it slowly and carefully, letting the shavings accumulate in a small pile in the middle of his desk.

OCCUPATIONAL ROLE STRAINS: THE AMERICAN ELECTIVE PUBLIC OFFICIAL
WILLIAM C. MITCHELL

An important subject for behavioral research is the interplay between organizational structure and personality, between the peculiar conditions or demands of given occupations and the kinds of accommodations that individuals make to them. This analysis is concerned with the strains and conflicts associated with elected political office in the United States. Unfortunately Weber's classic essay on politics as a vocation has not been widely read, nor is it influential among American political scientists.[1] Politics is widely and intensively studied, but the practice of politics as an occupation has received little more than anecdotal treatment by journalists.[2] In this study role theory and role analysis are used to explore certain facets of the elective public official's occupational role.

More precisely the paper is concerned with the development of a "middle-range" conceptual scheme for the analysis of the strains engendered by elective public office.

ROLE STRAINS

Briefly, we can define strain as the resultant of attempts to meet expectations that cannot be fully met either by a person or a social system. Neither social systems nor persons can ever be free of the problems of adjustment to new and difficult situations. Strain in some form will therefore accompany the process of adjustment.

The strains to which a person is subject are not randomized in the social system. Rather these strains are patterned along the structure of the roles or norms that make up the system. All incumbents of a particular role will therefore be subject to the same role strains, even though they may respond quite differently to them. If we know the role or norm structure of a given social system we ought to be able to predict where and how role strains will occur.

CREDIT: Reprinted, slightly abridged, by permission of author and publisher from *Administrative Science Quarterly*, September, 1958, pp. 219–228. [*Some footnotes renumbered.*]

[1] A translation of Weber's "Politik als Beruf" can be found in H. H. Gerth and C. Wright Mills, eds. and trs., *From Max Weber* (London, 1948).

[2] The best but by no means the only writings of this type are those of Frank Kent, *Political Behavior* (New York, 1928), and J. H. Wallis, *The Politician* (New York, 1935).

Whether a particular occupational strain is consciously felt by a given individual is problematical. Some politicians may recognize the existence of a strain for a colleague but not be personally bothered by that same strain. Certain personality types may demonstrate an immunity to strains that cause great anxiety among others. But even in the case of the person who does not recognize or admit to being disturbed by some strain, we have to recognize the possibility that his failure to do so is itself a response to the strain. Self-awareness of a role strain is not a criterion of its existence. If it were, psychoanalysis would have little to do.

The role strains of politics are not simply acquiesced in by the politician any more than is the case with other persons in the social structure. A variety of responses is possible, including passive acceptance and deviance; but typically the politician attempts to effectuate some control over the situation, even if only a partial form. Efforts, of course, are also made to reform the situation so that the strain can be eliminated, but for the most part politicians attempt to gain only a partial control as the more realistic course of action. Periodically rather full-scale transformations of the political situations are completed; one such transformation was the Legislative Reorganization Act of 1946, which made some significant changes in the situation of congressmen and senators.

I shall consider seven general sources of strain for the elected public official. The categories used are by no means exhaustive, but they are primary in the sense that any other role strains are products of those selected for discussion. In the order in which they will be analyzed they are (1) insecurity of tenure; (2) conflict among public roles; (3) conflict of private and public roles; (4) ambiguities in political situations; (5) diffused responsibility and limited control of situations; (6) time and pressure of demands; (7) and status insecurity. Finally, it should be clear that I am writing not as a psychologist, but as a political sociologist. No attempt will be made, therefore, to analyze the effects of role strains upon the personality. My concern is solely with sources.

SOURCES OF STRAIN

Insecurity of tenure

No occupational role guarantees perfect security of tenure, least of all, perhaps, that of the politician. The turnover in the ranks of elected public officials is very great as the investigations of Charles S. Hyneman have demonstrated.[3] His findings respecting tenure in ten state legislatures over a period of ten years (1925–1935) indicate that in only four of the twenty chambers studied had as many as 50 per cent of the members completed three sessions. And in seven chambers less than 25 per cent could show experience in three previous sessions. In "Tribulations of a State Senator" Duane Lockard claimed that "roughly half of the six thousand legislators you are going to elect will be entering the legislature for the first time. Most legislators cannot afford to

[3] Tenure and Turnover of Legislative Personnel, *Annals* 195 (Jan. 1938), 21–31.

serve more than one term." [4] Regardless of the reason fragmentary evidence indicates that tenure is far from being guaranteed in politics.

Although the insecurity of public office is a fact, it does, however, require an explanation. Whenever an occupational role is part of a competitive situation—as it normally is in politics—insecurity of tenure is bound to be felt. Tenure, of course, refers to the role itself and not to any other roles the person may occupy. A politician may have a guaranteed income from other sources so that his economic anxieties are allayed; yet his insecurity as a politician will force him to reduce the tensions of the political role. And this will not necessarily be done for selfish reasons. The reduction of tension will be an indicator of success as a politician, meaning that his work is being done more effectively. A person who has to devote considerable time and energy to the security of his tenure will be more responsive, both consciously and subconsciously, to the wishes of those governing his tenure than one who does not. The politician is in this position because he is elected. He is therefore peculiarly sensitive to the currents of public opinion in his constituency. The fickle nature of the crosscurrents of opinion adds to his insecurity, for the number of issues on which the constituency can be unified into significant, clear-cut majorities is rather small. The politician's mandate, then, is ambiguous on most issues and his insecurity heightened for that reason. No politician can ignore public opinion. Even when he feels it to be wrong, it is still a fact that he has to calculate when attempting to rule.

The strains of insecurity then stem from the periodic, usually rather short, terms of office that a politician can attain only by winning elections. Much of what a politician does can be viewed as varying forms of response to political insecurity. The very fact that American politicians respond more quickly and willingly to the demands of their constituencies than to those of their parties is a recognition, by them, of the source of the insecurity.[5] In devoting their attentions to the constituencies, they are hoping to relieve tension and its consequences.

Increases in salary and pension plans are also means of coping with the problem. Control over elections—ranging from the purely legal ones of intense campaigning and gerrymandering to the illegal buying of votes—are additional responses. Among the better-known means of control has been the resistance of politicians to the adoption of open primaries. Since the primary adds another hurdle, many politicians obviously opposed it; when they could no longer prevent its development, they then moved to minimize its effects. They were aided in this by an indifferent electorate. No politician encourages competition, and certainly not at the primaries. There the effort is to eliminate as many potential competitors as possible before the formal election and to reduce the effectiveness of those who escape during the campaign.

Democratic forms of procedure, however, are designed to promote

[4] Tribulations of a State Senator, *Reporter* (May 17, 1956), pp. 24–28.

[5] Julius Turner, *Party and Constituency: Pressures on Congress* (Baltimore, 1951), p. 179.

competition so that the politician can never be said to have complete control over his fate. And, as stated above, forces from without the constituency can and do affect tenure. Great social forces—and such well-known phenomenon as the "coattail" effect—all impinge upon the politician's tenure of office.[6] They are, almost of necessity, imponderable forces and difficult for the practical politician to control.

Role conflicts

The fact that most politicians serve in more than one role as elective public officials guarantees conflicts among norms of performance. Expectations emanating from a variety of sources impinge upon the politician every time he is to make a decision. Various persons and groups constantly attempt to influence the decisions and the premises of the politician so that the actual decision will satisfy the interests of the persons specifying the premises or decisions. . . .

If a politician chooses to accept or be guided in his decision making by one role in preference to another, he is forced to deemphasize other roles he might be expected by some to perform. This matter of choosing certain premises rather than others brings out the problem of role conflict.

We can illustrate the point by characterizing two roles, the administrative and the partisan. . . . The premises of action in each role are opposed. Whereas the administrator is expected to be affectively neutral, the

partisan is expected to be affectively involved in the situation. . . .

The norms or premises of action expected by others of the politician are not always in conflict. At some of the relevant junctures in decision making, the premises may be the same so that no role conflict ensues. We know that administrative and the judicial roles have much in common. The one role which, perhaps, conflicts the most with each of the other roles is that of the partisan. One should not deduce, therefore, that the partisan role is dysfunctional and to be suppressed. Whether it ought to be is a value judgment and not a scientific one. . . .

A fruitful question to pose at this time is: Under what conditions are role conflicts most likely to occur? On an impressionistic basis alone the answer suggests that the major variables are the office, the structure of the constituency, and the incumbent of the office.

Obviously those offices which combine the greater number of roles will engender the most conflicts, whereas the offices with the fewest number of roles develop the fewest conflicts. Offices such as the presidency, governorships, and mayoralties of the large cities are likely to be the source of more conflicts than both legislative and judicial offices. In the latter case litigants and interested persons or groups have conflicting expectations about the outcome of a particular trial or decision, but the role of the justice is so clear-cut, so isolated from the other role, and so protected from the public and retribution that role conflicts are minimized. The legislative and executive offices are not so

[6] See V. O. Key, Jr., *American State Politics: An Introduction* (New York, 1956), chs. ii and viii; Samuel Lubell, *The Future of American Politics* (New York, 1951).

protected; but since the legislator generally has fewer roles to play, he has fewer conflicts. His conflicts are of another type involving the same role, usually the partisan, in conflict with other partisans rather than with other roles. Republican and Democratic congressmen apply the same premises of action but come out with opposing decisions on a particular piece of legislation. One votes "yes" and the other "no."

It stands to reason that in the matter of constituencies, those districts which have the greatest heterogeneity in the voting population will cause the greatest number of conflicts for their elective public officials to resolve. Some voters will expect their officeholders to act as executives, and others will emphasize other roles. Generally speaking, the larger the constituency in terms of population, the greater will be the heterogeneity and the subsequent number of conflicts. Senators probably face more role conflicts than do congressmen, assuming other factors are constant. Because of the districting process some congressmen have larger constituencies than do many senators, so the former's problems may be magnified as a result. Congressman Celler is a good example, as he has more constituents than many western senators do. Among the executive offices role conflicts are greater on the national level than on the state and local levels.

Private versus public roles

The type of role conflict discussed in the previous section dealt with conflicts originating within or among the various roles that constitute an elective public office. But these are not the only

role conflicts a politician must face. The fact is that politicians while fulfilling public office must also play private roles, i.e., roles without formal public responsibilities. The distinction between the two types of roles is a convention, as are all roles, but it is a convention of the greatest significance in a democracy and especially in America.

In short, behavior which is regarded as acceptable or even admirable in private life may not be so regarded in public office. Let us compare, e.g., the role of the businessman with that of an elected public officeholder. The former is not only permitted to attempt to maximize his financial returns but is encouraged to do so; the public official, on the other hand, is not only discouraged from doing so but is sometimes required to divest himself of financial holdings. The politician is expected to work directly and at all times for the public interest, whereas the businessman is encouraged to serve his own ends. This contradiction between private, economic, and political roles would not be important if the politician could simply play one or the other role. In reality he must generally play both roles because public office seldom provides the incumbent his sole income. Insecurity of tenure and low salaries often force the politician to maintain other sources of income. As a result the politician has to live by a dual set of norms. To honor one set may mean the dishonoring of the other.

I should now like to consider another type of strain, one arising from this same source in the conflict of private and public roles. The previous illustration was one of a private and a public role conflict stemming from simultaneous adherence to both roles. Another type of strain results when a person transfers from one role to another but has difficulty in shedding his previous role and adopting the new one. This is particularly the case when at least one of the roles is sharply defined. A scholar, a military man, or a minister will probably have great difficulty in adjusting to the roles of a politician. Each role is not only sharply defined but defined in a way that is quite different from those of political life. Consider the notion of authority in each of these roles: the politician is expected to honor majorities; the minister the word of God; the scholar the canons of science; and the military man superior office or rank. A person who has devoted many years of obedience to any one set of these norms and who suddenly finds that he is expected to honor a new set is faced with very intense problems of adjustment. Political life subjects the person not only to a new set of norms but to different occupational problems, problems which it is not easy to prepare for through education or any other kind of experience. To be successful in a private role does not automatically guarantee success in public office. Illustrations are hardly necessary.

Ambiguities in political situations

Lest the discussion suggest that most political situations are characterized by clear-cut conflicting expectations, let me emphasize the fact that as many or even more are dominated by ambiguity. Instead of being pulled in opposite directions by well-known forces, the elected official is often in the position of a lost hunter seeking direction.

Both the administrative and partisan roles share in the ambiguity, but the latter experiences a somewhat different type. The ambiguities of the administrative role stem from a lack of knowledge concerning means, and the partisan has difficulty defining the goals of the community. Theoretically the former admit of scientific resolution; the latter only of compromise or power. Goals are, by definition, preferences, and in a democracy individual preferences are ideally weighted equally, as is testified by the practice of one man, one vote. While an administrator is concerned with the efficiency of means, the partisan focuses on the moral question of whether efficiency is the desired norm to apply. In a democracy efficiency may not be the proper end of societal action.

Yet the value problems confronted by the politician are not insoluble. Politicians do have some relatively stable reference points in the American value systems. The problem is one of the practical application of general norms to specific social problems. The task is not easy because standards change, constituency pressures are conflicting and powerful, and the authoritative documents, like the Constitution, are not always crystal clear. Politicians lack the certainty of scientifically valid answers, because political situations are concerned with values that do not admit of scientific treatment.[7]

---

[7] The assertion is premised upon the notion that political systems are primarily concerned with the specification of societal goals and the mobilization of support for their implementation. And, finally, it is maintained that such goals are statements of preference and not factual assertions about reality.

Response to ambiguous situations is uncertain response, whereas response to conflicting but unequal forces is generally certain. Politicians often have "no comment" to make when confronted by the former case. They are "waiting for the dust to settle," for the situation to clarify itself in terms of expectations and possibilities. Those situations in which the greatest amount of ambiguity exist are those in which both the greatest amount of strain and perhaps freedom are present. Depending upon the incumbent, the politician can either be immobilized or creative. Well-structured situations can permit independent action, as in a constituency where a given problem is of little concern; such is the case in many northern districts where the "Negro problem" is unimportant. But they may also deter independent action when the expectations are overwhelming in one direction. Such is the case with politicians in the South when faced with race issues.

Politicians react to ambiguity by attempting to reduce it. Public opinion polls, newspaper commentary, personal contact with constituents, reports from advisers, research bureaus, investigating committees, and "trial balloons" are a few of the methods used to counteract uncertainty. But while politicians are utilizing more scientific processes to gather factual data for the structuring of situations, in the final analysis the data is never complete, nor can it resolve value questions, because logically an "ought" statement cannot be deduced from an "is" statement. The politician's responsibility to define system goals will always be fraught with ambiguity.

Diffused responsibility and limited controls

Though the politician has to define his own sense of responsibility to some extent, it is probably safe to say that responsibility in all offices which have an executive role to play is diffused regardless of how the incumbent decides to structure his own role.[8] Executive responsibility is generalized rather than specific—as in most adminstrative roles or other nonpolitical, specialized roles. The focus in such a role is upon relationships with other persons rather than upon technical goals to be reached by the most efficient means. Men are to be treated less as instruments for the creation of things than as ends in themselves whose cooperation has to be sought before anything can be done. In a democracy diffused responsibility and limited controls over the situation are built into the situation of the leader. While the politician is often held responsible by someone for practically everything, he cannot control many of the variables that affect the outcome of the situation and its demands. This is, of course, more true of the executive role than of any other, and of national than of state and local offices. But politicians from all levels complain about the limited control they have to effectuate goals.

Most of the strain that comes from this disparity of responsibility and control relates to the structure of government in the United States. The American polity disperses power to such an extent that no one official is

[8] See Talcott Parsons, *The Social System* (Glencoe, Ill., 1951), p. 100.

able to accomplish a task without the co-operation of several other officials, who may have different values and goals and may, in addition, belong to a different party. Because the formal means for securing co-operation are not always sufficient, many informal means have grown up. I need not specify these means here, but merely indicate that role strains have encouraged them.

Politicians are constantly attempting to improve their control over their situations. Proposals are always being advanced to give the President more control, the Congress more control, the governors more control, and so on. I might quote a few politicians on the subject. Note how they claim inability to meet their functions as presently defined by themselves. Notice, too, that a simple reform of the structure of government is expected to improve their control. In general, while politicians always have good things to say about the American polity, they seldom deceive themselves about their own position within it. The governmental system, though outmoded in many respects, is never outmoded fundamentally. Efficiency can be introduced by enacting the necessary reforms.

Senator Kefauver has been quite articulate concerning reform of the governmental structure. In fact, he wrote a book on the subject, though restricting his analysis to the situation of congressmen. In the opening pages appears a straightforward statement about the strains of politics:

Like many an average freshman congressman, I had my ideals and plans for worthwhile legislation. . . . I was anxious that Congress be equipped for the part it would have to play.

As the years passed, the results were disappointing. I found that the outmoded legislative machinery made it difficult to get much done. I soon realized that the Congress, intended by the Founding Fathers to be the predominate branch of the government, was ill-equipped to chart the legislative program of the nation and was surrendering too many treasured powers to the Executive. I also discovered that the numerous other services expected of a congressman left me little time to study or analyze legislation.[9]

Later, Senator Kefauver speculates on the reasons why men leave active political careers. One of the reasons was the "feeling of frustration due to the inefficiency that results from trying to run a twentieth-century Congress without adequate tools." The frustrations of office outweighed the contributions one could make.

The volume of work and responsibility is simply too taxing for the legislator to accept his job with equanimity. Practically every student of the legislative process has commented upon this fact and suggested reforms to improve the condition. Senator Kefauver was one of these people. Senator La Follette was another.[10] Those who assisted La Follette and Senator Monroney in the legislative reorganization of Congress in 1946 also wished to reduce the demands upon the legislator stemming from organizational sources.

[9] Estes Kefauver and Jack Levin, *A Twentieth Century Congress* (New York, 1947), p. vii.

[10] Robert M. La Follette, Jr., "A Senator Looks at Congress," *Atlantic Monthly*, 172 (July 1943), 91–96.

Time and the pressure of demands

A persistent complaint of politicians at all levels is related to the number of demands being made on their time and influence. Voters commonly overestimate the influence of politicians; consequently they ask them to do the impossible. More burdensome are their time-consuming requests; the politician often feels this time could better be devoted to more important matters. Local politicians expect to perform chores and usually do not complain to the same extent as do politicians who are concerned with more significant policy matters. Senator Downey of California gives a vivid portrait of the burdens of a senator, burdens which, incidentally, are increasing:

Each day Senators have matters come before them which could, if they could spare the time, occupy their attentions for months . . . yet here we are compelled to dispose of weighty and complicated matters after being able to listen to arguments only for perhaps an hour or two. . . . Observe for a moment the volume of business that is done in my office alone. It is so great as almost to break me and my whole staff down. In mail alone we receive from 200 to 300 letters every 24 hours. And this in addition to telegrams and long-distance calls and personal visits. We do the best we can. We try to have every letter answered the day it is received. My staff is departmentalized. That is, each girl is an expert in some particular field. . . . If the office were not so organized, we could not possibly begin to carry the load. Yet, Mr. Chairman, I can say to you truthfully that even if I had four times the amount of time I have I could not possibly perform adequately and fully the duties imposed upon me as ambassador from my state. In the departments of government there are always delays or injustices or matters overlooked in which a Senator can be of very great assistance to his constituents. The flood of duties in my office has reached such proportions, and is so steadily increasing, that I am almost totally unable to enter into the study of any legislative matters. That means that frequently I have to inform myself concerning matters of importance by listening to arguments on the floor of the Senate. And yet even my presence on the floor is only intermittent, so great is the burden of my office duties if I am to efficiently carry out my responsibilities with respect to the state of California.[11]

Senator Fulbright adds his lament in the following words:

But the fact is that the multitude of requests for minor personal services comes close to destroying the effectiveness of a great many capable representatives. The legislator finds himself in a dilemma. If he refuses to see the constant stress of visitors or to give personal attention to their requests, they may become offended and withdraw their support. In addition, it is personally gratifying to be able to be of help to one's friends. On the other hand, if he does give his attentions to these matters, he literally has no time left for the intelligent study and reflection that sound legislation requires.[12]

The senator further states that voters often will not accept the services of secretaries but insist on the personal attention of the politician. "They [the voters] feel that they elected the Senator and they are, therefore, entitled to

[11] George B. Galloway, *Congress at the Crossroads* (New York, 1946), p. 279.

[12] J. William Fulbright, The Legislator: Duties, Functions, and Hardships of Public Officials, *Vital Speeches of the Day*, 12 (May 15, 1946), 470.

his personal attention." [13] Senator Kennedy adds:

If we tell our constituents frankly that we can do nothing, they feel we are unsympathetic or inadequate. If we try and fail—usually meeting a counteraction from other Senators representing other interests—they say we are like all the rest of the politicians. All we can do is retreat into the cloakroom and weep on the shoulder of a sympathetic colleague—or go home and snarl at our wives. [14]

Several of the quotations just given suggest rather strongly that politicians, at least those on the congressional level, feel frustrated in their mission by the press of time and conflicting demands in their situation. The politician often feels that he has a job of considerable responsibility and that petty demands prevent him from making the contribution which he was elected to do and ought to do. Young politicians are frequently disillusioned about politics in this respect. Senator Neuberger, then a newly elected state legislator in Oregon, wrote: "I arrived at our new marble Capitol expecting to spend most of my time considering momentous issues—social security, taxes, conservation, civil liberties. Instead, we have devoted long hours to the discussions of regulations for the labeling of eggs." [15]

Status insecurities

Adequate performance on the part of role incumbents requires some form of compensation or appreciation for the services rendered. Most men like to believe that what they are doing is a contribution to others and that the relevant others know this and are grateful. Politicians are no different in this respect than are other people; if anything, they are even more sensitive to opinion about their work than are many other groups in the community. Although politicians occasionally voice dissatisfaction with their monetary rewards, more often the complaint is about an assumed low social status. According to T. V. Smith and L. D. White, "The politician's faith in himself has been impaired by the people's distrust of him." [16] I have some doubts about the assumption of a low status for the politician, but the important point is the assumption in the case of the politicians themselves. If they feel they are appreciated, they may act accordingly. "If he [the politician] believes in himself he'll devote himself to his high mission," Smith and White conclude. [17]

Senator Robert La Follette, Jr., voiced a common complaint in respect to the status of Congressmen:

Congress has been a favorite target for the disgruntled, the disappointed, the intellectual snobs, and the doubters of democracy alike. But most of this criticism is not constructive. It springs from personal prejudice, political bias, and above all from an utter lack of knowledge of the workaday problems with which a great legislative body must deal. [18]

After stating that "a legislator, like other people, has an ego that re-

[13] Ibid.

[14] New York Times Magazine, Dec. 18, 1955, p. 34.

[15] I Go to the Legislature, Survey Graphic, 30 (July 1941), 374.

[16] Politics and Public Service: A Discussion of the Civic Art in America (New York, 1939), p. 228.

[17] Ibid., p. 229.

[18] La Follette, op. cit., p. 92.

quires expression and recognition if it is to avoid becoming warped and eccentric," Senator Fulbright went on to say:

Honorable men in public life can take the abuse that is heaped upon them by the public so long, and then they succumb to a sense of futility and frustration. It is true that some of the frustration that afflicts the Member of Congress is due to the antique and obsolete organization of the Congress itself, and it should be remedied. But of far greater influence upon the decision of good men to remain in politics is the attitude of those whom they seek to serve.[19]

Senator Neuberger has also been quoted as saying the vilification of politics is "one of the nation's basic problems."[20]

Status insecurities thus grow out of the ambivalent status accorded the politician by the voters. The politician is never quite certain whether he has a position of respect or not. If he is convinced that he has, he is still unsure about the reason for it. The reasons may not be particularly admirable ones, for the politician is subject to much selfish flattery. Some he can recognize, but not all. As a result many politicians are likely to manifest forms of behavior that indicate doubt about their prestige.

The foregoing quotations indicate some of the responses of the politician to his status insecurity. The first response is to give verbal expression to the fact, writing articles about the plight of the public official. Note, too,

that the writers assert vigorously that the politician is mistakenly abused and that he serves a vital function in society. Typical in this respect is an article by Governor Bradford of Massachusetts entitled, "Politicians Are Necessary Too."[21] A congressman and scholar has written an article on "The Magnitude of the Task of the Politician" to prove that the politician deserves better treatment.[22] In *Profiles in Courage* a well-known present-day senator, John Kennedy, has defended the politician by citing historical examples of great politicians who lived up to their principles. There is a certain defensiveness about such articles and books, indicating that the politician is not only interested in correcting the public's view of him but in sustaining his own conception of himself as a useful member of society.

Status insecurity can take other forms. One of the more obvious is for the politician simply to leave the realm of active politics. As noted earlier, Senator Kefauver believes some excellent congressmen are leaving government for precisely this reason. I have no statistics on the matter, but it seems certain that status insecurity does lead some men to leave politics. The writer knows of two individuals who participated in local politics but decided, with the approval of their wives, that they had taken enough abuse from unappreciative voters. Their resentment is considerable, even though other politicians have taken more abuse during the same period and in the same area.

[19] Fulbright, *op. cit.*, p. 472.

[20] Quoted by Maurice Klain, 'Politics'—Still a Dirty Word, *Antioch Review* (Winter 1955–1956), 464.

[21] *Harvard Business Review*, 32 (Nov.-Dec. 1954), 37–41.

[22] Frederich M. Davenport, in *Harvard Business Review*, 11 (July 1943), 468–477.

Politicians form a sort of informal mutual admiration society to compensate for their insecurities. The often exaggerated deference that politicians show for one another, in spite of party affiliations, suggests a latent function in terms of maintaining morale. The politicians who appear on television and radio to debate various issues always pay high tributes to their opponents and colleagues. The same is true of much of the debate that takes place in legislative assemblies. The contributions of one politician are always cited by other politicians in their public appearances. Incidentally the politician generally refers to his colleagues as "statesmen," and seldom, except during a campaign and only in regard to the opposition, as "politicians."

Still another means of coping with status insecurity is for the politician to adopt a cynical attitude toward those who are responsible for his situation, the voters. Not infrequently, the politician becomes tough-minded and cynical. By distrusting other people and their motives, he immunizes himself from criticism and disappointment. The politician may attempt to convince himself that he is uninterested in the attitudes of others. In fact, he cannot be, but the delusion is comforting.

Some politicians adopt a stoic view to handle their status problems. Presidents Roosevelt, Truman, and Eisenhower have all been known to say that the varying degrees of abuse to which each has been subjected is petty and unimportant compared to the criticism suffered by some of the greatest of American Presidents. The detractors are, so Truman is reported to have once said, soon forgotten. The historical-minded politician is more concerned with what future generations will think of him than what his contemporaries do. The conviction that what one is doing will be of lasting importance sustains the politician through the rocky present.

The role of humor ought not to be underestimated as a means for handling the strains of politics, including that of status insecurity. Politicians like the late Senator Barkley were not only renowned for their gift of humor but also honored for the use which they made of it during times of great stress. The politician, as Senator Wiley has shown, is quite capable of laughing at himself.[23] The fact that he can and does may constitute an effort to minimize the difficulties of political life.

CONCLUSION

I have indicated some of the major sources of strain in the occupation of the elected public official. Instead of summarizing them, I want, now, to list a few propositions or, better, hypotheses about role strains in the hope that others may be stimulated to further research. The hypotheses are stated in an unqualified manner and without supporting evidence.

Hypothesis 1. The more complex the social system, the more numerous are the possible sources of role strains.

Hypothesis 2. The more sharply roles are defined in a system the more intense will be the resultant strains where role conflict occurs.

[23] *Laughing with Congress* (New York, 1947).

Hypothesis 3. In the American polity executive offices are subject to more role strains than are legislative and judicial offices.

Hypothesis 4. Legislative offices are subject to more role strains than are judicial offices.

Hypothesis 5. The higher the office, i.e., in terms of the local, state, and national division, the more numerous the role strains.

Two further subjects deserve emphasis. The first concerns the practical use of any information which might result from further studies in the area of occupational role strains in politics. We know very little about the way in which public officials respond to the conditions under which they labor. Yet, as democrats, we want them to perform their functions in a responsive and responsible manner. Traditional political theory has not offered much help in devising conditions that will produce the desired behavior. Since much of political behavior is conditioned by the strains to which it is subject, we might inquire into those strains, their sources, and the resultant behavior. If we can understand and, perhaps, control the strains, we will be in a better position to make the ideals of democratic rule possible. I do not wish to be understood as pleading for a reduction of the strains of politicians, if indeed that were possible. American democratic theory has always empha-sized the desirability of subjecting public officials to various strains, and no doubt there is much to be said for this position. But empirical evidence on the point is rare, and the problem remains. In any case it is worth entertaining the view that the elected official's work, like that of other organizational members, might be improved by bettering his conditions of employment.

The final point I want to make relates to research on role strains. Relationships need to be established—if there are any—among types of offices, personalities, awareness of strains among politicians, and their behavior. The research apparatus of the social sciences is sufficiently advanced to handle most of the problems involved. Questionnaires and interviews can be used quite effectively in getting at a politician's awareness of his occupational problems and frustrations. Harold Lasswell long ago demonstrated some of the possibilities. More recently certain political scientists have shown how legislators respond to conflicting expectations when they cast their votes. And, of course, we have a rich background of historical and biographical writing from which to derive hypotheses and data. Burns's study of Roosevelt and the Georges' personality analysis of Wilson contain excellent material on the role strains of these two Presidents.

TRADITIONAL ROLE PERFORMANCE AND THE DEVELOPMENT OF MODERN POLITICAL PARTIES: THE INDIAN CASE
MYRON WEINER

The ineffectiveness of political parties has been an important factor in the collapse of many parliamentary regimes in the developing areas. In the immediate post-colonial era, nationalist movements in Asia and Africa were converted into political parties. Only in a few of these countries have parties proved capable of running relatively stable and effective governments in a competitive environment. More often, stability and order have been maintained at the price of eliminating competition; either one-party authoritarian states have been created or the governing party has been displaced by military rule. In still other countries, the failure of parties to maintain central authority has resulted in the near disintegration of the nation-state through civil war. Thus in the age-old attempt to balance stable authority and competitive politics, some countries such as Ghana and Guinea have moved toward stable authority

CREDIT: Myron Weiner, "Traditional Role Performance and the Development of Modern Political Parties: The Indian Case," *The Journal of Politics*, Vol. 26, No. 4, November 1964, pp. 830–849.

without competitive politics or, as in the Congo, competitive politics without stable authority. Relatively few countries—Nigeria, India, Malaysia and the Philippines come to mind—have been able to provide both.

An effective political party in a developing nation is not essential for the management of a government which can carry out the wide range and volume of decisions associated with the use of state power for maintaining national integration or stimulating economic development. But surely the existence of some cohesive national leadership with public support and coercive authority to carry out these self-imposed tasks is essential. A party organization is simply one means by which a leadership organizes itself for the dual purpose of controlling government and creating popular support. A successful party may perform many other important functions for a political system including recruiting personnel for government, political socialization, defining political issues, managing societal conflicts and linking public demands to public policy. But the performance of these functions for the political system is contingent upon the capacity of the party organization to satisfy certain internal functions essential to its own survival. That so many party organizations in the developing areas have not survived—or have only been able to do so by banning opposition—suggest that societies (and individuals) differ in their capacity to create and sustain complex political organizations.

Many theories have been suggested for explaining the origin and development of modern political parties and it is not our intent to survey these theories here.[1] The purpose of this article is to show how an analysis of traditional social and political roles in relation to the roles required by a modern political party can illuminate the problem of party organization-building in the new nations. Our starting point is to view organizations as composed of inter-related roles, that is, patterns of expected behavior. In a political organization such as a political party there exists a network of roles which must be performed if the party is to carry out its goals. The first goal of any organization is its maintenance. In addition, a party organization seeks to win power, or if it holds power, to maintain it. To fulfill these goals the party organization must be able to (1) recruit and train its personnel, thereby perpetuating itself as an organization, (2) win support (good will, money, votes, etc.) from the population or parts thereof, and (3) maintain internal cohesion. In

a successful party, there must be a distribution of party members into the various roles required by the party for the achievement of these functions. Theoretically, there may be a wide variety of possible roles for the performance of any given function; pragmatically and ideologically-oriented parties generally define these roles differently. But there must be well-defined roles for which party members are recruited and socialized which facilitate the achievement of the party's goals. In this article we shall attempt to show that in at least one type of modern political party organization, the roles performed within the party organization are those which have been readily adapted from the society at large to fit the role requirements of the party. We shall look at the actual roles performed within a local unit of a successful political party in one developing area to see first how the performance of the roles accounts for the party's success; secondly, to relate these roles to traditional role performance prior to the establishment of the party; and finally to suggest how the adaptiveness of the party limits its capacity to effect the society in which it operates.

ROLE PERFORMANCE IN THE CONGRESS PARTY OF INDIA

The Congress Party of India is one of the most successful party organizations to be found anywhere in the developing areas.[2] Its very success, that is, its

[1] For an analysis of these theories see Joseph LaPalombara and Myron Weiner (ed.), *Political Parties and Political Development* (Princeton: Princeton University Press, 1965).

[2] Field research for this article was conducted in India in 1961–62 under grants from the Guggen-

capacity to maintain a measure of internal cohesion and above all to win elections, has made it possible for India to sustain stable and relatively effective governments at the state and national level. The party, as is well known, developed during the pre-independence era and since the 1920s has extended its organization into all the districts of India. Today there is hardly a district in India which does not have a Congress party organization and a cadre of active party workers. In Belgaum district, the area selected for our study, there has existed a Congress organization since 1920. The district is located in Mysore state in South India and has nearly two million people in an area of 5500 square miles. During the nationalist era, party workers were engaged in agitational activities—organizing and participating in street processions, launching boycotts and civil disobedience movements, fighting with the police and going to jail. Since the nationalist movement was also concerned with social and economic reform, many party workers were concerned with encouraging peasants to produce handloom cloth, cease consuming

heim Memorial Foundation, the Rockefeller Foundation and the Center for International Studies at M.I.T. The district described in this article was one of five districts selected for an investigation of how the Congress party functions at the local level and adapts to differing local social, economic and political environments in which change is taking place. In this article we shall not try to analyze all aspects of the Congress party in the district, for we shall do that in a larger study now in preparation, but rather attempt to show how traditional roles have been adapted to the requirements of the local Congress party organization and in turn how the behavior of the party can be understood in terms of its adjustment to the social environment.

liquor, give up discrimination of untouchables, and other such reform activities generally classified under the rubric of "constructive work." Of these two important roles performed by workers in the nationalist movement in Belgaum (and elsewhere) before independence—agitational and constructive—the first role has disappeared and the other is of reduced importance. The transformation of the Congress from a mass nationalist movement, concerned with winning power from the British, into a political party, and its adjustment to the various changes which have taken place within the district is, in the final analysis, a transformation in the roles performed by the party membership.

The older roles were clearly inappropriate to the requirements of the Congress party after independence. The transfer of authority from the British to the Indians meant in effect a transfer of power to the Congress party. It meant a gradual increase in the power of the party vis-a-vis local district administration. Moreover, the new national and state governments also imposed a series of changes to which the local Congress party had to adapt. Firstly, the government announced the establishment of universal adult suffrage. By 1952, when the first general elections were held, the local Congress party had to nominate candidates and create a new election apparatus that would reach all the potential voters within the district. That same year the national government launched a new program, known as the Community Development Program, for the development of the country's rural areas. A new administrative machinery concerned with development activities was created in Belgaum district, as elsewhere, and here too the party had to make some major adjustments. Finally—and this is by no means a complete list—the state government passed land reform legislation which affected the position of tenants and landlords. Within Belgaum district, as elsewhere in the state, struggles often took place involving control over land, and to these conflicts again the party had to make an adjustment.

In short, the party now had to adjust to a new relationship to administration, had to develop a formal organization for the winning of electoral support, and had to still further refine and develop a machinery for dealing with conflict within the party and within the society at large. The party soon created roles for the performance of these functions and recruited and trained persons for the performance of these roles. We can now specify four such roles which developed within the party.[3]

Party, public and government: the expeditor

The decision by India's governmental elite to utilize and expand the governmental machinery for the purposes of economic development and social

changes has been the single most important factor in changing the role requirements of the local party organization. The expansion of government has in effect meant the expansion, both in numbers and functions, of local administration. Local administrative activities are at least of three types: (1) regulatory, (2) extractive, and (3) distributive. The regulatory functions involve placing limits upon what individuals can or cannot do without administrative approval: to open a shop or construct a factory, a businessman must first obtain a permit; legislation regulates the relationship between landlords and tenants, peasant proprietors and agricultural laborers. The extractive functions involve the taking of things from individuals: the government has imposed taxes on land, set rates for the use of water provided by the new irrigation schemes, imposed excise taxes on commercial sales, etc. Land reform legislation also permits the state to take land from those whose holdings exceed a legal ceiling, and under various circumstances land can be transferred from landlords to tenants. Finally, a vast number of government activities involve the distribution of goods and services to the population. Some, such as the construction of roads, schools, electrification, irrigation schemes and

[3] Approximately fifty party workers in the district were asked detailed questions concerning the kind of work they did for the party. They were also asked questions about the local political and social activities of their parents and grandparents. Those interviewed included the district members of parliament, the state legislative assembly, and the officers and most active cadres in the party. In addition, opposition politicians, members of the district administration, and other prominent people in the district were asked to describe the activities of party workers. The district party organization also generously made

available its party records, including profiles of the party's 1300 active members in 1959 and similar profiles for party membership in 1952. An analysis of the changing age, occupation, and residence of approximately half the party members has been performed, but it is not included here since it is largely irrelevant for an analysis of party roles. However, a casual examination of occupations and names (which are often indicative of positions in the land revenue system or village power structure) tends to support the conclusions based upon interviews.

the distribution of agricultural credit and fertilizers, are concerned primarily with economic growth. Others, such as the allocation of housing sites for Harijans (untouchables), the establishment of nursery school programs, the granting of scholarships to the poor for admission into colleges, and the reservation of jobs in government for classified "backward" communities are primarily concerned with providing social justice and social welfare.

The party has responded to this expansion of administrative activities by creating a class of "expeditors" who serve as a link between administrators and citizens. To say "create," however, implies a conscious decision and a program of action which is quite misleading. It is also misleading to assume that the role is a new one. To the contrary, there was a class of individuals under British rule who had access to local administration and used that access to further their own or their group's interests. But prior to 1937—when the Congress won control over the state government and for the first time shared power with the British at the state level—relatively few people within the Congress party performed this function.[4] When the party took

power those who performed expediting roles joined the party; and as the activities of government increased and the party became increasingly engaged in handling local grievances as well as using the administrative machinery for patronage purposes, more and more individuals within the party began to assume this role.

The elected representatives to the state legislative assembly from Belgaum district are important expeditors. Indeed, they are as a group more concerned with performing their roles as expeditors than they are in the legislative roles. A few legislators are concerned broadly with public policy problems, but most are concerned with "serving" their constituents and therefore much time is spent by the legislator in the office of the chief revenue officer (the *mamlatdar*) and the chief development officer (the Block Development Officer) in his constituency. But apart from the legislators, there are many prominent party officials who engage in expediting administrative activities for local people. In fact, a conscious criteria by the party for the selection of candidates to the state and national legislative assemblies is whether the prospective candidate is skillful at performing this role.

---

[4] Until 1936 the non-Brahmin communities in Belgaum district did not actively support the Congress movement, but were instead active in their own political organization which had won control of the District Local Board and other popularly elected bodies in the district. In 1936 the non-Brahmins joined the Congress and took control away from the Brahmins. Congress then won control over the District Local Board and other local bodies or, perhaps more accurately, those who controlled local bodies had now taken power within Congress. Until 1936 every district President of the Congress party was a Brahmin lawyer; thereafter every President has been a non-Brahmin. From 1947 to 1960 all three Presidents were agriculturalists and all belonged to

one non-Brahmin community known as the Lingayats. Though the Brahmin Congress Presidents were all substantial landowners, they lived in Belgaum town and practiced the profession of law. The new non-Brahmin leaders were, with a few exceptions, men of less wealth and less education, with roots in the small taluka towns and in the countryside, and without professional occupations. The pleaders continued to wield influence, if only because their work kept them in touch with landowners involved in law suits throughout the district, but those who lived in the taluka towns and villages had much more intimate knowledge of local conditions and greater opportunities to build up pockets of local power.

There are a few men of humble origins who perform this role, but in the main the expeditors are men of some means whose families were part of the local rural agricultural gentry. Lawyers, professional people and townsmen generally are not the classes from which this role is recruited, unless these individuals come from rural gentry backgrounds. A few of the expeditors come from families of large land-owners (known locally as *inamdars* and *watandars*). Many of these families, and others as well (but always those who were landowners if not landlords) held positions of authority within the village. Two such officers were particularly important. The hereditary village land record keeper (the *kulkarni*) kept the village accounts, wrote up landholder receipt books, and prepared the findings of village juries. He was paid partly in land and partly in cash by the British government. The village headman (the *patel* or *gauda*) was generally in charge of actually collecting revenue and in performing certain police functions. His position was also hereditary and his source of profit was generally an allotment by government of rent-free land. Both village functionaries, occupying as they did hereditary offices of profit, often became the largest landowners in their villages. Through a process of family fragmentation, many of the large landowners no longer hold positions as village officers, but they were almost always related to those who did.

Inamdars, watandars, kulkarnis, gaudas, patels or their descendents—to use the local terminology to refer to landlords and to village officers—abound in the local Congress party. In the past those who held these positions exercised great influence within local administration, for themselves, for their families, for their village faction or caste group or, though less often, for the village as a whole. Though in the past local administration was more concerned with the extractive functions than the developmental and distributive function, it has not been difficult for this class to extend its influence from the revenue to the new developmental departments of local government. It is not simply that these individuals—or their sons who join the Congress party—have knowledge as to how the government administration works, or even that they have access by virtue of their past power or their present wealth—though of course these factors are at work. But these men are also psychologically capable of dealing with local and state administration. In a hierarchically stratified social system such as India's, those who are low in the hierarchy find it difficult even to converse, much less make demands upon those in positions of high authority. There are low-caste people in the Congress party organization in Belgaum district, but it is rare that they perform expediting roles. In the main, those who fill these roles come from the higher castes and most often are the descendents of those who are landlords and as village officers were frequently engaged in dealing with local and state administration.

Party and public:
the "constructive worker"

Since independence, much social service work which had previously been completely voluntary now receives governmental support. Today private schools, cooperatives, Harijan welfare activities and other social service organizations receive government support and often take on a quasi-governmental character. The production of *khadi*—handspun, hand-loomed cotton cloth—which before independence was primarily a non-governmental activity engaging the attention of many nationalist workers, now receive official encouragement from the Khadi and Village Industries Board, a statutory body. In Belgaum district, this Board is controlled by a local Congressman. The chairmen of most of the cooperative banks in the district are also Congressmen. There are also a number of schemes to develop the woolens industry in the district and these are under the control of government-supported, Congress-controlled cooperatives. The School Board is controlled by Congress and the District Local Board and the Taluka (a unit of the district) Development Boards are controlled mainly by Congressmen.

Many of the men once engaged in constructive work on a voluntary basis are thus now engaged, often on salary, in governmental or quasi-governmental bodies. Much of what is still called "constructive work" in the district is now of this nature. Today the term constructive worker refers to the party worker engaged in aiding those who are particularly needy, whether or not the activity is wholly non-governmental. Thus one prominent constructive worker is secretary of a boarding and lodging hostel for poor students in the district. Another is active in organizing the Kurubars, a caste of shepherds and weavers, into

cooperatives to further the production of woolen blankets. Another is the head of the Congress-sponsored Women's Congress, concerned with the education of women, developing children's centers, ladies' clubs and a milk-distribution program.[5]

The emphasis in this role is on service—to help those who cannot otherwise help themselves. Though some of this work involves dealing with government administrators—and is therefore indistinguishable from the role of expeditor—the conduct of constructive work in the main is related to the tradition of philanthropy found in the district. Indeed, many of those who are described locally as constructive workers are essentially philanthropists operating within the framework of the Congress party. A prominent Jain (a religious community in the district) businessman constructed a hostel for Jain students. Several other leading Congressmen, now with some government assistance, are building a hostel for poor college students just outside of Belgaum town. One member of parliament, a prominent local landlord, has for many years (even before he joined Congress) been active in building and maintaining a local boys' school. Moreover both the President of the District Congress Committee and the senior member of parliament from the district are active in religious sects and temples (*mats*) in and around Belgaum. Thus the philanthropic tradition lends itself easily to the "con-

5 Among the fifteen members of parliament and the state legislative assembly from Belgaum listed in published *Who's Whos*, more than half report that they are engaged in "constructive work," "social reform," or "philanthropy."

structive" work program of the local party.

This is not to say that all those who are engaged in constructive work came from wealthy families who have engaged in philanthropic activities. Far from it. Quite a few of the constructive workers come from families of modest means. A few are younger men who have been assigned by the party leadership to engage themselves in constructive work. A few are given salaried jobs as secretaries of cooperatives or student hostels. But the institutions for which they work are often the creations of those whose families have been benefactors to the local temples and leaders of social reform and educational activities within the district, even before the Congress party and the nationalist movement developed. The existence of a philanthropic tradition within the district thus provides a model for the creation of the constructive work role.

Dispute settlement: the mediator

One approach to the study of political parties is to view them as organizations concerned with adjusting and balancing divergent views into sufficient agreement for action. This interpretation has largely been applied to the American party system in contrast to the supposed managerial functions of the British party system (party as a manager of government) or the party functioning as an organizational weapon as is characteristic of parties in totalitarian systems (party as a means of inducing change within the society). In practice, of course, all parties perform what is loosely called an aggregative function. For the purpose of this analysis this function might be

thought of in terms of two related problems faced by all parties: (1) how to maintain internal cohesion and (2) how to operate in an environment of conflict. Conflicts within the larger social system often spill over into the party. The party may attempt to resolve these conflicts, or isolate itself from them, but in some fashion it must react. We may ask of all party organizations: how do they go about dealing with conflict, and are there any specialized roles within the party concerned with the resolution of conflict?

At one level, conflict is handled by taking a "position." The party may declare itself and press for a governmental policy. Most of us tend to view parties as a machinery for taking "positions," as the aggregators of divergent interests. The party may have a pragmatic orientation, in which case it seeks to reconcile conflicting interests so as to minimize conflict and above all minimize the disruptive consequences for the party. Or alternatively, the party may be ideologically oriented and may seek to resolve conflict in accordance with some predetermined ideological framework concerned with restructuring the social, economic and political order.

Actually, only one level of conflict enters into the public arena and is "resolved" by a policy decision within the party. At another level conflicts persist and cannot be resolved through general policy. Outside the party there may be conflicts between individual landowners and tenants, businessmen and their customers, factory owners and their workers, children and their parents, and involving all kinds of social groupings: castes, tribes, kin groups, factions, etc. As modernization proceeds, these conflicts increase. Even when they enter the arena of public policy few are ever completely resolved. In time, modern societies develop structures for the management of conflict: churches, social work agencies, courts, and voluntary associations of all kinds, including political parties.

The extraordinary degree of politicization prevalent in most developing societies, the high degree of social conflict, and the absence of a wide variety of non-political structures for the resolution and management of conflict place a heavy load on political organizations. As the party becomes overloaded with these burdens in most of the developing areas, one of two tendencies usually develops. Either the party copes with growing internal dissension by moving in the direction of a greater concentration of authority within the organization (internal authoritarian or oligarchical tendencies) or centrifugal forces grow and the party becomes so fragmented that it is no longer able to provide any acceptable degree of effective government.

The Indian Congress Party wavers between these two tendencies although in the main it has been dominated more by the centrifugal than by authoritarian tendencies. But perhaps more than other parties in Asia and Africa it has been able to develop ways of resolving conflict which have made it possible to continue as a relatively effective and cohesive organization without moving in an authoritarian direction. There are many reasons for this but we shall try to show here that an analysis of roles at the local party level, and the relationship of these

roles to traditional roles, may help us to understand how one party in a developing area may cope with the problem of maintaining internal cohesion. Let us first turn to some of the conflicts in Belgaum district.

The passage of land reform legislation has, in Belgaum district as elsewhere, resulted in conflicts between medium-size and large landowners and their tenants. Many of these disputes arise when landowners attempt to resume the right of personal cultivation from their tenants, and either seek to evict their tenant or reduce him to a wage laborer. The Congress party organization in the district can hardly ignore these conflicts because tenants constitute a substantial part of the voting population and landlords constitute a substantial portion of the political leadership in the party. It is therefore in the interests of the local party to resolve such disputes without either political agitations or court litigations. Several leaders of the party are therefore involved in attempts to mediate disputes between landowners and tenants.

Disputes between landlords and tenants are not the only disputes within the villages. There are boundary disputes between landowners, fights over stray cattle, and criminal accusations. All of these may be handled by a local Congress politician. One such politician engaged in resolving these conflicts summed up his role as follows:

"We have a saying here that people fight over *honnu* (gold), *henno* (women) and *mannu* (land). We try to settle these disputes out of court. Sometimes we bring the disputes to the panchayats (elected village councils) but mostly we try to bring the two sides together. It is a matter of giving satisfaction to both sides."

When the party worker hears of a local dispute, he generally visits the opposing parties. Often he is asked to do so. As a local man he invariably knows the local situation, not simply the dispute at hand but the pattern of relationships which surrounds the dispute. But the mediator is not selected because he is a Congress party worker. In Belgaum a class of people exists from which those who perform the role of mediator are recruited. In most disputes involving members of different castes, it is generally a Lingayat,[6] a socially and politically dominant community in the region, who serves to mediate or arbitrate the dispute. A large and respected landowner or a local grain merchant, irrespective of his caste, may also be asked to perform this role. What is important to the participants is that the mediator (1) not be a party to the dispute, (2) that he be a man of high status, (3) that he understand the whole complex of interrelated conflicts which actually make up the dispute, not simply the issue at hand, and (4) that he be a man of such local power that the disputants would hesitate to ignore his advice for fear of retribution.

In the main the mediators inside the Congress party have been successful at resolving disputes involving economic relationships, but quite unsuccessful at coping with disputes involving the two major linguistic communities in the district. Though a majority of the district speaks Kannada, the predominant language in Mysore state, approximately one-third of the district speaks Marathi, the language of the neighboring state of Maharashtra. Until the states of India were reorganized in 1956, largely along linguistic lines, Belgaum district was located within Bombay state. The Congress party organization in the district was torn between those who wanted the entire district to be in the state of Mysore and those who wanted the district partitioned so that the Marathi-speaking areas would be placed in the newly-formed state of Maharashtra. As linguistic loyalties grew, the rift within the party intensified until the bulk of the Marathi-speaking members left the Congress party. Since the two communities live in different parts of the district and only intermingle at the cultural borders, each had their own mediators within the party. Everyone of political importance in the district was committed to one side or the other and therefore no one within the party could attempt to bring the two groups together. Moreover, the Mysore and Bombay state party organizations were committed to opposing positions and were in no position to serve a mediating role. The effect of the dispute was to disrupt the Congress party in the Marathi-speaking portions of the district—and therefore to lose assembly seats in those areas—but to strengthen the party in the remaining Kannada-speaking areas of the district. The dispute continues but the Lin-

[6] Though the Lingayats are often described as a caste, they are more accurately a group of castes who are often considered to be a separate religious community outside the Hindu fold. The Lingayats are the largest single ethnic group in the district, constituting approximately 30% of the Kannada-speaking community which itself constitutes about 63% of the district population. The Lingayats are the politically dominant group in the present Mysore government.

gayats, who now provide most of the prominent mediators for the party, cannot resolve this dispute for the obvious reason that they are a party to it.

In Belgaum district the role of mediator is a traditional one. For reasons we need not examine here, but which are related both to cultural patterns and traditional social organization, contending parties have always sought external intervention for the resolution of conflict. When the Lingayats entered the nationalist movement in the 1930s, the Congress now had within its ranks the single most important community containing individuals capable of settling disputes.

Those who perform this role, whether within the party or outside, are not only *exercising* power by settling a dispute, but at the same time are *increasing* their power. Those who successfully resolve one conflict are called upon to resolve others. There is respect for the man's "impartiality" and a sense of obligation is incurred by those who benefitted from his intervention in the dispute. During elections to local bodies and to state and national assemblies, the mediator may return to the village to exercise his influence.

There are some individuals who can effectively mediate within villages, but lack the skill or sufficient status and power to do so within the party. But more often a man who is powerful enough to handle societal conflicts also has the power and influence to serve as a mediator within the party. There are conflicts at all levels within the party organization: in the smallest mandal committees, through the taluka, district, and state organizations. Caste conflicts, factional feuds, personal animosities and rivalries are commonplace within the organization. The prevailing pattern for settling disputes within any given level of the organization is for the disputants or their friends to seek intervention from a mediator in another unit of the party, most often a higher level of the party. Thus a dispute within a mandal committee will generally be handled by a mediator in the taluka committee, and a taluka dispute by someone in the district committee and so on upwards until the Congress party president or the prime minister may be asked to mediate.

The national Congress party leadership has great respect for those in its ranks who can deal with conflicts in the state party organization, and in the state there is great respect for local party leaders who can deal with district party conflicts. Though one may find mediators holding many offices in the party at all levels, there are certain offices which are especially reserved for those who have these skills. In the national office in New Delhi, the general secretaries devote much of their time to the management of intra-party conflict, and in the state and district offices the local secretaries are also engaged in such work. The Congress party is as viable as it is—and here we are implying a comparison with parties in other developing areas rather than in the West—not because there is little conflict within it but because there are legitimized and institutionalized roles for the handling of conflict. To generalize from the Indian case, one might say that the internal viability of a party organization is not a function of the amount, kind, or intensity of internal conflicts but of whether or not there is a socially accepted mechanism for the resolution of conflict. This is not to imply, of course, that this mechanism always works in India's Congress party, for in fact there is considerable internal breakdown, but the important point is that such a mechanism does exist and it does work more satisfactorily to resolve disputes than one commonly finds in other parties in developing areas.

Housekeeping:
the party organizer

The performance of the mundane and routine tasks of political organization —the recruitment of membership, maintenance of party records, the transmission of information and instructions from one level of the party to another, the raising of funds, and the running of a party office, are all *sine qua non* of a modern political party. When these tasks are not well performed, a party may degenerate into a loose association. There are 1,312 people listed in the party rolls in Belgaum district as active party workers, of whom only about 200 or 250 are actually party cadres. Most of the cadres are engaged in work in the local cooperatives, district and local boards, and the schools. These cadres recruit members for the party and are active in the various elections which take place in the district. Except for recruitment and election work, it is often difficult to say when a man is working for the party or functioning in an individual private capacity. But Congress leaders rightfully point out that a man engaged in cooperative organizations

commands considerable voter support during the election. The cadres also actively recruit members into the party since their ability to win elections for party office depends upon the number of votes they can solicit from primary party members. But few are particularly interested in working in the party office itself, or at making more efficient the structure of the organization.

None of the local offices of the Congress party keep records efficiently and the party is often lax in replying to correspondence. The state party organization complains that reports requested are rarely sent. Although active members of mandal committees —the most local unit of the party —naturally do their party work in their own area, there is actually no formal allocation of geographical responsibilities to party workers as there is in the precinct organizations of American political parties. During the elections, some villages may be neglected through oversight, though this is less likely now than a decade ago. But even now, after several elections, most of the local party units in Belgaum have not developed the machinery for conducting elections that one finds not only in American parties, but even in some other units of the Congress party in other parts of India.

The party does employ several full-time paid workers. Several party secretaries are on salary. There is a paid district organizer for the Congress youth group, and there are several full-time but unpaid organizers in the women's and youth sections of the party. But by any standards such organizational work as there is, it is not well performed.

While the modern party roles of

arbitrating disputes, expediting requests through local administration and conducting constructive work are variations of traditional roles, the role of party organizer is essentially a new one. Perhaps that is why this role is performed least effectively. Almost no one has experience on how to maintain effective party records, prepare reports on activities for the state office and most importantly, assign responsibilities to workers throughout the district to carry out the complex organization necessary for the conduct of elections. For these, after all, are new skills, and traditional experience is of little avail. Moreover, so long as the local Congress party in Belgaum district is not presented with any continuous challenge by any strong opposition party, there is little pressure on Congress to improve its organizational skills or innovate with new organizational techniques. If there is complacency and low performance in this area, it is in part because the party is not threatened from outside.[7]

TRADITIONAL AND MODERN POLITICAL ROLES: THE CONSEQUENCES OF CONGRUENCE

It takes more than a particular kind of traditional social organization to make a modern political party. Increased monetization of the economy, a

[7] Opposition from the Marathi community constitutes no threat to the party in the bulk of the district where the Marathi community does not live. As we have noted, the effect of the Marathi attack is to strengthen the Congress hold in the Kannada-speaking areas; ethnic loyalties have thus reduced the need for improving organization.

growth in literacy and education generally, an improvement of mass communication, the expansion of governmental activities, and above all, the existence of a legal framework which permits people to organize, sets in motion the process of political organizing. In Europe, those new forces which entered politics destroyed or modified traditional monarchical systems; in Asia and Africa their main thrust has been nationalistic—to eject the colonial rulers, then take power for the purpose of creating modern nations. Liberalism, communism, nationalism—these have been the ideological vehicles for a process of social change which has brought new elements into the political arena, either as amorphous movements or as political organizations.

But the process which leads people to participate in the political system does not necessarily lead them to create effectual political organizations. By effectual, we mean the capacity to establish sufficient internal cohesion and external support to play some significant role in the decision-making or decision-implementing process. A multiplication of ineffectual political organizations (in Indonesia, for example) tends to result either in a highly fragmented unintegrated political process in which government is unable to make or implement public policy, or in a political system in which the authoritative structures make all decisions completely independently of the political process outside of government. In the latter case we have a dual political process, one inside of government which is meaningful, and one outside of government which, in policy terms, is meaningless.

We have tried to suggest here that one factor which may make for effectiveness in the performance of a political organization is the adaptiveness of traditional political roles and skills to the requirements of the organization. The expansion of governmental functions in India could so readily and so effectively be utilized by the Congress party because the role of political expeditor linking populace to bureaucracy is a traditional one. And the role of constructive worker as a political role within the party could be built upon the traditional notions of philanthropy.

In the absence of such traditional roles the Congress party would have had to be a very different kind of party. If specialists in dispute settlement were not so readily available at all levels of the party organization, then internal cohesion might have been maintained through a highly authoritarian, highly oligarchic central organization. And if a linkage role had not existed between populace and bureaucrats, then the struggle between bureaucrats and politicians so characteristic of other post-colonial countries might have been intense and disruptive. If a tradition of service as a means of linking the party to the populace were not present, then the party might have had to build its support through a program of class struggle. The decentralized, administration-oriented (as distinct from policy-oriented), non-ideological character of the Congress party is in part an adaptation to the social milieu in which it operates.

One may well ask, however, of a party which adapts well to its environment whether it can readily attempt to change that environment. Can a party which aggregates also propagate? Can a party whose major support comes from well established social and economic groups take any measures which would reduce the power of its supporters?

To answer these questions it is first necessary to note that not all the individuals who perform the roles described here belong to the landed classes and the high castes. The proportion of agriculturalists who are active party members (most of whom are landowners) has actually increased from 56.6% in 1952 to 64.2% in 1959, but only a small portion of these are large property owners from "well-established" families. During this same period there was a considerable diversification of non-agricultural occupations practiced by active party members. It is also important to note that the roles described here have become institutionalized. While there have been some changes in recent years as to *who* performs the roles described here, there has been little change in *how* these roles are performed. Nonetheless, it would be quite accurate to say that the most active party members of the Congress party in Belgaum come from those families which in the past have wielded local power. It would be appropriate to say also that the continuity of roles in the party is still in the main a reflection of the continuity of power and rank. The character of the local party's active membership does place limitations as to the kind of role the party can play in efforts to change the social and economic system. In matters of crucial importance to the established party leadership—control over land—these men exercise overwhelming influence on local officials. They have no objection to the government's development program, for it in no way threatens their position of power. In fact, they readily share in the work of the Block Development officers; they are willing to form cooperatives; they welcome the establishment of small-scale cottage industries; they press for more wells and irrigation channels and when necessary, they give financial support to help finance village schools, roads and panchayat halls. None of these activities threaten their positions of power. Indeed, their positions are strengthened by participating in the work of the government and of the party.

Belgaum is a relatively poor district—poor even by the standards of the rural areas of India. Nearly a half million people in the district are agricultural laborers and tenants, or their dependents. Both their literacy and their aspirations are low and their capacity to express their interests through political action is also low. Thus far, only the landowners, both small and large, the mercantile community and a few engaged in professional and white collar occupations are actively participating in political party life. Some members of the shepherd caste (the Kurubars) have begun to enter political party life in the district, but thus far they have been under the leadership of Congressmen. There have been economic conflicts within the district, but these largely involve individual tenants or laborers and their landlords and are generally successfully mediated by local leaders. There has been no mass discontent— least of all in the areas which have regularly experienced famine. One can find in Belgaum district ample evidence for the hypothesis that there is a level of living beneath which it is difficult to sustain voluntary political organization. Congress thus recruits its active members and its leaders from the small merchant community, the professionals and the five percent of the landowning population with more than 30 acres of land. We have tried to suggest in this article that these men have a high capacity to create and sustain a modern political organization largely because the tasks which the organization must perform to win are those which its leaders can perform readily. Philanthropy, the mediation and arbitration of local disputes, and liaison between the cultivator and the administration are activities which preceded the creation of the Congress party and the men (or their families) who performed these activities in the district are often those who subsequently joined the Congress. Even the modern version of patronage—helping a man get a license, or his son to get a job, or admission into a local school or college—has its precedents within the district. With the expansion of governmental activities within the district and the transfer of much power from appointed officials to elected representatives there has been some change in the channels and a considerable increase in scale, but the roles are still much the same.

The Congress party of Belgaum district has failed to integrate the two major linguistic groups in the district, but then the local Kannada leadership never attempted to do so. The local party leadership has not pressed for a redistribution of land and many of the large landowners have successfully evaded enforcement of the state legislation imposing ceilings on landholdings—but then there are no strong forces, at the moment at least, within the district to press for an enforcement of the legislation. The fact is that so long as electoral victory is the aim of the Congress party—as it is bound to be while there are free elections—then there is little choice but to welcome into the party the men of local power who can win popular support and make the party organization work. In the 1962 election Congress won twelve out of the eighteen state assembly seats and both of the parliamentary seats (one with 53.5% and the other with 67.7% of the vote). Outside of the predominantly Marathi-speaking portions of the district, Congress lost only one assembly seat in the 1962 elections. By so handsomely winning elections in the district, the local Congress party thus contributes to the maintenance of orderly government at the state and national level.

Our analysis of one district organization of the Congress Party of India suggests that traditional patterns of social life can be congruent with the needs of a developing modern party organization. We have also suggested that continuity with the past places limitations on the performance of the local party and is an important element in the creation of a non-ideological aggregative party. So long as the party's leadership is based largely on those who wield local power and their modes of operation are derived largely from the past, it is unlikely that the Congress party in Belgaum district could become revolutionary. But then it is wise to recall that the changes which often occur under the leadership of those linked with the past may be no less revolutionary than those which occur under the banner of self-acclaimed revolutionaries.

FOR FURTHER READING

BIDDLE, Bruce and Edwin J. Thomas (Eds.), *Role Theory: Concepts and Research* (New York: Wiley, 1966).

GOFFMAN, Erving, *The Presentation of Self in Everyday Life* (New York: Doubleday, 1959).

GROSS, Neal C., Ward S. Mason, and Alexander W. McEachern, *Explorations in Role Analysis: Studies of the School Superintendency Role* (New York: Wiley, 1959).

GROSSMAN, Joel B., "Role Playing in the Analysis of Judicial Behavior: The Case of Mr. Justice Frankfurter," *Journal of Public Law,* 1962, pp. 285–309.

GOULDNER, Alvin W., "Cosmopolitans and Locals: Toward an Analysis of Latent Social Roles," *Administrative Science Quarterly,* December, 1957; March, 1958, pp. 281–306, 444–480.

HOMANS, George, *Social Behavior: Its Elementary Forms* (New York: Harcourt, Brace, and World, 1961).

HUITT, Ralph K., "The Outsider in the Senate: An Alternative Role," *American Political Science Review,* September, 1961, pp. 566–575.

LINTON, Ralph, *The Study of Man* (New York: Appleton-Century, 1936).

MEAD, George H., *Mind, Self and Society From the Standpoint of a Social Behaviorist* (Chicago: University of Chicago Press, 1934).

MERTON, Robert K., "The Role Set," *British Journal of Sociology,* June, 1957, pp. 106–120.

SARBIN, Theodore R. and Vernon L. Allen, "Role Theory" in Gardner Lindzey and Elliot Aronson (Eds.), *The Handbook of Social Psychology* (Reading, Mass: Addison–Wesley, 1968), Vol. 1, pp. 488–567.

WAHLKE, John C., Heinz Eulau, William Buchanan and Leroy C. Ferguson, *The Legislative System* (New York: Wiley, 1962).

WILENSKY, Harold C., *Intellectuals in Labor Unions: Organizational Pressures on Professional Roles* (Glencoe: Free Press, 1956).

PART THREE: GROUP

Group theory follows from role theory in a very direct way. To put the matter most simply, a group is a network of roles. Role concepts are, therefore, commonplace in the analysis of groups. Newcomb, Turner, and Converse are very clear on this point: "Since a group *is* what its role relationships are, our descriptions and explanations of any group as a whole must be stated in terms of its entire network of role relationships. . . . The general principle, apparently applicable to any kind of relatively stable role system, is that the ways in which group resources are mobilized and organized through role relationships determines the group's properties. . . . Just as group properties are maintained by role relationships, the latter are maintained by group norms." [1]

The first American to use such group concepts as his principal point of departure for the analysis of politics was Arthur F. Bentley. Writing in 1908, he made a strong plea for a change of focus in the study of politics. Rather than concentrate on *man* and the *state,* as philosophers had done for centuries, Bentley urged consideration of another "raw material." What "we study is never found in one man by himself, it cannot even be stated by adding men to men." [2] The "action" in government, according to Bentley, was to be found in the activity of *groups.* "The collections, or groups, of men are composed of thinking and feeling actors. They act through a thought-and-feeling process. . . . The balance of the group pressures *is* the existing state of society. . . . In the broadest sense—a very broad sense indeed—government is the process of adjustment of a set of interest groups in a particular distinguishable group or system without any differentiated activity, or 'organ,' to center attention on just what is happening." [3] For Bentley, the process of government—the raw material of politics—consisted of "groups of people pushing other groups and being pushed by them in turn." [4]

We should not assume, of course, that Bentley sparked an interest in groups which had lain totally inert or undiscovered for centuries. Emphasis on "man the social animal" had come from Plato and Aristotle. The medieval notion of *Genossenschaft,* or the corporation, lying midway between the individual and the state, yet organically bound up with the latter, places much emphasis upon man's

---

[1] Theodore M. Newcomb, Ralph H. Turner, and Philip E. Converse, *Social Psychology: The Study of Human Interaction* (Holt, Rinehart, and Winston, 1965), pp. 350, 355.

[2] *The Process of Government—A Study of Social Pressures* (Chicago: University of Chicago Press, 1908), p. 176.

[3] *The Process of Government,* pp. 176, 258, 260.

[4] Peter H. Odegard, "A Group Basis of Politics, A New Name for an Ancient Myth," *The Western Political Quarterly,* September, 1958, p. 690.

association with man. The seventeenth century political philosopher James Harrington relies heavily on the notion of Interest—primarily property interests or groups—as "the Foundation of Government." And the idea that groups, or "factions," vie for shares of political resources flowed as clearly from James Madison, Alexis deTocqueville, and John C. Calhoun as it did from Arthur F. Bentley.

Yet Bentley's *The Process of Government* marks the beginning of an era. For Bentley, the process of government could be explained in relatively precise *analytic units*—or raw materials—and the most important of these was the group. Bentley's work marks the beginning of conceptualization about groups.

> The term "group" will be used throughout this work in a technical sense. It means a certain portion of the men of a society, taken, however, not as a physical mass cut off from other masses of men, but as a mass activity, which does not preclude the men who participate in it from participating likewise in many other group activities. . . . There is no group without its interest. . . . The group and the interest are not separate. There exists only the one thing, that is, so many men bound together in or along the path of a certain activity.[5]

Bentley viewed groups, then, as more than mere additions of men to men: men were "bound together" through common *interest* to form or perpetuate a group. As we shall discover, social scientists now express this common interest in terms of attitudes. Furthermore, Bentley was the first to note some of the important group properties such as size, intensity, and techniques.

Arthur F. Bentley is known more for his "group basis of politics" than for serious conceptualization about groups. Further effort in the latter by political scientists did not come for several decades.

Amplification of the "group basis of politics" came in 1928 in E. Pendleton Herring's *Group Representation Before Congress,* hailed as another "pioneer work." Herring was the first to apply the idea that politics is essentially a group struggle to a study of the United States Congress. In a later volume, comprised of a series of case studies, Herring explained how administrators responsible for regulating business make decisions:

> This increase in administrative discretion, while making possible the more understanding application of rules to concrete situations, nevertheless places a heavy duty on the administrator. . . .
> Although it is clear that the official must balance the interests of the conflicting groups before him, by what standards is he to weigh their demands? . . . Acting in accordance with this subjective conception and bounded by his statutory competence, the bureaucrat selects from the special interests before him a combination to which he gives official sanction. Thus inescapably in practice the concept of public interest is given substance by its identification with the interests of certain groups. . . . [T]he public interest can be realized only through promoting certain special interests.[6]

[5] Bentley, *The Process of Government,* p. 211.

[6] E. Pendleton Herring, quoted in Glendon A. Schubert, Jr., " 'The Public Interest' In Administrative Decision-Making: Theorem, Theosopy, or Theory?" *American Political Science Review,* June, 1957, pp. 360–361.

Although Herring never mentioned Bentley, it is clear that each had placed a high premium on the same raw materials. In succeeding years, several other imaginative political scientists made contributions to the burgeoning group basis school. Space precludes a close examination of these advances, but we should at least note the major contributions of Peter Odegard with *Pressure Politics* in 1928, E. E. Schattschneider with *Politics, Pressures and the Tariff* in 1935, Oliver Garceau with *The Political Life of the American Medical Association* in 1941, and Stephen K. Bailey with *Congress Makes a Law* in 1950.

Relying on the tenets of the group basis of politics developed by these scholars, Earl Latham in 1951 reiterated the argument that politics is a reflection of group conflict—with organized groups serving as "structures of power . . . forms of private government different from forms of public government principally in that public governments possess the characteristic of officiality." [7] Latham examined the Cement Institute in its struggle with such groups as the Maple Flooring Manufacturers' Association and the Southwestern Lumbermen's Association in the 81st and 82nd Congresses. Much like Bentley, Latham spoke of a "community of interest" among group members.

Jack W. Peltason was the first to depict the judicial process—from constitutional interpretation to administration of criminal justice—as a group struggle. "The functions of judges and the conditions under which they do their assigned tasks are determined by and are not above the group struggle. To win judicial support is a strategically important step for any interest. It brings the prestige of the judges, their opinions, and their sanction to enforce a desired policy. . . . A judicial decision is but one phase in the never-ending group conflict, a single facet of the political process." [8]

Accepted as a "milestone toward a systematic formulation of the dynamics of government," [9] David B. Truman's *The Governmental Process,* in 1951, reunited the strands that had appeared first in Bentley's treatise: (1) the group basis of politics; and (2) group as a precise analytic concept. Truman's work, it must be emphasized, is not simply a reworking of Bentley's basic ideas. Much more rigorous in its approach, it seeks to relate the many dimensions of group behavior to the political process. Truman's work marks the acceptance of the group paradigm in political science.

In our first selection, "A Group Interpretation of Politics," Truman begins by discussing "groups of all kinds." His definition of the group concept is much more detailed and systematic than Bentley's maiden effort. In many ways, this definition reflects the pioneering work of Theodore Newcomb and Conrad Arensberg studying the same concepts. Just one year earlier, Newcomb had published *Social Psychology.* By 1951, then, political scientists and sociologists were coming to an essential agreement on the definition of the concept.

According to sociologist A. Paul Hare, for a group to exist five conditions must be met:

[7] *The Group Basis of Politics, A Study in Basing–Point Legislation* (Ithaca, New York: Cornell University Press, 1952), p. 14.

[8] Jack W. Peltason, *Federal Courts in the Political Process* (New York: Random House, 1955), pp. 8, 63–64.

[9] Avery Leiserson, "Book Review of *The Governmental Process: Political Interests and Public Opinion,*" *American Political Science Review,* December, 1951, p. 1192.

1. There must be *interaction* of the members;

2. The members share (i.e., having the same attitudes about) one or more *motives* or *goals* which determine the direction in which the group will move.

3. The members develop a set of *norms*, which set the boundaries within which interpersonal relations may be established and activity carried on.

4. If interaction continues, a set of *roles* becomes stabilized and the new group becomes differentiated from other groups.

5. A *network of interpersonal attraction* develops on the basis of the "likes" and "dislikes" of members for one another.[10]

These conditions distinguish a group from a "grouping"—or mere conglomerate or collection of persons. In fact, we may place each, a group and a grouping, at opposite ends of a continuum:

grouping   group

Then, the degree to which these conditions are met indicates the extent to which one may move to the right on the continuum.

Truman places much emphasis upon the sharing of attitudes within a group (what Bentley called the sharing of "interest"). This sharing holds the group together (i.e., makes it cohesive) and facilitates intra-group equilibrium. If, on the other hand, several persons possess similar attitudes, *without* sharing them through an interactive process, we say that they are living in a state of "pluralistic ignorance."[11] There may be consensus on attitudes among these several persons; but as long as there is no conscious sharing, achieved through personal interaction, a group does not yet exist. For Truman, these persons constitute a potential interest group.

There is also much emphasis upon equilibrium: . . . the . . . expected patterns of interaction that make up the institutional group are normally in balance, or in a state of equilibrium. . . . An equilibrium must be worked out within an institutionalized group . . . if it is to survive. It is characteristic of such balanced groups that if the equilibrium is disturbed by some event outside the group, the equilibrium will be restored when the disturbance is over. . . . The existence of the equilibrium and its stability presumably can be measured by observing the consistency of interaction patterns."[12]

Sidney Ulmer[13] has demonstrated this tendency toward equilibrium on the United States Supreme Court.

By learning more about group behavior, it is possible to understand more

[10] A. Paul Hare, *Handbook of Small Group Research* (New York: The Free Press of Glencoe, 1962), pp. 9–10.

[11] Newcomb, Turner, and Converse, *Social Psychology*, p. 371.

[12] David B. Truman, *The Governmental Process* (New York: Knopf, 1951), p. 27.

[13] "Homeostatic Tendencies in the United States Supreme Court," in S. Sidney Ulmer (Ed.), *Introductory Readings in Political Behavior* (Chicago: Rand McNally, 1961), pp. 167–188.

fully the effect of groups on politics. Herein lies Truman's major contribution. With social scientists agreed on a definition of the concept, by the end of the decade, political scientists turned increasingly to empirical studies of group behavior. The chief work came from Sidney Verba,[14] Robert Golembiewski,[15] Harmon Zeigler,[16] and Samuel Patterson.[17]

Professors Truman and Latham had placed renewed emphasis upon the group in politics. Opposition gathered; its most articulate spokesmen were Peter Odegard and Stanley Rothman.

Odegard attacked what he called the "ambiguity" of the Group Theory of Politics—the failure of Bentley and Truman to define precisely what they meant by "group," "interest," "equilibrium," "feelings," and so on. Increased consensus about group theory terms among social scientists has taken the edge off much of this attack. Yet one persistent criticism lingers: "Group theorists, like the early radical behavioralists, have all but banished reason, knowledge, and intelligence from the governmental process. . . . Anyone familiar with the decision-making process knows that pressure, force, intimidation, self-interest, and, heaven knows, group interests, account for no small fraction of the decisions that are made. But they do not account for them all. Reason and logic are by no means strangers to the decision-making process." [18]

In other words, Professor Odegard refused to accept the idea that *all* political decisions result from the tug and pull of contending groups; and the idea that all demands upon the political system come from groups. In addition to suggesting the possibility of a rational decision, Odegard insisted that "political scientists must take account of the values no less than the process of allocation." [19]

Rothman's criticism of *The Governmental Process* dealt less with the inadequacies of explanation in the group approach. Instead, Rothman charged, "Truman's attempt to reduce human behavior to patterns of group interaction and their disturbance blinds him to all sorts of dimensions of human experience." [20] Many attitudes, Professor Rothman pointed out,[21] are derived from society, or what Gabriel Almond calls "political culture." [22] In essence, he was asking that political scientists pay attention to attitude-formation at the macrolevel as well as the microlevel. Rothman concluded that "the study of politics must not only involve the study of groups and individuals; it must also involve . . . the study of

[14] *Small Groups and Political Behavior—A Study of Leadership* (Princeton: Princeton University Press, 1961).

[15] *The Small Group* (Chicago: University of Chicago Press, 1962).

[16] *Interest Groups in American Society* (Englewood Cliffs, N.J.: Prentice-Hall, 1964).

[17] Among several excellent articles, see "Patterns of Interpersonal Relations in a State Legislative Group: The Wisconsin Assembly," *Public Opinion Quarterly*, Spring, 1959, pp. 101–109 and "The Role of the Deviant in the State Legislative System: The Wisconsin Assembly," *Western Political Quarterly*, June, 1961, pp. 460–472.

[18] Odegard, "A Group Basis of Politics," pp. 699–700.

[19] *Ibid.*, p. 701.

[20] Stanley Rothman, "Systematic Political Theory: Observations on the Group Approach," *American Political Science Review*, March, 1960, p. 31.

[21] *Ibid.*, See footnote 23, pp. 18, 23.

[22] Gabriel A. Almond and G. Bingham Powell, Jr., *Comparative Politics—A Developmental Approach* (Boston: Little, Brown, 1966), pp. 23–25.

the patterns of normatively oriented political action which characterize a given social system." [23]

Let us turn now away from the "group basis of politics" to a more detailed analysis of the group concept. As an example of a small primary group (one in which there is direct, face-to-face interaction), let us use a nine-man collegial court.[24] (You may wish to consider this the United States Supreme Court.) This court is depicted in Figure III-1. The circles indicate the position of associate justice; the larger circle, the position of chief justice; {Z} refers to the set of attitudes of any justice. The solid lines indicate paths of interpersonal attraction or dislike; arrows indicate direction of interaction; valence indicates liking or disliking; and valence quantity (the number of plusses or minusses) indicates intensity of feeling. These lines of interpersonal attraction form a "sociometric structure" which also serves as the basic group structure.

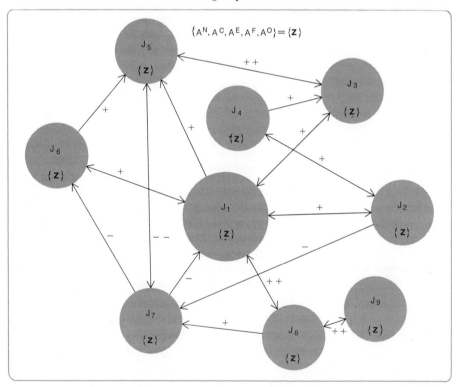

Figure III-1.   A collegial court

Since the "structure of anything refers to the relationships among its parts, . . . the attraction structure of a group is thus a description of interpersonal relationships of attraction and aversion among its members." [25] The structure of

[23] Stanley Rothman, "Systematic Political Theory: Observations on the Group Approach," *American Political Science Review*, March, 1960, p. 32.

[24] See Walter F. Murphy, "Courts as Small Groups," *Harvard Law Review*, June, 1966, pp. 1565-1572.

[25] Newcomb, *et al.*, *Social Psychology*, p. 292.

a group builds up (and stabilizes) as members interact with each other. Liking leads to positive interaction; disliking leads to negative interaction. Both are related, of course, to the *attitudes* that any one member has about his fellow members.

Each member of the court has a *set* of attitudes which are uniquely his own. This set includes attitudes about rules of behavior, or norms (A^N); attitudes about environment (A^E); attitudes about other members of the court (A^O); and general policy or interpretative attitudes, for example, attitudes about civil liberties (A^C) or federalism (A^F). We might represent many more attitudes. The set of all attitudes is represented by $\{Z\}$.

The extent to which one member's attitude coincides with another's is a strong determinant of structural attraction. That is, if two judges have similar attitudes about the efficacy of trespassing laws applied to civil rights advocates or about the constitutionality of wiretapping, or even about how each perceives his role on the Court, then it is likely that these judges will be attracted to each other. Diverse attitudes may engender negative attractions and, if diverse enough, animosities. Similarity of attitudes accounts for the strong attraction of, say, Oliver Wendell Holmes, Louis Brandeis, and Harlan Fiske Stone on the Taft Court; or of Pierce Butler, Arthur Sutherland and Willis Van Devanter on the Hughes Court.

With this knowledge of group structure, it is not difficult to link group behavior and leadership. That group member for whom most members have positive attraction—or that group member for whom most hold favorable attitudes—generally assumes the role of leader. This role may *not* coincide with a formal position (such as chief justice). If the chief justice fails to perceive himself as a leader, or if other members are negatively attracted to him, he may never become a leader even though he is in a leadership *position*. This was the case with Chief Justice Harlan Fiske Stone. Our group model indicates the relationship between sociometric considerations and leadership. As we can see, the chief justice (J_1) appears to be a strong leader.

Samuel C. Patterson has sought to link leadership with group and subgroup structures (depicted with sociometric diagrams) in the Wisconsin Assembly. As we shall see in our second selection, "Patterns of Interpersonal Relations in a State Legislative Group: The Wisconsin Assembly," Patterson found a "clear relationship between the extent of friendship perception and leadership." Like Patterson, Sidney Verba has sought a more rigorous definition of group leadership. He has concluded that several factors "influence the probabilities that an individual will assume a leadership role . . . (1) an individual's structural position within a group [e.g., whether a person is chief justice or majority leader]; (2) his status in the cultural environment external to the group; (3) his personality traits; and (4) his motivation to assume the leadership role." [26] The third and fourth factors hinge upon attitudes about others and about the job (task) that all are performing.

As our court model indicates, group members (or justices) possess attitudes about norms (A^N)—attitudes about how to behave. The object of these attitudes becomes regularity of behavior, or how members expect themselves and others to behave. We say that "a group norm exists insofar as a set of group members share

[26] Verba, *Small Groups and Political Behavior,* p. 128.

favorable attitudes toward such a regularity. . . . The principal characteristic of group norms as distinct from other shared attitudes is that they represent shared acceptance of a rule, which is a prescription for ways of perceiving, thinking, feeling, or acting." [27] Homans adds that "statements of expected behavior are considered norms only if behavior that violates them is followed by punishment." [28]

What is the purpose of a group norm? Norms provide stability, predictability, and orderliness in group behavior. Norms guide the process of interaction toward goals. Finally, norms have a restraining effect on individual members' deviant behavior. "Members of a group who, by such processes of sharing, subscribe to its norms are powerfully influenced by those norms, and thus the group may be said to have power over its members." [29] This "group power" is called normativeness. Failure to conform, of course, can lead to group sanctions.

Norms play an important part in the ability of a leader to control his group. In fact, according to Verba, group leaders are probably under greater pressure to conform to the expectations of the group than are the other members.[30] The leader represents the group. In his role as group representative before nonmembers of the group, he will be expected to some extent to symbolize the values and standards of the group.[31]

In our third selection, "Rules of the Game in the Canadian House of Commons," Allan Kornberg explains how many informal rules govern parliamentary behavior in Canada and facilitate goal achievement. Generally Kornberg found Canadian M.P.'s less aware of informal rules than their U.S. counterparts; and he found less reliance upon group sanctions for deviant behavior than John Wahlke and others [32] had discerned in state legislatures. Those behavioral norms and sanctions Kornberg did find worked for maximization of goal achievement and for maintenance of the parliamentary system itself.

The impact of informal rules of behavior on group members applies as well to collegial court judges as it does to legislators. For example, in the early years of the Taft Court, it became an informal norm that in the interest of unanimity a justice would minimize his dissenting opinions. To keep colleagues in line, justices would often try to "head off" dissents. Chief Justice Taft once wrote a colleague: "My dear Brother Stone: I am quite anxious, as I am sure we all are, that the continuity and weight of our opinions on important questions of law should not be broken any more than we can help by dissents. . . ." [33] Mr. Justice Stone gave in, writing only a concurring opinion. As Walter Murphy has explained, the "two major sanctions which a justice can use against his colleagues are his vote

---

[27] Newcomb, *et al., Social Psychology,* p. 229.

[28] George Homans, *The Human Group* (New York: Harcourt, Brace, 1950), p. 123.

[29] Newcomb, *et al., Social Psychology,* p. 246.

[30] Verba, *Small Groups and Political Behavior,* p. 185.

[31] *Ibid.,* p. 189.

[32] John C. Wahlke, Heinz Eulau, William Buchanan, and Leroy C. Ferguson, *The Legislative System—Explorations in Legislative Behavior* (New York: Wiley, 1962).

[33] Walter F. Murphy, *Elements of Judicial Strategy* (Chicago: The University of Chicago Press, 1964), p. 47.

and his willingness to write opinions which will attack a doctrine the majority or minority wishes to see adopted." [34]

All groups exist to achieve goals; to reach these goals they must resolve problems. According to Robert Bales, all group problems can be classified as task or social. Task problems relate to efficient and speedy movement toward goals; social problems relate to maintenance of harmony with a group. David J. Danelski has utilized this task-social distinction in the fourth selection, "Task Group and Social Group on the Supreme Court." On the Court, Danelski found that members clustered into subgroups oriented toward task or social functions. Leadership in these subgroups provided informal roles on the Court. On the Taft Court, for example, Mr. Justice Van Devanter became the task leader, whereas the Chief Justice was the social leader. Each in his own role guided the interaction of justices. Leadership and achievement are inextricably bound: "A stable leadership structure is important if the group is to accomplish its instrumental task. . . . Insofar as the group can achieve some satisfactory balance between the instrumental and the affective aspects of its interaction and a stable leadership structure is developed, the group will be effective and contribute to the satisfaction of its members." [35]

We have said that the sharing of attitudes aids group cohesion, and that these shared attitudes may include a predisposition to perceive members of other groups in a negative way. This is prejudice. Since prejudice is learned, group attitudes and behavior are self-reinforcing. "Attitudes of prejudice toward others differ from favorable attitudes in two principal respects: they involve the tendency to keep people at a distance rather than to have close relations with them, and the tendency to injure rather than help them." [36] Donald R. Matthews and James W. Prothro in the fifth selection, "Living Together as Strangers," examine Southern Negro and white attitudes toward each other.

In order to reduce inter-group prejudice, four conditions must be met:

1. The norms of Group A concerning Group B must be changed.
2. The norms of Group B concerning Group A must be changed.
3. The members of Group A must perceive that Group B's norms concerning Group A are changing.
4. The members of Group B must perceive that Group A's norms concerning Group B are changing.[37]

Since norms result from attitudes about behavior (A^N), it is obvious that attitude change is a necessary requisite for reduction of inter-group conflict. This is what Matthews and Prothro have found: "We have identified four factors— education, mass communications, geographic mobility, and armed service experience—that appear to decrease segregationist sentiment. Increasing numbers of Southern whites have been exposed to all these experiences. . . ." [38] Yet if there

[34] *Ibid.*, p. 54.

[35] Verba, *Small Groups and Political Behavior*, p. 159.

[36] Newcomb, *et al.*, *Social Psychology*, p. 430–431.

[37] *Ibid.*, p. 458.

[38] Donald R. Matthews and James W. Prothro, *Negroes and the New Southern Politics* (New York: Harcourt, Brace & World, 1966), p. 349.

has been some change in the first and second conditions necessary to reduce inter-group prejudice, lack of progress is most noteworthy in the third and fourth categories. In fact, Matthews and Prothro found "great inaccuracy of whites in estimating the views of Negroes. . . ." [39] Similar findings were attributed to Southern Negroes. Such misperception leads to an explosive situation, and the possibility of increased inter-group strife.

In the final selection, "British M.P.'s and their Local Parties: The Suez Cases," Leon D. Epstein demonstrates the relationship between group behavior (viewed through constituency associations) and the political process. In 1956–1957 Conservative Members of Parliament who expressed doubt about the necessity of military action or doubt about the withdrawal—those who expressed doubt about the handling of the Suez crisis by the Eden government—suddenly found themselves beyond the bounds of behavior acceptable to their local associations. The power of constituency associations to take action against deviant M.P.'s, such as Nigel Nicolson, indicates the extent to which agreement about group norms exists. Without the support of his constituency association, the M.P. finds himself deprived of a power base, like "a general without an army." As Epstein clearly shows, sanctions were a very real possibility, derived from the associations' power to select candidates.

Epstein also demonstrates the relationship between constituency groups and the parliamentary leadership group:

> Unquestionably national party leaders are aware of and grateful for the service performed by local units in maintaining parliamentary cohesion. . . . [T]he constituency associations . . . view their role as that of supporting their national leaders. . . . In other words, the British model of constituency association–M.P. relations is an integral part of the nation's working form of parliamentary government.[40]

[39] Donald R. Matthews and James W. Prothro, *Negroes and the New Southern Politics* (New York: Harcourt, Brace & World, 1966), p. 352.

[40] Leon D. Epstein, "British M.P.'s and Their Local Parties: The Suez Crisis," *American Political Science Review*, June, 1960, pp. 386, 389.

A GROUP INTERPRETATION OF POLITICS
DAVID B. TRUMAN

If the uniformities consequent upon the behavior of men in groups are the key to an understanding of human, including political, behavior, it will be well to specify somewhat more sharply what is involved when the term "group" is used. An excessive preoccupation with matters of definition will only prove a handicap. "Who likes may snip verbal definitions in his old age, when his world has gone crackly and dry." [1] Nevertheless, a few distinctions may be useful.

We find the term "group" applied in two broad senses. Both popularly and in much technical literature it is used to describe any collection of individuals who have some characteristic in common. These are sometimes known as categoric groups. In this sense the word is applied to persons of a given age level, to those of similar income or social status, to people living in a particular area, as Westerners, and to assortments of individuals according to an almost endless variety of similarities—farmers, alcoholics, insurance men, blondes, illiterates, mothers, neurotics, and so on. Although this sense of the word may be useful, it omits one aspect of peculiar importance. The justification for emphasizing groups as basic social units, it will be recalled, is the uniformities of behavior produced through them. Such uniformities do not depend immediately upon such similarities as those mentioned above, but upon the relationships among the persons involved. The significance of a family group in producing similar attitudes and behaviors among its members lies, not in their physical resemblance or in their proximity, as such, to one another, but in the characteristic relationships among them. These interactions, or relationships, because they have a certain character and frequency, give the group its molding and guiding powers. In fact, they are the group, and it is in this sense that the term will be used.

A minimum frequency of interaction is, of course, necessary before a group in this sense can be said to exist. If a motorist stops along a highway to ask directions of a farmer, the two are interacting, but they can hardly be said to constitute a group except in the most casual sense. If, however, the motorist belongs to an automobile

CREDIT: From *The Governmental Process*, by David B. Truman. Copyright © 1951 by Alfred A. Knopf, Inc. Reprinted by permission of the publisher. [*Footnotes renumbered.*]

[1] Arthur F. Bentley, *The Process of Government* (Chicago: The University of Chicago Press, 1908), p. 199.

club to the staff of which he and the other members more or less regularly resort for route information, then staff and members can be designated as a group. Similarly, groups in the first sense—collections of people with some common characteristic—may be groups in the proper sense if they interact with some frequency on the basis of their shared characteristics. If a number of mothers interact with one another as they tackle problems of child training, whether through a club or through subscription to a mothers' periodical, they have become a group, though the two forms differ in structure and frequency of interaction. If the members of any aggregation of blondes begin to interact as blondes, alcoholics as alcoholics (or former addicts), people over sixty as aged—they constitute groups. That is, under certain recurring conditions they behave differently with each other than with brunettes, teetotalers, or the young. In fact, the reason why the two senses of the term "group" are so close is that on the basis of experience it is expected that people who have certain attributes in common—neighborhood, consanguinity, occupation—will interact with some frequency. It is the interaction that is crucial, however, not the shared characteristic.[2]

These groups, or patterns of

[2] George A. Lundberg, *Foundations of Sociology* (New York: The Macmillan Company, 1939), pp. 340–341, 360–361. For further definitions from the same general viewpoint, see Muzafer Sherif and Hadley Cantril, *The Psychology of Ego-Involvements* (New York: John Wiley and Sons, 1947), p. 280; William F. Ogburn and Meyer F. Nimkoff, *Sociology* (Boston: Houghton Mifflin Company, 1946), p. 250. Cf. Amos H. Hawley, *Human Ecology: A Theory of Community Structure* (New York: The Ronald Press, 1950), chapter 12.

interaction, vary through time in a given society, and they obviously differ sharply in different societies. Why this variation occurs has been only incompletely ascertained, since comparative studies of simple cultures are relatively few and competent comparative analyses of complex cultures are virtually nonexistent. The most satisfactory hypothesis, however, indicates that the relative complexity of such interactions depends upon the degree of diversity in the everyday business of living. The latter in turn reflects refinement in the techniques by which the society adapts to its environment and the degree of specialization and division of labor that these techniques involve.[3] In a simple society in which all activities—economic, religious, political—are carried on within the family, the division of labor is rudimentary, the techniques are simple, and the patterns of interaction are few and standardized. The latter become more complex as the routine activities of existence alter in conformity with altered techniques for dealing with the environment.

Variations in the division of labor are nowhere more striking than in the activity of house building. An Eskimo igloo is usually constructed by a single family, each man erecting the structure of snow blocks with the aid of his wife and sons. Division of labor is slight, and the interactions among the participants—the patterns of superordination and subordination—are simple. Frequently among a sedentary farming people, however, such as the

[3] Eliot D. Chapple and Carlton S. Coon, *Principles of Anthropology* (New York: Henry Holt & Company, Inc., 1942), pp. 443–62; Sherif and Cantril, *Psychology of Ego-Involvements*, p. 47.

Riffians of North Africa, relatively elaborate and permanent dwellings are constructed by work parties in which a fairly complex division of labor occurs, based upon more developed techniques and differences in the skill with which particular individuals can perform the various operations:

Among Riffians, some of the men will bring stones, others will nick them into shape and set them in the walls, while still others puddle clay for the mortar. When the walls are up, two men . . . climb up and set the ridgepole and rafters in place. Meanwhile other men have been cutting young alders and other small saplings near the stream; they peel these and hand them up in bundles. Most of the men have now climbed to the roof, and they tie these sticks to the rafters to form a foundation for the clay.[4]

It is a considerable step from this moderately complex division of labor to the elaborate activities necessary in the construction of an ordinary American house. The collection, preparation, and transportation of materials, the elaborate behavior involved in procuring and readying the site, and the welter of specialities that contribute to its erection bespeak a series of complicated interaction patterns.

The complexity and variation of group life among human cultures apparently grow out of the daily activities of their participants and reflect the kinds of techniques that the cultures have developed for dealing with the environment. These techniques, however, are not confined to those directly utilized in providing food, clothing, and shelter. The invention of

a written language and its diffusion through a population include techniques of at least equal importance. Similarly, group patterns in a culture in which the priest, or *shaman,* deals with the crises and problems arising from birth, sickness, death, flood, drought, earthquakes, thunderstorms, and eclipses of the sun and moon will be far simpler than the group patterns of a culture where these crises are separately dealt with by various specialists. The activities of the shaman, and those of his functional descendant, the specialized scientist, consist of techniques for adjustment to the environment fully as much as do those of the farmer, the weaver, and the bricklayer. The skills of shaman and scientist are parts of different group patterns and their resulting attitudes and behavioral norms.[5]

THE EQUILIBRIUM
OF INSTITUTIONALIZED GROUPS

In any society certain of these group patterns will be characterized by "a relatively high degree of stability, uniformity, formality, and generality. . . ." These are customarily designated by the term *institution.*[6] The word does not have a meaning sufficiently precise to enable one to state with confidence that one group is an institution whereas another is not.[7] Ac-

[4] Chapple and Coon, *Principles of Anthropology,* p. 105.

[5] Ibid., p. 459.

[6] Lundberg, *Foundations of Sociology,* p. 375.

[7] A more precise, but slightly different usage is employed in Chapple and Coon, *Principles of Anthropology,* p. 287. This usage corresponds to what in the present instance will be called institutionalized groups.

cepted examples, however, include the courts, legislatures, executives, and other political institutions, families, organized churches, manufacturing establishments, transportation systems, and organized markets. All of these, it will be noted, are rather highly organized (formality); examples of the same type of institution show the same patterns (uniformity); and these patterns are characteristic of, though not necessarily peculiar to, a particular society, such as the American (generality).

The institutionalized groups that exemplify these behavior patterns, and the patterns themselves, represent almost by definition an equilibrium among the interactions of the participants.[8] In a typical American family, for example, it will be accepted almost unconsciously and without discussion that the male parent will almost always make certain kinds of decisions for the family group, such as what kind of automobile tires to purchase, whether they can afford a new washing machine, and how much money can be spent on the family vacation. He will be expected to take the lead in such actions, and the rest of the family will accept his decisions. The mother will make many more decisions affecting the children than will the father. The husband, moreover, will follow her lead in such things as home decoration, the color of a new car, and the guests to be included at a dinner party. These and the other expected patterns of interaction that make up the institutional group are normally in balance, or in a state of equilibrium. The same situation applies to any institutionalized group, although perhaps in a somewhat more complicated fashion, whether political, economic, or religious.

An equilibrium of this sort must be worked out within an institutionalized group or an institution if it is to survive. That is, the equilibrium must be achieved along standardized lines if the pattern is not to be radically altered or if the particular group is not to be irrevocably disrupted, as, for example, in the case of a family by the separation or divorce of man and wife. It is characteristic of such balanced groups that if the equilibrium is disturbed by some event outside the group, the equilibrium will be restored when the disturbance is over. This tendency to maintain or revert to equilibrium is what is meant by the stability of an institution. The existence of the equilibrium and its stability presumably can be measured by observing the consistency of interaction patterns. Although such observations have been made for simple groups and in a general way for more complicated ones, the possibilities in this area are largely still to be explored. The basic propositions, however, have been sufficiently tested to give them strong presumptive validity.[9]

[8] The following section is based largely upon Chapple and Coon, *Principles of Anthropology*. Some writers use the term "integration" to convey approximately the meaning of the word "equilibrium" intended by Chapple and Coon, although the latter has somewhat more explicit methodological meanings. See Ralph Linton, *The Study of Man* (New York: D. Appleton-Century Company, Inc., 1936), chap. 20.

[9] See E. D. Chapple and C. Arensberg, "Measuring Human Relations," *Genetic Psychology Monographs*, Vol. 32 (August, 1940), pp. 3–147; Chapple and Coon, *Principles of Anthropology, passim*; W. Lloyd Warner and Paul S. Lunt, *The Social Life of a Modern Community* (New Haven: Yale

Although institutionalized groups are characterized by stability, that is, by the tendency to revert to an equilibrium among the interactions of the participants following a disturbance from outside the group, not all disturbances are followed by a return to such a balance. If the disturbance is of great intensity or if it persists over a long period of time, a quite different pattern of interactions is likely to be established in place of the previous one. How serious the interruption must be and how long it must last in order to produce an alteration of the pattern are matters for careful observation, precise or approximate depending upon the use to which the observations are to be put.

An obvious example can be seen in the case of a family that loses one of its members through death. Since the remainder of the group can no longer interact with the deceased, any subsequent stable interaction pattern in the group will differ sharply from the preceding one. The possibilities of establishing a new and stable pattern will depend in part upon the role of the deceased in the previous balance. That is, it will be far more difficult if a parent or an only child has been withdrawn from the group, since relationships with a parent or only child will have constituted a very large segment of the total behavior pattern of the remaining members of the family. The death of one of eight or ten children,

however, may be far less disruptive, since almost inevitably a major portion of the total interactions in the group will not have depended upon one of eight or ten children.

If the removal of one member of a family group is not permanent, but temporary, a quite different situation will result. If the male parent is obliged to be away from the rest of the family for a short period of time or if his breadwinning activities temporarily require him to spend less time in the family than has been customary, the equilibrium of the group will be disturbed. The pattern and frequency of interactions will be altered. When the husband-father has returned from his travels, however, or when his duties permit him again to participate in the group with normal frequency, the previous balance probably will be restored.[10]

In the strictly political sphere there are obvious parallel instances of the effects of disturbances in established patterns of interaction. Thus the death or unexpected resignation of the "boss" of a highly organized political "machine" constitutes a serious disturbance to the group. It will be followed by a more or less prolonged tussle among aspiring successors. Unless some stable new pattern is established under the leadership of one of the previous "boss's" henchmen, the group will disintegrate into competing factions. Similarly, take the case of a trade association whose principal function is

University Press, 1941) and *The Status System of a Modern Community* (New Haven: Yale University Press, 1942); William F. Whyte, *Street Corner Society* (Chicago: University of Chicago Press, 1943); William F. Whyte (ed.), *Industry and Society* (New York: McGraw-Hill Book Company, Inc., 1946).

[10] For a careful critique of the concept *stable equilibrium* and for a discussion of change as a function of a great number of interdependent factors whose effects are cumulative, see Gunnar Myrdal, *An American Dilemma* (New York: Harper and Brothers, 1944), pp. 1065–70.

the fixing of prices. If it finds its methods outlawed as a result of government action, this disturbance will result in the disappearance of the group unless equilibrium is re-established in one of three ways. First, the group may secure the repeal of the disturbing decision. Second, new methods of performing the function may be developed. Third, an entirely different set of functions may be developed. The first of these results in a restoration of the disturbed pattern, whereas the second and third produce new patterns of interaction.

An important point must be kept in mind in talking of patterns, equilibriums, and the like. These terms do not refer to a mystical entity like a "group mind" that suffers, changes, and dies. A group is "real" in the sense that the interactions that are the group can be observed, and these terms are convenient ways of describing interactions. But one is dealing with the activities of individuals too. To draw any other inference is to become involved in the literally false and disastrously misleading distinction between "the individual" and "society." When men act and interact in consistent patterns, it is reasonable to study these patterns and to designate them by collective terms: *group, institution, nation, legislature, political party, corporation, labor union, family,* and so on. Similarly, it is reasonable for some purposes to study particular individuals, as do the clinical and individual psychologists. But these are merely two approaches to the same thing, not separate entities. Men exist only in society; society is the interactions of men.

It follows, therefore, that when one speaks of a disturbance in an institutional pattern, one refers as well to a disturbance in the individual organisms whose activities have made up the pattern. One of the features of an institutionalized group, as has been noted, is its persistence. It may be thought of as a habit and as being made up of certain habitual activities of a number of individuals. When the pattern is interrupted, there is disturbance or frustration in varying degrees of the habits of the participants, a circumstance that is always unpleasant and may be extremely painful. One may study the consequences for the affected individuals or the changes in the interaction patterns or both, but "the equilibrium of the internal environment [the organism], the equilibrium of the individual in relation to others, and the equilibrium of the group are similar and related phenomena." [11]

When the equilibrium of a group (and the equilibriums of its participant individuals) is seriously disturbed, various kinds of behavior may ensue. If the disturbance is not too great, the group's leaders will make an effort to restore the previous balance. As we shall see in more detail later, this effort may immediately necessitate recourse to the government. Other behaviors may occur if the disturbance is serious to the point of disruption. These may be classified in various ways for different purposes. In the present context three broad types of behavior may be distinguished on the basis of their effect upon the existing or poten-

[11] Chapple and Coon, *Principles of Anthropology*, p. 47. On this section generally see also Lundberg, *Foundations of Sociology*, chapters 1 and 5, especially pp. 163–173.

tial groups involved.[12] In the first place, the participants may individually engage in various kinds of inappropriate or aberrant or compensatory substitute activities: complaining, rumor-mongering, phantasies, alcoholism, drug addiction, indiscriminate aggression, and the like. Thus, in a revolutionary situation where the equilibriums of a wide range of institutions have been disturbed or disrupted, there is a constant possibility that large segments of the populace will engage in undisciplined loafing, irresponsible violence, or other activities useless to a successful revolutionary movement. It is the task of revolutionary leadership to limit such behavior by providing new and "constructive" forms of interaction in the place of those that have been disrupted.[13] Similarly, a sudden change in the relations (interactions) between management and workers in a factory, initiated by the former, may at first result in gossiping, griping, and picking on scapegoats.[14] The adolescent, whose roles are in a highly fluid state alternating between those of an adult and those of a dependent child and necessarily involving disequilibrium, will frequently indulge in daydreams

and phantasies. These substitutive activities may be harmless or may have neurotic consequences, depending on the situation.

Secondly, the disturbed individuals may increase their activities in other groups in order to restore some sort of personal balance. Thus a state of disequilibrium in the family group may be compensated for by increased interaction in the work group (longer hours at the office) or in a recreational group (increased attendance at meetings of a bowling league, woman's club, and the like).

The third type of behavior that may result from a serious disequilibrium is the formation of new groups that may function to restore the balance. For present purposes this type is the most important of the three, especially if a considerable number of individuals is affected, since these new groups are likely to utilize political means of achieving their objectives. They are likely to become political groups, although they need not do so. Adolescents who cannot establish a stable set of relationships in family groups may join others of the same age level in informal or formal clubs or gangs. This behavior is particularly likely where the adolescent adjustment is made more difficult by special problems such as arise for American-born children of immigrant parents, or for young men and women who are unable to establish stable and satisfactory relationships in an economic group.[15]

---

[12] A suggestive experiment concerning some of these problems is reported in John Arsenian, A Study of Reactions to Socio-Economic Frustration (unpublished Ph.D. dissertation, Harvard University, 1945).

[13] See Harold D. Lasswell, "The Strategy of Revolutionary and War Propaganda," in *Public Opinion and World Politics* (ed. by Quincy Wright, Chicago: University of Chicago Press, 1933), p. 202; Sherif and Cantril, *Psychology of Ego-Involvements*, pp. 283–4.

[14] Gordon W. Allport, "The Psychology of Participation," *Psychological Review*, Vol. 53 (May, 1945), p. 122.

[15] Whyte, *Street Corner Society*; Sherif and Cantril, *Psychology and Ego-Involvements*, chaps. 9 and 10; F. M. Thrasher, *The Gang* (Chicago: University of Chicago Press, 1927); H. W. Zorbaugh, *The Gold Coast and the Slum* (Chicago: University of Chicago Press, 1929).

Among adults new groups are likely to develop or old ones to grow and increase their activity where a serious disequilibrium is produced in family and work groups by a depression or similar economic crisis. Farm movements throughout American history have developed and reached their peaks of strength in times of great economic distress, such as the 1870's and the early 1920's.

When Japanese Americans and Japanese aliens resident on the West Coast were ruthlessly uprooted from their homes in early 1942 and sent to relocation centers, the disruption of established equilibriums was profound. In his distinguished study of the relocation camp at Poston, Arizona, Leighton found ample evidence to this effect: "Although social patterns did exist, some new and some old, more prominent was disarticulation and the *absence of the accustomed habits of human relationship.* People were strangers to each other in a strange situation and *did not know what to expect.*"[16] (Italics added.) This imbalance involved not only the family groups, work groups, and neighborhood groups but more inclusive institutions such as the nation itself. That is, the attitudes and behavior of wide segments of the American people, especially in the West, with whom Niseis in particular had been accustomed to interact peacefully and on a basis of considerable equality, sharply contradicted what most of the victims had been accustomed to expect.[17] The imbalance was not tempo-rary or minor, but persistent and inclusive: "Most aspects of life were lived with acquaintances made since coming to Poston and every individual and every family was trying to adjust to a society that had no framework and no stability. Hardly anyone had a confident expectation as to how anybody with whom he worked or had contact would behave from week to week."[18] Out of this situation a series of new groups emerged, some spontaneously and some under the guidance of the camp's administrators. Among the former were gangs that administered beatings to alleged informers.[19]

Examples of the emergence of new groups in compensation for disturbances in the equilibrium of existing institutionalized groups can be drawn from simpler societies as well as the more complex. When government officials and missionaries arrived in the Papua Territory, New Guinea, in the 1920's, they attempted to alter the ways of the natives and particularly to keep them from holding some of their customary religious ceremonies. The resulting disturbance in the established patterns of interaction was followed by the development of a series of religious movements that spread over New Guinea.[20]

When one views any society as a sort of mosaic of groups, one is confronted with a bewildering array of groups that may be classified in different ways. Thus various characteristic activities seem to be carried on in one group that make it different from an-

---

[16] Alexander H. Leighton, *The Governing of Men* (Princeton, N. J.: Princeton University Press, 1945), p. 140.

[17] Ibid., pp. 143 ff.

[18] Ibid., p. 158.

[19] Ibid., pp. 149–50, and chaps. 7–9 and 18, generally.

[20] Chapple and Coon, *Principles of Anthropology*, pp. 401–2.

other in that particular respect. The examples used in the preceding paragraphs are sufficient illustration. Similarly, although it is an observable fact that all groups involve the same fundamental process, the interaction of individuals, they seem to differ from one another in the form that this process takes—for example, in the degree of formality. In the pursuit of meaning and understanding, students of society, particularly sociologists, have classified groups on these and other bases, distinguishing and defining classes of groups. These efforts have varied with the purposes, skills, and insights of the classifiers. In addition to the category "institution," which has been examined briefly above, various sub-categories have been designated on the basis of fairly obvious differences of function—the family, economic groups, political groups, and religious groups. On somewhat different bases distinctions are drawn among crowds, publics, assemblies, organizations, mobs, primary groups, secondary groups, in-groups, out-groups, and a host of others.[21]

INTEREST GROUPS

Various of these established designations will be useful from time to time, but one identifying term, which was used without definition in the previous chapter, may be discussed at some length, since it involves the central

concern of these pages, the term "interest group." Like so many terms associated with the processes of government, it has been used for the purposes of polemics so freely that it has acquired certain emotional connotations which may render it ambiguous when used in analysis. *Political, partisan,* and even the word *politics* itself share with *interest, vested interest, special interest,* and *interest group,* among others, a connotation of impropriety and selfishness that almost denies them the neutral precision requisite to careful discussion.

As used here "interest group" refers to any group that, on the basis of one or more shared attitudes, makes certain claims upon other groups in the society for the establishment, maintenance, or enhancement of forms of behavior that are implied by the shared attitudes. In earlier paragraphs of this chapter it was indicated that from interaction in groups arise certain common habits of response, which may be called norms, or shared attitudes. These afford the participants frames of reference for interpreting and evaluating events and behaviors. In this respect all groups are interest groups because they are shared-attitude groups. In some groups at various points in time, however, a second kind of common response emerges, in addition to the frames of reference. These are shared attitudes toward what is needed or wanted in a given situation, observable as demands or claims upon other groups in the society. The term "interest group" will be reserved here for those groups that exhibit both aspects of the shared attitudes.

The shared attitudes, moreover,

[21] See, for example, Lundberg, *Foundations of Sociology,* chap. 5; and Ogburn and Nimkoff, *Sociology,* chap. 9 and *passim.*

constitute the interests. It has been suggested that a distinction be made between the two terms, reserving the latter to designate "the objects toward which these . . . [attitudes] are directed." [22] Such a distinction may be highly misleading. If, for example, reference were made to oil interests, one would presumably be referring, among other things, to certain elements in the physical environment, petroleum and its by-products. These features, however, have no significance in society apart from the activities of men. There were no oil attitudes prior to the time when the productive behaviors of men led them to do something with petroleum.[23] As a consequence of the use of oil, an array of attitudes with respect to that use has developed —that it should not be wasted, that it should be marketed in a particular way, that it should be produced by many small groups or enterprises, that it should be controlled by an international organization, and so on. Some of these attitudes are represented by interest groups asserting that the behaviors implied by the attitudes should be encouraged, discouraged, or altered. The physical features of oil production have no significance for the student of society apart from the attitudes, or interests, and the behaviors that they suggest.

Definition of the interest group in this fashion has a number of distinct advantages in the task of political analysis. In the first place, it permits the identification of various potential as well as existing interest groups. That is, it invites examination of an interest whether or not it is found at the moment as one of the characteristics of a particular organized group. Although no group that makes claims upon other groups in the society will be found without an interest or interests, it is possible to examine interests that are not at a particular point in time the basis of interactions among individuals, but that may become such. Without the modern techniques for the measurement of attitude and opinion, this position would indeed be risky, since it would invite the error of ascribing an interest to individuals quite apart from any overt behavior that they might display.[24] In the scientific study of society only frustration and defeat are likely to follow an attempt to deal with data that are not directly observable. Even the most insistent defenders of the scientific position, however, admit that, although activity is the basic datum of social science, a "becoming" stage of activity must be recognized as a phase of activity if any segment of a moving social situation is to be understood. There are, in other words, potential activities, or "tendencies of activity." [25] These tendencies are the central feature of the most widely accepted social psychological definition of attitude. Gordon W. Allport, after examining a series of definitions, arrived at his own generally used statement: "An attitude is a mental and neutral *state of readiness*, organized through experience,

[22] Robert M. MacIver, "Interests," *Encyclopaedia of the Social Sciences*. Cf. Avery Leiserson: *Administrative Regulation: A Study in Representation of Interests* (Chicago: University of Chicago Press, 1942), pp. 1–10.

[23] Cf. Bentley, *The Process of Government*, pp. 193–4.

[24] Ibid., p. 213.

[25] Ibid., pp. 184 ff.

exerting a directive or dynamic influence upon the individual's response to all objects and situations with which it is related." [26] On the basis of widely held attitudes that are not expressed in interaction, therefore, it is possible to talk of potential interest groups.

In the second place, as these statements suggest, this concept of interest group permits attention to what Lundberg calls the "degree of integrative interaction." [27] The frequency, or rate, of interaction will in part determine the primacy of a particular group affiliation in the behavior of an individual and, as will be indicated in more detail later, it will be of major importance in determining the relative effectiveness with which a group asserts its claims upon other groups. This approach affords all the advantages and none of the disadvantages that once accrued to the sociologists' concepts of "primary groups" and "secondary groups," meaning by the former face-to-face interaction as opposed to indirect contacts such as those made through the media of mass communication. Before the enormous expansion and development of the latter techniques, and still in societies where they have not penetrated, it was a verifiable fact that solidarity of group behavior depended largely upon physical proximity. Frequent face-to-face contact in no small measure accounted for the influence of such primary groups as the family, the neighborhood, and the like. As the social func-

tions performed by the family institution in our society have declined, some of these secondary groups, such as labor unions, have achieved a rate of interaction that equals or surpasses that of certain of the primary groups. This shift in importance has been facilitated largely by the development of means of communication that permit frequent interaction among individuals not in face-to-face contact or not continuously so.

In this connection note the confidence that James Madison, in seeking restraints upon the "mischiefs of faction" (interest groups), placed in "the greater obstacles opposed to the concert" of such groups by the "extent of the Union." [28] Such faith in physical dispersion had some basis in a period when it took a week to travel a distance of three hundred miles. It would not be true to say that primary groups no longer achieve the integration once ascribed to them. A recent study has indicated, for example, that the prolonged resistance of the German army in the face of repeated defeat in 1944 and 1945 was a result largely of the solidarity and continued structural integrity of such primary groups as the squad.[29] It is primarily from the degree of interaction that the face-to-face group fosters, however, that its influence is derived. A high degree may also be achieved through secondary means.

In the third place, this concept of the interest group permits us to evalu-

[26] Gordon W. Allport, "Attitudes," in Carl Murchison (ed.), *A Handbook of Social Psychology* (Worcester, Mass.: Clark University Press, 1935), chap. 17.

[27] Lundberg, *Foundations of Sociology*, p. 310.

[28] *The Federalist*, No. 10; see also No. 51 for similar arguments.

[29] Edward A. Shils and Morris Janowitz, "Cohesion and Disintegration in the Wehrmacht in World War II," *Public Opinion Quarterly*, Vol. 12 (Summer, 1948), pp. 280–315.

ate the significance of formal organization. The existence of neither the group nor the interest is dependent upon formal organization, although that feature has significance, particularly in the context of politics. Organization indicates merely a stage or degree of interaction.[30] The fact that one interest group is highly organized whereas another is not or is merely a potential group—whether the interest involved is that of affording more protection to consumers, greater privileges for brunettes, or more vigorous enforcement of civil rights—is a matter of great significance at any particular moment. It does not mean, however, that the momentarily weaker group, or interest, will inevitably remain so. Events may easily produce an increased rate of interaction among the affected individuals to the point where formal organization or a significant interest group will emerge and greater influence will ensue. The point may be illustrated by noting that this increased rate of interaction is usually what is meant when the journalists speak of "an aroused public opinion."

Finally, this use of the concept also gives a proper perspective to the political activities of many interest groups that are the principal concern of this book. Although a characteristic feature of these groups is that they make claims upon other groups in the society, these claims may be asserted or enforced by means of a variety of

techniques and through any of the institutions of the society, not merely the government. An interest group concentrating upon replacing the valuable shade trees in a village adjacent to a large gentleman's farm may achieve its objective by prevailing upon the baronial family to purchase the trees and pay for their planting. A group interested in the protection of certain moralities among the younger generation may secure the behaviors they desire in part through inducing motion picture producers to permit its officers to censor films before they are released.[31] Whether a group operates in such fashions as these or attempts to work through governmental institutions, thereby becoming a political interest group, may be a function of circumstances; the government may have primary or exclusive responsibility in the area involved, as in the war-time allocation of scarce materials. Or the choice between political and other modes of operation may be a function of technique; it may be easier or more effective to achieve temperance objectives through the government than by prevailing upon people to sign pledges. The process is essentially the same whether the interest group operates through other institutions or becomes political.

To summarize briefly, an interest group is a shared-attitude group that makes certain claims upon other groups in the society. If and when it makes its claims through or upon any of the institutions of government, it becomes a political interest group.

---

[30] For an influential characterization along similar lines of the phenomenon of organization, see John M. Gaus, "A Theory of Organization in Public Administration" in John M. Gaus, Leonard D. White, and Marshall E. Dimock, *The Frontiers of Public Administration* (Chicago: University of Chicago Press, 1936), pp. 66–91.

[31] Ruth A. Inglis, *Freedom of the Movies* (Chicago: University of Chicago Press, 1947), chaps. 3–5.

These are the meanings that we shall attach to these terms throughout this book. At times it will be convenient to omit the modifying term "political" in discussing interest group activity in the government. In such instances it will be clear from the context whether we are dealing with political interest groups or with groups that are making claims otherwise than through or upon the institutions of government.

It follows that any group in the society may function as an interest group and that any of them may function as political interest groups, that is, those that make their claims through or upon governmental insitutions. An economic group, such as a corporation, that seeks a special tax ruling is in that respect functioning as a political interest group. Trade associations, labor unions, philatelic societies, world government societies, political parties, professional organizations, and a host of others can and do seek to achieve all or a portion of their objectives by operating through or upon the institutions of government. Even a family group, whose prestige or financial interests approach imperial proportions, may make such claims. It will be useful and significant to identify or classify such groups according to the regularity or the success with which such claims are advanced through these channels. Even the casual observer will give somewhat different places to the philatelic society that prevails upon the Postmaster General to provide special handling for letters bearing a new stamp issue and a trade association that seeks legislation to protect it against its competitors. These may sensibly be placed in separate subcategories, but they both display the fundamental characteristics of such groups.

Seen in these terms, is an interest group inherently "selfish"? In the first place, such judgments have no value for a scientific understanding of government or the operation of society. Schematically, they represent nothing more than the existence of a conflicting interest, possibly, but not necessarily, involving another group or groups.[32] Judgments of this kind are and must be made by all citizens in their everyday life, but they are not properly a part of the systematic analysis of the social process. Secondly, many such political interest groups are from almost any point of view highly altruistic. One need only recall those groups that have consistently risen to defend the basic guarantees of the American constitution, to improve the lot of the underprivileged, or to diffuse the advantages stemming from scientific advance. Evaluations such as these may be made of particular groups, depending on the observer's own attitudes, but, as was indicated in the preceding chapter, they will not facilitate one's understanding of the social system of which the groups are a part.

Where does the term "pressure group" fit into this scheme? This expression, perhaps more than any other, has been absorbed into the language of political abuse. It carries a load of emotional connotations indicating selfish, irresponsible insistence upon special privileges. Any group that regards itself as disinterested and altruis-

---

[32] See, for example, the transparent interest preferences involved in the interesting popular treatment by Kenneth G. Crawford, *The Pressure Boys: The Inside Story of Lobbying in America* (New York: Julius Messner, Inc., 1939).

tic will usually repudiate with vigor any attempt to attach this label to it, a fact that suggests that the term has little use except to indicate a value judgment concerning those groups of which one disapproves. Some writers, however, in a courageous effort to reclaim for the term a core of neutral meaning, use it as a synonym for "political interest group." [33] This usage has certain disadvantages aside from the obvious possibility that many readers will be unable to accept the suggestion that "the objectives of the pressure group may be good or bad; the group may be animated by the highest moral purpose or it may be driving for the narrowest kind of class gain." [34] If the word "pressure" has more than a simply figurative meaning, it suggests a method or a category of methods that may be used by an interest group to achieve its objectives.[35] Even if the methods implied can be described precisely, unless we can demonstrate that all political interest groups use them, the term "pressure group" will indicate merely a stage or phase of group activity and will not serve as a satisfactory equivalent for "interest group" or "political interest group," as these have been defined.[36]

In view of the improbability of satisfying the conditions specified, it will be avoided in these pages in favor of the more inclusive and more nearly neutral term.

DIFFICULTIES IN A GROUP INTERPRETATION OF POLITICS

Since we are engaged in an effort to develop a conception of the political process in the United States that will account adequately for the role of groups, particularly interest groups, it will be appropriate to take account of some of the factors that have been regarded as obstacles to such a conception and that have caused such groups to be neglected in many explanations of the dynamics of government. Perhaps the most important practical reason for this neglect is that the significance of groups has only fairly recently been forced to the attention of political scientists by the tremendous growth in the number of formally organized groups in the United States within the last few decades. It is difficult and unnecessary to attempt to date the beginning of such attention, but Herring in 1929, in his groundbreaking book, *Group Representation Before Congress*, testified to the novelty of the observations he reported when he stated: "There has developed

---

[33] See, for example, V. O. Key, Jr., *Politics, Parties and Pressure Groups* (2nd edition, New York: Thomas Y. Crowell Company, 1947). Key, however, uses the terms somewhat more narrowly, confining them to "private associations formed to influence public policy" (p. 15). A similar use of the term will be found in Ogburn and Nimkoff, *Sociology*, p. 287.

[34] Key, *Politics, Parties, and Pressure Groups*, pp. 16–17.

[35] Robert M. MacIver, "Pressures, Social," *Encyclopaedia of the Social Sciences.*

[36] Mary E. Dillon specifies the method of propaganda as the distinguishing characteristic of the

pressure group, a usage that does not make it the equivalent of the political interest group. "Pressure Groups," *American Political Science Review*, Vol. 36 (June, 1942), pp. 471–81. The best case for a specific meaning of the term "pressure" can be made in connection with the effect of a group on its own membership rather than on those outside its boundaries.

in this government an extra-legal machinery of as integral and of as influential a nature as the system of party government that has long been an essential part of the government. . . ." [37] Some implications of this development are not wholly compatible with some of the proverbial notions about representative government held by specialists as well as laymen, as we have earlier noted. This apparent incompatibility has obstructed the inclusion of group behaviors in an objective description of the governmental process.

More specifically, it is usually argued that any attempt at the interpretation of politics in terms of group patterns inevitably "leaves something out" or "destroys something essential" about the processes of "our" government. On closer examination, we find this argument suggesting that two "things" are certain to be ignored: the individual, and a sort of totally inclusive unity designated by such terms as "society" and "the state."

The argument that the individual is ignored in any interpretation of politics as based upon groups seems to assume a differentiation or conflict between "the individual" and some such collectivity as the group. Those who propose this difficulty often state or imply the view that society is a series of individual persons "each assumed to have definite independent 'existence' and isolation, each in his own *locus* apart from every other." [38] They further assume that when this individual is a part of a group he becomes a different person in some obscure fashion, that his "complex character" experiences "a degeneration or simplification." [39]

Such assumptions need not present any difficulties in the development of a group interpretation of politics, because they are essentially unwarranted. They simply do not square with the kind of evidence concerning group affiliations and individual behavior that we presented in the preceding chapter. We do not, in fact, find individuals otherwise than in groups; complete isolation in space and time is so rare as to be an almost hypothetical situation. It is equally demonstrable that the characteristics of any interest group, including the activities by which we identify it, are governed by the attitudes and the circumstances that gave rise to the interactions of which it consists. These are variable factors, and, although the role played by a particular individual may be quite different in a lynch mob from that of the same individual in a meeting of the church deacons, the attitudes and behaviors involved in both are as much a part of his personality as is his treatment of his family. "The individual" and "the group" are at most merely convenient ways of classifying behavior, two ways of approaching the same phenomena, not different things.

The persistence among nonspecialists of the notion of an inherent conflict between "the individual" and "the group" or "society" is understandable in view of the doctrines of

[37] E. Pendleton Herring, *Group Representation Before Congress* (Baltimore: The Johns Hopkins Press, 1929), p. 18.

[38] Arthur F. Bentley, *Behavior Knowledge Fact* (Bloomington, Indiana: The Principia Press, Inc., 1935), p. 29.

[39] E. F. M. Durbin, *The Politics of Democratic Socialism* (London: George Routledge & Sons, Ltd., 1940), p. 52.

individualism that have underlain various political and economic conflicts over the past three centuries. The notion persists also because it harmonizes with a view of the isolated and independent individual as the "cause" of complicated human events. The personification of events, quite apart from any ethical considerations, is a kind of shorthand convenient in everyday speech and, like supernatural explanations of natural phenomena, has a comforting simplicity. Explanations that take into account multiple causes, including group affiliations, are difficult. The "explanation" of a national complex like the Soviet Union wholly in terms of a Stalin or the "description" of the intricacies of the American government entirely in terms of a Roosevelt is quick and easy.

We need not reckon with such notions of personal causation except as data on the behavior of certain segments of the society. Similarly, we need not accept at their face value the assertions of an inherent conflict between "the individual" and "society." The latter are merely the terms in which protests against particular social formations, such as the mercantilist system and a limited franchise, gained advantage by being clothed in the language of universals. They are not verified propositions about society in general.

It is not intended, however, that we should reject the general human values asserted in the militant doctrines of individualism. Since we have assumed the task of developing a conception of the political process in the United States that will enable us to determine the bearing of group organa-

nization upon the survival of representative democracy, we have in fact assumed the importance of those values. Far from leaving them out of account, we are primarily concerned with their place in the process of group politics.

We do not wish, moreover, to deny that individual differences exist or that there is evidence to support the notion of individuality. This assertion would be nonsense. No conception of society or of the political process would be adequate if it failed to accommodate the hard facts of personality differences. Although we shall have to deal quite explicitly with these, nevertheless, they should offer no insuperable obstacles. We have already admitted the essential facts of individuality when we have noted the infinite variations in biological inheritance and when we have pointed out that the experiences, the group experiences, of no two persons can be identical in all significant respects. It follows that the personality of any reasonably normal individual is not wholly accounted for by any single group affiliation. This proposition not only must be accepted; it must be a central element in any satisfactory explanation of the political process in group terms.

The second major difficulty allegedly inherent in any attempt at a group interpretation of the political process is that such an explanation inevitably must ignore some greater unity designated as society or the state. Thus MacIver sees such sharply different schools of political thought as the *laissez-faire* Spencerians, the Marxists, the pluralists, and group interpretations such as Bentley's, as being alike in one respect: "that they denied or rejected the integrating function of the state." [40]

Many of those who place particular emphasis upon this difficulty assume explicitly or implicitly that there is an interest of the nation as a whole, universally and invariably held and standing apart from and superior to those of the various groups included within it. This assumption is close to the popular dogmas of democratic government based on the familiar notion that if only people are free and have access to "the facts," they will all want the same thing in any political situation. It is no derogation of democratic preferences to state that such an assertion flies in the face of all that we know of the behavior of men in a complex society. Were it in fact true, not only the interest group but even the political party should properly be viewed as an abnormality. The differing experiences and perceptions of men not only encourage individuality but also, as the previous chapter has shown, inevitably result in differing attitudes and conflicting group affiliations.[41] "There are," says Bentley in his discussion of this error of the social whole, "always some parts of the nation to be found arrayed against other parts." [42] Even in war, when a totally inclusive interest should be apparent if it is ever going to be, we always find pacifists, conscientious objectors, spies, and subversives, who reflect interests

opposed to those of "the nation as a whole."

There is a political significance in assertions of a totally inclusive interest within a nation. Particularly in times of crisis, such as an international war, such claims are a tremendously useful promotional device by means of which a particularly extensive group or league of groups tries to reduce or eliminate opposing interests. Such is the pain attendant upon not "belonging" to one's "own" group that if a normal person can be convinced that he is the lone dissenter to an otherwise universally accepted agreement, he usually will conform. This pressure accounts at least in part for the number of prewar pacifists who, when the United States entered World War II, accepted the draft or volunteered. Assertion of an inclusive "national" or "public interest" is an effective device in many less critical situations as well. In themselves, these claims are part of the data of politics. However, they do not describe any actual or possible political situation within a complex modern nation. In developing a group interpretation of politics, therefore, we do not need to account for a totally inclusive interest, because one does not exist.

Denying the existence of an interest of the nation as a whole does not completely dispose of the difficulty raised by those who insist that a group interpretation must omit "the state." We cannot deny the obvious fact that we are examining a going political system that is supported or at least accepted by a large proportion of the society. We cannot account for such a system by adding up in some fashion the National Association of Manufac-

[40] Robert M. MacIver, *The Web of Government* (New York: The Macmillan Company, 1947), p. 56.

[41] For a trenchant criticism of this notion see Walter Lippmann, *Public Opinion* (New York: The Macmillan Company, 1922), chapter 1.

[42] Bentley, *The Process of Government*, p. 220.

turers, the Congress of Industrial Organizations, the American Farm Bureau Federation, the American Legion, and other groups that come to mind when "lobbies" and "pressure groups" are mentioned. Even if the political parties are added to the list, the result could properly be designated as "a view which seems hardly compatible with the relative stability of the political system. . . ." [43] Were such the exclusive ingredients of the political process in the United States, the entire system would have torn itself apart long since.

If these various organized interest groups more or less consistently reconcile their differences, adjust, and accept compromises, we must acknowledge that we are dealing with a system that is not accounted for by the "sum" of the organized interest groups in the society. We must go farther to explain the operation of such ideals or traditions as constitutionalism, civil liberties, representative responsibility, and the like. These are not, however, a sort of disembodied metaphysical influence, like Mr. Justice Holmes's "brooding omnipresence." We know of the existence of such factors only from the behavior and the habitual interactions of men. If they exist in this fashion, they are interests. We can account for their operation and for the system by recognizing such interests as representing what in the preceding chapter we called potential interest groups in the "becoming" stage of activity. "It is certainly true," as Bentley has made clear, "that we must accept a . . . group of this kind as an inter-

est group itself." [44] It makes no difference that we cannot find the home office and the executive secretary of such a group. Organization in this formal sense, as we have seen, represents merely a stage or degree of interaction that may or may not be significant at any particular point in time. Its absence does not mean that these interests do not exist, that the familiar "pressure groups" do not operate as if such potential groups were organized and active, or that these interests may not move from the potential to the organized stage of activity.

It thus appears that the two major difficulties supposedly obstacles to a group interpretation of the political process are not insuperable. We can employ the fact of individuality and we can account for the existence of the state without doing violence to the evidence available from the observed behaviors of men and groups. The development of this interpretation must wait until we have examined more closely the operation of groups and government. It is important to bear in mind, however, that any complete conception of the political process must incorporate the facts of individual differences and must reckon with the inclusive system of relationships that we call the state.

GROUP DIVERSITY AND GOVERNMENTAL COMPLEXITY

For all but those who see in the growth of new groups the evil ways of individ-

---

[43] Robert M. MacIver, "Pressures, Social," *Encyclopaedia of the Social Sciences.*

[44] Bentley, *The Process of Government*, p. 219. On this general point see pp. 218–220 and 371–372.

ual men, it is obvious that the trend toward an increasing diversity of groups functionally attached to the institutions of government is a reflection of the characteristics and needs, to use a somewhat ambiguous term, of a complex society. This conclusion stems necessarily from the functional concept of groups presented in the preceding chapter. Not all institutions of a society necessarily become complex simultaneously or at an even rate, of course. The religious institution may be highly complicated, for example, whereas economic institutions or the family may remain relatively simple. The political institutions of any culture are a peculiarly sensitive barometer of the complexity of the society, however, owing to their special function. Since they operate to order the relationships among various groups in the society, any considerable increase in the types of such groups, or any major change in the nature of their interrelationships, will be reflected subsequently in the operation of the political system. For example, as the Tanala of Madagascar shifted from a dry-land method of rice growing to a method based on irrigation, a series of consequent changes in the culture gradually took place. Village mobility disappeared in favor of settled communities, since the constant search for fertile soil was no longer necessary; individual ownership in land emerged, since the supply of appropriate soil was sharply limited; a system of slavery was developed; and the joint family was broken up into its constituent households. Finally, as a result of these changes in relationships and interests, and with the introduction of conflicts stemming from differ-

ences in wealth, the decentralized and almost undifferentiated political institution became a centralized tribal kingship.[45]

Alterations in response to technological or other changes are more rapid and more noticeable in a complex society in which a larger number of institutionalized groups are closely interdependent. Changes in one institution produce compensatory changes in tangent institutions and thus, inevitably, in government. A complex civilization necessarily develops complex political arrangements. Where the patterns of interaction in the society are intricate, the patterns of political behavior must be also. These may take several forms, depending upon the circumstances. In a society like ours, whose traditions sanction the almost unregulated development of a wide variety of associations, the new patterns are likely to involve the emergence of a wide variety of groups peripheral to the formal institutions of government, supplementing and complicating their operations.

This kind of complexity seems to stem in large measure, as was suggested in Chapter 2, from the techniques employed in the culture and especially from the specialization that they involve. This situation is so familiar that it hardly needs explanation, yet its very familiarity easily leads to a neglect of its basic importance. The specialization necessary to supply a single commodity such as gasoline may provide a miniature illustration:

An oil operator brings oil to the surface of the ground; the local government prevents the theft of oil or destruction of

---

[45] Linton, *The Study of Man*, pp. 348–54.

equipment; a railroad corporation transports the oil; State and Federal Governments prevent interference with the transport of oil; a refining company maintains an organization of workers and chemical equipment to convert the oil into more useful forms; a retail distributor parcels out the resulting gasoline in small quantities to individuals requiring it; the Federal Government supplies a dependable medium of exchange which allows the oil operator, the railroad, the refining company, and the retailer to act easily in an organized fashion without being under a single administrative authority, and enforces contracts so that organizing arrangements on specific points can be more safely entered into; finally, government maintains a system of highways and byways which allow an ultimate consumer to combine the gasoline with other resources under his control in satisfying his desire for automobile travel.[46]

The intricacies of what are ordinarily thought of as economic behaviors by no means exhaust the picture, of course. One has only to think of the specialities appearing in various kinds of amusement and recreation to realize that these characteristics pervade the society. Professionalized sports such as baseball and an increasing number of others, the motion pictures with their wide range of "experts" of all sorts, not to mention the specialists necessary to the operations of the press—all illustrate the basic fact.

These specializations are created by the various techniques with which we meet the challenges and opportunities of the physical environment, and they are allocated to individuals, at least in such simple forms as in the house-building examples discussed in Chapter 2, roughly on the basis of differences in skill. They produce a congeries of differentiated but highly interdependent groups of men whose time is spent using merely segments of the array of skills developed in the culture.[47] Men are preoccupied by their skills, and these preoccupations in large measure define what the members of such groups know and perceive about the world in which they live. As has been remarked in a slightly different connection: "Machines . . . make specifications, so to speak, about the character of the people who are to operate them."[48] Under favorable circumstances groups form among those who share this "knowledge" and the attitudes it fosters. Both the nature of the techniques utilized in the society and the interdependencies that they imply dictate the amount and kinds of interaction of this sort. Where the techniques are complex, the interactions must be also.[49]

It is unnecessary here to attempt to trace historically the increasing diversity of groups. MacIver sees the "dawn of modern multi-group society" in the splitting of the single church in the sixteenth century, the consequent struggles over religious toleration, and the demands of the middle economic classes.[50] It is obvious that the process has been greatly accentuated by tre-

[46] U. S. National Resources Committee, *The Structure of the American Economy, Part I: Basic Characteristics* (Washington, D.C.: Government Printing Office, 1939), p. 96.

[47] See Linton, *The Study of Man*, pp. 84, 272–3.

[48] U. S. National Resources Committee, *The Problems of a Changing Population* (Washington, D.C.: Government Printing Office, 1938), p. 244.

[49] Chapple and Coon, *Principles of Anthropology*, pp. 140, 250–1, 365.

[50] MacIver, *The Web of Government*, pp. 52, 71.

mendous technological changes, well meriting the appellation "industrial revolution," which inevitably produced new contacts, new patterns of interaction, and new "foci of opposing interests." [51]

A precondition of the development of a vast multiplicity of groups, itself an instance of technological change of the most dramatic sort, is the revolution in means of communication. The mass newspaper, telephone, telegraph, radio, and motion pictures, not to mention the various drastic changes in the speed of transportation, have facilitated the interactions of men and the development of groups only slightly dependent, if at all, upon face-to-face contact. This factor in the formation of groups was noted by De Tocqueville when the first-named medium had scarcely appeared on the American scene:

In democratic countries . . . it often happens that a great number of men who wish or want to combine cannot accomplish it because they are very insignificant and lost amid the crowd, they cannot see and do not know where to find one another. . . . These wandering minds, which had long sought each other in darkness, at length meet and unite. The newspaper brought them together, and the newspaper is still necessary to keep them united.[52]

The revolution in communications has indeed largely rendered obsolete, as we have observed in another connection, Madison's confidence in the dispersion of the population as an ob-

stacle to the formation of interest groups.

Among other influences greatly facilitating group formation are such major national efforts as a war mobilization or a collective attack upon the problems of an industrial depression. In recruiting the national resources for such an emergency, the Government stimulates interaction throughout the nation. It is no accident, for example, that the periods of most rapid growth of trade associations in this country have included the years of World War I and the vigorous days of the ill-starred N.R.A.[53] Once the habit of associated activity was established under the stimulus of government encouragement, most such groups tended to persist and to invite imitation.

CONCLUSION

Stating the argument of this chapter in general terms, we find that any society is composed of groups, the habitual interactions of men. Any society, even one employing the simplest and most primitive techniques, is a mosaic of overlapping groups of various specialized sorts. Through these formations a society is experienced by its members, and in this way it must be observed and understood by its students. These group affiliations, with varying degrees of completeness and finality, form and guide the attitudes and therefore the behavior of their partici-

[51] MacIver, *The Web of Government*, p. 52.

[52] Alexis de Tocqueville, *Democracy in America* (ed. by Phillips Bradley; New York: Alfred A. Knopf, 1945), Vol. II, pp. 111–112.

[53] Herring: *Group Representation Before Congress*, pp. 51–2; U. S. Temporary National Economic Committee: *Trade Association Survey* (Monograph No. 18, Washington, D.C.: Government Printing Office, 1941), p. 368.

pants. How completely and finally a particular group controls the attitudes and behavior of its members is a matter to be determined through observation of the degree to which habitual patterns of interaction persist. The frequency and persistence of interactions within a group will determine its strength. The groups that form this mosaic emerge from the particular techniques of the society. Some, especially associations, which constitute a major concern of these pages, develop more immediately out of crises and disturbances within those groups in which the basic techniques of the society are institutionalized. The moving pattern of a complex society such as the one in which we live is one of changes and disturbances in the habitual subpatterns of interaction, followed by a return to the previous state of equilibrium or, if the disturbances are intense or prolonged, by the emergence of new groups whose specialized function it is to facilitate the establishment of a new balance, a new adjustment in the habitual interactions of individuals.

PATTERNS OF INTERPERSONAL RELATIONS IN A STATE LEGISLATIVE GROUP: THE WISCONSIN ASSEMBLY

SAMUEL C. PATTERSON

Traditionally, legislative bodies have been studied in terms of the formal structure of the legislative group— the structure of formal leadership or of committee organization, and legislative decision-making typically has been analyzed in terms of "pressures" or "vectors" which influence the decision-making process. The pattern of informal organization of legislative groups based on a variety of interpersonal relationships among legislators has been frequently recognized, but seldom investigated systematically.

The Assembly, the lower house of the Wisconsin State Legislature, consists of one-hundred members elected from single-member districts apportioned on the basis of population. Assemblymen are elected in November of even-numbered years, and the Assembly meets in biennial session for about six months in odd-numbered years. The formal organization of the Wisconsin Assembly with respect to the election and powers of elected officers, the organization of committees, and the formal legislative procedure is similar in most respects to the practices in many other states.

During the months of February, March, and April 1958, members of the 1957 session of the Wisconsin Assembly were systematically interviewed by means of a schedule of questions.[1] Seventy per cent of the members were interviewed personally, and an additional 17 per cent were interviewed by mail. Data were therefore available for 87 per cent of the members of the 1957 Assembly.

With respect to the patterns of interpersonal relations in the Assembly, sociometric techniques were employed to determine (1) what the informal pattern of organization was in the 1957 Assembly, and (2) whether, as other social-psychological research has indicated, legislators who have leadership status tend to receive more

[1] The complete study is reported in Samuel C. Patterson, "Toward a Theory of Legislative Behavior: The Wisconsin State Assemblymen as Actors in a Legislative System," unpublished Ph.D dissertation, Madison, Wis., University of Wisconsin, 1958.

CREDIT: Reprinted by permission of author and publisher from the *Public Opinion Quarterly*, Spring, 1959, pp. 101–109. [*Figures and tables renumbered.*]

friendship choices than non-leaders; that is, whether leaders tend to be "overchosen."

The method employed by some social scientists to identify and analyze the interpersonal relations of members of a social group is that of interaction process analysis, a technique which was developed by Bales.[2] Interaction process analysis is, however, fairly strictly limited in its application to small-group research and certainly would be a monumental, if not an impossible, task for a researcher with limited facilities if it were attempted on a body as large as the Wisconsin Assembly.

The outstanding illustration of an effort to analyze the interpersonal relationships of members of a legislative group in the literature of political science is the classic study of Routt, who counted the number of interactions between members during the first fifteen minutes of each daily session of the 1937 Illinois Senate.[3] Routt's analysis was confined to a sample of eleven senators, and interactions were counted during eighty-six sample periods. This technique is, as Routt himself maintained, limited in its utility to a small group of members who could be observed manageably by the researcher.

Systematic interviewing of members of a legislative body provided an opportunity, however, to analyze the interpersonal relations among members by means of sociometric techniques which have been highly developed by the social psychologists.[4] In the Wisconsin study, members were asked to nominate their closest personal friends within the Assembly— members whom they liked the best and spent the most time with outside the legislative chamber. The analysis of the data was accomplished by the manipulation of a matrix which indicated the friendship choices of members. Members were listed on the top and on the side of the matrix, and friendship choices were then plotted on the matrix. The matrix was squared to reveal mutual choices between members and, finally, cubed to reveal cliques. The procedure is not difficult even with a 100-man legislative group, and is fully and adequately described in Festinger et al., Social Pressures in Informal Groups.[5]

The sociometric, or friendship, score for each member was computed simply by totaling the number of sociometric choices for the member. These data were utilized to show a relationship between high friendship scores and leadership status.

The role of friends

Friendship is not a well-defined concept, and for the most part Assemblymen were encouraged to define it for themselves in designating their closest friends in the Assembly. Clearly,

[2] Robert F. Bales, *Interaction Process Analysis: A Method for the Study of Small Groups* (Cambridge, Mass.; Addison-Wesley, 1950).

[3] Garland C. Routt, "Interpersonal Relationships and the Legislative Process," *The Annals of the American Academy of Political and Social Science*, Vol. 195 (1938), pp. 129–136.

[4] Sociogram analysis is, of course, far more refined than the simple application of it here illustrated. The principal reference is J. L. Moreno, *Who Shall Survive?* (New York: Beacon House, 1953).

[5] Leon Festinger, Stanley Schachter, and Kurt Back, *Social Pressures in Informal Groups: A Study of Human Factors in Housing* (New York: Harper, 1950), pp. 132–150.

friendship among members of any social group can develop in a variety of ways. In the Assembly some friendships develop between members from the same geographical areas in the state who regularly ride together from their homes to the capitol. Others are developed between seatmates—members who sit next to each other in the Assembly.[6] The most important friendships for this analysis are those that reflect a community of interests and attitudes among members who share norms.

Legislators have the usual expectations with respect to their friends. They expect them to be honest with them, keep their confidences, and demonstrate compatible psychological characteristics. With respect to the legislative process, by and large Assemblymen expect their friends to support their bills unless there is some compelling reason why they cannot. If a member cannot support a friend's bill, he is expected to tell his friend why he cannot "go along" before he votes against the bill, and to explain why he must vote as he does. Otherwise, his friend will most likely automatically "count" on him, and an unwarned adverse vote may sever the friendship relationship. Since members tend to select persons of like minds as their friends, this problem does not create

serious difficulty. A member will be most frequently "forgiven" for voting against his friend if his reason is based on the nature of his district, that is, if he cannot "go along" because of district pressure.

The informal substructure of the assembly

The analysis of perception of friends in the Assembly revealed a total of 81 mutual choices between members, that is, in 81 cases members chose each other reciprocally. In 18 per cent of these cases, the members who chose each other were seatmates, so that it can be hypothesized that friendships in the Assembly are sometimes a function of sitting together in the chamber. In a few other cases friendships can be attributed to the fact that the members often rode back and forth together from Madison to their homes, although these friendship relationships probably did not result in a high frequency of interaction while the members were in Madison. One instance of this kind resulted in a three-

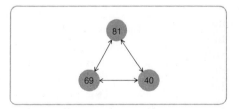

Figure III-2. Sociometric diagram of members from Green Bay area

way choice, which can be schematically illustrated by means of a simple sociometric diagram (Figure III-2).[7]

[6] This analysis of friendship in the legislative group considers primarily the question of who tends to form friendships with whom, and not the process through which these patterns develop. An attempt to study friendship as a process rather than a product is illustrated by the studies of Paul F. Lazarsfeld and Robert K. Merton, "Friendship as a Social Process: A Substantive and Methodological Analysis," in Monroe Berger, Theodore Abel, and Charles H. Page (editors), *Freedom and Control in Modern Society* (Princeton, N. J.: Van Nostrand, 1954), pp. 18–66.

[7] The numbers in the diagrams refer to interview code numbers.

These three members were all from the Green Bay area, one a Democrat and two Republicans.

The most interesting sub-groups, or cliques (which is the term the Assemblyman uses), revealed by an analysis of reciprocal choices are those among Democrats.[8] A third of the members of the 1957 Assembly were Democrats. The Democratic membership of the Assembly was divided into two principal cliques: the Milwaukee County clique and the Dane County clique. The Milwaukee County clique consisted of six Democrats who were referred to by members as the "Unholy Six," and included the Democratic floor leader (Figure III-3). The Un-

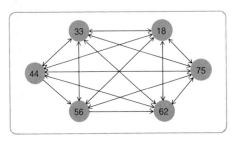

Figure III-3. Sociometric diagram of the "Unholy Six"

holy Six were Democrats who tended to see their role as one of cooperating with the majority party as much as possible in order to get their own legislation passed. Also, these members expected the floor leader to play down partisanship and cooperate with the Republican leadership. The Unholy Six were limited partisans. Three other Milwaukee Democrats comprised an additional sub-clique which

[8] A clique is operationally defined as any combination of three or more members who mutually choose each other, plus other related members.

was often allied with the Unholy Six (Figure III-4). In some respects, however, this smaller clique represented a dissident element among Milwaukee Democrats, expressing some dissatisfaction with the party leadership.

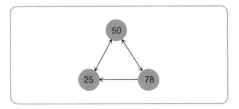

Figure III-4. Sociometric diagram of other Milwaukee Democrats

The Dane County clique was composed of the four Democratic members from the county in which the capitol is located, plus their allies (Figure III-5). Both the Democratic assistant floor leader and the caucus chairman were members of this clique. These members were more partisan in their role expectations, and tended to see the floor leader as a "party hatchet man." This group was able to defeat

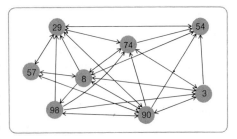

Figure III-5. Sociometric diagram of the Dane County clique

Pellant of the Unholy Six, the 1955 session assistant floor leader, for reelection and elect Hardie, one of their allies. The Dane County clique saw

Molinaro, the caucus chairman, as the "real" party leader, although he is himself from Kenosha. Molinaro was the Democratic candidate for speaker of the 1957 session, and he lost by a straight party vote to the Republican candidate, Marotz. In addition to the Dane County members, the clique included one Assemblyman from Racine, one from Kenosha, and two from northwestern rural Wisconsin.

An examination of roll-call votes indicates considerable difference in the voting behavior of the Dane County clique and the Unholy Six. The Dane County members were strongly influenced, and to some extent limited, by the editorial policy of one Madison newspaper, *The Capitol Times,* and were less likely to vote for legislation introduced by Republican members than were the Unholy Six. The same was true to a lesser extent of the northwestern Wisconsin Democrats in areas where the circulation of that newspaper is considerable.

The clique structure of the Democratic contingent in the 1957 Assembly reflects the statewide division between Milwaukee County and the rest of the state in the political behavior of Democratic activists. In this way the state Democratic convention is regularly divided, both in terms of platform policy and, to a greater extent, in the election of officers and the support of candidates.

The friendship clique structure of Republican members was not as spectacular. Interestingly enough, there were no three-way choices among the six members of the Republican steering committee, the group which comprised the primary Republican leadership of the Assembly, although these members met regularly as a group. The best-defined Republican clique had its own name: "Murderers' Row" (Figure III-6). This clique was com-

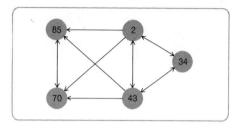

Figure III-6. Sociometric diagram of "Murderers' Row"

posed of members who sat together in the Assembly, who voted together most of the time, and who "caucused once in a while" if a member of the clique "got out of line." Three pairs of seatmates made up the clique, plus one other mutual choice and four single choices. Two of these members were chairmen of important committees, and one was Assembly chairman of the powerful joint finance committee.

Another Republican clique consisted of what might be referred to as the younger leadership group, which had as its center the relationship among Grady, the floor leader, Pommerening, Heider, and Bidwell (Figure III-7). This clique had friendship ties with other cliques close to the center of leadership in the Assembly. In terms of friendship expectancies, the clique was related to Rice, the powerful chairman of the agriculture committee, and through him to Stone, chairman of the finance committee and member of Murderers' Row. Heider, one of the members of this clique, sometimes sat in on meetings of the steering committee when one of

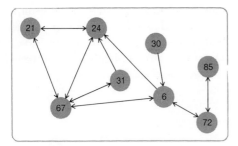

Figure III-7. Sociometric diagram of young Republican leader clique

1957 session members of this clique suggested the possibility of new leadership and the necessity for reforms in legislative procedure.

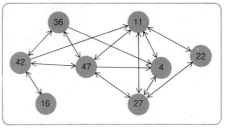

Figure III-8. Sociometric diagram of the "new member" clique

the regular members was not able to attend. Also, most of the members of this clique had supported Grady for speaker in the initial Republican caucus when Grady lost the speakership election to Marotz. Pommerening was Grady's campaign manager. These members constituted the core of the members who had, during the 1955 session, opposed the dominating tactics of Speaker Catlin, and these members believed at the opening of the 1957 session that the Catlin influence was being continued under the speakership of Marotz, who had been floor leader when Catlin was speaker.

Another clique of young Republican members which can be identified from the friendship patterns in the Assembly is a group, principally of new members, who were not related to the leadership by friendship ties and who were critical of certain aspects of the way the leaders performed (Figure III-8). This "new member" clique consisted of Assemblymen who had not been affected by the Catlin leadership in the Assembly, and who thought the legislative process was too cumbersome and inefficient. They believed that it was largely because of the unwillingness of older members that it had not been streamlined and at the end of the

The remaining Republican clique as determined by friendship patterns illustrates a different kind of relationship among members who mutually perceive each other in the role of friend. This clique consisted of Rice, former speaker and chairman of the agriculture committee, and two other southern Wisconsin farmerlegislators (Figure III-9). These two

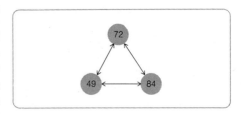

Figure III-9. Sociometric diagram of the Rice clique

farmer-legislators were new members, and one had been urged to run for the Assembly by Rice, with whom he was well-acquainted before he became an Assemblyman. For these two members Rice was, in effect, a role model. He "took them under his wing" during the session.

These patterns of interpersonal relationships in the Assembly in terms of friendship choices illustrate the structure of the informal organization of the legislative group. But the data with respect to friendship choices can be used not only to illustrate the patterns of influence and communication in a group, but also to indicate what kinds of individuals tend to get the most choices.

Friendship and leadership

The data on sociometric choices among legislators can be used to test the hypothesis: If a member has leadership status, then he will tend to be chosen as a friend by more members than will a non-leader. Leaders in the Assembly tend to be the prototypes of their group in a variety of ways: they tend to function as norm models, they tend to be the ideological prototypes of their group, and they tend to be more loyal to group-defined goals.[9] Since they also occupy positions of higher status in the legislative group than non-leaders, it should follow that leaders are perceived as friends by more members than are non-leaders.

Such a hypothesis is supported by the data from the Wisconsin Assembly. There is a clear relationship between the extent of friendship perception and leadership. Among members of both parties, leaders are seen as friends by more members than are the rank-and-file party members. Table III-1 shows that more members selected Republican steering committee members (primary leaders) for the role of friend than other Republican members.

TABLE 1 Relationship Between Republican Leadership and Friendship Perception (N = 67)

Leadership status	6 or more friends	Fewer than 6 friends
Steering committee	5	1
Other Republicans	8	53

$X^2 = 12.9; p. < .001$

The same relationship is true of the Democratic party members in the Assembly (Table III-2). Democratic

TABLE III-2 Relationship Between Democratic Leadership and Friendship Perception (N = 33)

Leadership status	6 or more friends	Fewer than 6 friends
Leaders	3	1
Other Democrats	2	27

$X^2 = 7.9; p. < .01$

leaders are seen in friendship roles by more members than rank-and-file Democrats.[10] It appears likely that members identify psychologically with their leaders and thus frequently see

[9] These are general characteristics of leadership, but they are borne out in the Wisconsin Assembly. See Patterson, *op. cit.*, chapter 9, "Leadership Roles in the Assembly."

[10] Similar findings with respect to other kinds of social groups can be found in the literature of social psychology. See Henry W. Riecken and George C. Homans, "Psychological Aspects of Social Structure," in Gardner Lindzey (editor), *Handbooks of Social Psychology*, Vol. 2 (Cambridge, Mass.: Addison-Wesley, 1954), pp. 786–832.

them not only as leaders but also as friends.[11]

CONCLUSION

Friendship roles are functional roles in the legislative group. No social group can be maintained if there are not significant and persistent interpersonal relations among members, and large groups like a legislature tend to be broken down into sub-groups on a friendship basis.[12] Friendship roles designated by the reciprocal choices among friends can be used to explore the informal organization of a legislative group. Perception of friendship by members can be related to leadership in the sense that leaders will tend to be perceived as playing friendship roles by more members than non-leaders.

Friendship roles are not only functional for the maintenance of the legislative group but also for the reso-

lution of political conflict. The legislator is not simply the "pawn of contending forces" who seek access to the legislative group in order to get their concepts of the public interest accepted as public policy. The legislator brings to the decision-making process not only his own sociological and psychological make-up and his multiple-group memberships, but also his informal associations within the legislative group. He is part of the informal social structure of the legislative group, and is affected by the norms of these informal groups in his own decision-making behavior.[13]

Individuals who assume the legislative role have diverse backgrounds and diverse social, political, and economic experience, and different reference groups are salient for them. The informal friendship structure of the legislature tends to lessen such differences, to mitigate against the development of potential conflicts, to provide channels of communication and understanding among members who share goals, and to facilitate logrolling.

---

[11] Routt found that interpersonal contacts "tended to center around individuals who by other indices were shown to play important roles in the process of legislation." See *op. cit.*, p. 132.

[12] A variety of related social-psychological research is analyzed in Harold H. Kelley and John W. Thibaut, "Experimental Studies in Group Problem Solving and Process," in Lindzey, *op. cit.*, pp. 761–770.

[13] In this connection, see the very valuable recent study of David B. Truman, "The State Delegations and the Structure of Party Voting in the United States House of Representatives," *American Political Science Review*, Vol. 50 (1956), pp. 1023–1045.

RULES OF THE GAME IN THE CANADIAN HOUSE OF COMMONS
ALLAN KORNBERG

Although, as Aristotle observed, man is a social animal, in any group there exist certain norms of behavior which structure the interactions of the individual in that group so as to enable it to achieve its purposive goals and/or maintain its viability. Such norms may be formal ones which require certain types of behavior or they may be informal expectations, conventions or obligations. The latter no less than the former set forth the expectations that the group has for its members and define appropriate and inappropriate actions.

The formal rules which govern the functions of and procedures within legislative bodies have long been subjects of study of political scientists. It has been relatively recently, however, that the attention of the discipline has focused on the informal norms of legislative behavior. David Truman has pointed out the importance of these informal "rules of the game" for understanding legislative behavior:

A legislative body has its own group life, sometimes . . . it has its own operating structure which may approximate or

CREDIT: Allan Kornberg, "Rules of the Game in the Canadian House of Commons," *The Journal of Politics*, Vol. 26, No. 2, May 1964, pp. 358–380. [*Tables and some footnotes renumbered.*]

differ sharply from the formal organization of the Chamber. When a man first joins such a body, he enters a new group. Like others, it has its standards and conventions, its largely unwritten system of obligations and privileges. To these the neophyte must conform, at least in some measure, if he hopes to make effective use of his position.

. . . .

Failure to learn the ways of the legislative group, to play ball with his colleagues is almost certain, especially in a large body like the U. S. House of Representatives, to handicap the proposals in which the freshman legislator is interested and to frustrate his ambitions for personal preferment.[1]

The only systematic empirical investigations of these informal behavioral norms have been those carried out by Donald R. Matthews in his study of the Senate,[2] and by John Wahlke and his colleagues in their study of American State legislators.[3]

[1] David Truman, *The Governmental Process* (New York: Alfred A. Knopf, 1960), pp. 343–345.

[2] Donald R. Matthews, *U. S. Senators and Their World* (New York: Vintage Books, 1960). Matthews lists six categories of rules of the game recognized by Senators: Apprenticeship; Legislative Work; Specialization; Courtesy; Reciprocity; and Institutional Patriotism.

[3] John Wahlke *et al., The Legislative System: Explorations in Legislative Behavior* (New York:

Our intentions were to determine what the rules of the game are for the Canadian House of Commons,[4] to make some meaningful comparisons of these rules with those discovered by the Wahlke group in their study, and to ascertain whether independent variables such as experience, party affiliation and so forth effect both the legislators awareness of rules of the game and sanctions and the types of rules and sanctions they articulated. In order to carry out the first two intentions, the legislators were asked the following question:[5]

We have been told that every legislature has its unofficial rules of the game, certain things members do and certain things they must not do if they want the respect and cooperation of fellow members. What are some of these rules that a member must observe to hold the respect and co-operation of his fellow members?

Since it was assumed that the primary functions of group behavioral norms are to maintain the viability of the group and to enable it to achieve its goals,[6] it was felt that the rules of the

game in the Canadian House of Commons would serve primarily three functions. These would be: (1) to expedite the flow of legislative business, (2) to channel and mitigate conflict, (3) to defend members against external criticism.

The first assumption is based on the knowledge that all democratic legislatures have had to handle an increasingly large volume of work in this century. As the positive functions of government, particularly national governments, have increased, the amount of legislation with which legislators have had to deal has increased correspondingly.[7] In Canada, every major piece of legislation introduced in Parliament is almost always commented on by the leaders and the relevant subject matter specialists of *each* of the *four* parties,[8] a practice which consumes large quantities of the time in the House of Commons. The problem is further aggravated by the custom of allowing freshmen members to make at least one fairly lengthy speech during the course of a legislative session. One result of these practices, taken together with an increased work load, has been the continuous lengthening of legislative sessions since

John Wiley & Sons, Inc., 1962). Wahlke and Ferguson have categorized the rules of the game according to the functions they perform. These are: Rules that promote group cohesion and solidarity; rules which promote predictability of legislative behavior; rules which channel and restrain conflict; rules which expedite legislative business; rules which serve primarily to give tactical advantages to individual members and desirable personal qualities cited as rules.

[4] This report is part of a larger statistical study carried out by the author in 1962 at which time a weighted stratified sample of 165 Members of Parliament were interviewed.

[5] This question was taken directly from the questionnaire employed by Wahlke and his colleagues in their study of State Legislators.

[6] See Dorwin Cartwright and Alvin Zander, *Group Dynamics: Research and Theory* (Evanston: Row, Peterson and Company Inc., 1953) for a complete discussion of the functions of group norms.

[7] For a discussion of the effects of the increase of the volume of legislation on the formal rules of Parliaments see Gilbert Campion, *Parliament: A Survey* (London: Allen and Urwin, 1952).

[8] The four parties in Canada fall quite naturally along the traditional left-right political continum: The New Democrats, the party of the far left had a house membership of nineteen; the Liberals, the party of the Left-Center had a membership of one hundred; the Progressive-Conservatives, the party of the Right-Center had a membership of one hundred and sixteen and formed the minority government for Canada's twenty-fifth Parliament; while the Social Credit, the party of the far right had a membership of thirty.

World War II. It therefore seemed reasonable to assume that some of the informal rules would encourage members to help speed the legislative process.

A democratic legislature necessarily presupposes that formal decisions will be made only after the opposition has been given a hearing and had an opportunity not only to influence the policy proposals under discussion but also to present alternative proposals. Of necessity then, democratic legislative decision-making generates conflict. In the United States this conflict is in part mitigated by the loosely disciplined parties which permit the crossing of party lines and the development of inter-party alliances. Such an arrangement is precluded by the nature of the Canadian party system. It was assumed that if conflict, a "normal" product of the democratic decision-making process which presumably is intensified by Canada's disciplined parties, was allowed to remain unchecked, it would be capable of obstructing the attainment of legislative goals and perhaps destroying the system itself. It appeared therefore, that an important function of the rules of the game in the House of Commons would be to help soften and channel conflict.

Like legislators in most countries with free speech and a free press, the Canadian legislator is a vulnerable, and sometimes an extremely attractive target for the barbs of a discontented group, or a newspaper seeking a boost in circulation by headlining a tale of supposed legislative misdeeds.[9] It was assumed that such criticism would tend to promote legislative solidarity regardless of party, and establish norms designed to discourage behavior which might bring the system and its members under attack from outsiders.

The data showed that the rules of the game in the Canadian Parliament appear to perform these three functions and in addition that they *also* appear to reinforce formal House rules, to propagate the system of disciplined parties, to mitigate intra-party conflict, to encourage members to become subject-matter experts and to perform the necessary labor required from a member of Parliament.

CANADIAN PERCEPTIONS OF RULES OF THE GAME

Rules listed by respondents fall into general categories: those which apply to behavior in the House itself and those which apply to behavior outside the House Chambers but within Parliament itself or to behavior entirely outside of Parliament. The charts on pages 250 and 251 contain the rules given by the legislators themselves grouped under these two headings and further categorized according to the functions they seem to perform in the legislative system.

Unlike the American State legislators studied by Wahlke and his colleagues, a considerable proportion of Canadian legislators seemed to perceive no rules. Fully 16.1% said they were

---

[9] For example during the months of November and December when these interviews were taken, Canadian Members of Parliament came under fire in the nation's press for their conduct and performance at the NATO meetings in Paris, for their conduct during a tour of some of the new African states and for excessive drinking and absenteeism.

not aware of any rules "in the House" and 17.4% were unaware of rules "outside of the House." If rules of the game are in part learned by experience the high percentage (38.7) of Freshman legislators may in part account for this large proportion of legislators who were "ignorant" of the rules. However, the data show that there are no appreciable differences among Freshman and other legislators in their awareness of the rules of the game. Another more cogent reason may have been a suspicion on the part of some of the respondents that the acknowledgment of such existing rules might be construed and reported unfavorably by the interviewer, that is, that such rules might be perceived as being underhanded, or operating to the advantage or disadvantage of some members. Hence they may have been reluctant to commit themselves.

Response typical of legislators who said they were unaware of such rules were:

"What do you mean, rules of the game, what rules?

Rules in the House Chamber by Primary Functions

A. Rules to decrease conflict   N=57   % =35.2

1. No personal attacks on a member, never bring personalities into debate
2. Don't be overly or stupidly partisan
3. Be generous in your praise of opponents at the proper time

B. Rules to expedite legislative business   N=16   % =10.0

1. Do not speak too often
2. Do not speak too long
3. Do not be a bore
4. Do not speak without proper knowledge of the subject

C. Rules which discourage conduct that would invite criticism   N=18   % =10.9

1. Don't curse or use improper language
2. Always be neatly dressed, shaved, properly attired
3. Never enter the House inebriated

D. Rules which encourage propagation of the party system   N=23   % =14.0

1. Maintain party solidarity
2. Don't break party ranks
3. Don't make a speech in the House you know will offend some of your party colleagues

E. Rules which encourage expertise and performance of labors   N=16   % =10.4

1. Do your homework before you speak, know what you are talking about
2. Do your proper share of the work
3. Attend House sessions, do not be absent too often

F. Rules which reinforce respect for formal rules   N=7   % =3.4

1. Know the proper rules of debate, observe the rules of debate
2. Extend the proper courtesies
3. Know the correct forms of address

Rules Outside of the Chamber by Primary Functions

A. Rules to decrease conflict	N = 35	% = 21.3

   1. Do not be rude or arrogant with other members
   2. Be friendly, courteous, respect other members in your relations outside the House
   3. Do not bring your partisanship out of the House, do not be partisan at social affairs, mix with everybody

B. Rules which discourage conduct that would invite criticism	N = 81	% = 48.9

   1. Be discrete in your comments to the press
   2. Do not pass on confidential information to the press
   3. Be honorable, honest, trustworthy, never make another member look bad, do not get another member in trouble with your remarks to the press
   4. Have good manners, behave yourself, act the same way you would in any good social club

C. Rules which encourage work	N = 10	% = 6.2

   1. Attend party caucus, do your share of assignments, pull your weight with your colleagues

D. Rules which discourage intra-party conflict	N = 10	% = 6.2

   1. Do not be too pushy, overaggressive
   2. Do not try too hard to advance yourself over your party colleagues

---

I've been around here for a long time and if there are any rules I don't know of them."

or "There are no rules, none that I've ever heard of."

or "Well there may be but I'm not aware of any. I haven't really been here long enough to know. I suppose I'll learn."

or "No, no rules except that you are honest in your dealings with people."

or "No, there are no rules, but you should know the House rules."

SANCTIONS

Although a majority of the legislators were aware of the rules of the game, only a relatively small number were cognizant of existing sanctions to enforce the observance of the rules. In contrast to the American State legislators, all but 11% of whom mentioned specific sanctions available, *83.6% of the legislators were unaware of sanctions that could be applied in the House itself and 47.5% were unaware of any available sanctions outside the House.*

In response to the statement, "I imagine things would be made rather difficult for someone who didn't follow the rules?" typical responses were:

"No!"

or "I don't know of anything."

or "Not necessarily! It depends on whose toes you step on. You can be popular with the leaders and unpopular with the members or vice versa. If you're popular with the leaders, there isn't much that can be done to a guy!"

or "Maybe, but I haven't been here long enough to find out what."

or "Unfortunately, no!"

or "I don't think so! Anyone who ignores the rules is so egotistical or has such a thick skin, it's impossible to get through to him at all."

or "No. If you win big, if the party needs you, you can get away with anything. —————— is the biggest boor in the world but he's tolerated!"

Legislators who replied to the statement in the affirmative were asked "Can you give me some examples of those things?"

The responses again could be classified into those sanctions applied in the House Chamber and those applied outside of the House.

There were two types of sanctions applied in the House, one by the members, the other by the Speaker. Examples of the first type of sanction were:

"Yes, there are. If you get up to speak, everyone suddenly starts to leave or if they stay they heckle, laugh, hoot at you. You get the idea."

or "Yes, people will whisper and talk when you try to speak in the House."

or "He'd lose status in the House. People will rise, walk out on him when he tries to speak. They wouldn't listen, they'd jeer."

Illustrative of the second type of sanction employed were:

"Mr. Speaker has a blind eye for such people. When he gets up to speak someone gets up with him and the Speaker recognizes the other person."

or "Oh sure, the Speaker will make sure he doesn't get the floor. Then when he goes to the Speaker, he will be told off!"

or "Such people are simply ignored by the Speaker."

There were four types of sanctions employed outside the House: (1) social ostracism, (2) sanctions from the offender's party, (3) sanctions from members outside the offender's party, and (4) sanction from the constituency. The following are illustrative of these sanctions.

'Certainly. Fortunately, this type doesn't last very long. They're usually defeated. Here they simply ignore you socially. It's like anywhere else. Who's going to like you if you won't go along? You certainly aren't going to get much consideration from the party or the Ministers if you don't play ball."

or "I have watched people who have built up a pretty good political image by being a maverick. But then there comes a time when the House becomes adamant and you as a maverick get no consideration from your own party or the government. Oh, the Liberals and Conservatives have ways—no campaign funds, no patronage, keep him from the nomination. They're very adept at this."

or "You just don't invite the guy in for a drink. You don't have lunch with him, you ignore him. It's like any other social group."

or "Yes! He wouldn't have the respect of his colleagues for one thing. He'd feel it. For another he'd get no consideration from his colleagues. If he were a member of the Government he'd have real trouble getting through to certain key people."

or "He is socially kept out of it. He isn't invited to certain functions. He gets the cold shoulder. He's on the awkward squad!"

The question arises as to why such a large percentage of the legislators either were unaware of, or stated emphatically that there were no sanctions in existence. It is suggested that there are three possible explanations for this phenomenon.

If we define a sanction as *an action which is deemed punitive or detrimental to the incumbent of the legislative position,* the key words are "deemed punitive or detrimental." In other words in order for the sanction to

constituents may not agree on the kinds of legislative behavior an M.P. should avoid. For example, one constituency may approve of behavior that draws the attention of the mass media to their representative because they may feel he is putting them "on the map." Another constituency, however, may feel that similar behavior on the part of their legislator should be punished by switching their support to another candidate. Similarly a member's rigid adherence to the demands

TABLE III-3   Sanctions Employed in the Canadian House of Commons

	N.	*%*
Sanctions Applied in the House		
1. Sanctions from colleagues	19	11.7
2. Sanctions from the Speaker	7	4.7
Sanctions Applied Outside the House		
3. Social ostracism	53	31.7
4. Sanctions from the party	13	7.6
5. Sanctions from members	19	11.8
6. Sanctions from the constituency	2	1.3

be effective, it must first be *perceived* by the legislator as being harmful or detrimental to him. Either through inexperience or individual personality differences, what one individual deems detrimental to him, for example social ostracism, may not be so perceived by another individual, who prefers to be left largely alone.

Another factor may be that the sanction system for enforcing adherence to the informal behavioral norms in the Canadian House of Commons may not be working effectively because of a lack of consensus about the Canadian legislators' role. That is, his party, the other legislators, and his

of party leaders may be approved of by the members of one party, while similar actions elicit only scorn from the members of another party.

Yet another reason for failing to recognize the existence of a system of sanctions may stem from the desire of the legislator to project a favorable image of himself and the group to the interviewer. By acknowledging the existence of a system of sanctions he implicitly acknowledges that his "correct conduct" as a legislator is motivated more by an anticipation of possible punishment than by some intrinsic virtue. Similarly his loyalty to the system of which he is a part may preclude him from acknowledging the existence of, what in reality, are extra-legal measures, and which may therefore be perceived by the "outsider" (the interviewer) as being somewhat sinister or undemocratic.

THE BASES OF RULES AND SANCTIONS

Wahlke and Ferguson suggest that legislators' occupations have a greater impact upon a legislator's ability to articulate rules than do either education or the demographic characteristics of the legislators' constituencies.[10] Furthermore, their data did not demonstrate that the length of a legislator's experience had any marked impact on his ability to articulate rules of the game. Since in this study not more than two of the responses were coded the analytic concern here is with legislators' ability to perceive rules and sanctions and the types of rules and sanctions they perceived, rather than with the *number* of rules that a respondent mentioned.

Our data support Wahlke's finding that the length of a legislator's service had little impact upon his ability to articulate rules (if the ability to perceive rules and sanctions is considered a criterion of articulative facility). It seemed reasonable to assume that the longer the legislator's period of service in the House, the more he would be aware of the rules, and the sanctions available to enforce the rules. However, the data show that although slightly more long-service legislators than Freshmen were aware of the rules, *one quarter of all legislators who had at least six years of experience were unaware of any sanctions available in the House to enforce adherence to the rules. In addition there was a higher proportion of legislators with seventeen years or more of service than there were Freshmen legislators who were unaware of any sanctions invoked outside the House Chamber.* Nor were there any really significant differences among them in the types of rules or sanctions that they perceived.

Other significant independent variables we should expect to find related to the legislators' awareness of rules and sanctions and the types of rules and sactions to which they were sensitive are party affiliation, positions of leadership,[11] differences in education, and the legislators' positions on the conflict indices.[12]

[10] Our own data (not shown) offer only partial support for this finding. Although, like Wahlke we found that differences in the demographic characteristics of the legislators' constituencies had little relation to their sensitivity to rules and sanctions, we found that differences in awareness of rules and sanctions that could be attributed to occupational differences were both insignificant and inconsistent. For example, although a higher percentage of legislators with blue collar occupations were unaware of rules outside the House than were legislators with professional or managerial occupations, the former were more sensitive than managerial types to rules in the House and more sensitive to sanctions both in and out of the House than either legislators with professional or business-managerial occupations.

[11] All Cabinet Ministers, Parliamentary Secretaries, party and deputy-party leaders, former Cabinet Ministers, Caucus chairmen and party Whips who fell within the sample were classified as party leaders. All others were classified as non-leaders regardless of any positions held in the party organization outside of Parliament.

[12] To facilitate analysis, a number of indices were constructed which attempt to measure the effect of certain cultural and political variables on the

TABLE III-4   Sensitivity to Rules and Sanctions by Experience

	Perceived no rules in the House	Perceived no rules out of the House	Perceived no sanctions in the House	Perceived no sanctions out of the House
Freshmen	18.7%	17.4%	85.5%	54.5%
"Diefenbakers" *	12.2	21.3	82.7	53.5
6–10 Years Service	25.4	11.9	93.2	57.7
11–16 Years Service	13.3	0.0	76.7	53.3
17 plus Years Service	13.3	13.3	63.3	66.7

* By "Diefenbakers," we mean those legislators who were first elected in the narrow Conservative victory of 1957 at which time Mr. John Diefenbaker became Prime Minister, and then re-elected in the overwhelming Conservative sweep of 1958.

The assumptions underlying the selection of these variables were:

1. The New Democrats, being the most politically sophisticated group of legislators,[13] would be more aware of the

values, attitudes and behavior of Canadian Members of Parliament. The codes for all variables were 0, 1, 2. If a respondent did not fit the description of the variable he was coded "0," if the information had not been ascertained he was coded "1," and if he fit the description, he was coded "2." Since excessively high variance together with low correlations to other items was not a factor for any of the variables employed, no special weighting was required and a respondent's position on any index was arrived at simply by summing his coded responses. The Tau Gamma rank order correlation test indicated that all correlations among the variables for each index were high enough to be judged significant. The constituency conflict index was constructed of five variables and measures the extent to which a legislator perceives conflict between himself and his constituents on goals, expectations for legislative position, and position, on certain policy issues. The four categories of the index are No Conflict, Low Conflict, Moderate Conflict and High Conflict. The Party conflict index is made up of three variables and measures the degree to which the legislator perceives himself in conflict with his party on three policy issues. The categories of the index are No Conflict, Some Conflict and High Conflict.

[13] By political sophistication we mean that the legislators had been raised in highly politicized environments, that is, their families were active

rules and sanctions in existence. The corollary of this would also be true, that is, the Liberal and Social Credit groups, the least politically sophisticated would be the least aware of rules and sanctions.

2. The Conservatives, the Government party, would most often mention rules that tend to expedite legislative business.

3. The New Democrats, the most party-oriented of the legislators [14] would mention rules that help propagate the party system.

4. Leaders would be more aware of rules and sanctions than those who were not leaders because of their greater political sophistication.[15]

5. Leaders would more often mention rules that mitigate intraparty conflict

politically, politics was frequently discussed at home and so forth. In addition they had held public and party offices at various levels before becoming candidates for Parliament.

[14] Party oriented legislators were those legislators who asserted: a) a party caucus decision was always binding; b) it is *always* necessary to vote with your party; c) one had to choose the party over the constituency in the event of conflict between the two. The Tau Gamma statistic indicated that there was a significant relationship among these variables.

[15] Data not shown.

and that encourage legislators to work at their jobs.

6. Legislators in the high conflict categories on the constituency conflict index would be less aware of sanctions available, since they would most likely perceive sanctions coming from their legislative districts.

7. Legislators with a college education, and who have been exposed to educational institutions outside of their own province would theoretically be more aware of rules and sanctions than either college educated legislators whose education had been confined to their own provinces or legislators who have less than a college education.[16]

Examination of the data confirmed some, but not all of these assumptions. With respect to party affiliation, for example (see Table III-5), the New Democrats *were* the party generally most aware of the existence of rules and sanctions. However, although the Social Credit members were least aware of rules in the Chamber and sanctions outside of it, the Conservatives, rather than the Liberals, were the party least sensitive to rules and sanctions. Also, contrary to our assumption, it was the New Democrats, rather than the Conservative who had the highest proportion of members who mentioned rules that help expedite legislative business.

Similarly, it was the Conservative and Social Credit parties', rather than the New Democrats, who mentioned rules that help propagate the party system in the legislature. The Social Credit party were almost alone in mentioning rules that function to reinforce the formal rules of debate. In addition they had the highest percentage of legislators who perceived sanctions emanating from the Speaker.[17] It would appear, therefore, that although differences in party affiliation affect the legislators' sensitivity to both rules and sanctions and the type of rules and sanctions they are aware of, these differences do not always coincide with theoretical expectations.

This was also found to be the case when we tried to explain differences in awareness and sensitivity to certain types of rules and sanctions in terms of the occupancy of leadership positions. For example, the data [18] only partially support the assumption that leaders are more sensitive to rules and sanctions than those who are not leaders. Contrary to expectations, leaders did not mention rules that discouraged intra-party conflict or encouraged members to work at their jobs more often than non-leaders.

However, a substantially higher percentage of leaders (48.7%) mentioned rules that tend to soften the conflict between the parties and leaders (40.5%) were also more sensitive to the possibility of social ostracism than were those not in leadership positions. Except for these differences, the occupancy of formal leadership

---

[16] For a discussion on the relationship between education and democracy see Seymour M. Lipset, *Political Man* (New York: Anchor Books, 1963), pp. 39–42.

[17] The concern of the Social Credit group with formal rules and sanctions from the Speaker may have been related to the fact that during the first session of the twenty-fifth Parliament, a number of Social Credit members clashed frequently and sharply with Mr. Speaker. The latter actually had one of these legislators temporarily expelled from the House, an event which occurs very infrequently in the Canadian House of Commons.

[18] Data not shown.

positions did not appear to have an appreciable impact on this aspect of legislative behavior.

Perceptions of conflict appeared to be a more important determinant of the legislator's ability to perceive rules

TABLE III-5   Relation Between Rules of the Game and Sanctions Available and Political Parties

	S.C.	*Conserv.*	*Liberal*	*N.D.P.*
Rules in the House				
Not aware of rules	21.1%	18.0%	16.1%	0.0%
Rules that decrease conflict	21.1	28.6	40.9	61.5
Rules that expedite business	9.9	10.6	6.5	23.1
Rules that discourage criticism	4.3	5.9	17.4	15.4
Rules that propagate party system	22.5	22.7	4.8	0.0
Rules which encourage expertise and hard work	0.0	14.2	11.7	0.0
Rules which reinforce formal rules	21.1	0.0	2.6	0.0
TOTAL	100.0	100.0	100.0	100.0

(Chi Square = 218.72   D.F. = 21   P < .005)

Rules outside the House

	S.C.	*Conserv.*	*Liberal*	*N.D.P.*
Not aware of rules	8.5%	25.5%	13.5%	7.6%
Decrease conflict	18.3	20.7	22.6	23.1
Discourage criticism	60.5	41.3	49.1	69.3
Encourage work	8.5	4.7	8.7	0.0
Discourage intra-party conflict	4.2	7.8	6.1	0.0
TOTAL	100.0	100.0	100.0	100.0

(Chi Square = 63.92   D.F. = 18   P < .005)

Sanctions in the House

	S.C.	*Conserv.*	*Liberal*	*N.D.P.*
Not aware of sanction	77.5%	87.5%	84.4%	75.0%
Sanctions from members	12.7	11.0	11.3	16.7
Sanctions from Speaker	9.8	1.5	4.3	8.3
TOTAL	100.0	100.0	100.0	100.0

(Chi Square = 14.14   D.F. = 6   P < .025)

Sanctions outside the House

	S.C.	*Conserv.*	*Liberal*	*N.D.P.*
Not aware of sanctions	62.0%	48.6%	42.2%	46.2%
Social ostracism	4.2	31.0	39.6	38.5
Sanctions from party	21.1	6.3	6.4	0.0
Sanctions from members	12.7	14.1	8.3	15.3
Sanctions from constituency	0.0	0.0	3.5	0.0
TOTAL	100.0	100.0	100.0	100.0
	(N = 23)	(N = 66)	(N = 63)	(N = 13)

(Chi Square = 66.18   D.F. = 12   P < .005)

and sanctions. Generally, the more conflict he perceived with his district the unaware he was of the rules (see Table III-6). Such legislators were also less aware of sanctions outside the House than were those in the No Con- flict category. One would expect that his constituency would be a salient factor for a legislator who perceived himself in conflict with it, and his tendency to be less aware of the rules may be related to the fact that "his

TABLE III-6   Relation Between Rules of the Game and Sanctions and Legislators' Positions on District Conflict Index

	No	*Low*	*Moderate*	*High*
Rules in the House				
Not aware	10.6%	18.9%	17.2%	18.1%
Expedite business	11.8	9.1	11.0	8.0
Decrease conflict	34.2	34.2	35.1	37.6
Discourage criticism	9.9	11.0	17.3	5.1
Propagate party-system	9.9	12.8	11.0	23.2
Encourage work and expertise	14.3	12.2	8.4	5.8
Reinforce formal rules	9.3	1.8	0.0	2.2
TOTAL	100.0	100.0	100.0	100.0
(Chi Square = 76.45 D.F. = 21 P < .005)				
Rules outside the House				
Not aware	13.7%	15.2%	18.6%	23.2%
Decrease conflict	13.7	20.1	21.4	31.9
Discourage criticism	54.7	53.7	49.0	36.2
Encourage work	11.7	4.3	5.5	2.9
Discourage intra-party conflict	6.2	6.7	5.5	5.8
TOTAL	100.0	100.0	100.0	100.0
(Chi Square = 60.39 D.F. = 18 P < .005)				
Sanctions in House				
Not aware	86.0	75.6	86.9	89.1
From colleagues	11.5	13.4	13.1	8.7
From Speaker	2.5	11.0	0.0	2.2
TOTAL	100.0	100.0	100.0	100.0
(Chi Square = 30.37 D.F. = 6 P < .005)				
Sanctions outside the House	*No*	*Low*	*Moderate*	*High*
Not aware	55.9%	48.8%	37.2%	47.1%
Social ostracism	27.3	37.2	29.0	33.3
From party	8.1	6.7	9.7	5.8
From colleagues	8.7	7.3	18.6	13.8
From constituents	0.0	0.0	5.5	0.0
TOTAL	100.0	100.0	100.0	100.0
	(N = 48)	(N = 45)	(N = 35)	(N = 37)
(Chi Square = 46.05 D.F. = 12 P < .005)				

mind is on his district." Assuming that this is the case one would also expect him to perceive sanctions emanating from his district. However, it was the legislator on the Moderate rather than on the High position of the Conflict index who tended to perceive the possibility of district sanctions.

High conflict legislators were most sensitive to rules that decreased conflict and those which tended to maintain the party system. Conversely, *they were least aware of the rules which function to avoid criticism. Perhaps one reason they perceive themselves in conflict with their constituents is that they are more likely to behave in ways that evoke criticism from their constituents.*

A considerably higher percentage of legislators who were in conflict with their *parties* were unaware of the rules outside the House Chamber than those not in conflict (see Table III-7). These legislators were also less aware of the possibility of sanctions operating outside the Chamber.

As was the case with the legislators in conflict with their districts, those in conflict with their parties also were more sensitive to rules that decreased inter-party conflict both in and out of the House. They were also *less concerned with rules that encourage legislators to work and rules whose function is to encourage "good" behavior.* One can speculate *that their perceived differences with the party may be related in part at least to this seeming indifference to both work and good behavior.*

Another factor, the assumption that a university education and exposure to an environment which differs from the one in which a legislator is

socialized would be manifested in an increased awareness of both the rules and sanctions was generally supported by the data (see Table III-8). The "cosmopolitan" college graduates were more aware of the rules and sanctions in effect outside the House than were the other two categories of legislators. However their "provincial" colleagues who also attended institutions of higher learning were more aware of sanctions in effect within the House. Legislators who were not college men, aside from their lack of sensitivity to the rules and sanctions were not *markedly* different in the emphasis they placed on those rules and sanctions which they did articulate than were their better educated colleagues.[19]

CONCLUSIONS

A study of the informal behavioral norms and sanctions in operation in the Canadian House of Commons reveals that such rules appear to be functional both for the maximization of the goals of the system and for the maintenance of the viability of the system itself. Essentially the rules expedite the flow of legislation, encourage members to work hard and become somewhat expert in different areas, maintain the party system and the strength of the parties and foster respect for the formal rules of the House. Members are at the same time urged to keep their conflict and animosities within certain limits and to avoid behavior that may draw criticism to both them and the institution of Parlia-

[19] Data not shown.

ment. To enforce adherence to these norms, the members are made aware that deviations will provoke sanctions from other members, from colleagues in the party, from officials in the system, and even from constituents.

Some rules receive more emphasis than others. Inside the House, stress is placed on rules which mitigate personal conflict and channel it into conflict between the parties. In other words conflict is legitimized and made predictable so that the stability of the system is not threatened as it might be

TABLE III-7   Relation Between Rules of the Game and Sanctions and Legislators' Positions on Party Conflict Index

	No	*Moderate*	*High*
Not aware	14.2%	19.6%	16.3%
Expedite business	9.5	9.2	14.0
Decrease conflict	35.5	30.4	44.2
Discourage criticism	10.9	14.0	3.5
Propagate party system	15.1	10.3	17.4
Encourage work	10.4	13.0	4.6
Reinforce formal rules	4.4	3.3	0.0
TOTAL	100.0	100.0	100.0

(Chi Square = 45.11   D.F. = 14   P < .005)

Rules outside the House

Not aware	11.2	19.0	38.4
Decrease conflict	19.6	20.6	30.2
Discourage criticism	52.9	49.4	31.4
Encourage work	8.9	4.3	0.0
Discourage intra-party conflict	7.4	6.7	0.0
TOTAL	100.0	100.0	100.0

(Chi Square = 72.48   D.F. = 12   P < .005)

Sanctions in House

Not aware	84.1	85.3	81.4
From colleagues	12.0	8.7	14.0
From Speaker	3.0	6.0	4.6
TOTAL	100.0	100.0	100.0

(Chi Square = 4.90   D.F. = 4   P < .500)

Sanctions outside House

Not aware	42.6%	54.3%	52.3%
Social ostracism	22.7	31.5	24.4
From party	9.2	3.8	9.3
From colleagues	21.1	10.4	14.0
From constituents	2.4	0.0	0.0
TOTAL	100.0	100.0	100.0
	(N = 92)	(N = 50)	(N = 23)

(Chi Square = 17.85   D.F.   P < .025)

if conflict was personal, intermittent and unpredictable.[20]

The relatively little emphasis placed on rules that expedite the flow of legislation is surprising but probably stems from the fact that in the Canadian system the program of legislation before the House is almost entirely the responsibility of the Government. Hence, the essential responsibil-

the group against a perceived external threat. Second, by keeping outside criticism to a minimum, demands for changes in the system by those outside it, are also kept to a minimum.

Although in articulating the rules outside the House, a smaller proportion of the legislators emphasized rules that mitigate conflict, such rules are still salient for the members. Since

TABLE III-8   Relations Between Awareness of Rules and Sanctions and Legislators' Educational Backgrounds

	College and some education out of the province	*College in province*	*No college and all education in province*
Not aware of rules in House	6.2%	18.0%	23.5%
Not aware of rules out of House	10.2	21.1	19.4
Not aware of sanctions in House	89.8	75.5	91.6
Not aware of sanctions out of House	41.9	49.8	50.0

ity for controlling both the type of legislation and the speed with which it is considered is probably also perceived as primarily a function of the government party.

Outside the House Chamber, the rules most often stressed were those which encouraged the type of conduct that does not invite criticism. Such rules apparently function in two ways to maintain the viability of the system. First, by making the legislators aware of the fact that they face the criticism and hostility of "outsiders," they (the rules) serve to promote the solidarity of

most of the social activities that legislators attend result chiefly from their official status as members of Parliament, they tend to interact almost as much outside, as in the House. Tensions built up in the House, which ordinarily would dissipate if legislators were not brought into continuous contact, tend to remain. Therefore, the rules require that all members are to be treated courteously, with deference and so forth. The rule requiring members not to bring their partisanship outside the House doors indicates that even "legitimate" party conflict must be restricted.

In contrast to the American Senate, relatively little attention is focused on the necessities of controlling intra-party conflict. This may arise

[20] Wahlke and Ferguson found that the function of certain informal rules in the State Legislatures was to make legislators' behavior predictable. Wahlke *et al., The Legislative System,* p. 160.

from the fact that unlike the Senate, seniority is not a major determinant in the selection of leaders. Since members are encouraged to believe that individual ability and industry, meritorious service to the party, and not primarily seniority will result in the granting of preferred position, they are less likely to feel frustrated by the requirement of a long apprenticeship period. Consequently there is not here the same necessity for emphasizing the virtues of serving an apprenticeship, of not being overly-aggressive and of waiting one's turn, that there is in a system governed by the seniority rule.

Examination of the sanctions available to enforce compliance with the rules indicates that the sanctions were perceived as coming essentially from informal rather than formal sources. For example the most powerful and/or frequently employed sanction was the social ostracism of the offender by other members. The next most frequent sanction employed outside the House was both a formal one, in the sense that members of the opposition parties felt that they would receive little consideration from Ministers, and an informal one, in that they perceived the offender as not being able to secure understanding, help, or co-operation from the other members.

The only official sanctions that were mentioned were perceived as emanating either from the party, from the Speaker, and in a few instances, the constituency. One would assume that in a national legislature with disciplined parties, the initiative in enforcing the rules of the game would come from official sources rather than from

individuals. This is not the case, it is suggested, because of the essentially extra-legal nature of the rules. Official sources can play only a limited part in securing their enforcement since the assumption by legal sources such as the Speaker, parliamentary disciplinary committees, or the heads of government departments, of too active a role in invoking sanctions might outrage the expectations of those outside the system, and endanger the system itself.

In attempting to assess the impact of different independent variables on both a legislator's awareness of rules and sanctions and the types of rules and sanctions of which he was aware, it was found that party affiliation, perceptions of conflict with party and constituency and to an extent, the length and type of education a legislator had enjoyed seemed fairly significant. On the other hand, leadership positions, occupation and length of experience in the Commons appeared relatively unimportant.

These findings suggest that the types of rules and sanctions that a legislator is sensitive to in any particular legislative system are primarily determined by what Professor Wahlke termed "circumstantial variables," [21] that is, variables which are transitory and are relative to a particular point in time but which may be particularly salient to the legislators being studied. For example, the data show that the Social Credit and Conservative legislators were more sensitive than were the Liberals or New Democrats to rules which promote party solidarity and propagate the party system. This is

[21] *Ibid.*, pp. 18–20.

particularly interesting since the members of the latter two parties were more party oriented. Why then should a considerably larger percentage of the former two parties emphasize rules that function to promote party solidarity?

It is suggested that circumstantial variables, that is, the Conservative's minority government position and the Social Credit internal troubles made such rules particularly salient for them. The life of the minority Government which the Conservatives formed was continually threatened by the possibility that the opposition parties might unite against them on a vote of confidence or that dissatisfaction with the party would result in sufficient numbers of Conservatives abstaining on a vote to bring down the government. The minority position of the Conservatives may also account for their failure to articulate rules which function to expedite the flow of legislation through the House. We had expected this to be particularly important to the Conservatives since they formed the government and the latter is charged with the responsibility for introducing most of the legislation the House will consider. However as a minority government their chances of being defeated by the opposition parties were directly related to the amount of legislation they introduced, since the more legislation they tried to push through the greater the probability that on a particular bill a coalition would form which would defeat them. Consequently rules which function to expedite the flow of legislation may have been the farthest thing from their minds at the time.

For the Conservatives, then, any informal rules which functioned to promote party unity or solidarity were particularly salient at that time while those which expedite legislation were not. This might not have been the case had the Conservatives been a majority rather than a minority Government party.

Rules that tend to promote party solidarity may have been even more important to the Social Credit group who were made up of a majority wing of twenty-six members from Quebec and a minority wing of four members from the far western provinces of Alberta and British Columbia. Even before the twenty-fifth parliament assembled it became evident that party leader Robert Thompson would have a difficult time controlling either the Quebec wing or their ebullient leader, Real Caouette. The latter frequently issued public statements which were diametrically opposed to the "official" party policy enunciated by Mr. Thompson. Subsequent votes of confidence during the parliamentary session indicated that there were serious internal divisions within the party.[22]

Similarly, the high percentage of members from both minority parties who mentioned rules that function to discourage public criticism may have been related to the widespread criticism of the Social Credit Deputy-Leader occasioned by some of his rather intemperate remarks to the press, and by the unwanted attention

[22] As this was being written, Mr. Caouette formally disavowed the leadership of Mr. Thompson and with eleven other Social Credit members from Quebec formed a new party, Le Ralliement des Creditistes.

the New Democrats received as a result of remarks about the new African States by one of their veteran parliamentary members.[23]

Still another finding which leads us to feel that circumstantial variables are important determinants of the types of rules articulated is the fact that not one of the respondents in the two minor parties mentioned rules which encourage expertise and hard work while 14.2% of the Conservatives and 11.7% of the Liberals articulated such rules. Since the Conservatives formed the government and the Liberals were the only party with a real chance of displacing them, such rules were understandably important for respondents who perceive hard work and expertness in a field as a potential vehicle to a Cabinet post but less so for members of parties with virtually no chance of forming a government in the immediate future.

Finally, the emphasis placed by legislators in conflict with party and constituency on rules that function to mitigate conflict, the concern of Social Credit members with rules that reinforce formal rules and the higher percentage of their members who perceived sanctions emanating from the Speaker, reinforce the feeling that circumstantial variables which are salient to the legislator determine the type of rules and sanctions he articulates.

[23] Mr. Harold Winch's statements to the press on his return to Canada from a visit to Africa, in which he expressed alarm and concern over both the lack of democratic practices in the new African States and the racist attitudes of some African elites, received considerable attention in the national press. It was felt by some that Mr. Winch's statements were also tinged with "racism."

The findings from this study lend support for Wahlke and Ferguson's feeling that rules of the game exist in every legislature. Although there is a remarkable similarity in the types of rules articulated in the House of Commons, the American Senate, and the four State legislatures studied previously, there are also some differences, primarily the significantly higher proportion of Canadian legislators who are unaware of the rules and the sanctions available to enforce adherence to them.

Although only further studies can definitely establish why these differences should exist, we suggest that they may in part be related to the fact that the Canadian House of Commons is a parliamentary system modeled on the British.

In the American Senate and in the State legislatures studied by Professor Wahlke and his colleagues the individual legislator is much more of a "free agent" and has considerably more opportunity to influence the output of the legislative system than in the Canadian Parliament. In the latter system the individual is much more of a "bit player" and the party as a whole the actor who plays the leading roles. Since the individual American legislator has more "to do" in helping the system attain its primary goal—the making of authoritative decisions in the form of legislation—he may be more aware of the informal behavioral norms which are related to that purpose. Another factor *may* be the relative lack of political sophistication of Canadian Members of Parliament in comparison with their American counterparts. The considerably smaller proportion of public offices available to potential aspirants in Canada as compared to the United States coupled with the rise of multipartyism since the thirties has manifested itself in the following situation: Four parties must recruit candidates in two hundred and sixty five districts, in which frequently two or even three of them have little chance of winning. This forces them to frequently recruit "amateurs" [24] whose chief virtues may be that they have sufficient resources to help pay part of the campaign costs and/or be able to maintain two homes on the relatively modest salaries paid

Members of Parliament.[25] The fact that the least amateur of our respondents, the members of the New Democratic party were *all* aware of rules in the House while only one of them was not aware of rules outside the House offers some support for this assumption.

Much more difficult to explain is the lack of awareness of sanctions among Canadian legislators. A number of suggestions have been made as to why this should be the case, not the least important of which may be that an imperfect consensus exists there as to what constitutes a sanction. This is certainly an area which requires further empirical study.

[24] For example, 54.4% of our respondents had never held a public office before becoming a candidate for Parliament, 26.6% had never held an office in their party and 17.8% had never held either a public or a party office. In addition 34.5% were socialized in an environment almost devoid of any mention of politics and 54.8% said they did not seek the office but were recruited by the parties.

[25] At the time these interviews were taken Canadian Members of Parliament were being paid an annual salary of ten thousand dollars. Since then the salary has been increased to eighteen thousand dollars.

TASK GROUP AND SOCIAL GROUP ON THE SUPREME COURT
DAVID J. DANELSKI

The Chief Justice of the United States has a unique opportunity for leadership in the Supreme Court. He presides in open court and over the secret conferences where he usually presents each case to his associates, giving his opinion first and voting last. He assigns the Court's opinion in virtually all cases when he votes with the majority; and when the Court is divided, he is in a favorable position to seek unity. But his office does not guarantee leadership. His actual influence depends upon his esteem, ability, and personality and how he performs his various roles.

IN CONFERENCE

The conference is the matrix of leadership in the Court.[1] The Court member

CREDIT: From *Courts, Judges and Politics,* Walter F. Murphy and C. Herman Pritchett, editors. © Copyright 1961 by Random House, Inc. Reprinted by permission.

[1] This study is based largely on private papers of members of the Supreme Court from 1921 to 1946. The theory of conference leadership is derived primarily from the work of Robert F. Bales. See his "Task Roles and Social Roles in Problem-Solving Groups" in Eleanor E. Maccoby, Theodore M. Newcomb, and Eugene L. Hartley (eds.), *Readings in Social Psychology* (New York: Holt, 1958), pp. 437–447.

who is able to present his views with force and clarity and defend them successfully is highly esteemed by his associates. When perplexing questions arise, they turn to him for guidance. He usually makes more suggestions than his colleagues, gives more opinions, and orients the discussion more frequently, emerging as the Court's task leader. In terms of personality, he is apt to be somewhat reserved; and, in concentrating on the decision of the Court, his response to the emotional needs of his associates is apt to be secondary.

Court members frequently disagree in conference and argue their positions with enthusiasm, seeking to persuade their opponents and the undecided brethren. And always, when the discussion ends, the vote declares the victor. All of this gives rise to antagonism and tension, which, if allowed to get out of hand, would make intelligent, orderly decision of cases virtually impossible. However, the negative aspects of conference interaction are more or less counterbalanced by activity which relieves tension, shows solidarity, and makes for agreement. One Court member usually performs more such activity than the others. He invites opinions and suggestions. He attends to the emotional needs of his associates by affirming their value as individuals and as Court members, especially when their views are rejected by the majority. Ordinarily he is the best-liked member of the Court and emerges as its social leader. While the task leader concentrates on the Court's decision, the social leader concentrates on keeping the Court socially cohesive. In terms of personality, he is apt to be warm, receptive, and responsive. Being liked by his associates is ordinarily quite important to him; he is also apt to dislike conflict.

As presiding officer of the conference, the Chief Justice is in a favorable position to assert task and social leadership. His presentation of cases is an important task function. His control of the conference's process makes it easy for him to invite suggestions and opinions, seek compromises, and cut off debate which appears to be getting out of hand, all important social functions.

It is thus possible for the Chief Justice to emerge as both task and social leader of the conference. This, however, requires the possession of a rare combination of qualities plus adroit use of them. Normally, one would expect the functions of task and social leadership to be performed by at least two Court members, one of whom might or might not be the Chief Justice. As far as the Chief Justice is concerned, the following leadership situations are possible:

	Task Leadership	*Social Leadership*
I	+	+
II	−	+
III	+	−
IV	−	−

In situation I, the Chief Justice is a "great man" leader, performing both leadership functions. The consequences of such leadership, stated as hypotheses, are: (1) conflict tends to be minimal; (2) social cohesion tends to increase; (3) satisfaction with the conference tends to increase; (4) production, in terms of number of decisions for the time spent, tends to increase. The consequences in situations II and III are the same as in I, particularly if the Chief Justice works in coalition with the associate justice performing complementary leadership functions. However, in situation IV, unless the task and social functions are adequately performed by associate justices, consequences opposite to those in situations I, II, and III tend to occur. . . .

Situation II prevailed in the Taft Court (1921–1930): Chief Justice Taft was social leader, and his good friend and appointee, Justice Van Devanter, was task leader. Evidence of Van Devanter's esteem and task leadership is abundant. Taft, for example, frequently asserted that Van Devanter was the ablest member of the Court. If the Court were to vote, he said, that would be its judgment too. The Chief Justice admitted that he did not know how he could get along without Van Devanter in conference, for Van Devanter kept the Court consistent with itself, and "his power of statement and his immense memory make him an antagonist in conference who generally wins against all opposition." At times, Van Devanter's ability actually embarrassed the Chief Justice, and he wondered if it might not be better to have Van Devanter run the conference himself. "Still," said Taft, "I must worry along until the end of my ten years, content to aid in the deliberation when there is a difference of opinion." In other words, Taft was content to perform the social functions of leadership. And he did this well. His humor soothed over the rough spots in conference. "We are very happy with the present Chief," said Holmes in 1922. "He is good-humored, laughs readily, not quite rapid enough, but keeps things moving pleasantly."

Situation I prevailed in the Hughes Court (1930–1941): task and social leadership were combined in Chief Justice Hughes. He was the most esteemed member of his Court. This was due primarily to his performance in conference. Blessed with a photographic memory, he would summarize comprehensively and accurately the facts and issues in each case he presented. When he finished, he would look up and say with a smile: "Now I will state where I come out." Then he would outline his views as to how the case should be decided. Sometimes that is all the discussion a case received, and the justices proceeded to vote for the disposition suggested by the Chief. Where there was discussion, the other Court members gave their views in order of seniority without interruption, stating why they concurred or dissented from the views of the Chief Justice. After they had their say, Hughes would review the discussion, pointing out his agreement and disagreement with the views expressed. Then he would call for a vote.

As to the social side of Hughes' leadership, there is the testimony of Justice Roberts: never in the eleven years Roberts sat with Hughes in conference did he see him lose his temper. Never did he hear him pass a personal remark or even raise his voice. Never did he witness him interrupting or engaging in controversy with an associate. Despite Hughes' popular image of austerity, several of his associates have said that he had a keen sense of humor which aided in keeping differences in conference from becoming discord. Moreover, when discussion showed signs of deteriorating into wrangling, Hughes would cut it off. On the whole, he was well-liked. Justice Roberts said: "Men whose views were as sharply opposed as those of Van Devanter and Brandeis, or those of Sutherland and Cardozo, were at one in their admiration and affectionate regard for their presiding officer." Roberts could have well added Justices Holmes, Black, Reed, Frankfurter, Douglas, McReynolds, and perhaps others.

Situation IV prevailed during most of Stone's Chief Justiceship (1941–1946). When Stone was promoted to the center chair, Augustus Hand indicated in a letter to Hughes that Stone did not seem a sure bet as task leader because of "a certain inability to express himself orally and maintain a position in a discussion." Hand proved to be correct. Stone departed from the conference role cut out by Hughes. When he presented cases, he lacked the apparent certitude of his predecessor; and, at times, his statement indicated that he was still groping for a solution. In that posture, cases were passed on to his associates for discussion. Court members spoke out of turn, and Stone did little to control their debate. Instead, according to Justice Reed, he would join in the debate with alacrity, "delighted to take on all comers around the conference table." "Jackson," he would say, "that's damned nonsense." "Douglas, *you* know better than that."

In other words, Stone was still acting like an associate justice. Since he did not assume the Chief Justice's conference role as performed by Hughes, task leadership began to slip from his grasp. Eventually, Justice Black emerged as the leading contender for task leadership. Stone esteemed Black, but distrusted his unorthodox approach; thus no coalition occurred as in the Taft Court. Justices Douglas, Murphy, Rutledge, and, to a lesser degree, Reed acknowledged Black's leadership which he was able to reinforce by generally speaking before them in conference. Justices Roberts, Frankfurter, and Jackson, however, either looked to Stone for leadership or competed for it themselves.

The constant vying for task leadership in the Stone conference led to serious conflict, ruffled tempers, severe tension, and antagonism. A social leader was badly needed. Stone was well-liked by his associates and could have performed this function well, but he did not. He did not use his control over the conference process to cut off debates leading to irreconcilable conflict. He did not remain neutral when controversies arose so that he could later mediate them. As his biographer, Alpheus T. Mason, wrote: "He was totally unprepared to cope with the petty bickering and personal conflict in which his Court became engulfed." At times, when conference discussion became extremely heated, Justice Murphy suggested that further consideration of certain cases be postponed. Undoubtedly others also performed social functions of leadership, but in this regard, Stone was a failure.

A consideration of the personalities of the task and social leaders on the Court from 1921 to 1946 is revealing. Of his friend, task leader Van Devanter, William D. Mitchell said: "Many thought him unusually austere, but he was not so with his friends. He was dignified and reserved." Of task leader Black, his former law clerk, John P. Frank, wrote: "Black has firm personal dignity and reserve. . . . [He] is a very, very tough man. When he is convinced, he is cool hard steel. . . . His temper is usually in close control, but he fights, and his words may occasionally have a terrible edge. He can be a rough man in an argument." On the other hand, social leader Taft was a warm, genial, responsive person who disliked conflict of any kind. Stone had a similar personality. He, too, according to Justice Jackson, "dreaded conflict." Hughes' personality contained elements conducive to both task and social leadership. He was "an intense man," said Justice Roberts; when he was engrossed in the work of the Court, "he had not time for lightness and pleasantry." Nonetheless, added Roberts, Hughes' relations with "his brethren were genial and cordial. He was considerate, sympathetic, and responsive."

The consequences of the various Court leadership configurations from 1921 to 1946 are summarized in the chart on page 270.

Except in production, the Taft Court fared better than the Courts under his two successors. The consequences of leadership in the Stone Court were predictable from the hypotheses, but Hughes' "great man" lead-

	Taft (II)	*Hughes (I)*	*Stone (IV)*
Conflict	Present but friendly.	Present but bridled by CJ.	Considerable; unbridled and at times unfriendly.
Cohesion	Good; teamwork and compromise.	Fair; surface personal cordiality; less teamwork than in Taft Court.	Poor; least cohesion in 25-year period; personal feuds in the Court.
Satisfaction	Considerable.	Mixed; Stone dissatisfied prior to 1938; Frankfurter, Roberts, and others highly satisfied.	Least in 25-year period; unrelieved tension and antagonism.
Production	Fair; usually one four- to five-hour conference a week with some items carried over.	Good; usually one conference a week.	Poor; frequently more than one conference a week; sometimes three and even four.

ership should have produced consequences more closely approximating those in the Taft Court. The difference in conflict, cohesion, and satisfaction in the two Courts can be perhaps attributed to the fact that Taft was a better social leader than Hughes.

OPINION ASSIGNMENT

The Chief Justice's power to assign opinions is significant because his designation of the Court's spokesman may be instrumental in:

1. Determining the value of a decision as a precedent, for the grounds of a decision frequently depend upon the justice assigned the opinion.

2. Making a decision as acceptable as possible to the public.

3. Holding the Chief Justice's majority together when the conference vote is close.

4. Persuading dissenting associates to join in the Court's opinion.

The Chief Justice has maximal control over an opinion when he assigns it to himself; undoubtedly Chief Justices have retained many important cases for that reason. The Chief Justice's retention of "big cases" is generally accepted by his associates. In fact, they expect him to speak for the Court in those cases so that he may lend the prestige of his office to the Court's pronouncement.

When the Chief Justice does not speak for the Court, his influence lies primarily in his assignment of important cases to associates who generally agree with him. From 1925 to 1930, Taft designated his fellow conservatives, Sutherland and Butler, to speak for the Court in about half of the important constitutional cases [2] assigned to associate justices. From 1932 to 1937, Hughes, who agreed more with Roberts, Van Devanter, and Sutherland than the rest of his associates during this period, assigned 44 per cent of the important constitutional cases to Roberts and Sutherland. From 1943 to 1945, Stone assigned 55.5 per cent of those cases to Douglas and Frankfurter. During that period, only Reed agreed more with Stone than Frankfurter, but Douglas agreed with Stone less than any other justice except Black. Stone had high regard for Douglas' ability, and this may have been the Chief Justice's overriding consideration in making these assignments.

It is possible that the Chief Justice might seek to influence dissenting justices to join in the Court's opinion by adhering to one or both of the following assignment rules:

Rule 1: Assign the case to the justice whose views are the closest to the dissenters on the ground that his opinion would take a middle approach upon which both majority and minority could agree.

Rule 2: Where there are blocs on the Court and a bloc splits, assign the opinion to a majority member of the dissenters'

bloc on the grounds that (a) he would take a middle approach upon which both majority and minority could agree and (b) the minority justices would be more likely to agree with him because of general mutuality of agreement.

There is some evidence that early in Taft's Chief Justiceship he followed Rule 1 occasionally and assigned himself cases in an effort to win over dissenters. An analysis of his assignments from 1925 to 1930, however, indicates that he apparently did not adhere to either of the rules with any consistency. The same is true for Stone's assignments from 1943 to 1945. In other words, Taft and Stone did not generally use their assignment power to influence their associates to unanimity. However, an analysis of Hughes' assignments from 1932 to 1937 indicates that he probably did. He appears to have followed Rule 1 when either the liberal or conservative blocs dissented intact. When the liberal bloc dissented, Roberts, who was then a center judge, was assigned 46 per cent of the opinions. The remaining 54 per cent were divided among the conservatives, apparently according to their degree of conservatism: Sutherland, 25 per cent; Butler, 18 per cent; McReynolds, 11 per cent. When the conservative bloc dissented, Hughes divided 63 per cent of those cases between himself and Roberts.

Hughes probably also followed Rule 2. When the left bloc split, Brandeis was assigned 22 per cent of the cases he could have received compared with his 10 per cent average for unanimous cases. When the right bloc split, Sutherland was assigned 16 per cent of the decisions he could have received compared with his 11 per cent

---

[2] "Important constitutional cases" were determined by examination of four recent leading works on the Constitution. If a case was discussed in any two of the works, it was considered an "important constitutional case."

average for unanimous cases. He received five of the six cases assigned the conservatives when their bloc split.

Of course, there are other considerations underlying opinion assignment by the Chief Justice, such as equality of distribution, ability, and expertise. It should be noted that opinion assignment may also be a function of social leadership.

UNITING THE COURT

One of the Chief Justice's most important roles is that of Court unifier. Seldom has a Chief Justice had a more definite conception of that role than Taft. His aim was unanimity, but he was willing to admit that at times dissents were justifiable and perhaps even a duty. Dissents were proper, he thought, in cases where a Court member strongly believed the majority erred in a matter involving important principle or where a dissent might serve some useful purpose, such as convincing Congress to pass certain legislation. But, in other cases, he believed a justice should be a good member of the team, silently acquiesce in the views of the majority, and not try to make a record for himself by dissenting.

Since Taft's conception of the function of the dissent was shared by most of his associates, his efforts toward unity were well received. Justices joining the Taft Court were indoctrinated in the "no dissent unless absolutely necessary" tradition, most of them learning it well. Justice Butler gave it classic expression on the back of one colleague's opinions in 1928:

I voted to reverse. While this sustains your conclusion to affirm, I still think reversal would be better. But I shall in silence acquiesce. Dissents seldom aid in the right development or statement of the law. They often do harm. For myself I say: "lead us not into temptation."

Hughes easily assumed the role of Court unifier which Taft cut out for him, for his views as to unanimity and dissent were essentially the same as Taft's. Believing that some cases were not worthy of dissent, he would join in the majority's disposition of them, though he initially voted the other way. For example, in a 1939 case involving statutory construction, he wrote to an associate: "I choke a little at swallowing your analysis, still I do not think it would serve any useful purpose to expose my views."

Like Taft, Hughes mediated differences of opinion between contending factions, and in order to get a unanimous decision, he would try to find common ground upon which all could stand. He was willing to modify his own opinions to hold or increase his majority; and if this meant he had to put in some disconnected thoughts or sentences, in they went. In cases assigned to others, he would readily suggest the addition or subtraction of a paragraph in order to save a dissent or a concurring opinion.

When Stone was an associate justice, he prized the right to dissent and occasionally rankled under the "no dissent unless absolutely necessary" tradition of the Taft and Hughes Courts. As Chief Justice, he did not believe it appropriate for him to dissuade Court members from dissenting in individual cases by persuasion or otherwise. A Chief Justice, he thought, might admonish his associates generally to exercise restraint in the matter of dissents and seek to find common ground for decision, but beyond that he should not go. And Stone usually went no further. His activity or lack of it in this regard gave rise to new expectations on the part of his associates as to their role and the role of the Chief Justice regarding unanimity and dissent. In the early 1940's, a new tradition of freedom of individual expression displaced the tradition of the Taft and Hughes Courts. This explains in part the unprecedented number of dissents and separate opinions during Stone's Chief Justiceship.

Nonetheless, Stone recognized that unanimity was desirable in certain cases. He patiently negotiated a unanimous decision in the Nazi Saboteurs case.[3] It should be pointed out, however, that this case was decided early in his Chief Justiceship before the new tradition was firmly established. By 1946, when he sought unanimity in the case of General Yamashita,[4] the new tradition of freedom was so well established that Stone not only failed to unite his Court, but the dissenters, Murphy and Rutledge, apparently resented his attempt to do so.

The unprecedented number of dissents and concurrences during Stone's Chief Justiceship can be only partly attributed to the displacing of the old tradition of loyalty to the Court's opinion. A major source of difficulty appears to have been the free-and-easy expression of views in conference. Whether the justices were sure of their grounds or not, they spoke up and many times took positions from which they could not easily retreat; given the heated debate which sometimes occurred in the Stone conference, the commitment was not simply intellectual. What began in conference frequently ended with elaborate justification as concurring or dissenting opinions in the United States Reports. This, plus Stone's passiveness in seeking to attain unanimity, is probably the best explanation for what Pritchett characterized as "the multiplication of division" in the Stone Court.

CONCLUSION

Interpersonal influence in the Supreme Court is an important aspect of the judicial process which has been given little attention. Of course, the "why" of the Court's decisions cannot be explained solely or even predominantly in those terms. Yet interpersonal influence is a variable worthy of consideration. Take, for example, the Court's about-face in the flag salute cases. With task leader Hughes presiding in 1940, not a single justice indicated in conference that he would dissent in the Gobitis[5] case. Subsequently, Stone registered a solo dissent, but such militant civil libertarians as Black, Douglas, and Murphy remained with Hughes. Only three years later, the Court reversed itself in the Barnette[6] case with Black, Douglas, and Murphy voting with Stone. One might seriously ask whether the presence of Hughes in the first case and not

---

[3] *Ex parte Quirin* (1942).

[4] *In re Yamashita* (1946).

[5] *Minersville School District* v. *Gobitis* (1940).

[6] *West Virginia* v. *Barnette* (1943).

in the second had something to do with the switch. Much more work has to be done in this area, but it appears that in future analyses of the Court's work, task and social leadership will be useful concepts.

The importance of the Chief Justice's power to assign opinions is obvious. Equally if not more important is his role in unifying the Court. Taft's success in this regard greatly contributed to the Court's prestige, for unanimity reinforces the myth that the law is certain. In speaking of the Court in 1927, Hughes said that "no institution of our government stands higher in public confidence." As Court unifier, he sought to maintain that confidence after his appointment in 1930. That the Court's prestige is correlated with unanimity was demonstrated in Stone's Chief Justiceship: as dissent rose, the Court's prestige declined.

Thus the activity of the Chief Justice can be very significant in the judicial process. If he is the Court's task leader, he has great influence in the allocation of political values which are inevitably involved in many of the Court's decisions. More than any of his associates, his activity is apt to affect the Court's prestige; this is important, for ultimately the basis of the Court's power is its prestige.

LIVING TOGETHER AS STRANGERS
DONALD R. MATTHEWS AND JAMES W. PROTHRO

On September 15, 1964, the people of Tuskegee, Alabama, trooped quietly to the polls to vote in a city election. Otherwise life went on much as before in the run-down and sleepy-looking little town in the midst of Alabama's black belt. But by nightfall it was apparent that a momentous event had occurred that day in Tuskegee: among the men the voters had elected to the city council were the Reverend K. L. Buford and Dr. S. H. Smith. Both were Negroes—the first members of their race to be elected to public office in the state of Alabama since Reconstruction.[1]

The Tuskegee story is too long and involved to repeat here.[2] If Booker T. Washington had not established Tuskegee Institute there in 1881, if the Supreme Court of the United States had not outlawed an outrageous racial gerrymander of the city in 1960, if the United States Congress had not passed the Civil Rights Act of 1957, if the United States Justice Department had not intervened to ensure that local Negroes were given a reasonable chance to become registered voters, the outcome of the 1964 municipal election would have been very different. The complex of events and forces that resulted in a Negro majority among the town's voters is not likely to occur frequently in the South.

Even so, the Tuskegee municipal election of 1964 is a symbol of revolutionary change. Politics is no longer just a white man's game in the South. Throughout most of the region, politics is now biracial. It has been that way in Piedmont County for decades and in Camellia County for years; Negroes in Bright Leaf County are becoming a political force to be reckoned with. Only in Crayfish County, and other counties like it, do the old rules of southern politics still hold. This, too, will change in time. In the new southern politics Negroes have political power, and their power is growing. In this and subsequent chapters we shall try to determine what this seem-

CREDIT: From *Negroes and the New Southern Politics* by Donald R. Matthews and James W. Prothro, © 1966 by Harcourt, Brace & World, Inc. and reprinted with their permission. [*Figures, tables, and some footnotes renumbered. The title of this selection was the title of an editorial in the Norfolk, Virginia, Pilot, September 26, 1962, stimulated by an earlier report of the findings of Professors Matthews and Prothro.*]

[1] *New York Times*, September 16, 1964; *Birmingham News* (Alabama), September 16, 1964. Four additional Negroes were elected to county office on November 4 of the same year. See Bernard Taper, "Reporter at Large: A Break with Tradition," *New Yorker*, July 24, 1965, pp. 58ff., for a description of subsequent events.

[2] Much of the history and background of the Tuskegee story may be found in Bernard Taper, *Gomillion versus Lightfoot* (New York: McGraw-Hill, 1962).

ingly irreversible change means for the future of the South.

WHAT NEGROES WANT

The basic fact about the new southern politics is that most southern Negroes desperately want something that most southern whites are adamantly unwilling to give—equality. Philosophers have argued endlessly about the meaning of the word, but to southern Negroes equality has a clear and simple meaning. They want to be treated as men, not as Negroes. They want a world, as one Negro college student from Virginia put it, in which "race is just about as important as eye color," a world in which a "human being is a human being regardless of race or color." This vision is widely shared. When asked if they prefer "integration, strict segregation, or something in between," 65 per cent of southern Negroes chose integration.

Southern whites, on the other hand, just as strongly want strict segregation; 64 per cent of them chose this alternative when presented with the same question.[3] When we present the distribution of these preferences graphically, as in Figure III-10, the magnitude of the Negro-white conflict in the South emerges dramatically. On the question of segregation—which is the pivot around which all else revolves in the South—the southern population is divided into two hostile groups, with solid support for segrega-

[3] In order to facilitate interviewing, we reversed the alternatives for white respondents to read "strict segregation, integration, or something in between."

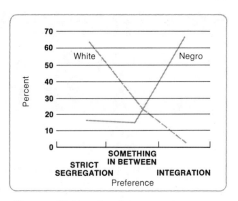

Figure III-10. Southerners' preferences on integration-segregation

tion by whites and for integration by Negroes.

Perhaps the most startling aspect of this awesome division is that Negroes support integration as solidly as whites support segregation. For three and a half centuries they have been treated as inherently inferior beings. All this time, they have been under great pressure to accept dominant white values. And they have done so in most areas—from cosmetics to religion. But not many have succumbed to the white image of proper race relations.

This sharp racial division would not be so frightening if these conflicting opinions were not so deeply felt and intensely held by both races. On most policy questions, a sizable portion of the citizenry has no opinion; this is especially true in a region of relatively low education such as the South. But on this question only 1 per cent of the whites and 4 per cent of the Negroes gave a "don't know" response. In addition, people who don't much care tend to choose "in between" rather than extreme responses to survey questions. Despite the fact that our question used the term *"strict* segregation," only 28 per cent of the whites and 14 per cent of the Negroes took the "in between" position.

But we need not rely solely on these inferences to judge the intensity with which southerners—both Negro and white—hold their incompatible racial views. Let our respondents speak for themselves. "They 'minds me of a rattlesnake," a 78-year-old Negro farmer in Camellia County said, referring to his white neighbors. "Sometimes you can get by one, then again you bound to get struck." A Negro man in Capital City was more vehement and explicit: "The Lord needs to kill every last one of them." "It's not but one way for them [Negroes and whites] to live together and get along," a Negro yardman living hundreds of miles away said, "and that's for the Old Jim Crow race to die out." "I couldn't imagine that," a Negro watchman in Piedmont County said, when asked to describe the best race relations possible, " 'cause white folks would kill us before they'd let that happen."

Hatred flows both ways. A white dairyman in Crayfish County defined his ideal of race relations as, "Back to slavery! That would put them [Negroes] where low-down white trash from the North couldn't make them believe they are better than southern white people." A truck driver in rural Georgia expressed his ideal just as starkly: "Give all the whites a shotgun!"

These attitudes, fears, and hatreds are not new. But in the past the awesome gap between Negro and white aspirations could safely be ignored—the white man ran the South in his own way, and the rest of the nation was not disposed to do anything about it. The politically effective part of the South—the white part—was united on racial policy and Negroes could do little about it—except to move North. Now the situation is very different. Increasingly, the southern Negro is armed with the vote; he enjoys at least some political power; his attitudes and aspirations count. The political future of the South will be dominated by a deep and bitter division along racial lines on the major problem of the region.

Leaders of each race thus have a minimum of maneuverability on racial issues. On most other issues, the predominance of moderate opinions and of popular indifference affords a cushion of ambiguity that permits leaders to act. They can work out compromises without knowing for certain what the popular response will be— or that any response at all will follow. In the South today the white leader who contemplates a tentative step toward accommodating Negro demands can expect to be labeled a "nigger-lover"; the Negro who cooperates with white leaders can expect to be labeled an "Uncle Tom." Indeed, we seriously wonder whether a viable political system in the South will be possible, granted the extreme polarization of opinion, without one race being dominated by the other.

This situation is more severe in some parts of the South than in others. In Figure III-11 the race-relations preferences of Negroes and whites are presented for the four communities we studied in detail. In Piedmont and Camellia counties, the conflict between the two races is severe. In the

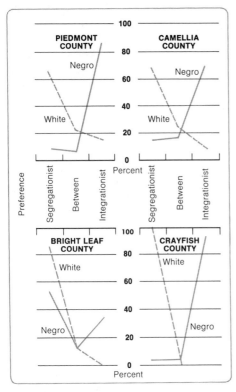

Figure III-11. Southerners' preferences on integration-segregation, by community

upper South county, 86 per cent of the Negroes want integration while 63 per cent of the whites prefer strict segregation; in Camellia County, the whites are somewhat more likely to be segregationists (67 per cent), but a somewhat smaller proportion of the Negroes (68 per cent) are committed to integration than in Piedmont. In both counties, however, fairly sizable minorities of whites are "moderates" (22 per cent in Piedmont and 24 per cent in Camellia) and a small but significant number are integrationists (15 per cent in Piedmont and 9 per cent in Camellia). One out of every three white adults in Piedmont is not a seg-

regationist; in Camellia County one third of the Negroes are not integrationists. Both communities, then, have at least some middle ground; the consensus *within* each race is not monolithic.

The two rural counties we studied differ from Piedmont and Camellia and from each other as well. The Bright Leaf County Negroes are less committed to the goal of integration than the Negroes in the other communities—only a third of them chose this alternative while half said they preferred race relations as they were. Apparently the paternalism of the whites in the county has resulted in a more contented Negro population than is found in either of the urban counties or in Crayfish. Thus, while the Bright Leaf whites are overwhelmingly in favor of strict segregation (87 per cent), the conflict between white and Negro preferences is relatively mild. The figures for Crayfish, on the other hand, show almost complete consensus *within* each race and almost complete discord *between* them: only 8 per cent of the Negroes and 2 per cent of the whites fail to go along with the majority of their own race. The middle ground of opinion has disappeared. The potential for racial conflict in this situation is almost absolute. The accommodation of such a vast conflict through democratic political processes seems virtually impossible.

But perhaps we are overstressing the potential for racial conflict in these communities and in the South as a whole. Gunnar Myrdal, in his *An American Dilemma,*[4] placed heavy stress on a tension-reducing mecha-

[4] (New York: Harper, 1964), ch. 3, part 4.

nism, called "the rank order of discriminations," which we have not yet considered. White people, "nearly unanimously" according to Myrdal, rate some types of racial discrimination above others, with the bar against intermarriage and sexual relations between Negro males and white females at the top, and discrimination in the courts, by the police, or in routine economic transactions near the bottom. And, Myrdal says, "The Negroes' own rank order is just about parallel, but inverse, to that of the white man." [5] Thus the areas of life in which Negroes most want desegregation are the areas in which white men are most likely to give in to their demands, and vice versa. Obviously the effect of this happy congruence is greatly to reduce the conflict stemming from the South's clashing racial attitudes.

But Myrdal's theory was based, as he was the first to point out, on unsystematic impressions. And a very great deal has happened to American race relations since Myrdal wrote his classic. Can we count on the "rank order of discriminations" to reduce the politico-racial tensions in the South today and in the future?

We can explore this question by looking at how Negroes and whites define and describe "the very best way that Negroes and white people could live in the same place together," and its opposite, the worst possible arrangement of a biracial community. The frequency with which Negroes and whites mentioned specific realms of life in answering this open-ended question provides a measure of the value they attach to each; these figures

5 *Ibid.*, p. 61.

are presented in Table III-9. In Table III-10 the percentage of whites favoring strict segregation and of Negroes favoring rapid integration of these same areas of social life are juxtaposed.

The first thing to notice in Table III-9 is that very few Negroes, as compared to whites, mentioned specific areas of community living. This cannot be dismissed merely as the reflection of lower levels of education among Negroes; these same Negro respondents proved as voluble and articulate as whites in responding to other open-ended questions about subjects of less emotional import to them at other points in the interview. Rather, the Negroes tended not to refer to concrete areas of life in describing their pictures of the best (and worst) of all racial arrangements because they wanted equality in all of them. Unlike the whites, they felt little need to specify, qualify, or explain. Thus, for example, a junior at Florida A. and M. University said:

I would say an ideal situation would be for Negroes and whites to repress the idea of skin coloration to such an extent that one neighbor would be regarded with the same esteem as any other; become Mary, the next door neighbor, not Mary, the white neighbor or vice versa. Period, amen, amen.

Negroes tend to think about segregation and desegregation in these global terms rather than in any rank order of preferences.

The whites, on the other hand, seem to have been considerably more anxious about the possible desegregation of some areas of life than others. At the time of our interviews, the desegregation of the public schools was uppermost in their minds—six out of

TABLE III-9 Percentage of Whites and Negroes Mentioning Specific Areas of Life in Describing Best Possible and Worst Possible Race Relations

	White	*Negro*
Public schools	60%	9%
Housing and residential patterns	55	13
Sex and marriage	52	14
Churches and religion	36	6
Public accommodations	32	5
Personal relationships	30	13
Jobs and employment	12	8

TABLE III-10 Percentage of Whites and Negroes Mentioning Specific Areas of Life Favoring Strict Segregation and Rapid Integration of Area Mentioned

	Whites favoring strict segregation	*Negroes favoring rapid integration*
Sex and marriage	98%	1%
Churches and religion	92	50
Housing and residential patterns	85	13
Public schools	83	34
Public accommodations	75	53
Personal relations	65	55
Jobs and employment	44	45

every ten white respondents volunteered some comment about what the racial composition of the schools should be. Eighty-five per cent of those mentioning the matter were opposed to even token desegregation. "What puzzles me is that they are so dirty . . . ," a housewife in Texas said. "I wish they could change and be more like we are. Of course I wouldn't want a child like that, all dirty and filthy, in school with my children." A brick mason in Arkansas made another popular argument—"They [Negroes] don't want to have schools together any more than we do." And a college professor in Capital City, who was among the small minority of whites who favored token desegregation of the schools, explained why he was reluctant to go beyond that point. "I'd say I was for complete integration," he reported, "but I know what a financial strain it would put on me to send my children to private schools. . . . I think under present [conditions] the intellectual loss to my children [resulting from wholesale desegregation] would be too great."

Almost as many whites—55 per cent—mentioned housing and residential patterns as mentioned the schools, and the opposition to "mixing" in this realm was equally strong. "Put a high fence around them," a 35-year-old man in Little Rock said. "I don't want them anywhere around. . . . They need to have separate schools, separate neighborhoods, and separate everything!" In rural Georgia a young man with a high-school education defined his ideal of race relations as "Just like it is—separate schools, housing, separate social life. Can you imagine living close to a nigger juke joint?"

But the young wife of a labor-union official in Florida, an avowed integrationist, was able to see Negroes as something more than an undifferentiated mass. "I wouldn't want my children going to school or church or anywhere with 'trash' whether they were white or colored," she said. "I wouldn't care if they [Negroes] lived next door to me if they lived the same as I did—clean, and kept their properties up, etc. . . . They should be able to live in a social class that they are able to afford." Very few southern whites are able to draw such elementary distinctions about Negroes.

Over half (52 per cent) of the whites were worried about intermarriage and sexual relations across race lines—and 98 per cent of these were steadfastly against it. "I know a Negro man over here," a white dairy farmer in Crayfish County said, "who is living with his daughter and having a child every year for 'The Welfare' to take care of—now you know white people don't do things like that. The worst thing would be intermarriage." A middle-aged housewife in Arkansas said: "I just can't feature my daughter and son dancing with niggers even if Mrs. Roosevelt did." Another housewife, this one in Georgia, was convinced that intermarriage "would bring on a war between the Negroes and white people." An elderly lady in a neighboring state disagreed:

Some people are scared to death [that] their children will marry niggers but any white boy or girl that's that big a fool—there's no use worrying about. If they have to go to a school together, it doesn't necessarily follow they'll marry! That's silly. People ordinarily marry people with similar backgrounds and those that go overboard—let 'em!

Interestingly enough, sexual relations and intermarriage were the areas of life most often mentioned by Negroes, too—although only 14 per cent of them did so. Almost all Negroes mentioning the matter did so to express resentment at the white males' traditional access to Negro females and to deny their interest in intermarriage. A college sophomore in North Carolina said: "Most people think when you integrate a community you want intermarriage, and this isn't so." "When I say integration," a 45-year-old Negro carpenter in Texas explained, "I mean equal opportunity for jobs, [equal access to] public places, tax-supported places, not necessarily social contact."

The sexual exploitation of Negro women by white men rankled some of the older Negroes. One of them, a farmer in Georgia, defined the worst possible race relations as ". . . the white man sneaking around the colored women. . . ." A Negro housewife in Alabama, who would no doubt be classified by the educational authorities as functionally illiterate, gave our interviewer a little lesson in southern semantics: "When white folks say 'mix' they mean some white man having him a colored woman. That's all 'mix' means to them."

Very few Negroes—only about 1 per cent of those mentioning the issue

—agreed with the freshman at Bethune-Cookman College who said that integration inevitably involved intermarriage ". . . because marriage produces the families and families make the communities."

No other areas of life concerned the whites quite so much as the public schools, housing and residential patterns, and sex and marriage. However, about one third of the whites did mention churches or religion, public accommodations, and personal relationships and racial etiquette. They expressed overwhelming disapproval of moves to integrate the region's churches (92 per cent) or public places (75 per cent), or to do away with traditional modes of treating Negroes in personal relationships (65 per cent). Very few whites mentioned jobs and employment practices at all— apparently this is not a highly salient issue for them. Moreover, this is the only area of life in which a majority of the whites who do think about it favor some policy other than strict segregation.

We see, then, that Myrdal's insight about a "rank order of discriminations" holds only partially true. True, intermarriage and racially integrated housing are highly salient issues among southern whites, and very few southern Negroes are inclined to push rapidly for either one. Equal job opportunities for Negroes do not seem to worry white southerners— indeed, most of them seem to favor the idea. But the conflict potential in all other realms of life is still exceedingly high. In these areas, as can be seen in Table III-10, large majorities of whites still oppose what most Negroes want very badly. The "rank order of dis-

criminations" may have eliminated some troublesome problems from the political arena for the time being, but the organization of most of the social life in the South still remains at issue. And the willingness of southern Negroes to postpone efforts at integrating some areas of life is solely a matter of expediency, of political tactics. In the long run, they insist that southern whites become colorblind.

FAREWELL TO UNCLE TOM

Although a large majority of southern Negroes are deeply committed to the goal of racial integration, about one in every three Negroes is not. Sixteen per cent of the Negroes interviewed indicated a preference for "strict segregation" and another 15 per cent for "something in between" strict segregation and integration. This is a significant minority of opinion. Perhaps this group may be able to convert other Negroes to a less militant racial stance in the future. Perhaps, in league with the tiny group of moderate and integrationist whites, they will be able to bridge the gap between white and Negro majorities.

Even the most casual examination of these Negroes rules out this possibility. Table III-11 compares the social and economic characteristics of the Negroes who are not integrationists with the characteristics of those who are. The Negro "Uncle Toms" [6] and,

---

[6] A logical possibility is that some Negroes who prefer segregation are not "Uncle Toms" but believers in black supremacy of the type espoused by the Black Muslims. An examination of the Negro respondents favoring segregation, however,

TABLE III-11   Social Characteristics of Southern Negroes Preferring Strict Segregation, Integration, and "Something in Between"

Respondent characteristics	*Racial preference*		
	Segregation (N=94)	*In between* (N=89)	*Integration* (N=400)
Blue-collar occupation	99%	91%	87%
Grade-school education or less	88	53	51
Income less than $2,000 a year	86	56	48
Female	71	69	56
Grew up on farm	71	51	57
Over 60 years of age	34	22	23
Never been outside of South	45	38	35
Lives in Deep South	46	48	38

NOTE: The numbers indicate the percentage of Negroes with a given racial attitude who possess the characteristics listed in the lefthand column. Thus 99 per cent of the Negro segregationists have blue-collar occupations.

to a lesser degree, the Negroes who are "in between" prove to be a miserable lot, ill equipped to provide the kind of leadership needed to ameliorate the South's politico-racial cleavage. Almost all of them are blue-collar workers with a grade-school education at best and with a family income of less than $2,000 a year. They tend also, in disproportionate numbers, to be elderly women with rural backgrounds and limited exposure to the patterns of life outside the American South. The proportion of them to be found in the Deep South is slightly larger than on the edges of the region, but the harshness of Negro life in the Deep South apparently has produced very little "payoff" in more frequent Negro acquiescence to white supremacy. The southwide resistance to white preferences in race relations is the more impressive in view of the great differences between the Deep South and the Pe-

reveals so few potential black nationalists that this group can safely be assumed to consist almost entirely of old-style "Uncle Toms."

ripheral South in Negro political participation and in white attitudes.

A look at the political and psychological characteristics of Negroes not committed to racial integration underscores this picture of ignorance, poverty, and apathy (see Table III-12). Seventy per cent of the Negro segregationists (as compared to 41 per cent of the integrationists) are "not much interested" in politics; 80 per cent (compared to 50 per cent of the integrationists) have never voted. Negro Uncle Toms are very poorly informed about public affairs—62 per cent as compared to 47 and 28 per cent of the uncommitted Negroes and integrationists answered fewer than three questions correctly on our information test. They tend to be relatively resistant to the idea of change and relatively unconcerned about the fate of other members of their own race.

Segregationist sentiment among Negroes cannot be expected to have political importance. The politically active segment of the Negro popula-

TABLE III-12 Political and Psychological Characteristics of Southern Negroes Preferring Strict Segregation, Integration, and "Something in Between"

	Racial preference		
Respondent characteristics	Segregation (N=94)	In between (N=89)	Integration (N=400)
Has never voted	80%	69%	50%
Not much interested in politics	70	56	41
Poorly informed about politics (0–2 correct)	62	47	28
Highly resistant to idea of change (Types V–VI)	68	46	40
Not much interested in other Negroes	23	8	5
Has participated beyond voting (PPS types IV–V)	19	25	45

NOTE: See note to Table III-11.

tion in the South is far more devoted to integration than is the total Negro population. If we consider the racial views of only politically active Negroes (PPS types III, IV, and V), we find 78 per cent (as compared to 65 per cent for the total Negro population) devoted to integration; thus the effective gap between white and Negro opinions is actually greater than that indicated in Figure III-9. Negro segregationists are not likely to become political activists in the future because their social, economic, and psychological characteristics seem largely incompatible with this role. Even fewer possess the training, interest, and skills needed for political leadership.

Moreover, the Uncle Tom is rapidly disappearing from the southern scene. Between 1961 and 1964, the proportion of voting-age Negroes preferring "strict segregation" to "integration" or "something in between" was cut in half; the percentage dropped from 16 to 8. During the same period, those favoring desegregation increased

from 65 to 71 per cent; those preferring "something in between," from 15 to 18 per cent.[7]

The few Negro segregationists who remain are pathetic survivors of an era that has gone and will never return. So far as their direct and personal influence on the future of southern politics is concerned, they might as well not be there. At least one of them, a 78-year-old Negro woman in Capital City, realizes it. After reporting that she personally favored segregation she remarked, by way of clarification:

I don't think I'll be in this world long so I'd just as soon it stayed like it is, for peace's sake. But the world can't wait for me to die, so let the young folks go on fight

[7] The 1964 figures were collected by the Survey Research Center of the University of Michigan in its presidential election study of that year. The question wording in 1964 was identical to ours of 1961 save for the substitution of "desegregation" for "integration" as one of the three options provided the respondent. Although a meaningful distinction can be drawn between "integration" and "desegregation," few respondents are likely to have drawn such a fine distinction.

for their rights. . . . Well, I guess *all* us old ones better die so we can't teach and influence the young ones with what used to be. Then God's word [will] come to pass. He said he would raise up a nation that would obey and that men would study war no more. And if we old ones, whites more than black, was to stop influencing the young ones, then God's word *would* come about.

INFLUENCES ON WHITE RACIAL ATTITUDES

If centuries of slavery and segregation have convinced only a pathetic minority of Negro southerners that they should accept inferior status, today's milder forms of suppression cannot be expected to accomplish the task. Indeed, southern Negroes will, in all probability, become even more militantly dedicated to racial equality in the future. Thus, only a substantial change in white attitudes can narrow the frightening gap between the objectives of the two races. But, as a Negro

laborer in Arkansas said, ". . . when a person has gone so long thinking he is superior, it's pretty hard for them to change. . . ." Will these changes occur? And, if so, will they occur soon enough to diminish the South's politico-racial crisis? By identifying the characteristics of white strict segregationists, moderates (those who say they favor "something in between"), and integrationists, and by considering the prospects for an increase or decrease in the incidence of these characteristics, we should be able to estimate the possibility of these changes occurring.

Numerous studies have shown that racial prejudice and discrimination tend to be related to low levels of formal education. If southern segregationist sentiments are linked to the low educational levels of the region, then a continued increase in the average schooling of southerners could be expected to lead to a basic modification of attitudes. The impact of education on racial attitudes is clearly demonstrated by the findings in Table III-13.

TABLE III-13   Level of Education and Racial Attitudes of White Southerners

Amount of schooling	*Racial attitude*					
	Strict segregation	*In between*	*Integration*	*Don't know, refusal, no answer*	*TOTAL*	*N*
0–6 years	89%	9	0	2	100%	91
Junior high school	75%	19	3	3	100%	114
Incomplete high school	70%	26	1	3	100%	95
Complete high school	66%	30	3	1	100%	152
Complete high school plus other (non-college) training	54%	36	8	2	100%	61
Some college	50%	36	14	0	100%	108
Complete college	41%	45	14	0	100%	49
College and post-graduate training	11%	47	42	0	100%	19

The proportion of whites who are strict segregationists decreases with every increase in formal education. Whites with no more than grammar-school education are *eight times* as likely as those with postgraduate college training to be strict segregationists. But a careful examination of the findings suggests that they provide no basis for expecting large-scale change in southern attitudes within the near future. The combined number of moderates and integrationists does not exceed the number of strict segregationists within any education level below completion of college—and only 8 per cent of the southern whites have a college degree. Although the proportion of college graduates in the region will certainly continue to increase, it will not soon move from 8 per cent to a majority of the population. Education decreases dedication to strict segregation, but extremely high levels of education are apparently necessary to produce actual acceptance of integration. Even among those whose formal education terminated with a college degree, only 14 per cent favor integration. To find substantial support for integration, we must look to those with graduate-school training—and these "eggheads" constitute not quite 3 per cent of the white adults of the South.[8]

We would be going too far if we were to assume that a majority of southern whites would have to hold college degrees before increased education could significantly modify southern racial patterns.[9] More modest

increases in the general level of education in the South might have some effect. The whites with incomplete college training are evenly divided between strict segregationists and those with moderate or integrationist views. Such a division, even though it includes only a small portion of integrationists, could certainly be expected to produce a different pattern of politics. With more and more whites going beyond high school, then, the size of the strict segregationist majority can be expected to decrease.

In addition to formal schooling, the informal education that comes from exposure to different racial ideas and customs may be a potential source of change. The white South's most important window on the world outside is provided by the mass media of communications. . . . [W]e found that mass media tend to encourage political participation by southern Negroes. Do the same communications also encourage southern whites to accept standard American racial values rather than their more repressive regional variant?

Table III-14 suggests that the answer is yes, but that the effects of the media are limited. As we see in Table III-14, the proportion of southern whites who are "strict segregationists" declines from 88 per cent to 58 per cent as regular exposure to the media increases from little or none to a good deal. On the other hand, the mass

[8] Of this 3 per cent, almost half grew up outside the South.

[9] The relationship between higher education and integrationist attitudes probably is as much the result of differential recruitment into colleges and universities as of changed attitudes flowing from what the students learn while attending them. If so, the relationship between having a college education and possessing pro-Negro attitudes would be substantially reduced if more than half the southern whites were to attend college. We have assumed that the association is not *entirely* the result of selective recruitment.

TABLE III-14   Number of Mass Media Channels Exposed To, and the Racial Attitudes of White Southerners

Number of different media exposed to regularly	Racial attitude				
	Strict segregation	In between	Integration	TOTAL	N
0–1	88%	12	0	100%	57
2	80%	16	4	100%	132
3	59%	32	9	100%	279
4	58%	36	6	100%	213

media do not seem so effective in producing full-fledged integrationists as does higher education; heavy media exposure is associated with growing racial moderation, not acceptance of the Negro position. And, of course, sizable majorities of southern whites still prefer strict segregation regardless of how much they read newspapers and magazines or listen to TV and radio.

Even this much impact by the media on southern racial attitudes is, in fact, an exaggeration. The better-educated tend to expose themselves more to mass communications than do other whites; they also tend to have more liberal racial attitudes. When the relationship between mass-media exposure and white racial attitudes is examined with education controlled, the apparent impact of the media is further reduced (see Table III-15). Formal education clearly has a greater impact on white racial attitudes than do mass communications.

Actual experience with different racial outlooks and customs, as distinct from the largely vicarious experience of the media, may have a greater impact on southern whites. As southerners share in the increasing mobility of all Americans, will their exposure to integrated public facilities elsewhere

weaken or reinforce their dedication to the peculiar institutions of the South? White southerners who have been outside the South are much more likely than those who have never left the region to believe in integration or moderate segregation. Indeed, not a single integrationist was found among respondents who have never been outside the South. And the farther the individual has been from the South, the more likely he is to have attitudes atypical for the region. Geographical mobility presumably means exposure to different customs, and such exposure apparently modifies the values of southerners. The more foreign the exposure, the more likely the modification.

Either of two possibilities might render these inferences invalid. First, travel may be associated with some other characteristic, such as high education, in such a way that education rather than travel would turn out to be the real source of the link between travel and nonsegregationist views. Second, self-selection may lie behind the apparent effect of travel; those who hold southern views least strongly may be most inclined to travel outside the region.

An examination of the relationship between formal schooling and

TABLE III-15   Exposure to the Mass Media of Communications, and Racial Attitudes of White Southerners, with Education Controlled

Racial attitude	Number of media 0–1 Education			Number of media 2 Education		
	Low	Medium	High	Low	Medium	High
Strict segregation	90%	85%	—	91%	74%	60%
In between	10	15	—	9	24	20
Integration	0	0	—	0	2	20
TOTAL	100%	100%	—	100%	100%	100%
N	41	13	2	58	54	20

NOTE: Low education = grade school or less; medium education = some high school; high education = some college training.

TABLE III-15   Cont.

	Number of media 3 Education			Number of media 4 Education		
	Low	Medium	High	Low	Medium	High
Strict segregation	75%	63%	39%	80%	62%	44%
In between	22	32	40	17	34	45
Integration	3	5	21	3	4	11
TOTAL	100%	100%	100%	100%	100%	100%
N	71	125	83	30	111	71

travel reveals that people with more education are, as suspected, much more widely traveled than those with less education. But this does not necessarily mean that travel itself has no independent influence on racial attitudes. When we make our comparisons between people with the same amount of education, as in Table III-16, the strength of the relationship between travel and racial attitudes decreases but by no means disappears. At every level of education, those who have been outside the South are less likely to be strict segregationists than those who have never left the region.

Although Table III-16 shows that geographical mobility has an independent effect on racial attitudes when education is "partialed out," it also reinforces our confidence in the role of formal education itself. The difference between those with high and low education is greater, regardless of the amount of their travel, than the difference between the well-traveled and the nontraveled, regardless of the amount of their education. Moreover, the nature of the response to travel varies according to the level of one's education. At every level of education, greater mobility means a decrease in strict-segregationist views, but only for those with high education is much of the shift to integrationist beliefs. For those at the low or medium level of education the shift is to a moderate position between strict segregation and integra-

tion. Increasing white education holds out the prospect of a decrease in segregationist attitudes, and the increasing mobility of white southerners reinforces and adds to that prospect. Again, however, the prospect is for an

TABLE III-16   Geographical Mobility and Racial Attitudes of White Southerners, with Education Controlled

	Farthest place respondent has been					
	Outside North America			Outside U.S.A.		
	Education					
Racial attitude	Low	Medium	High	Low	Medium	High
Strict segregation	71%	54%	35%	57%	46%	45%
In between	22	38	41	29	42	45
Integration	5	8	24	5	8	10
Don't know, refusal, no answer	2	0	0	9	4	0
TOTAL	100%	100%	100%	100%	100%	100%
N	41	39	58	21	24	31

NOTE: Low education = grade school or less; medium education = some high school; high education = some college training.

TABLE III-16   Cont.

	Farthest place respondent has been					
	Outside South			Within South		
	Education					
Racial attitude	Low	Medium	High	Low	Medium	High
Strict segregation	72%	60%	46%	89%	86%	57%
In between	25	35	36	8	14	43
Integration	1	4	18	0	0	0
Don't know, refusal, no answer	2	1	0	3	0	0
TOTAL	100%	100%	100%	100%	100%	100%
N	119	106	72	117	43	14

increase in moderate views rather than for an early conversion to integrationist values.

The relationship between geographical mobility and racial attitudes does not disappear when we control for the important third variable, education. But what about the self-selection problem—the possibility that those with nonsegregationist values choose to travel rather than that those who travel modify their values? A simple test of this possibility seems to be offered by the fact that involuntary travel in the armed services has been a common experience for the present generation of adult American males. If travel while in the armed services modifies racial sentiments, we can fairly safely reject the possibility that our findings are a result of the self-selection process. Again the data support the inference that exposure to nonsouthern customs has an independent effect on racial attitudes: the percentage of veterans favoring integration increases from 0 to 7 to 11 as the locus of service shifts from the South only to the United States outside the South to the world beyond the United States.

But the effect of travel in the service is confined to increasing the proportion of integrationists at the expense of the proportion of moderates. The proportion of strict segregationists among southern veterans is the same regardless of where they served. Travel in the service is less important than the fact of service itself for the percentage favoring strict segregation. Only 55 per cent of all white veterans in the South favor strict segregation, as compared with 63 per cent of all adult white males and 65 per cent of all

adult white females in the region.

We conclude not only that self-selection does not account for all the effect of travel on racial attitudes but also that military service itself—a largely nonvoluntary act—may decrease dedication to racial inequality.

We have identified four factors—education, mass communications, geographical mobility, and armed service experience—that appear to decrease segregationist sentiment. Increasing numbers of southern whites have been exposed to all these experiences, and more of all four—certainly of the first three—may reasonably be expected in the future. Granted the great importance of formal education, and the fact that each new generation receives more schooling, we may expect young white southerners to be less committed than their elders to segregation. Moreover, studies of other populations have consistently found that conservatism—in the same sense of accepting ethnic and other group norms—increases with age. But the relationship between age and the racial attitudes of white southerners does not correspond to these expectations. If the young adults of the South represent the hope of the future, they may be the hope of the strict segregationists rather than of anyone else.

Rather than a steady increase in segregationist sentiment with advancing years, the proportion of strict segregationists declines as we move from the youngest white southern citizens through those in their thirties and forties. Only with the 50-year-old group does the percentage begin to ascend, reaching a high point with those in their sixties and seventies. The percentage of strict segregationists within each age group of southern whites is: [10]

21–29	65%
30–39	61%
40–49	62%
50–59	66%
60–69	71%
70+	74%

The great commitment of the very old to segregation is, of course, in keeping with expectations created by the normally conservative effect of aging. But the greater adherence to strict segregation of the very young than of those in their thirties and forties deserves examination. It is the more impressive in view of the fact that more people have a high level of education in the youngest group than in any other. Because of their greater schooling, an equal proportion of strict segregationists among the very young would have been mildly surprising; the slightly greater proportion that was found therefore has more meaning than the size of the difference would suggest. When we hold education constant and confine the comparison of age groups to people with the same amount of education, the youngest southern whites include more segregationists than the middle-age groups at every level of education. Indeed, within the low- and medium-education categories, the largest percentage of strict segregationists is found in the 21-to-29 age group, and, within the high-education category, only those

over 60 years of age include more strict segregationists than the very young.

Why do more restrictive racial views turn up among the very young than among those in early middle age? Three factors contribute to the difference: more southern whites in their thirties and forties were brought up outside the South, more of them have served in the armed forces, and more have been exposed by travel to non-southern customs. Another factor may be the *nature* of the greater education to which the youngest age group has been exposed. These people were between the ages of 14 and 22 at the time of the Supreme Court's school-desegregation decision in 1954. Since the "black Monday" of that decision, white youths in the South may have been subjected to a more concentrated indoctrination in the merits of segregation.

Nevertheless, we need not agree with the middle-aged Negro maid in Urbania who concluded that "the way those white folks hate us, it's going to take God to change them." For between 1961 and 1964 [11]—and without divine intervention—the distribution of white racial attitudes changed in small but hope-inspiring ways. The proportion of adult whites preferring "strict segregation" declined from 64 to 51 per cent; whereas the proportion of moderates increased from 28 to 39 per cent, and of integrationists, from 7 to 9 per cent.[12] These

---

[10] We eliminated the 18-to-20-year-olds in our sample from this analysis, because all of them came from a single Deep South state, Georgia. The voting age is 21 elsewhere in the region. Hence persons under 21 are not included in our sample for the other states.

[11] See footnote 7.

[12] Herbert H. Hyman and Paul B. Sheatsley, "Attitudes Toward Desegregation," *Scientific American*, Vol. 221 (1964), pp. 16–23, report, on the basis of longitudinal studies conducted by the National Opinion Research Center, significant increases in integrationist attitudes among both

shifts did little to narrow the awesome gap between Negro and white ideals, because Negro militancy and commitment to integrationist goals increased during the same period.[13] But they do demonstrate that change is possible.

The above analysis suggests that future changes in white racial attitudes, though perhaps modest, should continue in the direction of eventual reconciliation.

THE DISTANCE BETWEEN RACES

The prospects for major changes in white racial attitudes seem to be fairly good only if we take a long-range view. But Negro leaders have made it abundantly clear that they are unwilling to wait for slow processes gradually to erode segregation. "We want our freedom *now;* we want it *all;* we want it *here."* The words are those of the Reverend Martin Luther King; the sentiments they express are shared by most black southerners. The South must somehow ameliorate—if not "solve"

northern and southern whites since 1942. Their operational definition of the South includes Delaware, the District of Columbia, Kentucky, Maryland, Oklahoma, and West Virginia, which are not included in our definition; hence their results are not directly comparable with ours. However, the magnitude of the 20–year increases in integrationist sentiment found within their extended definition of the region is a good sign.

[13] Changes in Negro racial attitudes were as follows:

Respondent's preference	1961	1964
Strict segregation	16%	8%
In between	15	18
Integration (desegregation)	65	71
Don't know, etc.	4	3
TOTAL	100%	100%
N		615	918

—its racial problems *before* the millennium has arrived, *before* the hearts and minds of most white men have been won to the cause of equality.

If this sort of accommodation is to be made, southerners must first realize the depth and extent of their differences. Knowledge of the conflicting views that divide southerners along racial lines seems a necessary if not sufficient condition for coping with these differences through democratic political processes.

How well aware are white and Negro southerners of the differences that divide the races on the question of segregation? Most nonsoutherners would probably assume that neither race could exist in the midst of such strongly divergent opinions without being aware of their existence. And they might be joined by social scientists: survey data have revealed a reasonable measure of success among citizens who were asked to estimate the position of various groups on questions that divide the groups less sharply and about which they have less intense opinions.

But other findings leave open the possibility that southerners might actually be ill informed about their differences. In the first place, communication crosses caste lines in a highly imperfect fashion; hence, one or both races may receive inaccurate impressions of the preferences of the other. In the second place, selective perception, through which an individual's perceptions of the views of others are influenced by his own values, may lead to a distortion of the information that is communicated. These are mutually reinforcing phenomena in public opinion, and southern race relations is a ripe field for the operation of both.

Table III-17 indicates that, regardless of the overwhelming preference of Negroes for integration and of whites for strict segregation, neither group can correctly estimate the views of the other. Although both races are misinformed, the estimates of whites are much more inaccurate than those of Negroes. Only 22 per cent of the

the relative lack of information among whites.

The great inaccuracy of whites in estimating the views of Negroes is not surprising. Inaccurate information about the views of the subordinate group may be considered one of the prices the superordinate group must pay for a repressive social system. Or, rather than viewing misinformation as

TABLE III-17   Southern White and Negro Estimates of the Other Race's Attitudes on Segregation and Integration

Estimated number of white strict segregationists or of Negro integrationists	Negro estimates of white opinion	White estimates of Negro opinion
All	21%	4%
Most	26	18
About half	21	21
Less than half	20	39
Practically none	0	1
Don't know, refusal, no members of other race in area	12	17
TOTAL	100%	100%
N	615	685

whites recognize that most Negroes favor integration, but 47 per cent of the Negroes recognize that most whites favor segregation. The greater inaccuracy of whites can also be seen by comparing the proportion of whites who say that "less than half" or "practically none" of the Negroes prefer integration with the proportion of Negroes who perceive equally small numbers of whites as favoring segregation. Such grossly inaccurate estimates occur among whites at twice the rate at which they occur among Negroes. The greater frequency of "don't know" responses among whites than among Negroes is a more direct expression of

a liability, one could say that the communication process permits the dominant group the luxury of ignorance about the wishes of those who are dominated. The percentage of Negroes who favor integration actually exceeds the percentage of whites who favor strict segregation. But the communication of Negro views is blocked in various ways. In almost all forms of activity in the South, Negroes are required by law to behave in conformity to segregationist values, whatever their opinions. Negroes in some localities may be afraid to express their dissatisfactions. In some cases, behavioral conformity may not be enough; white employers may elicit assurances from their Negro employees that they prefer segregation. Although the pressures from the dominant white majority have not succeeded in molding Negro opinions, then, they have succeeded in inducing many Negroes to refrain from expressing those opinions—or even to express contrary opinions—in contacts with local whites.

the conspicuous evidence to the contrary.

Selective perception characterizes whites as well, as Table III-18 demonstrates. White integrationists are three times more likely than segregationists and twice as likely as those in between to perceive correctly the portion of Negroes favoring integration. White integrationists are better able to per-

TABLE III-18   Percentage of Southern Whites and Negroes Aware of Other Race's Attitudes on Segregation and Integration, by Racial Attitude

Respondent's racial attitude	Negro awareness of white opinion	White awareness of Negro opinion
Strict segregation	53% (94)	18% (443)
Something in between	44 (89)	25 (194)
Integration	48 (400)	50 (44)

NOTE: The percentages in the first column indicate the portion of Negroes with a given racial attitude who say that "all" or "most" whites favor strict segregation; the second-column percentages indicate the proportion of whites with a given racial attitude who say that "all" or "most" Negroes favor integration.

Southern Negroes, on the other hand, live under a system of segregation that is a constant institutional reminder of the segregationist beliefs of the white majority. Local police and judges stand ready to correct any misperceptions on which Negroes begin to act. How, then, can we explain the fact that only a minority of southern Negroes—albeit a very large minority—recognize that most southern whites favor strict segregation? The answer must lie in selective perception. Their personal preference for integration must lead southern Negroes to underestimate the degree of white hostility to integration, despite

ceive Negro preferences, not necessarily because they are better informed but because they hold the same preferences.

The opinions of Negroes similarly tend to influence their estimates of the other race's preferences, although to a less extreme degree. Over half the Negro segregationists recognize that all or most whites also prefer segregation, whereas somewhat less than half of the Negro integrationists make such an accurate estimate. But this contrast (53 per cent to 47.5 per cent) is not nearly so great as that between white integrationists and white segregationists (50 per cent to 18 per cent). Just as the pattern of communication in the South leaves the superordinate group as a whole less informed about the other race's aspirations, so does it permit them greater freedom to project their own views to others.

From the Negro's vantage point, however, the preferences of whites are less ambiguous. The harsh realities of segregation set bounds that usually leave little room for selective perception; the more severe the repression, the more narrow the limits of misperception. Thus the Negroes in Piedmont County—the least segregated and most "liberal" of the counties we studied in detail—have the *least* accurate picture of white attitudes in their area; only 43 per cent realize that most local whites prefer segregation. In Bright Leaf and Crayfish, these figures are 53 and 58 per cent, respectively. And in Camellia County, which has a long, bitter, and largely abortive experience in racial protest, 73 per cent of the Negroes are realistically aware of the structure of white attitudes.

Although each race in the South is surprisingly ignorant of the other's point of view, the failure of southern whites to realize how discontented their Negro neighbors are is a more serious stumbling block to racial accommodation. Even in the midst of sit-ins, boycotts, and freedom rides, a majority of southern whites did not realize in 1961 that Negroes were bitterly unhappy about segregation. Let us examine the 22 per cent of southern whites who did recognize deep-seated Negro resentment then. Are their characteristics such as to suggest early recognition by other whites of the nature of Negro demands?

To begin with, we must face the possibility that correct information on Negro attitudes is simply one manifestation of a generally superior level of information. When we analyze the results of our political-information test with the racial views of the respondents held constant, we find that general political information has no relation to awareness of Negro racial attitudes.[14] Among the strict segregationists, those who are ignorant of Negro preferences actually have slightly higher information scores than those who are aware of Negro attitudes. Among the moderates, the difference is reversed, but in both cases the differences are minute. Although we may expect modern modes of mass communication to raise the general information level of southern whites, then, such an improvement will apparently have no direct effect on white perceptions of Negro attitudes.[15]

When we look at the level of formal schooling rather than at the level of political information, the sense of stability in white misperceptions is even stronger. Table III-19 reveals that, with white racial views held constant, more education makes no contribution at all to greater white aware-

[14] The mean number of questions answered correctly by each group of southern whites was: strict segregationists aware of Negro attitudes, 4.4; strict segregationists unaware, 4.5; moderates aware, 5.2; moderates unaware, 4.9; integrationists aware, 5.3. Too few integrationists were unaware to permit computing a mean score for this group.

[15] Although exposure to the mass media of communications does tend to weaken white commitment to segregation, it does *not* contribute to an awareness of Negro views. The percentage of whites "aware" of Negro racial attitudes varies thus according to the number of media they are regularly exposed to: none or 1, 23 per cent; 2, 17 per cent; 3, 25 per cent; 4, 21 per cent.

TABLE III-19   Percentage of White Southerners Aware[a] of Negro Racial Attitudes, by Racial Attitude and Education

White racial attitudes	White education		
	Low	Medium	High
Strict segregation	29%	29%	27%
In between	45	41	37
Integration	b	b	89
N	173	134	111

[a] The view that "all" or "most" Negroes favor integration is counted as "aware"; the view that "less than half" or "practically none" favor integration is scored as incorrect. Other responses—"about half," "don't know"—and failures to respond are excluded from this and subsequent tabulations related to white awareness of Negro racial attitudes.

[b] Too few cases for percentaging.

ness of Negro attitudes. Indeed, for strict segregationists there is a slight decrease in awareness as education goes up, and for moderates, a fairly sizable decrease. The assumption that white perceptions of Negro demands might be changed more quickly than white attitudes gets no support from these findings.

If white ignorance of Negro attitudes does not stem directly from lack of information or education, perhaps it results simply from lack of contact with Negroes. The most common form of close contact between whites and Negroes in the South is in an employer-employee relationship, but contact with Negroes as employees is associated with a lower level of awareness of Negro attitudes when we compare whites with the same racial attitudes. Because the employer-employee relationship places the Negro in the familiar role of subordination, such white contact with Negro employees seems to reinforce inaccurate views of Negro attitudes.

Contact with Negroes as fellow shoppers is probably the type of association in the contemporary South most nearly akin to contact in the use of integrated public facilities. But, again, whites with a given racial attitude are less likely to be aware of Negro attitudes if they report contacts with Negroes as fellow shoppers than if they report no such contacts.[16]

Like education and information, contact with Negroes does not contribute directly to white awareness of Negro attitudes. The effect of travel and of military service on white awareness, when preference is controlled, is similarly nonexistent or unimpressive. Ironically, each of these factors *does* contribute directly to more moderate or integrationist sentiment. Contrary to our expectations, white misperceptions of Negro preferences may be harder to change than white attitudes themselves.

The general conditions under which whites may become aware of Negro attitudes are suggested by the

[16] For a more detailed analysis of the importance of different kinds of contact on racial attitudes, see John Orbell, "Social Protest and Social Structure: Southern Negro College Student Participation in the Protest Movement" (Ph.D. dissertation, University of North Carolina, 1965).

contrast in awareness between whites in the Deep South and whites in the Peripheral South. This is the only variable we have examined in this chapter that serves, in clear independence of white preferences, to increase awareness of Negro preferences. Among strict segregationists, 32 per cent in the Peripheral South compared to 22 per cent in the Deep South realize that Negroes prefer integration (see Table III-20). And the difference be-

for us to say that the actual situation in the Peripheral South should call forth more white estimates that most Negroes prefer integration. Despite this difference, the fact remains that most Negroes, even in the Deep South, are integrationists.

A second factor underlying the subregional difference in awareness is that Negroes in the Peripheral South are more articulate about their opinions. With more Negroes voting, some-

TABLE III-20 Percentage of White Southerners Aware of Negro Racial Attitudes, by Racial Attitude and Subregion of Residence

	Subregion of respondent's residence	
Racial attitudes of whites	*Deep South*	*Peripheral South*
Strict segregation	22%	32%
In between	31	42
Integration	—	88
N	105	315

tween moderates in the two subregions is slightly greater. The Peripheral South contains a much larger proportion of moderates and integrationists than the Deep South does, but these are differences between people with the same personal preferences.

The greater ability of whites in the Peripheral South to recognize the preference of most Negroes for integration appears to be supported by three factors, all of which are important for the future race relations and politics of the region.

First, more of the Negroes in the Peripheral South than in the Deep South actually do prefer integration. The difference is not great (68 per cent to 60 per cent), but it is large enough

times supported by active and efficient political organizations, and with public and private expressions of discontent over segregation, the muting effects of the Deep South's pressures for conformity are decreased. Even whites who are appalled at Negro demands may be forced at least to recognize that the demands exist.

Finally, the whites in the Peripheral South are not nearly so close to consensus on segregation as are those in the Deep South. With a large minority of fellow whites rejecting strict segregation, even the strongest segregationist may be forced to recognize that Negroes must also reject segregation.

Thus, in a county like Crayfish,

the local whites are almost entirely ignorant of Negro racial attitudes—only 8 per cent of the whites there realize that most of the local Negroes are integrationists! In Camellia County, which actually contains a smaller proportion of Negro integrationists than Crayfish but where the Negroes are more aggressive, articulate, and active, and where they have the support of a minority of whites, 28 per cent of the whites have a reasonably accurate picture of Negro aspirations and goals. In Piedmont County, where white integrationists and moderates are more numerous than in Camellia and where the Negroes are more effectively organized, 38 per cent of the whites are adequately aware of Negro attitudes. But only in Bright Leaf County, of those we studied in detail, did a majority (63 per cent) of the whites correctly assess Negro attitudes, and there only because a majority of the Negroes preferred what the whites wanted them to—segregation.

Despite all the southern whites' talk about understanding "our niggers," and all the southern Negroes' stories about knowing "our white folks," the two races truly are "living together as strangers." *This situation is getting worse, not better.* In 1961, 22 per cent of southern whites had a reasonably accurate view of predominant Negro racial attitudes: over three years later they could do no better. Indeed, they did a little bit worse (21 per cent). In the meantime, however, a burst of optimism seems to have swept the Negro communities of the South. In 1961, 21 per cent of the Negroes believed that "all" southern whites favored "strict segregation"; in 1964, only 4 per cent of them did. In 1961, 26 per cent of the Negroes interviewed said that "most" southern whites were segregationists; three years later 14 per cent of them did. As southern Negroes gain power and concessions in the region, as the federal government intervenes in the racial struggle more and more strenuously on their behalf, they too fall prey to the selective perception and wishful thinking which in harsher days were almost impossible—except for white people.

So long as this mutual underestimation of the seriousness of the conflict persists, the new biracial brand of southern politics promises to be a dangerous version of blind man's bluff.

BRITISH M.P.S AND THEIR LOCAL PARTIES: THE SUEZ CASES
LEON D. EPSTEIN

Most students of British parties have accepted the view that the mass organizations are decidedly subordinate to parliamentary leadership. Mainly this has meant rejection of the idea that policy is imposed by a party conference, or its delegated executive, in the Labour party as in the Conservative party. But it may also lead one to ignore or depreciate the role of the constituency units which compose the national organizations.[1] That it is a mistake to do so is now suggested by the activities of local party associations during the Suez crisis of 1956–57. Research material derived from this experience provides the bases for altering the common model of the constituency party as a unit in the mass service organizations sustaining the parliamentary leadership.[2] True enough, the as-

sociation of dues-paying partisans is primarily service rather than policy-making. However, the Suez experience indicates that this service includes a partly self-generating function in relation to the maintenance of parliamentary party cohesion, going beyond the well-known earlier instances of local Labour units simply following national orders to drop candidates who were suspected Communists.

I. INTRODUCTION

The power of constituency associations to take action against their M.P.s derives from their power to select candidates in the first place. Within very broad limits set by the national party, whose advice is often so much resented that it is withheld, the local dues-paying membership, and in practice

CREDIT: Reprinted by permission of author and publisher from *American Political Science Review*, June, 1960, pp. 374–390.

[1] As I have probably done in "Cohesion of British Parliamentary Parties," *American Political Science Review*, Vol. 50 (June 1956), pp. 360–377.

[2] R. T. McKenzie, *British Political Parties* (London: Heinemann, 1955), p. 588. In this useful work there are good descriptions of local party structures. Briefly, the usual Conservative pattern is for authority to be exercised by a 40- to 70-member executive council consisting of officers elected by the association at its annual meeting and of representatives elected by various ward and branch units. A smaller finance and general pur-

poses committee, containing most of the important leaders, often expresses general policy. The divisional Labour party, technically not bearing the name of "association," has no annual meeting open to the entire membership, but it has a general management committee comparable in size, in elected representativeness and in practical authority with the Conservative executive council. In the Labour case, the general management committee also elects a small and influential local executive committee.

its most active leaders, does the choosing. In approximately two-thirds of the parliamentary seats, safe for one party or another, such local party selection practically means election of the M.P. But the logical inference that this power to select carries with it the power, at a subsequent election, to reject the M.P. came to be disregarded, on the ground that it was a power the associations on their own rarely used, and then for personal rather than ideological causes.[3] Thus the use of this power by several associations over the Suez issue, admittedly a most emotional phase of British political history, may seem exceptional. And it has to be granted that what happened then is hardly typical of the everyday working of the political system; parliamentary cohesion, for instance, is ordinarily maintained without reference to the associations. Yet this admission does not materially reduce the significance of the Suez experience. The way in which political institutions work in a crisis has an obvious importance of its own. It is then that ultimate sources of power may be revealed, to participants as well as to observers, so as to have an impact on future behavior.

Studying M.P.-constituency association relations requires an intrusion into business which, as one M.P. wrote in response to my inquiry, is "private, personal and confidential." Candidate selection, for example, is a closed affair

at all its important stages, and the observer has much less chance to learn the political forces at work than he has even at an American nominating convention, not to mention the direct primary. The press, as well as political scientists, usually get no more than bare announcements of resolutions and actions taken. The procedure was really no different during the Suez crisis, but then there was enough public controversy to draw attention to the constituency relations of M.P.s who deviated from their parliamentary party's position. In these cases, it has been possible to secure fairly full information from newspaper accounts, particularly local ones, and from interviews with M.P.s and other informed persons. A detailed presentation cannot be attempted in a journal article, and therefore the case material is summarized briefly in the next section, after a description of the political setting in 1956–57. General hypotheses and evaluation are reserved for later sections.

II. SUEZ POLITICS AND THE DEVIANT CASES

1. Political background

By late October 1956, the Conservative party had been in office for five years, having been returned with a majority increased to 60 in the general election of May 1955. That election, held just after Eden succeeded Churchill as prime minister, marked a high point in Eden's fortunes. In the next year, before the Suez crisis, the Conservative government's popularity slumped, Eden was denounced as a

---

[3] Of course, this was not Ostrogorski's view. In his famous alarmist study of the rise of the Liberal party "caucus," it was precisely the power of the local units of the new national party organizations that he deplored. *Democracy and the Organization of Political Parties*, Vol. I, chaps. 4–5 (London: Macmillan, 1902). *Cf.* McKenzie, *op. cit.*, p. 253.

"ditherer" even in his own party, and rank-and-file Conservatives were frustrated by their government's unwillingness to liquidate "socialism" more rapidly and to reverse the postwar policy of "scuttling the Empire." Eden himself had been suspect since it was he, as foreign secretary in 1954, who had committed Britain to the evacuation in early 1956 of the Suez Canal military base. Nasser's sudden announcement in July 1956 of his nationalization of the canal was the last straw for rank-and-file Conservatives, who desperately wanted the Conservative government to stand up for Britain's "rights." Therefore, they welcomed Eden's strong reactions to Nasser in the summer of 1956; and the party's annual conference, in early October, enthusiastically resolved to support a tough line against Nasser.[4]

On the Labour side, Attlee had retired in late 1955 to the House of Lords and he was succeeded as leader by the much younger Hugh Gaitskell. When the Suez crisis came, Gaitskell was still in the process of consolidating his position, particularly by assimilating Aneurin Bevan, his former rival, to the leadership group. Bevan was elected party treasurer at Labour's conference in the early fall, and subsequently, during the Suez crisis, he returned to the shadow cabinet, eventually to become its foreign affairs spokesman. Gaitskell, like Eden, had been suspected of a weak moderation by his more extreme followers, and his original apparent agreement with the Conservatives, in denouncing Nasser's seizure of the canal in mid-summer

1956, had not diminished those suspicions.[5] However, in the subsequent months, notably in the October-November crisis, Gaitskell became as vigorous an opponent of the Conservative government's use of force in Egypt as the most zealous, pacifist-inclined, anti-imperialist socialist could have wanted.

One other political matter should be mentioned because of its proximity to the Suez crisis. The most controversial and most widely debated issue of the preceding parliamentary session had been capital punishment. The proposal to abolish hanging had been introduced as a private member's bill by a left-wing socialist, and the Conservative government allowed the House a free vote on the measure in February 1956. Enough Conservative M.P.s, 47 to be exact, joined a virtually solid Labour party to pass the bill in the Commons.[6] Both before and after this vote, rank-and-file Conservative party members displayed, in many constituencies, sharp dislike for the anti-hanging stand taken by some of their M.P.s, and there is no doubt that Conservative M.P.s were subject to considerable constituency association pressure despite the fact that loyalty to parliamentary leadership was not involved on a free vote. In the end, incidentally, after the House of Lords refused to agree to abolition, the government later in 1956 presented a compromise, retaining hanging for a few special murder offenses, and on a party division rather than a free vote secured its enactment.[7] The issue left

---

[4] *76th Annual Report* of the Conservative Conference (1956), pp. 28–37.

[5] 557 *H. C. Deb.* 1609–17 (2 Aug. 1956).

[6] 548 *H. C. Deb.* 2645–56 (16 Feb. 1956).

[7] 560 *H. C. Deb.* 1144–1259 (15 Nov. 1956).

many Conservative party activists with a pre-Suez grievance against particular M.P.s for what was regarded as a weak, liberal and Labour-oriented reluctance to employ the full force of the state against criminals.

The actual circumstances of Britain's attempt, with France, to reoccupy the Suez Canal must be briefly told. Military preparations had been made during the unsatisfactory negotiations from July to October, but the occasion for action followed Israel's invasion of Egypt. Britain and France announced that they wanted to separate the Israeli-Egyptian forces and so safeguard the canal. On October 31, after Egypt's rejection of a one-day ultimatum, the Anglo-French attack was launched, first by air bombardment and later by landings at the northern end of the canal. The military action lasted only through November 6, at which point the British and French agreed, under immense pressure from the United States, the United Nations and some Commonwealth member nations, to halt their action, well short of its goal, and accept a United Nations force in the canal zone. Britain did not actually withdraw all of its troops until December, and the government continued to advise British shipowners to avoid using the canal until May 1957. Thus the controversy was prolonged in British politics through the period of Prime Minister Eden's illness—involving a month in Jamaica and ultimately his resignation early in January—and into the early months of the administration of the new prime minister, Harold Macmillan.

During this period of intense parliamentary argument, several important divisions strained the loyalties of M.P.s, particularly in the Conservative party. The first was a sudden parliamentary division on October 30, when Eden announced the Anglo-French ultimatum and the strength of both parties was low because there had not been the usual notice of the whips for an important vote. The second was a set of divisions on November 1, when the Labour opposition attacked the government during the actual military action. The third was a crucial vote on November 8, when after the cease-fire the Labour party made its most serious effort to defeat the government. Fourth, on December 6 came a division on the government's announcement that it was finally going to withdraw its troops from the canal. And fifth, there was another vote, along similar lines, in May 1957, when Prime Minister Macmillan announced, in effect, that British ships would use the canal now firmly in Egypt's hands.[8]

Of these five occasions, the first three, in the October-November period, involved support of the Eden government's military action; this is true even of the vote of November 8, after the action stopped, because the question was essentially whether the government's policy of the previous week should be upheld. But the divisions in December and the following May involved approval of the liquidation of Eden's Suez intervention, first by his own government during his absence in Jamaica and then, in May, by the government of Macmillan, who had him-

[8] Records of the five sets of parliamentary divisions are at 558 *H. C. Deb.* 1377–82 (30 Oct. 1956), 558 *H. C. Deb.* 1729–44 (1 Nov. 1956), 560 *H. C. Deb.* 403–08 (8 Nov. 1956), 561 *H. C. Deb.* 1577–86 (6 Dec. 1956), and 570 *H. C. Deb.* 697–704 (16 May 1957).

self been publicly (and privately, too, it was thought) a strong original supporter of the military action.

Accordingly there were two very different lines of Conservative deviation, one stemming from doubt about the military action and the other from doubt about the withdrawal. Neither deviation, it should be stressed, turned out to be so large as to destroy the essentially inter-party form which the Suez issue assumed in British politics.[9]

2. Anti-Suez Conservatives

The most important line of deviation, actually and potentially, was by members of the Conservative majority against their government's action in October-November 1956. If numerous and willing enough, they could have helped the Labour opposition to destroy the Eden government, or less drastically, by threats to abstain or to vote with the opposition, could have pressured the government to change its policy. Logically, then, signs of such deviation were regarded most seriously by the loyal Conservatives of the constituency associations.

Exactly how many Conservative M.P.s were against their government's Suez action is hard to specify. Varying degrees of such opposition ranged from widespread misgivings to thorough going antagonism. Estimates of the number sufficiently con-

cerned to meet together to organize means to stop the Suez action range from 25 to 50, and it is widely believed that this group, largely by informal personal communication to parliamentary leaders, did add its pressure to the international forces seeking to bring Eden's Egyptian intervention to a halt. Certainly 25 to 50 Conservative M.P.s could have constituted a vital pressure, but most of them never became publicly identified with the opposition cause. In fact there was not even a partial group demonstration until the division of November 8, by which time military action had been halted anyway. In that division, there were eight known Conservative abstentions. In addition, two other anti-Suez Conservatives have been identified because their views became publicly known, although they always voted in the government lobby. In these ten cases, then, it is possible to observe the reactions of Conservative constituency associations to their M.P.s' deviations against the Eden government's Suez action.

NICOLSON. The leading case is that of Nigel Nicolson, who abstained on November 8 after attacking Eden's action the night before in a speech to a distinctly non-Conservative UN Association meeting. His was a very safe constituency, Bournemouth East and Christchurch, a growing south-coast resort community populated by many retired middleclass citizens (including former military officers). Nicolson's troubles were the most publicized, partly because they were drawn out over two years and partly because Nicolson himself had both the opportunity and the ability to dramatize his cause. He wrote a book covering all

---

[9] This was true to a large extent outside of parliament as well. British Institute of Public Opinion polls (made available through the courtesy of the Gallup organization) showed that during the first two days of November 76 per cent of Conservative voters agreed with Eden's policy and 72 per cent of Labour voters disagreed. About a week later, Conservative support had strengthened to the remarkable point of 89 per cent agreement with Eden, while Labour disagreement had dropped to 63 per cent.

but the final climactic events of his experience,[10] and he received the support of most of the national press and of the intellectual community generally. To this community, he himself belonged both by inheritance—as the son of the distinguished Sir Harold Nicolson—and by his own work as an author and publisher. Moreover, Nicolson was a "liberal" intellectual who, as Bournemouth's M.P. since 1952, had previously offended his old-guard supporters by a moderate view of Aneurin Bevan and by opposition to the death penalty.

Nicolson's acute trouble with his association, which began promptly after his opposition to Suez became known, led his 55-member executive committee, by mid-November, to adopt a resolution charging that he had chosen to act so as to "a) cause embarrassment to the Prime Minister and Government; b) misrepresent the views of the vast majority of his supporters in the constituency; and c) encourage and delight the Opposition."[11] Then in early December a general meeting of the association voted, 298 to 92, its lack of confidence in Nicolson and its instruction to the executive to begin the process of selecting a new prospective parliamentary candidate for the next general election.[12] By February 1957, this new candidate had been selected, although Nicolson and a minority in the association continued to try to reverse the verdict.[13]

Nicolson's effort to fight back, despite the national publicity it secured, would have been entirely futile were it not for the fact that the new Conservative candidate was shown, in early 1959, to have foolishly and covertly collaborated with an extreme right-wing organization, the League of Empire Loyalists, whose campaign to save the Empire included attacks on Prime Minister Macmillan as a "traitor." With the expedient resignation of this prospective candidate, subsequent to his exposure,[14] it was possible for Nicolson to revive his cause in circumstances which made his enemies in the association leadership seem very poor judges of candidates.[15] Under pressure from the Conservative national office, by now so embarrassed by the adverse Bournemouth publicity as to overcome its previous and customary reluctance to intervene in a constituency matter, a postal ballot of all members of the Bournemouth association was held on the question of re-adopting Nicolson. This ballot Nicolson lost by the very close vote of 3,762 to 3,671.[16] He ended up deprived of his safe seat for the next general election, just as his association first intended and would normally have been able to accomplish with much less time and trouble. Nicolson's second opportunity, in the 1959 mail ballot, was fortuitous.

MEDLICOTT. The results of Sir Frank Medlicott's abstention on November 8, and of a critical letter he wrote to Eden, are the same as the consequences of Nicolson's defection; Medlicott also ceased to be his association's candidate for the next general

---

[10] Nigel Nicolson, *People and Parliament* (London: Weidenfeld and Nicolson, 1958).

[11] *Bournemouth Daily Echo*, 15 Nov. 1956, p. 1.

[12] *Ibid.*, 6 Dec. 1956, pp. 1, 20.

[13] *Ibid.*, 12 Feb. 1957, pp. 1, 16.

[14] *Times* (London), 15 Jan. 1959, p. 8.

[15] *Daily Telegraph* (London), 26 Jan. 1959, p. 15.

[16] *Times* (London), 27 Feb. 1959, p. 9.

election. However, the history is different. Medlicott had represented his largely rural, fairly safe Norfolk constituency since 1939. He did so technically as a National Liberal, under a curious arrangement made in the 1930's by the Conservatives to accommodate their allies among right-wing Liberals. Medlicott did have some views derived from his own nonconformist Liberal origins, such as opposition to hanging, blood sports and the horse-killing Grand National, on which he disagreed with his Tory landowning constituents. Nevertheless, as a Conservative-voting member of the Commons, he had maintained amiable relations with his almost entirely Conservative association.

This amiability ceased abruptly after Medlicott's Suez defection. In mid-November the local Conservative executive council passed a resolution dissociating itself from Medlicott's view,[17] and in subsequent months the association effectively froze its M.P. out of his normal constituency relations. Medlicott received no Christmas-recess invitations to address meetings of the several units of his association; five of the six principal local party officers made speeches against him; and he was subject to much personal unpleasantness. Although the association neither demanded Medlicott's resignation nor actually decided to start the procedure to select a new candidate, despite some hints that it might, Medlicott chose to withdraw, in May 1957, from consideration for subsequent re-selection.[18] He might well

have survived, not by defending his Suez views but by swallowing his pride and trying to gloss over the affair with some assurances about the future. Even so he would not have been sure of winning, and many M.P.s, even if less sensitive than Sir Frank, would have responded similarly when they were suddenly frozen out by their constituency associations.

NUTTING. Resembling Medlicott's case in the apparently voluntary withdrawal of the M.P. was the affair of Anthony Nutting. Since 1945, he had represented a comfortably Conservative constituency in rural Leicestershire, which was his family's home. Nutting was a protege of Eden's and had risen to be Minister of State for Foreign Affairs. It was from this position that he resigned in a widely publicized letter to the prime minister during the Suez crisis; furthermore Nutting was absent, and deliberately so, from the Commons during crucial parliamentary divisions. He had informed his constituency association officers of what he was doing, asking the local leaders to refrain from taking any public stand until he could appear to explain why he opposed the Suez action. This request the finance and general purposes committee of the association refused to observe, and it sent a telegram during the crisis to the prime minister pledging its support.[19] Then, on November 14, without taking the opportunity to explain his stand to the association, Nutting announced that he was resigning his seat (immediately, that is, not just withdrawing as had Medlicott from consideration as a can-

---

[17] *Eastern Daily Press* (Norfolk), 17 Nov. 1956, p. 1.

[18] *Ibid.*, 2 May 1957, pp. 1, 4.

[19] *Melton Mowbray Times*, 9 Nov. 1956, p. 1.

didate for the next election).[20] Nutting claimed that for him to have tried to stay on, once his association's leaders were committed against his Suez stand, would have caused a split in the association. Or, put differently, Nutting would have had a Bournemouth-type fight on his hands. He was not in the most ideal personal circumstances for such a fight. Between his resignation from the government and his resignation of his parliamentary seat, Nutting's separation from his wife and his friendship with a prominent American woman had been sensationally displayed by a popular pro-Suez Sunday newspaper.[21] Whether this did in fact play a part in Nutting's decision is not certain. What is clear is that he did not want to fight the leaders of his constituency association. And, as a resigned Foreign Office minister, he could not and would not treat his views on Suez as something which could be compromised by agreement with his association.

BOYLE. As the only other rebel to have resigned a governmental position, as well as to have abstained from parliamentary voting, Sir Edward Boyle demands special notice, and not least because he survived his deviation. Representing since 1950 a mixed middle-class and working-class Birmingham constituency, whose election majorities look securely Conservative despite a shifting urban population pattern, Boyle was very much a brilliant young junior minister (Economic Secretary to the Treasury) at the time of the Suez crisis. His constituency re-

lations had been excellent, and especially so personally with his local party agent and chairman. Although known to be against hanging, Boyle had had no great local difficulty. But during the Suez crisis when he resigned his governmental post and abstained in the division of November 8, trouble began. As in the other cases, virtually all of the association's leaders intensely disliked the M.P.'s anti-Suez position, and there was a faction which wished to use this disagreement to try to get rid of Boyle. However, when the local executive met with Boyle on November 16, it adopted a moderate resolution (subsequently endorsed by the association's general meeting) expressing disagreement with the M.P.'s views but acknowledging his right to "act in accordance with his sincere convictions." [22] There is no question that this resolution was a triumph attributable to the unusually high personal regard which leading officers had for Boyle, even though disagreeing on this issue, and to the accidental fact that the very competent and popular local agent happened himself to sympathize with Boyle's views. Consequently, Boyle remained as M.P. and, despite prolonged ill feeling still expressed two years afterwards, he was re-adopted as parliamentary candidate. Furthermore there was also a national seal of forgiveness in that Macmillan, when forming his government in January 1957 and trying to conciliate all Conservative factions, took Boyle back as a junior minister. Still, no matter how definite Boyle's survival of this deviation, it is assumed in the con-

[20] *Ibid.*, 16 Nov. 1956, p. 1.

[21] *Sunday Express* (London), 11 Nov. 1956, p. 5.

[22] *Birmingham Post*, 17 Nov. 1956, p. 7.

stituency that he would not be forgiven a second major break with party orthodoxy.

ASTOR. Here the complication is that the M.P., John Jacob Astor of *the* Astor family, had announced before Suez that he would not stand for parliament again. Since 1951 he had represented the distinctly marginal Plymouth seat which had first been his father's and then for many years his famous mother's. However, Labour had won the seat in 1945 and 1950. The constituency reflected the west country's traditional non-conformist liberalism, and Astor's anti-hanging position had not seriously disturbed his good local relations. On Suez, joining his family's onslaught on Eden— notably by one brother's Sunday newspaper, the *Observer,* and by another brother's stand in the Lords— Astor on November 8 spoke against the government in the Commons and abstained from voting. His association's 80-member executive, after hearing Astor's exposition of his views on November 23, re-affirmed its confidence in Eden, and said nothing officially one way or the other about Astor. Only the chairman said ominously of Astor after the meeting: "We hope he will remain loyal." [23] Nevertheless, despite the sharp disagreement over Suez, Astor not only stayed to serve out his term as M.P. but suffered no "freeze-out" from association affairs. There was really no point in retaliating against an M.P. who was to retire anyway, unless of course his resignation was to have been forced almost immediately. But only the Labour party wanted a by-election in this marginal seat over the Suez issue; and anyway, Astor would not have resigned even if asked.

BOOTHBY. Representing the same heavily Conservative Scottish constituency since 1924, having been a robust and popular champion of its local herring industry, and having achieved national fame as an independent-minded backbencher, broadcaster and journalist, Sir Robert Boothby was in a particularly good position to ride out any constituency association storm. Moreover, Boothby's personal relations with his association had been satisfactorily maintained despite his liberal views on many subjects, including hanging. But his abstention on November 8 caused him trouble, eventually patched up. Boothby explained his abstention to his executive on November 23, after which the executive, unconvinced on the merits, issued the following statement: "The executive committee accepted his explanation and, while confirming his right to hold and to express his own views on matters of public policy, was of the opinion that his abstention on this occasion was an error of judgment. Sir Robert accepted this opinion." [24] Cryptic as is the last sentence, especially since Boothby did not make clear in other contexts that he regarded his abstention as a mistake, the outcome looks like no more than a mild rebuke. Not only could it be survived, with only slight loss of pride, but a well-entrenched person-

[23] *Western Evening Herald* (Plymouth), 24 Nov. 1956, p. 5; *Times* (London), 24 Nov. 1956, p. 5.

[24] *Buchan Observer* (Peterhead), 27 Nov. 1956, p. 4.

ality like Boothby might even have survived another such occasion. However, his status was by 1956 nearly unique among M.P.s, and in 1958 he left the Commons for one of the new life peerages. Not long after entering the Lords he gave up his party ties altogether.

YATES. In the case of William Yates, since 1955 a young representative for a very marginal urban-rural Shropshire constituency, the deviant M.P. (although also anti-hanging) is not clearly identified with the liberal intellectual gentility characteristic of the anti-Suez rebels already discussed. Yates deviated for his own reasons and in his own way. Based on his earlier experience as a British government official in the Middle East and on subsequent discussion with Nasser himself, Yates opposed Eden's use of force against Egypt in the belief, once widely fashionable among Conservatives, that Britain should work with Arab nationalism. He was bold enough to say as much in early October in a Cairo press conference and at the Conservative party conference, where he was howled down.[25] Then during the Suez intervention itself and before the other Conservative rebels revealed themselves, Yates indicated in the Commons his belief that the government was involved in a conspiracy.[26] His abstention on November 8 was thus anti-climactic, and he had his open constituency association difficulties earlier, before the crisis period itself. On that occasion, while there was a stormy executive committee meeting

with Yates and general disagreement with his Middle East position, an uneasy toleration of Yates's deviation was announced and evidently adhered to through the crisis itself.[27] Subsequently Yates remained the candidate for the next general election. Yates would not have resigned if asked, and any attempt to displace him would have been politically dangerous for the Conservative cause. Yates, a vigorous campaigner, had won the seat by only 478 votes in 1955, after Labour had held it in the previous three elections.

BANKS. The case of Cyril Banks, a middle-aged business man representing since 1950 a fairly safe Conservative seat in a small Yorkshire borough, stands apart from the other cases both because of its simplicity and because Banks, even more than Yates, was separated from the liberal intellectual opposition to Eden's action. Banks was a personal friend of Nasser's, whom he frequently visited as an economic adviser, and he believed that Britain could and should come to terms with Egypt, despite Nasser's seizure of the canal. Banks abstained as early as September from supporting the Eden government's strong line; at that time his association executive indicated its disagreement with Banks and also, but in a close vote, its toleration of Banks's deviation.[28] That Banks's subsequent abstention during the crisis itself would thus have been tolerated seems unlikely. At any rate, Banks did not wait to have this question squarely decided. Immediately after abstaining

[25] *76th Annual Report* of the Conservative Conference (1956), pp. 33–34.

[26] 558 *H. C. Deb.* 1716–17 (1 Nov. 1956).

[27] *Wellington Journal & Shrewsbury News,* 27 Oct. 1956, p. 18.

[28] *Pudsey & Stanningley News,* 27 Sept. 1956, p. 7.

on November 8, he resigned the Conservative whip and became an Independent M.P. Treating this as its opportunity to secure a new prospective candidate, even though this is not often done when Conservatives simply renounce the whip, Banks's association started the selection procedure in mid-November and at the same time reaffirmed its support of the government.[29] As occurred elsewhere in the replacement of anti-Suez rebels, the association chose an outspoken and unmistakeably pro-Suez man as its new candidate.[30] It happened that this candidate as well as his successor had subsequently to withdraw for personal reasons, but Banks, although he resumed the Conservative whip while serving out his term, was not reconsidered as a candidate.

SPEARMAN. In this case and the next, the M.P.s definitely belonged to the main body of anti-Suez Conservatives. But unlike those first discussed, all of whom at least abstained on November 8, these two voted with the government in all crucial divisions. Sir Alexander Spearman, to take his case first, did make an anti-Suez parliamentary speech November 8,[31] and this was enough to raise the wrath of his association, in a heavily Conservative resort and rural constituency of Yorkshire which Spearman had represented since 1941. In mid-November the association's executive committee heard Spearman's explanation, and accepted particularly, in his defense, that he had always voted with the government. In this circumstance, the execu-

tive took no formal action against him, but asked its chairman to address a private letter to the M.P. containing their views.[32] It is fair to say that Spearman was let off with this and other personal unpleasantness, stretching over time. The impression was left that the association had warned, at least by implication, of what was expected in the future: certainly no abstentions on important issues.

KIRK. Here the M.P., Peter Kirk, did not even make a critical parliamentary speech. The fact that he was anti-Suez reached his association through a letter to a Labour constituent, which was made public, through his personal conversation in the constituency, and probably also through the party's national leadership. The consequent pressure was sufficient to dissuade Kirk from making an early statement of his anti-Suez views; for it he substituted an equivocal criticism after the immediate crisis.[33] Nor did Kirk abstain on November 8, as once he had intended to do. Thus his experience provides an instance of association pressure anticipating, and playing some part in preventing, an M.P.'s open deviation. Even his more or less private deviation caused Kirk to have trouble conciliating his association's leaders. To some, especially older Conservative party activists, Kirk was suspect anyway as a young liberal intellectual, and particularly as one who had led the Conservative anti-hanging bloc. But, in another way, Kirk's constituency position was strong. He was a liberal Conservative in a distinctly

[29] *Ibid.*, 22 Nov. 1956, p. 7.

[30] *Ibid.*, 14 March 1956, p. 6.

[31] 560 *H. C. Deb.* 369–70 (8 Nov. 1956).

[32] *Scarborough Evening News*, 19 Nov. 1956, p. 5.

[33] *Gravesend & Dartford Register*, 24 Nov. 1956, pp. 1, 6.

marginal seat, Gravesend (near London), and he had first won the seat from Labour in 1955 partly due to the presence of the ex-Labour M.P. as an Independent candidate in addition to the official Labour candidate.

3. Pro-Suez Conservative extremists

As members of the old 40-man Suez rebel group of 1954, which had opposed Britain's original withdrawal from its Suez base,[34] the "pro-Suez Conservative extremists" had welcomed Eden's action of 1956 as a belated and happy conversion to their cause. The basis for their subsequent deviation arose in December 1956 and May 1957 when they were asked to vote in support of their government's successive surrenders of its strong anti-Nasser line. Then their deviations, though varying in manner and degree, were always in content farther from the Labour party's position than from that of their own party leadership. Moreover, they were deviating in accord with the expressed convictions of the Conservative rank-and-file activists, most of whom also thought that the principal trouble with Eden's Suez intervention was that it had stopped. The pro-Suez extremist M.P.s could claim to be more Conservative than their parliamentary leadership. And they could expect considerable tolerance of their position particularly after January 1957 when their own favorite Harold Macmillan became prime minister and took a leading pro-Suez extremist and December abstainer, his son-in-law Julian Amery, into the government. More than that,

they could well have suspected that Macmillan would find it convenient, in dealing with other countries, to claim that he could not go too fast in withdrawing from Suez because of his pro-Suez rebel group.

Nevertheless the pro-Suez M.P.s did break with parliamentary discipline in significant ways, and their subsequent treatment by constituency associations provides a useful comparison with that of the anti-Suez deviants. There were 15 deliberate abstentions by Conservatives on December 6, 1956, on the vote on the government's withdrawal of troops from the canal zone; and on May 16, 1957, there were 14 abstentions (including nine repeaters from the first 15) on the vote over the government's decision to advise British shipowners to use the canal on Nasser's terms. Of the 14, in the latter instance, eight went farther than abstaining and resigned the party whip in order to sit as Independent Conservatives. Altogether 20 individual M.P.s were involved: the nine repeaters plus six in December only and five in May only.[35]

The vital point about this whole pro-Suez group is that no one lost his seat because of abstention, single or repeated. And in only one doubtful case can it be suspected that even going so far as to resign the whip contributed to

---

[34] 531 *H. C. Deb.* 495–504 (28 July 1954); 724–822 (29 July 1954).

[35] The fifteen abstainers in December were Biggs-Davison, Fell, Hinchingbrooke, P. F. Maitland, Maude, Turner, P. G. Williams, Hyde, McLean, Amery, T. H. Clarke, Horobin, Nabarro, Teeling, and Waterhouse. The first nine of these also abstained in May, and they were joined by Raikes, J. Eden, G. Howard, Lambton and N. Pannell. The first seven plus Raikes constituted the group resigning the whip in May. *Times* (London), 7 Dec. 1956, p. 10; 14 May 1957, p. 10; 17 May 1957, p. 12.

an M.P.'s loss of his seat. This is especially remarkable since of the eight who formed the Independent Conservative "cave," to oppose Britain's "weak foreign policy," five remained without the whip until June 1958. Despite their support for the government on other issues, these lingering Independent Conservatives sorely tried their party's patience, as a general election was thought to be near and there was a desire to have candidates in technically good standing. No doubt there was pressure on the Independents from the constituencies, and in at least one case this pressure did have something to do with an M.P.'s resumption of the whip.[36] Continued irregularity, even in a cause cherished by the rank-and-file, exposed an M.P. to attacks from local opponents, who occasionally wanted the seat for another candidate. However, to be pressured to rejoin one's parliamentary party is less significant than the fact that the local parties refrained from any more serious action during the whole year that Independent status was maintained.

The one doubtful case is that of Lawrence Turner, M.P. for Oxford city, who counted himself an Independent Conservative until June 1958 after having abstained in both the December and May divisions. In May 1958, just before resuming the whip, Turner announced his withdrawal from consideration as a candidate for the next general election, and one might guess that this withdrawal was

not entirely voluntary from the fact that his Oxford constituency association had almost simultaneously informed Turner that it was to start the process of considering candidates.[37] However, Turner's announced reason for withdrawal, namely medical advice, had a basis in fact. Furthermore, it was evidently Turner's own uncertainty about standing again, plus his continued delay in resuming the whip, which finally caused his association, over a year after the M.P.'s deviation, to consider other candidates. There were other reasons, too, for the association to reconsider Turner's situation. Over the years, since becoming Oxford's M.P. in 1950, he had deviated from his parliamentary leadership on certain economic issues, in a right-wing direction, as well as on foreign policy. These positions, plus a certain blunt businessman's outlook, tended to alienate the university element among Conservative voters. This could have been consequential even though Oxford was a reasonably safe Tory seat. However, it is probable that Turner's pro-Suez extremism, while unpopular with a Conservative minority (mainly outside active party circles), would not in itself have cost him his seat. In fact, his association executive voted Turner its full support after he addressed its meeting, in June 1957, to explain why he had abstained and joined the cave.[38]

One other pro-Suez rebel was subsequently deprived of his seat, but much more clearly than in Turner's case it was for reasons unconnected with his Suez stand. The M.P. was

[36] *Daily Telegraph* (London), 25 June 1958, pp. 1, 15. The five hold-outs were Biggs-Davison, Turner, Hinchingbrooke, Fell and Williams. One of the Independent Conservatives, Maitland, resumed the whip late in 1957, and two others, Maude and Raikes, had left Parliament.

[37] *Times* (London), 22 May 1958, p. 4.

[38] *Oxford Mail*, 12 June 1957, p. 1.

Montgomery Hyde, a prolific author with wide intellectual interests who represented a very safe Belfast constituency, as a Conservative-affiliated Ulster Unionist, since 1950. Without joining the cave, Hyde had abstained both in December 1956 and May 1957. But this evidence of pro-Suez extremism did Hyde no more harm than it did other M.P.s of the same group. The move against Hyde's readoption did not take place until 1959, and the list of grievances against him consisted entirely of deviations in very different directions. Specifically, Hyde was disliked in his association because he was against hanging, for a liberal approach to homosexual offenses and for the return of a legally disputed set of pictures from a London to a Dublin gallery.[39] Besides he was said to have too many outside interests to be a good Northern Ireland M.P. After a prolonged fight, almost rivalling Bournemouth's in interest, Hyde's association went ahead to choose another candidate.[40]

Putting aside Turner and Hyde, 18 other pro-Suez cases remain. Three of these M.P.s voluntarily retired from parliament in the years following Suez, two of them, Waterhouse and Raikes, appropriately to business in Britain's African dependencies, and Angus Maude to the editorship of an Australian paper. All three may have been disgusted with Conservative politics, but in none of the three cases was there any evidence that their associations were disgusted with them. In fact,

Maude, who stayed on in parliament the longest, until mid-1958, and was a member of the cave, was treated as a hero by the local Conservatives in his safe London suburban constituency.[41] Similar if less enthusiastic support was publicly accorded at least six other pro-Suez extremists. These included, besides Maude, five of the other eight Independent Conservatives, namely Fell, Paul Williams, Patrick Maitland, Lord Hinchingbrooke and Biggs-Davison (despite a notable restiveness in the latter's new and marginal constituency).[42] These cases, counting Maude's, of announced official local confidence account, along with Turner and Raikes (apparently supported too, if not publicly) for all of the 8-member cave. Theirs was really the only form of pro-Suez deviation usually taken seriously enough for the question of local confidence to be raised, although at least one simple abstainer of May 1957, John Eden, also received his association's public vote of confidence.[43] Ordinarily pro-Suez abstention, unlike anti-Suez abstention, was locally not even controversial.

Perhaps the most convincing way to show the tolerance of a constituency association for the pro-Suez extremist is to cite the case of Lord Hinching-

[39] Belfast Telegraph, 9 Jan. 1959, p. 2; 13 Jan. 1959, p. 2.

[40] Times (London), 4 April 1959, p. 4.

[41] Middlesex County Times & West Middlesex Gazette, 8 Dec. 1956, p. 2; 1 June 1957, p. 1; 8 June 1957, p. 12; and 7 Dec. 1957, p. 1.

[42] On each of the five M.P.s, see, in order, Eastern Daily Press (Norfolk), 14 May 1957, p. 1; Sunderland Echo, 22 May 1957, p. 8; Glasgow Herald, 14 May 1957, p. 8; Dorset Daily Echo, 18 May 1957, pp. 1, 7; and Chigwell Times & West Essex Star, 6 Sept. 1957, p. 1.

[43] Times (London), 25 May 1957, p. 4.

brooke. This highly individualistic, almost eccentric, son of the Earl of Sandwich functioned as leader of the Independent Conservative cave, and he abstained both in December 1956 and May 1957. The reaction of his association, after 500 local members heard Hinchingbrooke's explanation in May, was a vote of confidence, with only six dissenting votes, the singing of "For He's a Jolly Good Fellow," and the hope that "the foreign policy of Her Majesty's Government will enable him again to accept the Whip in the near future." [44] This overwhelmingly favorable outcome looks all the more significant by comparison with the other occasion, in 1952, when Hinchingbrooke, in the same fairly safe, largely rural Dorset constituency, had faced the consequences of a parliamentary deviation. Then, after Hinchingbrooke had spoken against and abstained from supporting the Conservative government's approval of German rearmament, his local executive adopted a resolution of no-confidence in its M.P. Only with much effort did Hinchingbrooke get a majority of the association, at a general meeting, to reverse this executive decision. [45] One may fairly speculate that the difference in treatment between 1952 and 1957 can be attributed not only to improved personal relations with a new executive, but also to the fact that Hinchingbrooke's later deviation was an essentially Conservative one close to the imperialist nerve-center of party activists, instead of one which, like his

opposition to German rearmament, happened to place him in the same camp with left-wing socialists.

4. Labour M.P.s

The Conservative party's two-way deviations over Suez had no parallel in the parliamentary Labour party. In fact, there was no group break, in any direction, from Labour's thoroughgoing opposition to the Eden government's military intervention. Suez provided common ground for Labour's right-wing leadership, mainly liberal internationalist in outlook, and its left-wing socialists, erstwhile Bevanites. Perhaps, as was widely believed, there were doubts among trade-union M.P.s, reflecting the views of a considerable share of working-class voters, but they remained loyal in the crucial divisions. So did all of the 17 Jewish M.P.s in the Labour party,[46] although some maintained such close ethnic, religious or social ties with the Jewish community that they were certainly cross-pressured to abstain from their party's all-out attack on Britain's intervention which, despite Eden's denials, appeared to be on Israel's side.[47] Yet all 17 voted in the Labour

---

[44] *Dorset Daily Echo, loc. cit.*

[45] *Times* (London), 6 Oct. 1952, p. 2; 10 Oct. 1952, p. 3; and 31 Oct. 1952, p. 6.

[46] The 17 names are from the list in the *Jewish Chronicle* (London), 9 Nov. 1956, p. 8. The same story names two Jews among Conservative M.P.s. Only a few of the M.P.s represented heavily Jewish constituencies.

[47] Zionist pressures are reported in the *Jewish Chronicle*, 9 Nov. 1956, pp. 5, 16, 23, in the form of sharp criticism of the Jewish M.P.s for voting with the Labour party. Consider particularly the case of Barnett Janner, M.P. for a non-Jewish constituency but the president of both the Zionist Federation and the Board of Jewish Deputies. To the latter, Janner had to justify his support of Labour's Suez stand before receiving a vote of

lobby on November 1, and except in the unwhipped division on October 30 there were no deliberate abstentions among the Jewish M.P.s. The closest any of the 17 came to public deviation was in remarks by two M.P.s.[48] Accordingly, the single clear-cut Labour deviation, that of Stanley Evans, was an individual affair. Evans, a self-made business man representing a working-class constituency in the black country of the midlands, simply had his own views of Suez. His constituency experience is well worth examination.

EVANS. M.P. for Wednesbury since 1945, Stanley Evans had already followed an individualist course in some respects before Suez. He had achieved a kind of fame in 1950 when, almost immediately after his appointment by the Attlee government as parliamentary secretary to the Ministry of Food, Evans referred to the government's farm subsidies as "featherbedding." [49] This refreshingly frank but foolish remark cost him his junior ministerial status. Subsequently, as a back-bench M.P., he continued to make statements at odds with his party's policy, particu-

larly on foreign and colonial issues. Some of these statements were made in the Commons and some in his constituency, often to business groups with whom Evans appeared to enjoy an increasing rapport as compared with the active leaders of his constituency party. Before Suez, however, Evans was tolerated by the Wednesbury party, for despite a general feeling of neglect and some antagonism from particular individuals there was no issue so sharply drawn as to cause the trade unionists, who dominated the local organization, to break from the normal loyalty to their M.P. After all, Evans's offenses had chiefly been those of outspokenness on issues of little direct concern to non-intellectuals, and his parliamentary record had remained sound enough on economic matters of interest to urban workers.

Evans's Suez deviation was especially sharp and open. On October 30, when Labour attacked Eden's ultimatum, Evans spoke against his party leadership's decision to divide the House and then he subsequently abstained from voting.[50] Also on November 1 Evans made a parliamentary speech distinguishing his position from Labour's, and then again abstained from voting on Labour's censure motion despite the three-line whip.[51] Although Evans returned to the fold in the party divisions of November 8, he had deliberately and surely made himself a conspicuous rebel. Some party reaction could be expected. Significantly, however, it did not come from the parliamentary leadership, which could well afford to tol-

---

confidence. *Ibid.*, 23 Nov. 1956, p. 1. Of course, it was possible to disapprove of Britain's action, on principle, and yet defend Israel.

[48] Harold Lever, who had not voted on October 30, defended Israel's action but still ambiguously refused to support Britain's action. 558 *H. C. Deb.* 1481–97 (31 Oct. 1957). Emanuel Shinwell, also a non-voter on October 30, went a little farther by issuing pro-Eden statements during his subsequent Far Eastern tour. In consequence, despite Shinwell's status as a former minister, a Labour activist of 53 years and an M.P. almost continuously from the 1920's, he had to explain his statements to his constituency executive. *Times* (London), 12 Jan. 1957, p. 6. But, like Lever, Shinwell could correctly claim that he had voted with his party when it really mattered.

[49] *Times* (London), 17 April 1950, p. 4.

[50] 558 *H. C. Deb.* 1287 (30 Oct. 1956).

[51] 558 *H. C. Deb.* 1681–86 (1 Nov. 1956).

erate but one rebel and so reap favorable national publicity for relative broad-mindedness. A willingness to forgive, if not forget, which did in fact characterize the attitude of both the parliamentary party and Labour's national executive committee, was not to be found in the Wednesbury divisional Labour party. On November 17, after Evans had explained his views to a special meeting of the general management committee (the 48-member body of delegates representing the whole local membership), this committee found a "deep conflict of basic principles" and voted unanimously to ask for Evans's resignation as an M.P.[52] This extreme reaction is partly explained by the strong feeling that Evans had been disloyal to an important party cause and partly by the fact that in September, when the Suez crisis was brewing, Evans had already been told that the management committee's views were different from his.

The local party's request for Evans's resignation, unlike a decision simply to look for another candidate for the next general election, was technically unenforceable. Constitutionally, meaning customarily, most M.P.s could and did resist any such demand. Moreover there was every sign that Labour's national leadership preferred Evans to resist since his ouster involved unwelcome publicity (but no danger from a by-election to the party's hold on the safe Wednesbury seat). At any rate, before any effective national intervention could have taken place, Evans complied with his local party's request by announcing his resignation

from the House of Commons although he remained a member of the Labour party. In leaving his seat immediately, Evans no doubt correctly anticipated his subsequent removal as a general election candidate. As he said in explaining why he chose not to stay on through his term: "A general without an army, and what is worse living on borrowed time, seldom wields much influence and lacks all dignity." [53]

III. TENTATIVE GENERALIZATIONS

From the fairly numerous experiences of Suez deviants, certain general hypotheses about M.P.-constituency relations can be attempted—though always with the proviso that what is being generalized about is behavior during a political crisis.

1. Effectiveness of constituency association pressure

That the constituency association is able and willing to use its power against an M.P. deviating from its political opinions is evident enough from the cases of the anti-Suez Conservatives and of Stanley Evans. This power is basically the refusal to readopt, rather than the unenforceable and often politically inexpedient demand for immediate resignation. But the threat of not readopting, combined with personal and political unpleasantness, can produce an M.P.'s withdrawal (subsequently as for Medlicott, if not immediately as for Nutting and Evans). Deprived of his association's support as of its confidence, an M.P.

[52] *Midland Advertiser & Wednesbury Borough News,* 24 Nov. 1956, p. 1.

[53] *Ibid.,* 24 Nov. 1956, p. 5.

finds himself in the untenable position, as Evans said, of "a general without an army," or as Ostrogorski wrote years ago, of "an excommunicated sovereign in the Middle Ages, whose subjects, so devoted to him the day before, are released from their loyalty to him." [54] The fact that an M.P. cannot fight back effectively from outside the party association makes him dependent on its continued good-will. Therefore, any policy dispute, even one that is eventually patched up, may appear menacing to an M.P., who understandably fears that he cannot afford another such dispute.[55] Or, for that matter, an M.P. may well think that he cannot afford even one such dispute, and consequently curb an intended deviation.

One qualification has to be made about the effectiveness of constituency association pressure. The Suez evidence indicates only that such pressure is effective when local party opinion is in line with that of the national party leadership, as it certainly was during October and November 1956. It is doubtful that an association could punish an M.P. for voting contrary to local party views if, in so doing, he was following the national party leadership. Indeed when a few local Labour parties had reacted against their M.P.s for supporting German rearmament, the national Labour leadership intervened to protect the M.P.s.[56] Of course,

such a circumstance is unlikely even to arise, especially in Conservative ranks, given the association's role as the custodian of national party orthodoxy.

2. Ideological extremism

Pressure from constituency associations, insofar as it is self-generating, tends to be that of relatively extreme partisans. The voluntary and amateur nature of these associations ensures that they attract zealots in the party cause, and particularly so at the local leadership level where there are many routine political chores which only the devoted are likely to perform. Principles, not professional careers, are what matter here. It is no wonder, then, that Conservative activists showed a tolerance for the pro-Suez deviants that was denied the anti-Suez M.P.s. The basis for tolerance was the same as that which had prevailed a few years earlier in local Labour parties for the Bevanite M.P.s who had deviated from their national leadership and, like the pro-Suez rebels, in a direction away from the opposition party's line. The very fact that extremists are attacked by the other party, instead of being praised as the anti-Suez Conservatives were by Labour, convinces local supporters of their essential soundness on party doctrine.

Clearly it is the M.P. whose deviation from national leadership is toward the center, away from traditional party orthodoxy, who encounters trouble in his constituency association, and primarily from the 40 to 100 most active leaders of the association who, in the nature of party organizations everywhere, tend to manage affairs. It is these activists who are truly "more royal than the king," as

---

[54] *Op. cit.,* p. 449.

[55] The impact of a local party's vote of no-confidence in its M.P. is vividly portrayed in the novel *No Love for Johnnie* (London: Hutchinson, 1959), written by the late Wilfred Fienburgh, himself a Labour M.P.

[56] Peter G. Richards, *Honourable Members* (London: Faber & Faber, 1959), p. 21.

was demonstrated by the fact that their zeal to punish Suez deviants like Nicolson and Evans appeared to outrun what national leaders regarded as the limits of prudence. Indeed their zeal may well have gone beyond that of the rank-and-file dues-paying membership which the local leaders are elected to represent. So it appeared at Bournemouth, where Nicolson's near 50 per cent of the 1959 mail ballot of party members contrasts sharply with the absence of any support at all on the 55-member executive body of his association. Similarly in the Stanley Evans case, but without the statistical verification, there were rank-and-file Labour supporters of Evans against his ouster by the unanimous action of the local party executive.[57] Also in accord with the same expectation, the pro-Suez Conservative deviant found his local *opponents* outside the association executive.[58]

3. Reinforcement of parliamentary party leadership

As amply illustrated, the tendency of constituency association pressure is to reinforce the leadership of each parliamentary party. Even without being stirred to action by the respective whips or central offices, as on occasion they are suspected of being, the associations are capable on their own of reacting sharply against an M.P.'s deviation. And the significance of this reaction is not lessened by the fact that the reaction is only against M.P.s who deviate toward the center. That, after

all, is the deviation important to the parliamentary leadership. Joined to the opposition, it can seriously embarrass or even bring down a government. Deviation toward the extremes, if only occasional, is annoying but not potentially fatal, for in the end the deviants have nowhere to go but back or out.

Unquestionably national party leaders are aware of and grateful for the service performed by local units in maintaining parliamentary cohesion. This is so even though they may regard the methods, especially at Bournemouth, as too drastic and uncivilized, as well as too unattractive a party image to put before marginal voters on a national scale. There was little effort by national leaders to interfere with the self-generating course of constituency politics. The only apparent intervention came at Bournemouth and then in a most unusual situation which occurred after more than two years of a constituency dispute. This chariness to intervene owes something to a general reluctance to dictate to voluntary local workers, but something also to a particular reluctance to try to keep an association from enforcing the line which was that of the national leaders themselves. The local zealots might not be genteel enough, but they help to maintain the parliamentary discipline on which the fortunes of the leaders rest.

In an important way, the constituency associations do view their role as that of supporting their national leaders. The M.P. is chosen to support the party in the House of Commons, and aside from personal services for constituents it is not clear that the association expects him to have any other important functions. Surely the

---

[57] *Midland Advertiser and Wednesbury Borough News,* 24 Nov. 1956, p. 1.

[58] *Chigwell Times & West Essex News,* 6 Sept. 1957, p. 1.

ordinary M.P. is not expected to pit his own judgment against that of the leaders whom the association is organized to support. On Suez, local Conservative activists, most plainly, thought it important to support Eden and not their deviating M.P.s.[59] Not only did this reflect a greater confidence in Eden's knowledge than, say, in Nigel Nicolson's. It also reflected a quite realistic appreciation of the British political system: what does count is the maintenance of parliamentary cohesion.

4. The attitude of the individual M.P.

Granted that greater experience and status may insulate certain M.P.s more than others from constituency pressures, it still appears generally true that a backbencher finds it dangerous to exercise in the division lobbies his individual judgment contrary to his national leaders *and* his local party. By so doing, to the extent of abstaining on a critical question, the M.P. may find himself without effective political support, and with only the sympathy of the liberal national press and of his fellow M.P.s. The attitude of the latter group is symptomatic of the state of affairs. Most M.P.s, at least backbenchers, do sympathize with each other's constituency association prob-

lems. At Bournemouth, for example, Nicolson secured the help of both pro-Suez and anti-Suez Conservative M.P.s, while the association executive could not, at the end, get any M.P. to speak on its platform. The local officers even complained of a "trade-union" of M.P.s.[60] Undoubtedly M.P.s individually and collectively resent their associations' efforts to keep them in line, more so than they resent the more gentlemanly persuasion of the parliamentary whips. The whips are members of the same club, and so more understanding of a deviation than are the more rigid and less "political" local activists. Furthermore, an M.P.'s resentment of his local party's reaction may be sharpened by a contempt for the opinions of party activists. This contempt is at least as evident in the attitudes of upper-class Conservative M.P.s toward their middle-class supporters, often housewives and widows, as it is in the views of intellectual Labour M.P.s toward their working-class activists. In conversation, one Conservative M.P. referred to constituency associations as "dreadful things," and another, with all the bite of an English public school background, called his local chairman "a small man."

5. Conservative and Labour party differences.

The one clear Labour deviant during the Suez crisis was so promptly disposed of that even the larger number of Conservative cases cannot lead toward any conclusion about greater effectiveness of local pressure in one

[59] In the words of a local women's Conservative leader addressing a Plymouth party meeting: ". . . the leader knows best because he has proved himself able to speak to the world on behalf of the nation." *Western Evening Herald* (Plymouth), 14 Nov. 1956, p. 3. Incidentally every account of local Conservative reactions indicates that women, especially important in Conservative association work, had the strongest and most bitter feelings against their anti-Suez M.P.s, and the greatest loyalty to Eden—long a "Prince Charming" figure for the loyal ladies.

[60] *Bournemouth Evening Echo*, 12 Feb. 1959, p. 15.

party than the other. However, there now seems little basis for the older belief that Conservative M.P.s enjoy much more freedom from their associations than do Labour M.P.s. Not only did the Suez period record the pressure of several Conservative associations, but there is also a growing awareness that local Conservative parties are usually more highly developed organizationally than are local Labour parties. This is especially true of associations in safe seats. Labour's seats are mainly in working-class areas where, with occasional exceptions, local parties have few active individual members but consist heavily of less interested trade-union affiliated memberships. Conservative seats, on the other hand, are concentrated in constituencies where there is a large middle-class citizenry from which political activists are always drawn. In these circumstances, Conservative associations are not just larger. They are also likely to consist of members with sufficient economic status and education to feel self-confident in dealing with their M.P. To them he is not clearly an educated "better," but perhaps as Nicolson seemed to his association executive, a man whose intellectual refinements are merely superior enough to be disliked by middlebrows.

A little less speculative is the question of whether association pressures have been increasing. In the Conservative party, at any rate, there is a widespread belief that this is the case. Furthermore it is attributable to the large postwar development of a new mass Conservative organization, and in particular to the reform which severely limited the amount of money which an M.P. or a candidate could contribute to his local association. Before this reform, instituted by the Maxwell-Fyfe committee,[61] many Tory M.P.s virtually bought their seats through the payment of a large part of the local association's campaign expenses, thereby rendering a large dues-paying organization unnecessary. Obviously the M.P.s of means, as were most Conservatives, then stood in a stronger position with respect to their associations than now when they no longer pay the bills.[62]

6. Internal constituency association factors

Within both major parties, there is a good deal of variation in the size and character of local units. In the Suez cases it was generally the large and vigorous associations which reacted against deviant M.P.s, but this does not necessarily exclude the possibility that small and otherwise uninterested associations would, given the opportunity, have reacted in the same way. However, this possibility is not strong, A priori, one would expect an M.P. to have an easier time with local party leaders who were doing rela-

[61] *Interim and Final Reports of the Committee on Party Organization, 1948 and 1949* (London: National Union of Conservative and Unionist Associations, 1949).

[62] Perhaps the survival of prewar Conservative deviants was easier for other reasons. The cases of the approximately 20 M.P.s who abstained at the time of Munich do evidently contrast with the experiences of the anti-Suez Conservatives. None of these, despite the fact that their leaders made particularly sharp attacks on the Chamberlain policy (339 *H. C. Deb.* 26–562; 28 Sept.–6 Oct. 1938), appear to have been dropped by their local associations. However, a number (including Winston Churchill and Alfred Duff-Copper) had to do some explaining to their associations. *Times* (London), 5 Nov. 1938, p. 7; 12 Oct. 1938, p. 14.

tively little to build the organization. Their absence of zeal in that respect would seem likely to correspond with absence of zeal generally. Such scattered testimony as is available from M.P.s is in accord with this supposition, and particularly with the view that in Labour constituencies where trade unions are strong and where there is little incentive to build an active party organization the M.P. may be subject to less pressure on most issues.

Whether there is a difference in behavior between urban and rural associations does not emerge from the Suez experiences. Most of the constituencies concerned were urban—as indeed are most British constituencies—but two rural associations, Nutting's and Medlicott's, also reacted sharply against their M.P.s Nor is it possible, beyond urban-rural differences, to do any more generalizing about the nature of constituencies. It is true that on Suez it was the association at Bournemouth, a resort area containing many retired military officers, which dealt most vigorously with its M.P. But in the other cases it was not so clear that older retired people were more decidedly against the anti-Suez M.P.s. Even if they were, the reaction could be accounted for by the fact that the particular issue was especially emotive for an older imperialist generation of Conservatives.

7. Safeness of the seat

Here the generalization, though hardly conclusive, can start with a widely believed view: The safer the seat, other things being equal, the more vulnerable the M.P. to local party pressure.[63] The logic is apparent. The more nearly the association can regard its candidate-selection as the bestowal of a parliamentary seat, the more confident can it afford to be that it owes the M.P. little while he owes it much. In a safe seat, the association knows it can win the constituency with someone else about as easily as with the current M.P. since no particular candidate is calculated to be worth more than about 500 votes above what the party can obtain for anybody. And in a very safe seat even the intervention of a third candidate, either a Liberal or the rejected M.P. standing as an Independent, would not decisively affect the result. Nor in such a case would the association be greatly worried by a by-election brought about by its M.P.'s resignation under pressure.

Bournemouth supplies the classic example of this generalization. Here the Conservative majority was so large that the association could, and did, ignore local repercussions. Even two or three intervening candidacies by Liberals or Independents could not upset an election result. Marginal or floating voters were of no local importance no matter how much they sympathized with the M.P. Clearly Nicolson was dispensable. So, in their safe constituencies, were Nutting, Banks, Medlicott and Evans, the four other M.P.s whose Suez deviations cost them their seats. Nevertheless, along with

[63] This is more applicable to Conservative seats than to Labour's since in the latter cases, as noted, the influence of a large party majority may be counteracted by the fact that in many safe Labour seats the local organization is small and nonmilitant. Conservative associations, however, are likely to be large in safe districts as well as in marginal ones.

this impressive fact that the five M.P.s actually forced out all came from safe seats, it has to be appreciated that some of the surviving deviants, even among the anti-Suez Conservatives, also came from safe seats. In other words, a large party majority was not in itself *sufficient* to account for the fate of M.P.s who deviated on the Suez issue. On the other hand, safeness of the seat did appear in the anti-Suez Conservative cases to have been a *necessary* condition for removal of an M.P. Not only were just those with safe majorities actually purged, but the three (Yates, Astor and Kirk) in distinctly marginal constituencies survived. Granting that their survival could be accounted for in other ways as well, it is significant that each of these three M.P.s, in personal interviews, stressed the marginal character of his constituency in explaining how he rode out his association difficulties.

8. Compounded offenses

Some of the Suez deviants, it was noted, committed other earlier offenses against party orthodoxy, as interpreted by their constituency associations. These, especially their anti-hanging stands, had been important in rousing local opposition to most of the Conservative M.P.s who were later attacked for being anti-Suez. Perhaps there were some local critics who disliked their M.P. more for his stand on hanging than on Suez, and Suez might then have provided the opportunity for retaliation that the parliamentary free vote on hanging had not. Or it is possible that either offense could have been tolerated, but not both. In the words cruelly attributed to Bournemouth Conservatives: "Nicolson

didn't want the blood of either Englishmen or Arabs. What's a Tory M.P. for?"

However, the hanging question complicates the analysis only because it was another emotional issue which had arisen at about the same time as Suez. It was important but not a prime determinant of what happened to the anti-Suez Conservatives. Some who were also against hanging survived both offenses, and some did not; and two of the anti-Suez Conservatives who had not been anti-hanging lost their seats. More significant is the consideration that an M.P.'s local critics, when aroused as they were in the Suez cases, could be expected to find other offenses to charge against an M.P. If it were not the hanging issue, there would almost certainly be something else in the M.P.'s record to hold against him along with the immediate deviation. The "something else" could be his personal life, his relations with constituents, or his campaigning, as well as his parliamentary record. To be sure, another actual deviation of recent origin is the most serious way for an offense to be compounded, but it is not the only way.

9. Personal relations

This is the variable hardest to estimate, but the M.P.'s purely personal relations with his local party leaders do apparently help to account for some of the consequences of the Suez deviations. For instance, one (Boyle) of the substantial anti-Suez deviators who survived association displeasure was especially well liked personally by key local officers. And in the case of one non-surviving deviator (Nicolson), relations with the local chairman had al-

ready been strained before Suez.
However, the same sort of evidence is
not available concerning the background in the other cases where Conservative M.P.s paid the ultimate political penalty for their deviation, and
in at least one such case (Medlicott's)
personal relations appeared particularly good over many years. Anyway
the importance of good personal relations as an independent factor ought
not be exaggerated. Obviously they are
easier to maintain if there is no important political difference between an
M.P. and his local supporters. And
even if an unusual degree of friendship
does exist there is nothing to suggest
that it would be sufficient to enable an
M.P. to survive more than one deviation.

Furthermore it must be stressed
that it is often quite accidental for an
M.P. to have close personal friends in
his constituency at all, not to mention
his association. Without the American-
style residential requirement, in principle or in practice, the M.P. often
starts as a stranger in his constituency.
His acquaintances then become numerous, but their basis is political. By
moving his residence to the constituency, an M.P. may develop some non-
political ties. But few do this on a full-
time basis.

IV. SUMMARY EVALUATION

When the Suez experiences displayed
the local associations' self-generating
pressure for parliamentary conformity
to the national party leadership, these
associations were severely criticized by
the British intellectual establishment,
including academics, M.P.s themselves
and leader-writers for most of the serious national press. The editorial comment of the *Times* was typical: the
Bournemouth affair, it said, left "a
nasty taste in the mouths of all who are
concerned to see representatives of integrity, and no mere delegates, sitting
in the House of Commons." [64] And the
Times quoted Burke, as did almost all
critics of the associations. Plainly,
however, this Burkean view of how
M.P.s should function does not correspond to the realities of contemporary
British party politics; nor, as Burke
himself learned, did it correspond with
the way politics worked even in late
18th century Bristol.[65] True, the modern British Burkeans would not deny
the democratic electorate's power
eventually to get rid of an M.P. whose
convictions differ from its own. What
is objected to is that the small portion
of the electorate composing a local
party's leadership should have this
power, and that it should use it in the
manner of a lynch mob in immediate
retaliation against a deviating M.P.
This latter point about method, while
much was made of it concerning Nicolson and Evans, does not seem crucial.
The association's power would be as
great if it waited a few extra months
before formally rejecting its M.P., or
even if it merely threatened to do so.

[64] 3 Oct. 1958, p. 7.

[65] What actually happened to Burke is worth
looking at along with his more familiar classic
apologia. There is a most judicious account by
Ernest Barker, "Burke and His Bristol Constituency, 1774–1780," in his *Essays on Government*
(London: Oxford Press, 1951), ch. vi. More details
are supplied in a somewhat antiquarian manner
by G. E. Weare, *Edmund Burke's Connection
with Bristol, From 1774 till 1780* (Bristol: Wm.
Bennett, 1894).

Anyway there is a strong practical reason for an association, once dissatisfied with its M.P., to secure quickly a new prospective general election candidate to fill the role which a locally-disowned M.P. can no longer play at party meetings.

Accordingly, the significant question is whether the associations should have the power at all to reject their M.P.s for their deviations. Once posed this way, the answer—given the British political system—has to be yes. It would be ridiculous to suggest that the groups which select candidates should not be able to reject them. If one wants to take away the power to reject, then the power to select must be shifted as well. It makes little sense to say that an M.P., when he is being rejected by the same group which selected him, should be able to appeal beyond this group to a larger section of the local electorate. Unless the British critics wish to substitute something like an American-style primary method of candidate selection—and they assuredly do not—then the power of constituency associations has to be borne.

More significantly, any shift in power from the associations might alter the basic arrangement for carrying on British parliamentary government. That arrangement, resting as it does on virtually complete party cohesion in the Commons, appears incompatible with a method of candidate selection which would transfer an M.P.'s loyalty from the zealous faithful of his association to those who are merely party voters. Such a transfer would have the effect, as it does in those American states where the primary is really effectual, of freeing the legislator from a complete dependence on party supporters for his political survival. This would not only allow an M.P. to use his own judgment; it would also subject him increasingly to the cross-pressures of various local interest groups. Both results would tend to work against parliamentary cohesion.

In other words, the British model of constituency association-M.P. relations is an integral part of the nation's working form of parliamentary government. Only the dislike of many Englishmen for the way that model functioned during the Suez crisis obscured this principle. However, even at the time, it was not obscure to an old hand at the maintenance of parliamentary party cohesion. Thus Earl Attlee, in a magazine debate with one of the anti-Suez Conservatives, wrote that there are "few, if any, Members who get into Parliament on account of their own qualities. They are elected because the politically active citizens select them as expressing broadly their views, and because these same citizens have worked to persuade a majority of the electors to support them." [66] So, Attlee continued, if an M.P. fails to support the government or fails to act with the opposition in its efforts to turn the government out, he acts contrary to the expectations of those who have put their trust in him. It follows, for Attlee, that when in disagreement with his party on a major issue an M.P. should submit the issue to his local as-

[66] "Party Discipline is Paramount," *The National and English Review*, Vol. 148 (Jan. 1957), p. 15. Attlee's piece is published along with Sir Edward Boyle's case for only a slightly looser interpretation of party discipline—one just loose enough to justify his own Suez deviation.

sociation and resign if the association so wishes. However, such a situation, as Attlee indicates, arises but rarely. The rules of the game are too well understood by almost all of the participants. M.P.s know what their parties expect by way of loyalty to the national cause, and they know that such loyalty is of the essence of British politics. In Attlee's words, the party leader requires disciplined troops "unless one is prepared to lose the battle." [67] In this perspective, constituency associations are only the ultimate sanction for rules usually observed for other reasons.

One can agree with Attlee about the role of constituency associations in preserving parliamentary party cohesion without sharing the dismay, first reflected by Ostrogorski and now by British liberals, concerning the power of the associations. Really how one regards this power depends on how one values the strong parliamentary party cohesion to which it contributes. And it is hard to see how British cabinet government, in contrast to the American style independent executive, can function satisfactorily in modern times without such party cohesion.

[67] *Ibid.,* p. 16.

FOR FURTHER READING

BALES, Robert F., *Interaction Process Analysis: A Method for the Study of Small Groups* (Reading, Mass.: Addison-Wesley, 1950).

BARBER, James D., *Power in Committees: An Experiment in the Governmental Process* (Chicago: Rand McNally, 1966).

COLLINS, Barry E. and Harold Guetzkow, *A Social Psychology of Group Processes for Decision Making* (New York: Wiley, 1964).

FENNO, Richard F., *The Power of the Purse* (Boston: Little, Brown, 1966).

GOLEMBIEWSKI, Robert T., *The Small Group* (Chicago: University of Chicago Press, 1962).

HARE, A. Paul, *Handbook of Small Group Research* (New York: Free Press, 1962).

HARE, A. Paul, Edgar F. Borgatta, Robert F. Bales (Eds.), *Small Groups: Studies in Social Interaction* (New York: Knopf, 1965).

HOMANS, George C., *The Human Group* (New York: Harcourt, Brace, 1950).

LATHAM, Earl, *The Group Basis of Politics* (Ithaca: Cornell University Press, 1952).

TRUMAN, David B., *The Congressional Party* (New York: Wiley, 1959).

TRUMAN, David B., *The Governmental Process* (New York: Knopf, 1951).

VERBA, Sidney, *Small Groups and Political Behavior* (Princeton: Princeton University Press, 1961).

ZEIGLER, Harmon, *Interest Groups in American Society* (Englewood Cliffs: Prentice-Hall, 1964).

PART FOUR: ATTITUDE

An understanding of attitudes is essential to a real grasp of role theory or group theory. Attitudes about the behavior expected of a person playing a role are a most important part of any role definition. The shared attitudes of members of a group, whether concerning the norms of the group, the goals of the group, or the environment in which the group finds itself, distinguish the group and help us understand its behavior. This we have already seen. In subsequent sections of the book, we shall learn that the attitudes of persons sending and receiving messages have much to do with the ability to communicate, and for this reason attitudes are important in the exercise of influence. Hence this location for the selections dealing directly with attitudes is not accidental. Attitudes link together what has gone before with what is yet to come.

The study of attitudes is relatively well developed, in part because work on them has been going forward for some time. Four phases, more or less following one another, can be distinguished. In the last decades of the nineteenth century and the first of the twentieth, the concept of attitude was coming into use in psychology. Once the concept was established, professional attention was given to the development of operational definitions which could be used to measure attitudes. This was followed by further descriptive and theoretical work. In this third phase the single concept of attitude gave way to a series of related concepts, each of which concerned some particular attitudinal property. And these more detailed descriptions and theories led in the last decade to more elaborate real world studies of cognitive dynamics. The interrelationships between theory and measurement have, of course, been much more complex than these four phases suggest, but thinking in these terms does not distort that involved intellectual history more than simplifications usually do.

Political scientists began to give explicit attention to attitudes in the 1930's after psychologists such as L. L. Thurstone and Rensis Likert had worked out successful measurement techniques. These methods, some of which became widely known with the establishment of the Gallup Poll, had obvious application in the study of public opinion. Continued impetus for the study of attitudes came in the 1940's with the work of Paul Lazarsfeld and Louis Guttman. The work of Lazarsfeld and his colleagues in *The People's Choice,* an early voting study, came to the attention of many political scientists, and Guttman scaling techniques were to find wide use in studies of legislative and judicial attitudes.

Our first selection illustrates the developing interest in a more detailed description of the properties of attitudes which came during the post-war years. In one of the best studies to be done in this third phase, M. Brewster Smith, Jerome S. Bruner, and Robert W. White, all psychologists, gathered comprehensive information about the personal lives of ten men and their attitudes toward the

Soviet Union in 1947. Their principal interest was with the personal setting of a public opinion. They wanted to know how a person's opinions and beliefs were linked to his basic personality and to the informational environment in which he lived. But they also sought to "develop a coherent framework for conceptualizing these relations, and to illustrate this framework sufficiently to encourage more systematic investigation of the research problems to which it gives rise." [1] Their conscious interest in concept development makes this study particularly valuable to us. From the excerpts in this book, we first learn what Smith, Bruner, and White's concepts are. Next, in two sketches of the men they studied, we see how very limited information about the Soviet Union was sufficient for the personal needs of a factory operative called Sam Hodder, and how an amiable real estate agent was able to absorb a wide range of information about Russia without his basic outlook being altered in any fundamental way. Then, having shown that attitudes thus conceptualized can be related to individual personalities, Smith, Bruner, and White use their set of concepts to describe the opinions of all ten men. One can see that these concepts can be related to each other to construct a theory of attitudes, and that they have been operationalized so they can be applied either to individuals or, if the data are available, to the attitudes of a large population. It is therefore no surprise that saliency, differentiation, time perspective, and so forth, have found wide use in subsequent studies.

Research done in the years since the publication of Smith, Bruner, and White's *Opinions and Personality* has resulted in many changes in our understanding of attitudes. Robert Zajonc concluded a recent survey of cognitive theories with the statement: "There is almost no overlap between the present chapter and [a similar survey published in 1954]. The changes in the field have been remarkable and one observes with amazement how little we have in common with the previous generation of social psychologists." [2] The key change is the current emphasis on *cognitive organization*. In Theodore Newcomb's *Social Psychology*, published in 1950, an attitude was defined as a state of readiness to be motivated. In the 1965 edition of *Social Psychology*, Newcomb, Turner, and Converse added another definition with a different emphasis: "From a cognitive point of view, an attitude represents an organization of valenced cognitions." [3] Research such as that done by Smith, Bruner, and White called our attention to cognitive structuring, to questions of how the components of one's mental world were related to one another. Current research is using these concepts in order to investigate questions of cognitive dynamics.

An understanding of the importance of cognitive organization has given us a different view of perception. The pioneering work of Paul Lazarsfeld and his colleagues had made selective perception a very important concept for political scientists. Their view, unchallenged for a score of years, was: "From his many past experiences shared with others in his economic, religious, and community groups, (the voter) has a readiness to attend to some things more than others. . . . Voters somehow contrive to select out of the passing stream of stimuli those by

---

[1] *Opinions and Personality* (New York: Wiley, 1956), p. v.

[2] "Cognitive Theories in Social Psychology" in Gardner Lindzey and Elliott Aronson (Eds.), *Handbook of Social Psychology*, 2nd ed. (Reading, Mass.: Addison-Wesley, 1968), vol. 1, p. 391.

[3] Theodore M. Newcomb, Ralph H. Turner, and Philip E. Converse, *Social Psychology: The Study of Human Interaction* (New York: Holt, Rinehart and Winston, 1965), p. 40.

which they are more inclined to be persuaded."[4] But a recent review of the studies on selective perception led to a different interpretation.

> This research suggests a change of emphasis in our thinking about how people deal with discrepant information. It has generally been assumed that selective exposure and other processes that bar information reception are prime mechanisms by which people resist influence. . . . [But] perhaps resistance to influence is accomplished most often and most successfully at the level of information evaluation, rather than at the level of selective seeking and avoiding information.[5]

"Information evaluation" is the last sentence in this quote refers to cognitive dynamics. We are led to ask what subjective meaning is given to a bit of newly acquired information because of the recipient's already established cognitive organization.

Ralph K. White's "Misperception of Aggression in Vietnam" raises essentially this question. Professor White, a psychologist who has worked for many years on propaganda, how nations perceive each other, and other foreign policy topics, points out that both sides see the other as the aggressor in Vietnam. The reasons Americans perceive the North Vietnamese to be the aggressors—sending troops to the South, a campaign of assassination against South Vietnamese leaders—are quite familiar, and Professor White has examined the American perception of the war elsewhere.[6] In this article, he asks why the North Vietnamese perceive Americans to be the aggressors. He points to eight bits of evidence, eight valenced cognitions as Newcomb, Turner, and Converse would refer to them, "that when strongly focused upon by a Communist mind and interpreted with a Communist frame of reference could seem to substantiate his charge of American aggression." It is not the presence or absence of information,[7] nor any intrinsic meaning that information may contain, that leads to a particular perception. Rather it is a question of which bits of information are salient, and how a person organizes the information that is important to him.

Robert E. Lane is particularly suited to study the way one organizes information about his political world. He is a fine political scientist who has had professional training in psychotherapy as well. Before writing *Political Ideology,* the 1962 book from which "Political Cognition in Eastport" is taken, he conducted extensive depth interviews with fifteen lower middle class and working class men. The opening sentence of his book—If we are to talk about the human mind, let us start with human beings.[8]—suggests Professor Lane's approach. He has

[4] Paul Lazarsfeld, *The People's Choice,* 2nd ed. (New York: Columbia University Press, 1948), pp. 81–82.

[5] David O. Sears and Jonathan L. Freedman, "Selective Exposure to Information: A Critical Review" *Public Opinion Quarterly,* Summer, 1967, p. 213.

[6] Ralph K. White, "Misperception and the Vietnam War," *Journal of Social Issues,* July, 1966, pp. 1–167.

[7] Obviously, there is some *de facto* perceptual selectivity which shapes North Vietnamese thinking as well. Radio Hanoi does not present the American view of the conflict, and this produces an informational environment in which a North Vietnamese is likely to encounter new information which supports the view he already has.

[8] *Political Ideology* (New York: The Free Press of Glencoe, 1962), p. 1.

enough empathy with his subjects to be able to show how their cognitions are related to their underlying personalities and to their daily experiences in Eastport. And with this foundation, Lane is also able to indicate the consequences of their "typical" mode of conceptualization for the larger political system.

The men of Eastport, Professor Lane finds, are not political theorists who use broad social concepts easily and pursue ideas to their logical conclusions. Often single units of information remain discrete and isolated from one another. When concepts are used, they are apt to be narrow and close to their personal work-a-day experiences. "They have differentiated and easily articulated concepts about money, work, and consumption, but their conceptualization of their religious beliefs, the duties of the church, and the purposes of life are blunt and unsophisticated." [9] Their cognitions about politics (and other matters at some remove from the central experiences of their lives) tend to be undifferentiated and unstructured. This cognitive style, of course, may be quite appropriate for the needs of a person of modest education who is confronted with a complex and rapidly changing environment. If the Eastport workingman does not relate his actions as, say, a consumer and a voter to one another, he will not be troubled by a need to rationalize his behavior in the light of any particular economic doctrine. And the same characteristics that give a formlessness to his thought also guarantee that it will not be frozen. "Without the blockages of strong emotion, or the walls of ideological defensiveness, their minds, like the society itself, seem pluralistic, with both liberal and conservative roots to which new ideas can attach themselves and grow." [10]

"The Cognitive Structuring of John Foster Dulles" provides a sharp contrast. If the cognitive patterns of Eastport workingmen tended to be relatively unstructured and undifferentiated, here we see a cognitive pattern marked by such clear organization that it survived over a very long time. Ole R. Holsti, the author of this piece, has a particular interest in the perceptions of those in policy-making positions, and has done considerable work with content analysis. The assertions Professor Holsti advances about Secretary Dulles's point of view in fact rest on a content analysis published in *Enemies in Politics*.[11]

John Foster Dulles had decided opinions. Both his grandfather and his uncle had served as Secretaries of State, and his personal experience in diplomacy and international law extended over half a century. But it should be stressed that his views were *not* abnormally rigid. Our interest in his thinking stems from the fact that the data on Secretary Dulles are rich enough, and Professor Holsti's analysis is good enough, to enable us to interpret his attitude system in the light of what we now regard as normal cognitive dynamics. During the 1950's there was a great deal of exciting new work in this area. Fitz Heider's earlier (1946) principle of structural balance was developed into a theory of cognitive congruity by Charles Osgood and Percy Tannenbaum. Leon Festinger published his seminal *Theory of Cognitive Dissonance*. Robert Abelson and Milton Rosenberg presented a mathematical model based on eight rules of symbolic psycho-logic. There are some important technical distinctions between these theories, but they all imply that incongruent or dissonant information tends to be rejected. An existing attitu-

[9] *Political Ideology*, p. 362.

[10] *Political Ideology*, p. 363.

[11] David J. Finlay, Ole R. Holsti, and Richard R. Fagen, (Chicago: Rand McNally, 1967).

dinal system, on the other hand, tends to remain in balance. It is this point which Professor Holsti develops in the case of John Foster Dulles. Because each of his cognitions about the Soviet Union were supported by others, his attitudinal system was very stable. Massive evidence was necessary before Secretary Dulles finally changed his belief in Russian economic weakness. *All* of the other cognitions described by Holsti remained unaltered until Dulles's death.

These theories of cognitive organization also cast light on questions of attitude change, the focus of Herbert Hyman and Paul B. Sheatsley's "Attitudes toward Desegregation." We know that the acquisition of some new bit of information concerning the attitude object is necessary for an attitude to change, but we also know that this is by no means a common occurrence. Indeed, one well-known study on which Professor Hyman, a distinguished sociologist, and Mr. Sheatsley, a pollster long associated with the National Opinion Research Center, also collaborated, was entitled "Some Reasons Why Information Campaigns Fail." Their evidence was drawn from surveys about foreign policy taken during the immediate post-war period. Among other things, Hyman and Sheatsley found that there exist a hard core of chronic "know-nothings," that those who paid the closest attention to information campaigns were those who already were interested in foreign policy and had well developed attitudes, and that, as we would now put it, people often use dissonance-reduction mechanisms to keep incongruent information from causing any change in existing cognitive structures. Despite fanciful popular writing about attitude "manipulation," the weight of the evidence is that substantial attitude change is relatively unusual.

"Attitudes toward Desegregation" is of interest because it is a study of just such a substantial attitude change. In fact, another study has shown that the magnitude of this attitude shift is among the highest of which we have record.[12] Why should this be so? Answering this question permits some conclusions about the conditions which facilitate attitude change. First, if the topic is not important to a person (if it is psychologically remote), it is easy to ignore it. But as Hyman and Sheatsley state, "plainly the conflicts of integration had immediacy for the young Southerners." Second, new information is more likely to be accepted if it comes from a trusted source or if it is based on firsthand observation. Hyman and Sheatsley find that attitudes accommodated themselves to integration *after* official action has been taken in one's own community. This, of course, makes it possible to learn from one's own friends what has happened, or, better yet, to judge for oneself. For similar reasons of the trustworthiness of information, Southerners who have lived in the North are more likely to have changed their attitudes in a pro-integration direction. And a "moderate level of inconsistency [in one's cognitive organization] may be conducive to a better reality orientation and to greater combinatorial resourcefulness."[13] What this suggests is that new information may not immediately alter the general character of an attitude system, but may be incorporated as inconsistent information. If this happens frequently enough, however, the attitude system may be weakened to a point where some major change is possible. Something of this nature may have happened to American

[12] Karl W. Deutsch and Richard L. Merritt, "Effects of Events on National and International Images" in Herbert C. Kelman (Ed.), *International Behavior* (New York: Holt, Rinehart and Winston, 1965), pp. 172–173, 180–181.

[13] Deutsch and Merritt, "Effects of Events on National and International Images," p. 159.

attitudes about desegregation. At some point in the past, there was a coherent structure of racist attitudes. Acceptance of some initial bit of incongruent information, for example, the observed fact that the local schools continued to function after they had been integrated, was the first step in a sequence which eventually could lead to a modification of the whole system of attitudes about race.

In Philip E. Converse's "The Nature of Belief Systems in Mass Publics," we see microconcepts used in an elegant discussion of ideology. This is of special interest because one frequently hears statements made that ideas (liberty, the public interest, and so on) are the root of political life, and concepts such as those in this book cannot be employed to study this most important subject matter.[14] The problem with such statements is that they are usually made by individuals who do not have any personal experience using microconcepts, and who do not have, therefore, a very precise idea of what is and is not possible. Professor Converse, who is perhaps best known to political scientists as co-author of *The American Voter* and *Elections and the Political Order,* does have the requisite qualifications. He is quite sensitive to theoretical questions, but, in addition, he has shown great ingenuity in devising operational measures which can be used with real-world data.

Professor Converse begins with a careful definition of a belief system as "a configuration of ideas and attitudes in which the elements are bound together by some form of constraint or functional interdependence." [15] (This definition, incidentally, means that the diagram of a conceptual network in Figure I-1 may be used to visualize a belief system.) He then proceeds to an analysis of easy macro-level statements such as "The country is becoming more conservative." by looking for manifestations a belief system should exhibit if it in fact exists in the minds of members of the general public. He reviews data on the levels of conceptualization found characteristic of the American public, then looks at the number of constraints linking attitudinal elements and the stability of these cognitions over time contrasting political elites and mass publics on these points. Essentially he finds that the elites have coherent belief systems such as that of John Foster Dulles while the belief systems of the mass public are closer to the vague theories shown by the workingmen of Eastport. "A realistic picture of political belief systems in the mass public," he tells us, "is not one that omits issues and policy demands completely, nor is it one that presumes widespread ideological coherence; it is rather one that captures with some fidelity the fragmentation, narrowness, and diversity of these demands." [16]

Converse's major finding, however, is that the differences between elite and mass are sufficiently great that it is a mistake to think of mass behavior in primarily ideological terms. A better hypothesis is that there is a discontinuity in political movements as they gain true mass support; the movements' new supporters may have quite different beliefs than those which animated the founding elite.

---

[14] See, for example, the freewheeling attack of Russell Kirk and the much more carefully thought out strictures of Mulford Q. Sibley in James C. Charlesworth (Ed.), *The Limits of Behavioralism in Political Science* (Philadelphia: American Academy of Political and Social Science, 1962).

[15] "The Nature of Belief Systems in Mass Publics" in David E. Apter (Ed.), *Ideology and Discontent* (New York: The Free Press of Glencoe, 1964), p. 207.

[16] "The Nature of Belief Systems in Mass Publics," p. 247.

Professor Converse closes by showing there is evidence to support this hypothesis in the origin of the Republican party in the United States and in the electoral success of the Nazi party in Germany. He thus provides us with a fine example of the use of microconcepts to yield a more richly detailed analysis of macrolevel behavior.

SOME PROPERTIES
OF ATTITUDES
M. BREWSTER SMITH,
JEROME S. BRUNER,
AND ROBERT M. WHITE

DESCRIBING AN OPINION

It follows from [knowledge] of personality functioning that we must define an attitude in such a way as to take into account its presumed interrelation with other aspects of personality. With this in mind we define an attitude as a predisposition to experience a class of objects in certain ways, with characteristic affect; to be motivated by this class of objects in characteristic ways; and to act with respect to these objects in a characteristic fashion. In brief, an attitude is a predisposition to experience, to be motivated by, and to act toward, a class of objects in a predictable manner.

We shall not be fussy about the word used to denote the phenomenon described in our definition. Attitude, opinion, sentiment—all of these terms refer to the kind of predisposition we have in mind. The permanence of such a predisposition is less a

problem of definition than of measurement. Although it is true that most of the attitudes in which the social psychologist and student of personality are interested are relatively long enduring, we would emphasize the continuity between supposedly short-term "sets" and more long-term "attitudes." Finally, the class of objects around which a sentiment is organized—the object that one is predisposed to experience, to be motivated by, and to act toward in a characteristic manner—need not be restricted as in some definitions of attitude to "social objects" or "controversial issues." For an attitude as we have defined it can be related to any class of objects which exist in the person's life space: moral issues, lifted weights in a psychological experiment, Russia, prime numbers, or what not. The specification of objects is again an empirical matter, not a matter for definition.

The reader will sense that our rather broad definition of attitude or sentiment is in the tradition of Shand and McDougall, and conforms in the main to the usage of most contemporary writers such as Murray, Krech and Crutchfield, and Newcomb. In all honesty we must confess that we do not think the time is ripe to be theoretically solemn about the definition of an attitude. Definitions are matters of convenience, and they attain high status only in the advanced stages of a science. In time, greater precision will come. In the meantime we think that little is served by quarreling about definition in the abstract.

Now let us sketch our descriptive apparatus for distinguishing the *object* of an attitude. As we have indicated, it may be anything in the life space of the individual. In less technical terms, it may be anything which exists for the person.

One problem in the use of words can be set aright here. It is important to distinguish the object as it exists for the person and the object as we designate it in common speech. When the object of a sentiment is specified in terms of some social referent, we shall speak of the *topic* of an attitude. A man, let us say, has a highly negative attitude toward "Russia-as-it-exists-for-him." "Russia-as-it-exists-for-him" is the *object* of his sentiment. When, however, we speak of this man's attitude toward "the Soviet Union" or "Russia" or some other socially defined entity, we shall be speaking of the *topic* of his attitude. Perhaps the use of these two terms will keep us from the pitfall of assuming that attitudes have as their objects the socially defined entities of the history books and newspaper columns.

We may distinguish various characteristics of the object of a sentiment: *differentiation, saliency, time perspective, informational support,* and *object value.* We shall consider each of these in turn.

Differentiation

An attitude toward Russia may be focused upon a highly amorphous subjective impression of that country or upon a highly differentiated one. One person will see Russia as a highly complex phenomenon comprising many *aspects;* Russia as a social experiment, Russia as an aggressor, Russia as a country capable of producing many of the great literary figures of the 19th century, Russia as an approach to Orwell's *1984,* Russia as a veritable basin of natural resources, Russia as anti-Zionist—all of these may be aspects of one man's view of Russia. To another man, Russia is a collectivity of ignorant peasants guided by a small ruthless band of radical agitators and "trouble-makers"—and that is about all. Not only is the object of an attitude differentiated into various aspects; it also varies with respect to its *organization.* "Degrees" of structure are not readily specified, and we shall not attempt to scale such a dimension. One can, however, specify the manner in which a differentiated object of opinion is organized. In the second hypothetical case cited above, the major, organizing aspect of our man's view of Russia might be the sensed absence of personal liberty in that country, and all other parts of the picture might be subordinated to it. We shall see at least one case of this sort in the case histories of the following chapters. In sum, then, the object of an attitude varies in its differentiation; and given any particular order of differentiation, it also varies in the manner of its organization.

Saliency

By this term we indicate the extent to which a particular object or class of objects is central in the everyday concerns of a person. Russia and Communism were matters of the most personal concern and central attention for one of our subjects—almost the most important things in his life. For another, it was of the most marginal interest.[1] We may also speak of the saliency of various differentiated aspects of a man's view of Russia—saying, for example, that Russian anti-religious activity for a given person is more salient than Russian aggressiveness.

Time perspective

Here we mean the temporal frame of reference applied to the object of a sentiment. In our analysis of cases we found this to be an inescapable and vital characteristic of an attitude. Characterizing time perspective systematically is difficult. Yet if we are to predict anything about the way in which the person will guide his actions, it is essential that we do so. Again in terms of Russia, one person will regard Russia as a matter of only momentary, transitory concern: something that erupts into the headlines for a while and then is gone. Another will take, as one of our subjects did, a long-term view, the essential theme of which was: "Russia is an unreasonable child; if we remain firm, she will eventually grow up." Still another will

[1] A recent survey of the American public concludes as one of its principal findings that the threat of Communism is very low in saliency for most Americans. See S. A. Stouffer, *Communism, Conformity, and Civil Liberties* (New York: Doubleday & Company, 1955).

adopt a short-term climactic point of view in which Russia is seen as making tremendous inroads into our strength which, unless stopped immediately, will drive us to disaster. Such characterizations of time perspective are, to be sure, highly qualitative and will undoubtedly vary widely as one goes from one kind of attitude to another. Although we do not pretend to have reached an adequate way of handling time perspective, we are convinced that it is a vital aspect of a person's sentiment.

Informational support

Strictly speaking, this term does not characterize the object itself, but rather the knowledge an individual possesses that is relevant to his attitude. It merely identifies the amount of information a person is capable of bringing to bear in appraising the topic of an attitude. In our studies, for example, we have used rather primitive information tests to determine how much the individual "knows" about various phases of Soviet life and society. We recognize, of course, that there is a very close relationship between the amount of differentiation of an attitude and the amount of its informational support. Differentiation refers to an analysis of the person's subjective conception of Russia (which is based upon many things aside from information): while informational *support* refers merely to the amount of the available information that may go into the building of this conception.

Object value

Here we refer to the affective tone of an object. We had considered the term "object *affect*," our choice of "value" being dictated primarily by the importance of value in the sense of positive, negative, and neutral. For the first thing we usually ask about the object of a person's sentiment is whether it appears as disagreeable, pleasant, or neutral. It goes without saying, of course, that when one has said that Russia is a negatively toned symbol for a given person, one has said very little. One must also specify certain other affective qualities: whether, for example, it is seen as threatening or simply as annoying.

So much for the general description of objects about which people have sentiments. One could doubtless multiply categories in terms of which description can be carried out. We have wanted merely to construct a minimum set of variables which might guide us in our exploration. The task of expanding or contracting our modes of description and of rendering them quantitatively scalable remains, of course, for future work.

Orientation

Our next task is to characterize the action tendencies aroused by the object: what we shall call the *orientation* of an attitude. Given a person's subjective view of Russia, we may ask how he orients himself action-wise. In abstract terms, we may speak of three possible action tendencies: *approach, avoidance,* and *hostility.* Concretely, and again in terms of an attitude toward Russia, approach may mean a wish to go to Russia, the act of taking books out of the library to find out more about Russia, joining the Communist Party, buying the *Daily Worker* to find out about its side of the story, or what not. Avoidance again may take varied

forms: anything from motivated indifference to an actual active avoidance of anything having to do with Russia. Hostility we know to be a subtle and complex form of behavior. By it we mean any act whose objective is injury, debasement, or any other form of harm to the object: advocating a preventive war, voting for a rabidly anti-Communist candidate, or even fantasying a counterrevolution in Russia.

Policy stand

The translation of one's orientation into a preference for a particular proposal for collective action (such as a given foreign policy), we shall call the *policy stand* of the person. *Policy stand* indicates preference for a socially defined policy and may or may not be identical with the individual's own *orientation.* So a person may say, "I'm in favor of taking Russia's veto power away, but what I'd really like to do is to take the whole damned Politburo and dump them into the middle of the Atlantic Ocean." Most of the work done in public opinion polling is designed to discover the policy stands of cross-sections of the population. And one of the major differences between the regular polls and the open-ended surveys is that the latter try to determine the orientation of their respondents in addition to their stand on policies.

THE EXPRESSIVE NATURE OF OPINIONS

A person's behavior is marked by a certain self-consistency or congruency. Expressive movement, speech, intensity of striving, style of thinking, "temperament"—all of these things and many others seem to constitute a congruent pattern which we think of as typical of the individual. How one comes to know this flavor or style in another person is one of the neglected problems in psychology. Yet in spite of the fact that correlational studies designed to uncover consistency between selected facets of behavior have left unresolved the basis of their congruence, there is no gainsaying that this congruence is one of the primary facts of human behavior.

How much of this consistency can be attributed to innate or constitutional endowment and how much can be referred to the distinctive pattern of adjustment achieved by the person in coping with the world is not a particularly fruitful kind of inquiry. Given a person with certain initial endowments of energy and cognitive equipment, there inevitably develops a style of adjustment to the world which is shaped and limited both by constitution and by the intervening opportunities the person has had for learning and adapting.

Opinions, like any other form of complex behavior, are involved in such a pattern of consistency. They reflect the man's style of operating. When we speak of "the expressive nature of opinions" we refer not to any need for expression, but rather to the simple fact that a man's opinions reflect the deeper-lying pattern of his life—who he has become by virtue of facing a particular kind of world with a particular kind of constitution.

In our analysis of concrete opinions, we explain little by saying that a given opinion is "expressive" of the man. Yet there are times when one can do no better than this. A person, let us say, has as one of his most salient cognitive characteristics an inability to deal with abstractions. He must solve all his problems on the level of mulling over the concrete details of events. Perhaps he got that way in the course of adjusting to the conditions of his life. Yet examination of his intellectual functioning shows a definite limit in his intellectual capacities. We find in this individual's opinions the same lack of generality, the same preoccupation with minor detail that is characteristic of his performance in a mental test. To put the matter in dynamic or functional terms—to say, for example, that his opinions serve the function of keeping the informational environment cut down to manipulable size—would be to stretch things considerably. Granted that this preference for detail may serve a function in the *economy* of his personality, it seems to us evident that his detail-oriented opinions are also to be understood as expressive of the over-all *style* of the person.

Another person, let us say, has a history from earliest childhood of meagre energy and a low fatigue threshold. The adult pattern of life of such a person may reflect an adjustment to this deficit, marked among other things by a lack of interest in affairs of the world outside the immediate circuit of routine daily activities. We may find that this man at age forty is markedly indifferent toward the issues of Russia and foreign policy. Again, one can put the matter in dynamic terms: his opinions are a function of needs to conserve energy. But at the simplest level of analysis one must also note that indifference toward world political affairs in this man is expressive of a more pervading indifference toward the world outside his immediate personal orbit.

We do not want to make an issue of the difference between analysis in terms of "need fulfillment" and description in terms of expressive "consistency." For we shall utilize both approaches. Rather, there are certain points in our study where it seems to us that parsimony is on the side of shunning the dynamic explanation in favor of the less glamorous description. The expression of temperamental traits is one such case. A man of generally vivid affect is likely to feel more vividly than others about his opinions. We shall not seek to find dynamic explanations for it, granting nonetheless that in other kinds of personality research one might be primarily concerned with the psychodynamic origins of vivid affect. The same is true of intellectual functioning. We feel no strong urge to explain the gratifications accruing to the unintelligent man by virtue of having poorly informed opinions. Again, in another context, stupidity may be the object of dynamic analysis. Should the vivid man be apathetic toward a major event or the dull person reveal a fastidiously equipped storehouse of reasoned knowledge on a complex issue —then we too shall be more concerned about the dynamics involved.

SAM HODDER

Sam Hodder was casual about union participation, little interested in long-range plans for social betterment, quite contented with his position in life even though he earned only about $2700 a year. His education extended only through six years of grade school, and his scores on tests of intellectual ability were the lowest of our group, though still within the "bright normal" range. His forty-eight years had been spent in ways so diverse and helter-skelter that it was almost impossible to reconstruct the order of events. From fifteen to forty-five he had used alcohol with great freedom, but for the last three years his allegiance had been given to Alcoholics Anonymous.

Hodder provided us with our best opportunity to examine opinions in a person little given to reading, reflection, or the more abstract operations of mind. His speech was ungrammatical, disjunctive, full of slang and profanity; the limits of his vocabulary often demanded a rewording of instructions. Many of the verbal coins used in the exchange of opinions were unfamiliar to him, so that we had to learn his views without relying on such standard pieces as "Socialism," "Liberalism," "veto," and "isolationism." It was plain from the tests, however, that Hodder was a man of better than average potentiality. His performance on the *Wechsler-Bellevue Test* yielded an I.Q. of 113. At a concrete level he functioned effectively, showing good common sense and practical judgment. It was in the realm of abstraction that his limitations were most marked. On the *Vigotsky Test,* for instance, his performance was primitively concrete, and in the *Argument Completions* he found it impossible to marshal arguments, though he sometimes put forth a fairly sound overall conclusion. He never read books, rarely listened to the radio, and did little more than scan such newspapers and magazines as came his way. Both his information and his opinions were arrived at almost wholly through channels of conversation.

In all his contacts with us Hodder was completely at ease, good-humored and cheerful. After a brief warming-up period he obviously came to consider all the interviewers as good friends with whom he could have an enjoyable time, even when they involved him in baffling tasks or, as in the *Stress Interview*, unaccountably expressed nonsensical opinions. He took them as partners into each situation, pleasantly sharing with them his reminiscences, opinions, and reactions to the tests. He did not try to impress us, nor was he overimpressed by us. When his views were challenged he asserted himself vigorously yet without hostility. In the interviews he was almost always open and frank, conspicuously free of defensiveness. While acknowledging his educational and intellectual shortcomings with some regret and condemning his past life as a heavy drinker, he discussed these matters with little sign of sensitivity or guilt. His interest in our project was at the start purely financial, but he came to enjoy the sessions for the fun that he could get, and give, in social interaction.

When Hodder was three months old his mother, a dressmaker, turned him over to her parents for upbringing. From this circumstance and from his evasiveness when questioned about his father we inferred that the relationship between his parents might have been of the most transient character. Although the mother lived near the grandparents, she apparently had little contact with her child and was content to leave him in safe hands. Hodder described his grandmother with some warmth as a kindly woman who took good care of him, fed him well, and set him the pattern of a devout Roman Catholic. She was probably a most satisfactory mother during his infancy, but she got beyond her depth when it came to understanding and guiding an active growing boy. He remembered that she dressed him in clothes that brought ridicule and that she tried to keep him from playing with other children on Sunday. Her attempts at restraint soon became ineffective; he did pretty much as he pleased, getting out of school and church attendance and living largely outside the home. The grandfather, a shoemaker and a drunk, was equally ineffective. Though he sometimes attempted control and sometimes helped get Sam out of scrapes, he inspired neither admiration nor fear and provided no model after which, or against which, the boy could fashion himself. From the time Sam was six or seven years old his grandparents had no influence that could compete with that of the boys who roamed freely in the run-down neighborhood.

It was in the gang that Sam developed the main outlines of his present personality. Tall, lean, and strong, he met group standards as a fighter and probably exercised his share of leadership in the daily program of adventure and mischief. Gang activities were a constant source of pleasure and excitement, and his belongingness gave a solid ground of security. Absorption in the activities of these groups together with the defiance of authorities prescribed by group mores contributed to his neglect of school. Against school authorities, truant officers, and the police he learned to conduct a guerrilla warfare of trickery, cheating, and defiance. The police were the enemies most feared, but their influence and threat were effectively annulled by their own attitude of joking and kidding between occasions of punishment. The activities of the gangs changed with age. Games and mischief, inter-gang fights and petty stealing evolved in the direction of more serious delinquency, and the program was progressively enriched by gambling, drinking, and sexual exploits. It is interesting to note that the gang members themselves felt a certain parting of the ways during adolescence. A few members joined forces with older delinquents and embarked on criminal careers; the others found employment and began the painful process of settling down. Sam Hodder rejected the higher walks of delinquency but postponed settling down in favor of going to sea as a sailor.

After a few years at sea, having visited many parts of the world and participated in many adventures, he came ashore again and supported himself by a succession of small jobs. For a two-year period he had his own business delivering coal and ice. At the age of 32 he obtained a job with the company for which he has worked ever since, a large and stable concern offering a considerable sense of security. Describing his work, he mentioned as its chief asset the pleasurable company provided by the team of fellow-workers, among whom there was a constant exchange of banter and horseplay. He valued also a certain sense of power over authority—the team could easily make or break a foreman—and a feeling that the work was important and responsible, inasmuch as carelessness might lead to the spoiling of expensive materials. He had taken a part, though not a prominent one, in the unionizing of the plant. According to his account, this step was not stubbornly opposed by the management, which maintained the most cooperative relationship with the union.

Hodder believed that he was "about 25" when he married. He "married for love" and in retrospect considered his marriage entirely satisfactory. His wife, a woman of quiet tastes, kept the house well and reared their daughter into a "splendid young lady." He gave his wife credit for preserving the marriage in spite of his heavy drinking. She was helped in this by the support of her mother who lived in the same building, and by the fact that he never spent the housekeeping money nor was violent toward her while drunk. Hodder spoke of his wife with kindness and affection, just as he spoke of his daughter with approval and pleasure, but we got the impression that his family life really meant less to him than the companionship of his numerous men friends. Even at the time of the study, when he had not been drinking for three years, almost all of his free time was spent away from home, sometimes in the activities of Alcoholics Anonymous, sometimes in other forms of community enterprise, sometimes even at bars where he took soft drinks and endured, perhaps even enjoyed, the jibes of unconverted drinking companions. Wherever he was, it was always in company.

In attempting to understand Sam Hodder's career we are probably justified in assuming an original basis of security laid by the maternal ministrations of his grandmother. It was perhaps his love for her and respect for her values that left him with an enduring counterweight against serious delinquency and hopeless alcoholism. His mother's rejection, which he probably dealt with by some combination of repressive and counter-rejective tactics, seemed very much a thing of the past in his mind but may have contributed to his forming no deep attachments to women, even his wife. The influence of adults early ceased to be paramount in his childhood; instead, an identification with age equals became the main source of his attitudes, goals, and ideals. This influence was reflected in his indifference to ideals of achievement, getting ahead, improving one's status, and in his accent on excitement, adventure, and the code of fair dealing and mutual help among equals. Perhaps the lack of absolutism and severity in his conscience resulted from its formation chiefly through membership in informal groups of equals. At all events it was in neighborhood gangs that he developed his main pattern of strivings: friendly sociability and companionship. The pursuit of these central satisfactions also served as a means of adjustment and defense. Sociability and companionship probably disposed of any feelings of weakness, inadequacy, and anxiety. We ourselves witnessed his skill in creating an atmosphere of friendliness and the consequent ease with which he met what might otherwise have been the frightening demands of our study.

It was in the light of this analysis that we tried to understand his alcoholism. Drinking began as a group activity at around 10 or 11 years, when some of the boys were hired to help on a beer delivery truck. Hodder continued drinking with sailors, friends, coworkers, and casual companions. He drank to excess and was hospitalized twice, once with a severe attack of delirium tremens. Marriage produced a moratorium of only eight months, and later, when prevailed upon by wife or priest to take a pledge, he merely waited impatiently for the time to be up. It is important to bear in mind that although most of his spare time was spent in drinking he never drank alone, never abused his family, always managed to keep his job, and was able at forty-five to abandon the lifelong habit. He described himself as a happy drinker, not one who sought alcohol to get over worries. There was little evidence that his drinking served to narcotize anxieties and provide satisfaction for repressed needs. Its primary service seemed to be that of reinstating the happy-go-lucky, irresponsible atmosphere of the boyhood gangs, thus easing the strain of settling down to respectable middle-class adulthood. Such an interpretation is supported by the highly social nature of the cure. He and his chief drinking companion both became worried about their health, his friend's condition being somewhat ominous. While in this frame of mind they followed advice to make contact with Alcoholics Anonymous, and their skepticism was melted when they realized that the woman who greeted them knew all about drinking. They were soon involved in the many social activities of the organization, which seemed to provide Hodder with an adequate substitute for the companionship he had formerly sought to stimulate by drinking. He became thoroughly identified with Alcoholics Anonymous and felt no danger of real relapse.[2]

If we make explicit the beliefs that seem to be implied in Hodder's disjointed conversations, we arrive at the following picture of the world as he saw it. There is a Higher Being who has placed man in this world and who tells him, through religion and church, what is right and wrong. Hodder had either forgotten or felt incompetent to discuss any specific teachings of the Roman Catholic Church, but in spite of this paucity of content it was clear that religion had for him the definite function of sanctioning meaning and order in the world. The good life as he saw it had both an individual and a social aspect. The individual man should be a thinking, orderly human being, who tries to see where he stands in the world—not a fool who behaves on impulse, who takes no responsibilities, who may even come to live like an animal in dirt and disorder. This ideal of rationality and order as the basis of human dignity was a value which Hodder had doubtless entertained for some time but formulated more explicitly after joining Alcoholics Anonymous. The social order he saw as requiring people to give the other fellow a fair chance, not to be just out for themselves. This requirement did not exclude shrewd dealings, but it definitely put limits on them. Such limits

[2] For a fuller discussion of this feature of the case see E. Hanfmann, "The life history of an exalcoholic, with an evaluation of factors involved in causation and rehabilitation," *Quarterly Journal of Studies on Alcohol*, Vol. 12 (September 1951), pp. 405–443.

he characteristically formulated not in terms of abstract moral principles but with reference to the behavior of the other person. If he himself were unfair, for example, it would be proper for others to cheat him. Most people, however, he considered to be decent, therefore deserving of decent treatment and of help when they needed it. A generally fair social system run by decent people he perceived not simply as an ideal but as existing, as "human nature," with only a minority not conforming to it. One can sense in this part of his outlook an extension of the code of fair dealing among members of a group which he had learned on the streets in his boyhood.

Hodder's genial, unambitious way of life allowed him to extend his philosophy to specific issues without finding many objects of bitterness. The friendly relation obtaining between management and workers in his plant, and his own sense of having been dealt with fairly, set the pattern for his acceptance of the American economic system. He wholeheartedly favored all social security measures, especially those designed to counteract the effects of unemployment. His image of the international scene emphasized trading and competing for material benefits, and though hazy about details he favored international cooperation and fair dealing with the help of the United Nations. Aside from a certain cautious attention to our own self-interest, inasmuch as some nations still demanded more than their fair share, his view of the world would have been remarkably benign except for one thing—the Communists.

To Hodder the Communists represented that small portion of humanity which is not fundamentally decent. The Russian people he perceived as just like people anywhere, but they were duped and enslaved by their Communist leaders, a small but powerful group which was the source of all evil. The real Communists, he said, were "ruthless people, out for themselves and down with everything," seeking all the power and wealth they could grab, unwilling to give the other fellow an equal chance. Rejecting the basic give-and-take of cooperation, denying the axiomatic value of religion, they functioned as a destructive force in all human affairs, local, national, and international. His ideas about Communists had been formed many years before when as a sailor he encountered members of the I.W.W. whose fanatical violence outraged him; later, he had met Party members in union work whose tactics of disturbance increased the antipathy. Conceived in such a pattern, the Communists formed a living negation of all the values he held to be important.

Hodder's current attitude toward Russia followed from his basic idea about Communist intentions. He distinguished various aspects of the problem: the impairment of freedom, the economic system run for the benefit of Party members, the atheistic bias, the grasping international attitude, the ruthless methods; but he was against them all. His feeling was intense, and all aspects of Russia seemed to engage the same central values in him. His information was quite defective so that few contradictory facts embarrassed his forthright vehemence. That the Russian plans included a social welfare state, for example, was not part of his fund of knowledge, and he accepted a test item which stated that private property was restricted to Party members. For our own policy he advocated a vigilant firm stand, helping Greece, Turkey, and other threatened nations, opposing Russia wherever she created disturbance.

Ever since Hodder emerged from his thoughtless alcoholic days he had been trying to think rationally about the world and his place in it. His views on Russia formed a part of this recent attempt at *object appraisal*. He used the Communists as a way of explaining anything that seemed to disturb his generally satisfactory world. His own ambitions did not extend beyond repairing his home and perhaps earning a few more dollars a week; his daughter would soon be taken care of by marriage. His main desire was to find the world open, friendly, and fair-minded, a suitable medium for his central strivings. Contented as he was with his immediate world, he felt it to be not perfectly secure, and the Communists were his hypothesis, so to speak, as to the source of danger. It was not easy to estimate the extent to which *social adjustment* entered his views. In his largely Catholic milieu and in his not very radical union his opinions created no disharmony, but it was also true that discussion of opinions was not in his circle a particularly acceptable social technique. We exerted ourselves to overlook no way in which his sentiments could be thought of as representing the *externalization of inner problems,* but our catch was somewhat small. The drives he attributed to the Communists seemed either absent from himself—he showed little urge toward power and wealth even at covert levels—or so readily admitted by him, as in the case of aggression and trickery, that an assumption concerning defensive projection became superfluous. The one way in which externalization possibly functioned was that by picturing the Communists as really dangerous enemies of society he sharpened the contrast between them and his own career of less sinister delinquency, thus bolstering his none too secure position as an advocate of decent living.

Viewing Hodder's opinions in their *expressive* aspect it was easy to perceive the influence of his limited education, weakness in abstract operations, and lack of the discipline of reading and serious discussion. His intellectual shortcomings made it easy for him to focalize the evil in the world uncritically upon the actions of certain people. Because of his affiliative needs he could not attribute evil to human nature as such or to any sympathy-awakening minority, but because of his concrete thinking he could not place it in an abstract construct such as the economic order. A group of people defined merely by their greater selfishness and wrong-headedness satisfied the demands of his intellect and conveniently accounted for evil both at home and abroad.

DANA OSGOOD

The last of our subjects was a man of 38, a partner in a small real estate and insurance office in South Newton. His somewhat fluctuating income had reached $10,000 in the previous year, when business was particularly active. With his growing family he occupied a pleasant home in the prosperous sub-urb where he himself had grown up and where now his office carried on most of its business. An outstanding characteristic of his life was its dedication to community service. He was on so many boards of so many useful and charitable community organizations that only one or two evenings a week were left free from engagements. The motive of service was largely responsible for his willingness to participate in the study. Generally satisfied with his position and happy in his personal associations, he nevertheless sometimes thought that his life had merely drifted along instead of being pointed toward definite goals. Some discontent on this score, together with a strong need to feel acceptance and respect, probably accounted for his marked curiosity afterwards to know what we had made of him.

Dana Osgood opened his written autobiography with the following sentence: "I was one of those children born to parents who were in a position to send me to private schools and college and to give me the advantages of dancing school, music lessons, and all the things that go with a 'correct' bringing up." This sentence, including the quotation marks around "correct," forms a good starting point for the understanding of his personality. The economic and social status occupied by his parents came to his mother by inheritance but was achieved by his father only after an early career marked by ill health and frequent changes of occupation. It was in fact when recovering from an illness several years after his marriage that he drifted into the real estate business which finally brought him financial success in his own right. The home in which Dana and his sisters grew up was never without servants, including a nurse when the children were small. In this respect one is reminded of Grafton Upjohn's childhood home, but in spirit the two families were poles apart. The Osgoods cared little for entertaining or displays of affluence. They were loyal and active members of the Universalist Church, pillars of the community, much interested in providing a good home and sound influence for their children.

Osgood remembered his mother as completely dedicated to her children. No outside activities interfered with their needs, and she seemed to be "always there" when they wanted her. He praised her qualities of patience and kindness, but well remembered also her firmness on issues such as wearing rubbers or telling the truth. Memories of the father included certain genial moments, as when he told exciting stories about a western ranch he had visited, but there were also incidents in which Dana's desire to be helpful came to grief because of the father's high standard of orderliness in whatever he undertook. The atmosphere of the home was well-mannered and high-minded. Standards of conduct were clear, and the expectation that they would be met was so compelling that Dana remembered very little actual punishment. For all their devotion, the parents were felt to be somewhat unapproachable. Dana could not imagine confiding his troubles to them, especially to his mother who always seemed "far above" such things. Neither parent ever spoke a word to him on the subject of sex. This blend of devotion, high expectations, and

reticence created certain difficulties for Dana in the management of rebellious impulses. Overt hostility achieved poor results, while the covert form left feelings of guilt. The parents sometimes used a technique of silent disapproval and seemed always to have difficulty in making their positive feelings explicit. Thus there was a shortage of reward for the expected good behavior, together with an all-too-good chance to magnify one's feelings of wickedness and inferiority. In a curious father-and-son story on the *Thematic Apperception Test* Osgood made the father watch his son's accomplishments with silent admiration; when at last he expressed his feeling, the boy received the praise "ruefully," for he was not happy in the work and had really been wanting to do something else. As a boy Dana was often uncertain as to whether he was pleasing his parents and as to whether he was pleasing himself.

Although the home involved certain difficulties, Dana found opportunities for a more adventurous life among his friends in the neighborhood. His happiest memories were of times spent with his cousin, a boy a year younger about whom he said, "We always used to click, no matter what we did. He was a little bolder than I was, a better athlete than I was, yet I seemed to be steadier than he was and we balanced each other beautifully." He sought companionship wherever it could be found, sometimes straying outside the neighborhood approved by his parents. Repeatedly he emphasized that he was not outstanding in groups: "just another player" in sports and "fumbling" with radio sets, for example. Apparently he got from the other boys what he got from his cousin: acceptance, encouragement to do "bad" things like breaking windows on Hallowe'en, and in general an initiative and zest which he could not muster from his own resources. Meanwhile his piano practice went badly, and at dancing school he was not only awkward but became, at about 12, extremely shy with girls. His parents struggled vainly to prevent the dwindling of his more formal social life. Feeling that something had gone wrong with his local adjustment they sent him away to a boy's boarding school.

The first venture from home resulted badly. Dana felt inferior to the rich boys at the school and was humiliated when his parents came to see him in a Model T Ford. His shyness persisted even when the other boys urged him to go out with girls. But when he went to a small college many miles from home he suddenly came into his element. Here his economic position was not inferior, he knew no one, he was on his own and had his own way to make. In his social life he at once began to make up for lost time. His dancing and conversation improved with remarkable speed. He threw himself energetically into a round of campus activities. Studies were merely a "great chore which had to be done," and they were done so carelessly that he finally needed an extra term to graduate. When his parents protested he replied, feeling his oats a bit, with the well-chosen argument that if they did not like his grades he would leave college and look for a job. This threat of downward mobility brought his

parents into line, and in the end his father rescued him from all financial miscalculations by sending him whatever funds he requested.

After this period of freedom and happy development he returned home and began in random fashion to look for an occupation. Eventually he was offered a position in the office which had been his father's, though by this time his father had sold his share in the business and was in no way responsible for the offer. Osgood thus followed in his father's footsteps, but he was able to feel that his progress in the office was the result of his own efforts. From the start he enjoyed the work. Disliking routine application, at which he continued to be somewhat careless, he took pleasure in the constant variety and flexible hours of his business day. Above all, he found major satisfaction in meeting people, talking with them, helping them to find the kind of homes they wanted, and receiving their gratitude. "I enjoy people immensely," he said in an interview, and later, "I don't think there's anything quite as pleasant as to have people thank you ever so much and send their friends to you and so on." He became an anchorage point for clients new in the neighborhood, who often called him to the rescue if anything went wrong with their houses. He liked this trouble-shooting and found that he got "particular satisfaction out of helping older people." He had, in short, fallen into a kind of work which gave him contentment: "I'm very happy where I am and I expect and hope to stay in my present position."

Osgood was married at the age of 32 after a long and somewhat stormy engagement. His wife fitted into his background and shared his ideals; harmony reigned in the establishment of a home in which the children would be given love and a chance for self-expression yet not allowed to dominate the household or render it unfit for adult habitation. In her devotion to the children Osgood saw a similarity between his wife and his mother. In relation to himself, however, he emphasized especially her zest and capacity to make him feel more deeply the experiences of everyday life. He took pleasure in the children and also valued his home as a place of rest and as a place for genial social gatherings. Home life was interrupted during World War II when Osgood, having been rejected in attempts to enlist for officer training, became subject to the draft. At the very top of the age range, he was pleased to discover that he could take the rigors of training, even though he lost much weight in the process. He was not sent overseas and regained his weight quickly when returned to domestic life.

With the exception of Sam Hodder, no subject in our group cared so much about his friends as Dana Osgood. His friendship with his cousin was only one of several childhood attachments that continued into adult life. He had made new friendships along the way, generally with men of considerable ability whose company he found stimulating and exciting. In the Army, for instance, he developed a warm feeling for an alert and brilliant Jewish refugee who showed him new beauties in music, pictures, and scenery. Besides this quality of stimulating him above his usually placid level, the friendships always involved

mutual esteem and appreciation. Osgood felt liked and respected by his friends. He felt free to exchange mildly aggressive banter, which he could both give and take without creating hard feelings.

Osgood's work for community organizations constituted another major source of satisfaction. Like his parents he was active in the Universalist Church, but otherwise his participations were of his own making rather than the continuing of family traditions. Part of the satisfaction came from being with people, but "more than that," he said, "I feel that if you are living in a community you are duty bound to belong to social agencies." Out of his experiences he had developed a general ideal of service, embodied in his statement: "I'd like to devote my life to helping others." As his career of service lengthened he began to receive certain outward marks of distinction, but it was evident that community activities appealed to him mainly for other reasons. Here he could work for clear and concrete goals, associate with others in enterprises of indubitable worth, and receive the thanks, always implicit and often explicit, due to those who give their time in unpaid public service. In community work he could be certain that he was pleasing people.

We would overlook the creative element in Osgood's life if we charged his devotion to service entirely to the conscience generated in his childhood home. We were careful to note, as was he, that both his vocation and his community work, close as they lay to lines of parental interest, were substantial achievements of his own. To a large extent they were the heirs of his campus activities at college and his group activities with the boys of the neighborhood, neither of which had enjoyed particular parental blessing. Indeed there was reason to believe that his conscience itself, admittedly a strong contemporary guide, had been partly shaped by his interest in being accepted by the boys who served to counterbalance the restraints of his home. Most of Osgood's submission to strictly parental goals showed earmarks of half-heartedness. He practiced the piano badly, danced clumsily, suffered shyness with girls, got poor school grades and groaned at the "great chore" of college studies. On those of our tests which most resembled school tasks he put forth a limited amount of energy, impressing one examiner as a "not too conscientious" worker. We judged that this withholding of energy had been the one possible mode of resisting parental pressures. As an adult he regretted some of the things he had not learned and not accomplished, wishing in particular that his father had been more strict and prevented him from feeling that everything came easily. His failure to work hard for parental goals was the basis of his idea that his life might have had more point and less drift. But through his friends, through his way of handling his business, and through his community activities he had achieved a way of life which was certainly not a piece of half-hearted conformity. The claims of conscience had come to be satisfied in a setting of gratifying social relationships.

In order to understand Osgood's general values it is necessary to bear in mind that he had little personal reason for wanting a change in the social order. It was natural for him to hope that his children would have the same advantages and economic security that he and his parents had enjoyed. Social and economic change would be likely to have only an adverse effect on his personal situation. Within the existing framework he was by no means an enemy of improvement. He attached great importance to the liberal and independent tradition of his church. He was interested in bettering child training and in alleviating the condition of the poor through community enterprises. But in politics and economics all his sentiments were conservative. He called himself a "dyed-in-the-wool Republican." He felt threatened by government interference, the trend toward Socialism, the power of labor, and especially the threat of inflation. When pressed he conceded that government ownership was in certain respects desirable, but for the most part he automatically rejected the idea. His interest in public affairs outside the community was rather small. Calling himself "not an original thinker" on such topics, he had borrowed his views first from his father, later from his immediate associates. One could properly say that he had a collection of views rather than an organized philosophy, and the collection had been made largely through such personal channels as lunch-time conversation with his business friends.

As regards Russia Osgood classed himself among those "optimists" who believed that war was not inevitable. Peace could be maintained if we took a strong stand against Russian expansion and at the same time aided the democratic governments in Europe. He found two things to praise about

Russia: her stalwart *part in World War II* and her rapid *internal development* with respect to manufacturing, agriculture, education, and improvement of the condition of the poor. These strong points were badly outweighed by things which he could only deplore. Russia's *role in international relations* he believed to be inspired by a wish for expanded influence and power, the spreading of Communist doctrine being merely a secondary consideration. Her statesmen knew what they wanted, were playing a close hand, and in trying to achieve their power goals would stop at nothing except a counter display of force. Her *methods of spreading influence* received his vehement condemnation. He believed that a small number of dangerously fanatical Russian agents were responsible for our most serious labor toubles. *Restriction on individual freedom* he considered highly undesirable, causing a decay of individual initiative and responsibility and reflecting an attitude that human life was cheap. He was particularly outraged by Russian brutality in killing off political opponents. As regards *religion and morality* he was poorly informed, but what he knew he perceived as a threat to the family: the "foundation of any country," and as destroying a person's right to freedom of worship. When it came to specific policies he did not like the Truman Doctrine but nevertheless considered it inevitable: conditions required that we participate in Europe and show strength toward Russia. He admired the tough line taken by Secretary of State Byrnes and favored our maintaining superiority in crucial arms and in productive capacity. Along with this we should not relax our efforts to demonstrate the superiority of democracy, nor should we overlook any opportunity to proceed by peaceable means.

In examining the *expressive* character of Osgood's opinions about Russia we noticed first, as in several other cases, that because of a lack of interest in theory and abstraction he took no account of Marxism as an element in Soviet policy. For him the activities of the Communists were motivated by a desire for power uncomplicated by any interest in doctrine; this made it difficult for him to see any difference between Communists and Nazis. Another characteristic of his opinions was their lack of sharp definition. When confronted with a topic he was apt to give a series of sentiments without feeling impelled to resolve the contradictions that usually appeared. He was also wedded to a kind of fair-minded detachment which in the end sometimes obscured his viewpoint. Though occasionally downright on specific questions, in extended discussion he typically began with mild and noncommittal evaluations which later seemed scarcely representative of his true feelings. These two traits, the mild detachment and the lack of sharp definition, we thought reflected his habitual mode of social interaction. As one who aimed to please, he had no urge to form harsh-edged opinions and little practice in forging weapons for altercation. His opinions were designed to avoid strife, in form as well as in content.

As already remarked, Osgood's *object appraisal* was dominated by a desire for as little social-economic change as possible. He was a beneficiary of the economic order, and everything in which he was interested—home, neighborhood, church, real estate business, community services—was predicated on the continued existence of considerable private wealth. This caused him to see no good in the Russian system except the points of resemblance to our own country: internal development of economic and educational resources, and a stout fight against Nazi tyranny. His poor opinion of Russia did not cause him to think war inevitable, but he felt that only a counter display of strength would check Communist imperialism. Osgood's *social adjustment* was an important and successful part of his life. It was not, however, an assertive adjustment, nor did argument nor even the taking of clear stands play an essential part in the kind of relationship he generally sought to establish. Although he accepted the social responsibility of having opinions on important topics, he took pleasure in agreement, and the few issues on which he showed vehemence were those on which we felt safe in deducing that his chief business associates were vehement. His views on Russia were in full accord with those of the people around him. We judged that he would need them to be so even if circumstances had not made it happen almost as a matter of course. Osgood's opinions about Russia did not strike us as being strongly colored by the *externalization of inner problems*. Only two points deserve mention. His dwelling on Russian brutality and his focussing of criticism upon it suggested the problem of repressed aggression, for which some of our material offered independent evidence. His admiration for strength

and assertiveness, whether displayed by America or by the Russians—for it was clear that he admired the position of power they had made for themselves in world affairs—we judged to be the product of a sense of personal shortcoming which he made some effort to repair. Apart from these two individual accents the content of his views grew almost wholly from his needs for object appraisal and for social adjustment.

The impression generally left by a series of intensive case studies is one of almost boundless individual variation. If the studies are faithful to their subject matter they show us living people who are as distinctive as the ones we meet in everyday life. Such descriptive abundance is requisite in order to show the lawfulness within each personality. It is thus an essential step on the way to more general propositions about fundamental processes. The very wealth of individuality, however, looms as an obstacle to generalization. The comparative study of cases—the comparison of individual lives that differ in so many particulars—can be successfully carried out only when variables have been selected which draw attention to significant generalities beneath the crowding multitude of surface features. Generalities of this kind we have sought in our descriptive and functional analysis of opinions. [But now] we shall undertake to gather and appraise our findings. What have we learned from our attempt to describe the opinions held by our ten men? What have we learned by examining the expressive nature of their opinions? What have we learned by considering their opinions with respect to object appraisal, social adjustment, and externalization? What have they taught us about the commerce between men's opinions and their informational environment?

In order to summarize the information in such a way that it can be taken in at a glance, we shall set out our findings in six tables. These tables consist simply of condensed statements of relevant findings for each subject; they will serve as points of departure for our discussion of what we believe we have learned.

DESCRIBING AN OPINION

In selecting men to serve in our study, it was our aim to include a wide variety of opinion about Russia. At the outset, the idea of representing the positions of our respondents on some spectrum of favorableness or unfavorableness was appealing. Variety we achieved, as the summary of opinions in Table IV-1 attests, but our notion of a simple spectrum soon faded. At best, such a spectrum is constructed by pooling or ordering an arbitrary set of expressed

TABLE IV-1   Summary Description of Opinions about Russia

Chatwell   Object characteristics: moderate salience; high differentiation; long-range optimistic time perspective, vaguer in short range; major aspects: *police state* (−), advocate of world Communism (−), developing nation (+)
Orientation: approach-hostility (counteraction and interdependence)
Policy stand: strengthen UN; reassure Russia from U.S. position of strength

Lanlin   Object characteristics: low moderate salience; rather low differentiation; time perspective, easy optimism; major aspects: *evil leaders seeking world domination* (−), backward country of great resources and ignorant people (−)
Orientation: *avoidance,* hostility, approach (make friends but keep powder dry)
Policy stand: vigorous U.S. stand if Russia refuses to be reasonable

Sullivan   Object characteristics: very high salience; high cognitive (but low affective) differentiation; optimistic historical time perspective, vague short-run perspective; major aspects: *experiment in social welfare* (+), alternative to moribund capitalism (+), ideological opponent of U.S. (+), temporary police state (±)
Orientation: *approach*
Policy stand: opposed to actual U.S. policy and any conceivable one; has no positive stand

Daniel   Object characteristics: moderate salience; considerable differentiation; broad time perspective; major aspects: *social welfare state* (+), limitations on freedom and democracy (−), religion and morality (−)
Orientation: *approach*-avoidance
Policy stand: favors U.S. stand from position of strength; opposes cooperation that might jeopardize security

Hodder   Object characteristics: very low salience; very little differentiation; time perspective restricted to present; major aspects: *Communists as*

destructive, grasping, atheistic force of evil (−), impairment of freedom (−); international menace (−)
Orientation: *avoidance*-hostility
Policy stand: favors U.S. stand from position of strength, opposing Russia
wherever she creates disturbance

Clark   Object characteristics: very low salience; very little differentiation; narrow
time perspective; major aspects: *international greed* (−), atheistic
immorality (−)
Orientation: *avoidance*
Policy stand: confused; call Russia's bluff, with preventive war if necessary—but also trade, cooperation on live-and-let-live basis; probably
no real policy stand

Kleinfeld   Object characteristics: considerable salience; considerable differentiation;
rather narrow, pessimistic time perspective; major aspects: *world
domination* (−), social welfare state (+), limitations on freedom and
democracy (−), treatment of Jews and minorities (±)
Orientation: *avoidance*-hostility
Policy stand: cooperation to avoid provocation; avoidance of war at all
costs

Rock   Object characteristics: rather low salience; little differentiation; time perspective, long-run pessimism—expects Communistic Europe; major
aspects: *religion and morality* (−), threat of war (−), restriction of
personal freedom (−)
Orientation: *avoidance*-hostility
Policy stand: diplomacy from U.S. position of strength

Upjohn   Object characteristics: low salience, little differentiation; narrow time perspective; major aspects: *greedy expansion and threat of war* (−), religion and morality (−), restriction of freedom (−), material progress
and contribution to World War II (+)
Orientation: *avoidance*-hostility
Policy stand: diplomacy from position of strength, risking war if necessary

Osgood   Object characteristics: low salience; moderate differentiation; time perspective, long-run optimism; major aspects: *disruption in international
relations and U.S. domestic conflict* (−), restriction in individual freedom (−), part in World War II (+), internal development (+)
Orientation: *avoidance*
Policy stand: maintain peace by strong stand against Russian expansion,
aid to democracies

---

opinions in the interest of giving an individual an overall "score." Whether one uses a Guttman scale for performing the operation, i.e., determining what the scale shall be and then placing the subject along it, or uses some other method, the result in the present case would be stunting and artificial. For demographic purposes, perhaps, it might be worth knowing that Hodder, Lanlin, Upjohn all had about the same position on a "Communism Scale." Our interest lay elsewhere. The question we posed was "How may a man's opinion on an issue be fruitfully described?"

Object characteristics.

The Russias to which our ten men were reacting were different objects, differently composed. That these objects of opinion shared common features reflecting world events and constancies in the information environment is evident. But the first and most striking impression we got in talking with our respondents was that the Russia to which each referred was a conception selectively fashioned, a reflection of individuality. It was soon apparent to us that we could not begin describing an attitude until the qualitative pattern of its object had been set forth.

First as to content.

To the majority of our subjects Russia was conceived as a disruptive force in the international scene and as a threat to the United States. But only to Chatwell and Sullivan did the challenge of Russia assume a markedly ideological character. Greedy aims of world domination, concrete and personified, were seen by others. The aims, the evil, the immorality of Rusia sensed by most of our subjects were properties of specific men or of cliques, not of a system or of a set of ideas called Marxism. Restriction in individual freedom figured importantly in the image most of the men had of Russia. It had no place, however, in the impoverished conception held by Clark, whose own feeling of freedom was so poorly defined. Lanlin took cognizance of the authoritarian features of the Russian system, but his version of the business ethic was concerned with the uses to which dictatorial power is put rather than with its bare existence; this feature of Russia did not stand out

for him. The ideological Sullivan, exposed as he was to unquestionable facts about the Russian police state, took embarrassed notice of them, assigning them a subsidiary and well-rationalized place in his image of the land of hope.

A few of our men found a place in their conceptions for the social welfare aspirations of Russia. This feature stood out, for example, in Sullivan's image, less so in Daniel's. For most, it was an aspect of Russia that had little centrality.

Not only were the objects of our men's attitudes constructed of different content, but they were differently organized. The men varied greatly in the extent to which Russia presented a *differentiated* image in their thinking. At one extreme was Chatwell with his many-faceted view of Russia. Clark and Hodder provide the contrast in the barren poverty of their conceptions. But there were interesting variations that defy alignment on a single dimension. Sullivan, for example, vied with Chatwell in the detail with which his picture of Russia was sketched; cognitively speaking, Russia was well differentiated for him. But so imperative was his need to see the Soviet Union as the promised land that he assimilated every feature, even the least tractable, to an affectively dominated totality of incarnate good.

To speak of differentiation is, however, insufficient. For in each man's conception, *hierarchically organized* as it was, some features dominated the picture at the expense of others. For Chatwell, several themes jostled for the central positions, while in the less differentiated opinions of Clark and Hodder the single theme of evil malice occupied an otherwise empty stage. The single aspect that we judged to be most dominant in each case is italicized in Table IV-1.

These aspects were not conceived in neutral tones. Each of the aspects of Russia to which our men attended presented itself laden with what we have termed *object value,* an immediate and self-evident goodness or badness, desirability or fearsomeness. The signs ($+$, $-$) in the lists of major aspects in Table IV-1 represent our rough categorization of the value that each of these object features had for the men. It is interesting to observe that whenever "world domination" occurs as a differentiated aspect, it receives negative valuation; similarly with "religion and morality" and with "impairment of freedom," Sullivan being the sole exception in regard to the latter.

What of the overall value set on Russia? It is difficult to describe with any precision save to say that the picture each had of Russia as a totality grew out of those few dominant features that stood at the top of his hierarchy of attention. It was as if, in each case, certain features were the principal determinants of the image as a whole. Abridgment of freedom, persecution of religion, threat to peace— from these the larger view grew. Some of our men could tolerate aspects of Russia that were discordant with their overall view; others could see nothing discrepant. Chatwell could see good things, but they did not dilute his overall negative valuation based on what he conceived as the major issues. If he could do this by virtue of the highly articulate image he had constructed, Osgood could do the same by virtue of the loose-knittedness of his

image. To Sullivan, on the other hand, every seeming Russian cloud was a threat to his favorable views until he found its silver lining.

Two other object characteristics that we distinguished were *salience* and *time perspective.* With the exception of Sullivan and to a lesser degree Kleinfeld, Russia was not particularly salient in the lives of our men; there were many other matters that preoccupied them more. There was for most of them, therefore, little occasion to elaborate a highly developed time perspective on Russian affairs. Two of our subjects, Chatwell and Sullivan, showed a longer perspective, the former in terms of explicit events, the latter in terms of a rather unarticulated conception of historical necessities. For the rest, time perspective was little more than generalized optimism or pessimism.

Orientation.

The orientations of our men toward Russia, how they were set to react, may be described in terms of *approach, avoidance,* and *hostility.* This classification recommended itself to us on grounds of logical comprehensiveness and as preferable to the stock "pro-con" distinction, but we take little satisfaction in it. Only Sullivan among our subjects was set squarely in the direction of approach. Two of the men seemed straightforwardly avoidant: Clark and Osgood. Each of them viewed Russia with repugnance, but in neither were there appreciable tendencies to punish or destroy her. More common was some balance of avoidant and hostile orientations, with the accent on the former. Predominant in the feelings of Hodder, Rock, and Upjohn was the desire to be freed from the threat they saw Russia posing. If necessary they would support, though reluctantly, hostile action toward Russia. Daniel and Kleinfeld shared an ambivalence between avoidance and approach, with different emphases. Each was drawn toward some features of Russia, repelled by others, but there was little hostility in the orientation of either. No subject is harder to place in terms of this scheme than Chatwell, whose ideal was an interdependent world in which Russia would have a major place, a state of affairs unfortunately prevented by Russian policies. If anything, his orientation harmoniously combined approach and hostility: military preparedness in the context of firm internationalism.

In spite of the negative value with which Russia appeared in the attitudes of most of our men, none of them could be classified as primarily destructive in his orientation. We suspect that unalloyed hostile orientations were and are a rarity in peacetime American attitudes.

Policy stand

Here we consider the "final common path" taken by a person's attitudes into publicly formulated issues. Put crudely, the issue of the day was: Should the United States attempt to "cooperate" with Russia, in the hope that cooperation in the spirit of give-and-take would evoke a reasonable response, or should the United States "get tough" with Russia, negotiating only from a position of strength? Under Secretaries Byrnes and Marshall, the country was becoming increasingly committed to the latter alternative, after unfortunate experience with the former.

All but a few of our subjects stood firmly behind this emergent American policy, though with individual qualifications such as, for instance, Chatwell's prior emphasis on support of the United Nations. Only Sullivan as an acknowledged deviant was entirely out of step—so much so that his policy stand could only be a negative one.

It is when one observes the compression of rich individual opinions into the "yeas" and "nays" of policy stand that one senses the relatively narrow range of alternatives by which individual opinion can express itself on public matters. It is no surprise to find a plenitude of different motives bringing men together in a common stand on policy. What strikes one forcibly, however, is the complexity of attempting to link deeper-lying motives with position on such specific matters as the Truman Doctrine. In many ways, the policies upon which these men must take a stand have little directly to do with the substance of their opinions: the question always is whether a given policy proposal will serve as an adequate channel through which the more amorphous underlying opinions may be expressed.

We regard the rubrics under which we have described the opinions of our ten men as a minimum list. There are many and varied categories which might be applied to such a task. Our objective has been to choose descriptive terms that keep contact with those commonly found in the opinion literature and that can also be related to descriptions of more general psychological functioning.

In most general terms, our description has been threefold. First, to characterize the phenomenology of an opinion in terms of the object toward which it was directed. About *what* was the opinion? The "what" in this case refers to the object as experienced: not Russia as a political entity but as a psychic entity, one man's Russia. Eventually, the transmutation of the external events that constitute Russia into an individual impression of Russia will be rendered more comprehensible by psychological research on the higher mental processes. Even prior to such elucidation, we feel that a description of opinion is empty unless it includes a description of the object of the opinion.

The second aspect of opinion to be described is what we have called orientation: the readiness of the individual to approach, avoid, or attack the object of his opinion. The specific forms of carrying out these orientations are many where Russia is concerned. The general rubrics we have used may serve to remind the analyst of opinion that one must go beyond describing orientation in the language of "pro" and "con."

Finally, there is the question of how the rich complexity of an attitude is fitted to the final common path of a stand on some particular policy. We have sought to underline the subtlety of this process in our description of policy stand.

MISPERCEPTION OF AGGRESSION IN VIETNAM
RALPH K. WHITE

In the Vietnam war each side declares that it has to fight because of obvious, self-evident "aggression" by the other side. On each side there are images of a Hitler-like enemy, brutally, calculatingly bent on conquest. On each side there is a feeling that it would be weak and cowardly to let the enemy's aggression be rewarded by success; each side feels: "If we are men we cannot let this aggression go unpunished."

The thesis of this article is that both are wrong. There has been no aggression on either side—at least not in the sense of a cold-blooded, Hitler-like act of conquest. The analogies of Hitler's march into Prague, Stalin's takeover of Eastern Europe, and the North Korean attack on South Korea are false analogies. There is a better analogy in the outbreak of World War I, when, as historical scholarship has shown, both sides stumbled and staggered into the war in a spirit of self-defense (or defense of national pride against "intolerable humiliation") rather than in a spirit of deliberate conquest. . . . In Vietnam each side, though by no means free from moral guilt, is far from being as diabolical as

its enemies picture it, since both believe that whatever crimes they may commit are justified by the magnitude of the emergency. Each knows that it has not "willed" this war. On each side ordinary human beings have become gradually entangled, hating the war and all the suffering associated with it, honestly believing that their manhood requires them to resist the "aggression" of the enemy. But the enemy's "aggression," in the sense in which it has been assumed to exist, has not existed.[1]

For reasons that will be discussed, it follows that the only honorable peace would be a compromise peace in which each side could feel it had held out against the aggressor's onslaught and had managed to preserve at least the bare essentials of what it was fighting to defend.

CAN THEY BELIEVE IT WHEN THEY CALL US "AGGRESSORS"?

President Johnson has said, "The first reality is that North Vietnam has at-

CREDIT: Reprinted by permission of author and publisher from the *Journal of International Affairs*, Number 1, 1967, p. 123–140.

[1] A much more detailed and documented presentation of this thesis is contained in Ralph K. White, "Misperception and the Vietnam War," *Journal of Social Issues*, Vol. 22, Number 3 (1966), pp. 1–167.

tacked the independent nation of South Vietnam. Its object is total conquest. . . . Let no one think for a moment that retreat from Vietnam would bring an end to the conflict. The battle would be renewed in one country and then another. The central lesson of our time is that the appetite of aggression is never satisfied." [2] Secretary McNamara has said, "The prime aggressor is North Vietnam." [3] Secretary Rusk has repeatedly declared that the whole purpose of our intervention would disappear the moment the North Vietnamese decided to "let their neighbors alone."

The great majority of the American people do not seriously doubt these statements; even among those who doubt the wisdom of our attempting to resist aggression in Southeast Asia there are many who do not doubt that Communist aggression has occurred. Those who do feel that it is our responsibility to resist the aggression that they regard as self-evident are likely to have ready answers to what they suppose to be the arguments against this belief. They may ask: "Can you deny that North Vietnam has sent troops and weapons to the South? Can you deny that the Viet Cong cadres are Communists, controlled by other Communists in Hanoi and perhaps in Peking? Can you deny that war by assassination in the villages is aggression, in principle, as much as is war by invasion of troops across a border?" And when they find that their opponents, while making certain qualifications (e.g., with regard

to the completeness of the control of the Viet Cong by Hanoi), do not try to deny the essential truth of any of these things, they are likely to feel that their case is well established and that Communist aggression is indeed self-evident.

A visitor from Mars would be struck by the close parallel between all of this and the attitudes that are continually expressed on the other side. According to Ho Chi Minh, "It is crystal clear that the United States is the aggressor who is trampling under foot the Vietnamese soil." [4] According to Chou En-lai, "America is rapidly escalating the war in an attempt to subdue the Vietnamese people by armed force." [5] And according to Leonid Brezhnev, "Normalization of our relations [with the U.S.] is incompatible with the armed aggression of American imperialism against a fraternal Socialist country—Vietnam." [6] To the extent that they mean what they say, aggression by us seems as obvious to them as aggression by them seems to us.

That, then, is the essential question: to what extent do they mean what they say?

To most Americans, probably, the charge that *we* are aggressors seems like outrageous nonsense, so transparently false that honest men all over the world must put it down immediately as a propaganda trick by the Communists to cover up their own aggression.

[2] Johns Hopkins speech, Apr. 7, 1965.

[3] Speech before the National Security Industrial Assn., Mar. 26, 1964.

[4] Interview with Felix Greene, quoted in *The Washington Post*, Dec. 14, 1965, pp. A 1, A 16.

[5] Speech in Peking, reported in *The New York Times*, May 1, 1966, p. 4.

[6] Speech to the Central Committee of the CPSU, reported in *The Washington Post*, Sept. 30, 1965, A 16.

The thief is crying "Stop thief!" and must be doing it simply to distract attention from his own crime.

It is precisely here, though, that the perceptions of most Americans are, in my judgment, basically mistaken. The charge that we have been aggressors—inadvertent aggressors, without for a moment intending to be—is not outrageous nonsense. It is no more false than our charge that the Communists have been aggressors. Both charges are psychologically false, since neither side has committed conscious, deliberate, Hitler-like aggression. But both charges are in a less essential sense true, since both sides, in the belief that they have been defending themselves, have engaged in certain actions which the other side, seeing them within a radically different frame of reference, could easily perceive as aggressive.

That this is true on the American side needs no demonstration. Certain actions of the Communists, notably the campaign of assassination in the villages and the sending of troops from the North to the South, have seemed to most Americans, interpreting them within an American frame of reference, to be flagrantly, self-evidently aggressive. What most Americans have almost wholly failed to realize is that we too have done things which, when perceived within the Communists' radically different frame of reference, have probably seemed to them to be just as flagrantly and self-evidently aggressive. This failure to see how our own actions are perceived by the Communists is the essence of our misperception.

Most of the rest of this article will be devoted to an exploration of the reasons for believing that the Communists do see our behavior as aggressive. The argument is twofold. (1) There are at least eight important kernels of truth in the Communist case against us—eight types of evidence that, when strongly focused upon by a Communist mind and interpreted within a Communist frame of reference, could seem to substantiate his charge of American aggression. (2) There is ample reason to believe that the lenses through which the Communists see reality have a high enough degree of refraction to do the rest of the job. They are quite capable of focusing strongly on these kernels of truth, interpreting them solely within a Communist frame of reference, failing to realize that we see them within a quite different frame of reference, ignoring or misinterpreting all the kernels of truth on our side, and therefore coming up with a black-and-white picture in which their role is wholly defensive and ours is aggressive. The chief reason to think they are capable of this much distortion lies in the fact that most American minds—presumably less dogmatic, more evidence-oriented—have been capable of a similar degree of distortion in the opposite direction. The very fact that so many Americans have denied, misinterpreted, softpedaled or simply ignored these eight important kernels of truth on the Communist side is sufficient evidence that the capacity to misperceive in this way is not inherently Communist. It is human. In other situations the Communists have, on the whole, shown much more of it than we have, but in the case of Vietnam the amount of distortion that apparently exists in Communist minds, i.e., the amount of it that they would need in order to believe most of what they say, is no greater than the amount in the minds of most Americans.

What is needed, then, is a careful examination of the "eight kernels of truth." We can hardly understand either the sincerity of Communist thinking or the distortions and blind spots in our own until we focus steadily on the facts that to them seem decisively important.

THREE REASONS WHY THEY THINK SOUTH VIETNAM "BELONGS" TO THEM

The usage of the term "aggression" in the Communists' discourse suggests that in their minds, as in ours, it is applied when either or both of two conditions exist: (1) when they believe, rightly or wrongly, that country A is using force to take land that "belongs" to country B; and (2) when they believe, rightly or wrongly, that most of the people on that land want to be part of country B. The "eight kernels of truth" mentioned above include three types of evidence that, in my judgment, actually do tend to support their claim that South Vietnam "belongs" to them (reasons other than the belief that the people are on their side) and five types of evidence supporting their claim that most of the people are on their side.

Perhaps it should be repeated: this is not an argument that South Vietnam *does* "belong" to them, or that most of the people *are* on their side. It seems to me that the first of these propositions, when closely ana-

lyzed, is largely meaningless, and that the second, though very meaningful, cannot be clearly answered on an empirical basis and is probably somewhat less than half true, since most people in South Vietnam probably do not want to be ruled either by Hanoi or by Saigon. This is simply an argument that the facts are complex and ambiguous enough to disprove completely our prevailing American assumption that there has been deliberate, unequivocal Communist aggression, and to make it highly probable that the Communists *think* South Vietnam belongs to them and the people are on their side.[7]

What does "belonging" mean, psychologically? On what grounds does any group come to feel that a certain piece of land obviously "belongs" to it and not to someone else? Though at first glance the concept seems simple, on closer examination it turns out to be extraordinarily complex and elusive. Such an examination is needed, too, in view of the fact that an endless amount of bad blood and of violent conflict has been generated at the places in the world where two or more groups have had conflicting assumptions about what belongs to whom: the Thirteen Colonies, the Confederate States, Cuba, Bosnia-Herzegovina, Alsace-Lorraine, Austria, the Sudetenland, the Polish Corridor, Danzig, the Baltic states, Taiwan, Quemoy, Tibet, the Sino-Indian border, Indochina, Algeria, Kashmir, Cyprus, Israel. When the territorial self-image of one country overlaps with the territorial

[7] For a more balanced picture of the evidence on both sides, see White, *op. cit.*, especially pp. 19–44, 46–50, 89–90, and 106–16.

self-image of another, trouble seems to be almost inevitable, and such overlapping is hard to avoid because nations differ in their criteria of what constitutes ownership or "belonging." Sometimes, as in our American feeling about the Revolutionary War and the Southern feeling about the Civil War, the criterion is a belief about what most of the people in the area want. Sometimes, as in the British feeling about our Revolutionary War and the Northern feeling about the Civil War, it is a compound of habit, respect for tradition and legality, national pride, beliefs (which may be very deeply held) about what is best for all concerned, including minority groups such as the slaves in the American South or the Catholics in South Vietnam, and perhaps anxiety about what may happen elsewhere if violent attacks on the legally established order are allowed to succeed. There is always a tendency to accept whatever definition of "belonging" makes a given piece of land clearly belong to one's own nation or to an ally.

If we ask ourselves why most Americans assume that South Vietnam belongs to the Saigon Government and does not belong to the Viet Cong or to the Communist Government in the North, perhaps the best single answer would be that since 1954 we have regarded this as an established, accepted fact. Since 1954 we have had a mental image of Vietnam as having been divided, as Korea was, between a Communist North and a southern portion that was still part of the free world—perhaps precariously so, but for that reason all the more in need of being shored up and defended. Probably in the minds of most well-informed

Americans there has been no belief that most of the people in South Vietnam want the kind of government they have had in Saigon. On that score there have been embarrassing doubts. But the doubts have usually been fairly well resolved in various ways, e.g., by the belief that most of the people in South Vietnam belong to a large, politically apathetic middle group that only wants peace and would gladly go along with whichever side seems likely to be the winner—from which many infer that there is no popular will which needs to be considered, and that we are therefore free to decide the matter on other grounds. Or the doubts may be resolved by the belief that in the long run a government sponsored by us would permit a genuine development of democracy and national independence, whereas no Communist government would do so; or by the belief that permitting a Communist use of force to succeed in South Vietnam would encourage the "wars of liberation" favored by Communist China and therefore endanger both peace and freedom throughout the world. But all of these points also encounter controversy, and when tired of such controversy many Americans, including Dean Rusk, fall back on the solid, simple, and (they feel) unanswerable proposition that there are Communist soldiers fighting on land that does not "belong" to them. "We will stay until they decide to let their neighbors alone." And the seeming obviousness of this "belonging," since it cannot be based on assumptions about what the people want, is probably based primarily on the fact that for at least twelve years there has been, on our maps and in our minds, a division between the Communist North and the non-Communist South. We see this as the established, accepted, natural order of things.

In doing so we ignore three facts that in Communist minds are much more important than the division of the country that occurred in 1954.

1. *The division of the country has its only legal basis in the Geneva Conference of 1954, and at that conference it was explicitly agreed that it would last only two years.* The Communist-led Viet Minh stopped fighting on the basis of what seemed to be a firm agreement that there would be an all-Vietnamese vote in 1956 (which they fully expected to win) that would unify the country, establishing both unity and full independence without further bloodshed. According to the respected French historian Philippe Devillers, "The demarcation line was to be purely provisional; the principle of Vietnamese unity was not questioned, and the idea of partition was officially rejected with indignation by both sides. When military forces were regrouped and administrative divisions laid down, national unity would be restored by free general elections." [8]

Informed Americans are now embarrassingly aware (though a great many reasonably well-informed Americans were not clearly aware of it until perhaps two or three years ago) that in 1956 Diem, apparently with American backing, refused to permit the elections that had been provided for by the Geneva Agreement. To be sure, neither he nor we had signed those agree-

ments, and there were other persuasive reasons for not permitting the elections at that time or at any time since then. But that is not the present point at issue; the point is that, having in effect rejected the Geneva Agreement by not carrying out one of its key provisions, Diem and the United States deprived themselves of any right to invoke the Geneva Agreement as a legal or moral sanction for the division of the country. With Diem's decision not to press for a plebiscite under international supervision even in "his own" southern part of the country, he forfeited—at least in Communist eyes—not only all claim to the kind of legitimacy that genuine popular endorsement would have provided, but also all claim to invoke the Geneva Conference's endorsement of the 17th Parallel as a basis for his own rule in the South. In effect he proclaimed *de facto* control—"possession is nine-tenths of the law"—as his sole basis of legitimacy.

In the same year—and this is a fact that very few Americans know, though it is of great importance to the villagers in South Vietnam who became members of the Viet Cong—Diem abolished the fine old semi-democratic Vietnamese system of electing village councils and mayors, which had survived even during the period of French rule. Both of these actions by Diem must have seemed to the Communists to be flagrantly anti-democratic, anti-Vietnamese, and a violation of the agreement on the basis of which they had laid down their arms. It was only *after* both had occurred, in 1957, that the Viet Cong began their campaign of assassination of government-appointed officials in the villages. From their standpoint,

[8] Philippe Devillers, "The Struggle for Unification of Vietnam," *China Quarterly*, No. 9 (1962), pp. 2–23.

the decisive acts of armed aggression against them occurred in 1956, and anything they have done since then has only been defensive.

2. *In the years between 1950 and 1954, when the United States was supplying money and arms on a large scale to the French, the French were fighting against a clear majority of the Vietnamese people.*

The years before 1954 represent another major blind spot in the thinking of most Americans, though they are probably ever present in the thinking of the Vietnamese Communists. For them those years were as terrible and as heroic as the years of World War II were for the Communists in the Soviet Union.

Few Americans realize that in 1945 and 1946, when the postwar world was settling down to its present division between East and West, Vietnam was not so divided. Instead, it was enjoying the first flush of what seemed to be independence from the rule of France, under Ho Chi Minh's leadership. Since he was a Communist, this meant that the boundary between the two worlds was at that time the boundary of Vietnam itself. Vietnam as a whole had in a sense "gone Communist" when it accepted Ho's leadership. It was, then, the West that stepped over the boundary and used force on the far side of it. France began then, and continued until 1954— with massive American financial help after 1950—to try to reimpose her rule. Although there was talk of a new autonomous role for the three states of Indochina within the French Union, the anti-French majority of the Vietnamese could be forgiven for regarding this war as naked aggression on the

part of France, aided greatly by the United States. The term "imperialist," which sounds so strange in American ears when applied to ourselves, does not sound so strange in the ears of Vietnamese who regarded French rule as imperialist and had much reason to associate alien intruding Frenchmen with alien intruding Americans. As for the word "aggressor," it is difficult to escape the conclusion that, by any definition of the term, we were committing aggression in Vietnam from 1950 to 1954. We were financing the use of force on land that did not "belong" to us—or to the French—by any criterion that we would now accept, and we were doing it against what now clearly seems to have been a majority of the people.

On this last point we have the testimony of many people, including President Eisenhower. As he put it in a much-quoted passage, "I have never talked or corresponded with a person knowledgeable in Indochinese affairs who did not agree that had elections been held as of the time of the fighting, possibly 80 per cent of the populace would have voted for the Communist Ho Chi Minh as their leader rather than Chief of State Bao Dai." [9]

Since President Eisenhower's statement has often been misinterpreted it should be noted that he did not say that Ho Chi Minh would probably have won by 80 per cent in the elections that Diem refused to hold in 1956. He said "possibly;" he carefully said "had elections been held as of the time of the fighting," i.e., in 1954

---

[9] Dwight D. Eisenhower, *Mandate for Change* (Garden City, N.Y.: Doubleday and Co., Inc., 1963), p. 372.

or earlier, not in 1956, when Diem's prospect of victory would have been much brighter; and he specified as Ho's hypothetical opponent Bao Dai, who was generally regarded as a weak French stooge, rather than Diem, who at that time was regarded even by many of his enemies as an honest man and a staunch anti-French patriot. But on the point that is now at issue— whether the help we gave to the French was in effect a use of force against a majority of the Vietnamese people—President Eisenhower's statement would seem to be decisive.

Why did we do it? Our reasons were understandable if not valid. In 1950 the Communists had just won in China; they were starting the Korean war, and it looked as if desperate measures were necessary in order to keep all of East and Southeast Asia from succumbing to the Communist juggernaut. Perhaps President Truman was honest enough to say to himself that even aggression against the Vietnamese was justified by the magnitude of the emergency. If present-day Americans are able to be equally honest and to remember clearly the situation as it was then, it will help them to understand how present-day Vietnamese Communists could really regard us as aggressors.

3. *The Communist-led majority of the Vietnamese people had actually won their war for independence in 1954.*

Though they were supported to some extent by arms from China, the arms their enemies gained from the United States and from France were far more formidable. Consequently, one of the clearest indications that a large majority of the Vietnamese people did support Ho lies in the fact that his ragged, relatively poorly armed troops did finally win. The battle of Dienbienphu was decisive, and it was generally agreed at the time that if the Viet Minh had wanted to fight a few months more they could have had the whole country.

This is an important part of the psychological background of the Geneva Agreements, and of everything that has happened since. In this respect the situation was very different from the situation in Korea in 1945, when the boundary at the 38th Parallel was first established, or in Korea in 1953, when a military stalemate finally led to a new and roughly similar truce line. In 1953 there was a military stalemate in Korea and the Communists had no basis at all for setting their hearts on unifying the country on their terms. In Vietnam they did. The Vietnamese Communists and the many non-Communists who fought with them had every reason to feel that the prize for which they had struggled and sacrificed through nine heartbreaking years of war was finally theirs: a unified, independent country. Then, by what must have seemed to them a form of chicanery, with the face of America appearing where the face of France had been, and with both Diem and John Foster Dulles blandly claiming that they were not bound by the decisions made at Geneva, a full half of the prize they felt they had fairly won was snatched from them.

Apart from any question of what the people want, then, the Vietnamese Communists have three additional reasons for feeling that South Vietnam "belongs" to them and not to the government established and maintained by us in Saigon: the artificial division of the country at the 17th Parallel was legally and morally invalid after 1956; their war for independence was supported by a large majority of the people; they won that war.

FIVE REASONS WHY THEY THINK THE PEOPLE OF SOUTH VIETNAM ARE ON THEIR SIDE

Since Communists have repeatedly said that any people has a right to fight a "war of liberation" against colonial overlords, no matter how much the rule of the overlords may be sanctioned by tradition and legality, it is clear that their decisive criterion of "aggression" (if they are consistent with their official statements) must be whether "the people" oppose it or not. The following five types of evidence, of which they are probably much more aware than the average American, are therefore relevant to the question of their sincerity on this point.

1. *There are many reasons to think that Vietnamese nationalism is now mobilized, and has been mobilized for some twenty years, much more in favor of Ho Chi Minh than in favor of the French-backed or American-backed government in Saigon.*

In Vietnam, perhaps more than in any other developing country, the Communists have apparently succeeded in fusing Communism with nationalism, and especially with the cause of national unity. The long and finally victorious struggle against the French was conducted primarily under Communist leadership by peasants who regarded their leaders more

as patriots than as Communists.[10] President Eisenhower's statement, quoted above, is very relevant here.[11]

It should be noted too that the more and more conspicuous role of America on the Saigon Government side since 1960 has been such as to mobilize the xenophobic nationalism of the Vietnamese in a new way. Since 1960 American aid to Saigon has become far greater and more obvious, while Chinese aid to the Communists has been on a much smaller scale. There are many big-nosed white faces now on the Government side of the war, while those on the Viet Cong side are authentically Vietnamese, even though now a considerable and very potent fraction of them have come down from the North. The Viet Cong guerrillas have been helped by their own countrymen, while the Government has incurred what is probably a much greater stigma by accepting massive help from white foreigners who cannot even speak Vietnamese.

2. *The peasants want land, and many of them have had land taken away from them by the Government.*

Although there is a village-centered peasant nationalism, it may well be that another motive—hunger—is even more basic in the typical peasant's make-up. He wants to safeguard the bowl of rice that represents

[10] Bernard Fall, *The Two Vietnams* (New York: Frederick A. Praeger, 1964), pp. 104–29; Ellen Hammer, *The Struggle for Indochina* (Stanford: Stanford University Press, 1954); Jean Lacouture, *Vietnam Between Two Truces* (New York: Random House, 1966), pp. 5, 8, and 32.

[11] On the importance and nature of Vietnamese nationalism, see George A. Carver, Jr., "The Real Revolution in South Viet Nam," *Foreign Affairs*, Vol. 43, Number 3 (1965), especially pp. 399 and 403.

his next meal, and the rice field that represents next year's meals for himself, his wife, and his children. From the standpoint of many peasants in the southern part of South Vietnam, especially the Mekong Delta, their rice and their rice fields have been under attack not only by the crop-destroying chemicals that have been dropped (in some areas) by Government planes, but also by the absentee landlords who have in many instances demanded between thirty and fifty per cent of the crop. This fact of absentee landlordism in the South is little known in the United States. It has been estimated that in South Vietnam proper (Cochin China, roughly the southern one-third of the country) only two per cent of the people owned forty-five per cent of the land before 1945.[12] Land reform since then has not greatly changed the situation. Some has occurred under Diem and his successors, but it was preceded by a drastic reclaiming of land that the Viet Minh, when it was in control of large areas in South Vietnam, had given to the peasants outright. Land reform by the present government has been a pale imitation of land reform under the Communist-led Viet Minh.

3. *Probably much more physical suffering has been imposed on the peasants by the Government and its American allies than by the Viet Cong.*

On this point Americans have had misperceptions of two quite different kinds. On the one hand there is the misperception of those Americans who, shocked by occasional television pictures of weeping mothers, roughly handled prisoners, and deliberately burned villages, have failed to realize that the atrocities of the Viet Cong, less accessible to Western photographers and less vividly depicted, are just as real. Public disembowelment of "enemies of the people" and of their wives and children is only one of the revolting procedures employed by them, and it has seldom found its way to our American newspaper pages or television screens. On the other hand, there is the misperception of those Americans who, focusing primarily on the widely discussed Viet Cong assassinations of teachers, health workers, and Government-appointed village officials, have often remained ignorant of the highly probable fact that, because of the nature of guerrilla and counter-guerrilla war, the sheer volume of suffering inflicted by the Government has been considerably greater than that inflicted by the Viet Cong.

There are two reasons for this. The more familiar one is that the present process of using American firepower and mobility to break the back of the Viet Cong has meant—despite genuine efforts to minimize it—a large amount of killing, maiming, and sometimes napalming of villagers who, whether "innocent" from our point of view or not, certainly regard themselves as innocent.[13] In a culture that values family loyalty as much as the Vietnamese culture does, this deeply affects not only those who have suffered from it themselves but also those who have seen a parent or other relative suffer or die.

The less familiar reason for it is that, in the conduct of counter-

[12] Fall, *op. cit.*, pp. 308–311.

[13] Major-General Edward G. Lansdale, "Viet Nam: Do We Understand Revolution?" *Foreign Affairs*, Vol. 43, Number 1 (1964), p. 81.

guerrilla operations, it is urgently necessary to obtain intelligence about the identity of the guerrilla fighters and where they are hiding. South Vietnamese soldiers have interpreted this as justifying a large-scale use of torture to obtain information not only from captured Viet Cong prisoners themselves but also from wives and relatives of men suspected of being in the Viet Cong. There is the water torture, the electric-current torture, the wire-cage torture—all widely used—and there are other kinds even less well-known in the United States (perhaps chiefly because of unofficial self-censorship by most of our information gatherers in Saigon) but well documented by observers such as Bernard Fall, Malcolm Browne, and Robin Moore.[14]

The ignorance and apathy of the great majority of the American public with regard to this ugliest aspect of the war represent in themselves a puzzling and very disturbing psychological phenomenon. Bernard Fall in 1965 spoke about "the universally callous attitude taken by almost everybody toward the crass and constant violations of the rules of war that have been taking place. . . . To me the moral problem which arises in Vietnam is that of torture and needless brutality to combatants and civilians alike."[15] But the fact of widely used torture has not been cited here as an accusation against the United States. As we have seen, some of the Viet Cong atrocities have been at least as bad. The direct participants in the torture have as a rule been South Vietnamese, not Americans, and during the past year (partly as a result of the article by Bernard Fall quoted above) the American military authorities have provided American troops with clear instructions not only as to the applicability of the 1949 Convention on the humane treatment of prisoners but also as to the long-run counterproductive character of the torturing of prisoners and their relatives. The fact is cited here because it provides such an emotionally compelling kernel of truth in the Communist case against the Saigon Government, as well as for the Communist thesis that the common people *must* hate that government. Simply by focusing on this and ignoring similar atrocities on the Communist side a Communist could arrive at that conclusion.

4. *There has been a great deal of inefficiency and corruption on the part of the local officials appointed by the Saigon Government.*

The tradition of exploitation and cheating of the peasants by Government-appointed officials is perhaps no worse than in a number of other Asian countries, including pre-Communist China; but it is very bad,[16] and it does contrast with the Viet Cong's tradition of comparative honesty and concern with the welfare of the rank-and-file peasants.[17] Inefficiency is also clearly very common, in contrast with the

[14] Bernard Fall, "Vietnam Blitz: A Report on the Impersonal War," *The New Republic*, Oct. 9, 1965, pp. 18–21; Malcolm W. Browne, *The New Face of War* (New York: Bobbs-Merrill, 1965), pp. 114–18; Robin Moore, *The Green Berets* (New York: Avon Books, 1965), pp. 46–50.

[15] Fall, *ibid.*, pp. 19–20.

[16] M. Mok, "In They Go—To the Reality of This War," *Life*, Nov. 26, 1965, p. 71.

[17] Malcolm Browne, *op. cit.*, pp. 121–28; Viet Cong Soldiers' Diaries, quoted in *The Vietnam Reader*, ed. by M. G. Raskin and Bernard Fall (New York: Random House, 1965), p. 227.

quite extraordinary efficiency (in some ways) of the Viet Cong; and in many relatively inaccessible villages the choice is not between the Viet Cong type of village government and that of the Saigon officials, but between Viet Cong government and virtually no government at all. In these villages the Viet Cong cadres fill a political vacuum and provide an alternative to anarchy. To be sure, they themselves have helped to produce the anarchy by assassinating Government-appointed village leaders. But their tactics have not been the only cause of anarchy, and they themselves are probably more aware, indeed inordinately aware, of their own comparative honesty and efficiency, which "must" bring the peasants over to their side.

None of this, it may be noted, is incompatible with the fact, now well documented, that in the years since 1963 the Viet Cong's high-handed methods of taxation and recruitment among the peasants have become more and more burdensome. The comparative honesty and efficiency of Viet Cong functionaries are linked with an essentially authoritarian attitude and a willingness to subordinate peasant welfare to the progress of the war. But *in their minds* the peasant's resentment of such tactics is probably underestimated, while his appreciation of their more positive contributions is probably overestimated.

5. *The Viet Cong has a record of remarkable military success against enormous obstacles, and it seems unlikely that such success could have been achieved without widespread popular support.*

Americans sometimes forget or underestimate the great advantage that the anti-Communist forces have enjoyed from the standpoint of weapons, especially since America began in 1950 to give large-scale material help to the French. The total amount of such help has clearly been much greater than the material help the Viet Cong has received from the North. Moreover, few Americans realize that the rebellion did not begin in the part of South Vietnam near Laos and the Ho Chi Minh Trail, where an appreciable amount of help from the North might have been possible. It began primarily in the far South, in the Mekong Delta, where it was necessary to use mainly homemade or captured weapons. The rebels therefore had to make up in organization, dedication, and extent of popular support for the Government's great advantage in material equipment.[18] Still another fact frequently forgotten in America (or never learned) is that the rebellion began to a significant extent in 1957,[19] at least three years before its surprising success—with little outside help— led the Communist authorities in the North to give it a significant amount of material help.

It is true that one major compensating advantage possessed by the Viet Cong has been the tactical advantage of concealment and surprise that has led to the conventional estimate that counter-guerrilla forces must have a ten-to-one numerical superiority over guerrilla forces in order to defeat them. But what is sometimes forgotten is that the guerrillas' tactical advantage exists to this high

[18] Fall, *The Two Vietnams,* p. 317; Lacouture, *op. cit.,* pp. 21–23.

[19] Carver, *op. cit.,* p. 406.

degree only when they have the active support of most of the people (which they could hardly get by intimidation alone) in helping them to conceal themselves, in helping to supply them with the intelligence they need in order to have the full advantage of surprise, and in denying to the counter-guerrilla forces the same kind of intelligence.

Here too there are important counterarguments on the anti-Communist side. In particular the use of intimidation by the Viet Cong to clinch their hold on the peasants must account for much of the peasant co-operation that has occurred. But here again it is important to note that the Communists themselves are probably overinclined to discount or ignore those counterarguments. The military successes of the Viet Cong against far better armed opponents have been remarkable enough to enable Communists to say to themselves: "The people *must* be on our side."

*   *   *   *

There are at least five reasons, then, to think that the Communists believe most of the people are on their side: nationalistic resentment of intrusion by white Americans, land hunger, resentment of torture and other physical suffering caused by the Government, the corruption of officials, and the military success of the Viet Cong against great material odds.

Together with the three additional reasons reviewed earlier for thinking they feel that South Vietnam is part of "their" country, these five seem quite adequate to make it probable that doctrinaire Communists, already predisposed against the United States, do believe it when they call us "aggressors." However mistaken this proposition may be (and I happen to think it is largely mistaken, on the basis of evidence that has hardly been touched upon here), the Communists probably *believe* it is true.[20]

A SENSIBLE AND HONORABLE COMPROMISE

The preceding discussion is a diagnosis of the problem, not a prescription for its solution. In the light of this diagnosis, though, my own feeling is that the most sensible and honorable policy for the United States is to seek a compromise peace. It is the only kind of peace that would allow *both* sides to feel that they had preserved from the aggressor's grasp the bare essentials of what they were fighting to defend.

It could take various forms. One is a coalition government, with efforts by other countries to keep the coalition from being dominated by the organized, dedicated Communist minority within it. Such a coalition could be the outcome of negotiations, if genuine negotiations become possible, or it might conceivably be set up by our side unilaterally, with a real effort to give the Viet Cong and all other elements of the population power commensurate with their actual strength. Or it could take the form of a partition of the South along lines reflecting the

[20] Douglas Pike, *Viet Cong* (Cambridge, Mass.: M.I.T. Press, 1966), p. 378. Although Pike is very skeptical of the proposition that most of the people support the Viet Cong, he speaks of the party's "mystic belief in the power *and loyalty* of the people." Italics added.

balance of military power at the time the partition occurs. This too could be done with negotiations if possible but without negotiations if necessary— unilaterally, by a decision to concentrate our military strength on consolidating non-Communist control of large contiguous areas (not small "enclaves") while withdrawing from overexposed, hard-to-hold areas elsewhere. Free migration into and out of each area might follow, as it did in the partition that followed the 1954 agreement.

As to the relative merits of different types of compromise peace there are complex pro's and con's, and this is not the place to discuss them. What is argued here is that a search for *some* feasible form of compromise peace is the only sensible and honorable policy for the United States.

When each side believes the other to be the aggressor, both are sure to regard any compromise as unsatisfactory, since each will see a compromise as granting to the aggressor some part of his ill-gotten gains. Each wants to ensure that the aggressor is not rewarded by any expansion whatsoever. In this case, for instance, we Americans and our Vietnamese allies would hate to accept a compromise that we defined as granting to the Communists any expansion of power, either by gaining some land south of the 17th Parallel or by gaining some power in a coalition government. The Communists would similarly regard with dismay a compromise peace that left the American "aggressors" still firmly ensconced on Vietnamese soil and still (as they would see it) ruling a large part of the country through their lackeys in Saigon. To them it would seem like a

bitter and futile end to their twenty years of struggle to drive the alien white intruders into the sea.

As long as both sides rigidly adhere to this principle, a compromise is clearly impossible. However, *if* there is no clear break in the present military stalemate and the bloody, inhuman war continues with no end in sight, each side may lower its sights and begin to consider seriously whether some form of compromise would necessarily be cowardly and dishonorable. Probably both sides would even then be grimly determined never to surrender. "Surrender is unthinkable." But each side might become aware that it had a hierarchy of preferences. Three choices might emerge instead of only two: surrender (unthinkable), a compromise peace, and unending war, instead of surrender (unthinkable) and victory. Among these three choices a compromise peace might then seem the least intolerable.

What are the bare essentials of what each side is fighting to defend? Are they incompatible? Or would it be possible for both sides simultaneously to preserve what they care about most?

On our side, it seems to me, there are two things that a large majority of the American people regard as essential: to avoid a significant "domino" process in other parts of the world, and to preserve a tolerable life for our anti-Communist friends in Vietnam. The first of these is believed to be a matter of defending both freedom and peace: the freedom of other countries that are vulnerable to the Chinese strategy of takeover by "wars of liberation," and the peace that would be endangered elsewhere if a Communist victory in Vietnam led Communists everywhere to be more aggressive. The second is more a matter of honor and commitment. We feel that our words and actions have established a commitment to our anti-Communist allies, and that if we abandoned them to the untender mercies of the Viet Cong we would be doing a shameful thing. The validity of these two points will not be debated here; it is necessary only to recognize that most of the Americans who would be involved in the decision do care about both of them, and care deeply.

On the Communist side there are as yet no verbal indications of a hierarchy of preferences. On the surface there is only a fervent, monolithic insistence that the American aggressors must be wholly eliminated from the scene; and since we feel that any complete withdrawal by us would both accentuate the domino process and leave our anti-Communist friends helpless in the face of the organized, dedicated, vengeful Viet Cong, there is little chance of a compromise on this basis. It seems likely, though, that beneath the surface they do have a hierarchy of preferences. Perhaps, if convinced that the alternative is not victory but unending war, they would prefer peace with undisturbed control of some large fraction (say a half) of the population of South Vietnam. This would mean that they could stay alive, go back to the increasingly urgent business of cultivating their rice paddies, and preserve the way of life in which they have invested so much effort and sacrifice. The Communists in the North would be spared further bombing and the danger of a wider war, and although they would have failed in their great objective of unifying the country under their own control, they could salvage some pride in the thought that they had held their own against a much more powerful aggressor.

On each side, then, a compromise peace might be interpreted as salvaging the bare essentials of what that side was fighting to defend. It therefore seems psychologically feasible if we pursue it intelligently and persistently.

It also seems more honorable than any other alternative. By keeping the American flag flying in South Vietnam and stubbornly refusing to retreat from our present power position we would be balancing the power of Communist China on its periphery and fulfilling our obligation to the small non-Communist countries that are threatened by Communist takeover. We would also be fulfilling our obligation to preserve the life and livelihood of our non-Communist friends in Vietnam itself. But if we attempted by force of arms to conquer the parts of South Vietnam in which most of the people regard us as alien aggressors—and the evidence suggests that a very large proportion of the people in certain areas see us in that light—we would be in conflict with the principle of self-determination. It is not in the American tradition to impose abject surrender on brave men who believe, rightly or wrongly, that they are defending their homeland against aggression by us.

POLITICAL COGNITION IN EASTPORT
ROBERT E. LANE

PRINCIPLES AND PRAGMATISM

Tocqueville thought that "the Americans are much more addicted to the use of general ideas than the English and entertain a much greater relish for them." The English, he says, were concerned only with "particular facts" and "only generalize in spite of themselves." On the other hand "Among the French . . . the taste for general ideas would seem to grow to so ardent a passion that it must be satisfied on every occasion." [1] André Siegfried says of the French, "Principles and ideals are the very heart and soul of our politics." [2] But of the Americans no one has repeated Tocqueville's observation; on the contrary they are said to be as pragmatic and as addicted to facts as Tocqueville says the English were some 120 years ago.

The discussion of this issue is loose; it is complicated by the fact that every explanation of an event requires, implicitly or explicitly, a set of generalizations. Thus one interpretation of these alleged differences is that some people tend to *describe* situations rather than to explain them. If this were the allegation with respect to the American pragmatism—that it is a discourse based on description—the evidence from Eastport would tend to refute it. In the discussion of "major problems," of the causes of war and poverty, of the functioning of government, and elsewhere, there is a marked tendency to explain, a focus on why things happen the way they do.

But a causal explanation has two main ingredients. Popper says, "To give a *causal explanation* of an event means to deduce a statement which describes it, using as premises of the deductions one or more *universal laws,* together with certain singular statements, the *initial conditions.*" [3] When the French, with their alleged emphasis upon principles, explain an event, they may elaborate the universal laws, generalizing about the nature of men and society, and they may slight the statement of particulars, the facts, or, in Popper's phrase, the initial conditions. When Americans explain an event—and certainly this is true in Eastport—they may assume the uni-

CREDIT: Reprinted with permission of The Macmillan Company from *Political Ideology* by Robert E. Lane, pp. 348–363. Copyright © 1962 by The Free Press of Glencoe, a Division of The Macmillan Company. [*Footnotes renumbered.*]

[1] Alexis de Tocqueville, *Democracy in America,* Phillips Bradley, ed. (New York: Knopf, 1945), II, 14.

[2] André Siegfried, *France: A Study in Nationality* (New Haven: Yale University Press, 1930), p. 25.

[3] Karl R. Popper, *The Logic of Scientific Discovery,* 2nd ed. (New York: Basic Books, 1958), p. 58, his emphasis.

versal laws and focus upon the initial conditions, the facts that characterize the situation. It is, indeed, true, that the man of Eastport tends to explain matters in terms of latent principles and manifest facts, and when he argues the argument more often turns on the characteristics of the situation, not on the rules that govern the universe. But, of course, he has ideas about these rules, ideas that remain part of his somewhat inarticulate and often unconscious assumptions of the nature of things.

The latency of the principles employed in social explanations tends to be supported by two other features of the American ideology. In the first place there stands the belief that most men are more or less the same; thus the rules governing human behavior are intuitively known through introspection. They are assumed, not discussed. Second, the common unchallenged assumptions about government derive from the almost universal acceptance of the same Lockean model, as Louis Hartz has pointed out.[4] One consequence of this latency is that the American finds it difficult to argue about political principles, and there is little doubt that one reason why Americans become so furious over the arguments of the Communists is that their own political principles are hard to tear from their native bed in the unconscious.

MORSELIZING AND CONTEXTUALIZING

"Our way," said Edith Hamilton of contemporary civilization, "is to con-

sider each separate thing alone by itself." On the other hand, she says, "the Greeks always saw things as parts of a whole, and this habit of mind is stamped upon everything they did. It is the underlying cause of the difference between their art and ours."[5] Others, too, have spoken of the fragmentation of the world in modern times. Yet one of the features of what is sometimes called "understanding" is to grasp the context of an event, that is, temporally to know what went before and what is likely to follow, spatially to know the terrain, in human terms to see the play of the many motives involved. To understand an event in this way is to *contextualize* it; not to do this is to *morselize* it, to see it isolated from the surrounding features that give it additional "meanings." What education does for a man is to help him to contextualize events, particularly public events, but the unusual man, as we shall see, can capture some of this context without formal education.

In Eastport, as elsewhere, some men morselize the political world and some contextualize it. We can see how this works by stripping their discourse bare of the "I don't knows," the repetition, the false starts, and giving a summary outline of the ideas presented by three men as they discuss Soviet-American relationships. DeAngelo, who left school in the seventh grade but who is now shop steward of his plant and a hard-working factory operative, sets forth the following ideas on this subject: "It doesn't seem like you can negotiate with them [because] they've just got their minds set." "We're trying to do things with

[4] Louis Hartz, *The Liberal Tradition in America* (New York: Harcourt, Brace, 1955).

[5] Edith Hamilton, *The Greek Way to Western Civilization* (New York: New American Library, 1948), p. 169.

'em peacefully." "We are keeping them surrounded with air bases, kind of keeping them in check." "They'll start trouble somewhere." "It's not our fault." "It's just like Germany—they want to conquer the world." "There's no religion . . . if a man doesn't believe in anything, you can't bargain with him." "I don't know who's behind the Russians," "We must protect ourselves." "The whole world today is all fouled up." There is no dearth of ideas here; DeAngelo, with his tongue getting in the way of his speech, is a rough, untrained observer, but not unintelligent.

McNamara finished high school and went to night school to learn bookkeeping. He says: "Inflation and defense policy are related." "Russia's come a long way in twenty years," "No one knows what the Russians have accomplished." "It appears they are ahead of us in the science field." "You've got to be careful." "They're probably now as powerful as Germany was, and Germany stirred up a lot of trouble." "Our policy is pretty well set: go along carefully and every once in a while pass out a few threats; a display of power here and there doesn't hurt." "We are now in a scientific race." "Barriers between nations don't help; perhaps we should open up more trade." "We're making the same mistakes with them we made with Germany." "War may not be inevitable."

Flynn, who did finish high school but never had any training beyond that, except what he picked up as a young assistant on a water-company survey, says: "The trade problem and the defense problem are related." "Mutual scaring of each other by us and the Russians is risky." "The philosophy of disarmament runs into the difficulty that the Russians won't compromise." "A firmer foreign policy ten years ago would have prevented some of this." "While we have been building up other countries, the Russians have been building up their military strength." "You will never get disarmament until each side is certain of armament parity." "Full-scale disarmament is too idealistic." "We believe that you can't trust the Russians, and they believe they can't trust us." "Agreement is difficult because of the many nations involved." "War is probably inevitable, but the horror of nuclear war may prevent it." "Agreements are worthless in preventing atomic warfare." "We set the precedent for dropping the bomb."

What do we learn from this? It is a pretty fair sampling of the way these men wrestle with a policy problem somewhat more remote from their experience than the problems they like to deal with. In the first place, there is a wonderful "off the cuff" quality to it; judgments are made with an abandon that terrifies and paralyzes the analytic mind. (How would you, the reader of this book, analyze and meet the proposition: "It's just like Germany—they want to conquer the world"?) There is not in any of the three a real argument, a building up of a case. Instead their statements represent a series of impressions. Third, there is a marked difference among them that reflects something we have said about the scope of the concepts involved; for DeAngelo, these are somewhat narrow and tied to the specific instances involved (a defense policy defined by bases, negotiation as a function of religious faith). McNamara seems to broaden out this straitened view somewhat so that the instances of the present case fall into a larger context. For one thing the idea of Russia is not limited to Russia *now;* it is a part of the larger notion of historical and developing Russia; then too, an important link between domestic and foreign policy is forged, and the concept of a broader fiscal-defense unit of thought is created. Still, the thinking is fairly instance-specific; the conceptual setting is rather meager. With Flynn, however, it broadens again. Like McNamara he links several problems together, for example, defense and trade, and our foreign aid and Russia's rapid advance. His conceptualization includes the Russian side —when he speaks of how we see them he adds how they must see us; it is a conceptualization that embraces one more step then, a feedback concept. He refers not simply to disarmament, but to "the philosophy of disarmament," including by reference, then, a much broader concept of an idea, one to which he is opposed at this time. Like McNamara, his conceptualization includes a time perspective—American foreign policy over the past ten years. He broadens the conceptualization to include other nations: negotiations, he understands, cannot be only bipartite anymore. His concept of a problem and a policy, then, is topically broader, spatially more inclusive, and has historical depth. But more of the men are like DeAngelo than like Flynn, or even McNamara.

If one does not see the instance in its context, the man in his setting, the event in a pattern of events, he misses the significance of what he sees, and missing this, he has no adequate means of dealing with the relevant social or political problems. Sokolsky tells of juvenile delinquency where the deli-

cious details are the focus of his attention and the limit of his observation; Woodside, a railroad guard, sees it in a broader framework; he sees it as falling within a class of minor crimes likely to happen in two or three familiar parts of the city and to be committed by youth with certain characteristics; Farrel, the educated man who slipped into our panel by the processes of randomization, sees it as a part of a social pattern with a broad metropolitan distribution, certain family and psychological correlates, and consequences affecting educational programs and school-leaving age requirements. This treatment of an instance in isolation happens time and again and on matters close to home: a union demand is a single incident, not part of a more general labor-management conflict; a purchase on the installment plan is a specific debt, not part of a budgetary pattern—either one's own or society's. The items and fragments of life remain itemized and fragmented—at least at the conscious level.

Contextual political thinking, then, is not just pigeonholing, not labeling, not in any necessary way associated with the "ismatic" terminology of today (Fascism, Communism, Federalism.) It reflects a configurative and relational turn of mind—in several ways. One way is to picture an event as part of a stream of events; that is, it is historical. Another is to compare and contrast events so as to group them in some way that sheds light on their common characteristics. Still another is to bring the event into contact with a conceptual framework such that it may be seen to illustrate or modify or rebut some part of that framework. Yet it is true that any one of these ways of placing "figure against ground," "contextualizing" an event or an idea, often reaches beyond the experience of the individual in time or place; they are not encouraged by a quality of thought that is characteristic of Eastport workingmen: the tendency to keep concepts narrow and close to personal experience. For while this intellectual sobriety may ensure that the men know the evidential basis for their observations, it deprives them of some of the sources of interpretation that make an event meaningful. And in a curious sense this itemization may then mean that they derive their interpretation of an event from a free associative fantasy process rather than through the social and historical context to which the isolated events may be said to "belong."

CONTEXTUALIZING AND IDEOLOGIZING

Now, the very morselizing tendency that prevents these men from discovering the pattern and significance of an event also prevents them from ideologizing. While they do not place events in the context of a pattern of history or policy, neither do they place them in the context of some more or less rigid and exclusive interpretation of world affairs, a forensic ideology. They do not make events illustrate a predetermined theory of the way the world lies for the simple reason that they do not have such a theory; rather, they have several conflicting theories with vague referents.

Only in one or two instances did it seem to me that these men of Eastport attempted consciously to increase their understanding of an event by explicitly placing it in the context of a forensic ideology, though of course the individual, private, latent ideology of each man served as a constant sentinel at the gate of his mind. Sokolsky, arriving in an angry mood because of his brush with the supervisor on his part-time janitorial job, argues against equal income for everyone regardless of occupation on several personal and pragmatic grounds ("I look with horror on everybody exactly the same"), but he finds room for one more argument of an ideological sort: "I think that would be swinging a little toward your Communists, wouldn't it?" This is more window dressing than anything else, but it illustrates what it is that, on a larger scale and with more emotional force, and with greater elaboration, might be the central characteristic of a political debate. (The fact that we must use this slender example for illustration is significant in itself.)

Consider the difficult case of Sullivan, an over-the-road truck driver, with a laconic but penetrating style of discourse. His argument must be read with the understanding that four out of five of the Eastportians hold that Communists should have no right to free speech in the United States. He does not suffer fools gladly, and while in the Army nearly beat a man to death because he talked after "all quiet" (and brought down punishment on the barracks). Turning to the question of whether or not Communists should be allowed to speak, he says: "Well, [pause] it's a hard thing to say 'no' to, because—I mean I'm not too happy about it, but [pause] you can't very well have a democracy, and freedom of speech, if you don't let them, even though it's [pause] it's not something you agree on or particularly like. There's not too much you can do without changing the policy or the foundation of the country. [pause] I wish there was, but I guess there just isn't something." The logic is clear. This son of a former Jesuitical student argues: freedom of speech for Communists is a necessary part of the general class of things included in the concept "democracy." Since democracy is established by law, and not subject to change, freedom of speech for Communists is not subject to change—and probably shouldn't be. Substitute the right of an employer to contract individually with each of his employees for the rights of free speech for Communists, and substitute "due process" for "democracy," and you have the reasoning of the Court in *Hammer* v. *Dagenhart* and other child-labor cases.

When is a person contextualizing and when is he ideologizing? In each case he adds to his understanding by bringing additional material to bear upon a single event; in each case he must select which material to use; in each case he is guided either explicitly or implicitly by a theoretical construct. The difference centers on the need to confirm the pattern of ideas employed in this process; if the event is used and needed to support an emotionally involved theory or interpretation, the tendency is toward ideologizing. Moreover this frame of mind protects the sacred theory by admitting ideas only from approved sources. The ideologue takes his cue on the interpretation of information from its source; the contextualist is more open to information from all sources. Furthermore, the

ideologue keeps the things he believes quite separate from those he doesn't believe so that their colors, their whiteness and blackness, do not mingle; the contextualist permits a shading in his pictures of the world. For the contextualist information is a positively useful tool, an enjoyment; for the ideologue information is a threat, and therefore suspect, unless it can be made familiar by attaching it to a known system of ideas.[6]

Judged by these standards, Sullivan's wrestling with the problem of civil liberties for Communists by placing the problem in the context of democratic principles could not be said to be ideologizing, for instead of forcing an event into a preferred interpretation he is reluctantly yielding a preferred position to the logic of an over-all pattern of ideas. But Sullivan is exceptional only in the explicitness of the conflict; the others not infrequently confront an event with a cherished principle and tolerate the conflict. Those who believe that unions advance working-class interests accept evidence of their abuse; lifelong Democrats admit that it is unfair to blame the recession on Republicans; 100 per cent American "working-class capitalists" admit that the Russian people are better off these days. Theories of the advantages of unions, Democratic administrations, capitalist economies make room for contrary evidence. Thus in two senses we must say that Eastport tends not to ideologize: first, the use of forensic ideologies, of theoretical constructs with well-

---

[6] Some of these distinctions derive from the excellent discussion in Milton Rokeach, *The Open and Closed Mind* (New York: Basic Books, 1960), pp. 54–82.

defined referents, is minimal; second, the smaller and vaguer theories, the segments of ideologies employed, are used more as guides to interpretation than as defenses against the real world.

RIGIDITY AND COMPROMISE

Closely allied to the concept of ideologizing is that of rigidity, the inflexible mind, whether because it is doctrinaire (ideologized) or merely stubborn, willful, unyielding. Perhaps these men are, in this sense, rigid; that is, they may tend to uncompromising assertion in the face of contrary evidence and argument. Uncertainty of the kind modern men face sometimes produces rigidity. There is good psychoanalytic evidence for this, and some further evidence that it is exactly when their faith seems most at odds with the evidence that religious sectarians become most assertive about their beliefs.[7] I cannot say that I found the men of Eastport rigid, for, of course, I did not argue with them, but rather supported and rewarded the views they brought out themselves to create the most permissive atmosphere possible. But, as mentioned earlier, my associate James D. Barber did arrange for some debate among them in a room where a recording apparatus had been set in motion (with the knowledge of the men) and where the men were then left alone to thrash out a problem by themselves. There were two groups of three; one group was selected because of the prickly personalities of the men, and

[7] Leon Festinger, Henry Reicken, and Stanley Schacter, *When Prophecy Fails* (Minneapolis: University of Minnesota Press, 1956).

another group for their rather more easygoing dispositions. They argued a half-hour each on four topics. I have taken the last topic discussed, on the grounds that by then the men were most heated and free; as it turns out this is also the most controversial topic: "Are unions doing a good job?" The angry, prickly group (whose members I shall not identify, since they have met each other) includes one who recently knocked down a man for a slighting remark, another who nearly beat a man to death in the Army, and a third, who not long ago punched someone in the face for an alleged slur on his mother. At the end of the fourth half-hour argument, Number One, a member of a strong trade union, has been defending the union; Number Two has just been telling of how unions caused his brother-in-law to go bankrupt by "stalling along on the jobs." Number Three finds abuses everywhere but generally thinks unions are a good thing. Here are their summary statements:

NUMBER ONE: Well, I'd say that [pause] the unions are good. You have to have them—the workingman has to have them, and well, I think they're a little too strong, some of them, now. And some of them are a little bit too lax, too. But on the whole, they're good, and on the whole I think [pause] any man that's a union member is getting paid what he's worth. And every union man's got a right to make a little bit more than a nonunion man. . . . A nonunion man just sits back, and when the unions get raises for other members he just falls right in.

NUMBER TWO: Well, I think that unions are a necessity. We've got to have them. But then, again, I think they're getting out of hand. I think they should be controlled, for one thing. I think they're lax—the union itself is lax, as they do allow certain undesirable elements into the union that shouldn't be there, and as a whole I don't think they're doing a good job. I think they're taking advantage of this organization, and just running hog-wild, right now.

NUMBER THREE: [after some critical comments about unions and a statement of agreement with number one— "where they do need unions"]: Yes and no—I think it's just about fifty-fifty.

During the course of the prior discussion, which revealed some real differences of opinion and some strong feeling, there was a tendency to accept part of the opponent's argument, just as there is in the summing up just quoted.

The theme that these three men are working out in these passages, not quite rising above their passions, might be stated as "there is good and bad in unions." Indeed, this general theme could be emblazoned on Eastport's crest: "There is good and bad in everything." When a man speaks evil of something, he will retract it a little later on by saying something good. In Anna Freud's phrase, we are always "undoing" the evil that we do. On the other hand, there is little glorification, either. The exposed evaluative position is rarely rigidly defended—there is, instead, a search for neutral ground.

There are several routes to the "neutral ground" they seek.[8] One is to *deny that there are real differences* of interest among men, and this often follows from their position on the reality of a true public interest. Another is to stress the reconciliation of apparent differences by *bringing the conflicting partisans together.* Johnson discloses this penchant in his belief that the "race problem" might be solved by bringing the parties together. Discrimination in certain areas is "not the American way of doing it," he says, and, in a pleading and rather desperate tone, he adds, "But I should think there should be some way of bringing it out between them." It is his vain hope that the Negroes could be persuaded to accept a segregated arrangement, and thus relieve him of what is really a rather bad conscience. DeAngelo gives the idea of bringing labor and management together a classic expression. He has just said that he believes union pressure is partly responsible for the high cost of living, and continues: "Well, I don't know; the union—they won't press for wages unless, y'know, things keep goin' up. I mean, [pause] I think the government, big business, unions— they gotta get together and straighten the thing out, as best they could. Y'know what I mean? Talk it over; see what the hell they can do about it. [pause] I mean, I don't know, it's gotta be settled some way—if—I think the only way they can settle it, they gotta get together and settle it."

But for these men in their difficult tasks of suggesting policy, the main device is to pursue a kind of *centralist* tendency, something like the one described by Alfred Jones in Akron, Ohio, some twenty-five years ago.[9]

---

[8] For a discussion of basic roots as well as routes of this flexible nondoctinaire theme in America, see Erik Erikson, *Childhood and Society* (New York: Norton, 1950), pp. 275–277.

[9] Alfred W. Jones, *Life, Liberty, and Property* (Philadelphia: Lippincott, 1941).

Given three policy choices the men will choose the "middle" one; given two choices they will yield a little on each, borrow something from the other, obscure the differences. You see this in the concluding statements of the three men on the unions; it is true of many other situations as well. This holds for "feeling strongly," too. On tests where they are given an option to state how strongly they agree or disagree with a proposition, they tend to squash their feelings down into a middle range. Inevitably this produces a certain uniformity of opinion, roughs off the edges and idiosyncrasies, factors that may have caused Bryce to remark how "Americans appear to vary less, in fundamentals, from what may be called the dominant American type, than Englishmen, Germans, Frenchmen, Spaniards, or Italians do from any types which could be taken as the dominant type in any of those nations." [10]

Something might be said here of how this search for neutral ground, this tendency to try to adjust between apparently disparate positions, produces, in the end, that minimal speculation and originality characteristic of Eastport's common man. If everyone is trying to be a broker of opinion and to bring other people's opinions into harmony, none will range far in the pursuit of new ideas. In a way, this represents the substitution of "goodwill," a quality Laski says Americans believe will solve all problems,[11] for hard thinking. For the functioning of a political system, of course, both are

required, but in Eastport, at least, the balance is in favor of goodwill; the common man there is likely to be only a middle man.

Perhaps this is a condition of any successful democracy; perhaps it is more specially American. A hundred and twenty years ago, Tocqueville argued that "the great privilege of the Americans does not consist in being more enlightened than other nations, but in being able to repair the faults they may commit." [12] We are able to acknowledge our mistakes and to correct our errors—something incompatible with rigid thinking. If, as Riesman says, there are penalties to the loss of inner-direction and the conscientious knowledge of what is right, flexibility and the lack of rigidity are the contrasting benefits.

DIFFERENTIATION

There is an economy in stereotypes, says Walter Lippmann. "For the attempt to see things freshly and in detail, rather than as types and generalities, is exhausting, and among busy affairs practically out of the question." [13] Stereotypes are the mind's shorthand for dealing with complexities. They have two aspects: they are much blunter than reality; they are shaped to fit a man's preferences and prejudgments. Thus two principles are involved: differentiation or its lack, and biased preferential perception. "An attitude toward Russia may be focused upon a highly amorphous

[10] James Bryce, *The American Commonwealth* (New York: Macmillan, 1910), II, 886.

[11] Harold Laski, *The American Democracy* (New York: Viking, 1948), p. 708.

[12] Alexis de Tocqueville, *op. cit.*, I, 231.

[13] Walter Lippmann, *Public Opinion* (New York: Penguin, 1946), p. 66.

subjective impression of that country or upon a highly differentiated one. . . . The object of an attitude varies in its differentiation. . . ." [14] This is our problem for the moment.

There are many reasons for ·a blunted differentiation, of which we distinguish three: insufficient information (cognitive bluntness), blockage by strong emotion, especially anger (emotional bluntness), and remoteness from one's own beliefs and values (ideological bluntness). Dempsey, who never advanced beyond the sixth grade, illustrates the first of these. He says the word "government" suggests to him, "Well, someone to govern, to rule over, probably [pause] to guide people in the right way." While interesting for many reasons, not the least of which is the passive and dependent tone of this response, it is certainly a blunt and undifferentiated idea of government. The next "witness," a week later, said: "To me it means organization. [pause] It brings to mind, at least, a society which is regulated, that is, it's governed by a set of rules and a governing body." This is our friend Flynn speaking, a white-collar worker who has completed high school. Dempsey's comment has the bluntness of tautology, with the "guidance" feature added; Flynn breaks down the idea into three, still large but more explicit ideas: organization, the rules of law, an organ through which government acts. Flynn goes on later to develop these ideas, while Dempsey has little more to say. (I ask him what kinds of things the

government ought to do, and he responds, "That I couldn't say; I'm not up on that.") This is what we call a cognitive difference in differentiation based upon information, but there are others.

Rapuano, a volcanic man with the burden of his Americanism lying heavily across his broad but stooping shoulders, answers the same question, after a pause and some heavy breathing, as follows, "Government? What do I think of?" He pauses again. "Politics, for one thing. Oh, yes, [pause] politics is about all I could think of. [pause] There ain't anything that's unpolitical that's not—that's government. Everything that seems to be government is politics." I ask him what kind of things the government ought to do, and he answers after another short pause: "Well, that's hard to say. I mean, I'm not that smart. Let's see what the hell they should do." But he can find things for them to do; he almost finished high school, has an active mind, and is interested in political affairs. What accounts for the bluntness in this case, of course, is the emotional reverberations that echo so loudly in his mind that, so to speak, "he cannot hear himself think." This, then, is a case of emotional bluntness.

This pattern is marked in the cases of four men (Rapuano, Ferrera, Sokolsky, and Kuchinsky) and observable in others. But as we said above, in Eastport the level of indignation is generally low; the flow of affect is moderate; the responses to "things in the news that made me mad" are not very "mad"; the tendency to avoid blaming keeps emotion at a modest level; the adjustive strategies make the nursing of anger dysfunctional, and all

[14] M. Brewster Smith, Jerome S. Bruner, and Robert W. White, *Opinions and Personality* (New York: Wiley, 1956), pp. 34–35.

in all emotional bluntness is kept at a minimum. As a system, the American low-keyed political style keeps open the windows of perception and differentiation to a remarkable degree.

The third type of failure to differentiate, ideological bluntness, is based on the principle that the further away from a person's beliefs and values a group of objects lies, the less significant do the differences between those objects appear. Rokeach illustrates this with the difficulty a follower of Senator McCarthy had in distinguishing between Communists, Socialists, and advanced liberals.[15] In the same way, in 1961 liberals found the distinction between positions held by the *National Review*, the John Birch Society, and Barry Goldwater hard to discern, although conservatives saw important differences. Now, it is significant that a search through the discussion of "subversives in America," "big business," "Russia," "the causes of war and poverty," and other areas of discourse where rejected groups or conspiracies or evil systems have their abode does not discover much blunting of perception. The measure for blunted differentiation includes: (1) an increased use of derogatory labels instead of descriptive terms, such as "a crazy bunch," "madmen," "bloodsuckers," and so forth; (2) a substitute of programs of quick violent action prior to, or probably instead of, description and analysis; (3) dismissal of a problem or group with a phrase, refusal to treat it seriously, contemptuous withdrawal. Only in the case of the domestic Communists was there much evidence of undifferentiated perception and quick

[15] Milton Rokeach, *op. cit.*, pp. 38–39.

prescription—and not by any means in all such cases. Here, for example, is the way Costa begins his discussion of subversive elements in America. Costa is a frequent and militant defender of "the American way." He says:

Well, I think there are too many. Too many leaks, too much of our secret information gets out. I don't know whether that's because we're a democracy or whether there's just people—I mean, I can think of several things, like the Rosenbergs, for one, like that Dr. Fuchs over in England. . . . Are you asking me does Russia have an organized [group]? I think they do.

In the context of Costa's usual level of differentiation there is no loss of differentiated thinking here, no ideological bluntness. Thus the over-all impression (the reactions of about half of the men to domestic Communism excepted) is one of continuity of perception, differentiation, conceptualization—each at his own level—as one moves from areas of belief and support to areas of disbelief and opposition.

Differentiation, as the anthropologists tell us with respect to language, is a measure of social focus, a clue to what the society cares about. Speaking loosely, and about this stratum of lower- middle- and upper-working-class men, I would say the American political mind is differentiated more in terms of rights than duties—almost all men mention and illustrate the various rights that Americans enjoy; they had more trouble in explaining the nature of citizenly or patriotic duties—here the terms were more global and more derivative. Secondly, their capacities to distinguish and deal intellectually with the problems of race relations were greater than those of interclass relations—they had thought more about the one than about the other. Third, their concepts of appropriate means of social adjustment, of how to behave in different situations, are elaborate and clear in their minds—much more elaborate and clear than their pictures of themselves. If one may be elliptical to make the point: each person knows more about *what* he should do than about *who* he is. The American tendency to objectify, rather than subjectify, the world is reflected here. They have differentiated and easily articulated concepts about work, money, and consumption, but their conceptualization of their religious beliefs, the duties of the church, and the purposes of life are blunt and unsophisticated. It is as though they put forth a special effort to homogenize all religious and moral thought. When it came to commentaries on the dogmatic beliefs of their churches, the products were indeed a meager gleaning; and, as we noted before, their time perspectives are differentiated by short-range matters, which may account, in a way, for the optimism of the American outlook. It is only in a perspective that encompasses the period of death that a profound sense of tragedy is likely to develop.

We have said that the political mind of Eastport tends to emphasize one of the ingredients of an explanation, the initial conditions, at the expense of the other, the universal laws. Eastportians tend to morselize their knowledge rather than to contextualize it, thus losing much of the significance or meaning of an event. On some intercultural ideologizing scale, I would guess that they would be "low"; they use events to confirm or defend a world view less frequently than others. They avoid exposed positions, yield quickly in an argument, seek middle ground, and compromise where they can. And while they often use stereotypes and blunted perceptions of events, these tend to flow from lack of information rather than from disagreement or anger.

There are other characteristics of their thought with consequences for the political system: they rarely *organize* their views. Kuchinsky begins his interview as follows: "We have a lot of problems today, and, um, in this country concerning the other side, [Europe] uh, which I think, uh, this country's really gone overboard on a lot of things—I mean throwing a lot of money away." About four sentences later he is speaking of the rent increase in Hilltop—it is a kind of stream of consciousness. On the other hand Flynn begins his interview: "The major problems? Of course that means defining, Number One, what the major problems are. They're in two areas, I guess, foreign and domestic." He turns to the domestic first and discusses this before he moves on for a fuller treatment of the foreign problems. The group mode is closer to Kuchinsky than it is to Flynn; there is an almost complete lack of an effort to think through a question before attempting to answer it; it is a rare moment when a man speaks of the "areas," "levels," "stages," or "phases" of a problem, or uses the apparatus of analysis of component elements of a complex affair, treating them one by one.

These men rarely acknowledge a difference between the speculative and the known, making a point of the *dif-*

ferences in certainty or familiarity. One blends into the other without a break. There is no *strategy* to their discourse, no attempt to persuade through such a logical development that if one admits one point, the next must follow. In short, their discussion is not self-conscious, not planned; it has a kind of "free form" associative quality. In this sense they are open to new information, open to experience. Without the blockages of strong emotion, or the walls of ideological defensiveness, their minds, like the society itself, seem pluralistic, with both liberal and conservative roots to which new ideas can attach themselves and grow.

THE COGNITIVE STRUCTURING OF JOHN FOSTER DULLES
OLE R. HOLSTI

I

It is a basic theorem in the social sciences that "if men define situations as real, they are real in their consequences." Stated somewhat differently, the theorem asserts that an individual responds not only to the "objective" characteristics of a situation, but also to the meaning the situation has for him; the person's subsequent behavior and the results of that behavior are determined by the meaning ascribed to the situation.[1]

This theorem can be applied more specifically to the concept of the enemy. Enemies are those who are defined as such, and if one acts upon that interpretation, it is more than likely that the original definition will be confirmed: "It is an undeniable privilege of every man to prove himself in the right in the thesis that the world is his enemy; for if he reiterates it frequently enough and makes it the background of his conduct, he is bound eventually to be right."[2]

If the concept of the enemy is considered from the perspective of attitudes, one interesting problem is the manner in which attitudes about the enemy are maintained or changed. The history of international relations suggests two contradictory tendencies. On the one hand, just as there are no permanent allies in international relations, there appear to be no permanent enemies. During its history, the United States has fought wars against Britain, France, Mexico, Spain, Germany, Italy, and Japan, all of which are currently allies to some degree. Even the most enduring international antagonisms—for example, between France and Germany—have eventually dissolved. Thus, it is clear that attitudes toward enemies do change.

Although hostile relationships at the international level are not eternal, it is also evident that they tend to en-

CREDIT: Reprinted by permission of author and publisher from Ole R. Holsti, "Cognitive Dynamics and Images of the Enemy," *Journal of International Affairs*, Number 1, 1967, pp. 16–39. [*Figures renumbered. This paper is drawn from sections of a full-scale study published in David J. Finlay, Ole R. Holsti, and Richard R. Fagen, Enemies in Politics (Chicago: Rand-McNally, 1967). Owing to space limitations, quantitative content-analysis data used to test a number of propositions have been omitted from this paper. The reader interested in the data and techniques used to obtain them should consult the book.*]

[1] Robert K. Merton, *Social Theory and Social Structure*, rev. ed. (New York: The Free Press of Glencoe, 1957), pp. 421–22.

[2] "X" (George F. Kennan), "The Sources of Soviet Conduct," *Foreign Affairs*, Vol. XXV (1947), p. 569.

dure well past the first conciliatory gestures. This resistance to changes in attitudes may be attributed to a number of factors, not the least of which is an apparently universal tendency to judge the actions of others—and particularly of those defined as enemies—according to different standards than those applied to oneself. Because friends are expected to be friendly and enemies to be hostile, there is a tendency to view their behavior in line with these expectations. When the other party is viewed within the framework of an "inherent bad faith" [3] model the image of the enemy is clearly self-perpetuating, for the model itself denies the existence of data that could disconfirm it. At the interpersonal level such behavior is characterized as abnormal—paranoia. Different standards seem to apply at the international level; inherent-bad-faith models are not considered abnormal, and even their underlying assumptions often escape serious questioning.

This paper reports a case study of the cognitive dynamics associated with images of the enemy. The basic hypothesis—that there exist cognitive processes that tend to sustain such images—will be examined through study of a single individual, former Secretary of State John Foster Dulles, and his attitude toward a single "enemy," the Soviet Union. One point should be made explicit at the outset: there is no intent here to indicate that Secretary Dulles' attitudes or behavior were in any way "abnormal." It is precisely because of the assumption that his attitudes and behavior were within the normal range of high-ranking policy-makers that he was selected for intensive study. Thus, though Dulles was a unique personality in many respects, this research was undertaken on the premise that the findings may have implications for foreign-policy decision-making in general.

Primary data for this study were derived from the verbatim transcripts of all publicly available statements made by Dulles during the years 1953–1959, including 122 press conferences, 70 addresses, 67 appearances at Congressional hearings, and 166 other documents. This documentation was supplemented by contemporary newspapers, secondary sources, questionnaires sent to a number of Dulles' closest associates, and memoirs written by those who worked closely with him.[4]

II

The theoretical framework for this study has been developed from two major sources. The first and more gen-

[3] This term, derived from Henry A. Kissinger, *The Necessity for Choice* (Garden City: Doubleday & Co., 1962), p. 201, is used here to denote a conception of the other nation by which it is defined as evil *whatever* the nature of its actions—"damned if it does, and damned if it doesn't." The reverse model is that of appeasement; all actions of the other party, regardless of their character, are interpreted as non-hostile. Despite some notable examples of appeasement, such as the Munich settlement prior to World War II, misinterpretation deriving from the appeasement model seems to be relatively rare at the international level.

[4] For example, Sherman Adams, *Firsthand Report* (New York: Harper, 1961); Emmet John Hughes, *The Ordeal of Power* (New York: Atheneum, 1963); and Andrew Berding, *Dulles on Diplomacy* (Princeton: Van Nostrand, 1965). Berding, Assis-

eral of these is the literature on the relationship of an individual's "belief system" to perception and action. The belief system, composed of a number of "images" of the past, present, and future, includes "all the accumulated, organized knowledge that the organism has about itself and the world." [5] It may be thought of as the set of lenses through which information concerning the physical and social environment is received. It orients the individual to his environment, defining it for him and identifying for him its salient characteristics. National images may be considered as subparts of the belief system. Like the belief system itself, these are models that order for the observer what would otherwise be an unmanageable amount of information.

All images are stereotyped in the trivial sense that they oversimplify reality. It is this characteristic that makes images functional—and can render them dysfunctional. Unless the *content* of the image coincides in some way with what is commonly perceived as reality, decisions based on these images are not likely to fulfill the actor's expectations. Erroneous images may also prove to have a distorting effect by encouraging reinterpretation of information that does not fit the image; this is most probable with such inherent-bad-faith models as "totalitarian communism" or "monopolistic capitalism," which exclude the very types of information that might lead to a modification or clarification of the models themselves. Equally important is the *structure* of the belief system, which, along with its component images, is in continual interaction with new information. In general, the impact of this information depends upon the degree to which the structure of the belief system is "open" or "closed." [6]

Further insight and more specific propositions concerning the relationship between the belief system and new information can be derived from the theoretical and experimental literature on the cognitive dynamics associated with attitude change, and more specifically, from those theories that have been described as "homeostatic" or "balance theories." Among the most prominent of these are theories that postulate a "tendency toward balance," a "stress toward symmetry," a "tendency toward increased congruity," and a "reduction of cognitive dissonance." [7] Despite terminological differences, common to all these theories is the premise that imbalance between various components of attitude is psychologically uncomfortable.

tant Secretary of State for Public Affairs, took extensive shorthand notes that reveal a remarkable similarity between Dulles' public and private views. The Eisenhower and Nixon memoirs have also been consulted, but these are notably lacking in any insight into Dulles' personality or beliefs.

[5] George A. Miller, Eugene Galanter, and Karl H. Pribram, *Plans and the Structure of Behavior* (New York: Holt, 1960), p. 16. See also, Kenneth E. Boulding, *The Image* (Ann Arbor: University of Michigan Press, 1956).

[6] Milton Rokeach, *The Open and Closed Mind* (New York: Basic Books, 1960), p. 50.

[7] Fritz Heider, "Attributes and Cognitive Organization," *Journal of Psychology*, Vol. XXI (1946), pp. 107–12; Theodore M. Newcomb, "An Approach to the Study of Communicative Acts," *Psychological Review*, Vol. LX (1953), pp. 393–404; Charles E. Osgood and Percy H. Tannenbaum, "The Principle of Congruity in the Prediction of Attitude Change," *Psychological Review*, Vol. LXII (1955), pp. 42–55; Leon Festinger, *A Theory of Cognitive Dissonance* (Evanston, Ill.: Row, Peterson, 1957).

Attitudes, which can be defined as "predispositions to respond in a particular way toward a specified class of objects," consist of both cognitive (beliefs) and affective (feelings) components.[8] Beliefs and feelings are mutually interdependent. A person with strong positive or negative affect toward an object is also likely to maintain a cognitive structure consistent with that affect. The reverse relationship is also true. Thus new information that challenges the pre-existing balance between feelings and beliefs generates intrapersonal tension and a concomitant pressure to restore an internally consistent belief system by reducing the discrepancy in some manner, *but not necessarily through a change in attitude.*

A stable attitude about the enemy is one in which feelings and beliefs are congruent and reinforce each other. An interesting problem results when information incongruent with pre-existing attitudes is received. What happens, for example, when the other party is perceived to be acting in a conciliatory manner, a cognition that is inconsistent with the definition of the enemy as evil? According to the various balance theories, a number of strategies may be used to reduce this discrepancy between affect and cognition. The source of discrepant information may be *discredited,* thereby denying its truth or relevance. However, denial may be difficult if it involves too great a distortion of reality; denial is perhaps most likely to occur when the discrepant information is ambiguous, or when its source is not considered credible. Receipt of information not consistent with one's attitudes may lead to a *search for other information* that supports the pre-existing balance. The challenge to pre-existing attitudes about an object may lead a person to *stop thinking* about it, or at least to reduce its salience to a point where it is no longer uncomfortable to live with the incongruity. This strategy seems most likely if the attitude object has low ego-relevance for the person. It has been pointed out, for example, that the remoteness of international relations for most individuals places them under very little pressure to resolve incongruities in their attitudes.[9] The person whose beliefs are challenged by new information may engage in *wishful thinking* by changing his beliefs to accord with his desires. The new information may be *reinterpreted* in a manner that will conform with and substantiate pre-existing attitudes rather than contradict them. The process of reinterpreting new and favorable information about a disliked person is illustrated in the following dialogue:

Mr. X: The trouble with Jews is that they only take care of their own group.

Mr. Y: But the records of the Community Chest show that they give more generously than non-Jews.

[8] Milton J. Rosenberg, "Cognitive Structure and Attitudinal Affect," *Journal of Abnormal and Social Psychology,* Vol. LIII (1956), pp. 367–72; and Milton J. Rosenberg, "A Structural Theory of Attitude Change," *Public Opinion Quarterly,* Vol. XXIV (1960), pp. 319–40. The definition of attitude used here is derived from Rosenberg, Carl I. Hovland, William J. McGuire, Robert P. Abelson, and Jack W. Brehm, *Attitude Organization and Change* (New Haven: Yale University Press, 1960), p. 1.

[9] William A. Scott, "Rationality and Non-rationality of International Attitudes," *Journal of Conflict Resolution,* Vol. II (1958), pp. 8–16.

Mr. X: That shows that they are always trying to buy favor and intrude in Christian affairs. They think of nothing but money; that is why there are so many Jewish bankers.

Mr. Y: But a recent study shows that the per cent of Jews in banking is proportionally much smaller than the per cent of non-Jews.

Mr. X: That's just it. They don't go in for respectable business. They would rather run night clubs.[10]

Discrepant information may also be *differentiated* into two or more subcategories, with a strong dissociative relationship between them. Whereas strategies such as discrediting discrepant information appear to be most germane for situations of limited and ambiguous information, differentiation is likely to occur in the opposite situation. Abundant information "equips the individual to make minor (and hair-splitting) adjustments which minimize the degree of change in generalized affect toward the object. . . . Upon receipt of new information, a person is more agile in producing 'yes, but . . .' responses when he is well informed about an object than when he is poorly informed."[11]

Finally, the new and incongruent information may be accepted, leading one to *modify or change his preexisting attitudes* so as to establish a new, balanced attitude-structure.

One difficulty with balance theories as described to this point is that any and all data—attitude change or resistance to attitude change through a variety of strategies—appear to support them. If the theories are to be meaningful, they should enable the investigator to predict which of the outcomes discussed above is likely to take place under specified circumstances. At least four factors related to persuasibility have been identified: the *content* and *source* of the discrepant information, the *situation,* and the *personality* of the recipient.[12] A further discussion of these four factors in conjunction with their relevance to John Foster Dulles will permit the development of specific propositions about his attitudes toward the Soviet Union and the effects of new information on these attitudes.

Content factors

All discrepant information does not create an equal pressure to reduce dissonance. Attitudes about central values will be more resistant to change because of the introduction of discrepant information than those at the periphery of the belief system. Tolerance for incongruity is lowest and, therefore, the pressure for dissonance reduction is highest if the attitude object is highly salient for goal attainment. Attitudes that support important values, such as self-acceptance, tend to remain unchanged even in a high dissonance situation. Thus predictions concerning the effects of incongruent information about an attitude object presuppose some knowledge of the person's belief system and

[10] Gordon W. Allport, *The Nature of Prejudice,* quoted in Robert B. Zajonc, "The Concepts of Balance, Congruity, and Dissonance," *Public Opinion Quarterly,* Vol. XXIV (1960), p. 281.

[11] Theodore M. Newcomb, quoted in Richard E. Walton and Robert B. McKersie, *Attitude Change and Intergroup Relations,* Herman C. Krannert Graduate School of Industrial Administration, Purdue University, Institute Paper No. 86, Oct. 1964, p. 53.

[12] Rosenberg *et al., op. cit.,* pp. 215–21.

the relationship of the attitude object to central values in the belief system.

In his memoirs, Anthony Eden describes Dulles as "a preacher in a world of politics." [13] Of the many attributes in Dulles' belief system it is perhaps this "theological" world view that was most germane to his conception of the enemy. It is clear that the Soviet Union represented the antithesis of the values that were at the core of his belief system. An associate recalled that "the Secretary's profound and fervent opposition to the doctrine and ambitions of communism was heightened by the fact that communism was atheistic." [14] The distinction between moral and political bases for evaluating the Soviet Union was blurred, if not totally obliterated. The more Dulles' image of the Soviet Union was dominated by moral rather than political criteria, the more likely it would be that new information at odds with this model would be reinterpreted to conform with the image, leaving his basic views intact.

Situational factors

An individual may hold inconsistent attitudes without discomfort if he is not compelled to attend to the discrepancy. But he may find himself in a situation that continually forces him to examine both information at odds with his attitudes and any inconsistency arising therefrom.

That Dulles' position as Secretary of State constantly forced him to examine every aspect of Soviet foreign policy is a point requiring no further elaboration. As a result, any discrepancies in his attitudes toward the Soviet Union were continually brought to his attention, presumably creating some pressure to reduce the dissonance created by incongruent information. Persons who are required to express their attitudes in public may be under greater constraint to maintain or restore a balance between components of attitudes; this pressure may be heightened if the situation is one in which a high social value is placed on consistency.[15] Again it is clear that the office of Secretary of State required frequent public interpretations of Soviet policy. These statements were in turn scrutinized and evaluated for consistency by the press, Congress, interested publics, and allies. Thus situational factors would have made it difficult for Dulles to withdraw his attention from any discrepancies in those attitudes.

Source factors. Responses to new information are related to the perceived credibility of the communicator; the higher the credibility of the source and the more he is esteemed, the more likely is the audience to be persuaded.[16]

Dulles considered Soviet communicators to be generally unreliable, an opinion sustained both by the record of Soviet propaganda and by his judgment that "atheists can hardly be expected to conform to an ideal so high" [17] as truth. The fact that much of

[13] Anthony Eden, *Full Circle* (Boston: Houghton-Mifflin, 1960), p. 71.

[14] Berding, *op. cit.*, p. 162. See also, Hughes, *op. cit.*, 204–06.

[15] Rosenberg *et al.*, *op. cit.*, pp. 220–21.

[16] Carl I. Hovland, Irving L. Janis, and Harold H. Kelley, *Communication and Persuasion* (New Haven: Yale University Press, 1953), pp. 19–55.

[17] John Foster Dulles, *War or Peace* (New York: Macmillan, 1950), p. 20.

the information which might be at odds with Dulles' image of the U.S.S.R. originated with the Soviets themselves tended to diminish rather than enhance the probability of attitude change; unless the truth of the information was beyond question, it was likely to be discredited owing to its source.

Personality factors

Persuasibility exists as a factor independent of content.[18] That is, certain personality types can be more easily persuaded than others to change their attitudes. Individuals also appear to differ in their tolerance for dissonance and tend to use different means to re-establish stable attitudes. There is also evidence that persons with low self-esteem and general passivity are more easily persuaded to alter their attitudes. With such persons, "a previously stabilized attitude will be maintained at low levels of certainty and confidence. Such persons will also be more likely to 'submit' to others who claim for themselves some status as authority or expert." [19] On the other hand, persons with high self-esteem are inclined to decrease their search for information under stress.[20]

Data on attributes of Dulles' personality that might be relevant to the problem of attitude change are necessarily fragmentary and anecdotal

[18] Irving L. Janis *et al., Personality and Persuasibility* (New Haven: Yale University Press, 1959).

[19] Ivan D. Steiner and Evan D. Rogers, "Alternative Responses to Dissonance," *Journal of Abnormal and Social Psychology,* Vol. LXVI (1963), pp. 128–36.

[20] Margaret G. Hermann, *Stress, Self-Esteem, and Defensiveness in an Internation Simulation* (China Lake, California: Project Michelson, 1965), p. 77.

rather than systematic. The problem is perhaps compounded by the controversy that surrounded him. Both critics and admirers seem to agree, however, that Dulles placed almost absolute reliance on his own abilities to conduct American foreign policy. He felt, with considerable justification, that his family background and his own career had provided him with exceptional training for the position of Secretary of State. Intensive study of the Marxist-Leninist classics added to his belief that he was uniquely qualified to assess the meaning of Soviet policy. This sense of indispensability carried over into the day-to-day operations of policy formulation, and during his tenure as Secretary of State he showed a marked lack of receptivity to advice. One of his associates wrote:

He was a man of supreme confidence within himself. . . . He simply did not pay any attention to staff or to experts or anything else. Maybe in a very subconscious way he did catalog some of the information given him but he did not, as was characteristic of Acheson and several others of the Secretaries of State with whom I have worked, take the very best he could get out of his staff. . . .[21]

Using this summary of content, situational, source, and personality factors as a base, a number of specific predictions about Dulles" attitudes toward the Soviet Union can be derived. It seems clear that Dulles' role was one that placed a high premium on consistency between elements of his attitudes toward the Soviet Union. At the same time, despite information that might challenge his beliefs, any fundamental change in attitude would appear un-

[21] Letter to author, Aug. 25, 1961.

likely. As long as the Soviet Union remained a closed society ruled by Communists, it represented the antithesis of values at the core of Dulles' belief system. Furthermore, information that might challenge the inherent-bad-faith model of the Soviet Union generally came from the Soviets themselves—a low-credibility source—and was often ambiguous enough to accommodate more than one interpretation. Finally, the sparse evidence available is at least consistent with the theory that Dulles had a low-persuasibility personality.

Thus, on the basis of the theoretical framework developed earlier, three strategies for restoring a balance between his belief system and discrepant information appear most likely to have been used by Dulles: discrediting the source of the new information so as to be consistent with the belief system; searching for other information consistent with pre-existing attitudes; and differentiating between various elements in the Soviet Union.[22]

III

Dulles' views concerning the sources of Soviet foreign policy provide an almost classic example of differentiating the concept of the enemy into its good and bad components to maintain cognitive balance. His numerous statements indicate that he considered Soviet policy within a framework of three conflicting pairs of concepts:

[22] Only some of these techniques are illustrated in this paper. For further evidence, see Finlay, Holsti, and Fagen, *op. cit.*, Chap. 2.

ideology vs. national interest; party vs. state; and rulers vs. people.

After Dulles had been temporarily retired to private life by his defeat in the New York senatorial election in 1949, he undertook his most extensive analysis of Soviet foreign policy in his book *War or Peace*. The source of that policy, he stated repeatedly, was to be found in the Stalinist and Leninist exegeses of Marx's works. In particular, he cited Stalin's *Problems of Leninism,* which he equated with Hitler's *Mein Kampf* as a master plan of goals, strategy, and tactics, as the best contemporary guide to Soviet foreign policy. From a careful reading of that book, he concluded, one could understand both the character of Soviet leaders and the blueprint of Soviet policy. Characteristically, he placed special emphasis on the materialistic and atheistic aspects of the Communist creed, attributes that he felt ensured the absolute ruthlessness of Soviet leaders in their quest for world domination. By the time Dulles took office as Secretary of State in 1953 he had clearly adopted the theory that Soviet policy was the manifestation of ideology. His six years in office appear to have confirmed for him the validity of that view; it changed only in that it became stronger with the passing of time.

The second dichotomy in Dulles' thinking concerning the sources of Soviet foreign policy—the Russian state vs. the Communist Party—paralleled the concepts of national interest and Marxist ideology. He often pointed to the existence of a conflict of interests and, therefore, of policies between party and state. It was to the Communist Party rather than to the Russian state that he attributed Soviet aggressiveness, asserting that the state was simply the tool of the party. During his testimony at the hearings in early 1957 on the Eisenhower Doctrine for the Middle East, the following dialogue took place.

Secretary Dulles: I say countries controlled by international communism.

Senator Jackson: Yes. Well, they are synonymous [with 'Soviet'] but for the purpose—

Secretary Dulles: No, it is much broader . . . international communism is a conspiracy composed of a certain number of people, all of whose names I do not know, and many of whom I suppose are secret. They have gotten control of one government after another. They first got control of Russia after the first World War. They have gone on getting control of one country after another until finally they were stopped. But they have not gone out of existence. . . .

Senator Jackson: Would you not agree on this: that international communism has been used as an instrument of Russian foreign policy since 1918?

Secretary Dulles: I would put it the other way around. Russian foreign policy is an instrument of international communism.[23]

From the distinction between party and state Dulles deduced that Soviet hostility toward the United States existed only on the top level of the party hierarchy and that, but for the party, friendly relations between Russia and the United States could be achieved.

The third dichotomy in Dulles' theory of Soviet foreign policy was that of the Russian people vs. the Soviet

leaders. As in the case of the distinction between party and state, in which he equated the former with hostility toward the United States, he believed that the enmity of the Soviet leadership was in no way shared by the Russian people. At no time did he suggest anything but the highest degree of friendship between the Russian people and the free world. Typical of his view was the statement that: "There is no dispute at all between the United States and the peoples of Russia. If only the Government of Russia was interested in looking out for the welfare of Russia, the people of Russia, we would have a state of non-tension right away."[24] By asserting that the rulers of the Soviet Union, as Communists, enjoyed little public support, Dulles laid the groundwork for the further assumption that, were Soviet leaders responsive to Russian public opinion, Soviet-American differences would be negligible.[25]

---

[23] Senate Committees on Foreign Relations and Armed Services, *Hearings* (Jan. 15, 1957), pp. 176–77.

[24] John Foster Dulles, "Interview in Great Britain," *State Department Bulletin* (hereafter cited as *SDB*), Vol. XXXIX (Nov. 10, 1958), p. 734.

[25] This is precisely the position that the Soviet leaders have taken toward the nations of the free world. For example, after the U-2 incident Khrushchev stated: "Even now I profoundly believe that the American people, with the exception of certain imperialists and monopolist circles, want peace and desire friendship with the Soviet Union. . . . I do not doubt President Eisenhower's earnest desire for peace. But although the President is endowed with supreme executive power in the U.S.A., there are evidently circles that are circumscribing him." Nikita Khrushchev, "May 5 Report," *The Current Digest of the Soviet Press*, Vol. XII, No. 18 (June 1, 1960), pp. 17, 19. A detailed review of Soviet images of the United States may be found in Ralph K. White, "Images in the Context of International Conflict: Soviet Perceptions of the U.S. and the U.S.S.R.," *International Behavior*, ed. by Herbert C. Kelman (New York: Holt, Rinehart & Winston, 1965), pp. 236–76.

This theory, however, directly contradicted another of his propositions concerning Soviet foreign policy. Discussing Khrushchev's sensational revelations about the Stalin era in 1956, he commented that a Stalinist dictatorship was tolerated as long as it was gaining external triumphs, as was true from 1945 to 1950.[26] That interpretation, made in the course of a declaration that Soviet policy had gone bankrupt in the face of free-world

tion, consisted of the policy of the Russian state, grounded in a concern for Russia's national interest and representing the aspirations of the Russian people. Rarely, if ever, did he represent these as being hostile toward the free world. The second set of interests that Dulles felt were represented in actual Soviet policy were Marxist ideology, the international conspiratorial party, and the Soviet rulers. These factors had completely domi-

FIG. IV-1   Dulles' Conception of Conflict Between the Soviet Union and the Free World

Parties to conflict		*Level of conflict*	*Conflict resolution*
Free World	Soviet Union ruled by International Communists	Moral	No resolution possible
Free World	Russia ruled by national elites	Political	Resolved by traditional methods
Free World	Russian people	No conflict exists owing to moral consensus	

firmness, is not wholly compatible with a theory of absolute divergence of interests between people and rulers.

Dulles' views regarding the sources of Soviet foreign policy lend support to the proposition that a stable attitude-structure can be maintained by differentiating the concept of the enemy. Moreover, it was consistent with Dulles' proclivity for viewing the world in moral terms that the various characteristics of the Soviet Union were differentiated into the categories of good and evil. The former, which in his view played little part in actual Soviet policy-formula-

nated his thinking by the latter part of his term in office, and it was in them that he located the source of Soviet-American enmity.

A theory such as Dulles', which postulated a divergence of interests between party and state and between elites and masses, is pessimistic for short-term resolution of conflict. At the same time, the theory is optimistic for the long-term, for it suggests that competing national interests are virtually nonexistent. It assumes that, but for the intransigence of the Communist elite, Russia and the United States would coexist in harmony (Fig. IV-1). In this respect, his theory was in accord with what has been described as "the traditional American assumption that

[26] John Foster Dulles, "News Conference of June 27, 1956," *SDB*, Vol. XXXV (July 9, 1956), p. 48.

only a few evil leaders stood in the way of a worldwide acceptance of American values and hence of peace." [27]

IV

The proposition that information consistent with pre-existing attitudes is more readily accepted than that which is incongruent can be illustrated by a more detailed examination of Dulles' views concerning various elements of Soviet capabilities: military, technological, political, economic, popular support, and external support. Two further factors beyond Dulles' belief system must also be considered: How ambiguous was the information, and how easily could it be confirmed by data from sources other than the Soviet Union? Because Dulles considered the Soviets a low-credibility source, there should be a tendency to discount information on Soviet strength unless independent verification was available.

On the basis of Dulles' belief system it was predicted that information about those elements of Soviet strength that contribute to and sustain the inherent-bad-faith model and that can be verified would be accepted most readily. Technological and military elements of strength meet both requirements; such capabilities are compatible with the image of a hostile and threatening enemy, and are relatively easily verified by independent data. On the other hand, those attributes of the Soviet system about which information is most ambiguous, or which

[27] Eric F. Goldman, *The Crucial Decade—And After* (New York: Vintage Books, 1960), p. 250.

tend to lend "legitimacy" to the regime, would be perceived as weak. Such factors as morale, loyalty, prestige, and goodwill—all of which are implied in the categories of "internal support" and "external support"—are difficult to evaluate, in part owing to the paucity of independent sources of data. Moreover, a high assessment of Soviet strength on these factors would be at odds with that aspect of Dulles' image of the Soviet Union which predicted an absolute divergence between the Russian people and their Communist rulers. In summary, then, the hypothesis predicts an evaluation of Soviet capabilities that would be most compatible with the image of a garrison state with ample capabilities for aggression, but internally weak owing to the absence of economic strength, political stability, and support for the regime from within or without. A more precise explication of the hypothesis is presented in Fig. IV-2.

Dulles' evaluation of Soviet armed forces and military strength was consistently high. Without disregarding Soviet capabilities in atomic weapons, he repeatedly pointed to the huge land forces at the disposal of the Kremlin as the major threat to the West, a threat heightened by the mobility of these forces within the perimeter of the Sino-Soviet world. He felt that neither in size nor in mobility could the more dispersed armies of the West match those of the Soviet Union and its satellites. This assessment was in large part the underlying rationale for the Dulles doctrine of "massive retaliation," which was designed to neutralize the preponderant Communist strength for conventional and guerrilla types of warfare.

FIG. IV-2   Hypothesized Assessment of Soviet Capabilities

Element of Soviet power	Congruity with "inherent bad faith" model	Ambiguity of information	Sources of independent data	Hypothesized assessment by Dulles
Military	High	Low	Many	Strong
Technology	High	Low	Many	Strong
Economy	Intermediate	Intermediate	Intermediate	Intermediate
Political	Intermediate	Intermediate	Intermediate	Intermediate
Popular Support	Low	High	Few	Weak
External Support	Low	High	Few	Weak

If Dulles had any doubts about the military strength of the Soviet Union they were, as might be expected, with respect to its loyalty. In 1952 he stated that the "Communist leaders of Russia are almost as afraid of the Red Army as we are." [28] These doubts notwithstanding, Dulles' statements on the Soviet military are notably lacking in the ringing pronouncements of impotence that often characterized his assessment of other elements of Soviet power.

Dulles generally had a high regard for Soviet technology, particularly for that sector with implications for military strength. As with many Americans, any doubts about Soviet capabilities disappeared after the successful launching of Sputnik I in the autumn of 1957. In 1953 he had expressed some skepticism about the first Soviet claim to having exploded a hydrogen bomb, but four years later, when questioned about the veracity of the announced claim of a successfully tested intercontinental ballistic missile, he replied, "I would assume that there are facts which underlie this statement. *In general the Soviet statements in this area have had some supporting facts.*" [29]

During the middle years of his term in office, Dulles perceived Soviet strength as deteriorating markedly, a decline attributed largely to economic weakness. He insisted that the Soviet Union was staggering under an impossible economic burden that had forced its leadership to seek a respite in the cold war. It was in this area that Dulles located the major cause of the impending "collapse" of the Soviet regime; one of his associates recalled that Dulles "felt it [the Soviet system] would eventually break on the rigidities of its economic system." [30] This belief was clearly revealed in his Congressional testimony just before the Geneva summit meeting of 1955.

They [the Soviets] have been constantly hoping and expecting our economy was going to collapse in some way, due to what

[28] *Congressional Record*, 82nd Cong., 2nd Sess., p. 1801.

[29] John Foster Dulles, "News Conference, Aug. 12, 1953," *SDB*, Vol. XXIX (Aug. 24, 1953), p. 236 (italics added); and Dulles, "News Conference, Aug. 27, 1957," *SDB*, Vol. XXXVII (Sept. 16, 1957), p. 458.

[30] Letter to author, Aug. 25, 1961.

they regard as the inherent defects in the capitalistic system, or due to overexpenditure, and the like. *On the contrary, it has been their system that is on the point of collapsing.*[31]

Hence he was initially quite optimistic concerning the Soviet shift toward the use of economic tactics in foreign policy. His first reaction was that Soviet offers of aid to underdeveloped areas were a bluff to force the United States into bidding against the Soviet Union and, in the end, into spending itself into bankruptcy. He characterized that economic offensive as an admission of weakness rather than a sign of strength, stating that the Soviet Union had neither the intention nor the ability to carry out all of its foreign-aid commitments. At the December 1955 meeting of the NATO Council, Dulles predicted that the free world would defeat Soviet economic moves in the Middle East because the Soviet Union had a deficit in its balance of trade. Under these circumstances it was agreed to offer Colonel Gamal Abdul Nasser of Egypt a loan —eighty per cent to be financed by the United States—for building a dam at Aswan, in order to reap some of the propaganda advantages that had accrued to the Soviet Union through far less grandiose projects.

The Egyptian government, however, contracted for the purchase of Soviet-bloc arms, recognized the Peoples' Republic of China, and made unfriendly gestures toward both Israel and the Suez Canal. Although Dulles had been tolerant of Egyptian diplomacy only weeks earlier, stating that Nasser was "actuated primarily by a desire to maintain the genuine independence of the area," [32] Nasser's increasing reliance upon Soviet aid was not so easily forgiven.

With the tacit support of a Congress increasingly uncomfortable about the prospects of competition from higher Egyptian cotton production and the precarious survival of Israel, he decided upon Egypt as the place to call the bluff of Soviet economic aid. C. D. Jackson, a presidential foreign-policy adviser, revealed that the Aswan offer was cancelled to provoke a showdown with the Soviet Union.[33] Thus, partly on the basis of his evaluation of Soviet economic weakness, he abruptly cancelled the Aswan Dam offer, setting off a chain of events that was to culminate in the tripartite invasion of Egypt.

In many respects, Dulles' conduct during the Middle East crisis was most revealing of certain facets of his personality and belief system. It was based upon an almost unshakeable conviction that the Soviet Union was economically weak and upon a belief in the efficacy of "brinkmanship" to defeat Soviet policy. It was a period during which he relied largely upon his own instincts rather than upon the advice of others. Henry A. Byroade, American Ambassador to Egypt, was never consulted, perhaps because he had made known his opposition to the cancellation of the Aswan offer. In fact, Byroade did not know of the decision until he read of it in Cairo news-

---

[31] House Subcommittee of the Committee on Appropriations, *Hearings* (June 10, 1955), p. 10. Emphasis added.

[32] John Foster Dulles, "News Conference, Apr. 3, 1956," *SDB*, Vol. XXXIV (Apr. 16, 1956), p. 640.

[33] *Toronto Globe Mail*, Mar. 13, 1957, 1:2–5.

papers. Byroade called the Aswan Dam "a feasible project" that would be beneficial to our relations with Egypt and the Middle East, the cancellation of which was "a mistake." [34] The French Ambassador's attempts to warn Dulles of the probable consequences of his decision, two days prior to the cancellation, were greeted by Dulles with derision. The announcement of cancellation was made in such a manner as to maximize the humiliation of Colonel Nasser by casting doubts on the ability of the Egyptian economy to absorb the American aid. And finally, after the tragic episode had run full cycle, Dulles was prepared—as he had not been after his earlier "triumphs at the brink"—to give full credit to the Senate Appropriations Committee, which he claimed had forced him to cancel the Aswan offer.[35]

As much as a year after the Suez episode, Dulles was still adamantly insisting that the Soviet economy was weak because of serious imbalances. He was especially inclined to suggest that the effort to gain rocket and missile parity with the United States had placed an intolerable burden upon the economy, a contention for which, however, he relied upon such evidence as the low Russian automobile production figures. Thus, it was largely in the realm of economics that he located the "fatal weakness" in the Soviet regime.

Only during his final year in office was Dulles' estimate of Soviet economic strength revised upward. The continuing Russian economic offensive, which proved to be more than mere bluff, the increased evidence of a rising Russian standard of living, coupled with Premier Khrushchev's contention that he would "bury" the free world under the products of his economy, appear to have had a marked effect upon his attitude. By mid-1958, he referred to a Russian "economic breakthrough" and to the Soviet intention to become the world's greatest producer of consumer goods.

Why did Dulles' evaluation of the Soviet economy change so dramatically in 1958, while other aspects of his attitude remained constant? In terms of the typology presented in Fig. IV-2, the evidence beyond mere Soviet claims was so overwhelming that denial of its validity was no longer possible. Even Dulles must have recognized that his predictions of economic collapse, made only three years earlier, were no longer tenable.

Dulles' evaluation of Soviet political and diplomatic strength was an ambivalent one, in which he perceived both institutional strengths and weaknesses as well as varying capabilities among individual leaders. He felt that Soviet goals were institutionalized in the Communist Party and in the works of Marx, Lenin, and Stalin, and not, like those of the Nazis, dependent upon the idiosyncrasies of one unstable man. Following the death of Stalin, however, his estimate changed in that his attention was focused more on the intra-Kremlin cliques and the "despotic disarray" among Stalin's heirs. Dulles' reaction to such events was a curious mixture of hope and fear. On the one hand, he welcomed maneuverings for personal power

---

[34] Senate Committees on Foreign Relations and Armed Services, *Hearings* (Feb. 7, 1957), pp. 708, 714, 717, and 752.

[35] Senate Appropriations Committee, *Hearings* (Aug. 19, 1957), pp. 610–11.

within the Kremlin on two grounds: they tended to confirm his theory of weakness and instability within the Soviet Union, and he interpreted much of the infighting as a challenge by those who represented the forces of enlightenment within the Soviet Union (national interest and more consumer goods) against the forces of evil (international Communism and continued emphasis on heavy industry). On the other hand, he appeared to fear the consequences of de-Stalinization on the Western Alliance. When Beria was arrested in mid-1953, Dulles told the Cabinet: "This is the kind of time when we ought to be *doubling* our bets, not reducing them —as all the western parliaments want to do. This is the time to *crowd* the enemy—and maybe *finish* him, once and for all. But if we're dilatory, he can consolidate—and probably put us right back where we were." [36]

Dulles' most unequivocal assessment of Soviet weakness was in the area of popular and external support. Not one of his recorded statements indicates that he believed there was any support whatever by the masses of the Russian people for the Soviet regime. This was completely consistent with his prior assumption that there was no conflict of interest between the Russian people, who were basically friendly to the free world, and the United States. The corollary to this premise was that Soviet hostility and aggressiveness derived only from the designs of a small clique of leaders. Thus, the Russian people were assumed to be not only dissatisfied

with domestic conditions but also opposed to the Soviet orientation in foreign policy.

Dulles had mixed feelings about the increment added to Soviet power by other Communist nations. His most serious criticism of the Truman Administration during the 1952 campaign had been against the "sterile" policy of containment, which did not envision an offensive to liberate the captives of international Communism. The proclaimed policy was based upon the premise that moral support from the free world would enable patriots within the Communist world to bring "nationalist" regimes to power. Despite his sometimes intemperate language—he was reprimanded by General Eisenhower during the campaign for his failure to qualify his discussion of liberation with the word "peaceful" in one of his speeches [37]—it is highly unlikely that he ever intended the "rollback" to be accomplished by the force of arms.

The meaning of liberation received its first test in June 1953 when riots in East Germany threatened to destroy Soviet control of that satellite state. By October 1956, just prior to the Hungarian Revolution, Dulles spoke as one who, trapped by his own campaign slogan, had come to realize the truth in the London *Economist's* assertion that, "Unhappily, 'liberation' entails no risk of war only when it means nothing." On October 21, 1956, when questioned about events in Eastern Europe, Dulles devoted a great deal of time to emphasizing that the Soviet Union could *legally* as well as practi-

---

[36] Cabinet meeting of July 10, 1953, quoted in Hughes, *op. cit.*, p. 137. Emphasis in the source.

[37] Hughes, *op. cit.*, pp. 70–71; and Adams, *op. cit.*, p. 88.

cally move troops into the area and that there was little the United States was prepared to do in any eventuality. Six days later he made a special point of stressing peaceful American intentions in Eastern Europe. He refused, however, to consider any bargain that would involve Soviet withdrawal of troops from the area in exchange for some American concessions.[38] The events of November 1956 removed all doubts about the meaning of liberation, confirming what had become obvious in 1953 when the East German rioting was met with offers of Red Cross food packages to the Ulbricht government.

Thus Dulles' evaluation of Soviet capabilities was consistent with his thinking on other aspects of the Soviet Union. His assessment of Soviet military and technological capabilities was consistently high, and there is evidence that he interpreted new information, such as the breakthrough in Soviet rocketry, with a realism not always shared by his colleagues. As was suggested in the hypothesis, new information in the military area of Soviet power was least ambiguous and most easily verified by external sources. At the same time, such information was not inconsistent with his pre-existing attitude toward the Soviet Union.

On the other hand, certain other elements of Soviet capabilities were consistently rated as weak. Dulles'

overall evaluation of Soviet strength may have been valid in many respects. However, there is some question whether his views on the Soviet economy or popular support were totally realistic, even admitting the unevenness of Soviet economic development and the certainty of some dissatisfaction with Soviet dictatorship—be it of the harsh Stalinist type or of the more relaxed Khrushchevian model. In both cases, he appeared far more prone to accept information tending to confirm his beliefs of economic impotence and popular resistance than information to the contrary. He readily accepted, for example, almost any hint of agricultural trouble within the Soviet Union, but it was a long time before he regarded Soviet foreign aid as anything but a sign of weakness and failure. Not until long after the disaster of Suez did he reassess his earlier evaluation; only then did he conclude that the Soviet economy had achieved a "breakthrough." Whereas his attitude regarding the Soviet economy had changed by 1958, he never rejected his long-standing theory that the Soviet regime was wholly without support from the Russian people.

V

These findings concerning Dulles' views on the Soviet Union are generally consistent with research on attitude change carried out within the framework of "cognitive balance" theories under rigorous experimental conditions. But the relevance of either the theory or the findings for international politics is somewhat less evident.

---

[38] Hans J. Morgenthau, in *An Uncertain Tradition*, ed. by Norman A. Graebner (New York: McGraw-Hill, 1961), p. 293; John Foster Dulles, "Face the Nation," (Oct. 21, 1956), mimeo., pp. 1–7; Dulles, "The Task of Waging Peace," *SDB*, Vol. XXXV (Nov. 5, 1956), pp. 698–99; and G. Barraclough, "More than Dulles Must Go," *Nation*, Vol. CLXXXVI (Jan. 25. 1958), p. 69.

At the beginning of this paper it was asserted that "enemies are those whom we define as such." This is not to say, however, that images of the enemy are necessarily unrealistic or that they can be attributed solely to an individual's belief system.[39] Soviet policy itself was clearly an important source of Dulles' images, and his definition of the Soviet Union as an enemy was in many respects a realistic one. During his tenure of office, from 1953 to 1959, the Soviet Union did represent a potential threat to the United States; the cold war was not merely a product of Dulles' imagination, nor can the development of Soviet-American relations during the period be explained solely by reference to his belief system.[40]

Another question also arises: To what extent do policy decisions reflect attributes of those who made them? The assertion that personal characteristics are crucial to politics because political decisions are made by individuals is as trivial as it is true. If it were demonstrated that other factors (role, organization, culture, and the like) account for an overwhelming proportion of the variance in the formulation of foreign-policy decisions,

then findings about individual behavior would be peripheral to international politics.

Although a decision-maker carries with him into office a complex of personal values, beliefs, and attitudes, even a high-ranking official such as the Secretary of State is subject to bureaucratic constraints. These range from constitutional and legal requirements to informal, but nevertheless real, limitations rooted in the expectations of his associates. The organizational context may influence the premises and information upon which the incumbent makes his decisions in a number of ways: organizational goals tend to endure beyond the tenure of a single individual; pressures for policy continuity can affect the interpretation of new information; colleagues and subordinates can serve as important sources of values and information; and the tendency of groups to impose conformity on its members is well documented. These constraints establish boundaries that restrict to a greater or lesser degree the scope of the incumbent's decisions and the criteria used to make them.

How much latitude is there, then, within which a single official's values and attitudes may significantly affect foreign-policy decisions?[41] In part this may depend on the nature of the situation and the ambiguity of relevant information. Decisions requiring only

---

[39] Except, of course, in abnormal cases such as paranoia. These are, however, outside the scope of this paper.

[40] More generally, a socio-psychological approach would provide an all-encompassing theory of international politics only if the prior assumption was made that all conflict results from distorted images of nations. Such a premise—in effect denying the existence of contradictory and mutually exclusive interests—is clearly untenable. For further elaboration of this point, see Herbert C. Kelman, "Social-Psychological Approaches to the Study of International Relations: The Question of Relevance," in Kelman (ed.), *op. cit.*, pp. 565–607.

[41] The assumption that the individual decision-maker has no freedom of action is often one aspect of the stereotyped images that Russians and Americans have of each other. According to the orthodox Marxist view of American politics, political figures of both parties are interchangeable, for they all represent the narrow interests of the capitalist ruling class. Similarly, Americans often

the application of well-established procedures are likely to reflect institutional routines rather than personal values. On the other hand, during an unanticipated situation in which decision time is short and information is ambiguous, the attitudes of a small group or even a single official will take on added significance.

The manner in which each decision-maker interprets his sphere of competence and perceives constraints upon it is also important. If he defines his role in narrow terms—for example, if he perceives his primary responsibility to be that of administering the Department of State rather than the formulation of policy—his influence on many issues will be concomitantly decreased. On the other hand, by defining his sphere of competence in broad terms, the decision-maker can increase his authority.

Dulles' admirers and critics agree that his impact on American foreign policy was second to none. Richard Rovere's judgment that "Mr. Dulles has exercised powers over American foreign policy similar to those exercised by Franklin D. Roosevelt during the war" [42] is supported by most students of the Eisenhower Administration. His brilliant mind and forceful personality, combined with an almost total reliance upon his own abilities and the strong support of the President, served to magnify his influence.

Dulles was keenly aware of the power structure in which he operated and was a zealous guardian of his position within it. He was most careful to ensure that no competing centers of influence were established. All four of President Eisenhower's White House aids on foreign policy—C. D. Jackson, Nelson A. Rockefeller, William Jackson, and Harold Stassen—left the government after clashing with Dulles, who perceived that they might become a threat to his position; he "watched these specialists intently and, at the first sign of what he suspected to be a possible threat to the tight and straight line-of-command between himself and the President, he straightened out the difficulty." [43] Nor did he brook any competition within his own department. It was reported that Henry Cabot Lodge's direct access to the President, through his unprecedented invitation to attend Cabinet meetings, was a source of friction between Lodge and Dulles. Also indicative is Christian Herter's remark that as Undersecretary he had been "No. 2 man in a one-man show." [44]

Dulles' care in guarding the prerogatives of his office was neither unique nor by itself incompatible with the active enlistment of alternative sources of premises, values, and information into the policy process. But during his tenure traditional sources of information—ambassadors and foreign-service officers—played a markedly less significant role, partly

---

tend to assume that all Soviet leaders are interchangeable cogs in a monolithic party-state structure. Dulles himself seemed to alternate between this view of the Soviet political process and the theory that the Kremlin was split between factions representing the "friendly Russian nationalists" and "hostile Communists."

[42] Richard Rovere, "Dulles," *The New Yorker,* Vol. XXXV (Apr. 25, 1959), p. 95.

[43] Adams, *op. cit.,* p. 91. See also *The New York Times,* Feb. 25, 1953, 9:1, and Feb. 2, 1958, 1:4, 56:3.

[44] Thomas C. Kennedy, "The Making of a Secretary of State: John Foster Dulles," M.A. thesis, Stanford University, 1959, p. 21.

because he preempted some of their functions as the most widely traveled Secretary of State in history. Moreover, the Dulles-sanctioned "purge" of foreign-service personnel during the zenith of Senator McCarthy's power was a deterrent to accurate reporting by any but the imprudent or the very brave. The severe punishment—loss of careers and often public disgrace— meted out to those who had years earlier warned of difficulties in the Nationalist Government in China did little to encourage frankness in the foreign service. At any rate, there is considerable evidence that the advice of subordinates was neither actively sought, nor, when tendered, was it often of great weight in the making of policy decisions.

Although it is not implied that American foreign policy and the will of John Foster Dulles were identical, a number of factors tended to enlarge the influence of his beliefs on policy decisions. Dulles' conception of his role, buttressed by the consent and support of President Eisenhower, by frequent crises, by the ambiguity of information concerning the Soviet Union, and by his tendency to make decisions with little consultation provided him with wide latitude in the conduct of foreign policy. Consequently, his interpretation of the Soviet Union and its foreign policy assumed considerable importance.

The decision-maker also operates within the somewhat broader and less clearly defined limits delineated by public opinion. In many respects Dulles' attitudes toward the Soviet Union resembled those of the public; opinion surveys have consistently revealed a tendency to view the Soviet

Union in black-and-white terms not dissimilar to aspects of Dulles' views. This is not to say, however, that his attitudes merely reflected public opinion. Although public opinion may set broad limits on policy beyond which the decision-maker cannot move, it is also true that public attitudes are in large part shaped by decision-makers.

The role of "educator" was a challenge that Dulles recognized and accepted with characteristic vigor. His distaste for negotiation with the Kremlin derived in part from the fear that Soviet-American agreement on such matters as arms control might have an adverse effect on the public, which could lead to a relaxation of the American defense posture. Yet if his fear of uninformed public opinion was legitimate, his own contribution to its education was often niggardly. Even allowing a generous discount for political partisanship, there was more than a grain of truth in Senator Fulbright's complaint that in respect to the Soviet Union, Dulles "misleads public opinion, confuses it, feeds it pap, tells it that, if it will suppress the proof of its senses, it will see that Soviet triumphs are really defeats and Western defeats are really triumphs." [45] By painting a picture of the world in bold strokes of black and white, interlaced with periodic claims of spectacular American triumphs and calamitous Soviet defeats, he contributed to the latent tendency of the public to view the enemy of the moment in one-dimensional terms.

The extent to which Dulles' assessment of the Soviet Union was

[45] Quoted in *The New York Times*, Feb. 8, 1958, 7:2.

correct will become clearer with the passage of time; evaluations of his contemporaries ran from "unerring" to "absurd." [46] Yet some significant errors of judgment, *interpretations that appear to have derived directly from his belief system,* can be identified; these arose not from his "hardheaded" view of Soviet-American differences, but rather from inferences regarding developments in Soviet policy that did not appear to fit the model of an implacable enemy. The situation during the period from 1953 to 1959 was such that any American official would have regarded the Soviet Union as a major threat to the security of the United States; in this respect Dulles' initial premise coincided with those of even his most persistent critics. But no imperative of the situation, role, organization, or public opinion made other aspects of Dulles' beliefs about the Soviet Union inevitable. For example, his premise that Soviet and American interests were in deep conflict on most issues was surely accurate, but whether a similar conflict existed between the Soviet government and the Russian people is open to debate. Certainly, events in the Soviet Union during the years since Dulles' death have produced no evidence to support his conviction. The validity of his view that the Soviet Union possessed the military strength to threaten American security is beyond question, but his prediction that the Soviet system was on the verge of economic collapse— an estimate that contributed to the series of decisions leading to disaster at Suez—remains unfulfilled.

If, as the evidence appears to suggest, at least part of Dulles' attitudes about the Soviet Union can be traced to personal factors, how far can one generalize from these findings? It seems reasonable to suppose that his manner of perceiving and interpreting the environment is not unique among decision-makers. Like Dulles, many Soviet officials have interpreted their adversaries' actions within a rigid inherent-bad-faith model, that of "monopoly capitalism." Many other examples could be cited. If this premise is correct, the implications for international politics are somewhat sobering.

When decision-makers for both parties to a conflict adhere to rigid images of each other, there is little likelihood that even genuine attempts to resolve the issues will have the desired effect. Such a frame of reference renders meaningful communication with adversaries, much less resolution of the conflict, almost impossible. Even the British, whom Dulles tended to distrust, often found it difficult to get their views across to him by conventional methods: "As a result the British themselves occasionally felt bound to resort to non-diplomatic methods for getting their views across to the Secretary of State; one was to plant them on American secret service agents in the knowledge that they would then get back to Allen Dulles, who would pass them on to his brother, who would take them at their face value." [47]

[46] *Time,* Vol. XXVI (Feb. 4, 1957), p. 16; Senator Hubert Humphrey, quoted in V. M. Dean, "Two Worlds: Could Both Be True," *Foreign Policy Bulletin,* Vol. XXXV (Mar. 15, 1956), p. 104.

[47] Richard Goold-Adams, *The Time of Power: A Reappraisal of John Foster Dulles* (London: Weidenfeld and Nicolson, 1962), p. 309.

To the extent that each side undeviatingly interprets new information, even conciliatory gestures, in a manner calculated to preserve the original image of the adversary, they are caught up in a closed system with little prospect of changing the relations between them.

Because every decision-maker is in part a prisoner of beliefs and expectations that inevitably shape his definition of reality, to judge Dulles or any individual against a standard of omniscience or total rationality is neither fair nor instructive. Decisions based on less-than-perfect knowledge are unavoidable and will continue to be a source of potential danger as long as foreign policies are formulated by human beings. The avoidable hazards are those that arise from reducing complexities to simplicities, ruling out alternative sources of information and evaluation, and closing off to scrutiny and consideration competing views of reality. On these counts Dulles is open to legitimate criticism.

Modern technology has created an international system in which the potential costs of a foreign policy based on miscalculation have become prohibitive; one of the cruel paradoxes of international politics is that those decisions that require the most serious consideration of alternative interpretations of reality often carry with them the greatest pressures for conformity to stereotyped images. Wisdom in our world consists of maintaining an open mind under such pressures, for a realistic assessment of opportunities and risks in one's relations with adversaries appears to be at least a necessary, if not a sufficient, condition for survival.

ATTITUDES TOWARD DESEGREGATION
HERBERT H. HYMAN AND PAUL B. SHEATSLEY

Nearly eight years ago—in December, 1956—we summarized in these pages the main findings of 14 years of investigation by the National Opinion Research Center at the University of Chicago on the attitudes of white Americans toward Negro Americans. Those findings showed that a majority of white persons in the North favored racial integration of public schools, believed there should be no racial discrimination in public transportation and said they would have no objection to living near Negroes of their own income and educational status. In the South a majority of whites opposed each of these views.

Another finding, however, was that since 1942, when the studies had begun, white opinion in both the North and the South had moved steadily and in some cases strikingly toward the acceptance of integration. Underlying this long-term trend, it appeared from the surveys, were fundamental changes in old beliefs about the Negro —such as that he is innately inferior to whites—and a continued influx of better-educated and more tolerant young people into the population of white adults.

A retrospective look now makes it seem that at the time of our earlier article the pace of events in the area of race relations was slow, at least compared with the pace of events since 1956. Even then, however, school-integration conflicts in small communities such as Clinton and Oliver Springs in Tennessee, Clay and Sturgis in Kentucky and Mansfield in Texas had led to episodes of violence and drawn national attention. Since then developments have come frequently and dramatically: in 1957 the Little Rock conflict, the first Civil Rights Act to be passed by Congress since the Reconstruction and the first demands for school integration in the North; in 1960 the first "sit-in," which was conducted by Negro college students in Greensboro, N.C., and led to a wave of similar demonstrations in both Southern and Northern cities; in 1962 the riots at Oxford, Miss., and last year the march on Washington.

The pace and scope of the Negro protest movement have provoked intensified resistance to integration in some quarters and may even have alienated many whites who are basically sympathetic to the aspirations of Negroes. The surprisingly strong showing of George C. Wallace, the segregationist governor of Alabama, in several Presidential primaries this spring has been interpreted by some analysts as reflecting just such a reaction.

In the light of these developments it is reasonable to ask if the generally optimistic conclusions we drew in our 1956 article are still tenable and if the long-term trend toward the acceptance of integration has been halted or perhaps even reversed. We have a basis for providing some answers to those questions. Last year the National Opinion Research Center, aided by a grant from the Whitney Foundation, was able to make three surveys (in June, November and December) repeating some of the questions asked in the surveys on which the 1956 article was based. The new findings provide a measure of two significant things: the actual shifts in the attitudes of white adults as a result of the eventful developments in race relations since 1956, and the trends of opinion on integration over a span of more than two decades.

Before we discuss these findings we shall briefly describe how the surveys were made. Each survey was designed to include a representative sample of the nation's adult white population and for that purpose involved interviews with 1,200 to 1,500 individuals. The interviewers were white people trained for the task and living in the sample areas. Each interview resulted in a punched card containing the answers and pertinent information about the person interviewed: age, sex, education, place of residence and so on. In this way the National Opinion Research Center was able to compare the opinions of various groups, such as the elderly and the youthful, the highly educated and the poorly educated, and many others.

In discussing the findings we shall use the terms "South" and "North." "South" refers to three regions as defined by the Bureau of the Census: the South Atlantic region (Delaware, Maryland, the District of Columbia, Virginia, West Virginia, North Carolina, South Carolina, Georgia and Florida), the East South Central region (Kentucky, Tennessee, Alabama and Mississippi) and the West South Central region (Arkansas, Louisiana, Oklahoma and Texas). "North" refers to the rest of the country except for Alaska and Hawaii, where no interviews were conducted. Finally, we wish to emphasize that what we have sought to investigate over these 22 years is the trend of white opinion on racial integration. That is why the findings we shall discuss pertain only to the opinions of white adults and do not include the views of the more than 10 million Negro adults in the nation.

The dramatic changes throughout the nation are illustrated by the findings about school segregation, based on the question "Do you think white students and Negro students should go to the same schools or to separate schools?" In 1942 fewer than a third of all whites favored the integration of schools. The attitudes of Southern whites at that time were about as close to unanimity as one ever comes in surveys of the U.S. public: only 2 percent expressed support for integration. Among Northerners in that period integration also represented a minority view, endorsed by only 40 percent of white adults.

By 1956, two years after the Supreme Court decision against racial segregation in public schools, national approval of integrated schools had risen to approximately half of the total white population; in the North it had become the majority view, endorsed by three out of five white adults. Even the South was far from immune to the changing situation. Earlier only one person in 50 had favored school integration; in 1956 the proportion was one in seven. The most recent figures now show not only that the long-term trend has continued but also that in the South it has accelerated. Today a substantial majority of all white Americans endorse school integration. In the North the figure has continued its steady climb and now stands at approximately three out of every four adults. But whereas in the 14 years from 1942 to 1956 the proportion of Southern whites who accepted this principle rose only from 2 percent to 14 percent, the proportion has now risen to 30 percent in just seven years since that time.

That these are real changes rather than accidental results reflecting unreliability of the sampling method is indicated by other findings. In spite of the errors inherent in all sampling procedures, which may run as high as three or four percentage points in samples of the size used in these surveys, the figures for the total white population, in three separate surveys in 1956 and in three other separate surveys last year, did not vary by more than one percentage point. Even the findings for the separate regions, based on smaller numbers and therefore subject to an even larger sampling error, are highly stable.

The surveys repeated in 1956 and 1963 also establish that the changes in national opinion on this question represent long-term trends that are not easily modified by specific—even by highly dramatic—events. The survey last November was conducted within a week after the assassination of President Kennedy, but the national findings remained unchanged in spite of any soul-searching that may have been occurring in the North or the South. In 1956, between the June and September surveys, the attention of the nation had been focused on the first violent crises over school integration in a number of small towns in the border states and in Texas. Again the figures showed no change. The overall picture is thus one of a massive trend, unbroken by the particular news events of the day.

What accounts for the steady and strong rise in support for school integration? One important factor would seem to be the conversion of segregationists. The size of the "Don't know" vote in opinion surveys can be taken as a crude but fair measure of the intensity of the public's views. If large numbers report themselves as undecided, the opinions of the remainder are often lightly held. Conversely, if almost everybody has an opinion on the issue, it is probable that opinions are strong.

It could have been expected that in 1942—12 years before the Supreme Court decision and long before the great ferment in civil rights—a considerable number of Americans would have been undecided on the question of school integration. On most issues put to the U.S. public in surveys it is common to find that 10 percent or more of those interviewed are undecided. Yet in 1942 the "Don't know"

TABLE IV-2 Major Events in the Field of Relations During the Past Decade Are Listed Chronologically. They Indicate the Background Against Which Opinions of Whites Were Formed

Year	Event
1954	Supreme Court decision against school segregation
1955	Court ruling on school integration "with all deliberate speed" Federal order barring segregation in interstate transportation
1956	School integration conflict, Clinton, Tenn.
1957	First Civil Rights Act since Reconstruction; Little Rock conflict
1958	First use of Civil Rights Act in Negro voting case
1959	Closing of public schools in Prince Edward County, Va.
1960	Second Civil Rights Act; Start of "sit-in" movement, Greensboro, N.C.
1961	Freedom rides
1962	James Meredith at University of Mississippi
1963	March on Washington
1964	Congressional debate on third and strongest Civil Rights Act Supreme Court order on reopening Prince Edward County schools

group on the question of school integration amounted to no more than 4 percent of the total.

That group has remained at about 4 percent since 1942. Therefore the increased support for school integration cannot have come significantly from the ranks of the undecided, leaving the number of staunch segregationists virtually unchanged; nor can it be argued that a number of segregationists have become doubtful of their position and have moved into the ranks of the undecided. The greatly increased support for integration must have come mainly from segregationists who switched to the opposite camp.

There are other indications of the public's strong involvement in the issue of race relations. In last December's survey, prior to any specific questions about integration, respondents were asked: "What, in your opinion, are some of the most important problems facing the United States today?" More people mentioned civil rights and race relations than mentioned any other problem. Similarly, when respondents were asked to rate their degree of interest in a number of public issues, there were more people reporting themselves "very interested" in Negro-white relations than in Cuba or the forthcoming Presidential election.

In sum, the long-term trend toward school integration seems to be moving with considerable force. It has not been reversed even by highly dramatic events. Moreover, integration has been achieving its gains by converting persons with strongly held opposing views.

The problems of Negro-white relations involve many issues other than the integration of schools. For two of these—the integration of neighborhoods and of public transportation— detailed data are available on the trend of public opinion over the 22 years. The question asked concerning neighborhoods was: "If a Negro with the same income and education as you have moved into your block, would it make any difference to you?" The question was asked in this way to eliminate the factor of social class from the discussion and leave the respondent confronted only with the issue of his potential neighbor's color. Since the answer "It would make a difference" could include people who would positively welcome a Negro neighbor, supplementary questions clarified any ambiguity in the matter. The question asked about transportation was: "Generally speaking, do you think there should be separate sections for Negroes on streetcars and buses?"

On these questions the same fundamental trends and underlying processes appear as in opinions on school integration. Opinion has remained highly crystallized, with fewer than 4 percent unable to decide. And although these questions were asked in only one of the 1956 surveys, so that it was not possible to judge the impact of short-run events at that time, the fact that there was little change between June and December of last year again

suggests that attitudes are not greatly modified by such events.

The main findings, which are presented in more detail in Figure IV-3, are that support of residential integration rose from 35 percent in 1942 to 64 percent at the end of last year among all whites; that for Northern whites the increase was from 42 percent to 70 percent and for Southern whites from 12 percent to 51 percent, and that during the same period of more than two decades approval of integrated public transportation rose from 44 to 78 percent among all whites, 57 to 88 percent among Northern whites and 4 to 51 percent among Southern whites.

The uniformities in the long-term trends in both the South and the North should not be allowed to obscure certain regional differences in the pattern of opinion on schools, neighborhoods and transportation. For example, the North has been consistently less amenable to residential integration than to integration of public transportation, and the shift in the North over the 22 years has been smallest on the residential issue. Presumably these attitudes reflect the fact that in most of the North whites maintain a social distance from Negroes, although allowing them the legal right to use the same public facilities. This social pattern has contributed to the existence of *de facto* school segregation in the North, even though the great majority of white Northerners are now opposed to school segregation in principle. The pattern is illustrated by the comment of a retired mason in a town in eastern Pennsylvania. After expressing approval of integrated schools and transportation, he said he would object if a Negro of equal edu-

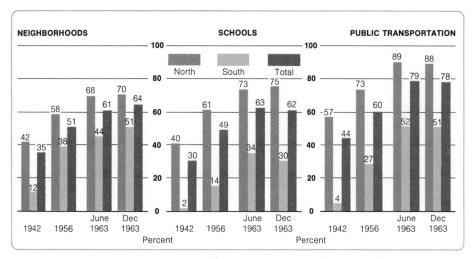

Figure IV-3.   White opinions on desegregation of public schools, public transportation and residential areas are charted for a period of more than two decades. In each case the bars represent the percentage of white adults favoring integration. The spaces above the bars, however, do not wholly represent persons opposed to integration, for on each issue about 4 percent of the respondents were undecided. Two other surveys in 1956 and one in 1963 produced results consistent with those shown, indicating the reliability of the sampling. The 1963 survey also showed that dramatic events, such as the assassination of President Kennedy, had little effect on the trend of opinion about integration.

cation and income moved into his block. He added: "I believe in equality, but not that much."

Having discussed the broad findings of the surveys of the National Opinion Research Center since 1942, we turn to some interpretive remarks and to certain aspects of the findings, particularly as they pertain to views about the integration of schools. We shall first discuss the validity of the responses on which the findings are based. Then we shall examine in some detail opinions about the intelligence of Negroes; the correlation between the support of school integration and the degree of school integration existing in the community; the views of Northerners who have lived in the South and of Southerners who have lived in the North; the correlation between degree of education and support

for integration, and the attitudes of different age groups.

It is sometimes argued that in public opinion surveys the respondents do not always reveal their true opinions but instead tend to give the answers they think are expected of them. According to this argument some of the opinion supporting integration is of this character because integration is now fashionable. In our view it is unlikely that such factors inhibited many of the respondents in the surveys we are discussing. The surveys show a substantial number of individuals, even in the North, who express opposition to integration, and the magnitude of the opposition is highest in just those spheres where independent evidence would lead one to expect it: the schools in the South and housing in the North.

On many other questions asked in the most recent surveys white respondents freely expressed opposition to full integration or voiced criticism of Negroes. An example is provided by a question asked last December: 'Do you think there should be laws against marriages between Negroes and whites?" To this 80 percent of Southern whites and 53 percent of Northern whites answered affirmatively.

Furthermore, many of the respondents seem to take full account of the moral issues involved and still end up on the segregationist side. For example, a mother in North Carolina gave this response to the question about school integration: "I have mixed emotions. I think they deserve the right, but when I think of my own children going with them, I don't know. . . . Well, I guess I'd say separate schools."

That the demonstrated decline in support of segregation reflects changes in fundamental beliefs is suggested by the long-term trend in white opinion about the inherent intelligence and educability of Negroes. (See Figure IV-4.) On several occasions since 1942 the National Opinion Research Center has asked the question: "In general, do you think that Negroes are as intelligent as white people—that is, can they learn things just as well if they are given the same education and training?" In the responses to that question there has been a striking change. In 1942 only 50 percent of Northern whites answered "Yes." Today the figure has risen to 80 percent. In the South today a substantial majority credits Negroes with equal intelligence, in contrast with only 21 percent in 1942.

This revolutionary change in belief goes far to explain the increased acceptance of school integration over the past two decades. It has undermined one of the most stubborn arguments formerly offered by whites for segregated schools. Figure IV-5 shows the relation between belief in the educability of Negroes and the support of

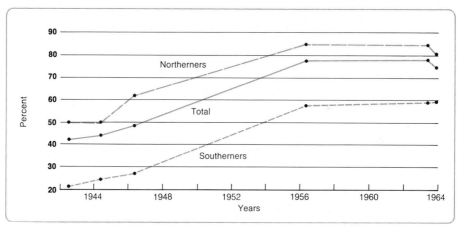

Figure IV-4.   Intelligence of Negroes in the opinion of whites is the subject of this chart. A series of polls in which whites were asked if they believed Negroes to be as intelligent and educable as whites produced the percentage of affirmative responses shown here.

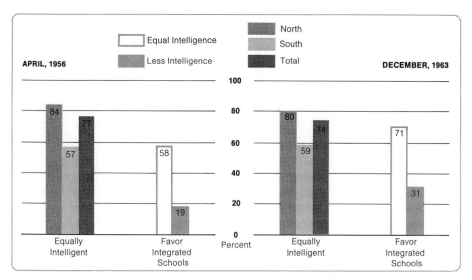

Figure IV-5. Correlation between belief in the comparability of Negro and white intelligence and support for integrated schools is indicated. The three bars at left in each set show details from chart on opposite page; colored bars, how support for integration of schools varies according to opinion of Negro intelligence.

integrated schools in the 1956 and 1963 surveys. As one might expect, those who regard the Negro's intelligence as equal to the white's are much more likely to favor integrated schools than those who regard the Negro as inferior in intelligence. There is more than this, however, to be said. Belief in the equal intelligence of Negroes, after rising steadily for 14 years, leveled off in 1956 and has remained stable since then. Support of integrated schools, however, has continued to rise. Plainly there are forces at work in the growing support for the integration of schools other than belief in the educability of Negroes.

Attitudes on school integration vary according to the degree of integration existing in a given area. This becomes apparent when one looks at particular Southern areas instead of regarding "the South" as a homogeneous region, as we have in this discussion up to now. The occurrence of racial crises in some Southern communities but not in others and the varying degrees of official compliance with Federal law suggest that there are large differences within the region. Our surveys bear this out. We divided our sample of Southern localities into three groups according to the amount of integration in the public schools: those with considerable integration, those with token integration and those that remain completely segregated. Since few Southern communities fall into the first classification, respondents living in those areas constitute a tiny fraction of the total, and the sampling error of this particular statistic could be substantial. To give greater strength to the findings we have pooled the results of the surveys in June and December, 1963, and as another check we have compared responses made when the Gallup Poll, at our request, asked Southern whites the question on school integration in June, 1963.

In Southern districts where considerable integration of schools has taken place 54 percent of white adults favor integration; in districts where token integration has occurred, 38 percent express favorable attitudes, and in segregated districts 28 percent favor integration. There is obviously some parallel between public opinion and official action, but which came first? In the desegregated areas did integration come about in response to a more favorable public opinion or did the more favorable public opinion develop only after the official act of desegregation?

Close analysis of the current findings, compared with those of the 1956 surveys, leads us to the conclusion that in those parts of the South where some measure of school integration has taken place official action has *preceded* public sentiment, and public sentiment has then attempted to accommodate itself to the new situation.

In the 1956 surveys of those Southern districts that had already achieved some integration of schools only 31 percent of white adults expressed approval of the idea. By 1963 the number of such communities had been increased by those districts that only belatedly and reluctantly accepted a measure of integration; in our current sample more than half of the Southern respondents living in communities now classified as integrated to any degree experienced such integration only within the past year, and none of those in areas of considerable integration were exposed to such a level of integration before 1962. One

might expect as a result that the proportion approving integration would be even lower than it was seven years ago. Instead approval of integration has risen in such areas from less than a third in 1956 to more than half of their white population today.

Similarly, it was found in 1956 that only 4 percent of white adults in Southern segregated districts favored the integration of schools. Since then some of these communities have reluctantly adopted a measure of integration, so that the segregated districts that remain might be described as the hard core of segregation. Within this hard core, however, approval of school integration has now risen to 28 percent of the white public. Thus even in the extreme segregationist areas of the South the tides of opinion are moving toward integration, and in the more progressive areas it seems that official action in itself is contributing to the speed and magnitude of popular change.

In this connection it is relevant to cite the results of the following question, asked repeatedly over the years by the Gallup Poll and included in the National Opinion Research Center survey of June, 1963: "Do you think the day will ever come in the South when whites and Negroes will be going to the same schools, eating in the same restaurants and generally sharing the same public accommodations?" In South and North alike, whether the community has segregated or integrated schools, more than three-quarters of the white adults believe that integration is bound to come. In contrast, only 53 percent of the respondents felt that way in 1957. Apparently the pattern is that as official action works to bury what is already regarded as a lost cause, public acceptance of integration increases because opinions are readjusted to the inevitable reality.

Data from the 1963 surveys also enable us to compare opinions in Northern communities that vary in the extent to which Negro and white children

percent favor integration; in Northern areas where schools are considerably integrated 83 percent favor the policy.

A similar pattern of support for integration growing with exposure to integrated situations appears in the findings about people who have moved between North and South. Figure IV-6 compares the opinions of four

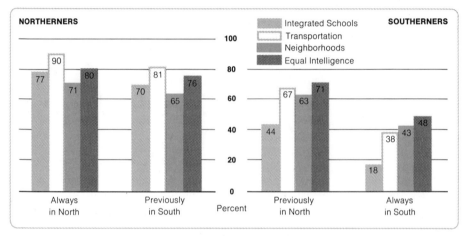

Figure IV-6. *Exposure to integration appears to increase white support for integration. Northern whites who previously lived in the South show nearly as much support for integration and as much belief in the comparability of Negro and white intelligence as whites who have always lived in the North. Southern whites with previous Northern residence show a markedly higher support for integration and belief in the equality of white and Negro intelligence than Southerners who have never lived outside the South.*

attend the same schools. As we have noted, such segregation in the North stems largely from patterns of residential housing rather than from law, but the comparisons with the South are nonetheless of interest. Again we find greater support for integration where integration actually exists and greater support for segregation where there is no integration. In both types of community, however, the overall level of support is much greater in the North than in the South. Among Northern whites living in districts that have segregated schools 65

groups: Northerners who have never lived in the South, Northerners who once lived in the South, Southerners who have never lived in the North and Southerners who did at one time live in the North. From the comparison it is apparent that Northerners who once lived in the South differ very little in their views from Northerners who have never been exposed to Southern life. They are only slightly less favorable to integration. In striking contrast, those Southerners who have previously lived in the North differ greatly from those who have always lived in the South. Except on the issue of school integration, the attitudes of Southerners with a history of earlier residence in the North are much closer to those of Northerners than to those of their fellow Southerners. Even on school integration the difference is substantial.

The influence of geographical

1963 surveys showed that the better-educated groups, North and South, were more favorable to integration of schools and public transportation than people of less education were. Between the two surveys, however, all subgroups have become more favorable to integration. (See Figure IV-7.) Since the number of cases in the South

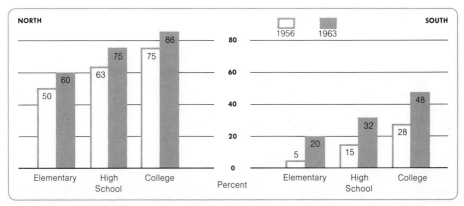

Figure IV-7.   Degree of education and attitudes toward integration of schools are compared. Each bar shows the percentage of whites in that category supporting integration of public schools. Although support for integration rises with degree of education and has gone up in all categories, even college-educated Southerners have yet to attain the level of support for integration of public schools shown in 1956 by Northerners of grammar school education.

mobility on Southern opinion may well account for a considerable part of the gross change in Southern attitudes over the recent decades. Although the rate of movement from South to North exceeds the rate from North to South, the Southern migrants represent a relatively small proportion of the Northern population, whereas among Southerners today a considerably larger proportion have had some Northern exposure. Thus the net effect of migration is to strengthen support for integration.

As for the relation between amount of education and support of integration, both the 1956 and the

is small, and since the subgroup estimates are subject to a larger sampling error, we have pooled the two recent surveys.

The most dramatic change of opinion has occurred in the best-educated segment of the Southern white population, where the proportion in favor of integration has increased from only about a fourth to almost half. Lest formal education appear to be a decisive factor, however, note that in 1963 the best-educated white Southerners were not as favorably inclined to integration as the least-educated white Northerners, and that by 1963 those Southerners had not yet reached the level of opinion already exhibited in 1956 by poorly educated Northerners.

In 1956 it was found that the segment of the white population represented by people 65 and older, in both the North and the South, was least favorable to integration, and the same finding is documented in the recent surveys. One would expect this result on the basis of education alone; inasmuch as the expansion of educational opportunity is a development of recent decades, the oldest adults are less likely than the younger ones to have had advanced schooling. Indeed, some of the long-term trends in attitudes toward segregation may simply represent the passing of the oldest generation and its replacement in the population by younger individuals of greater tolerance. The persistence of the difference in attitudes between the oldest group and younger groups would help to ac-

count for the further changes in public opinion in more recent years and would augur still more change in the future.

Since the analysis of differences between age groups is so relevant to an understanding of long-term opinion trends, the sample in last December's survey was designed to double the number of interviews with the youngest adults—those from 21 to 24. These extra interviews were not included in the tabulations except for this particular analysis, but by using them here we can place greater confidence in our findings for this age group, which otherwise would account for only a small portion of the national sample. In this way we are able to provide more evidence for a new finding that appeared in the survey of June, 1963, but then could be regarded only as suggestive. The finding, which is reflected in Figure IV-8, is that whereas

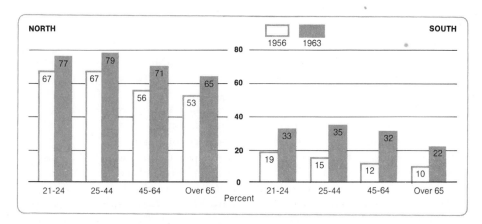

Figure IV-8. *Age groups vary in support for integration of public schools. The tendency is for older persons to show more opposition to integration. A different trend may be appearing, however, among Southerners of the youngest group. In 1956 that group showed more support for integrated schools than the next older group; it now shows less. Such a tendency might be attributable to the direct involvement of the youngest Southerners in the clashes of recent years over school and college integration.*

in 1956 the youngest adults were the most favorable to school integration, by 1963 the pattern—at least for the South—seemed to have changed. Although they were never as prosegregationist as the older age groups, the 21-to-24-year-olds appeared in the recent surveys to be less favorable to the integration of schools than the adults aged 25 to 44. The difference is admittedly small and could conceivably be due to sample variation. But the finding appeared in all of last year's surveys; unless it is disproved by subsequent studies one must accept as valid the evidence that the youngest adults are relatively less tolerant than formerly, in spite of the fact that on the average they are more highly educated.

The members of the youngest group in 1956 have, of course, now aged sufficiently to be included in the present 25-to-44 group and have added their earlier quantum of tolerance to that older group's attitudes. Those who are now in the 21-to-24 group were still children in 1956 and so were not included in the surveys of that time. But why, having arrived at the status of young adults, do they not exhibit the larger measure of tolerance characteristic of the equivalent age group in earlier years?

That the phenomenon is clearly evident only in the South suggests an explanation, because this newest group of young Southern adults has lived through experiences quite different from those of the generation of young adults studied in 1956. They have spent their high school and college years in the stormy decade since the Supreme Court decision, and it is they who have been most closely associated with the crises and dislocations that have accompanied the transition to integration in various communities. Actually few of them appear to have suffered directly from these events. They were asked "In what ways have you or any members of your family been affected by integration?" More than four-fifths reported no effects. It is noteworthy, however, that not a single Southerner of this age group spontaneously reported any kind of favorable effect, whereas among Northerners of the same age 5 percent volunteered an answer describing the personal effects of integration in favorable terms.

Plainly the conflicts of integration have had a great immediacy for the young Southerners. The issue of civil rights is more salient for them than for the older groups in our Southern sample. More of them spontaneously mention race relations as the biggest problem facing the country today. The youngest Southerners are more likely than the next older group to express themselves as believing the Negro protest movement is "violent" rather than "peaceful" and to voice the opinion that demonstrations and protests have "hurt the cause" of Negroes.

Other questions substantiate the likelihood that a change of attitude has occurred among young Southern adults. When asked if their views have remained the same in recent years or have become more favorable or less favorable to integration, it is this youngest group that is more likely than others to report both a change in attitude and a shift away from a favorable opinion. For example, the youngest adults in the South say they have shifted almost two to one against integration in recent years. The older groups report less change of attitude, and when it occurs, the shifts are about equal in both directions.

Apart from this tendency, about the extent or permanence of which we cannot yet be sure, it appears that the attitudes of white Americans of both the North and the South are continuing to shift toward greater acceptance of integration. We cannot be certain that future events will not reverse the course. But the unbroken trend of the past 20 years, and particularly its acceleration in the past decade of intensified controversy, suggest that integration will not be easily halted. In the minds and hearts of the majority of Americans the principle of integration seems already to have been won. The issues that remain are how soon and in what ways the principle is to be implemented.

THE NATURE OF BELIEF SYSTEMS IN MASS PUBLICS
PHILIP E. CONVERSE

Belief systems have never surrendered easily to empirical study or quantification. Indeed, they have often served as primary exhibits for the doctrine that what is important to study cannot be measured and that what can be measured is not important to study. In an earlier period, the behaviorist decree that subjective states lie beyond the realm of proper measurement gave Mannheim a justification for turning his back on measurement, for he had an unqualified interest in discussing belief systems.[1] Even as Mannheim was writing, however, behaviorism was undergoing stiff challenges, and early studies of attitudes were attaining a degree of measurement reliability that had been deemed impossible. This fragment of history, along with many others, serves to remind us that no intellectual position is likely to become obsolete quite so rapidly as one that takes current empirical capability as the limit of the possible in a more ab-

CREDIT: Reprinted with permission of The Macmillan Company from Philip E. Converse, "The Nature of Belief Systems in Mass Publics," in David E. Apter (Ed.), *Ideology and Discontent*, pp. 206–219, 227–229, 234–241, 245–256. Copyright © 1964 by The Free Press of Glencoe, a Division of The Macmillan Company. [*Figures, tables, and some footnotes renumbered.*]

[1] Karl Mannheim, *Ideology and Utopia* (New York, 1946), especially pp. 39 ff.

solute sense. Nevertheless, while rapid strides in the measurement of "subjective states" have been achieved in recent decades, few would claim that the millennium has arrived or that Mannheim could now find all of the tools that were lacking to him forty years ago.

This article makes no pretense of surpassing such limitations. At the same time, our substantive concern forces upon us an unusual concern with measurement strategies, not simply because we propose to deal with belief systems or ideologies, but also because of the specific questions that we shall raise about them. Our focus in this article is upon differences in the nature of belief systems held on the one hand by elite political actors and, on the other, by the masses that appear to be "numbered" within the spheres of influence of these belief systems. It is our thesis that there are important and predictable differences in ideational worlds as we progress downward through such "belief strata" and that these differences, while obvious at one level, are easily overlooked and not infrequently miscalculated. The fact that these ideational worlds differ in character poses problems of adequate representation and measurement.

The vertical ordering of actors

and beliefs that we wish to plumb bears some loose resemblance to the vertical line that might be pursued downward through an organization or political movement from the narrow cone of top leadership, through increasing numbers of subordinate officials, and on through untitled activists to the large base formally represented in membership rolls. It is this large base that Michels noted, from observations of political gatherings, was rarely "there", and analogues to its physical absence do not arise accidentally in dealing with belief systems. On the other hand, there is no perfect or necessary "fit" between the two orderings, and this fact in itself has some interest.

That we intend to consider the total mass of people "numbered" within the spheres of influence of belief systems suggests both a democratic bias and a possible confusion between numbers and power or between numbers and the outcomes of events that power determines. We are aware that attention to numbers, more or less customary in democratic thought, is very nearly irrelevant in many political settings. Generally, the logic of numbers collides head on with the logic of power, as the traditional power pyramid, expressing an inverse relation between power and numbers, communicates so well. "Power" and "numbers" intersect at only one notable point, and that point is represented by the familiar axiom that numbers are one resource of power. The weight of this resource varies in a systematic and obvious way according to the political context. In a frankly designed and stable oligarchy, it is assumed to have no weight at all. In such a setting, the

numbers of people associated with particular belief systems, if known at all, becomes important only in periods of crisis or challenge to the existing power structure. Democratic theory greatly increases the weight accorded to numbers in the daily power calculus. This increase still does not mean that numbers are of overriding importance; in the normal course of events it is the *perception* of numbers by democratic elites, so far as they differ from "actual" numbers, that is the more important factor. However this may be, claims to numbers are of some modest continuing importance in democratic systems for the legitimacy they confer upon demands; and, much more sporadically, claims to numbers become important in nondemocratic systems as threats of potential coercion.

SOME CLARIFICATION OF TERMS

A term like "ideology" has been thoroughly muddied by diverse uses.[2] We shall depend instead upon the term "belief system," although there is an obvious overlap between the two. We define a *belief system* as a configuration of ideas and attitudes in which the elements are bound together by some form of constraint or functional interdependence.[3] In the static case, "constraint" may be taken to mean the

[2] Minar has compiled a useful if discouraging survey of this diversity. See David W. Minar, "Ideology and Political Behavior," *Midwest Journal of Political Science*, 5 (November, 1961), pp. 317–331.

[3] Garner uses the term "constraint" to mean "the amount of interrelatedness of structure of a

success we would have in predicting, given initial knowledge that an individual holds a specified attitude, that he holds certain further ideas and attitudes. We depend implicitly upon such notions of constraint in judging, for example, that, if a person is opposed to the expansion of social security, he is probably a conservative and is probably opposed as well to any nationalization of private industries, federal aid to education, sharply progressive income taxation, and so forth. Most discussions of ideologies make relatively elaborate assumptions about such constraints. Constraint must be treated, of course, as a matter of degree, and this degree can be measured quite readily, at least as an average among individuals.[4]

In the dynamic case, "constraint" or "interdependence" refers to the probability that a change in the perceived status (truth, desirability, and so forth) of one idea-element would *psychologically* require, from the point of view of the actor, some compensating change(s) in the status of idea-elements elsewhere in the configuration. The most obvious form of such constraint (although in some ways the most trivial) is exemplified by a structure of propositions in logic, in which a change in the truth-value of one proposition necessitates changes in truth-value elsewhere within the set of related propositions. Psychologically, of course, there may be equally strong constraint among idea-elements that would not be apparent to logical analysis at all, as we shall see.

We might characterize either the idea-elements themselves or entire belief systems in terms of many other dimensions. Only two will interest us here. First, the idea-elements within a belief system vary in a property we shall call *centrality,* according to the role that they play in the belief system as a whole. That is, when new information changes the status of one idea-element in a belief system, by postulate some other change must occur as well. There are usually, however, several possible changes in status elsewhere in the system, any one of which would compensate for the initial change. Let us imagine, for example, that a person strongly favors a particular policy; is very favorably inclined toward a given political party; and recognizes with gratification that the party's stand and his own are congruent. (If he were unaware of the party's stand on the issue, these elements could not in any direct sense be constrained within the same belief system.) Let us further imagine that the party then changes its position to the opposing side of the issue. Once the information about the change reaching the actor has become so unequivocal that he can no longer deny that the change has occurred, he has several further choices. Two of the more important ones involve either a change in attitude toward the party or a change in position on the issue. In such an instance, the element more likely to change is defined as less central to the belief system than the ele-

system of variables" when measured by degree of uncertainty reduction. Wendell R. Garner, *Uncertainty and Structure as Psychological Concepts* (New York, 1962), pp. 142ff. We use the term a bit more broadly as relief from such polysyllables as "interrelatedness" and "interdependence."

[4] Measures of correlation and indices of the goodness of fit of a cumulative scale model to a body of data are measures of two types of constraint.

ment that, so to speak, has its stability ensured by the change in the first element.[5]

In informal discussions of belief systems, frequent assumptions are made about the relative centrality of various idea-elements. For example, idea-elements that are logically "ends" are supposed to be more central to the system than are "means." It is important to remain aware, however, that idea-elements can change their relative centrality in an individual's belief-system over time. Perhaps the most hackneyed illustration of this point is that of the miser, to whom money has become an end rather than a means.

Whole belief systems may also be compared in a rough way with respect to the *range* of objects that are referents for the ideas and attitudes in the system. Some belief systems, while they may be internally quite complex and may involve large numbers of cognitive elements, are rather narrow in range: Belief systems concerning "proper" baptism rituals or the effects of changes in weather on health may serve as cases in point. Such other belief systems as, for example, one that links control of the means of production with the social functions of religion and a doctrine of aesthetics all in one more or less neat package have extreme ranges.

[5] Definitions of belief systems frequently require that configurations of ideas be stable for individuals over long periods of time. The notion of centrality fulfills this requirement in a more flexible way. That is, once it is granted that changes in the perceived status of idea-elements are not frequent in any event and that, when change does occur, the central elements (particularly in large belief systems) are amply cushioned by more peripheral elements that can be adjusted, it follows that central elements are indeed likely to be highly stable.

By and large, our attention will be focussed upon belief systems that have relatively wide ranges, and that allow some centrality to political objects, for they can be presumed to have some relevance to political behavior. This focus brings us close to what are broadly called *ideologies,* and we shall use the term for aesthetic relief where it seems most appropriate. The term originated in a narrower context, however, and is still often reserved for subsets of belief systems or parts of such systems that the user suspects are insincere; that he wishes to claim have certain functions for social groupings; or that have some special social source or some notable breadth of social diffusion.[6] Since we are concerned here about only one of these limitations—the question of social diffusion—and since we wish to deal with it by hypothesis rather than by definition, a narrow construction of the term is never intended.

SOURCES OF CONSTRAINT ON IDEA-ELEMENTS

It seems clear that, however logically coherent a belief system may seem to the holder, the sources of constraint are much less logical in the classical sense than they are psychological—and less psychological than social. This point is of sufficient importance to dwell upon.

Logical sources of constraint

Within very narrow portions of belief systems, certain constraints may be

[6] Minar, *loc. cit.*

purely logical. For example, government revenues, government expenditures, and budget balance are three idea-elements that suggest some purely logical constraints. One cannot believe that government expenditures should be increased, that government revenues should be decreased, and that a more favorable balance of the budget should be achieved all at the same time. Of course, the presence of such objectively logical constraints does not ensure that subjective constraints will be felt by the actor. They will be felt only if these idea-elements are brought together in the same belief system, and there is no guarantee that they need be. Indeed, it is true that, among adult American citizens, those who favor the expansion of government welfare services tend to be those who are more insistent upon reducing taxes "even if it means putting off some important things that need to be done." [7]

Where such purely logical constraint is concerned, McGuire has reported a fascinating experiment in which propositions from a few syllogisms of the Barbara type were scattered thinly across a long questionnaire applied to a student population. The fact that logical contingencies bound certain questions together was never brought to the attention of the students by the investigator. Yet one week later the questionnaire was applied again, and changes of response to the syllogistic propositions reduced significantly the measurable level of logical inconsistency. The conclusion was that merely "activating" these ob-

jectively related ideas in some rough temporal contiguity was sufficient to sensitize the holders to inconsistency and therefore to occasion readjustment of their beliefs.[8]

On a broader canvas, such findings suggest that simple "thinking about" a domain of idea-elements serves both to weld a broader range of such elements into a functioning belief system and to eliminate strictly logical inconsistencies defined from an objective point of view. Since there can be no doubt that educated elites in general, and political elites in particular, "think about" elements involved in political belief systems with a frequency far greater than that characteristic of mass publics, we could conservatively expect that strict logical inconsistencies (objectively definable) would be far more prevalent in a broad public.

Furthermore, if a legislator is noted for his insistence upon budget-balancing and tax-cutting, we can predict with a fair degree of success that he will also tend to oppose expansion of government welfare activities. If, however, a voter becomes numbered within his sphere of influence by virtue of having cast a vote for him directly out of enthusiasm for his tax-cutting policies, we cannot predict that the voter is opposed as well to expansion of government welfare services. Indeed, if an empirical prediction is possible, it may run in an opposing direc-

[7] See A. Campbell, P. E. Converse, W. Miller, and D. Stokes, *The American Voter* (New York, 1960), pp. 204–9.

[8] William J. McGuire, "A Syllogistic Analysis of Cognitive Relationships," in Milton J. Rosenberg, Carl I. Hovland, William J. McGuire, Robert P. Abelson, and Jack W. Brehm *Attitude Organization and Change*, Yale Studies in Attitude and Communication, Vol. 3 (New Haven, 1960), pp. 65–111.

tion, although the level of constraint is so feeble that any comment is trivial. Yet we know that many historical observations rest directly upon the assumption that constraint among idea-elements visible at an elite level is mirrored by the same lines of constraint in the belief systems of their less visible "supporters." It is our argument that this assumption not only can be, but is very likely to be, fallacious.

Psychological sources of constraint

Whatever may be learned through the use of strict logic as a type of constraint, it seems obvious that few belief systems of any range at all depend for their constraint upon logic in this classical sense. Perhaps, with a great deal of labor, parts of a relatively tight belief system like that fashioned by Karl Marx could be made to resemble a structure of logical propositions. It goes without saying, however, that many sophisticated people have been swept away by the "iron logic" of Marxism without any such recasting. There is a broad gulf between strict logic and the quasi-logic of cogent argument. And where the elements in the belief system of a population represent looser cultural accumulations, the question of logical consistency is even less appropriate. If one visits a Shaker community, for example, one finds a group of people with a clear-cut and distinctive belief system that requires among other things plain dress, centrality of religious concerns, celibacy for all members, communal assumptions about work and property, antagonism to political participation in the broader state, and a general aura of retirement from the secular world. The visitor whose sense of constraint has been drawn from belief configurations of such other retiring sects as the Amish is entirely surprised to discover that the Shakers have no abhorrence of technological progress but indeed greatly prize it. In their heyday, a remarkable amount of group energy appears to have been reserved for "research and development" of labor-saving devices, and among the inventions they produced was a prototype of the washing machine. Similar surprise has been registered at idea-elements brought together by such movements as Perónism and Italian Fascism by observers schooled to expect other combinations. Indeed, were one to survey a limited set of ideas on which many belief systems have registered opposite postures, it would be interesting to see how many permutations of positions have been held at one time or another by someone somewhere.

Such diversity is testimony to an absence of any strict logical constraints among such idea-elements, if any be needed. What is important is that the elites familiar with the total shapes of these belief systems have *experienced* them as logically constrained clusters of ideas, within which one part necessarily follows from another. Often such constraint is quasi-logically argued on the basis of an appeal to some superordinate value or posture toward man and society, involving premises about the nature of social justice, social change, "natural law," and the like. Thus a few crowning postures—like premises about survival of the fittest in the spirit of social Darwinism—serve as a sort of glue to bind together many more specific attitudes and beliefs, and these postures are of prime centrality in the belief system as a whole.

Social sources of constraint

The social sources of constraint are twofold and are familiar from an extensive literature in the past century. In the first place, were we to survey the combinations of idea-elements that have occurred historically (in the fashion suggested above), we should undoubtedly find that certain postures tend to co-occur and that this co-occurrence has obvious roots in the configuration of interests and information that characterize particular niches in the social structure. For example, if we were informed that dissension was rising within the Roman Catholic Church over innovations designed to bring the priest more intimately into the *milieu* of the modern worker, we could predict with a high degree of success that such a movement would have the bulk of its support among the *bas-clergé* and would encounter indifference or hostility at the higher status levels of the hierarchy.

Of course, such predictions are in no sense free from error, and surprises are numerous. The middle-class temperance movement in America, for example, which now seems "logically" allied with the small-town Republican right, had important alliances some eighty years ago with the urban social left, on grounds equally well argued from temperance doctrines.[9] Nonetheless, there are some highly reliable correlations of this sort, and these correla-

tions can be linked with social structure in the most direct way. Developmentally, they have status similar to the classic example of the spurious correlation—two terms that are correlated because of a common link to some third and prior variable. In the case of the belief system, arguments are developed to lend some more positive rationale to the fact of constraint: The idea-elements go together not simply because both are in the interest of the person holding a particular status but for more abstract and quasi-logical reasons developed from a coherent world view as well. It is this type of constraint that is closest to the classic meaning of the term "ideology."

The second source of social constraint lies in two simple facts about the creation and diffusion of belief systems. First, the shaping of belief systems of any range into apparently logical wholes that are credible to large numbers of people is an act of creative synthesis characteristic of only a minuscule proportion of any population. Second, to the extent that multiple idea-elements of a belief system are socially diffused from such creative sources, they tend to be diffused in "packages," which consumers come to see as "natural" wholes, for they are presented in such terms ("If you believe this, then you will also believe that, for it follows in such-and-such ways"). Not that the more avid consumer never supplies personal innovations on the fringes—he is very likely to suppress an idea-element here, to elaborate one there, or even to demur at an occasional point. But any set of relatively intelligent consumers who are initially sympathetic to the crowning posture turns out to show more

[9] Joseph R. Gusfield, "Status Conflicts and the Changing Ideologies of the American Temperance Movement," in Pittman and Snyder, (Eds.), *Society, Culture and Drinking Patterns* (New York, 1962).

consensus on specific implications of the posture as a result of social diffusion of "what goes with what" than it would if each member were required to work out the implications individually without socially provided cues.

Such constraint through diffusion is important, for it implies a dependence upon the transmission of information. If information is not successfully transmitted, there will be little constraint save that arising from the first social source. Where transmission of information is at stake, it becomes important to distinguish between two classes of information. Simply put, these two levels are what goes with what and why. Such levels of information logically stand in a scalar relationship to one another, in the sense that one can hardly arrive at an understanding of why two ideas go together without being aware that they are supposed to go together. On the other hand, it is easy to know that two ideas go together without knowing why. For example, we can expect that a very large majority of the American public would somehow have absorbed the notion that "Communists are atheists." What is important is that this perceived correlation would for most people represent nothing more than a fact of existence, with the same status as the fact that oranges are orange and most apples are red. If we were to go and explore with these people their grasp of the "why" of the relationship, we would be surprised if more than a quarter of the population even attempted responses (setting aside such inevitable replies as "those Communists are for everything wicked"), and, among the responses received, we could be sure that the majority would be incoherent or irrelevant.

The first level of information, then, is simple and straightforward. The second involves much more complex and abstract information, very close to what Downs has called the "contextual knowledge" relevant to a body of information.[10] A well informed person who has received sufficient information about a system of beliefs to understand the "whys" involved in several of the constraints between idea-elements is in a better position to make good guesses about the nature of other constraints; he can deduce with fair success, for example, how a true believer will respond to certain situations. Our first interest in distinguishing between these types of information, however, flows from our interest in the relative success of information transmission. The general premise is that the first type of information will be diffused much more readily than the second because it is less complex.

It is well established that differences in information held in a cross-section population are simply staggering, running from vast treasuries of well organized information among elites interested in the particular subject to fragments that could virtually be measured as a few "bits" in the technical sense. These differences are a static tribute to the extreme imperfections in the transmission of information "downward" through the system: Very little information "trickles down" very far. Of course, the ordering of individuals on this vertical information

---

[10] Anthony Downs, *An Economic Theory of Democracy* (New York, 1957), p. 79.

scale is largely due to differences in education, but it is strongly modified as well by different specialized interests and tastes that individuals have acquired over time (one for politics, another for religious activity, another for fishing, and so forth).

Consequences of declining information for belief systems

It is our primary thesis that, as one moves from elite sources of belief systems downwards on such an information scale, several important things occur. First, the contextual grasp of "standard" political belief systems fades out very rapidly, almost before one has passed beyond the 10% of the American population that in the 1950s had completed standard college training.[11] Increasingly, simpler forms of information about "what goes with what" (or even information about the simple identity of objects) turn up missing. The net result, as one moves downward, is that constraint declines across the universe of idea-elements, and that the range of relevant belief systems becomes narrower and narrower. Instead of a few wide-ranging belief systems that organize large amounts of specific information, one would expect to find a proliferation of clusters of ideas among which little constraint is felt, even, quite often, in instances of sheer logical constraint.[12]

At the same time, moving from top to bottom of this information dimension, the character of the objects that are central in a belief system undergoes systematic change. These objects shift from the remote, generic, and abstract to the increasingly simple, concrete, or "close to home." Where potential political objects are concerned, this progression tends to be from abstract, "ideological" principles to the more obviously recognizable social groupings or charismatic leaders and finally to such objects of immediate experience as family, job, and immediate associates.

Most of these changes have been hinted at in one form or another in a variety of sources. For example, "limited horizons," "foreshortened time perspectives," and "concrete thinking" have been singled out as notable characteristics of the ideational world of the poorly educated. Such observations have impressed even those investigators who are dealing with subject matter rather close to the individual's immediate world: his family budgeting, what he thinks of people more wealthy than he, his attitudes toward leisure time, work regulations, and the like. But most of the stuff of politics— particularly that played on a national or international stage—is, in the nature of things, remote and abstract. Where politics is concerned, therefore, such ideational changes begin to occur rapidly below the extremely thin

---

[11] It should be understood that our information dimension is not so perfectly correlated with formal education as this statement implies. Since educational strata have a more ready intuitive meaning, however, we shall use them occasionally as convenient ways of measuring off levels in the population. In such cases, the reader may keep in mind that there are always some people of lesser education but higher political involvement who are numbered in the stratum and some people with education befitting the stratum who are not numbered there because their interests lie elsewhere and their information about politics is less than could be expected.

[12] There is a difference, of course, between this statement and a suggestion that poorly educated people have no systems of belief about politics.

stratum of the electorate that ever has occasion to make public pronouncements on political affairs. In other words, the changes in belief systems of which we speak are not a pathology limited to a thin and disoriented bottom layer of the *lumpenproletariat;* they are immediately relevant · in understanding the bulk of mass political behavior.

It is this latter fact which seems to be consistently misunderstood by the sophisticated analysts who comment in one vein or another on the meaning of mass politics. There are some rather obvious "optical illusions" that are bound to operate here. A member of that tiny elite that comments publicly about political currents (probably some fraction of 1% of a population) spends most of his time in informal communication about politics with others in the same select group. He rarely encounters a conversation in which his assumptions of shared contextual grasp of political ideas are challenged. Intellectually, he has learned that the level of information in the mass public is low, but he may dismiss this knowledge as true of only 10 to 20% of the voters, who affect the course of mass political events in insignificant ways if at all.[13] It is largely from his informal communications that he learns how "public opinion" is changing and what the change signifies, and he generalizes facilely from

these observations to the bulk of the broader public.[14]

ACTIVE USE OF IDEOLOGICAL DIMENSIONS OF JUDGMENT

Economy and constraint are companion concepts, for the more highly constrained a system of multiple elements, the more economically it may be described and understood. From the point of view of the actor, the idea organization that leads to constraint permits him to locate and make sense of a wider range of information from a particular domain than he would find possible without such organization. One judgmental dimension or "yardstick" that has been highly serviceable for simplifying and organizing events in most Western politics for the past century has been the liberal-conservative continuum, on which parties, political leaders, legislation, court decisions, and a number of other primary objects of politics could be more—or less—adequately located.[15]

---

[13] This observation is valid despite the fact that surveys showing ignorance of crucial political facts are much more likely to run in a range from 40–80% "unaware." At the height of the 1958 Berlin crisis, 63% of the American public did not know that the city was encircled by hostile troops. A figure closer to 70% is a good estimate of the proportion of the public that does not know which party controls Congress.

[14] In this regard, it was enlightening to read the stunned reactions of the political columnist Joseph Alsop when, during the 1960 presidential primaries, he left the elite circuits of the East Coast and ventured from door to door talking politics with "normal" people in West Virginia. He was frank to admit that the change in perceived political worlds was far greater than anything he had ever anticipated, despite his prior recognition that there would be some difference.

[15] The phrase "less adequately" is used to show recognition of the frequent complaint that the liberal-conservative dimension has different meanings in different politics at different times. More importantly, it takes into account the fact that in most politics new issues are constantly arising that are difficult before the fact to relate to such a yardstick. Some of these intrinsically "orthogonal" issues may remain unrelated to the di-

The efficiency of such a yardstick in the evaluation of events is quite obvious. Under certain appropriate circumstances, the single word "conservative" used to describe a piece of proposed legislation can convey a tremendous amount of more specific information about the bill—who probably proposed it and toward what ends, who is likely to resist it, its chances of passage, its long-term social consequences, and, most important, how the actor himself should expect to evaluate it if he were to expend further energy to look into its details. The circumstances under which such tremendous amounts of information are conveyed by the single word are, however, two-fold. First, the actor must bring a good deal of meaning to the term, which is to say that he must understand the constraints surrounding it. The more impoverished his understanding of the term, the less information it conveys. In the limiting

case—if he does not know at all what the term means—it conveys no information at all. Second, the system of beliefs and actors referred to must in fact be relatively constrained: To the degree that constraint is lacking, uncertainty is less reduced by the label, and less information is conveyed.

The psychological economies provided by such yardsticks for actors are paralleled by economies for analysts and theoreticians who wish to describe events in the system parsimoniously. Indeed, the search for adequate over-arching dimensions on which large arrays of events may be simply understood is a critical part of synthetic description. Such syntheses are more or less satisfactory, once again, according to the degree of constraint operative among terms in the system being described.

The economies inherent in the liberal-conservative continuum were exploited in traditional fashion in the early 1950s to describe political changes in the United States as a swing toward conservatism or a "revolt of the moderates." At one level, this description was unquestionably apt. That is, a man whose belief system was relatively conservative (Dwight D. Eisenhower) had supplanted in the White House a man whose belief system was relatively liberal (Harry Truman). Furthermore, for a brief period at least, the composition of Congress was more heavily Republican as well, and this shift meant on balance a greater proportion of relatively conservative legislators. Since the administration and Congress were the elites responsible for the development and execution of policies, the flavor of governmental action did indeed take a turn in a conservative di-

mension, and, if they become of intense importance, they can split existing parties and redefine alignments. More typically, however, elites that are known on some other grounds to be "liberal" or "conservative" ferret out some limited aspect of an issue for which they can argue some liberal-conservative relevance and begin to drift to one of the alternative positions in disproportionate numbers. Then, either because of the aspect highlighted or because of simple pressures toward party competition, their adversaries drift toward the opposing position. Thus positions come to be perceived as "liberal" or "conservative," even though such alignments would have been scarcely predictable on logical grounds. After the fact, of course, the alignments come to seem "logical," by mechanisms discussed earlier in this paper. Controversy over British entry into the European Common Market is an excellent example of such a process. Currently the conservatives are officially proentry, and Labour leadership has finally declared against it, but the reverse of this alignment had frequently been predicted when the issue was embryonic.

rection. These observations are proper description.

The causes underlying these changes in leadership, however, obviously lay with the mass public, which had changed its voting patterns sufficiently to bring the Republican elites into power. And this change in mass voting was frequently interpreted as a shift in public mood from liberal to conservative, a mass desire for a period of respite and consolidation after the rapid liberal innovations of the 1930s and 1940s. Such an account presumes, once again, that constraints visible at an elite level are mirrored in the mass public and that a person choosing to vote Republican after a decade or two of Democratic voting saw himself *in some sense or other* as giving up a more liberal choice in favor of a more conservative one.

On the basis of some familiarity with attitudinal materials drawn from cross-section samples of the electorate,[16] this assumption seems thoroughly implausible. It suggests in the first instance a neatness of organization in perceived political worlds, which, while accurate enough for elites, is a poor fit for the perceptions of the common public. Second, the yardstick that such an account takes for granted—the liberal-conservative continuum—is a rather elegant high-order abstraction, and such abstractions are not typical conceptual tools for the "man in the street." Fortunately, our interview protocols col-

lected from this period permitted us to examine this hypothesis more closely, for they include not only "structured" attitude materials (which merely require the respondent to choose between prefabricated alternatives) but also lengthy "open-ended" materials, which provided us with the respondent's current evaluations of the political scene in his own words. They therefore provide some indication of the evaluative dimensions that tend to be spontaneously applied to politics by such a national sample. We knew that respondents who were highly educated or strongly involved in politics would fall naturally into the verbal shorthand of "too conservative," "more radical," and the like in these evaluations. Our initial analytic question had to do with the prevalence of such usage.

It soon became apparent, however, that such respondents were in a very small minority, as their unusual education or involvement would suggest. At this point, we broadened the inquiry to an assessment of the evaluative dimensions of policy significance (relating to political issues, rather than to the way a candidate dresses, smiles, or behaves in his private life) that seemed to be employed *in lieu of* such efficient yardsticks as the liberal-conservative continuum. The interviews themselves suggested several strata of classification, which were hierarchically ordered as "levels of conceptualization" on the basis of *a priori* judgments about the breadth of contextual grasp of the political system that each seemed to represent.

In the first or top level were placed those respondents who did indeed rely in some active way on a relatively abstract and far-reaching con-

[16] All American data reported in this paper, unless otherwise noted, have been collected by the Survey Research Center of The University of Michigan under grants from the Carnegie Corporation, the Rockefeller Foundation, and the Social Science Research Council.

ceptual dimension as a yardstick against which political objects and their shifting policy significance over time were evaluated. We did not require that this dimension be the liberal-conservative continuum itself, but it was almost the only dimension of the sort that occurred empirically. In a second stratum were placed those respondents who mentioned such a demension in a peripheral way but did not appear to place much evaluative dependence upon it or who used such concepts in a fashion that raised doubt about the breadth of their understanding of the meaning of the term. The first stratum was loosely labeled "ideologue" and the second "near-ideologue."

In the third level were placed respondents who failed to rely upon any such over-arching dimensions yet evaluated parties and candidates in terms of their expected favorable or unfavorable treatment of different social groupings in the population. The Democratic Party might be disliked because "it's trying to help the Negroes too much," or the Republican Party might be endorsed because farm prices would be better with the Republicans in office. The more sophisticated of these group-interest responses reflected an awareness of conflict in interest between "big business" or "rich people," on the one hand, and "labor" or the "working man," on the other, and parties and candidates were located accordingly.

It is often asked why these latter respondents are not considered full "ideologues," for their perceptions run to the more tangible core of what has traditionally been viewed as ideological conflict. It is quite true that such a

syndrome is closer to the upper levels of conceptualization than are any of the other types to be described. As we originally foresaw, however, there turn out to be rather marked differences, not only in social origin and flavor of judgmental processes but in overt political reactions as well, between people of this type and those in the upper levels. These people have a clear image of politics as an arena of group interests and, provided that they have been properly advised on where their own group interests lie, they are relatively likely to follow such advice. Unless an issue directly concerns their grouping in an obviously rewarding or punishing way, however, they lack the contextual grasp of the system to recognize how they should respond to it without being told by elites who hold their confidence. Furthermore, their interest in politics is not sufficiently strong that they pay much attention to such communications. If a communication gets through and they absorb it, they are most willing to behave "ideologically" in ways that will further the interests of their group. If they fail to receive such communication, which is most unusual, knowledge of their group memberships may be of little help in predicting their responses. This syndrome we came to call "ideology by proxy."

The difference between such narrow group interest and the broader perceptions of the ideologue may be clarified by an extreme case. One respondent whom we encountered classified himself as a strong Socialist. He was a Socialist because he knew that Socialists stood four-square for the working man against the rich, and he was a working man. When asked, however, whether or not the federal government in Washington "should leave things like electric power and housing for private businessmen to handle," he felt strongly that private enterprise should have its way, and responses to other structured issue questions were simply uncorrelated with standard socialist doctrine. It seems quite clear that, if our question had pointed out explicitly to this man that "good Socialists" would demand government intervention over private enterprise or that such a posture had traditionally been viewed as benefiting the working man, his answer would have been different. But since he had something less than a college education and was not generally interested enough in politics to struggle through such niceties, he simply lacked the contextual grasp of the political system or of his chosen "ideology" to know what the appropriate response might be. This case illustrates well what we mean by constraint between idea-elements and how such constraint depends upon a store of relevant information. For this man, "Socialists," "the working man," "non-Socialists" and "the rich" with their appropriate valences formed a tightly constrained belief system. But, for lack of information, the belief system more or less began and ended there. It strikes us as valid to distinguish such a belief system from that of the doctrinaire socialist. We, as sophisticated observers, could only class this man as a full "ideologue" by assuming that he shares with us the complex undergirding of information that his concrete group perceptions call up in our own minds. In this instance, a very little probing makes clear that this assumption of shared information is once again false.

The fourth level was, to some degree, a residual category, intended to include those respondents who invoked some policy considerations in their evaluations yet employed none of the references meriting location in any of the first three levels. Two main modes of policy evaluation were characteristic of this level. The first we came to think of as a "nature of the times" response, since parties or candidates were praised or blamed primarily because of their temporal association in the past with broad societal states of war or peace, prosperity or depression. There was no hint in these responses that any groupings in the society suffered differentially from disaster or profited excessively in more pleasant times: These fortunes or misfortunes were those that one party or the other had decided (in some cases, apparently, on whim) to visit upon the nation as a whole. The second type included those respondents whose only approach to an issue reference involved some single narrow policy for which they felt personal gratitude or indignation toward a party or candidate (like social security or a conservation program). In these responses, there was no indication that the speakers saw programs as representative of the broader policy postures of the parties.

The fifth level included those respondents whose evaluations of the political scene had no shred of policy significance whatever. Some of these responses were from people who felt loyal to one party or the other but confessed that they had no idea what the party stood for. Others devoted their attention to personal qualities of the candidates, indicating disinterest in parties more generally. Still others confessed that they paid too little attention to either the parties or the current candidates to be able to say anything about them.[17]

ceptualization is summarized in Table IV-3. The array is instructive as a portrait of a mass electorate, to be laid against the common elite assumption that all or a significant majority of the public conceptualizes the main lines of politics after the manner of the most highly educated. Where the specific

TABLE IV-3   Distribution of a Total Cross-Section Sample of the American Electorate and of 1956 Voters, by Levels of Conceptualization

		Proportion of total sample	*Proportion of voters*
I.	Ideologues	2½ %	3½ %
II.	Near-ideologues	9	12
III.	Group interest	42	45
IV.	Nature of the times	24	22
V.	No issue content	22½	17½
		100%	100%

The ranking of the levels performed on *a priori* grounds was corroborated by further analyses, which demonstrated that independent measures of political information, education, and political involvement all showed sharp and monotonic declines as one passed downward through the levels in the order suggested. Furthermore, these correlations were strong enough so that each maintained some residual life when the other two items were controlled, despite the strong underlying relationship between education, information, and involvement.

The distribution of the American electorate within these levels of con-

hypothesis of the "revolt of the moderates" in the early 1950s is concerned, the distribution does not seem on the face of it to lend much support to the key assumption. This disconfirmation may be examined further, however.

Since the resurgence of the Republicans in the Eisenhower period depended primarily upon crossing of party lines by people who normally considered themselves Democrats, we were able to isolate these people to see from what levels of conceptualization they had been recruited. We found that such key defections had occurred among Democrats in the two bottom levels at a rate very significantly greater than the comparable rate in the group-interest or more ideological levels. In other words, the stirrings in the mass electorate that had led to a change in administration and in "ruling ideology" were primarily the

[17] This account of the "levels of conceptualization" is highly abbreviated. For a much more detailed discussion and rationale, along with numerous illustrations drawn at random from interviews in each stratum, see Campbell, *et al.*, *op. cit.*, Chapter 10.

handiwork of the very people for whom assumptions of any liberal-conservative dimensions of judgment were most farfetched.

Furthermore, within those strata where the characteristics of conceptualization even permitted the hypothesis to be evaluated in its own terms, it was directly disproved. For example, the more sophisticated of the group-interest Democrats were quite aware that Eisenhower would be a more pro-business president than Stevenson. Those of this group who did defect to Eisenhower did not, however, do so because they were tired of a labor-oriented administration and wanted a business-oriented one for a change. Quite to the contrary, in the degree that they defected they did so *in spite of* rather than *because of* such quasi-ideological perceptions. That is, their attitudes toward the respective interests of these groups remained essentially constant, and they expressed misgivings about an Eisenhower vote on precisely these grounds. But any such worries were, under the circumstances, outweighed by admiration for Eisenhower's war record, his honesty, his good family life, and (in 1952) his potential for resolving the nagging problem of the Korean War. Among respondents at higher levels (ideologues and near-ideologues), there was comparable attraction to Eisenhower at a personal level, but these people seemed more careful to hew to ideological considerations, and rates of Democratic defection in these levels were lower still. In short, then, the supposition of changing ideological moods in the mass public as a means of understanding the exchange of partisan elites in 1952 seems to have had little

relevance to what was actually going on at the mass level. And once again, the sources of the optical illusion are self-evident. While it may be taken for granted among well educated and politically involved people that a shift from a Democratic preference to a Republican one probably represents a change in option from liberal to conservative, the assumption cannot be extended very far into the electorate as a whole.

CONSTRAINTS AMONG IDEA-ELEMENTS

In our estimation, the use of such basic dimensions of judgment as the liberal-conservative continuum betokens a contextual grasp of politics that permits a wide range of more specific idea-elements to be organized into more tightly constrained wholes. We feel, furthermore, that there are many crucial consequences of such organization: With it, for example, new political events have more meaning, retention of political information from the past is far more adequate, and political behavior increasingly approximates that of sophisticated "rational" models, which assume relatively full information.

It is often argued, however, that abstract dimensions like the liberal-conservative continuum are superficial if not meaningless indicators: All that they show is that poorly educated people are inarticulate and have difficulty expressing verbally the more abstract lines along which their specific political beliefs are organized. To expect these people to be able to express what they know and feel, the critic goes on, is comparable to the fallacy of assuming that people can say in an accurate way why they behave as they do. When it comes down to specific attitudes and behaviors, the organization is there nonetheless, and it is this organization that matters, not the capacity for discourse in sophisticated language.

ter, however, this claim does not seem to be valid. Indeed, it is for this reason that we have cast the argument in terms of constraint, for constraint and organization are very nearly the same thing. Therefore when we hypothesize that constraint among political idea-elements begins to lose its range very rapidly once we move from the most sophisticated few toward the "grass

Table IV-4.   *Constraint between specific issue beliefs for an elite sample and a cross-section sample, 1958*[a]

	DOMESTIC					FOREIGN		
	Employment	Education	Housing	F.E.P.C.	Economic	Military [b]	Isolationism	Party Preference
Congressional Candidates								
Employment	—	.62	.59	.35	.26	.06	.17	.68
Aid to Education		—	.61	.53	.50	.06	.35	.55
Federal Housing			—	.47	.41	−.03	.30	.68
F.E.P.C.				—	.47	.11	.23	.34
Economic Aid					—	.19	.59	.25
Military Aid						—	.32	−.18
Isolationism							—	.05
Party Preference								—
Cross-Section Sample								
Employment	—	.45	.08	.34	−.04	.10	−.22	.20
Aid to Education		—	.12	.29	.06	.14	−.17	.16
Federal Housing			—	.08	−.06	.02	.07	.18
F.E.P.C.				—	.24	.13	.02	−.04
Economic Aid					—	.16	.33	−.07
Soldiers Abroad [b]						—	.21	.12
Isolationism							—	−.03
Party Preference								—

[a] Entries are tau-gamma coefficients, a statistic proposed by Leo A. Goodman and William H. Kruskal in "Measures of Association for Cross Classifications," *Journal of the American Statistical Association,* 49 (Dec., 1954), No. 268, 749. The coefficient was chosen because of its sensitivity to constraint of the scalar as well as the correlational type.

[b] For this category, the cross-section sample was asked a question about keeping American soldiers abroad, rather than about military aid in general.

If it were true that such organization does exist for most people, apart from their capacities to be articulate about it, we would agree out of hand that the question of articulation is quite trivial. As a cold empirical mat-

roots," we are contending that the organization of more specific attitudes into wide-ranging belief systems is absent as well.

Table IV-4 gives us an opportunity to see the differences in levels of constraint among beliefs on a range of specific issues in an elite population and in a mass population. The elite population happens to be candidates for the United States Congress in the off-year elections of 1958, and the cross-section sample represents the national electorate in the same year. The assortment of issues represented is simply a purposive sampling of some of the more salient political controversies at the time of the study, covering both domestic and foreign policy. The questions posed to the two samples were quite comparable, apart from adjustments necessary in view of the backgrounds of the two populations involved.

SOCIAL GROUPINGS AS CENTRAL OBJECTS IN BELIEF SYSTEMS

While for any unbiased sampling of controversial belief items we would predict that the relevant elite would show a higher level of internal constraint among elements than those shown by their publics, we would predict at the same time that it would be possible to bias a choice of issues in such a way that the level of constraint in the public could surpass that among the elites. This possibility exists because of the role that visible social groupings come to play as objects of high centrality in the belief systems of the less well informed.[18]

[18] Much of the ensuing passage can be read as a slight restatement of Herbert Hyman's insights concerning "reference groups." If we add anything at all, it is to suggest some of the circumstances under which groups *qua* groups are more or less likely to be central in individual belief systems (more or less potent as points of reference), as opposed to other kinds of belief object.

Such a reversal of the constraint prediction could be attained by choosing items that made it clear that a particular grouping, within the population and visible to most respondents, would be helped or hurt by the alternative in question. Consider, by way of illustration, the following set of items:

Negroes should be kept out of professional athletics.

The government should see to it that Negroes get fair treatment in jobs and housing.

The government should cut down on its payments (subsidies) on peanuts and cotton, which are raised mainly by Negroes in the South.

The government should give federal aid only to schools that permit Negroes to attend.

Even though it may hurt the position of the Negro in the South, state governments should be able to decide who can vote and who cannot.

If this country has to send money abroad, the government should send it to places like Africa that need it, and not to countries like Britain and France.

The strategy here is obvious. The questions are selected so that the same group is involved in each. In every case but one, this involvement is explicit. Some American adults would not know that Africa's population is largely Negro; for these people, the level of constraint between this item and the others would be relatively low. But the majority would know this fact, and the total set of items would show a substantial level of constraint, probably higher than the general level shown by the "mass" items in Table IV-4. Furthermore, the items are chosen to cut across some of those more abstract dimensions of dispute (states' rights, the strategy of economic development abroad, the role of the federal government in public education, and so forth) customary for elites, which means that constraint would be somewhat lowered for them.

The difference between the mass and elite responses would spring from differences in the nature of the objects taken to be central in the beliefs represented. For the bulk of the mass public, the object with highest centrality is the visible, familiar population grouping (Negroes), rather than questions of abstract relations among parts of government and the like. Since these latter questions take on meaning only with a good deal of political information and understanding, the attitude items given would tend to boil down for many respondents to the same single question: "Are you sympathetic to Negroes as a group, are you indifferent to them, or do you dislike them?" The responses would be affected accordingly.

While we have no direct empirical evidence supporting this illustration, there are a few fragmentary findings that point in this direction. For example, following the same format as the issue items included in Table IV-4, we asked our cross-section sample an attitude question concerning the desirability of action on the part of the federal government in the desegregation of public schools. Since we had also asked the question concerning fair treatment for Negroes in jobs and housing, these two items form a natural pair, both of which involve Negroes. The correlation between the two (in terms comparable to Table IV-4) is .57, a figure very substantially greater than the highest of the twenty-eight

intercorrelations in the "mass" half of Table IV-4. It seems more than coincidence that the only pair of items involving the fortunes of a visible population grouping should at the same time be a very deviant pair in its high level of mutual constraint.

A parallel question was asked of the elite sample of Table IV-4, although the comparability was not so great as for those items presented in the table. This question was, "If Congress were to vote to give federal aid to public schools, do you think this should be given to schools which are segregated?" While the question was worded in such a manner as to avoid responses based on attitudes toward federal aid to education, a number of elite respondents insisted on answering in the negative, not because they were necessarily against desegregation, but rather because they were against any kind of federal aid to education. (The additional element of federal aid to schools was not present at all in the item for the cross-section sample). Setting aside those respondents who gave indications that they were deviating from the intention of the question (7% of the elite sample), the correlation between the desegregation item and the F.E.P.C. item was nevertheless only .31, or very much to the low side of the elite intercorrelations on domestic issues, instead of being uniquely to the high side as it was for the mass sample.

We may summarize this situation in the following manner. Out of twenty-eight "trials" represented by the intercorrelations in Table IV-4, in only three cases did the mass sample show an intercorrelation between issues that was of the same sign and of greater absolute magnitude than its counterpart for the elite sample. Two of these "reversals" were completely trivial (.02 and .04), and the third was not large (.08). With respect to the only pair of items that explicitly involved the fortunes of a well-known social grouping, however, there not only was a reversal, but the reversal was large: The constraint for the mass sample, by a simple difference of coefficients, is .26 greater. This isolated test certainly provides some striking initial support for our expectations.

Up to this point, we have discussed two broad classes of findings. The first, as exemplified by Table IV-4 and our more recent elaborations on it, suggests that groups as attitude objects (groups *qua* groups) have higher centrality in the belief systems of the mass than of the elite. The second is exemplified by the many findings that the alignment of an individual's social-group membership (like class or religious membership) and his political behavior is sharpest among the most politically involved and sophisticated third of a mass sample and fades out progressively as involvement and sophistication decline.

In case these propositions do not seem to square perfectly with one another, Figure IV-9 provides a schematic view of the situation that may clarify the matter for the reader. Of course, the details of the figure (like the precise characters of the functions) are sheer fancy. But the gross contours seem empirically justified. The elite of Table IV-4 would naturally be represented by a line along the top of Figure IV-9, which would be thin to the vanishing point. The "relative elite" of the mass sample, which defines "the public" as perceived by most impres-

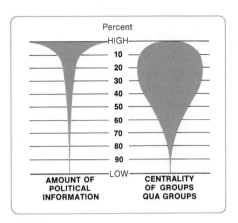

Figure IV-9. *Political information and the centrality of groups as objects in belief systems*

sionistic observers, might sweep in the top 2%, 5%, or 10% of the graph, as one chose. In the upper reaches of the group centrality graph, we have already seen glimmers of the inverse relationship between group centrality and sophistication in such diverse items as the falling-off of party loyalty at the very "top" of the mass sample or the lowered constraint for the Negro items in the elite sample.

On the other hand, why is it that when we work downward from the more sophisticated third of the population, the centrality of groups begins once again to diminish? We are already committed to the proposition that differences in information are crucial, but let us consider this point more fully. The findings that lead us to posit this decline come from a class of situations in which the actor *himself* must perceive some meaningful link between membership in a particular group and preference for a particular party or policy alternative. These situations are most typically those in which the link is not made explicit by the very nature of the situation (as we made it explicit in our battery of Negro questions above). In these cases, the individual must be endowed with some cognitions of the group as an entity and with some interstitial "linking" information indicating why a given party or policy is relevant to the group. Neither of these forms of information can be taken for granted, and our key proposition is that, as the general bulk of political information declines, the probability increases that some key pieces of information relevant to this group-politics equation will not show up.

The first item—the individual's cognition that a group exists—is a very simple one and may not even seem plausible to question. For certain groups at certain times and places, however, the possibility that such a cognition is absent must be recognized. All groups, including those that become important politically, vary in their visibility. Groups delimited by physical characteristics "in the skin" (racial groups) are highly visible, if specimens are present for inspection or if the individual has been informed in some rather vivid way of their existence. Similarly, groups that have buildings, meetings, and officers (church, congregation, and clergy for example) are more visible than groups, like social classes, that do not, although the salience of any "official" group *qua* group may vary widely according to the individual's contact with its formal manifestations.

Some groups—even among those to which an individual can be said to "belong"—are much less visible. Two important examples are the social class

and the nation. Where social class is concerned, virtually all members of a population are likely to have absorbed the fact that some people have more means or status than others, and most presumably experience some satisfaction or envy on this score from time to time. Such perceptions may, however, remain at the same level as reactions to the simple fact of life that some people are born handsome and others homely; or, as Marx knew, they may proceed to cognitions of some more "real" and bounded groups. The difference is important.

Much the same kind of observation may be made of the nation as group object. On the basis of our analysis, it might be deduced that nationalist ideologies stand a much better chance of penetrating a mass population than would, for example, the single-tax ideology of the physiocrats and Henry George, for nationalist ideologies hinge upon a simple group object in a way that single-tax notions do not. This kind of deduction is perfectly warranted, particularly if one has in mind those Western nations with systems of primary education devoted to carving the shape of a nation in young minds as a "real" entity. But Znaniecki has observed, for example, that the vast majority of peasants in nineteenth-century Tsarist Russia was "utterly unconscious that they were supposed to belong to a Russian society united by a common culture." Again he reports that a 1934–1935 study in the Pripet marshes showed that nearly half of those inhabitants who were ethnically White Ruthenian had no idea that such a nationality existed and regarded themselves as belonging at most to local communities.[19] The nation as a bounded, integral group object is difficult to experience in any direct way, and its psychological existence for the individual depends upon the social transmission of certain kinds of information. What is deceptive here, as elsewhere, is that decades or even centuries after the *literati* have come to take a nation concept for granted, there may be substantial proportions of the member population who have never heard of such a thing.[20]

While cognitions of certain groups are not always present, the much more typical case is one in which the interstitial or contextual information giving the group a clear political relevance is lacking. For example, a substantial proportion of voters in the United States is unable to predict that any particular party preference will emerge in the votes of different class groupings, and this inability is particularly noticeable among the least involved citizens, whose partisan behavior is itself essentially random with respect to social class.[21]

One important *caveat* must be offered on the generalization represented in Figure IV-9. From a number of points we have made, it should be clear that the figure is intended to represent an actuarial proposition and nothing more. That is, it has merit for most situations, given the typical state of distribution of political information in societies as we find them "in nature." In certain situations, however, the cues presented to citizens concerning links between group and party or policy are so gross that they penetrate rapidly even to the less informed. In such cases, the form representing group centrality in Figure IV-9 would taper off much less rapidly with declining over-all information in the lower strata of the population.

For example, the linking information that made religion particularly relevant in the 1960 election was extremely simple, of the "what goes with what" variety. It was expressible in five words: "The Democratic candidate is Catholic." Studies have shown that, once Kennedy was nominated, this additional item of information was diffused through almost the entire population with a speed that is rare and that, we suspect, would be impossible for more complex contextual information. The linking information that made social class unusually relevant after World War II was, however, precisely this vague, contextual type.[22]

[19] Florian Znaniecki, *Modern Nationalities* (Urbana, 1952), pp. 81–2.

[20] Even in the modern United States, there are scattered pockets of the population that are rather vague about national identity. We encounter respondents, for example, who when asked if they were born in the United States, answer "No, I was born in Georgia," in what is clearly ignorance rather than a throwback to secession or kittenish state pride.

[21] McClosky observes more generally: "Members of the active minority" [the political elite sample] "are far better able than the ordinary voter to name reference groups that fit both their party affiliation and their doctrinal orientation. . . . Clearly the political stratum has a much better idea than the public has of where its political sympathies lie and who its ideological friends and enemies are. The ability to recognize favorable or unfavorable reference groups is, on the

whole, poorly developed in the populace at large." McClosky, *op. cit.*

[22] With regard to the postwar increase in relevance of social class, see Philip E. Converse, "The Shifting Role of Class in Political Attitudes and Behavior," in E. L. Maccoby, T. W. Newcomb, and E. E. Hartley, (eds.), *Readings in Social Psychology* (New York, 1958), p. 388.

It can be readily demonstrated with our data that the impact of the religious link in 1960 registered to some degree in the behavior of even the least sophisticated Protestants and Catholics, while the incremental impact of social-class cues in the earlier period had not registered at these lower levels.

The precise form of the centrality function in Figure IV-9 depends heavily therefore upon the character of the linking information at issue in the special case. Furthermore, if we wished to "tamper," it would not be difficult to supply a poorly informed person with a very tiny increment of linking information, too small to change his over-all amount of political information visibly yet large enough to increase considerably the centrality of a specific group in a specific situation. However this may be, Figure IV-9 is valid in an actuarial sense, for in "natural" populations the probability that any given individual possesses such linking information declines as over-all information becomes less.

THE STABILITY OF BELIEF ELEMENTS OVER TIME

All of our data up to this point have used correlations calculated on aggregates as evidence of greater or lesser constraint among elements in belief systems. While we believe these correlations to be informative indicators, they do depend for their form upon cumulations among individuals and therefore can never be seen as commenting incisively upon the belief structures of individuals.

It might then be argued that we are mistaken in saying that constraint among comparable "distant" belief elements declines generally as we move from the more to the less politically sophisticated. Instead, the configuration of political beliefs held by individuals simply becomes increasingly idiosyncratic as we move to less sophisticated people. While an equally broad range of belief elements might function as an interdependent whole for an unsophisticated person, we would find little aggregative patterning of belief combinations in populations of unsophisticated people, for they would be out of the stream of cultural information about "what goes with what" and would therefore put belief elements together in a great variety of ways.

For the types of belief that interest us here, this conclusion in itself would be significant. We believe however, that we have evidence that permits us to reject it rather categorically, in favor of our original formulation. A fair test of this counterhypothesis would seem to lie in the measurement of the same belief elements for the same individuals over time. For if we are indeed involved here in idiosyncratic patterns of belief, each meaningful to the individual in his own way, then we could expect that individual responses to the same set of items at different points in time should show some fundamental stability. They do not.

A longitudinal study of the American electorate over a four-year period has permitted us to ask the same questions of the same people a number of times, usually separated by close to two-year intervals. Analysis of the stability of responses to the "basic" policy questions of the type presented in Table IV-4 yields remarkable results. Faced with the typical item of this kind, only about thirteen people out of twenty manage to locate themselves even on the same *side* of the controversy in successive interrogations, when ten out of twenty could have done so by chance alone.

While we have no comparable longitudinal data for an elite sample, the degree of fit between answers to our issue items and congressional roll-calls is strong enough to suggest that time correlations for individual congressmen in roll-call choice on comparable bills would provide a fair estimate of the stability of an elite population in beliefs of this sort. It is probably no exaggeration to deduce that, in sharp contrast to a mass sample, eighteen out of twenty congressmen would be likely to take the same positions on the same attitude items after a two-year interval. In short, then, we feel very confident that elite-mass differences in levels of constraint among beliefs are mirrored in elite-mass differences in the temporal stability of belief elements for individuals.

We observed much earlier that the centrality of a specific belief in a larger belief system and the relative stability of that belief over time should be highly related. From our other propositions about the role of groups as central objects in the belief systems of the mass public, we can therefore arrive at two further predictions. The first is simply that pure affect toward visible population groupings should be highly stable over time, even in a mass public, much more so in fact than beliefs on policy matters that more or less explicitly bear on the fortunes of these groupings. Second, policy items that do bear more rather than less explicitly upon their fortunes should show less stability than affect towards the group *qua* group but more than those items for which contextual information is required.

Figure IV-10 gives strong confir-

Figure IV-10 Temporal Stability of Different Belief Elements for Individuals, 1958–60[a]

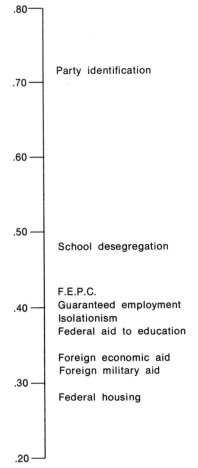

[a] The measure of stability is a rank-order correlation (tau-beta) between individuals' positions in 1958 and in 1960 on the same items.

mation of these hypotheses.[23] First, the only question applied longitudinally that touches on pure affect toward a visible population grouping is the one about party loyalties or identifications. As the figure indicates, the stability of these group feelings for individuals over time (measured by the correlation between individual positions in two successive readings) registers in a completely different range from that characterizing even the most stable of the issue items employed.[24] This contrast is particularly ironic, for in theory of course the party usually has little rationale for its existence save as an instrument to further particular policy preferences of the sort that show less stability in Figure IV-10. The policy is the end, and the party is the means, and ends are conceived to be more stable and central in belief systems than means. The reversal for the mass public is of course a rather dramatic special case of one of our primary generalizations: The party and the affect toward it are more central within the political belief systems of the mass public than are the policy ends that the parties are designed to pursue.

Figure IV-10 also shows that, within the set of issues, the items that stand out as most stable are those that have obvious bearing on the welfare of a population grouping—the

Negroes—although the item concerning federal job guarantees is very nearly as stable. In general, we may say that stability declines as the referents of the attitude items become increasingly remote, from jobs, which are significant objects to all, and Negroes, who are attitude objects for most, to items involving ways and means of handling foreign policy.

In short, all these longitudinal data offer eloquent proof that signs of low constraint among belief elements in the mass public are not products of well knit but highly idiosyncratic belief systems, for these beliefs are extremely labile for individuals over time. Great instability in itself is *prima facie* evidence that the belief has extremely low centrality for the believer. Furthermore, it is apparent that any instability characterizing one belief sets an upper limit on the degree of orderly constraint that could be expected to emerge in static measurement between this unstable belief and another, even a perfectly stable one. While an aggregate might thus show high stability despite low constraint, the fact of low stability virtually ensures that constraint must also be low. This kind of relationship between stability and constraint means that an understanding of what underlies high instability is at the same time an understanding of what underlies low constraint.

---

[23] The items portrayed in Figure IV-10 are the same as those in Table IV-4 and are described at that point.

[24] We regret that we did not get measures of pure affect for other groupings in the population, for all population members. A copious literature on intergroup attitudes in social psychology contains, however, much presumptive evidence of extreme stability in these attitudes over time.

ISSUE PUBLICS

Our longitudinal data on eight specific political issues permit us to sketch crudely the boundaries of a sampling of eight issue publics.[25] While details of specific publics are not appropriate here, the general picture that emerges provides some final confirming glimpses into the character of political belief systems in a mass public.

First, of course, these publics vary in size, although none embraces any clear majority of the electorate. As would be expected, relative size is almost perfectly correlated with the ranking of issue stability (Figure IV-10), and the smallest issue public (that associated with the "ideological" private-enterprise issue) includes less than 20% of the electorate.

Since all members of the same population fall either within or outside eight different issue publics, a second analytic question involves the structure that would be revealed were we to map several issue publics at once. What proportions of the electorate would fall at the intersection of two, three, or even more issue publics? One logically possible outcome of such mapping would be a set of concentric rings, suggesting that these issue concerns are cumulative in Guttman's sense. That is, the picture might show that, if a person fell within the bounds

of one fairly narrow issue public embracing only 20% of the population, then he would be nearly certain to fall within some other related issue public encompassing 40% of the population.

The reality does not approach such neatness, however. Memberships and overlapping memberships in issue publics are quite dispersed phenomena, although distribution is not entirely random. It can be shown, for example, that the number of respondents who warrant inclusion in all eight of the issue publics exceeds chance expectation by a factor greater than five. Exactly the same is true for the number of people who fall in none of the eight issue publics. Furthermore, the proportions of people who lie at the intersections of two or more issue publics tend to show increments above the chance level that, while much smaller, are nevertheless relatively large where the joint content of the issues would lead one to expect greater overlap. At any rate, the departure from a Guttman cumulative structure is extreme, and the simple conclusion seems to be that different controversies excite different people to the point of real opinion formation. One man takes an interest in policies bearing on the Negro and is relatively indifferent to or ignorant about controversies in other areas. His neighbor may have few crystallized opinions on the race issue, but he may find the subject of foreign aid very important. Such sharp divisions of interest are part of what the term "issue public" is intended to convey.

Since one of our early comparisons in this paper had to do with the general levels of constraint among an elite and a mass public on a sampling

[25] The definition of these boundaries is necessarily crude. While we have means of improving upon it in the future, it rests for the moment upon the exclusion of those people with unstable opinions, along with those who at one point or another confessed that they had no opinions. We know that each public, so defined, contains some respondents who give stable patterns of response by chance alone and therefore do not belong in the issue-public conceptually. On the other hand, for those issues where it is necessary to posit some small "third force" undergoing conversion on the issue, these people are inadvertently overlooked. Nonetheless, these two contingents appear to be small, and the issue-public boundaries are thus roughly accurate.

of belief elements, it is interesting to ask what degree of constraint can be found among the belief elements of those who fall at the intersection of any pair of issue publics. In such a case, we have some assurance that both sets of beliefs are important to the actor, and it is not therefore surprising that these correlations tend to be much stronger. A matrix of intercorrelations parallel to those of Table IV-4 for people at these respective intersections looks more like the elite matrix than like the mass matrix. Of course, this "intersection" matrix is a spurious one, representing no particular population: Very few people contribute to all of the intercorrelations, a substantial number contribute to none, and the set contributing to each cell is quite variable in composition. Nevertheless, the fact remains that removal from analysis of individuals who, through indifference or ignorance, lie outside the issue publics in question serves to close much of the gap in constraint levels between mass and elite publics.

SUMMARY

Our discussion of issue publics has brought us full circle, for there is an obvious relationship among the divisions of the common citizenry into relatively narrow and fragmented issue publics, the feeble levels of constraint registered among specific belief elements of any range, and the absence of recognition or understanding of overarching ideological frames of reference that served as our point of departure. For the truly involved citizen, the development of political sophistication means the absorption of contextual information that makes clear to him the connections of the policy area of his initial interest with policy differences in other areas; and that these broader configurations of policy positions are describable quite economically in the basic abstractions of ideology. Most members of the mass public, however, fail to proceed so far. Certain rather concrete issues may capture their respective individual attentions and lead to some politically relevant opinion formation. This engagement of attention remains narrow however: Other issue concerns that any sophisticated observer would see as "ideologically" related to the initial concern tend not to be thus associated in any breadth or number. The common citizen fails to develop more global points of view about politics. A realistic picture of political belief systems in the mass public, then, is not one that omits issues and policy demands completely nor one that presumes widespread ideological coherence; it is rather one that captures with some fidelity the fragmentation, narrowness, and diversity of these demands.

Such a description is not particularly economical, and the investigator is confronted by the fact that, in coping with a poorly constrained system, he must choose between parsimony and explanatory power. This dilemma confronts him only in the degree that he insists upon dealing with the issue or ideological base of mass politics. That is, the very diffusion of this issue base at the mass level means that many of the threads cancel themselves out and can be ignored at one level of description. With good information on basic party loyalties in a population, with knowledge of sudden disruptions of economic expectations, and with freedom to treat other short-term perturbations in mass political behavior in terms of such inelegant factors as candidate popularity, there is no reason to feel that mass political phenomena are difficult to understand or predict in relatively economical terms. But such accounts do not probe to the level that supplies for many the fundamental "why" of politics—its issue or ideological base.

If we insist on treating this base and choose economy over explanatory power, then we are likely to select one or two ideological threads to follow, with recognition that the consequences of substantial numbers of other threads must be ignored. If the limited threads are well chosen, this strategy has a number of strengths, and a "good" choice of threads is likely to involve visible and competing population groupings, for reasons sketched above.

This latter strategy is essentially that employed by Lipset in tracing the imprint of social class upon mass political behavior across time and nationality in *Political Man*. His choice of threads is good, in part because of the ubiquity of social-class differences historically and cross-nationally and in part because, among issue threads, social class is one of the more reliably prominent. Despite the great diversity of issue concerns in the American public in the 1950s, if one were required to pick the single thread of ideological relevance most visible and persistent, it undoubtedly would be related to social class.

On the other hand, there is a major sacrifice of explanatory power here. For example, when we argue that social-class concerns represent the most prominent, unitary "issue" thread in mass American politics in the past decade, the scope of our statement should not be overestimated. Given the diversity and number of such threads, it need only mean (as is probably the case) that such concerns have made some greater or lesser contribution to the significant political behaviors—for the mass, largely in voting—of 20 to 40% of the American population in this period. This contribution is enough, of course, to leave a clear imprint on mass political phenomena, although it does not constitute even substantial explanation.[26]

Furthermore, it may well be that, in pluralist societies with other highly visible group cleavages, these cleavages may often have greater penetration into mass publics than do class differences, as far as consequences for political behavior are concerned. Religious pluralism is a case in point. While class differences mark every society, not all current democracies contain fundamental religious differences. Where such differences exist and can in some measure be separated from social class differences—the Netherlands, Austria, and the United States are good examples—there is fair reason to believe that they are fully as important, if not more important, in

[26] And if we take as a goal the explanation of political *changes* touched off by movements in mass political decisions in this period, as opposed to questions of more static political structure, then the explanatory utility of the social-class threat is almost nil, for the ideological class voters were least likely to have contributed to these changes by corresponding changes in their voting patterns.

shaping mass political behavior than are class differences. Even in current France, one can predict with greater accuracy whether a citizen will be a partisan of the "left" or of the "right" by knowing his position on the "clerical question" than by knowing his position on the more central class issues typically associated with the left-right distinction. And this accuracy is possible despite several decades during which French elites have focused primary attention on other more gripping controversies and have frequently attempted to deflate the clerical question as a "phony" issue.[27]

Whatever problems are posed for description by the diffuseness of the issue base of mass politics, the most important insights are to be gained from the fact that ideological constraints in belief systems decline with decreasing political information, which is to say that they are present among elites at the "top" of political systems, or subsystems and disappear rather rapidly as one moves "downward" into their mass clienteles. We see the importance of this fact in a number of standard phenomena of both routine and crisis politics.

Perhaps the simplest and most obvious consequences are those that depend on the fact that reduced constraint with reduced information means in turn that ideologically constrained belief systems are necessarily

more common in upper than in lower social strata. This fact in turn means that upper social strata across history have much more predictably supported conservative or rightist parties and movements than lower strata have supported leftist parties and movements.

These facts have further bearing on a number of asymmetries in political strategy, which typically arise between elites of rightist and leftist parties. These elites operate under rather standard ideological assumptions, and therefore recognize their "natural" clienteles in the upper and lower strata of the society respectively. The cultural definitions that separate upper and lower in most if not all modern societies are such that the lower clientele numerically outweighs the upper. The net result of these circumstances is that the elites of leftist parties enjoy a "natural" numerical superiority, yet they are cursed with a clientele that is less dependable or solidary in its support. The rightist elite has a natural clientele that is more limited but more dependable.

Asymmetrical elite strategies therefore emerge. They are best summed up perhaps in terms of an increasingly *overt* stress on group loyalty and cohesion *per se* as one moves from right to left across party spectra in most political systems. This difference has a great number of concrete manifestations. For example, where political institutions encourage multiparty development, there is likely to be less party fragmentation on the left than on the right. Where political institutions permit interparty differences in the stringency of party discipline at the legislative level, it is common to

[27] P. E. Converse and G. Dupeux, "Politicization of the Electorate in France and the United States," *Public Opinion Quarterly*, 26 (Spring, 1962). For complementary evidence covering an earlier period, see Duncan MacRae, "Religious and Socioeconomic Factors in the French Vote, 1945–1956," *American Journal of Sociology*, 64 (November, 1958).

find a rather steady progression in strength of discipline exacted as one moves from right to left. At an electoral level, rightist candidates are more likely to run as individual *notables,* dissociating themselves from party *per se* or claiming positions "above the parties" and priding themselves on the independence of their consciences from party dictation.

Entirely parallel asymmetries arise in the relations between party elites and elites of organized interest groups based "outside" the political order as it is narrowly conceived. These relations tend to be more overtly close as one moves from the right to the left. Trade unions have with some frequency created or coalesced with leftist parties, and, where such coalition has not occurred, trade unions (and particularly those with the less politically sophisticated memberships) publicize political endorsements that link them rather unequivocally with specific leftist parties. Associations of professional and business people, to the degree that they perform public political activity at all, tend toward non-partisan exhortations to "work for the party of your choice" and in other ways maintain or are kept at a "proper" distance from rightist parties so far as self-publicized connections are concerned. All these differences flow from the simple fact that, for leftist parties, the transmission of gross, simple, group-oriented cues is a functional imperative. For rightist parties, there is much to lose and nothing to gain in such publicity, for the basic clientele can be counted on for fair support without blatant cues, and the tactical needs are to avoid the alienation of potentially large-scale "haphazard" support from the lower-status clientele.

These simple social biases in the presence of ideological constraints in belief systems thus register to some degree in the calculations of practical political elites. Fully as interesting, however, are the miscalculations that arise when the low incidence of these constraints in the middle and lower reaches of mass publics is forgotten. While this forgetting is more common among academic commentators than among practical politicians, it is sometimes hard to avoid—particularly where an elite with a distinctive ideology captures a broad surge of mass support. Here it is difficult to keep in mind that the true motivations and comprehensions of the supporters may have little or nothing to do with the distinctive beliefs of the endorsed elite. Yet we believe that such hiatuses or discontinuities are common and become more certain in the degree that (1) the distinctive elements of the elite ideologies are bound up in abstractions or referents remote from the immediate experience of the clientele; (2) and that the clientele, for whatever reason, is recruited from the less informed strata of a population. We shall close by applying these propositions to historical cases.

Abolition and the rise of the Republican Party

Historians have devoted a great deal of prose to the rise of abolitionist ferment in the North after 1820. Popular sentiment against slavery seems to have gathered momentum in the relatively unbroken line that is so typical of *successful* reform movements, from the persistent agitations of Lundy and

William Lloyd Garrison through the formation of antislavery societies in the 1830s, the development of the underground railroad, the birth of the Republican Party in the name of abolition, and its final electoral triumph in a popular majority for Lincoln outside the South in 1860. A number of figures are commonly cited to express the deep penetration of the ferment into the consciousness of the general public, including the membership of 200,000 attracted by the American Anti-Slavery Society in the seven short years after 1833 and the truly remarkable sales of *Uncle Tom's Cabin* in 1852 and after.

We obviously do not challenge the mountains of evidence concerning the high pitch of this controversy. We assume from the outset that this ferment among the elites and near-elites was in point of fact most noteworthy and has been accurately described. If we take the figures at face value, for example, we can compute that the Anti-Slavery Society's membership amounted to between 3 and 4% of the adult population outside of the South at that time.[28] Against what we have considered to be the commonly "visible" part of the political public (5 to 15% of the total adult public), this figure does indeed represent a vigorous development of antislave sentiment. What interests us instead is the gap between the figure of 4% indicative

[28] This figure is for 1840, and it undoubtedly advanced further in the next decade or two, although one deduces that the expansion of membership slowed down after 1840. Our estimates do not take into account, however, the standard inflation of claimed membership (intentional or unintentional) that seems to characterize all movements of this sort.

of a sturdy ideological movement, and the 46% of the nonsouthern popular presidential vote won by the Republican Party two years after its conception in Wisconsin and birth in Michigan under the pure banner of abolition. The question is, Essentially what part did beliefs in abolition play in attracting the votes of the mass base that made the Republican Party a political success?

The question seems particularly worth asking, for among events or causes that have commonly been assumed to have had some substantial resonance among the mass public in American history, few would strike us as less plausible than abolition. Panics, the promise of free land in the West, railroad charges for transportation of farm produce, and competition by immigrants for urban jobs could all be expected to have had some immediate impact on at least limited portions of the mass public. Similarly, the threat of abolition would have had some concrete and day-to-day meaning for many citizens in the South. But it is hard to imagine that the ordinary nonsoutherner in 1855 would have had reason to be concerned about the plight of his "black brother" in a land several days' journey away—certainly not reason sufficient to make any visible contribution to his political responses. Indeed, we are tempted to the heresy that there were very substantial portions of the nonsouthern population in that period who were only dimly aware that slavery or a controversy about it existed.

If this latter statement seems dubious in the light of the torrents of literature poured out on the subject in the 1850s, the reader might reflect upon the feeble impact registered in the mass public by "the communist hysteria" of the McCarthy era in the early 1950s. At an elite level, the controversy was bitter and all-pervasive for a considerable period of time. Yet, during the nationally televised hearings that climaxed the affair, Stouffer found that 30% of a cross-section public could not think of any senator or congressman investigating internal communism, and the low salience of the whole controversy for most of the public was clearly demonstrated in other ways as well.[29] In the 1952 presidential campaign, the Republican charges against the Democratic Party were summed up in the handy slogan "Corruption, Korea and Communism." Our materials drawn at the time from a mass electorate showed a strong spontaneous response to the issues of corruption and Korea (although there was little understanding of the "Great Debate" that was in full swing over how the Korean conflict should be terminated) but almost no response at all to the third item, even though it referred to a controversy that, like abolition in the 1850s, has tended to remain in elite minds as the principal struggle of its period.[30] And evidence of this lack of public recognition or resonance emerges despite the existence of a population that relative to that of 1850, was highly literate, leisured, and exposed to mass media of a speed, breadth, and penetration that simply had no counterpart in an earlier day.[31]

The controversy over internal communism provides a classic example of a mortal struggle among elites that passed almost unwitnessed by an astonishing portion of the mass public. Quite clearly, there is no necessary connection between the noise, acrimony, or duration of an elite debate and the mass penetration of the controversy, however automatically the equation is made. A better guide to penetration seems to be the character of the issue itself.

A student recently decided to analyze the contents of caches of letters from the 1850s and 1860s, which had been preserved by old families in the various attics of a small Ohio community. He was interested in tracing the development of abolitionist sentiment, and Ohio had been the first state to give the new Republican Party a mass base in the election of 1854. The problem was that no references to abolition were ever found in any of the letters, despite the fact that their writers necessarily represented the "upper" stratum of the community, the stratum that, by all odds, would be most likely to have some awareness of the controversy. In letters written on the eve of the Civil War, there were increasing "ideological" references to the disruption of the Union. Once political events had passed to the dramatic point at which the South was clearly in treasonable rebellion against the Union, the mass penetration of the controversy in the North is not difficult to understand. But it is likely that

---

[29] S. A. Stouffer, *Communism, Conformity and Civil Liberties* (New York, 1955).

[30] Campbell, *et al., op. cit.*, pp. 50–51.

[31] In 1954, the average circulation of daily newspapers amounted to about 20% more papers than households. In 1850, one newspaper had to stretch across five households. These estimates are calculated from Bureau of the Census figures in *Historical Statistics of the United States* (Washington, D.C., 1961).

this stage was reached at a mass level much later than is customarily assumed. And for the preceding period, the Ohio letters betrayed no concern for abolition.[32]

There is, furthermore, a major leap from some awareness that a controversy is in the air to opinion formation of a strength sufficient to register in an individual's own political behavior. Once again, modern data are instructive. Although civil rights and the race question have been primary controversies in the past five years and although a very large majority of the public was aware of the struggles at Little Rock and the University of Mississippi, opinion formation on the subject among a cross-section of nonsouthern whites was far from intense. While everybody responds to opinion items on the matter, the true issue publics are made up very disproportionately of Negroes and southerners. A sprinkling of nonsouthern whites shows some genuine interest in the issue, and the bulk of them is positively disposed toward the Negro. But a measure of the salience of the Negro question as a political problem stringent enough to register two-thirds of nonsouthern Negroes as intensely concerned leaves scarcely one nonsouthern white out of ten qualifying at the same level. It should be remembered that this indifference is evident at a time when the Negro has become an important problem in urban areas outside the South, a situation that did not exist in 1850 or 1860. Most northern whites with intense positive or negative concern also live in areas

where Negroes live or are inordinately interested in politics. In the hinterland, opinion is superficial or indifferent.

If the population of the hinterland that gave initial mass impetus to the Republican Party had indeed felt some deep humanitarian concern about the plight of the Negro in the South, then we would be forced to conclude that empathy in human nature has suffered an astonishing decline in the past century. In fact, however, there are enough anomalies in the voting records of the period to leave room for fair doubt about the nature of the Republican mass base in its first three years. Fringe votes for the earlier abolitionist parties (the Liberty and Free Soil Parties) were never strong in the urban centers—Boston and New York—which were generating much of the intellectual ferment about abolition, although they were concentrated in smaller towns in Massachusetts and New York outside these centers and probably reflect the lines of genuine if thinly sprinkled abolitionist feeling. When, however, the Whig Party no longer presented itself as an alternative to the Democrats and when broad-gauged mass support had to turn either to the Republicans or to the anti-Catholicism of the "Know-Nothing" American Party, the patterns were somewhat different. In 1856 the largest northeastern centers (excluding all but the potentially abolitionist North [33]), where intellectuals had pursued abolition most doggedly

---

[32] Informal communication from Professor Robert L. Crane.

[33] We set aside Pennsylvania, Delaware, and Maryland, all of which had been slow in moving towards complete abolition and which tended to follow southern voting patterns through the election of 1856.

and where Catholic immigrants were accumulating, gave the Know-Nothings their clearest mass support and the Republicans their weakest harvest of former Whig or Free-Soil votes. The capacity to move these votes into the Republican column was greater in those surrounding areas that had shown the strongest traces of support for the earlier abolition parties, although in many of these areas the Know-Nothings cut into the vote as well. The least blemished successes of the new Republican party lay in the deeper hinterland, which had given the feeblest support to abolition in preceding elections.[34]

While any evidence pertaining to the thoughts and motivations of the mass of citizens who did not make public speeches or leave written records must be circumstantial, it is worth suggesting that there was probably an important discontinuity between the intransigent abolitionism associated with the Republican Party at an elite level in its early phases and its early mass successes. How great this discontinuity was we do not and doubtless shall not ever know, although we have some confidence that, if the truth were known, the discontinuity would be large enough to shock many students of documents and data from more elite levels.

Of course, from the point of view of historical outcomes, all that is important is that this particular conjunc-

tion of circumstances occurred when it did and was interpreted as it was by political elites in both North and South. These facts shaped history and placed the abolitionist movement in the forefront of "popular" American reforms, set apart from other reforms that have either achieved general elite acceptance without need for mass support or have faded into semioblivion because times were not propitious for the capture of a mass base. Nonetheless, our understanding of history may be improved at some points if we recognize the possibility that such discontinuities can occur.

The mass base of the Nazi Party

The rise of the Nazi Party in Germany between the two World Wars entrained such a tragic sequence of events that the experience has provoked diagnoses from every school of thought concerned with people, politics, or societies. Typically, the question has been, How could the German people have lent support to a movement with an ideology as brutal and authoritarian as that of the Nazis? Some years ago, Bendix argued that it was important to differentiate between the top Nazi leaders, the party members, and the masses whose sudden surge of support at the polls converted the National Socialists from simply another extremist fringe group of the sort that many societies harbor much of the time to a prominence that permitted them to become masters of Germany soon after 1932.[35]

Few would now question that the

---

[34] A simple ordering of potentially abolitionist states according to apparent success in transfer of 1852 Free-Soil and Whig votes to the Republicans in 1856 is negatively correlated with an ordering of these states according to the relative amount of fringe support they had tended to contribute to the abolitionist parties of the 1840s.

[35] Reinhard Bendix. "Social Stratification and Political Power," in Bendix and S. M. Lipset, (eds.), *Class, Status and Power* (New York, 1953), pp. 596–609.

simple magnitude of economic collapse Germany suffered in the wake of
World War I was the critical catalyst,
both for the organizational strength
the cadre of Nazi activists had attained
prior to 1930 and for the sweeping successes they attained at the polls in that
year. Once this point is made, however,
we concur with Bendix that the explanatory paths for the mass and the
elite are likely to diverge. Our interest
here has to do solely with the relationship between the new-found mass of
Nazi voters and the ideology of the
movement they endorsed.

Who was particularly attracted to
this mass base? Once again, there is fair
agreement among analysts that there
was a significant connection between
the marked increase in voter turnout
and the sudden surge in Nazi votes
that marked the 1928–1932 period.
Bendix noted that the staggering increase of 5½ million votes picked up
by the Nazi Party in 1930 over its 1928
totals coincided with a rapid influx
into the active electorate of nearly 2½
million adults who had failed to vote
in 1928. These figures for new voters
are exclusive of the estimated 1,760,000
young people who became eligible and
voted for the first time, and there is
reason to believe that these young
people flocked to the Nazis in disproportionate numbers.[36] In addition,
there is convincing evidence from
Heberle and others that, among older
voters, the most dramatic shifts from
other parties to the Nazi Party occurred in rural areas and especially
among peasants.[37] We conclude there-

fore that, whatever the social backgrounds or motivations of the activist
cadre of the Nazis, its mass base was
disproportionately recruited from
among customary nonvoters, the
young and the peasantry.

Of course, chronic nonvoters
would lie at the bottom of any scale of
political sophistication or ideological
comprehension. . . . The young are
also the most politically unsophisticated age grade, despite their higher
average education. Finally, for American data at least, it is clear that political information and political involvement decline systematically with declining mean education from urban
areas to increasingly rural areas. Even
taken as a whole, farmers in modern
America are more remote from and
comprehend less of the normal political process than do the lower echelons
of the urban occupational hierarchy.[38]
Furthermore, the Heberle data for
Germany suggest that, among farmers,
it was the most isolated and the poorest
educated who shifted in the most dramatic proportions to the Nazi ticket in
the crucial years.[39] In sum, it seems

Nazism to Rural Areas," *American Sociological
Review*, 11 (December, 1946), 724–34.

[38] See Campbell *et al., op. cit.,* Chap. 15. The
above remarks on the Nazi movement are a condensation of a case study originally written as
part of this chapter.

[39] The most extreme shifts to the Nazis, arriving
at a peak of between 80 and 100% of the votes
in some hamlets, occurred in the central zone of
Schleswig-Holstein, the *Geest*. To the East and
West lay the sea, a somewhat more cosmopolitan
coast, better farmland with larger estates, and a
more stratified rural population. While the farmers of the *Geest* owned their own family farms
and have been designated as "lower middle class,"
they appear to have been subsistence farmers on
land that did not interest gentry. Heberle describes them as being "in mentality and habits
still more of a real peasant" than farmers in the

[36] Bendix, *ibid.,* pp. 604–5.

[37] Rudolf Heberle, *From Democracy to Nazism*
(Baton Rouge, 1945). See also Charles P. Loomis
and J. Allen Beegle, "The Spread of German

safe to conclude that the mass base of the Nazi movement represented one of the more unrelievedly ill-informed clienteles that a major political party has assembled in a modern state.

Heberle, who was anxious to show that Nazi popularity in Schleswig-Holstein was not the result of an ingrained antidemocratic bias, commented on how incredible it seemed that the Nazis should be so widely acceptable to these "generally soberminded and freedom-loving North Germans, who were not at all accustomed to a tradition of authoritarian government." He devoted a lengthy analysis to an attempt to find comparable belief elements in earlier ideational movements of Schleswig-Holstein that could explain the area's receptiveness to the new ideology. While occasional common threads could be discerned, their number was meager enough to be quite accidental, and antithetical elements predominated.[40] Heberle concluded that farmers and other rural people respond to politics less in terms of "ideologies and general political ideals" than in terms of "concrete advantages and disadvantages" of one party relative to another, and he closed with the hope that, under better circumstances, these rural people would "revert" to their more innocuous attitudes of the past.[41]

Even had the clientele of the Nazi Party been of average education and political sophistication, there would be strong reason to doubt the degree to which prior awareness of Nazi ideology among its voters could be claimed. In view of the actual peculiarities of its mass base, the question verges on the absurd. The Nazis promised changes in a system that was near collapse. Under comparable stresses, it is likely that large numbers of citizens in any society (and particularly those without any long-term affective ties to more traditional parties) would gladly support *ad hoc* promises of change without any great concern about ideological implications. And typically, they would lack the contextual information necessary to assess these implications, even if some stray details were absorbed. We believe this response would be true of any mass public and not only those that, like Germany, had experienced only a brief democratic tradition.[42]

---

other sectors, who regarded the *Geest* farmer "very much as the Southern hillbilly or redneck is looked upon by the planters." Heberle, *ibid.*, p. 39.

[40] Heberle and others have argued that the Nazi Party had particular appeal for villagers and rural people living in simple *gemeinschaft* societies because it demanded a degree of active and disciplined participation not required by other parties and such rural folk had a need to give themselves totally to a cause. At another point, however, Heberle implies that, although Schleswig-Holstein was the "most Nazi" province at the polls in both 1930 and 1932, it contributed but a meager share of activists or members to the party. See Heberle, *ibid.*, p. 87. What the mass base of the Nazi Party in its urban and rural segments seemed to share, in addition to a desperate desire for a change that would bring respite from economic duress, was low education or, in the case of the young, low political sophistication.

[41] Heberle, *ibid.*, pp. 100, 124.

[42] This is not to challenge the importance of a lengthening democratic tradition or of the bearing of its absence in the German case. But we suspect that once beyond the stabilizing influence of mass identifications with standard parties, the primary salutary effects of a longer democratic tradition are limited to elite political processes. Two hundred years of democracy and several decades of elementary civics courses in the United States have not given the model citizen much capacity to recognize antidemocratic maneuvers and movements, particularly when they occur "at home."

To the farmers in particular, the Nazis promised a moratorium on, if not an abolition of, all debts.[43] Furthermore, they had the disciplined and motivated party organization capable of disseminating such propaganda through the hinterland. While they had conceived of themselves as an urban party (which by origin and personnel they were), the Nazis appeared to have made a conscious discovery in the late 1920s that a golden harvest of votes had ripened in rural areas, and they set about to exploit this fact systematically, having become quite discouraged with their lack of progress in urban areas. The Communists had preceded them among the peasantry—but in an earlier and less propitious period—and they had relaxed their efforts. Furthermore, in view of Marxist dogma on the dubious political utility of the peasant, it is unlikely that their energies had ever been concentrated in quite the same manner. In principle, however, there is no reason to believe that, had the Communists instead of the Nazis arrived freshly on the rural scene at the same point and with similar vigor and sketchy propaganda, European history would not have taken a dramatically different turn. All evidence suggests that, in this historical case, the link between specific ideology and mass response was probably of the weakest.

CONCLUSION

We have long been intrigued, in dealing with attitudinal and behavioral materials drawn from cross-section

[43] Heberle, *ibid.*, p. 112.

publics, at the frequency with which the following sequence of events occurs. An hypothesis is formed that seems reasonable to the analyst, having to do with one or another set of systematic differences in perceptions, attitudes, or behavior patterns. The hypothesis is tested on materials from the general population but shows at best some rather uninteresting trace findings. Then the sample is further subdivided by formal education, which isolates among other groups the 10% of the American population with college degrees or the 20% with some college education. It frequently turns out that the hypothesis is then very clearly confirmed for the most educated, with results rapidly shading off to zero within the less educated majority of the population.

We do not claim that such an analytic approach always produces findings of this sort. From time to time, of course, the hypothesis in question can be more broadly rejected for all groups, and, on rare occasions, a relationship turns out to be sharper among the less educated than among the well-educated. Nevertheless, there is a strikingly large class of cases in which confirmation occurs only, or most sharply, among the well educated. Usually it is easy to see, after the fact if not before, the degree to which the dynamics of the processes assumed by the hypothesis rest upon the kinds of broad or abstract contextual information about currents of ideas, people, or society that educated people come to take for granted as initial ingredients of thought but that the most cursory studies will demonstrate are not widely shared. As experiences of this sort accumulate, we become increasingly sensitive to these basic problems of information and begin to predict their results in advance.

This awareness means that we come to expect hypotheses about wide-ranging yet highly integrated belief systems and their behavioral consequences to show results among relative elites but to be largely disconfirmed below them. It is our impression, for example, that even some of the more elaborate "ideological" patterns associated with the authoritarian personality syndrome follow this rule. Some recent results that have accumulated in connection with the Protestant-ethic hypothesis of Weber seem to hint at something of the same pattern as well.[44]

In this paper, we have attempted to make some systematic comments on this kind of phenomenon that seem crucial to any understanding of elite and mass belief systems. We have tried to show the character of this "continental shelf" between elites and masses and to locate the sources of differences in their belief systems in some simple characteristics of information and its social transmission.

The broad contours of elite decisions over time can depend in a vital way upon currents in what is loosely called "the history of ideas." These decisions in turn have effects upon the mass of more common citizens. But, of any direct participation in this history of ideas and the behavior it shapes, the mass is remarkably innocent. We do not disclaim the existence of entities that might best be called "folk ideologies," nor do we deny for a moment that strong differentiations in a variety of narrower values may be found within subcultures of less educated people. Yet for the familiar belief systems that, in view of their historical importance, tend most to attract the sophisticated observer, it is likely that an adequate mapping of a society (or, for that matter, the world) would provide a jumbled cluster of pyramids or a mountain range, with sharp delineation and differentiation in beliefs from elite apex to elite apex but with the mass bases of the pyramids overlapping in such profusion that it would be impossible to decide where one pyramid ended and another began.

---

[44] All investigators have had success in showing high "achievement motivation" among American Jews (a remarkably well educated group). Furthermore, some early findings confirmed Weber's thesis, in a modern setting, by showing higher achievement motivation among Protestants than among Catholics. Veroff, Feld, and Gurin, working with a national sample, were able, however, to replicate these findings only among higher-status Catholics and Protestants (with income the criterion) in the Northeast. This more sophisticated subpopulation is alleged to be the one within which the original confirmations were found. See J. Veroff, S. Feld, and G. Gurin, "Achievement Motivation and Religious Background," *American Sociological Review*, 27 (April, 1962), 205. While even poorly educated adherents of differing creeds can probably be counted on for fairly accurate knowledge of concrete matters of ritual and mundane taboos, they would be much less likely to absorb the broad and abstract theological conceptions that are the crucial "intervening variables" in the Weberian hypothesis.

FOR FURTHER READING

ALMOND, Gabriel and Sidney Verba, *The Civil Culture* (Boston: Little, Brown, 1963).

CAMPBELL, Angus, Philip E. Converse, Warren E. Miller, and Donald E. Stokes, *The American Voter* (New York: Wiley, 1964).

DREYER, Edward C. and Walter A. Rosenbaum (Eds.), *Political Opinion and Electoral Behavior* (Belmont, Calif.: Wadsworth, 1966).

FISHBEIN, Martin (Ed.), *Readings in Attitude Theory and Measurement* (New York: Wiley, 1967).

KATZ, Elihu and Paul F. Lazarsfeld, *Personal Influence* (New York: Dryden Press, 1954).

KEY, V. O., Jr., *Public Opinion and American Democracy* (New York: Knopf, 1962).

LUTTBEG, Norman R. (Ed.), *Public Opinion and Public Policy: Models of Political Linkage* (Homewood: Dorsey Press, 1968).

MATTHEWS, Donald R. and James W. Prothro, *Negroes and the New Southern Politics* (New York: Harcourt, Brace and World, 1966).

MILBRATH, Lester, *Political Participation* (Chicago: Rand McNally, 1965).

SCHUBERT, Glendon (Ed.), *Judicial Decision-Making* (New York: Free Press, 1963).

PART
FIVE:
COMMUNICATION

"Attitude change," we are told, "depends very generally on the receipt of *new information* that in some way or another is relevant to the attitude object from the point of view of the attitude holder." [1] This fact, the reasons for which were explored at some length in the last section, clearly points the way to communication theory. In terms of this theory, communication is considered to have taken place precisely when some *new information* is received.

Of all the theories we are considering in this book, communication theory has been developed most recently. The solution of the engineering problems of any age yields concepts which shape its thought, and these concepts, of course, leave a residue of metaphors in the language. "If the 17th and 18th centuries were the age of clocks, and the latter 18th and 19th centuries the age of steam engines, the present time is the age of communication and control." [2] And out of the solution of certain communication problems grew a theory which was seen to have wider application.

Every theory, of course, has antecedents. Communication theory, with its reliance on the statistical mechanics of Boltzmann and Gibbs, is no exception. But new theories are not discovered by being logically inferred from their predecessors. A crucial stage in the birth process of any theory is the recognition of certain concepts as being those around which a network of other concepts can be constructed to form a theory. The central concepts in communication theory were not recognized until recent decades.

Considerable research began to be devoted to communication with the advent of the telegraph and telephone. The sophistication of this work increased with the introduction of the more complex electronic systems of radio, television, radar, and computers. R. V. L. Hartley, writing in the *Bell System Technical Journal* in 1928, defined *information* as the successive selection of signs or words from a given list. He also showed that a logarithm could be used as a measure of a *quantity of information,* and that the transmission of such a quantity of information depended on bandwidth (*i.e.,* channel capacity) and time. [3]

More general realization of the importance of the concept of *information* came during the 1940's to a group of men associated with Norbert Wiener. Wiener was a Massachusetts Institute of Technology mathematician then concerned with the early development of computers, the solution of problems of air-

---

[1] Theodore M. Newcomb, Ralph H. Turner, and Philip E. Converse, *Social Psychology: The Study of Human Interaction* (Holt, Rinehart and Winston, 1965), p. 82. [Italics in original]

[2] Norbert Wiener, "Cybernetics" *Scientific American,* November, 1948, p. 14.

[3] For a discussion of these historical developments, see Colin Cherry, *On Human Communication* (New York: Wiley Science Editions, 1961), chapter 2.

craft tracking, and investigation of similarities between electrical systems and the human nervous system. As Professor Wiener later recounted the development,

> On the communication engineering it had already become obvious to Mr. Bigelow and myself that the problems of control engineering and communication engineering were inseparable, and that they centered not around the technique of electrical engineering but around the much more fundamental notion of the message, whether it should be transmitted by electrical, mechanical, or nervous means. . . . To cover this aspect of communication engineering, we had to develop a statistical theory of the amount of information, in which the unit—amount of information—was that transmitted as a single decision between equally probable alternatives. This idea occurred at about the same time to several writers, among them the statistician R. A. Fisher, Dr. Shannon of the Bell Telephone Laboratories, and the author. Fisher's motive in studying this subject is to be found in classical statistical theory; that of Shannon in the problem of coding information; and that of the author in the problem of noise and message in electrical filters.[4]

News about this concept spread rapidly through the scientific community, first through a series of professional "seminars," then more broadly with the publication of Norbert Wiener's *Cybernetics* in 1948.

The classic statement of communication theory per se came in *The Mathematical Theory of Communication* in 1949. This book consisted of two parts. First was a paper by Claude E. Shannon (who, incidentally, had been a student of Wiener's at M.I.T.) setting forth the statistical theory. This had been published the preceding year in the *Bell System Technical Journal.* The second part was an exposition of the theory in less technical language by Warren Weaver. Weaver, himself a mathematician and a leading figure in the American scientific community, has long been interested in making important ideas accessible to a wider public. He did exactly this in his contribution to the Shannon-Weaver volume. "The Mathematics of Communication," the first paper in this section, is based upon this work. Warren Weaver first explains the basic concepts of the theory, then turns to the range of its possible applications, and ends with a reflection on its aesthetic attraction.

The unit of measure devised for information is called *entropy*. This name is useful for suggesting a correspondence between communication theory and physics, but it might have been better if the unit had been called "amount of information transmitted." It is simply a statistical parameter (conventionally denoted by H) that indicates the probability of one particular message being sent (or received) from the set of all possible messages. Its value is zero if a given message is certain to be sent, and it assumes its maximum value if all messages in the set of messages have an equal probability of being sent. Hence, *in terms of this very special definition*, we say that no communication has taken place unless the recipient gets some new information, that is, some message whose content he could not have predicted in advance.

---

[4] Norbert Wiener, *Cybernetics* (Boston: The Technology Press, 1948), pp. 15–18. Wiener also acknowledges his indebtedness to the Russian mathematician, V. A. Kolmogoroff, but notes that (as frequently happens) his own work was far along before his attention was called to Kolmogoroff's work.

"The great central theorem for this whole communication theory," as Warren Weaver refers to it, concerns the possibility of devising a code for use on a noisy channel.[5] However, a relationship which is perhaps more significant for *interpersonal* communication concerns the rate of information transfer.[6]

$$R = H(source) + H(destination) - H(source, destination)$$

This says that the rate of information transmitted will be equal to the sum of entropy of the source and the entropy of the destination minus their joint entropy. In other words, the rate depends on the probability that person A will transmit a particular message, the probability that person B will receive it, and the (resulting) probability that the message can be transmitted between persons A and B. Now if a particular message is certain to be sent, H(source) = 0; and if a particular message is certain to be received, H(destination) = 0. Therefore if persons A and B are totally acquainted with each others' opinions, the rate of information transmission will be zero because the source and destination entropies both equal zero. If, on the other hand, persons A and B hold no opinions in common, the rate of transmission will also be equal to zero because when the source and destination probabilities are independent of each other,

$$H(source, destination) = H(source) + H(destination).$$

It follows that the relationship between the rate of communication and the extent of attitudinal agreement will be that shown in Figure V-1. There is no empirical work to confirm this,[7] but it is plausible if one thinks of persons A and B in terms

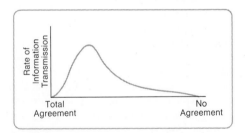

Figure V-1.   Information transmission and attitudinal agreement

[5] You may recall from the Introduction that noise refers to the presence of any signal in a channel other than those intended by the sender.

[6] R. Duncan Luce, "The Theory of Selective Information and Some of its Behavioral Applications" in R. Duncan Luce (Ed.), *Developments in Mathematical Psychology* (Glencoe, Ill.: The Free Press, 1960), p. 39.

[7] There are very difficult problems in operationalizing the concept of entropy for a human being. Think of yourself as an information source, and try to make a list of all the things you might say. The concept of probability does apply since you are very likely to say some things and very unlikely to say others. The complexity of the problem lies in the length of the list of things you might say, and the difficulty of assigning probabilities to all of them. And, of course, an interpersonal problem would be more difficult than an individual problem. The electronic networks that give rise to this theory are much simpler than human networks.

of their respective cognitive systems. If their attitudinal systems are identical, nothing is added to the cognitive structures of either A or B when either articulates one of their common thoughts. Hence no communication. If their cognitive structures are quite similar but each has some ideas of his own, A's ideas are likely to be expressed in a way so B can easily add them to his own cognitions. Hence communication would be quite easy. But if their cognitive structures were completely dissimilar in organization and content, A would not be able to say anything B could understand. Again the result would be no communication.[8]

Information theory is very suggestive, but relatively little research on politics has been consciously designed to test it. In Duncan Luce's phrase, it has proven to be "like a new mistress," full of promise, but elusive.[9] The payoff of the theory thus far has been largely heuristic. Our attention has been directed to the technical problem, the semantic problem, and the effectiveness problem as being crucial questions in communications. But what we *know* about communications rests on research such as that guided by the models of attitude change discussed in the last section and simulation along the lines of the Abelson–Bernstein model discussed in the Introduction.[10]

An admirable summary of our knowledge of interpersonal communication is found in "Communication in Organizations" by Harold Guetzkow, whose range of ability is suggested by the fact that he holds academic appointments in three different Departments (psychology, sociology, and political science) at Northwestern University. We can see that it is proper to conceptualize this information as referring to the technical problem—the accuracy of transference of information from sender to receiver—in the context of communication theory. Interpersonal communication does have certain fixed characteristics. In fact, one can sum up the studies surveyed by Professor Guetzkow by saying the technical problem in human communication derives from its being communication between *positions*. Here the concept of position has the same meaning as in role theory. A position is occupied by a person whose behavior is determined by certain role expectations. Consequently some of the distortion found in interpersonal communication stems from the information processing characteristics of all human beings; other more specific biases are introduced by the role behavior of the person occupying the particular position. We see the general human characteristics, for example, in D. T. Campbell's "Systematic Error on the Part of Human Links in Communication Systems," and in the discussion of the effects of cognitive structuring in the work of Charles Osgood and Robert Zajonc. Professor Guetzkow invites our attention to the biases introduced by those occupying specific organizational positions at many points including his reference to lack of candor in reports to hier-

---

[8] Additional plausibility is given to the curve in Figure V–1 because of its similarity to the hypothetical curve suggested by Newcomb, Turner, and Converse relating exposure to new information during a political campaign to the probability of attitude change. See *Social Psychology*, p. 81.

[9] Luce, "The Theory of Selective Information and Some of its Behavioral Applications," p. 51.

[10] For various simulation models incorporating present knowledge about communication, see William D. Coplin (Ed.), *Simulation in the Study of Politics* (Chicago: Markham, 1968); Hayward R. Alker, Jr., Richard Brody, and Benjamin Page, "A Model of the Electoral Process," (August, 1968, mimeographed); and Donald R. Matthews and James A. Stimson, "Decision-Making by U. S. Representatives: A Preliminary Model," a paper prepared for presentation at a Conference on Political Decision-Making sponsored by the Sperry-Hutchinson Foundation and the University of Kentucky Department of Political Science, April 10–11, 1968.

archical superiors, the systematic bias that is functional for certain staff positions, and what Richard Cyert and James March call "interpretive adjustment"— "counterbiases to adjust for such biases as they anticipate in the data they receive." The generality of these characteristics of interpersonal communication is seen in Professor Guetzkow's argument that they also can be employed to explain rumor transmission, a phenomenon which has been studied to isolate its supposedly unique characteristics.

"Semantic Difficulties in International Communication," by Edmund S. Glenn, a diplomat professionally concerned with problems of translation, deals with the particularly arduous chores faced by negotiators in finding words that will convey an accurate meaning to those coming from different cultures. Communication theory holds that the semantic problem is quite real, but it also assumes that a code can be devised if the would-be communicator is sufficiently patient. In international communication, however, two additional complications sometimes make it impossible for representatives of two cultures to convey their meaning to one another. When translating from one language to another, the word in the second language which corresponds most closely to the word in the first may have entirely different connotations. And one's cognitive structure is at least partly formed by his culture. If the typical thought patterns are different in the two cultures, the rate of expected information transfer between representatives of the two cultures may be very low indeed. As Glenn tells us, "the purely linguistic problem can be solved superbly, insofar as translation and interpretation may solve it, by the staff of the United Nations Secretariat." But the problems caused by differing connotations of words and differing cognitive structures remain.

Drawing on the work of Professor Karl Pribam, Mr. Glenn distinguishes between four patterns of thought: intuitional in which there are few apparent links between concepts,[11] nominalistic in which particular objects are linked together because experience has shown that it is convenient to do so, universalistic in which links run from general concepts to more particular ones, and dialectic thinking in which the links between historically opposed concepts determine new ones. Arguing that the nominalistic, universalistic, and dialectic cognitive structures are characteristic of the English-speaking, French, and Russian delegates, respectively, Glenn goes ahead to illustrate how these different modes of thinking complicate international communication by analyzing exchanges in the United Nations Security Council. Granting that the disagreement he analyzes has a substantive political basis as well as semantic roots, it is also apparent that the diplomats have been unable to devise a mutually understood code which will accurately convey their views to each other.

The third problem mentioned by Warren Weaver, communication effectiveness, is dealt with in "Ordeal by Debate" by Kurt and Gladys Lang, a team of sociologists who have done a great deal of work on the effects of mass media, particularly television. In this paper, they report a panel study (*i.e.*, a series of interviews) with New York City respondents to determine the impact of the 1960 debates between two men, John Kennedy and Richard Nixon, both of whom were to

[11] Glenn does not use this category of intuitional thought in his later analysis, but he does make the point that it is frequently associated with extreme nationalism. The lack of cognitive links between concepts may be a characteristic of many fringe movements in politics. Hence the emphasis in such movements in "belief in the Cause," and the difficulty in criticizing the ideology of members of fringe movements on a "rational" basis.

become Presidents of the United States. Here we see some things we could expect from our earlier readings. There was a considerable "surprise effect." Viewers had expected Vice President Nixon to do better than Senator Kennedy; signals about Senator Kennedy's ability therefore had a higher information value and were widely perceived. The information which was received was cognized in a way to be consistent with the respondent's dominant values. The Langs point to three techniques, isolation, selective perception, and personalization, which were used to reduce cognitive dissonance on the part of the respondents.

The desire of the candidates, of course, was to communicate to the voters so as to lead the voters to cast ballots for them. It is difficult to say that the "meaning conveyed to the receiver led to the desired conduct on his part," and that the communication was effective in this sense. The Langs tell us that Senator Kennedy "drew his added strength largely from weak Democratic party identifiers. . . . The majority [of the intra-campaign switchers] merely responded to inclinations which had clearly been present before the debates." [12] But it is also true that there was a net improvement in the respondents' evaluations of John Kennedy after watching the first debate, and that this change in their evaluation of the Massachusetts Senator coincided with the decision of several to vote for him. The Langs are much too careful in their statements to claim that this was the decisive influence in an election as close as 1960, but if the factors discerned in this New York City study operated elsewhere, then these communication effects were among the influences which made Richard Nixon delay his inauguration as President until January 20, 1969.

"Communication in Bureaus" by Anthony Downs covers some of the same material dealt with by Harold Guetzkow in "Communication in Organizations," and it is interesting to compare the two. Guetzkow's professional training was in social psychology while Downs's was in economics. These disciplines use different ways of conceptualizing the same phenomena. As William C. Mitchell puts it, "The political sociologist wants a great deal more simplicity for any small sacrifice of realism, while the economist will give up a great deal of realism to attain a small increment of simplicity." [13] Essentially social psychologists and economists accent different theoretical criteria. The social psychologists are more concerned with operational definitions for their concepts. Economists stress theoretical links between arbitrarily defined concepts. The result of these different accents is that it is often easier to apply the theories of social psychologists in the real world whereas it is often easier to perform logical operations with the simpler theories of the economists. These contrasts are very clear in the Guetzkow and Downs articles. The former is richly documented; the prose in the latter is lean and terse. Harold Guetzkow suggests many more possibilities about organizational communications. Anthony Downs is able to summarize all he wants to say in a series of twelve propositions.

Wilbur Schramm, whose "Communication in Crisis" closes this section, is the author of many distinguished works on communication research. This particular article introduces a collection of studies on the Kennedy assassination. A number of talented behavioral scientists were able to mount studies quickly

---

[12] Kurt Lang and Gladys E. Lang, "Ordeal by Debate: Viewer Reactions," *Public Opinion Quarterly*, Summer, 1961, p. 280.

[13] "The Shape of Political Theory to Come: From Political Sociology to Political Economy," *American Behavioral Scientist*, Nov.–Dec. 1967, p. 20.

enough to capture these fugitive data before they were lost; Professor Schramm draws their findings together into a general interpretation. These studies enable us to answer many of the questions suggested by communication theory. We know what happened. We know the rate at which this information was transmitted. We know the words and the pictures that were used to encode these complex messages. And we know the effects these messages had upon the persons who ultimately received them. Yet in the skilled hands of Professor Schramm, we learn much more. He tells us not simply about the assassination of a particular American President, but uses this event as a vehicle to write generally about "the powerful direct effects of which the mass media are capable," and to present some general theories about communications at the time of a disaster.

This paper is another example of how microlevel knowledge can provide a power explanation of system level phenomena. Schramm is explicit about his interest in systems.

> When a crisis interrupts the slow, ongoing rhythms of communication —scanning the environment, disposing of the day-to-day needs and problems of the system, filing away and sharing the increment of experience— the rate of information flow is enormously increased. A message signals the emergency. Information rushes to and from the point of crisis, which becomes a new focus of attention as the system strives to adjust to the problem. This is the case regardless of the size of the system. . . . Systems theory would describe the response to crisis as a sudden imbalance in the system, followed by emergency steps to restore balance, and then by a gradual restoration of normal functioning around whatever new balance is achieved.[14]

There are three clear stages in Professor Schramm's analysis: first, the initial shocking message from Dallas; second, the interruption of all regular programming to focus first on the events in Dallas and then on the mourning in Washington, D. C.; finally, an increasing number of messages stressing the theme that a normal transition had taken place, that a new Chief Executive was at the head of the government. But what gives this analysis real strength, is that Schramm is able to depict these stages at three analytical levels—the system level, the institutional level, and the individual level. He tells us how the total system responded, what the various media did, and a great deal about the feelings and behavior of American citizens. It is the incorporation of microlevel data that makes Professor Schramm's macrolevel explanation persuasive. "When the experience is seen in this way, it is somewhat easier to understand why the experience was so largely grief rather than anxiety, why Americans closed the book on an anxiety over conspiracy more quickly than Europeans did, and why the recovery after the weekend of grief came so comparatively soon, came with elements of rededication and reintegration rather than divisiveness and disquiet." [15] Thus, we have reason to conclude that microanalysis and macroanalysis are not rivals, but rather that microanalysis is a necessary component in a sufficient macroanalysis.

---

[14] Wilbur Schramm, "Communication in Crisis" in Bradley S. Greenberg and Edwin B. Parker (Eds.), *The Kennedy Assassination and the American Public* (Stanford: Stanford University Press, 1965), pp. 5–7.

[15] Schramm, "Communication in Crisis," p. 24.

THE MATHEMATICS
OF COMMUNICATION
WARREN WEAVER

How do men communicate, one with another? The spoken word, either direct or by telephone or radio; the written or printed word, transmitted by hand, by post, by telegraph, or in any other way—these are obvious and common forms of communication. But there are many others. A nod or a wink, a drumbeat in the jungle, a gesture pictured on a television screen, the blinking of a signal light, a bit of music that reminds one of an event in the past, puffs of smoke in the desert air, the movements and posturing in a ballet—all of these are means men use to convey ideas.

The word communication, in fact, will be used here in a very broad sense to include all of the procedures by which one mind can affect another. Although the language used will often refer specifically to the communication of speech, practically everything said applies equally to music, to pictures, to a variety of other methods of conveying information.

In communication there seem to be problems at three levels: 1) technical, 2) semantic, and 3) influential.

The technical problems are concerned with the accuracy of transference of information from sender to receiver. They are inherent in all forms of communication, whether by sets of discrete symbols (written speech), or by a varying signal (telephonic or radio transmission of voice or music), or by a varying two-dimensional pattern (television).

The semantic problems are concerned with the interpretation of meaning by the receiver, as compared with the intended meaning of the sender. This is a very deep and involved situation, even when one deals only with the relatively simple problems of communicating through speech. For example, if Mr. X is suspected not to understand what Mr. Y says, then it is not possible, by having Mr. Y do nothing but talk further with Mr. X, completely to clarify this situation in any finite time. If Mr. Y says "Do you now understand me?" and Mr. X says "Certainly I do," this is not necessarily a certification that understanding has been achieved. It may just be that Mr. X did not understand the question. If this sounds silly, try it again as "Czy pan mnie rozumie?" with the answer "Hai wakkate imasu." In the restricted field of speech communication, the difficulty may be reduced to a tolerable size, but never completely eliminated, by "explanations." They are presumably never more than approximations to the ideas being explained, but are understandable when phrased in language that has previously been made reasonably clear by usage. For example, it does not take long to make the symbol for "yes" in any language understandable.

The problems of influence or effectiveness are concerned with the success with which the meaning conveyed to the receiver leads to the desired conduct of his part. It may seem at first glance undesirably narrow to imply that the purpose of all communication is to influence the conduct of the receiver. But with any reasonably broad definition of conduct, it is clear that communication either affects conduct or is without any discernible and provable effect at all.

One might be inclined to think that the technical problems involve only the engineering details of good design of a communication system, while the semantic and the effectiveness problems contain most if not all of the philosophical content of the general problem of communication. To see that this is not the case, we must now examine some important recent work in the mathematical theory of communication.

This is by no means a wholly new theory. As the mathematician John von Neumann has pointed out, the 19th-century Austrian physicist Ludwig Boltzmann suggested that some concepts of statistical mechanics were applicable to the concept of information. Other scientists, notably Norbert Wiener of the Massachusetts Institute of Technology, have made profound contributions. The work which will be here reported is that of Claude Shannon of the Bell Telephone Laboratories, which was preceded by that of H. Nyquist and R. V. L. Hartley in the same organization. This work applies

in the first instance only to the technical problem, but the theory has broader significance. To begin with, meaning and effectiveness are inevitably restricted by the theoretical limits of accuracy in symbol transmission. Even more significant, a theoretical analysis of the technical problem reveals that it overlaps the semantic and the effectiveness problems more than one might suspect.

A communication system is symbolically represented in the drawing in Figure V-2. The information source selects a desired message out of a set of possible messages. (As will be shown, this is a particularly important function.) The transmitter changes this message into a signal which is sent over the communication channel to the receiver.

The receiver is a sort of inverse transmitter, changing the transmitted signal back into a message, and handing this message on to the destination. When I talk to you, my brain is the information source, yours the destination; my vocal system is the transmitter, and your ear with the eighth nerve is the receiver.

In the process of transmitting the signal, it is unfortunately characteristic that certain things not intended by the information source are added to the signal. These unwanted additions may be distortions of sound (in telephony, for example), or static (in radio), or distortions in the shape or shading of a picture (television), or errors in transmission (telegraphy or facsimile). All these changes in the signal may be called noise.

The questions to be studied in a communication system have to do with the amount of information, the capac-

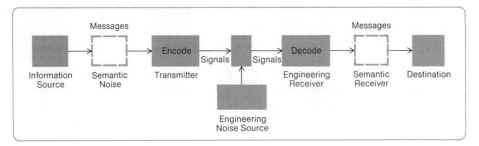

Figure V-2. Communication System. A communication system may be reduced to three fundamental elements. In telephony the signal is a varying electric current, and the channel is a wire. In speech the signal is varying sound pressure, and channel the air. Frequently, things not intended by the information source are impressed on the signal. The static of radio is one example; distortion in telephony is another. All these additions may be called noise. This diagram is adapted by Harold Guetzkow from a schematic diagram of a general communication system developed by Claude E. Shannon, with the suggestions (in dotted lines) of Warren Weaver. See Shannon and Weaver, The Mathematical Theory of Communication (*Urbana: University of Illinois Press, 1949), pp. 5, 115–116.*

ity of the communication channel, the coding process that may be used to change a message into a signal and the effects of noise.

First off, we have to be clear about the rather strange way in which, in this theory, the word "information" is used; for it has a special sense which, among other things, must not be confused at all with meaning. It is surprising but true that, from the present viewpoint, two messages, one heavily loaded with meaning and the other pure nonsense, can be equivalent as regards information.

In fact, in this new theory the word information relates not so much to what you *do* say, as to what you *could* say. That is, information is a measure of your freedom of choice when you select a message. If you are confronted with a very elementary situation where you have to choose one of two alternative messages, then it is arbitrarily said that the information associated with this situation is unity.

The concept of information applies not to the individual messages, as the concept of meaning would, but rather to the situation as a whole, the unit information indicating that in this situation one has an amount of freedom of choice, in selecting a message, which it is convenient to regard as a standard or unit amount. The two messages between which one must choose in such a selection can be anything one likes. One might be the King James version of the Bible, and the other might be "Yes."

The remarks thus far relate to artificially simple situations where the information source is free to choose only among several definite messages —like a man picking out one of a set of standard birthday-greeting telegrams. A more natural and more important situation is that in which the information source makes a sequence of choices from some set of elementary symbols, the selected sequence then forming the message. Thus a man may pick out one word after another, these individually selected words then adding up to the message.

Obviously probability plays a major role in the generation of the message, and the choices of the successive symbols depend upon the preceding choices. Thus, if we are concerned with English speech, and if the last symbol chosen is "the," then the probability that the next word will be an article, or a verb form other than a verbal, is very small. After the three words "in the event," the probability for "that" as the next word is fairly high, and for "elephant" as the next word is very low. Similarly, the probability is low for such a sequence of words as "Constantinople fishing nasty pink." Incidentally, it is low, but not zero, for it is perfectly possible to think of a passage in which one sentence closes with "Constantinople fishing," and the next begins with "Nasty pink." (We might observe in passing that the sequence under discussion *has* occurred in a single good English sentence, namely the one second preceding.)

As a matter of fact, Shannon has shown that when letters or words chosen at random are set down in sequences dictated by probability considerations alone, they tend to arrange themselves in meaningful words and phrases.

Now let us return to the idea of information. The quantity which uniquely meets the natural requirements that one sets up for a measure of information turns out to be exactly that which is known in thermodynamics as entropy, or the degree of randomness, or of "shuffledness" if you

will, in a situation. It is expressed in terms of the various probabilities involved.

To those who have studied the physical sciences, it is most significant that an entropy-like expression appears in communication theory as a measure of information. The concept of entropy, introduced by the German physicist Rudolf Clausius nearly 100 years ago, closely associated with the name of Boltzmann, and given deep meaning by Willard Gibbs of Yale in his classic work on statistical mechanics, has become so basic and pervasive a concept that Sir Arthur Eddington remarked: "The law that entropy always increases—the second law of thermodynamics—holds, I think, the supreme position among the laws of Nature."

Thus when one meets the concept of entropy in communication theory, he has a right to be rather excited. That information should be measured by entropy is, after all, natural when we remember that information is associated with the amount of freedom of choice we have in constructing messages. Thus one can say of a communication source, just as he would also say of a thermodynamic ensemble: "This situation is highly organized; it is not characterized by a large degree of randomness or of choice—that is to say, the information, or the entropy, is low."

We must keep in mind that in the mathematical theory of communication we are concerned not with the meaning of individual messages but with the whole statistical nature of the information source. Thus one is not surprised that the capacity of a channel of communication is to be described in terms of the amount of information it can transmit, or better, in terms of its ability to transmit what is produced out of a source of a given information.

The transmitter may take a written message and use some code to encipher this message into, say, a sequence of numbers, these numbers then being sent over the channel as the signal. Thus one says, in general, that the function of the transmitter is to encode, and that of the receiver to decode, the message. The theory provides for very sophisticated transmitters and receivers—such, for example, as possess "memories," so that the way they encode a certain symbol of the message depends not only upon this one symbol but also upon previous symbols of the message and the way they have been encoded.

We are now in a position to state the fundamental theorem for a noiseless channel transmitting discrete symbols. This theorem relates to a communication channel which has a capacity of C units per second, accepting signals from an information source of H units per second. The theorem states that by devising proper coding procedures for the transmitter it is possible to transmit symbols over the channel at an average rate which is nearly C/H, but which, no matter how clever the coding, can never be made to exceed C/H.

Viewed superficially, say in rough analogy to the use of transformers to match impedances in electrical circuits, it seems very natural, although certainly pretty neat, to have this theorem which says that efficient coding is that which matches the statistical characteristics of information source and channel. But when it is examined in detail for any one of the vast array of situations to which this result applies, one realizes how deep and powerful this theory is.

How does noise affect information? Information, we must steadily remember, is a measure of one's freedom of choice in selecting a message. The greater this freedom of choice, the greater is the uncertainty that the message actually selected is some particular one. Thus greater freedom of choice, greater uncertainty and greater information all go hand in hand.

If noise is introduced, then the received message contains certain distortions, certain errors, certain extraneous material, that would certainly lead to increased uncertainty. But if the uncertainty is increased, the information is increased, and this sounds as though the noise were beneficial!

It is true that when there is noise, the received signal is selected out of a more varied set of signals than was intended by the sender. This situation beautifully illustrates the semantic trap into which one can fall if he does not remember that "information" is used here with a special meaning that measures freedom of choice and hence uncertainty as to what choice has been made. Uncertainty that arises by virtue of freedom of choice on the part of the sender is desirable uncertainty. Uncertainty that arises because of errors or because of the influence of noise is undesirable uncertainty. To get the useful information in the received signal we must subtract the spurious portion. This is accomplished, in the theory, by establishing a quantity known as the "equivocation," meaning the amount of ambiguity introduced by noise. One then refines or extends the previous definition of the capacity of a noiseless channel, and states that the capacity of a noisy channel is defined to be equal to the maximum rate at which useful information (*i.e.*, total uncertainty minus noise uncertainty) can be transmitted over the channel.

Now, finally, we can state the great central theorem of this whole communication theory. Suppose a noisy channel of capacity C is accepting information from a source of entropy H, entropy corresponding to the number of possible messages from the source. If the channel capacity C is equal to or larger than H, then by devising appropriate coding systems the output of the source can be transmitted over the channel with as little error as one pleases. But if the channel capacity C is less than H, the entropy of the source, then it is impossible to devise codes which reduce the error frequency as low as one may please.

However clever one is with the coding process, it will always be true that after the signal is received there remains some undesirable uncertainty about what the message was; and this undesirable uncertainty—this noise or equivocation—will always be equal to or greater than H minus C. But there is always at least one code capable of reducing this undesirable uncertainty down to a value that exceeds H minus C by a small amount.

This powerful theorem gives a precise and almost startlingly simple description of the utmost dependability one can ever obtain from a communication channel which operates in the presence of noise. One must think a

long time, and consider many applications, before he fully realizes how powerful and general this amazingly compact theorem really is. One single application can be indicated here, but in order to do so, we must go back for a moment to the idea of the information of a source.

Having calculated the entropy (or the information, or the freedom of choice) of a certain information source, one can compare it to the maximum value this entropy could have, subject only to the condition that the source continue to employ the same symbols. The ratio of the actual to the maximum entropy is called the relative entropy of the source. If the relative entropy of a certain source is, say, eight-tenths, this means roughly that this source is, in its choice of symbols to form a message, about 80 percent as free as it could possibly be with these same symbols. One minus the relative entropy is called the "redundancy." That is to say, this fraction of the message is unnecessary in the sense that if it were missing the message would still be essentially complete, or at least could be completed.

It is most interesting to note that the redundancy of English is just about 50 percent. In other words, about half of the letters or words we choose in writing or speaking are under our free choice, and about half are really controlled by the statistical structure of the language, although we are not ordinarily aware of it. Incidentally, this is just about the minimum of freedom (or relative entropy) in the choice of letters that one must have to be able to construct satisfactory crossword puzzles. In a language that had only 20 percent of freedom, or 80 percent redundancy, it would be impossible to construct crossword puzzles in sufficient complexity and number to make the game popular.

Now since English is about 50 percent redundant, it would be possible to save about one-half the time of ordinary telegraphy by a proper encoding process, provided one transmitted over a noiseless channel. When there is noise on a channel, however, there is some real advantage in not using a coding process that eliminates all of the redundancy. For the remaining redundancy helps combat the noise. It is the high redundancy of English, for example, that makes it easy to correct errors in spelling that have arisen during transmission.

The communication systems dealt with so far involve the use of a discrete set of symbols—say letters—only moderately numerous. One might well expect that the theory would become almost indefinitely more complicated when it seeks to deal with continuous messages such as those of the speaking voice, with its continuous variation of pitch and energy. As is often the case, however, a very interesting mathematical theorem comes to the rescue. As a practical matter, one is always interested in a continuous signal which is built up of simple harmonic constituents, not of all frequencies but only of those that lie wholly within a band from zero to, say, W cycles per second. Thus very satisfactory communication can be achieved over a telephone channel that handles frequencies up to about 4,000, although the human voice does contain higher frequencies. With frequencies up to 10,000 or 12,-000, high-fidelity radio transmission of symphonic music is possible.

The theorem that helps us is one which states that a continuous signal, T seconds in duration and band-limited in frequency to the range from zero to W, can be completely specified by stating 2TW numbers. This is really a remarkable theorem. Ordinarily a continuous curve can be defined only approximately by a finite number of points. But if the curve is built up out of simple harmonic constituents of a limited number of frequencies, as a complex sound is built up out of a limited number of pure tones, then a finite number of quantities is all that is necessary to define the curve completely.

Thanks partly to this theorem, and partly to the essential nature of the situation, it turns out that the extended theory of continuous communication is somewhat more difficult and complicated mathematically, but not essentially different from the theory for discrete symbols. Many of the statements for the discrete case require no modification for the continuous case, and others require only minor change.

The mathematical theory of communication is so general that one does not need to say what kinds of symbols are being considered—whether written letters or words, or musical notes, or spoken words, or symphonic music, or pictures. The relationships it reveals apply to all these and to other forms of communication. The theory is so imaginatively motivated that it deals with the real inner core of the communication problem.

One evidence of its generality is that the theory contributes importantly to, and in fact is really the basic theory of, cryptography, which is of course a form of coding. In a similar way, the theory contributes to the problem of translation from one language to another, although the complete story here clearly requires consideration of meaning, as well as of information. Similarly, the ideas developed in this work connect so closely with the problem of the logical design of computing machines that it is no surprise that Shannon has written a paper on the design of a computer that would be capable of playing a skillful game of chess. And it is of further pertinence to the present contention that his paper closes with the remark that either one must say that such a computer "thinks," or one must substantially modify the conventional implication of the verb "to think."

The theory goes further. Though ostensibly applicable only to problems at the technical level, it is helpful and suggestive at the levels of semantics and effectiveness as well. The formal diagram of a communication system in Figure V-2 can, in all likelihood, be extended to include the central issues of meaning and effectiveness.

Thus when one moves to those levels it may prove to be essential to take account of the statistical characteristics of the destination. One can imagine, as an addition to the diagram, another box labeled "Semantic Receiver" interposed between the engineering receiver (which changes signals to messages) and the destination. This semantic receiver subjects the message to a second decoding, the demand on this one being that it must match the statistical semantic characteristics of the message to the statistical semantic capacities of the totality of receivers, or of that subset of receivers which constitutes the audience one wishes to affect.

Similarly one can imagine another box in the diagram which, inserted between the information source and the transmitter, would be labeled "Semantic Noise" (not to be confused with "engineering noise"). This would represent distortions of meaning introduced by the information source, such as a speaker, which are not intentional but nevertheless affect the destination, or listener. And the problem of semantic decoding must take this semantic noise into account. It is also possible to think of a treatment or adjustment of the original message that would make the sum of message meaning plus semantic noise equal to the desired total message meaning at the destination.

Another way in which the theory can be helpful in improving communication is suggested by the fact that error and confusion arise and fidelity decreases when, no matter how good the coding, one tries to crowd too much over a channel. A general theory at all levels will surely have to take into account not only the capacity of the channel but also (even the words are right!) the capacity of the audience. If you overcrowd the capacity of the audience, it is probably true, by direct analogy, that you do not fill the audience up and then waste only the remainder by spilling. More likely, and again by direct analogy, you force a general error and confusion.

The concept of information developed in this theory at first seems disappointing and bizarre—disappointing because it has nothing to do with meaning, and bizarre because it deals not with a single message but rather with the statistical character of a whole ensemble of messages, bizarre also because in these statistical terms the words information and uncertainty find themselves partners.

But we have seen upon further examination of the theory that this analysis has so penetratingly cleared the air that one is now perhaps for the first time ready for a real theory of meaning. An engineering communication theory is just like a very proper and discreet girl at the telegraph office accepting your telegram. She pays no attention to the meaning, whether it be sad or joyous or embarrassing. But she must be prepared to deal intelligently with all messages that come to her desk. This idea that a communication system ought to try to deal with all possible messages, and that the intelligent way to try is to base design on the statistical character of the source, is surely not without significance for communication in general. Language must be designed, or developed, with a view to the totality of things that man may wish to say; but not being able to accomplish everything, it should do as well as possible as often as possible. That is to say, it too should deal with its task statistically.

This study reveals facts about the statistical structure of the English language, as an example, which must seem significant to students of every phase of language and communication. It suggests, as a particularly promising lead, the application of probability theory to semantic studies. Especially pertinent is the powerful body of probability theory dealing with what mathematicians call the Markoff processes, whereby past events influence present probabilities, since this theory is specifically adapted to handle one of the most significant but difficult aspects of meaning, namely the influence of context. One has the vague feeling that information and meaning may prove to be something like a pair of canonically conjugate variables in quantum theory, that is, that information and meaning may be subject to some joint restriction that compels the sacrifice of one if you insist on having much of the other.

Or perhaps meaning may be shown to be analogous to one of the quantities on which the entropy of a thermodynamic ensemble depends. Here Eddington has another apt comment:

Suppose that we were asked to arrange the following in two categories—*distance, mass, electric force, entropy, beauty, melody.*

I think there are the strongest grounds for placing entropy alongside beauty and melody, and not with the first three. Entropy is only found when the parts are viewed in association, and it is by viewing or hearing the parts in association that beauty and melody are discerned. All three are features of arrangement. It is a pregnant thought that one of these three associates should be able to figure as a commonplace quantity of science. The reason why this stranger can pass itself off among the aborigines of the physical world is that it is able to speak their language, *viz.,* the language of arithmetic.

One feels sure that Eddington would have been willing to include the word meaning along with beauty and melody; and one suspects he would have been thrilled to see, in this theory, that entropy not only speaks the language of arithmetic; it also speaks the language of language.

COMMUNICATION IN ORGANIZATIONS
HAROLD GUETZKOW

EFFECTS OF COMMUNICATION SYSTEMS ON MESSAGE CONTENTS

Introduction

To this point, attention has been given to the way a communication system operates within an organizational context, stressing its network characteristics. But such flows consist of messages—messages which have meanings. Communication engineers have investigated technical problems involved in characterizing the informational contents of messages. They are concerned with the way that messages may be encoded into signals, then transmitted efficiently through channels (despite extrinsic sources of noise) to receivers for decoding into messages at a destination, as exhibited in the solid-lined parts of Fig. V-2.

The greater the extent to which an external environment provides multiple bases for the origination of communication, "the greater the differentiation of perceptions within the organization" (March & Simon, 1958, p. 127).[1] However, when one unit

holds an acknowledged monopoly over incoming messages, its communication to other parts of the organization tends to be uniform, thereby reducing contradictions within the organization. Vice versa, one may also speculate that when an organization provides multiple end-points for the reception of communication, the variation in interpretation of a given message is greater. Uniformity in reception would seem to depend upon the extent to which a common frame of reference exists within the organization, as such has developed over the years through training programs and the gamut of other devices which an organization uses to insure conformity to its norms.

Students of social communication, in contrast to the communication engineers, have stressed ways of characterizing the semantic contents of messages, being concerned with their affective and cognitive aspects. The work of Shannon on a theory of selective information is now being complemented by work on a theory of semantic information, as outlined by Carnap and Bar-Hillel (1953) and then developed further by Bar-Hillel (1954) alone. The semantic problem may be superimposed upon informational

CREDIT: Reprinted by permission of author and publisher from James G. March (Ed.), *Handbook of Organizations*, pp. 550–565, 568–569. Copyright © 1965 by Rand McNally & Company. [*Figures and tables renumbered.*]

[1] *Editors' Note:* Many scientists use this form of citation rather than footnoting. The information refers to articles and books listed in alphabetical order at the end of this selection. There are three parts in this citation: author(s), year of publication cited *in toto* in the list of references, and page number.

technology in a communication system, as has been done in the dotted lines that were added in Fig. V-2, upon the suggestion of Weaver (Shannon & Weaver, 1949, pp. 115–116). Because the message is processed and reprocessed at each node in the communication system, there is ample opportunity to transform the meaning of the message as it is communicated within an organization. The so-called General Semantics people also argue that attention for understanding "patterns of miscommunication" should be focused on "those which arise in the encoding and decoding phases of the process and which emanate in large part from certain faulty and often unconsciously held premises on the part of the communicator—be he sender and/or receiver" (Haney, 1960, p. 3).

In stressing the importance of "nonverbal communication," Ruesch and Kees discussed the organizational executive, remarking that

most of these men have rather limited contact with many of the processes they symbolically deal with or control. The danger of this remoteness from reality lies in the tendency to regard abstract principles as concrete entities, attributing body and substance to numbers and letters and confusing verbal symbols with actual events. Such a way of thinking is an almost inescapable occupational hazard to those who use words for purposes of control (1956, p. 193).

An attempt has been made by Harrah (1963) to formulate aspects of a theory of semantic information, with special emphasis upon the development of a model of the question-and-answer situation. Harrah is concerned with normative models of the "news-value" and the "message adequacy" of communication events. Although his fundamental work eventually may serve to induce focused, empirical follow-up, its multitude of quite rigorously stated refinements seem to be years ahead of present empirical work in the field. For instance, in discussing the shortcomings of his question-and-answer model when applied to the hierarchical situations found in a variety of communication nets, Harrah recognized that many meanings of the message must be considered, in addition to those he prescribed for analysis of noncommand messages (p. 94).

Thus, it seems infeasible to apply either the theory of selective or of semantic information in their present state to our concerns. We turn to problems involved in the semantics of the messages handled in a communication network, even though we lack the elegance of analytic tools being forged in both of these new areas of theory development.

Perhaps the central problem which characterizes the handling of contents in communication is: How may meanings be preserved without overloading the system? Communication systems become effective when they employ languages which carry larger amounts of meaning with relatively fewer symbols. Organizations find such things as blueprints, product number systems, and occupational jargons helpful in increasing the efficiency of their communications. The role of compact language in communication is illustrated by the Macy-Christie-Luce (1953) experiments with "noisy marbles." Using a Bavelas type of setup, participants in control groups were given marbles of different solid colors, with the task of finding who had which colors. Experimental groups were given streaked marbles whose colors were not easily described in conventional language. These latter groups were severely handicapped by their lack of an adequate technical vocabulary; only gradually did their performance equal that of the controls, as they succeeded in inventing a vo-

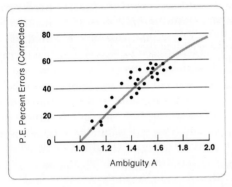

Figure V-3.   Prediction of errors from ambiguity. (Developed by Macy, Christie, & Luce, 1953, Fig. 7, p. 405; and Macy, 1956, Fig. 20, p. 464.)

cabulary for describing the streaked marbles and securing its acceptance throughout the group. The authors developed a measure of ambiguity in the terms used to describe the mottled marbles by counting the number of different marbles which were attached to a given name. The relation of this ambiguity measure of semantic noise to accuracy in sending correct answers to other members in the net is graphed in Fig. V-3.

The transformation of the contents of messages

When the symbols fail to carry the full contents of the messages, their semantic properties are transformed as they are handled within a communication flow—either by omission of aspects of the contents, or by the introduction of distortions. Let us consider each of these aspects of the transformation of messages separately.

1. Omission. The deletion of aspects of messages is a common phenomenon within social communication. Sometimes omission takes place at the point of message reception, in that the two or three levels of meaning of the communication simply are not grasped. Or, more grossly, the message may be neglected because of sheer overload in message-processing capability.

In pyramidal organizations, it is easy to understand why the few recipients at the upper levels of the organization are flooded with messages originating at numerous lower levels; and yet simultaneously they are unable to respond in a one-for-one fashion, as the situation demands. Donald (1959) obtained evidence on the asymmetric way in which communication takes place between the local and national-and-state headquarters units in her study of the League of Women Voters of the United States. The communication originating at the state and national levels for downward flow was quite constant, regardless of the size of the local unit. But there was asymmetry with respect to the relation of the officers of the local to their state and national offices. For example, in the case of the president and her communications to the state level, the product-moment correlation between size of her local unit and the amount of communication sent upward reached .50. In other words, the information ("facts and ideas") flowing downward from supra-local levels in the over-all organization was relatively standardized, free from the impact of local-unit size. However, as the local size varied from less than 100 to more than 400 members, the amount of information sent upward to both state and federal levels varied with size of local.

Although Shaw and his associates utilized the concept of "saturation" in explaining their failures to find continuing increases in message input and output as conducive to group effectiveness, they neglected to operationalize the concept, nor have they developed empirical analyses which bear more than indirectly upon their interpretation (Gilchrist, Shaw, & Walker, 1954; Shaw, 1955). Perhaps the clearest evidence on the impact of overload from increase in input is found in the experimental work of Lanzetta and Roby. In experiment after experiment, as load increased, the adequacy of group performance decreased (Lanzetta & Roby, 1956a; Lanzetta & Roby, 1956b; Lanzetta & Roby, 1957; Roby & Lanzetta, 1957). In discussing the effects of overload, they noted that the "overloaded individual is as likely to neglect obligations to other group members, thereby increasing their errors, as he is to neglect his own control responsibilities" (Roby & Lanzetta, 1957, p. 176).

In commenting on their experimental induction of overload in four-man groups by increasing the amount of problem-relevant information, Shelly and Gilchrist noted that overload results in "more or less self-perpetuating conditions of communication confusion." They speculated that, "Under pressure of greater amounts of required communication to be handled at once, the individuals in the group probably neglect to forward some problem relevant information and/or duplicate previously forwarded information; this in turn gives rise to information-seeking questions. These questions, because answers are required, further increase the communication load (a) leading to greater probability of neglecting to forward information and/or (b) forgetting to whom certain items have previously been sent, etc." (1958, p. 43).

Thus, one encounters a central problem in communication systems: How may fullness of meaning be carried without overload? Omission of detail, as messages are transmitted within organizations, may provide one means for reducing overload. As mentioned above, the degree to which knowledge may be transported throughout the organization depends on the extent to which details may be encapsulated within efficient languages, as in technical jargon. The more complicated the data, the earlier in the channel would one expect the message to be condensed by omission of detail. In other words, as the matter was stated by March and Simon,

The more complex the data that are perceived, and the less adequate the organization's language, the closer to the source of information will the uncertainty absorption take place, and the greater will be the amount of summarizing at each step of transmission (1958, p. 166).

As Cartwright pointed out,

Units which correspond to articulation points of a communication network are likely to carry a heavy load of communication, because certain pairs of units of the organization cannot communicate to each except through this unit. If such a unit becomes a "bottleneck" or if it systematically screens out certain types of information, parts of the organization will become poorly informed about matters that may be of importance to the organization as a whole (1959, p. 261).

Under conditions of overload of information input, demanding corresponding increases in outputs, J. G. Miller (1962) noted a number of mechanisms of adjustment. He conjectured that the proliferation of more channels of input or output ("Multiple Channels") is a typical way for organizations to make response—as "by putting more people on a job." Sometimes, however, response to overload is made by reducing the inflow, either by sporadic avoidance of processing ("Omission") or by "leaving the situation entirely" ("Escape"). When omission is systematic with respect to "certain categories of information," it is called "Filtering." These omitting devices may be obviated for moderate overloads by "Queuing," which involves "delaying responses during peak load periods and then catching up during lulls." In discussing output, Miller noted that the unit may adjust either by making "Error" or an "Approximation" to a more "precise or accurate response" (p. 64).

But the pressures of overload are not the only source of transformation of the communications by omission. Sometimes omissions may occur quite intentionally, as in the rules set up in the operation of security systems, in which dispersion of the message is highly restricted by such criteria as "need to know." Sometimes the press of crisis situations induces "bypass-

ing," so that usual linkages within the network are short-circuited in the transmission of messages within the organization, as has been noted by Baker, Ballantine, and True (1949, p. 127).

2. Distortion. Intimately associated with the processes of omission are those which transform the meanings of messages by distorting their contents in a wide variety of ways. March and Simon pointed out, "In our culture, language is well developed for describing and communicating about concrete objects. . . . On the other hand, it is extremely difficult to communicate about intangible objects and nonstandardized objects" (1958, p. 164). Organizations at times make provision to handle less objective communication contents. As explained by Cyert and March,

Any decision-making system develops codes for communicating about the environment. Such a code partitions all possible states of the world into a relatively small number of classes of states. . . . Thus, if a decision rule is designed to choose between two alternatives, the information code will tend to reduce all possible states of the world to two classes (1963, pp. 124–125).

But such rules for the codification of inputs themselves would seem, then, to introduce distortions.

Campbell (1958) has reviewed the literature of "systematic error"; the distortions take a number of quite regular forms, as exhibited in Table V-1. Campbell argued that person-to-person communication "involves, after all, only cumulation of individual processes" (p. 360). Hence, his impressive marshalling of evidence from the psychology of knowledge processes may be useful in providing under-pinnings for insights into the way that meaning is transformed, as symbols are transmitted and filtered in the context of other symbol complexes.

TABLE V-1 Propositions Adapted from Campbell's "Systematic Error on the Part of Human Links in Communication Systems"[a]

ERRORS SPECIFIC TO DUPLICATORY TRANSMISSION PROCESS

1. *Condensation:* "Output, if imperfect, will on the average be shorter, simpler, and less detailed than input . . . [yielding] an abbreviation of message with some retention of over-all form, a loss of minor detail with retention of major effects."
2. *Accentuation:* "distortion of message in the direction of dividing the content into clear cut 'entities,' reducing gradations both by exaggerating some differences and losing others," "regularizing asymmetric inputs, 'filling in' of gaps, enhancing contrasts, and categorization."

ERRORS RELATED TO ASSIMILATION OF CONTEXT WITHIN WHICH TRANSMISSION OCCURS

3. *Assimilation to Message Contexts:*
   —to Prior Message Inputs: "distortion of messages in the direction of identity with previous inputs . . . [with] a pervasive bias toward [substitution of] ordinary, typical, popular outputs."
   —to Expected Message Inputs: "errors in transmission will in general be in the direction of making output like expected, rather than different from expected input."
4. *Assimilation to Personal and Value Contexts:*
   —to Own Attitudes: "the human transmitter is prone to bias output away from input in the direction of the transmitter's own attitudes."
   —to Please Receiver: "transmitter's output may be expected to deviate from input in the direction of pleasing the recipient, avoiding causing distress, etc."
   —to Evaluative Coding: "tendency to distort coding assignments in direction of an affective coding . . . of the general nature of 'like' versus 'dislike,' . . . 'good' versus 'bad.'"

ERRORS RELATED TO FILTERING IN REDUCTIVE CODING

5. *Coding Relativism:* "Residues of recent inputs are combined in a mean net effect which provides the effective reference for any coding process. If the general input level lowers over a substantial period of time, the coding thresholds will similarly lower; if the mean input level rises, coding thresholds will similarly rise."
6. *Coding Contamination from Association Cues:* "inputs are usually complex and multidimensional. If in the past, two dimensions have varied together . . . both dimensions will come to contribute to coding decisions . . . to distort the coding so that the response goes along with the associated cue, the effect being the greater the more ambiguous the relevant input dimension."

[a] From Campbell (1958).

In organizations, messages are condensed and features within them are accentuated, as Allport and Postman (1947) have illustrated experimentally in their laboratory versions of the parlor game, "Pass Along to Your Neighbor." Allport and Postman described how transmitted messages were *leveled,* that is, "tended to grow shorter, more concise, and more easily grasped and told" and *sharpened,* that is, how there is the "selective perception, retention, and reporting of a limited number of details from a larger context" (Allport & Postman, 1954, pp. 146–148). As these experimenters put it, "The longer the time that elapses after the stimulus is perceived . . . also, the more people involved in a serial report, the greater the change is likely to be . . ." (Allport & Postman, 1954, p. 154). This tendency toward assimilation may be accentuated in an organization, as when individuals are signaled about the contents of communications that they are to receive. Allyn and Festinger have demonstrated experimentally that persons "who were forewarned of the nature of the communication changed their opinions less and rejected the communicated as biased to a greater degree than unprepared subjects" (1961, p. 40).

As Campbell's review hints (cf. Table V-1, Items 3 & 4), because different persons man different points of initiation and reception of messages, there is much assimilation of meanings to the contexts within which transmission occurs. Frames of reference at a multitude of nodes differ because of variety in personal and occupational background, as well as because of difference in viewpoint induced by the communicator's position within the organization. One of the experiments by Cyert, March, and Starbuck (1961) demonstrates the operation of assimilation bias in the case of the individual operating within such organizational contexts. Graduate students were asked to make estimates from *identical* figures, at one time assuming the role of the "chief cost analyst," and at another time assuming the role of the "chief market analyst." The empirical results clearly confirmed the experimenters' hypothesis that "costs

analysts will tend to overestimate costs and that sales analysts will tend to underestimate sales" (p. 256).

An exemplary demonstration of the way in which such distortion occurs is found in the work of Cohen (1958) on upward communication in experimentally created hierarchies, which constitutes a clarifying replication of an earlier experiment by Kelley (1951). Cohen created two kinds of persons of rank, some who merely had positions that were considered desirable, and others who not only had desirable positions but also had control over the advancement of individuals of low rank. The average number of messages with critical content sent by lows to highs, when no power was involved, was three times the quantity sent when the highs had both desirable position and power over the advancement of the lows (Table 3, p. 48). Critical comments were simply omitted by those whose fortunes depended upon those with higher hierarchical rank.

In a field study in three major industrial organizations, Read (1962) obtained complementary findings. "In industrial hierarchies, mobility aspiration among subordinate executives is negatively related to accuracy of upward communication" (p. 13), there being a correlation of $-.41$ between a measure of need for movement into higher-level positions and inaccuracy in communicating about major problems involved in work with one's superior. Read's interpretation that this negative relationship is a reflection of the subordinate's desire "to withhold or refrain from communicating information that is potentially threatening to the status of the communicator" (p. 13) is substantiated by his finding that among those who do and do *not* trust their superior's "motives and intentions with respect to matters relevant to the subordinate's career and status in the organization" (p. 8), the correlation between mobility need and inaccuracy in communication is $-.16$ and $-.66$, respectively (a difference significant at more than the .01 level) (Table 2, p. 10). This work constitutes a replication of the findings by Mellinger on 330 professional scientists, indicating that an individual who lacks trust in the person to whom he communicates tends to conceal his own attitudes, resulting in messages which are "evasive, compliant, or aggressive" (1956, p. 309).

There is evidence that a similar situation prevails with respect to horizontal communication. In a government laboratory, Shepard and Weschler (1955) found that positive affective relations among dyads were associated with less tendency to express awareness of actual difficulties in communication. Could it be in this situation of good feeling that there was inhibition of messages about communication failures, in order to avoid unpleasantness in an otherwise satisfactory relation?

Perhaps as fascinating is the impact on accuracy in communication of the very cognitive dimensions in terms of which messages are generated and received, as has been delineated by Osgood and his associates (Osgood, Suci, & Tannenbaum, 1957). Triandis' study (1959) in industry of "categoric similarity" found that boss-subordinate pairs could communicate more effectively when they similarly categorized particular people (such as the personnel director of their company and the vice-president of their divi-

sion), when responding to an adaptation of Kelly's (1955) Role Repertory Test. This work was replicated in the laboratory, in which dyads of students were found to communicate better with each other in a game situation when their previously measured categorizations of attributes were more similar (Triandis, 1960). This same finding had been obtained earlier by Runkel, using Coombs's "unfolding technique," in a classroom situation. Runkel (1956) found students received higher grades on quizzes when their responses to the contents of their introductory psychology course were "mediated by the same underlying attribute" as were their instructors'. The higher grades for students who were cognitively similar to their teachers "could not be accounted for by differences in scholastic ability as measured by A.C.E. scores, nor by conformity to a common attitude norm, nor by preference for the same attitude position as that held by the teacher" (p. 191).

More recently, Zajonc and Wolfe (1963) have used Zajonc's techniques (Zajonc, 1960) for the measurement of cognitive structures about a variety of characteristics of the company in their research with 42 members of an industrial firm, ranging in level from vice-presidents to production workers. Comparing employees who reported wide as contrasted with narrow informal communication contacts, they found no differences in such properties of cognitive structure as *differentiation* ("amount of information which the structure subsumes"), *complexity* ("variety and elaboration of the information dealt with"), *segmentation* ("degree to which the groupings within the cognitive structure are independent of one another"), or *organization* ("extent to which the cognitive structure represents a tightly knit whole"). However, those employees with wide contacts in their formal communications tended to be more differentiated, more complex, less segmented, and more organized in their cognitive structures than those with narrow contacts (Zajonc & Wolfe, 1963, Table 3, p. 13).

tant and significant (F-tests at $p < .001$) differences in both "amount of information" which the cognitive structures subsume and in the "variety and elaboration of the information dealt with" when they contrasted vice-presidents with production workers and clerks (p. 15). The vice-presidents described their companies in more differentiated and complex ways than did the workers. The finding with respect to cognitive organization, as portrayed

TABLE V-2   Properties of Cognitive Structures of Three Hierarchical Levels of Staff and Line Employees[a]

Property	Function	Heads	Hierarchical level supervisors	Workers	All
	Line	22.0	10.9	7.7	11.4
Differentiation	Staff	23.5	16.6	10.7	15.2
	Both	22.8	12.8	9.1	
	Line	59.0	23.5	18.2	27.2
Complexity	Staff	54.8	51.4	28.9	40.9
	Both	56.9	32.8	23.3	
	Line	.120	.245	.358	.321
Segmentation	Staff	.144	.146	.189	.167
	Both	.132	.212	.278	
	Line	42.53	29.58	15.76	25.98
Organization	Staff	223.59	49.28	19.89	73.32
	Both	133.06	36.14	17.72	

[a] From Zajonc & Wolfe (1963), Table 4, p. 16. The higher the index the more differentiation, complexity, segmentation, or organization.

In the Zajonc and Wolfe organizations, differences in cognitive structure were closely related to line and staff functions, as well as to differences in level of hierarchy, as shown in Table V-2. Their findings may contradict earlier speculation by Barnard, "When communications go from high positions down, they often must be made more specific as they proceed; and when in the reverse direction, usually more general" (1938, pp. 176–177). Zajonc and Wolfe found impor-

in the last lines of Table V-2 is intriguing. Zajonc and Wolfe asked the reader to

note that there is little difference between staff and line for lower hierarchical levels, but that this difference increases in favor of the staff function as we go up the hierarchical ladder. The degree of organization of the cognitive structure, we said, measures the extent to which cognitions are integrated around a single guiding principle.

Then the authors speculated,

Since staff provides more or less a service function to the line, and in many instances has the responsibility for the integration of data coming from various line activities, it requires a fairly stable frame of reference. A personnel officer or the vice-president in charge of finance and administration must view the activities of the company constantly in terms of some single implication—for instance, budget, expansion, labor relations, work standards, or the like. Thus, the high staff positions apparently deal with information in terms of specific goals of their responsibilities and with a fairly stable and specific frame of reference. We note therefore an extremely high level of cognitive organization on the part of staff heads (Zajonc & Wolfe, 1963, pp. 17–18).

Taking a broader perspective, such inaccuracies and systematic biasing perhaps are not always dysfunctional. The transformation may increase the motivation of the participants in the organization by introducing symbols that have more cathectic value. Or the omission and inaccuracy may merely increase the message's ambiguity. Because ambiguous messages are open to multiple interpretations, meanings more agreeable to the receiver may be attached. Although at times ambiguity results in slippage between sender and receiver, such slippage also may promote consensus and agreement, which have important value for organizational activity. The values of ignorance have been discussed in general terms by Moore and Tumin, who mentioned the usefulness of stereotypes in the operation of organizations (1949, p. 792). However, as Schneider (1962) discovered, despite the seminal nature of the earlier Moore and Tumin work, to date there has been no exploration of the functioning of ignorance in communication systems.

Maintenance and restoration of accuracy in message contents

The disadvantages emanating from the transformation of messages in organizations result in a number of devices for decreasing the omissions and increasing the accuracy of transmission. Two important mechanisms involved in these processes are those that provide for message repetition and for its verification. Yet, as is noted below, the very processes used for maintaining the accuracy of message contents themselves become new sources of omission or distortion.

1. Repetition. In repeating messages, by varying their form and at times even the channel used for their transmission, senders attempt to reduce omissions and to decrease the amount of distortion which may occur within message flows. By using written messages, which may be read and re-read, shifts in meaning over time can be reduced but not eliminated; different stations decode the stable message in varying ways, as situations change. But repetition itself may interfere with the functioning of the communication system as a whole by increasing the load of total messages which must be processed. And when redundancy at the reception point is high, due to constant repetition, further neglect of messages from particular sources may be induced by ennui.

Cyert and March noted, "One of the ways in which the organization adapts to the unreliability of information is by devising procedures for making decisions without attending to apparently relevant information"

(1963, p. 110). For example, the growth of specialized companies for gathering market-survey information may have originated, in part, as a device by product-producing organizations to reduce reliance upon contradictory information coming internally from segments of their own sales and shipping departments.

Macy, Christie, and Luce (1953) demonstrated the increase of symbol redundancy in their noisy marbles experiment. They discovered duplication in the coding scheme used to describe the mottled and streaked marbles when synonyms were developed for describing ambiguous objects. They found that a "reduction in the errors always came after this rise" of the average number of names used for describing the noisy marbles (p. 407).

Redundancy also can be achieved by the simultaneous use of multiple channels for essentially the same message. G. A. Miller remarked, "Because the network of communication channels in a social group permits each member to be connected with the source of information via several paths, the social situation provides its own kind of redundancy" (1951, p. 254). As Baker, Ballantine, and True indicated in their case studies of the transmission of information through management and union channels, "there were many evidences that for most subjects the use of only one channel or one medium of communication was inadequate . . ." (1949, p. 131). Thus, it would not be unreasonable to find a tendency for persons in organizations to use more than one channel, in order to assure delivery of important messages. The organizational

situation, however, may be such as to make the use of multiple channels needless. In their "games of agreement," Willis and Hale (1963) so structured both their competitive and cooperative situations that the "one-way feed-back condition supplied the S with as much *usable* information as the two-way feed-back condition" (p. 155).

Earlier, mention was made of the way in which the reward system of organizations interacts to reduce the effectiveness of communications in hierarchy. Even when the organization adds a staff channel to complement overloaded line channels, these rewards and punishments serve to reduce its effectiveness. As Blau and Scott pointed out,

The staff expert can submit accurate operational reports to management, but if he presents adverse information concerning the action of lower managers he will earn their antipathy and distrust, and these attitudes will prevent him from obtaining accurate information from them in the future. Alternatively, he can attempt to modify his report in order to maintain the good will of his informants, but in so doing he suppresses the information that reflects adversely on lower managers, making his report hardly more accurate than their own communications (1962, p. 173).

The proliferation of channels of communication at times may become so great as to change the organization's structure. Meier (1963) has described the operation of a university library organization which responded to its inadequacies by organizational elaboration. The library system used a variety of devices for reducing its inputs, such as queuing its requests with a "gate" at peak periods (pp. 534–535), setting priorities in the queue, and destroying those inputs given lowest priority (p. 535). The organization in overload is claimed to lose "its original simply defined territorial boundaries" through the proliferation of "Multiple Channels."

When interaction rate is very high, the short cuts and aids that expedite the flow of messages, such as priority assessment and "active files," create substructures in the vicinity of the boundary. The need to make and remake policy within the institution and to ascertain that it has the expected local outcomes leads to an accentuated headquarters unit, usually surrounded by a "home facility" that provides continuous support. The expansion of capacity results in a series of branches. These subsidary units are likely to have differentiated functions (p. 542).

Thus, the use of repetition to reduce the transformation of contents in communication takes a large variety of forms, from simple redundancy to the elaboration of organizational structure.

2. *Verification.* Sometimes messages of verification are sent merely to insure the accuracy of earlier messages. Then clashes in interpretation may be isolated. As Baker, Ballantine, and True found in their case analyses, there is need for "methods of communication which can, in the *process of communication,* test the degree to which the recipient *understands* what he is being told" (1949, p. 133, italics original). It would seem that one of the very important uses of the informational conference, which involves multiple-way discussion, is found in its ability to verify the extent to which participants understand the materials

communicated. Although one-to-many modes of communication may limit distortion in a message by eliminating the need for serial transmission of the message, feedback is severely restricted in such situations. Usually there are only limited amounts of time on the part of the one for response to the queries of the many.

Lack of feedback would seem a fertile way of increasing the proclivity of individuals within organizations to become centers of speculation. Willis and Hale (1963) noted in their "games of agreement" that the "no feedback condition produced almost twice as many hypotheses" as conditions with one- or two-way feedback. They interpreted their findings "as being due to the fact that, receiving no feedback whatsoever, these *Ss* were unable to disconfirm any of the hypotheses which occurred to them during the course of play" (p. 154). In their noisy marbles experiment described above, Macy, Christie, and Luce (1953) found that different communication nets permitted varying amounts of verification. Those groups in nets with sufficient interconnection to allow detection and correction of errors—that is, groups operating in open nets— clearly tended to reduce their errors (p. 408).

Cyert and March noted that one "cannot reasonably introduce the concept of communication bias without introducing its obvious corollary— 'interpretive adjustment.' Those parts of the organization receiving data include human beings accustomed to the facts of communicative life. In short, they ordinarily use counterbiases to adjust for such biases as they anticipate in the data they receive" (1963, p.

71). When teams of two persons were placed in a knob-adjusting situation so that feedback from each member was differentially weighted, Hall (1957) found that "it made little difference whether teammates contributed equally or in a 3 to 1 ratio to the team score that was used as feedback." The interpretation was made that the experimental setup simply permitted "one teammate to compensate for another's errors" (p. 303).

Working as experimenters with Starbuck, Cyert and March believed such counterbiases foiled their efforts to demonstrate experimentally the operation of conflicts of interests within miniature laboratory organizations. They attempted to create a series of situations in which biases, produced by different payoff schedules, would interfere with the accuracy of estimates made by a central decision-maker from biased information fed to him by subordinates. But the coordinator made interpretive adjustments so that the estimates over time converged toward the true values, regardless of the direction or combination of the original biases.

The experiment also included the consequences of feedback data, which were provided the central decision-maker after each estimate over a period of 30 trials, as exhibited for the six groups comprising each of six different conditions of bias in Fig. V-4 (Cyert, March, & Starbuck, 1961, Fig. 1, p. 262). Note the convergence of the estimations to the asymptote of about 15 per cent error. Members of the organization

tend to consider the decision for which the information is sought, the probable consequences of various potential biases in

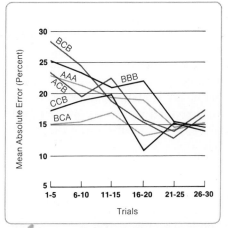

Figure V-4.   Consequences of Feedback on Performance Errors. (Developed by Cyert, March, & Starbuck, 1961, Fig. 1, p. 262.)

information, and the payoff to them for various possible decision results. They adjust the information they transmit in accordance with their perceptions of the decision situation (pp. 263–264).

There seems little doubt that feedback often improves group performance as was early demonstrated by Leavitt and Mueller (1951). Not only is feedback useful for messages about the substance of the task, as for communication of the geometric patterns used in the Leavitt and Mueller experiment, but it seems also helpful for the development of organizational relations. This procedural use of feedback is illustrated by Pryer and Bass (1959) in their study of groups estimating the size of cities in teams who "learned that one or two members were responsible for the most accurate groups' decisions," so that "in subsequent trials they delegated more authority to these persons" (p. 62).

In 1957, Hall distinguished feedback that directly reflects consequences from the action of the individual versus a "socially confounded feedback," in which knowledge of results is available, but as a composite group score. In a series of elegant experiments involving coordinated knob-turning by dyads (Rosenberg, 1959; Rosenberg, 1960; Rosenberg, 1962; Rosenberg & Hall, 1958), it was shown that the relative proportion of contribution of the feedback resulting from one subject's action rather than from another's importantly influenced the extent to which each participants' reinforcement was "confounded." Using a simple reaction time task, Zajonc (1962) was able to demonstrate quite clearly that "pronounced improvement occurs for a difficult group task when information about the performance of all team members as well as of the team as a whole is made available. When information about team performance alone (confounded feedback) is given, only slight improvement occurs" (p. 160).

But anticipated benefits of feedback can be erased by the circumstances under which the feedback is provided. In their experiment on semantic noise, Macy, Christie, and Luce (1953) provided one of their sets of groups with a closed communication system with direct feedback about errors. However, performance did not improve to the level of a more open system, they believed, because the net restrictions created a bottleneck at the center position. This made it impossible "for each S to participate actively in the noise reduction process" (p. 408). In work in Bavelas-type, all-channel nets, Shure and his associates (1962) contrasted "Separate-Planning" conditions, which permitted only delayed feedback between operating trials, with "Contemporal" condi-

tions, which allowed simultaneous, immediate feedback. These researchers found that immediate feedback displaced long-range planning, so that in the end, such direct feedback "proved more detrimental to performance than the delayed feedback" (p. 280). Another example of the dysfunctional effects of feedback is found in the empirical work of Bowman (1963) in four factories. His studies enabled demonstration that "decision rules derived from management's own average behavior" often yielded better results than that obtained in actual day-by-day operations by these same managers. When there is overload in feedback stimuli, Bowman hypothesized, the manager responds selectively to this overrich environment. "He may respond not at all up to some point and overrespond beyond that" (p. 316). Thus, although under many circumstances feedback may be helpful in improving the accuracy of communication, its side-effects may even be deleterious to over-all performance of the group.

Once again, the very reward characteristics of an organization tend to develop barriers to adequate communication. When channels prove to be reliable in their regularity, and when there seldom is omission or inaccuracy, these very channels will tend to be used more often. But this greater usage will increase the likelihood of the channel being overloaded, thereby making it less reliable and less accurate. Thus, not only do the very devices invented to alleviate communication difficulties tend to produce new sources of communication trouble, but even success in the surmounting of such difficulties itself produces new blockages in the already existing structures in organizations.

AN APPLICATION TO RUMOR TRANSMISSION

A number of the considerations developed in this chapter may be seen in interrelationship when one examines the operation of the grapevine, as it transmits rumors. There has been little systematic study of such dissemination of unofficial information with high interest value by informal, person-to-person communication within organizations. However, comparison is possible among a few observational studies (Caplow, 1946–1947; Davis, 1953b; Festinger et al., 1948) and two experimental studies (Back et al., 1950; Festinger, Schachter, & Back, 1963), all of which were conducted in field situations. These studies seem to reveal no characteristics which distinguish rumors in any fundamental way from other communications.

The three observational researches were made in a variety of field sites. Caplow reported his studies on rumors in a dozen company-size units, operating as a regiment for two years in the Pacific Theater during World War II. Davis made an intensive analysis of the grapevine in the "Jason Company," involving communication among 67 management employees in a moderately sized firm that manufactured leather goods. Festinger and his collaborators examined in some detail the evolution and demise of a rumor within a housing project, involving

assertions that professional community organizers in "Regent Hill" were "communists." The experimental studies, both by Festinger and his associates, featured the introduction of rumors into natural organizations. In one case, two comparable rumors were introduced in two courts of the "Westgate" housing project. The courts were similar, except for contrasts in the extent to which the residents favored community activities. Within 48 hours, the spread of the inserted information was checked by survey interviews of all 26 residents. In the other case, nine different rumors were planted over a period of four months in an ongoing organization employing 55 persons. The spread of the information was checked throughout the period by confederates, as well as through a terminal survey of all members of the organization.

Caplow indicated the cycle involved in the operation of rumor processes.

Typically, an interest-situation was created by circumstances (*e.g.*, the conclusion of one operation focussed interest on the next), a number of rumors then appeared and began to circulate . . . , until the interest-situation was terminated either by an official announcement or by the occurrence or nonoccurrence of the rumored event (1946–1947, pp. 301–02).

Despite preconceptions that the grapevine is a pervasive phenomenon, the empirical evidence within organizational settings suggests that rumors occur infrequently. Checking rumors throughout two years, Caplow reported, "The greatest number discovered in one month was seventeen, less than one per hundred men. During one period of two weeks, not a single new rumor could be discovered" (Caplow, 1946–1947, p. 299). This finding seems to be confirmed by the tendency for few within organizations to pass on information, once they have received it. For example, in Davis' field work he found that some 68 per cent of Jason executives had received information about a quality-control problem, but only 20 per cent transmitted it; in another instance, although some 81 per cent of the executives knew about an impending resignation, "only 11 per cent passed the news on to others" (1953b, p. 46).

Even in the experimental field situations, the dissemination of planted rumors was constricted. In Back's organizational study, seven rumors produced but 17 transmissions (Back et al., 1950, p. 311). In the Westgate housing-project study, the four residents with whom the rumor was planted communicated the information in 24 hours to only 13 others. This averages but slightly more than three persons per resident (Festinger, Schachter, & Back, 1963, calculated from Fig. 8, p. 122).

The five studies of rumor seem not to reveal features that significantly distinguish rumors from other kinds of communication within organizations. Reconsider my definition of rumor: dissemination of unofficial information with high interest value by informal, person-to-person communication. Although by this definition, rumors are "unofficial," they are not unique in this characteristic; for example, much staff communication lacks authoritativeness. By definition, rumors involve information of "high interest value";

so does much status-laden, official communication. By definition, rumors are carried informally, "person to person"; so is much information used in coordinating authorized, important management action, as is revealed in the studies by Burns (1954, p. 92). In general, the findings of these field studies show that the same communication processes are involved in rumor transmission as are involved in other kinds of organizational communication, both as to their structure and content.

Rumor communications seem similar to other forms of organizational communication in the characteristics of their message flows. The degree of structuring of the rumor channels varies, as is true for other organizational communications. Davis reported that there is "no evidence that any group consistently acted as liaison persons" (1953b, p. 46), while Caplow remembered that "most of the diffusion of rumors actually took place through a relatively small number of rather well-defined paths" (1946–1947, p. 299). The dissemination of rumors also follows gradients, as do other message flows. In Westgate, it was found that induced rumor "decreases as the distance between people becomes greater" (Festinger, Schachter, & Back, 1963, p. 124). Caplow observed, "During a given period, there appear to be certain centers from which most rumors emanate. Headquarters is always such a center and so is the front line during actual battle" (p. 299).

Caplow, Davis, and Festinger and his associates all agreed that rumors spread rapidly; for example, in Regent Hill, "Only four of those [30] who heard the rumor reported having heard it more than two months after its beginning" (Festinger et al., 1948, p. 477). The speed of rumor diffusion, however, may be merely an artifact of our definition, in requiring that the content of the rumor be of "high interest value." In one of the experimental situations, one of the implanted rumors was of special concern to a subgroup. Its content revealed that "some questionnaire data the morale committee had gathered were lost, . . . Within about fifteen minutes it had spread to the entire [six-member] committee. In four days, however, there was only one communication about it to anyone outside the committee," where its interest would be of less significance (Back et al., 1950, p. 311). Thus, in this characteristic, too, it would seem rumor flow is similar to other kinds of communication flow, varying from high speeds to a speed of zero.

In earlier parts of this chapter, distinctions were made between nets resulting from the authority, information, task, friendship, and status characteristics of organizations. Again, these same context characteristics seem to affect the transmission of rumors, as they influence other communications in organizations. For example, in the study of

the hostile rumor in Regent Hill, it was possible to divide the sample of people interviewed into three groups: (1) those who indicated that they had closer friends living in the housing project, (2) those having many acquaintances but not very close friends, and (3) those who reported they had no friends in the project. The percentages of people in these three groups who heard the rumor were 62, 42,

and 33 respectively (Festinger, Schachter, & Back, 1963, p. 126).

This finding exhibits similar gradient characteristics to those obtained by Rapoport (1953) in his study of friendship nets, discussed in an earlier part of this chapter.

The similarities between rumor and non-rumor communications hold with respect to the contents of the messages, as well as for the structure and context of their flows. In this the evidence is weaker, however, inasmuch as Caplow alone has been concerned with the transformation of contents in rumor processes. For example, he noted in rumor the widespread tendency for contents to be simplified. Caplow used some of the same processes to explain the maintenance and restoration of accuracy as have been invoked in earlier parts of this chapter. Presaging Homans' elaboration of "exchange" mechanisms (Homans, 1961), Caplow noted that the "customary *quid pro quo* for a rumor is either another rumor or a validity judgment upon the one received" (1946–1947, p. 300). Further, he observed that "increasing negative prestige was attached to the transmission of false rumors . . ." (p. 302). In fact, the troops at times would build into the message itself an accuracy judgment, in a "warning, such as, 'I don't believe a word of this, but . . .'" (p. 302). As Caplow summarized the matter, "Most of the tendencies toward distortion which were discovered in the classroom did exist in the theatre of operations, but that definite group devices developed to diminish their effect" (p. 302).

The "need-to-know" criterion

mentioned earlier in the discussion of secrecy barriers in communication is highlighted in the definition of rumor, inasmuch as only those messages of great relevance to the members of the organization are usually considered as material of rumor potential—the "hot stuff." In the Festinger group's work in Regent Hill, they found the hostile rumor, which was concerned with personnel involved in the formation of a cooperative nursery school, was differentially disseminated. "When the sample of people who were interviewed was divided into those who had children of nursery school age and those who did not have any such children, it was found that 62 per cent of the former group had heard the rumor, while only 28 per cent of the latter group had heard it." Communication was directed "toward those who are seen as being most affected by the information" (Festinger, Schachter, & Back, 1963, pp. 129–130). Earlier, it was noted that before the experimental implantation of rumors in Westgate, one of the courts was favorable to community activity, while the other was unfavorable. The rumors were concerned with magazine and radio publicity to be given to the activities of the tenants' organization in the housing project. In examining the spread of the rumors, Festinger and his associates found "a much more active process of communication existed about content favorable to the tenants' organization in the favorable court than existed in the unfavorable court" (p. 123).

Many believe with Knapp that "In any given group the amount of rumor being circulated is roughly in inverse proportion to the degree to which official information is viewed as trustworthy and satisfying" (1944, p. 27). But "need to know" may be more general in nature than is usually suggested. Caplow advanced the intriguing proposition that "the demand for particular information in a group of this kind can be satisfied by any other information not totally irrelevant, if presented in sufficient amount." He noted that the "demand for information by a group—upon which the rumor process depends—may be easily saturated" by the "amount of nonrumored information in circulation" (p. 300). Caplow related how a captain of an invasion convoy

made a practice of announcing over the public address system anything of interest that came to the bridge and would not be known on deck—such as a submarine search by escort vessels over the horizon. In this situation . . . , there were areas of immediate interest in which information was scant, but about which rumors would ordinarily have been expected, but the hourly bombardment of announcements on the convoy's progress seemed to satisfy the total demand for information (p. 300).

Do variations in over-all levels of need for information apply to both the rumor and nonrumor situation, as Davis has noticed? "Where formal communication was inactive at the Jason Company, the grapevine did not rush in to fill the void . . . ; instead, there simply was lack of communication. Similarly, where there was effective formal communication, there was an active grapevine" (1953b, p. 45). It may be that in organizational settings, as contrasted with rumor in the larger "publics," as observed through such groups as the Massachusetts Committee of Public Safety during World War

II, Allport and Postman's "insistence that rumor thrives only in the absence of 'secure standards of evidence' " is inapplicable (1947, p. x).

Thus, perhaps "need to know" influences rumor and nonrumor communication alike. In this, as in many other ways, rumor communication seems to be part and parcel of the communication system which exists within organizations, failing to be qualitatively differentiable. If the processes involved in grapevines are fundamentally similar to those involved in other aspects of organizational communication, it is understandable why no special literature about rumor has come into being.

In speculation on the communication of rumor in organizational contexts, one senses the sharp contrast which holds between the systems approach used in this chapter and the individual approach used by Allport and Postman (1947) in their study of the psychology of rumor. Their emphasis on the role of the factors of importance (or "high interest value," as our definition posits) and ambiguity of evidence—even when amended by the inclusion of the *"critical sense"* of the rumor transmitter (Chorus, 1953) —analyzes but a small segment of the rich process which occurs in rumor transmission.

SUMMARY

The organizational context in which communication systems develop induce transformations in the contents of the messages which constitute the flow. Such effects seem to stem, in the main, from the overload imposed on the system, due to such internal factors as bottlenecks in the communication structure, and inputs from the external environment beyond the capacity of the system.

1. The message contents are transformed through the use of omitting devices via delaying inputs through queuing (resulting in only temporary omission), by reducing contents through special encodings, via by-passing segments of the net, and by "escaping" through outright neglect of input.

2. The messages are also transformed by system distortion of contents by such biasing devices as leveling and sharpening, and by assimilation of meanings to the organizational context.

Counteracting this transformation of contents induced by devices for omitting and distorting messages are attempts made by the communication system to prevent or correct the alterations.

3. Accuracy is increased in organizational communication by repeating the contents of the message— through multiple channels in parallel or by mere redundancy.

4. Accuracy is increased in organizational communication by verifying message contents, often by devices of feedback.

Yet, both devices—repetition and feedback—tend to add to the communications load of the organization. Such additional overload induces further transformation of messages, whose contents in turn need to be corrected for omissions and distortions.

The interrelations between tasks and communication system within organizations are many. Two features of task were focused upon: (a) the ways in which information is distributed within the organization, and (b) the problem-solving techniques used in solving the task problem. The adequacy with which the communication system functioned, given the variations in task, proved to be highly conditional.

COMMENT

It may not be accidental that research in communication has lagged behind studies concerning other features of organizational life, such as authority, division of work, and status. The contingent nature of the findings is exhibited over and over again in each section of this chapter. For example, vertical flows of communication depend upon size of organization, but lateral flows seem to be independent of size. Such contingency is found also in the way the very reward system embodied in a communication system makes the use of rewarded channels punishing. As a final example, remember that the adequacy of a net for task performance could be completely reversed, when a change in problem-solving technique was permitted. Do we find in communications in organizations an area of study in which there is special richness in contingent, interactive effects? Or is it merely that a clarifying perspective —which would make the pieces fall more simply into the whole—remains hidden?

Allport, G. W., and Postman, L. *The Psychology of Rumor*. New York: Holt, 1947.

Allport, G. W., & Postman, L. The Basic Psychology of Rumor. In W. Schramm (Ed.), *The Process and Effects of Mass Communication*. Urbana: University of Illinois Press, 1954. pp. 141–155.

Allyn, Jane, & Festinger, L. The Effectiveness of Unanticipated Persuasive Communications. *Journal of Abnormal Social Psychology,* 1961, 62, 35–40.

Back, K., Festinger, L., Hymovitch, B., Kelley, H., Schachter, S., & Thibaut, J. The Methodology of Studying Rumor Transmission. *Human Relations,* 1950, 3, 307–312.

Baker, Helen, Ballantine, J. W., & True, J. M. *Transmitting Information Through Management and Union Channels*. Princeton: Princeton University, Department of Economic & Social Institutions, Industrial Relations Section, 1949.

Bar-Hillel, Y. Logical Syntax and Semantics. *Language,* 1954, 30, 230–237.

Barnard, C. I. *The Functions of the Executive*. Cambridge: Harvard University Press, 1938.

Blau, P. M., & Scott, W. R. *Formal Organization: A Comparative Approach*. San Francisco: Chandler, 1962.

Bowman, E. H. Consistency and Optimality in Managerial Decision-Making. *Management Science,* 1963, 9, 310–321.

Burns, T. The Directions of Activity and Communication in a Departmental Executive Group. *Human Relations,* 1954, 7, 73–97.

Campbell, D. T. Systematic Error on the Part of Human Links in Communication Systems. *Infor-*

mation & Control, 1958, 1, 334–369.

Caplow, T. Rumors in War. Social Forces, 1946–1947, 25, 298–302.

Carnap, R., & Bar-Hillel, Y. An Outline of a Theory of Semantic Information. Tech. Report 247. Cambridge: M.I.T., Research Lab of Electronics, 1953.

Cartwright, D. The Potential Contribution of Graph Theory to Organization Theory. In M. Haire (Ed.), Modern Organization Theory: A Symposium of the Foundation for Research on Human Behavior. New York: Wiley, 1959, pp. 254–271.

Chorus, A. The Basic Law of Rumor. Journal of Abnormal Social Psychology, 1953, 48, 313–314.

Cohen, A. R. Upward Communication in Experimentally Created Hierarchies. Human Relations, 1958, 11, 41–53.

Cyert, R. M., & March, J. G. A Behavioral Theory of the Firm. Englewood Cliffs, N. J.: Prentice–Hall, 1963.

Cyert, R. M., March, J. G., & Starbuck, W. H. Two Experiments on Bias and Conflict in Organizational Estimation. Management Science, 1961, 7, 254–264.

Davis, K. Management Communication and the Grapevine. Harvard Business Review, 1953, 31 (5), 43–49.

Donald, Marjorie N. Some Concomitants of Varying Patterns of Communication in a Large Organization. Unpublished doctoral dissertation, University of Michigan. (Dissertation Abstracts, 1959, 19: 3392; University Microfilms, Ann Arbor, Michigan, 59:2108.)

Festinger, L., Cartwright, D., Barber, Kathleen, Fleisch, Juliet, Gottsdanker, Josephine, Keysen, Annette, & Leavitt, Gloria. A Study of Rumor: Its Origin and Spread. Human Relations, 1948, I, 464–486.

Festinger, L., Schachter, S., & Back, K. Social Pressures in Informal Groups: A Study of Human Factors in Housing. Stanford, California; Stanford University Press, 1963.

Gilchrist, J. C., Shaw, M. E., & Walker, L. C. Some Effects of Unequal Distribution of Information in a Wheel Group Structure. Journal of Abnormal Social Psychology, 1954, 49, 554–556.

Hall, R. L. Group Performance under Feedback that Confounds Responses of Group Members. Sociometry, 1957, 20, 297–305.

Haney, W. Communication: Patterns and Incidents. Homewood, Illinois: Irwin, 1960.

Harrah, D. Communication: A Logical Model. Cambridge: M.I.T. Press, 1963.

Homans, G. C. Social Behavior: Its Elementary Forms. New York: Harcourt, Brace, & World, 1961.

Kelley, H. H. Communication in Experimentally Created Hierarchies. Human Relations, 1951, 4, 39–56.

Kelly, G. A. The Psychology of Personal Constructs. New York: Norton, 1955.

Knapp, R. H. A Psychology of Rumor. Public Opinion Quarterly, 1944, 8, 22–37.

Lanzetta, J. T., & Roby, T. B. Effects of Work-Group Structure and Certain Task Variables on Group Performance. Journal of Abnor-

mal Social Psychology, 1956, 53, 307–314. (a)

Lanzetta, J. T., & Roby, T. B. Group Performance as a Function of Work Distribution and Task Load. *Sociometry,* 1956, 19, 95–104. (b)

Lanzetta, J. T., & Roby, T. B. Group Learning and Communication as a Function of Task and Structure "Demands." *Journal of Abnormal Social Psychology,* 1957, 55, 121–131.

Leavitt, H. J., & Mueller, R. Some Effects of Feedback on Communication. *Human Relations,* 1951, 4, 401–410.

Macy, J., Jr. Processes Affected by Noise and Confusion of Meanings. In J. F. McCloskey & J. M. Coppenger (Eds.), *Operations Research for Management.* Vol. 2. Baltimore: Johns Hopkins Press, 1956, pp. 458–489.

Macy, J., Jr., Christie, L. S., & Luce, R. D. Coding Noise in a Task-Oriented Group. *Journal of Abnormal Social Psychology,* 1953, 48, 401–409.

March, J. G., & Simon, H. A. with Guetzkow, H. *Organizations.* New York: Wiley, 1958.

Meier, R. L. Communications Overload: Proposals from the Study of a University Library. *Administrative Science Quarterly,* 1963, 7, 521–544.

Mellinger, G. Interpersonal Trust as a Factor in Communication. *Journal of Abnormal Social Psychology,* 1956, 52, 304–309.

Miller, G. A. *Language and Communication.* New York: McGraw-Hill, 1951.

Miller, J. G. Information Input Over-

load. In M. C. Yovits, G. T. Jacobi, & G. D. Goldstein (Eds.), *Self-Organizing Systems.* Washington, D. C.: Spartan, 1962. pp. 61–78.

Moore, W. E., & Tumin, M. M. Some Social Functions of Ignorance. *American Sociological Review,* 1949, 14, 787–795.

Osgood, C. E., Suci, G. H., & Tannenbaum, P. H. *The Measurement of Meaning.* Urbana: University of Illinois Press, 1957.

Pryer, Margaret W., & Bass, B. M. Some Effects of Feedback on Behavior in Groups. *Sociometry,* 1959, 22, 56–63.

Rapoport, A. Spread of Information Through a Population with Socio-Structural Bias: I. Assumption of Transitivity. II. Various Models with Partial Transitivity. *Bulletin of Mathematical Bio-Physics,* 1953, 15, 523–533; 535–543.

Read, W. H. Upward Communication in Industrial Hierarchies. *Human Relations,* 1962, 15, 3–16.

Roby, T. B., & Lanzetta, J. T. Conflicting Principles in Man-Machine System Design. *Journal of Applied Psychology,* 1957, 41, 170–178.

Rosenberg, S. The Maintenance of a Learned Response in Controlled Interpersonal Conditions. *Sociometry,* 1959, 22, 124–138.

Rosenberg, S. Cooperative Behavior in Dyads as a Function of Reinforcement Parameters. *Journal of Abnormal Social Psychology,* 1960, 60, 318–333.

Rosenberg, S. Two-Person Interactions in a Continuous-Response

Task. In Joan H. Criswell, H. Solomon, & P. Suppes (Eds.), *Mathematical Methods in Small Group Processes.* Stanford, California: Stanford University Press, 1962, pp. 282–304.

Rosenberg, S., & Hall, R. L. The Effects of Different Social Feedback Conditions Upon Performance in Dyadic Teams. *Journal of Abnormal Social Psychology,* 1958, 57, 271–277.

Ruesch, J., & Kees, W. *Nonverbal Communication: Notes on the Visual Perception of Human Relations.* Berkeley: University of California Press, 1956.

Runkel, P. J. Cognitive Similarity in Facilitating Communication. *Sociometry,* 1956, 19, 178–191.

Schneider, L. The Category of Ignorance in Sociological Theory. *American Sociological Review,* 1962, 27, 492–508.

Shannon, C., & Weaver, W. *The Mathematical Theory of Communication.* Urbana: University of Illinois Press, 1949.

Shaw, M. E. A Comparison of Two Types of Leadership in Various Communication Nets. *Journal of Abnormal Social Psychology,* 1955, 50, 127–134.

Shelly, M. W., & Gilchrist, J. C. Some Effects of Communication Requirements in Group Structures. *Journal of Social Psychology,* 1958, 48, 37–44.

Shepard, C., & Weschler, I. R. The Relation between Three Interpersonal Variables and Communication Effectiveness: A Pilot Study. *Sociometry,* 1955, 15, 103–110.

Shure, G. H., Rogers, M. S., Larsen, Ida M., and Tassone, J. Group Planning and Task Effectiveness. *Sociometry,* 1962, 25, 263–282.

Triandis, H. C. Cognitive Similarity and Interpersonal Communication in Industry. *Journal of Applied Psychology,* 1959, 43, 321–326.

Triandis, H. C. Cognitive Similarity and Communication in a Dyad. *Human Relations,* 1960, 13, 175–183.

Willis, R. H., & Hale, J. F. Dyadic Interactions as a Function of Amount of Feedback and Instructional Orientation. *Human Relations,* 1963, 16, 149–160.

Zajonc, R. B. The Process of Cognitive Tuning in Communication. *Journal of Abnormal Social Psychology,* 1960, 61, 159–167.

Zajonc, R. B. The Effects of Feedback and Probability of Group Success on Individual and Group Performance. *Human Relations,* 1962, 15, 149–161.

Zajonc, R. B., & Wolfe, D. M. *Cognitive Consequences of a Person's Position in a Formal Organization.* Tech. Report No. 23. Ann Arbor: University of Michigan, Institute for Social Research, Research Center for Group Dynamics, 1963.

SEMANTIC DIFFICULTIES IN INTERNATIONAL COMMUNICATION
EDMUND S. GLENN

It is too often assumed that the problem of transmitting the ideas of one national or cultural group to members of another national or cultural group is principally a problem of language. It is likewise assumed that that problem can always be solved by the use of appropriate linguistic techniques—translation and interpretation. A constant and professional preoccupation with the problem of international communication has convinced me of the fallacy of this point of view.

PATTERNS OF THOUGHT

Both an eminent professional philosopher, Professor Max Otto, and a very prominent layman, President Eisenhower, have stated that each man has a philosophy, whether or not he is aware of that fact. This means of course that people think in accordance with definite methods or patterns of thought. The methods may vary from individual to individual and even more from nation to nation.

Philosophical controversy is a historical fact. It is a mistake to believe that philosophical differences of opinion exist only at the level of conscious and deliberate controversies waged by professional philosophers. Ideas originated by philosophers permeate entire cultural groups; they are in fact what distinguishes one cultural group from another. The individuality of, for instance, Western culture, or Chinese culture, cannot be denied. The fact that when speaking of the English, the Americans, the French, or the Spanish, we tend to use expressions such as "national character" should not blind us to the fact that what is meant by "character" is in reality the embodiment of a philosophy or the habitual use of a method of judging and thinking. Thus the French describe themselves as Cartesian; the English and the Americans seldom describe themselves, but still they act consistently in such a manner as to be described by others as pragmatic or empirical. Professor Karl Pribram writes,

Mutual understanding and peaceful relations among the peoples of the earth have been impeded not only by the multiplicity of languages but to an even greater de-

CREDIT: Reprinted by permission from *ETC: A Review of General Semantics*, Vol. XI, No. 3. Copyright © 1954 by the International Society for General Semantics.

gree by differences in patterns of thought —that is, by differences in the methods adopted for defining the sources of knowledge and for organizing coherent thinking.

No mind can function to its own satisfaction without certain assumptions regarding the origin of its basic concepts and its ability to relate these concepts to each other. These assumptions have undergone significant changes in the course of time and have varied more or less among nations and among social groups at any given time. These differences in methods of reasoning have generated tension, ill-feeling, and even hatred.

The determination of the relationship between the patterns of thought of the cultural or national group whose ideas are to be communicated, to the patterns of thought of the cultural or national group which is to receive the communication, is an integral part of international communication. Failure to determine such relationships, and to act in accordance with such determinations, will almost unavoidably lead to misunderstandings.

Soviet diplomats often qualify the position taken by their Western counterparts as "incorrect" *nepravilnoe*. In doing so, they do not accuse their opponents of falsifying facts, but merely of not interpreting them "correctly." This attitude is explicable only if viewed in the context of the Marxist-Hegelian pattern of thought, according to which historical situations evolve in a unique and predetermined manner. Thus an attitude not in accordance with theory is not in accordance with truth either; it is as incorrect as the false solution of a mathematical problem. Conversely,

representatives of our side tend to propose compromise or transactional solutions. Margaret Mead writes that this attitude merely bewilders many representatives of the other side, and leads them to accuse us of hypocrisy, because it does not embody any ideological position recognizable to them. The idea that there are "two sides to every question" is an embodiment of nominalistic philosophy, and is hard to understand for those unfamiliar with this philosophy or with its influence.

Or again, on a slightly different plane: a simple English "No" tends to be interpreted by members of the Arabic culture as meaning "Yes." A real "No" would need to be emphasized; the simple "No" indicates merely a desire for further negotiation. Likewise a nonemphasized "Yes" will often be interpreted as a polite refusal.

Not all patterns of thought, or rather not everything in patterns of thought, is due to the influence of well-defined methodologies. Association of ideas plays a great part in thought; thus, clearly, each man's thought is to a large extent a function of this man's past.

Thus for instance, the word "colonialism" carries particularly irritating connotations to most Americans whereas it carries no such connotations to most Englishmen, Frenchmen, or Dutchmen. The reason for this is obviously anchored in history. It may not necessarily be, on the part of the Americans, the effect of a fully thought out political theory, but may be a simple association of ideas based on verbal habits which describe the American Revolution as the rising of "colonies" against an "empire."

DENOTATION AND CONNOTATION

Problems of this type appear in a much more complicated form whenever two words in two different languages have the same denotation but different connotations.

Thus for instance, the French word *"contribuable"* and the English word "taxpayer" denote the same thing, but their connotations are not identical. "Taxpayer" is a word descriptive of physical action, of something which might have been seen with the eyes. It evokes the image of a man paying money at, for instance, a teller's window. *"Contribuable,"* on the contrary, embodies an abstract principle. It evokes not an image but a thought, the thought that all citizens must contribute to the welfare of the nation of which they are a part.

Let us consider for a moment the connotations of these two words in the context of the North Atlantic Treaty Organization. A normal reaction on the American side will be: Does the man who pays get a fair return on his money? Or, in other words, is the Mutual Assistance Program really the best way of getting the most security for the least cost? A typical reaction on the French side will be quite different: Does everyone contribute equally to the common cause? Are the Americans as deeply and personally involved as the French? I would be surprised if some of the differences of opinion which arose at various moments within NATO between the United States and France were not due to a large extent to this particular semantic difficulty.

THE ROLE OF LANGUAGE

The preceding paragraph showed how patterns of thought may influence language and in turn be influenced by it. Both "taxpayer" and *"contribuable"* are comparative neologisms. If a certain method of word formation—by intension—was chosen by the French, it is because it corresponded to the pattern of thought prevalent in France. If another method of word formation— by extension—was chosen by the English, it is because it corresponded to their most general pattern of thought. Thus, peculiarities of language may constitute good indications of the prevalent manner of thinking.

However, once created, words and expressions assume an active role and contribute to the fashioning of thought. Thus two types of situations arise:

1. Cases where a given language is capable of expressing various shades of meaning and where the pattern of expression selected by given individuals provides a clue for the determination of their pattern of thought.

2. Cases where a certain combination of denotation and connotation cannot be obtained in a simple manner in a given language.

An example of the first case may be found in the following expressions: "What should we do under the circumstances?" and "What does the situation require?" Although the denotations of these two questions are just about identical, the answers, influenced in part by connotations, may tend to be different. The point is that although one of these two forms will appear more natural than the other, the English language is capable of using both.

The following occurrence may be presented as an example of the second case: At an international conference which took place a few years ago and in which both the United States and the Soviet Union participated, it became rapidly apparent that the Soviet Union would not sign the agreement in preparation. The reason for it was a disagreement in substance, which would not be overcome. The Russians, however, continued to participate in the work of the various committees, and in particular of the drafting committee, mainly it seemed in order to preserve diplomatic niceties. Their representatives were seldom heard from.

Thus, considerable surprise was created when a seemingly unimportant proposal by the U.S. delegate resulted in an outburst of violent Soviet opposition. Even more surprising was the attitude of most Europeans and in particular of the French who publicly supported the United States but privately stated that it was a mistake to have backed the Soviets against the wall by an attitude which they described as rigid and overbearing. The proposal of the U.S. delegate consisted in inserting in the preamble to the proposed agreement a clause taken from another instrument and containing the expression "expanding economy."

I would suggest the following explanation for this incident: the expression "expanding economy" is neutral with respect to the aristotelian categories of accident and essence. An "expanding economy" may be an economy which happens to be expanding because of various outside influences, or else an economy which is expanding because of characteristics inherent to its nature.

In Russian "expanding economy" becomes *rasshiryayushchiyasya ekonomiya"* in which the reflexive form is used. Although it would be incorrect to say that *"rasshiryayushchiyasya"* has the denotation of the English expression "self-expanding" it unquestionably carries a connotation which will lead a Russian-speaking listener to conclude that "expanding economy" means an economy expanding for reasons inherent to its nature.

Thus in this case language itself directed the attention of the listener away from one possible explanation and in the direction of another. To compound the confusion the difference between accident and essence is much more important to a person whose mind follows the Marxist-Hegelian patterns than to a person whose mind follows an empirical or pragmatic bent. The fact that an economy is expanding may warrant a certain type of action in the eyes of the empiricist, whichever be the cause of the expansion of the economy. To a Hegelian an economy expanding for accidental causes is bound to reverse itself unavoidably and rapidly.

Now it so happens that Marxist theory rules that the economy of the Western world must contract and cannot expand. Thus the recognition of an inherently expanding character in this economy, and this is an official document, could not fail to appear completely unacceptable to a Soviet delegate.

CLASSIFICATION OF PATTERNS OF THOUGHT

The problem of defining, describing and analyzing patterns of thought is not the only one which needs to be faced in the field of international communications. Questions such as translation *proprio motu,* choice of media and levels of approach, etc., also deserve attention. However, as they have been less neglected than were the problems of basic philosophical, ethnical, anthropological and linguistic determinations, they will be considered outside the scope of this paper.

I will deal here only with the analysis of pronouncements made by persons belonging to the Western cultural world and using one of the European languages. I do not feel competent at the present moment to do any work which would extend beyond the boundary defined above. In consequence, the classifications suggested below will be such as to help in analyzing a field limited to one culture, albeit an important one. Three basic groups of criteria will be used in the sample analysis at the end of this paper.

1. PATTERNS OF REASONING. Professor Karl Pribram, who has pointed out the importance of linguistically determined assumptions in the formation of concepts, distinguishes, in his book *Conflicting Patterns of Thought,* the following four patterns of reasoning.

A. *Universalistic   reasoning.* Universalistic reasoning is based on the premise that the human mind is able to grasp directly the order of the universe. Reason is credited with the power to know the truth with the aid of given general concepts and to establish absolutely valid rules for the organization of human relationships in accordance with these concepts. Universalistic reasoning proceeds from the general to the particular; it believes that general concepts, or universals, possess a reality independent from those of their components or constituents. The best way to determine what will happen in a given case is to know what happens in a more general category and then to determine what particular modifiers make the case in question a slight exception to the general rule.

B. *Nominalistic, or hypothetical, reasoning.* Nominalistic philosophy rejects the belief that general concepts have a reality of their own; instead it considers them merely as names, as convenient categories, more or less arbitrarily established by human minds. Reasoning proceeds from the particular to the general. Any exercise in pure reason establishes merely a hypothesis which must be verified by concrete experience.

Although these descriptions of patterns of thought may give the impression of dealing with abstract and complex reasonings, the influence of the patterns of thought described above may be found also at very concrete levels. Thus, for example, French visitors to New York are in general highly critical of the New York subway. What repels them is not the dirt or the crowding, but the evident lack of comprehensive planning in the geographical distribution of lines. For instance, there is no subway line which would take one from the business district around Wall Street to the new business district around Rockefeller Center, or from the Cloisters to the Metropolitan Museum of Art. The argument that the New York subway is the one which carries the greatest number of persons the most rapidly over the greatest distances from home to work and from work home does not impress the French visitors overly much.

On the contrary, the Paris Métro covers all of Paris like a spider web. Convenient changeover stations make it possible to go from any monument to any other. At the same time the Métro strikes the American visitor as almost unbelievably slow. It does not reach very far into the suburbs, where many people live, and its routes do not necessarily follow the pattern of home-to-work and work-to-home connections.

I will put it that the Paris Métro is based on the universalistic concept of a means of transit designed to provide for the needs of a city, considered as such, or as a universal, a collective noun. Lines run from one point of interest to another, no part of the city being deprived of a means of communication with all of the other parts; at the same time considerations such as the density of traffic are almost completely disregarded. On the contrary the New York subway is nominalistic; there is no network planned to cover a collective entity, the city; on the contrary, lines are built in such a way as to do the most possible good to the greatest possible number of individuals considered as such. It is not much help

to those who want to go from one residential area to another—but then people go fairly seldom from one residential area to another. On the contrary, it is every day that people go from home to work and from work home, and the New York subway is planned according to this consideration.

The names selected in each case by popular usage express the same preoccupation as the planning. "Metro" is an abbreviation of *"métropolitain"* or "metropolitan." The French language has resources which would have enabled Parisians to have selected a name such as "subway," but they did not choose to do so. Likewise English has the word "metropolitan," and the official titles of the various subway organizations in New York include words such as "transfer," "transit," and "system," yet the names chosen by the public are "subway," "el," or in Britain, "underground" or "tube."

It might be noted that *"chemin de fer"* is etymologically as well as factually similar to "railroad." But then, French railroads have the same characteristics from the point of view of planning as does the New York subway. Rail lines follow lines of probable maximum density which in France means that they radiate from Paris to the provinces. At the same time the network is not completed by transversal roads; the shortest way of getting from one provincial town to another may very often be the long way through Paris. This state of affairs was always considered illogical by the French and was violently criticized by them. As a result of this criticism it has been corrected to a large extent. The same criticism might have been leveled against American railroads. I remember being told that the best way to get from Sheridan, Wyoming, to San Francisco was through Seattle. Yet the criticism which might have been leveled at the American roads are in fact never heard. The American public understands that it is not economical to provide trains for occasional travel along low-demand routes.

Now it so happens that the French railroads were started by English capital and planned under English inspiration: they even run on the left whereas everything else in France runs on the right. Thus even this exception seems to confirm the rule: the fact that France is by and large a universalistic country does not mean that nominalism is entirely without influence there.

C. *Intuitional or organismic reasoning.* This type of reasoning stresses intuition rather than systematic cogitation. It is thus in a position to ignore some of the basic opposition between nominalism and universalism. It considers that the relationship between a collectivity and its members may be compared to the relationship between a biological organism and its component cells. Organismic reasoning opposes intuitive to discursive consciousness and claims that reliance on one's intuition enables man to be "independent yet subject to one's duties" (Joel). It is often associated with extreme nationalism and is prevalent in Germanic and Slavic Central Europe.

D. *Dialectic reasoning.* Hegelian dialectics are derived from universalism and, like universalism, believe in the possibility of a full understanding of the universe through reason. "But, according to the principles of dialectics, comprehension of the ever-changing nature of the phenomena and the flux of events can not be achieved with the aid of rigid concepts, alleged to be implanted in the human mind. The course of events is believed to be determined by the operation of antagonistic forces and must be understood with the aid of concepts adjusted to the contradictions logically represented by these forces" (Pribram).

Marxist dialectic materialism follows the Hegelian pattern which it modifies by the dogma of the predominance of materialistic factors.

2. THE VERB "TO BE" AND THE VERB "TO DO." The classification described above has been used very successfully by Professor Pribram in the analysis of a broad historical evolution of the patterns of thought. Other types of classification may be useful in supplementing it in cases of a more concrete nature.

One such method of classification may be found in the difference which separates the logic of the verb "to do" from the logic of the verb "to be."

The logic of the verb "to be" is basically two-valued: things are either thus or not thus. Propositions are either true or false. Meaningless propositions may generally be eliminated and reasoning presented in such a way that a two-valued logic applies.

On the contrary the logic of the verb "to do" is essentially multivalued: one does not do things truly or untruly, one does them more or less well.

All men are confronted with situations in which they tend to reason in terms of the verb "to be" and with other situations in which they tend to reason in terms of the verb "to do." There are, however, still other situations which may be studied by either of the methods correlated with these two verbs. Choices made by various individuals are indicative of the patterns of thought followed by them.

Quite obviously a prevalence of reasoning in terms of the logic of the verb "to do" ties in with nominalism, while a prevalence of reasoning in terms of the logic of the verb "to be" ties in with universalism. Thus an analysis undertaken in terms of these two verbs will be helpful in detecting patterns of thought. More than that, such an analysis will also show why it is that in some cases nominalists and universalists reach different conclusions even when starting from identical premises.

Let us take as examples the two concepts of compromise and intervention. If A wishes to paint the wall black and B wishes to paint it white, they may reach an honorable compromise by painting it gray. If A now states that the wall is black, and B states that the wall is white, they may not compromise by calling it gray, as this would make liars of both of them. They may try to convince one another, they may try to fight it out, or they may drop the subject.

I believe that the instability of the French cabinets is due to the fact that, when faced with an issue, the French tend to ask themselves. "What is right?" That is why there are so many issues which often come up for debate and seldom reach the stage of solution. That is also why action can be undertaken only at the expense of excluding from the cabinet for the time being those who do not agree with the majority and who can compromise only by being absent, even temporarily.

It may be noted that the verb "to compromise" has a dual meaning both in French and in English, as for instance in "compromise the difference" and "compromise one's integrity." The first of these two meanings is by far the more frequent in English, the second one by far the more frequent in French.

Let us turn now to the concept of intervention. A and B intend to have lunch together but have not agreed on the choice of a restaurant. They discuss the question in terms of their likes and dislikes, one saying that he would like to go one place and the other that he would like to go to another. C, who has not been invited, overhears the conversation, steps in and tells them what to do. C's attitude would be unanimously considered extremely rude: the action taken by a group to which he doesn't belong, in a case when this action does not affect him, is none of his business.

Once more A and B intend to have lunch but are not in agreement on the choice of a restaurant. This time, however, they conduct their discussion in terms of the verb "to be," A saying that food is better at one place and B that it is better at another. C, who still has not been invited, again overhears their conversation, again steps in offering some factual information about either or both of the two places. This time C's attitude will probably be quite acceptable.

Yet in fact that is no difference between the two situations. If a person wants to have lunch at a certain restaurant, it is probably because the person in question believes that the food is good there. Conversely, to say that food is good at a place means simply that one likes what is served there. As for factual information, one might do well to remember Goethe's saying: that which we call facts are nothing but our own pet theories. Thus again the difference is not in the situation, but in the patterns of thought.

It may be noted that French has several words which more or less mean intervention, for instance *"intervention," "immixion," "ingérence."* The two latter have a pejorative meaning. If now we pass from the nouns to the verbs, we see that the verbs corresponding to the pejorative nouns take the reflexive form, thus: *"s'immiscer," "s'ingérer,"* but *"intervenir."* Thus clearly what brings in the pejorative meaning is an insistence on the intervener, the doer, as opposed to an insistence on the situation.

Let us now consider the hypothetical case of the country A which wishes another country B to take a certain step of a very controversial nature. Country A is basically nominalistic, country B is basically universalistic. Country A will not try to influence public opinion in country B; its government thinks of intervention in terms of the verb "to do" and considers it *a priori* as an unfriendly gesture. Country A will try to negotiate directly this issue at government level, offering perhaps some inducements in another field as basis for a compromise, which being nominalistic, it considers honorable. Unfortunately country B, being universalistic, cannot accept a barefaced compromise. At the same time it would not necessarily have resented an intervention, even addressed directly to its own public opinion, if such intervention were made in sufficiently theoretical and impersonal terms.

3. DENOTATION AND CONNOTATION. Of the two methods of classification suggested above, only one may be qualified as linguistic. Yet language may influence thought or else be used as an indication of an existing pattern of thought correlated with a pattern of expression in many more ways than one. Unfortunately the field of the mutual influence of language and thought is as yet largely unexplored. In consequence purely linguistic manners of classification will need to be developed slowly, through experience.

It appears clear, nevertheless, that a search for connotation as distinct from denotation may clarify many concrete situations. Some examples of situations of this kind have been given previously, some others will be found below.

In seeking to systematize the influence of connotations particular attention will have to be paid to the formation of names of sets or classes, or of representatives of sets, either through extension or through intension. Extensives or descriptive formation will generally indicate the prevalence of nominalist patterns and of multivalued logic. On the contrary, intensive formation will indicate the prevalence of universalistic patterns. Both types of word formation will be found in most languages. Areas in which words are formed by one or the other system will in general correspond to areas in which a corresponding type of reasoning is prevalent.

Analysis of connotations should go beyond simple words. It should also embrace sentence structure, set expressions made up of several words, current metaphors, proverbs, and manners in which groups of words may be formed around the same root.

For instance an expression such as *"faire faire,"* which can never be properly translated into English—"to have something done" lacks both spontaneity and generality—is in itself an indication of a certain contempt toward action and at the same time is an expression of respect toward the thought which precedes action; in other words it is an expression of universalistic thinking.

The use of the verb "to do" as the principle auxiliary verb in English is also a program in itself.

The systems of classification suggested above are not intended to cover the entire field. They are, rather, examples of lines which can be followed. No analysis should neglect the possibility of finding other explanations such as the ones which may be derived from the implications of history, even where those implications cannot be expressed in terms of semantic or philosophical categorization.

Thus, for instance, of all the great democracies the United States is the one which shows the greatest intolerance of domestic Communism. I believe that an explanation of this fact may be found in the very tradition of the beginnings of an American nationality. Most European countries are founded on a tradition of indigenous ancestry. There are naturalized Frenchmen and Britons, and other Frenchmen and Britons who are descendants of immigrants, but people of these descriptions constitute very small minorities of the citizens of their respective countries. In consequence it is difficult for European countries to consider unwelcome the exponent of any political ideology as long as he can point out a long line of indigenous ancestry. On the contrary, the United States as a nation was created by men and women who had come to a new continent in order to establish a society based on certain definite ideals. It may be interesting to note in that connection how much more important is for American tradition the settlement of the Pilgrims in 1620 than is the settlement of the Gentlemen adventurers of Virginia in 1607. The United States thus bases its tradition on the establishment of an ideology on virgin soil. It is thus quite normal for Americans to think that those who wish to establish some other ideology should go and do it somewhere else.

A DAY IN THE SECURITY COUNCIL

In the paragraphs below I will try to analyze the complete stenographic record of the first part of the one-hundredth meeting of the Security Council. The record used is in three languages—English, French, and Russian. Analysis will start in all cases with the consideration of statements in the original language, then pass on to the translations.

In that connection it should be noted that (1) the differences of opinion of the various representatives are due primarily to questions of a political nature the discussion of which falls outside the scope of the present paper. At the same time the type of arguments chosen by the participants and the manner in which those participants present their arguments are considered indicative of patterns of thought and will be the subject of the present analysis.

(2) The translations by linguists of the United Nations Secretariat are invariably excellent. Although I have spent many years in work of this type, there is not one single aspect of these translations on which I feel I could improve.

In order to facilitate reading the various points being analyzed will be numbered consecutively.

1. The President, a Belgian, says, *"Aucune proposition n'étant faite dans ce sens, j'en déduis. . . ."*

The last word becomes "I assume" in the English translation. "I deduce" would have been stiff, "I conclude" almost impolite, implying that no change of opinion or of interpretation on the part of the Assembly would be welcome. "I assume" is correct because that is the word which an English-speaking chairman would have chosen in all probability, and also because, in a nominalistic or hypothetical reasoning, one acts upon assumptions. Assumptions become certainties only after action has resulted in their verification.

The President could not have used the French equivalent of "I assume." If one considers that reason is capable of reaching entirely valid conclusions one does not act upon assumptions. *"Je suppose"* would have implied that the members of the Council have not made their positions sufficiently clear to allow the President to reach a clear conclusion.

The Russian translation uses *"zaklyuchaiyu"*—"I conclude." The strength of this word may be best evaluated if one realizes that the participle form *"zaklyuchonnyi"* means a prisoner and is often used in the subsequent remarks of the Russian delegate.

In that respect it may be interesting to note that Slavic languages tend to create groups of words using the same root with different prefixes and suffixes. Thus for instance *"zaklyuchit' "* to conclude, *"izklyuchit' "* to exclude, *"vyklyuchit' "* to switch off, *"vklyuchit' "* to switch on or to include. A still better example is found in the Polish verbs "to read." There is one such verb in English, and twelve in Polish, to wit:

czytać	to read
czytywać	to read habitually
przeczytać	to read completely
przeczytywać	to read completely and habitually
odczytać	to read aloud to a group, to communicate a written text
odczytwać	the same thing habitually
wyczytać	to read excerpts, to interpret (a meaning)
wyczytywać	the same thing habitually
wczytać	to read a meaning into a text
wczytywać	the same thing habitually
zaczytać sie	to bury oneself in one's reading

zaczytywać sie the same thing habitually

It is not difficult to imagine how such a manner of expression would encourage a manner of thinking prone to a certain subtlety in distinctions and to a certain rigidity of categorization. Situations should fall into one of several clearly defined patterns; whenever they fail to do so, they would be considered with disbelief or at least skepticism.

2. An intervention of the Australian delegate, who alludes to the need of investigating "the situation which is before us."

"Which is before us" becomes *"qui nous est soumise"* in French and *"rassmatrivayemym nami"* in Russian. "Which is before us" is neutral. *"Qui nous est soumise"* means literally "which is submitted to us" and implies the assumption of authority of a body of men—the Security Council—over a situation. The Russian expression means "which is under consideration" but with the connotation of "which is being taken apart" or "in regard to which the precise category into which it falls has to be determined." Both the establishing of a hierarchy and that of fixed categories are characteristic of universalism.

3. Where the Australian delegate says that the situation needs to be investigated, the Soviet delegate says that the question is already decided. It is the "same" situation as the one which was discussed before. The difference of opinion between the two delegates is due to the fact that the Australian looks at it from the point of view of procedure while the Soviet delegate looks at it from the point of view of substance. (Once again it is realized that they may have political reasons for adopting the attitude which they have taken. Nevertheless the manner of argumentation remains indicative of the pattern of thought.) An insistence on the procedural aspect is well in keeping with the nominalist attitude, as after all it is procedure which will determine the manner of action—if not necessarily the direction of such action—of a body such as the Security Council. On the contrary an insistence on the broad substantive aspects of the situation is well in keeping with a manner of thinking according to which historical development falls in a predetermined course, and the main task of the statesman is to recognize and diagnose correctly a substantive situation. The "correct" action to be undertaken will follow more or less automatically from a correct diagnosis.

4. The Soviet delegate claims that the present situation is part and parcel of a more general situation and should not be discussed separately. In doing so, he uses the expression *"opryedyel-yennaya stadiya"* which becomes *"phase nouvelle"* and "another aspect" in English. Literally it means "a well-defined phase." Even such an expression as "another phase" might have conveyed to an English-speaking listener the idea that special measures should be taken, as it is perfectly normal to treat each phase of a situation separately. An expression such as "a well-defined or well-determined phase" would have even accentuated this idea of separateness from the more general question, and thus expressed an intention exactly contrary to that of the speaker. *"Phase nouvelle"* is faith-

ful to the meaning but *"phase bien determinée"* would have again given the impression that this phase should be separated from the broader aspects of the problem. As a matter of fact the expression *"opryedyelyennaya stadiya"* would have conveyed an intention somewhat contrary to that of the speaker even to a non-Communist Russian listener. If used by the Soviet delegates it is because it fits in with the Marxist interpretation of history according to which evolution proceeds necessarily from one "well-determined phase" to another; the fact that the phase is well determined, and not merely vaguely outlined, proves that it is indeed an integral part of a correctly diagnosed and described over-all situation.

5. In the same intervention the Soviet delegate said that the decision of the Council *"dolzhen reshat'sya avtomaticheski."* As "should be reached automatically" is ambiguous in English, it becomes "the question settles itself automatically" in the English translation, and *"pouvons trancher d'office"* in the French translation. The English translation is a wee bit stronger than the original Russian, the French quite a bit weaker. But both convey clearly the dialectical meaning: once the correct diagnosis is reached, the manner of action is determined automatically.

6. The Australian delegation again takes the floor and spells out his meaning: the substantive situation is irrelevant for a moment as the Council must first of all settle a question "concerning the operations" of one of its subsidiary organizations.

7. The President, speaking in French, states that a commission has requested a certain government *"de faire ajourner"* certain measures. This becomes "requested to postpone" in the English translation. In French, a government acts directly only at a very high level. In regard to questions of a less exalted nature, it merely causes an action to be taken. Thus a clear hierarchy between principle and mere action is established. (In Russian this becomes "a request in regard to postponement.")

8. The United States delegate finds that the situation is clearly one of procedure. The question is "simple" because the "only concrete" action which may be taken is a procedural one. The procedural situation should not be "seized upon" in order to introduce long arguments about substance.

9. It might be noted that the expression "draft resolution" becomes *"projet de résolution"* in French and *"proyekt rezolyutsiyi"* in Russian. A draft is something you work upon and try to perfect. The implication is that it is only the final product which will be judged. A project is something which may be rejected *in toto;* the implication is that the desirability of such a project should be decided upon theoretically before any work is spent in trying to reach perfection.

10. The Soviet delegate reiterates that *"otvyet mozhet byt' tol'ko"*— there is but one answer to the question. Once again the Soviet delegate asks how is it possible to consider a question of procedure—about which nothing is said in the theory of historical evolution—independently from the question of substance, which is the one to which an answer can be found through dialectics.

11. The Russian *"utvyerzhdye-*

niye" appears as "assertion" in English and as *"avis"* in French. *"Avis"* means in this context merely "opinion." "Assertion" is stronger, but not as strong as "affirmation" which would be the closest to the original Russian. However the very strength of "affirmation" would tend to give it an ironical or even pejorative connotation. *"Utvyer-zhdyeniye"* is very strong; it derives etymologically from *"tvyerdyi"*— "hard" and the obsolete *"tyerdynya"* —"fortress." The contrast between the weakness of the French expression and the strength of the Russian one is particularly striking, the more so that we tend to consider both nations as following a more or less universalistic bent. Incidentally, it is quite as easy to express the meaning of "opinion" in Russian as that of "affirmation" in French. The present choice of words, on the part of the Russian delegate and on the part of the very competent French translators, is probably due to the absence in pure universalism and to the presence in Hegelianism of an element of systematic strife: thesis versus antithesis.

12. The Soviet delegate further states that he "cannot understand" how his opponents can consider a procedural aspect as being distinct from the more general question of substance.

13. The Russian *"sootvyetstvo-vat'"* becomes "to signify" in English and *"appeler"* in French. It literally and also etymologically means "to correspond" (*so-otvyet, cum—re-spondere*). This again shows a predilection for rigid categories.

14. The representative of France takes the floor. For obvious reasons he sides with the Australian and the American and gives his own very brief restatement of their position. The only thing which he introduces and which was not contained in the earlier speeches of the Western delegates is one little word: *"donc"*—"therefore." The effects of this little word will be seen in some of the subsequent remarks.

15. For the French delegate the question is *"la question dont il s'agit."* This is translated into Russian by the equally impersonal *"ryech idyet,"* but becomes in English "the question with which *we* are concerned" with a shift of emphasis from the situation *per se* to the people dealing with it.

16. *"Il est naturel"* remains "it is natural" in English but becomes *"yestyestvenno"* in Russian. This word derives from the root *"yestyestvo"* meaning "substance" and itself deriving from the word "to be." It is much closer in its connotations to the aristotelian original than is "natural."

17. There are two French words which correspond to the English word "probable." These are *"probable"* and *"vraisemblable,"* the latter containing the connotation of a judgment as to truth value which is absent from the first. It might be interpreted as meaning "something similar to the established scheme of truth." The one Russian word translating "probable," *"vyeroyatno,"* corresponds to the French word *"vraisemblable."*

18. The delegate of the United States takes the floor to "concur with the opinion expressed by the delegate of France." Now, as we have mentioned before, the delegate of France merely restated the position taken by the delegates of Australia and of the United States. He did, however, add

the little word "therefore," which made the position so much clearer and more forceful that it becomes from now on known as the French position.

19. The delegate of the United States presents a draft resolution for the purpose of "giving concrete form" to opinion and to enable "the Council to dispose of this matter." It would be "the acme of futility" to discuss questions of substance when there is need for an immediate procedural decision.

20. The President says, *"Je ne voudrais préjuger en rien la décision que le Conseil de sécurité va prendre."* *"Préjuger"* remains *"pryedugadyvat'"* in Russian (etymologically, "to guess before my turn") but becomes "to prejudice" in English, thus implying that prejudging by a President could not fail to influence the action of the Council. Once again emphasis is shifted from situation to action.

21. The delegate of Australia also expresses his agreement with the delegate of France.

22. "To have no claim" becomes *"ne pas pouvoir prétendre"* in French and *"nye imyeyet' prava,"* "to have no right," in Russian. The English word "claim" is extremely difficult to translate, as it expresses an entirely nominalistic idea: that of a juridical situation which is neither clearly white nor clearly black, but which on the contrary takes into account the legitimacy of practical adjustments.

In trying to present an over-all evaluation of the meeting described above, one should remember that the various delegates were faced indeed with difficult political problems. On the other hand, however, the men who engaged in the debate described were unquestionably far above the average in preparation for and experience in handling international communication.

The impression obtained is that whereas the French and the Belgian members of the Assembly on the one hand and the American and the Australian on the other have retained their individuality, communication between them has been established; in particular the Frenchman and the Belgian have conclusively shown that they understood not only the position, which would be a political matter, but also the reasoning, which is a semantic matter, of the Australian and the American. On the contrary, the degree of communication between the Soviet delegate and the delegates of Australia and of the United States appears to be nil. Once again political situations may not be disregarded. When the Soviet delegate states that he does not understand the attitude of his opponents, he may be simply seeking to gain some rhetorical advantage. At the same time, however, the very fact that this form of argumentation should have occurred to him shows that he genuinely believes that it is at least conceivable that people of good will might find the attitude of the Australian and the American delegates difficult to understand.

At the same time no attempt is made by anyone to explain the basis of his manner of thinking; all that the various speakers do is to present arguments which appear pertinent once a certain manner of thinking is accepted.

Thus for instance nobody has made a speech along these lines: "It is true that the basic problems which we are supposed to discuss here are the political problems of the world. Those problems, however, are complex, and their solution cannot be expected to be reached rapidly. In consequence we must separate from those problems questions pertaining to our day-to-day operations within the Council. If we did not do so, we would be unable to accomplish any useful work whatsoever."

Words—Returning from an International Conference

The converse was not heard either: "Operations can be fruitful only if they are in agreement with the substance of the situation to which they pertain. Thus it is better to postpone any action than to undertake an action which might make it more difficult for us to analyze the situation correctly and to take in the end such measures as the situation dictates." The precise point under dispute in this meeting was whether the delegates of certain nonmember countries should be invited to participate in the debate. This participation was at first opposed by the Australian delegate in extremely conciliatory terms. It does not appear to be necessary "for the present." The Council should however be ready to reconsider in accordance with possible developments. After the Soviet delegate has taken the floor to suggest that an invitation be extended, this invitation is again opposed by the delegates of the United States and Australia in terms much stronger than those used previously. The Soviet delegate had based his arguments on the subordination of the procedural aspects to substantive ones; as the non-member nations are interested in the substantive aspects, they should participate in all the discussions, and in fact the debate should bear on substance principally. The Western delegates reply that the question is one of procedure over which only members of the Council have jurisdiction. The increasing acrimony of the debate leads to the impression that the Australian and the American delegates oppose more the pattern of thought of the Soviet delegate, with his insistence on discussion and inaction, than they do the actual invitation which he champions.

To sum up, it appears that all difficulties of international communication have not been solved in the case above. The purely linguistic problem was solved superbly, insofar as translation and interpretation may solve it, by the staff of the United Nations Secretariat. The question of patterns of thought, however, does not appear to have been given any attention whatsoever.

CONCLUSION

In presenting this paper I do not wish to say that it is possible to arrive at a rigid classification of patterns of thought which would apply in all cases. Neither do I wish to imply that national or cultural groups are characterized by a rigid and constant adherence to definite patterns of thought. Nor again do I wish to imply that there is a rigid correspondence between languages and patterns of thought.

What I hope to have shown is:

1. That here exist correlations between patterns of thought and patterns of expressions and that those correlations may be used in the analysis of patterns of thought.

2. That patterns of thought will be more easily recognized through the connotations appearing in the patterns of expression than in the denotations of statements.

3. That forms taken by language tend in many cases to encourage certain patterns of thought and to discourage others.

4. That connotations appearing in language have at least as much a part in influencing thought as do denotations.

5. That even an imperfect method of classification may greatly help in analyzing patterns of thought as they appear in concrete cases, and thus to make it easier to overcome some of the obstacles inherent in international communications.

ORDEAL BY DEBATE: VIEWER REACTIONS

KURT LANG AND GLADYS E. LANG

Since John F. Kennedy's narrow election victory in 1960, observers, even while lacking clear data, have suggested that television was Richard M. Nixon's undoing. This article seeks neither to belabor nor to challenge the diagnosis that Kennedy could not have won had there been no television debates. To disentangle the influence of any single campaign event or issue on the outcome of an election is always difficult. In the case of the TV debates, it becomes a logical absurdity, since the narrow margin of victory indicates that to win Senator Kennedy needed every single one of the breaks he got. His victory is attributable only to a concatenation of all factors that worked in his favor. He needed the votes of Southern Negroes and obtained them apparently through his intervention for Martin Luther King. The support of New York's liberal Democrats—equally decisive—was obtained through the efforts of Eleanor Roosevelt, Herbert Lehman, and others in the party's reform movement. Labor's enthusiastic assist everywhere supplied a crucial balance. The rise in unemployment in the fall undoubtedly helped. There is no way of showing that the TV debates supplied the decisive margin of victory.

The issue of the impact of the televised debates can, however, be posed against a background of what has been fairly well established about the impact of mass communications during a political campaign.[1] They function primarily in two ways: (1) to increase the salience of party alignments and (2) to adjust and bring images of the men, issues, etc., into line with voting preferences. A change in alignment can be brought about by campaign events which crystallize the votes of one side more strongly than those of the other or which (a less likely eventuality) produce mass switches. The televised debates were different from the usual campaign materials in that they created "double exposure." There was no practical way for a viewer to expose himself to the personality and arguments of one candidate and not the other. Also, the debates drew top audiences.

CREDIT: Reprinted by permission of the publisher from *Public Opinion Quarterly*, Summer, 1961, pp. 277–288. [*Tables renumbered.*]

[1] Among a number of good summaries of the impact are the Appendix to B. R. Berelson, P. F. Lazarsfeld, and W. N. McPhee, *Voting* (Chicago: University of Chicago Press, 1954), and E. Burdick and A. J. Brodbeck, *American Voting Behavior* (Glencoe, Ill.: The Free Press, 1959), chapters 12 and 13.

This small-scale panel study of 95 New York viewers offered an opportunity to detail how some individuals responded to this double exposure. The observations do not warrant any statistical inference about a larger population, national or local. Twenty-four of the interviews are self-interviews by college seniors in a mass communications class at Queens College, a nonresident campus. The other 71 were obtained by these same students from voters outside the college community. Instructions were issued that would give us a fairly even distribution of potential Kennedy and Nixon supporters. But in no sense can the sample be treated as representative even of the New York population.[2]

Each respondent was interviewed three times: first, late in September just before the first debate, then immediately after that debate, and again after the fourth and last encounter. Although changes in voting intention unquestionably constitute the clearest measure of impact and interview schedules elicited data on such changes, the schedules were designed primarily to determine how viewers' images and comparisons of Kennedy and Nixon were directly influenced by the debates.

Among this panel there was an immediate and dramatic improvement of the Kennedy image right after the first debate, but this improvement was not accompanied by shifts in voting intentions of anywhere near compara-

ble proportions. Since the final vote did not depend on the outcome of the debate alone, this analysis discusses separately vote changes, which reflect decisions made, and the manner in which new perceptions, often disturbing ones, developed into a candidate image appropriate to electoral choices. The observations set forth here illustrate processes involved in communication effects. Inference beyond the specific cases depends on whether and how widely the general factors shown to determine impact in this sample operate elsewhere and not, to repeat, on statistical probability.[3]

VOTE SHIFTS

Three types of vote shift could be observed in the sample: the crystallization from "undecided" or abstention into a clear-cut preference for one of the two candidates, a switch from one candidate to the other, and a tempo-

---

[2] Altogether, 104 persons were interviewed before or after the debates. Ninety-seven were interviewed before the debates, while 7 more were interviewed after the first and fourth debates. References throughout the paper are only to those 95 persons with whom three interviews were successfully completed.

[3] Of the 97 interviewed before the debates, 13 were too young to vote, 23 were first voters, 19 were twenty-five to thirty-four, 33 were thirty-five to fifty-four, and 7 were fifty-five and over. The sample contained 50 persons of Jewish origin, 26 Protestants, 18 Catholics, and three who gave no answers. The seven respondents added were Catholic. The socio-economic level was somewhat above average: excluding the students and housewives, the respondents were divided rather equally among professionals, managerial and white-collar workers, salesmen and small businessmen, and blue-collar workers. Obviously, these characteristics do not reflect the larger American population but, insofar as political identification is the significant determinant of response to the telecasts (as we think it is *during a campaign*), then the atypicality of respondents should not make the findings completely atypical. We did employ a much-modified F scale to try to get at personality and viewing habits as a correlate of response, but this attempt was frankly a failure.

rary weakening of commitment without any actual change (wavering). Table V-3 summarizes the aggregate change within the sample. Most of it is due to a rally of uncommitted voters behind Kennedy.

right after the first debate. All three said they had been impressed by the Kennedy performance. The pro-Nixon switch recorded by the end of the debate series was not evident in any way after the initial television encounter.

TABLE V-3   Vote Decisions *

	Before debates	*After 1st debate*	*After 4th debate*
Decided for Kennedy	37	47	52
Leaning toward Kennedy	2	6	4
	39	53	56
Undecided	23	12	7
Leaning toward Nixon	2	2	1
Decided for Nixon	31	28	31
	33	30	32
TOTAL	95	95	95

* Based on respondents for whom three interviews were completed.

After the fourth debate, the votes of 23 persons initially uncommitted had crystallized in this way: 15 were either for Kennedy or clearly "leaning" his way, 3 had moved into the Nixon column, 5 were still undecided or determined not to vote. The decisive shift came immediately after the first debate, when 8 became decided for Kennedy and 4 more indicated a definite leaning toward him. Shifts toward Nixon did not become evident until sometime between the first and the last debates. Nor is there any clear evidence that the debates were a specific determinant in these gains for Nixon.

Four persons who had expressed a definite commitment before the debates switched by the latter part of October—three from Nixon to Kennedy and one from Kennedy to Nixon. The three pro-Kennedy switchers defected (or began to lean) to Kennedy

Six persons initially decided for Nixon wavered: one of these moved to the undecided group right after the first debate, and one after the series was over. The other four weakened in their preference, three of them immediately after the first debate, but they either continued to lean toward Nixon or had returned to Nixon at the end. The lone Kennedy waverer grew less sure of his preference for Kennedy after the first debate, but continued to lean toward him.

All told, there were then 22 intra-campaign vote changes, consisting of 18 crystallizers and 4 switchers. Kennedy drew his added strength largely (11 out of 18) from weak Democratic Party identifiers, 9 of whom had been too young to vote in 1956 and 2 of whom had defected to vote for Eisenhower in 1956. Only two persons—one self-styled Independent and one

Republican—can be said to have crossed party lines to vote for Kennedy. Nixon, on the other hand, won two votes from Democrats for Stevenson in 1956, together with one from a Democrat who had voted for Eisenhower and another from a new voter calling himself Independent. Therefore, when viewed against the voters' background of party identification and previous vote, very few of the intra-campaign shifts attributable to the debates are contrary to past political commitments. The majority merely responded to inclinations which had clearly been present before the debates.[4]

Nevertheless, the debates brought about a sharper polarization. Within this group, the first debate in particular crystallized some votes and reinforced others. Then, after that first impact, choices tended to remain firm in the face of new campaign developments. We can now examine in some detail how our viewers' images of the candidates were affected by exposure to the first "debate."

PRE-DEBATE IMAGES

Voting preferences are usually linked in various degrees with party identifications, orientation to political issues, and images of the candidates.[5] The last two are clearly the more variable and volatile and account for occasional

[4] The small sample prevents any meaningful statistical analysis of politically relevant background factors (like religion and occupation).

[5] Cf. A. Campbell, G. Gurin, and W. E. Miller, *The Voter Decides* (Evanston, Ill.: Row, Peterson, 1954).

crossovers that contradict party identifications. But since one can reasonably assume that the debates would highlight especially the competitive performance of the two candidates, one would expect any change in voting preference because of the debates to be mediated primarily through the image of the candidates.

Before the debate the image viewers had of Nixon was understandably much sharper than that of Kennedy, since Nixon had held national elective office and was far better known. Seventy per cent of the panel said they were "more familiar" with Nixon; 18 per cent said they were equally familiar (or unfamiliar) with both; only 12 per cent thought they knew Kennedy better. Yet certain well-defined images of each candidate were widely shared by the panel.

The image of Nixon

First, the impression that the Vice Presidency entailed more responsibility and afforded better preparation for the Presidency than serving in the Senate was accepted, at least tacitly, even by most Democrats. Second, Nixon was remembered as a roving political ambassador who had dealt with angry mobs in South America and debated with Khrushchev in Russia, though viewers assessed these accomplishments differently. Third, Nixon's formidability as a TV personality and debater was acknowledged by those both for and against his candidacy. Finally, respondents saw in Nixon an experienced and skilled politician; even opponents who heartily disliked him doubted he would ever again resort in public to the tactics which had been successful against some past political opponents, tactics which they distrusted and which made them distrust Nixon.

The image of Kennedy

The Kennedy image was simpler but also somewhat fuller. The dominant image of Kennedy, even among many intending to vote against him, was of a "fine young man" with some potential. He was most often viewed as competent and cool—an ambitious politician who knew how to build an organization, as evidenced by his nomination. Both those for and against him widely referred to Kennedy as "vigorous" or "vital." However, doubts were voiced about his convictions: many considered him too immature and inexperienced, though eager, to qualify for the Presidency. To a small minority of the panel who were strongly opposed to him, he was the embodiment of the stereotype of wealth. They called him "snobbish" and were highly suspicious of the political influence of his family and of his Catholicism. As an aside, it may be mentioned that the most unfriendly image of Kennedy was shared largely by the Catholic Republicans in the sample, of whom two were among the most outspoken in their opposition to a Catholic, especially one like Kennedy, in the White House.

Expectations of the debate

Respondents looked forward to the debates as a match of the candidates' forensic skills: their ability, as it was so often expressed, to "put their views across." It was to be an ordeal by TV through which the men could be put to the test. The partisan hoped to see his candidate perform effectively and thereby improve his chances of winning. Most of those interviewed thought the debates might affect the voting decisions of others but discounted in advance any effect on themselves.

There was, however, a significant difference between the expectations of Nixon partisans and Kennedy partisans (Table V-4). Two-thirds of Nixon partisans felt confident of their candidate's superior debating skills; only 4 out of 33 thought Kennedy might do better. Among Kennedy partisans, Nixon held his own at least. A reading of the interviews reveals that only a few Kennedy partisans expressed real confidence that their man was a match for Nixon. By their evasion of a flat prediction, many implied that they were worried by Nixon's reputation as a political in-fighter.

Respondents who thought they "might be influenced" by the debates put special stress on the image the candidates would project. A number intended to look specifically for "the way the candidates answered" as apart from what they might say. "I want to see," said one, "whether they hem and haw before they answer, whether they mean what they say, and whether they are sincere." Others said they would look for signs of knowledgeability and an ability to stand up "courageously."

Finally, many who were undecided and a number of party faithfuls lukewarm to their party's candidate said they would seek information on how the candidates stood on important issues. The debates offered a unique opportunity for an "instantaneous reply." Viewers expected that the candidates would force each other

TABLE   V-4   Expectations and Actual Performance in First Debate,* by Political Preference

Political preference before 1st debate	Nixon better	About the same	Kennedy better	D.K. no answer
		Expectations of performance		
Nixon (33)	22	7	4	0
Undecided (23)	9	8	4	2
Kennedy (41)	13	12	13	3
TOTAL	44	27	21	5
Per cent	45%	28%	22%	5%
		Actual performance		
Nixon (30)	8	10	12	0
Undecided (22)	0	2	20	0
Kennedy (39)	2	9	28	0
TOTAL	10	21	60	0
Per cent	11%	23%	66%	0

* Based on 97 respondents for whom pre-debate and the first post-debate interviews were available. Six respondents re-interviewed did not watch.

into clear-cut statements on future policy and expose their past records.

IMPACT OF THE FIRST DEBATE

Eighty-nine per cent of those who watched or heard the first television encounter thought Kennedy had bested Nixon in debate or at least fought him to a draw.[6] The single most important result of the debate lay in its destruction of the image, so widely held, of Richard Nixon as champion debater and television politician par excellence. This reevaluation of the comparative ability of the two men as performers helped crystal-

[6] Of a national sample of approximately 1,000 viewers interviewed by the Gallup Organization during the week Sept. 27 to Oct. 4, 1960, about twice as many thought Kennedy did better than thought Nixon did better (release of Oct. 12, 1960).

lize the vote of undecideds and caused partisans to revise their images of the men as "persons" and as presidential timber.

Changes in the images of candidates as "persons" following the first encounter were generally in the direction of greater consonance between preference and image. But, as Table V-5 shows, Kennedy scored net gains, creating a more favorable personal image for himself. His unexpectedly able performance dissolved many doubts about his maturity and experience even among Nixon partisans. The deterioration of the Nixon personal image was most evident among the Democrats in the panel and the undecideds but affected also 5 of the 30 Nixon partisans. On the other hand, Nixon's own partisans who thought him well-informed before the debates found him even better informed after the first debate, and this gain more

TABLE V-5   Percentage Change in Candidates' Image After First Debate *

	Better	*Unchanged*	*Worse*	*No answer*
Kennedy personal image	45	45	5	4
Nixon personal image	20	47	29	4
Kennedy—informedness	41	53	3	3
Nixon—informedness	14	67	11	8

* Based on 91 respondents.

than offset the loss Nixon suffered among the pro-Kennedy group.

A judgment of over-all attitude toward the two candidates was made from answers to questions about what viewers had found out about each man. Table V-6 uses the categories "Improvement" and "Deterioration" with regard to general image. The categories "Favorable (Unfavorable) Validated" were added to indicate persons who changed in that they became more sure of their judgment.

As expected, many partisans validated a favorable image of their own candidate and an unfavorable image of his opponent. Improvements and deteriorations in images interest us more. The Kennedy image improved markedly among those initially uncommitted and only somewhat less among Kennedy partisans; the improvement extended even to Nixon supporters. The over-all image of Nixon generally deteriorated. Even among his partisans, 1 out of 5 reported impressions that were less favorable to Nixon than they had been before.[7]

[7] Among a test audience recruited in the Trenton, New Jersey, area, the proportion who held a very favorable image of Kennedy increased 16 per cent following the debate compared with an increase of 4 percent for Nixon (Gallup Organization Release, Oct. 2, 1960).

CUMULATIVE IMPACT

Once firmed up in response to the initial debate, the images of the two candidates changed very little thereafter, even though many of the perceptions about that encounter must have been dissonant or incongruous with commitments. Both candidates had, for example, scored some gains in over-all image among persons supporting their opponent. Exposure to such invalidating information, one would expect, forces viewers to gear their subsequent communications behavior to the reestablishment of balance.[8] It is possible to do this in a number of ways other than a change in preference: (1) by refusing to watch any further debates, (2) by turning to sources of information more "favorable" to one's candidate, and (3) by continuing to look in subsequent debates for clues reaffirming one's original convictions.

1. Among our sample there is no evidence that dissonance introduced by the first debate led either to a general curtailment or to an increase of exposure. The number of debates

[8] Cf. L. Festinger, *A Theory of Cognitive Dissonance* (Evanston, Ill.: Row, Peterson, 1957).

TABLE V-6   Changes In Over-All Evaluation of Candidates After First Debate, by Political Preference

Political preference before 1st debate	Improvement	Favorable validated	No hange	Unfavorable validated	Deterioration
		Kennedy evaluations			
Nixon (30)	10	1	7	12	0
Undecided (22)	11	0	9	2	0
Kennedy (39)	19	15	4	0	1
TOTAL	40	16	20	14	1
Per cent	45%	18%	22%	15%	1%
		Nixon evaluations			
Nixon (30)	1	16	7	0	6
Undecided (22)	2	0	9	3	8
Kennedy (39)	6	0	13	14	6
TOTAL	9	16	29	17	20
Per cent	10%	18%	32%	19%	22%

watched was unrelated to initial candidate preference, judgment of who had won the first debate, amount of change in image, or education. The availability of alternate techniques for reducing dissonance, besides avoidance, militates against the emergence of a clear relationship to exposure.

2. Responses after the fourth debate showed rather clearly how much persons had come to rely on interpretations they had read in newspapers and news magazines, usually publications reflecting their own views. Later observations lacked the originality that had characterized viewers' responses after the first debate and exhibited considerable uniformity. From this it appears that journalistic interpretations and personal conversations supplied a frame of reference permitting the assimilation of information from subsequent debates without stirring new doubt or conflict.

3. An important way of reducing the strain between image and voting preference involved a reassessment of the various component elements that

make up a candidate's political personality as dramatized by TV. Such TV appearances entail a television *performance,* here performance as "debater," a political appearance in a *political role,* and a *personal image* of the performer and candidate (a conception of the kind of human being he is, the "real" person).[9] The appeal of a political personality is a function of the way he projects along each of the three dimensions and of the way they are related or isolated in the viewer's cognition. The relationship between performance, on the one hand, and personal image and political role, on the other, is similar in certain respects to the relationship between information and the attitudes on which the information supposedly bears.[10] The remainder of this paper takes up the

[9] The authors, in a previous paper, showed that three elements are clearly separable. "The Television Personality in Politics," *Public Opinion Quarterly,* Vol. 20, 1956, pp. 103–113.

[10] Cf. J. T. Klapper, *The Effects of Mass Communication* (Glencoe, Ill.: Free Press, 1960), pp. 84–90. Cf. also G. Lindzey (editor), *Handbook*

question of how new cognitive elements introduced so dramatically by the first debate were later related to ideological preferences.

Even though partisans wanted their man to "win," few viewers on either side would have seriously proposed before the first debate that a candidate's ability to score points under the rules agreed for the debate was a test of fitness for office. Yet by his unexpectedly good performance in that debate Kennedy established among his potential supporters his character as well as his "right" to the candidacy. Viewers developed an image of Kennedy more congruent with the political role he was playing as a candidate because—as some put it—"He seemed to know all the time where to refute Nixon," "He never fumbled," etc. Some lukewarm supporters became enthusiastic: "People could see he was qualified," or, "I've switched from an anti-Nixon Democrat to a pro-Kennedy Democrat." These same respondents, many of whom expected their man to be "beaten," had been prepared to isolate competitive performance from their evaluation of the candidates' qualifications. At the same time, Nixon's avowed competence as performer was a focus for many negative perceptions about Nixon's political role. But failure on Nixon's part to measure up to expectations did not destroy the negative image supposedly derived from such performances. On the contrary, it was from his poor performance (for example, the "way he fumbled, ingratiated himself, appeared nervous and not quite rational") that some Ken-

of *Social Psychology* (Cambridge, Mass.: Addison-Wesley, 1954), chapter 17, for a review of literature on person perception.

nedy supporters now drew explicit inferences about whether he could be entrusted with the leadership of the country. Six Kennedy supporters, on the other hand, improved their overall image of Nixon. They did so largely out of a deep-seated distrust about the spontaneity of the performance. The encounter was personalized, and they extended their sympathy to the apparent victim without their electoral choice being in any way affected.

As far as Nixon supporters are concerned, disappointment with their candidate's performance in the debate moved into the Kennedy column only those few whose intention to vote for Nixon had been based on rather weak party identifications, as among the self-styled Independents. The majority countered the strain that perceptions of Nixon's shaky performance introduced into their image by one or more of three devices: *isolation, selective perception,* and *personalization.*

Isolation (in the sense of denying the relevance of information to behavioral commitment) has already been noted in the pre-debate responses of Kennedy backers. The pro-Nixon group who had viewed their candidate as a person in terms of his past performances and supported their judgment of his qualifications by reference to his debating skills ceased to stress debating and performing skills when his performance proved disappointing.

Selective perception is illustrated by claims that both candidates had been "primed beforehand," an observation often documented by "Kennedy's ability to rattle off figures." That Kennedy "handled himself nicely" was often admitted, but a pro-Nixon respondent would add that "what he said and what he stands for are two different things." Nixon's claim to the Presidency was most often justified after the debate by his long advocacy of "sound policies." The candidate's performance was ignored, while the policies advocated were singled out for attention. Since, presumably, Nixon supporters were in agreement with what their candidate believed, they could, by focusing on the political content of his statements, define him as the winner. One said, "I think Nixon did better but of course I'm prejudiced." Others thought that reporters were favoring Kennedy, feeding him easier questions. Kennedy was also accused of breaking the rules by taking notes and, in subsequent debates, of reading from notes.[11] Different evaluations of performance thus are a function of the elements singled out for attention and of the context in which they are interpreted.

The technique of *personalization* is perhaps a special case of selective perception in that it involves also the reinterpretation of intrinsically ambiguous person perceptions into a personal image that imputes to persons with whom one is in disagreement unfavorable personal traits, and vice versa. A number of Nixon supporters contrasted Kennedy's "self-praising attitude" with Nixon's "thoughtfulness and cautious modesty." Others agreed with the respondent who thought "Kennedy came over nicely if you like his type. He was snide and impolite to

make notes while Nixon was speaking." Nixon, it was said, though a target of Kennedy's "brashness," "never likes to offend anybody."

Personal images were also related to capacity to fill the office of President, as illustrated by a reference to Kennedy as "quick-acting, but if he'd talk to Khrushchev, he'd say something he later would regret." Nixon, according to several, was not at his best in the first debate because he had recently been hospitalized for an infected knee. He had shown great fortitude. "Nixon could stand up to Kennedy. That shows he could stand up to the Russians," was the way one person summed it up after the fourth debate.

SUMMARY AND IMPLICATIONS

Data from intensive interviews with a panel of New York City viewers indicates that exposure to the televised debates resulted in some rather dramatic changes in candidate image, but vote intentions changed much less. Instead, images were adjusted to preference by turning to congruent sources of information and by isolation, selective perception, and personalization.

In balance, the impact of these debates, as observed on this panel, appears to have favored Kennedy more than Nixon. But when viewed against the backgrounds of voters, the majority of whom had identified themselves with or voted for the Democratic Party in the past, Kennedy's gain depended as much on past traditions as on his ability to identify himself with these traditions.

---

[11] These accusations illustrate also how a charge taken up by the press helped Nixon supporters to maintain an image congruent with their preference. They had "seen" how Kennedy "cheated" to best Nixon. Nixon's dissociation from the charge is irrelevant.

Our observation that Kennedy, the less well-known of the candidates, was helped by his performance to project a favorable image is supported by other research. It must not, however, be extended too far, for some of the very elements in the Kennedy performance operating in his favor among this group of viewers might produce different responses in other surroundings. Attention is drawn to the personal hostility Kennedy's smooth performance aroused among some Nixon voters. Thus, in communities where attitudes prevail that were rarely encountered among this sample (such as strong anti–"big city" sentiment or fundamentalist views) the distribution of responses might differ greatly.

Though the evidence from this study does not suggest that dramatic and immediate changes in votes can be expected from such TV spectacles in the middle of a campaign, there may nevertheless be important sleeper effects not observed by the methods employed. The image of Nixon, for example, as viewers remembered it from past telecasts or as they remembered it from what they read about those telecasts afterwards, was an important element in the reactions to these debates. Furthermore, interviews with campaign workers showed that the Kennedy performance sparked the organization of viewing groups, generated enthusiasm, and perhaps led to greater campaign efforts, all of which might ultimately be reflected in votes.

COMMUNICATIONS IN BUREAUS
ANTHONY DOWNS

TYPES OF COMMUNICATION COSTS

Communication requires definite costs.[1] Every message involves the expenditure of time to decide what to send, time to compose the message, the resource-cost of transmitting the message (which may consist of time, money, or both), and time spent in receiving the message. Also, if the message passes over a channel operating near its capacity, it may cancel or delay other messages.

Since the time of each official is limited, the more he spends in searching or communicating, the less he has for other types of activity. His capacity for absorbing and using information is also limited. Hence every individual has a saturation point regarding the amount of information he can usefully handle in a given time period.

To achieve reasonable efficiency, the communications network in any organization must not normally load any individual beyond his saturation point. If he becomes overloaded, he will be unable to comprehend the information given to him well enough to screen it efficiently, or to use it.

The number of persons from whom any official can effectively receive messages in a given period is inversely related to the average length of the messages. This limitation does not apply to his transmitting information if the messages sent to all concerned are identical. However, if he must transmit different messages to each recipient, then the inverse relationship between number of recipients and size of message also holds true.

Because messages are costly, only a limited amount of all available information is either collected or used by any organization. This means that the particular methods used by the organization to collect, select, and transmit information are critically important determinants of its behavior.

FORMAL, SUBFORMAL, AND PERSONAL COMMUNICATIONS NETWORKS

Following the classification set forth by William M. Jones in *On Decision-making in Large Organizations*, we distinguish among three types of com-

CREDIT: From *Inside Bureaucracy* by Anthony Downs, pp. 112–123. A RAND Corporation Research Study. Copyright © 1967 by The RAND Corporation. Reprinted by permission of the publisher, Little, Brown and Company, and The RAND Corporation. [*Figure renumbered.*]

[1] For extensive references to the literature on communications in large organizations, see Peter M. Blau and W. Richard Scott, *Formal Organizations* (San Francisco: Chandler Publishing Co., 1962), pp. 116–139, and Albert H. Rubenstein and Chadwick J. Haberstroh (eds.), *Some Theories of Organization* (Homewood, Illinois: Irwin-Dorsey, 1960), pp. 229–322.

munications networks within a bureau and among different bureaus.

Formal communications

The formal communications network transmits messages explicitly recognized as "official" by the bureau. At this level, one finds published organization charts, standing operating procedures, formal orders and directives, periodic reports, official correspondence, and so on. Formal messages make certain actions, decisions, or policies "legal" within the framework of the bureau's powers.

Therefore, in almost all large organizations, the formal channels of communication substantially coincide with the formal authority structure.

Subformal communications

Subformal channels transmit those messages arising from the informal authority structure existing in every organization. Every member of the bureau must know and observe informal rules and procedures about what to communicate to whom. Such rules are rarely written down, and must be learned by experience and example. This creates frequent difficulties for newcomers and outsiders, including bureau customers. In fact, the classic feeling of "getting the run-around" from bureau officials often arises from the average citizen's ignorance of how a bureau's informal communications channels are structured.

Subformal communications are of two kinds: those that flow along formal channels, but not as formal communications; and those that flow along purely informal channels. Both types have the great advantage of not being official; hence they can be withdrawn,

altered, adjusted, magnified, or canceled without any official record being made. As a result, almost all new ideas are first proposed and tested as subformal communications. In fact, the vast majority of all communications in large organizations are subformal.

As a rule, subformal channels of communication spring up whenever there is a functional need for officials to communicate, but no formal channel exists. Formal channels are normally vertical, following the lines of the formal authority structure. Consequently, most of the gap-filling subformal lines of communication are horizontal, connecting peers rather than subordinates and superiors. Even when subformal channels link officials of different ranks, the informality of the messages exchanged plays down variations in status. This is important because men are more prone to speak freely and openly to their equals than to their superiors.[2] Thus, subformal communications normally evoke much more forthright and candid responses than formal communications.

The prevalence of subformal channels means that formal networks do not fully describe the important communications channels in a bureau. Therefore, it is futile for persons designing an organization to set up the formal channels they want and assume that those channels will in fact carry most of the messages. On the contrary, the more stringently restricted the formal channels, the richer will be the flowering of subformal ones. Thus, within every organization there is a straining toward completeness in the overall communications system.

[2] This point is discussed at length in Blau and Scott, *Formal Organizations,* pp. 116–139.

Even though the subformal system strains toward filling the gaps in the formal one, the leaders of an organization can severely restrict the development of the former. This can be done by ordering subordinates not to communicate with each other, by physically separating people, by requiring prior clearance for any communication outside a certain bureau section, or by hiring only reticent subordinates.

An even more important determinant of a bureau's subformal network is the nature of the bureau's functions, as shown by the following relationships:

— The greater the degree of interdependence among activities within the bureau, the greater will be the proliferation of subformal channels and messages therein.
— The higher the degree of uncertainty inherent in a bureau's function, the greater will be its proliferation of subformal channels and messages. When the environment is relatively unpredictable, men cannot logically deduce what they should be doing simply by referring to that environment. Hence they tend to talk to each other more to resolve ambiguities.
— If a bureau is operating under great time-pressure, it will tend to use subformal channels and messages extensively, since there is often no time to check formal procedures and follow them. Thus, in a crisis, top-level decision-makers will reach out for information whenever they can get it, whatever the channel structure involved. They will also tend to rely on other officials in whom they have great confidence, even if those other officials are not formally connected with the subject of the crisis (for example, Robert Kennedy's role in the Cuban missile crisis).[3]
— Sections of a bureau in strong conflict will tend to eschew subformal channels and communicate only formally; whereas closely cooperating sections will rely primarily upon subformal communications. Thus strong rivalry has important communications drawbacks.
— Subformal communications networks will be more effective if bureau members have stable relationships with each other and with other persons outside the bureau than if these relationships are constantly changing. This means that newly established, fast growing bureaus are likely to have less effective subformal networks than well established, slower growing ones.

Personal communications

According to Jones, a personal communication is one in which "an organization functionary, in communicat-

[3] William M. Jones, *On Decisionmaking in Large Organizations* (Santa Monica: The Rand Corporation, RM–3968–PR, March 1961), pp. 17–20.

ing with an insider or an outsider, deliberately reveals something of his own attitude toward the activities of his own organization." [4] Jones sets forth the following points about personal communications:

— Personal channels are almost always used for reports rather than directives.

— Since personal messages are transmitted by officials acting as persons rather than as office-holders, they do not bear the responsible weight of the office emitting them. In this respect, they differ from subformal messages, which are transmitted by individuals acting in their official capacity—but not for the record.

— The personal network can transmit messages with amazing speed because there is no verification mechanism to slow down their dissemination. In his investigation of "Rumors in War," Theodore Caplow also found a very high degree of accuracy in the rumor network, even for messages that had passed through hundreds of persons. [5]

— Before an official takes action on the basis of information received through personal channels, he will usually verify that information organizationally through either subformal or formal channels.

[4] *Ibid.*, p. 5.

[5] A. H. Rubenstein and C. J. Haberstroh, *Some Theories of Organization*, pp. 280–287.

The impact of subformal communications on inter-bureau relations

In many instances, formal communications between bureaus are inappropriate for several reasons. First, it takes a long time for a formal message from a low-level official in one bureau to pass to a similar official in another. Second, formal messages are on the record; whereas the officials concerned may want to discuss things tentatively. This is especially important in the generation of new ideas. Third, low-level officials may not want to expose their ideas to their superiors for the time being, even in rough form; yet any formal communication is immediately routed through the originator's superior.

Thus subformal communications play important roles in the relationships between bureaus. However, an official in one bureau is rarely familiar with the subformal communications networks or authority structures in other bureaus. This often makes it difficult for officials of different bureaus to communicate subformally.

The difficulty can be easily overcome, however, if the official concerned can establish some type of subformal or personal relationship with just one official in the other bureau, who can quickly steer him to the right man to talk to. This explains why smart officials eat as many lunches with counterparts in other bureaus as they do with colleagues in their own bureaus.

Inter-bureau obstacles to communication are not so easily bypassed when two bureaus are in strong conflict. Then the informal networks of one may be substantially closed to members of the other by orders of top-echelon officials, a feeling of mutual hostility at all levels, or a tactical need to keep procedures and ideas concealed so as not to yield any competitive advantage in the conflict. Jones contends that all large, interacting organizations are in partial conflict with one another; hence these obstacles to informal communications always exist to some degree.[6] However, substantial closure of informal communications channels probably occurs only when two bureaus (or two parts of one bureau) are in an unusually strong direct conflict.

TULLOCK'S MODEL OF HIERARCHICAL DISTORTION

. . . [I]ndividual officials tend to distort information passing through them. But how does this affect the bureau's communication system as a whole? A first step toward answering this question has been set forth by Gordon Tullock.[7] His argument focuses on upward flows of formal messages in a bureau hierarchy, but it is also relevant to the primarily horizontal flows of subformal and personal messages described in the previous section. True, the average distortion per message is probably greater in vertical flows than horizontal ones. The former involve superior-subordinate rela-

[6] W. M. Jones, *On Decisionmaking in Large Organizations*, p. 6.

[7] Gordon Tullock, *The Politics of Bureaucracy* (Washington, D.C.: Public Affairs Press, 1965), pp. 137–141.

tions, whereas the latter usually involve relations among equals. Nevertheless, the following analysis concerning aggregate message distortion and antidistortion devices applies in an important sense to all messages in a bureau.

To illustrate Tullock's argument, let us postulate a hierarchy of authority containing seven levels. A part of this hierarchy is shown in Figure V-5. We assume that officials on the lowest (G) level are actually out in the field. Officials on all other levels depend upon secondary sources and information forwarded by G-level officials. All the information so forwarded is sent to their F-level superiors, who then screen it and relay the most salient parts to *their* superiors on the E-level, who in turn screen that information and forward it to D-level officials, and on up the line. Eventually, the information reaches the top man in the hierarchy after having been screened six times in the process.

There are two major features of this winnowing process worth examining in detail. First, condensation of information is an essential part of the bureau's communications process. Otherwise the top man would be buried under tons of facts and opinions. Let us assume that the information gathered by each official on the G-level in a single time period can be set equal to 1.0 units of data. If we further assume that the average span of control in the bureau is four, then there are 4,096 officials at the G-level. This means that 4,096 units of data are gathered during each time period. The quantity that actually reaches the A-level depends upon the percentage omitted at each screening. For exam-

FIGURE V-5   Model Hierarchy

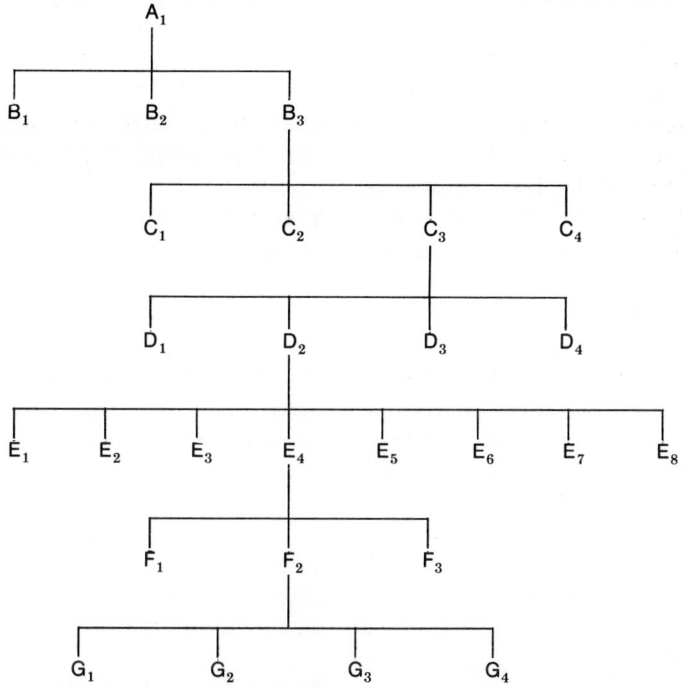

ple, if the average official screens out only half the data given to him by his subordinates, then A will receive a total of 1/64 of all the information, or 64 units per time period. The winnowing process will have omitted 98.4 per cent of the data originally gathered.

Second, the quality of information finally received by A—that is, its substantive content—will probably be very different from that originally put into the communications system at the lowest level. The selection principles used by officials below A to determine which data to pass on and which to omit will always differ from those of A himself. Their self-interest gives them goals different from A's, their specialized modes of perceiving reality vary from his, their stocks of current information are not the same as his, and they may altruistically identify themselves with a certain part of the bureau rather than the whole structure under A. In fact, the selection principles used by officials at each level are likely to be different from those used by other levels for the same reasons. Hence, the information that finally reaches A has passed through six filters of different quality and the "facts" reported to A will be quite different in content and implication from the "facts" gathered at the lowest level.

To illustrate the potential magnitude of the resulting distortion, we will use an admittedly oversimplified and ambiguous mathematical analogy. In spite of its serious limitations, it is useful as a means of providing at least some quantification to our analysis of the quality of information reported to A. Let us assume that each screening destroys a certain fraction of the true meaning of the information from A's point of view. If this fraction is 10 per cent, by the time the information passes through all six filters, only about 53 per cent of it will express the true state of the environment as A would have observed it himself. If we assume another 5 per cent distortion due to errors of transmission and poorer quality of personnel at lower levels, then the fraction of truth reaching A will be only about 38 per cent. Under such conditions, the leakage of information caused by frictions in the communications system is enormous. It may be so large that the majority of information A receives is not really information at all from his point of view, but noise—error introduced into the signals he receives by the operation of the signalling apparatus.

This process will tend to distort information in such a manner that A receives reports that tell him primarily what his subordinates believe he wants to hear, and indicate that his bureau should probably be expanded, but certainly not contracted. The first of these conclusions stems from distortions originated by the climbers in the network. They tend to tell their superiors what would please them most, so that the climbers themselves can win fast promotions. The second conclusion is derived from our hypothesis that many officials in the bureau are likely to be advocates. Both advocates and climbers will seek to expand the power of the bureau; hence they will tend to distort information so as to show that the bureau needs more resources.

ANTIDISTORTION FACTORS IN THE COMMUNICATION SYSTEM

The above observations are based upon a useful but oversimplified model of hierarchical communications. This model neglects many important forces that limit the amount of distortion the bureau's communications system will produce. Tullock himself pointed out some of these antidistortion forces, and we will add a few more. Altogether, they tend to reduce the degree of information distortion likely to occur in a bureau considerably below that indicated above, but they do not eliminate it.

Redundancy: the duplication of reports for verification

Whenever A receives information from his own bureau that he believes is distorted, his desires as a consumer of data are being ignored by his monopolistic supplier, the bureau. The classic antidote for monopoly is competition. Therefore A will try to establish more than one channel of communication reporting to him about the same events and topics.

From one point of view, this approach is wasteful, since he must maintain duplicate (sometimes triplicate or quadruplicate) communications facilities covering the same area of activity. Yet only in this way can he check up on the accuracy of his own bureau and, by using the threat of such checks, force the bureau to give him information selected by principles close to his own.

There are several methods by which an official can produce such redundancy. Among them are the following:

Use of information sources external to all bureaus

Merely by reading several good newspapers each day, and letting all his subordinates know he does, a top official can produce a marked reduction in the distortion practiced by his own bureau. The absence of a free press in dictatorial countries undoubtedly makes this verification process much more difficult than in democratic societies.

However, no successful top-level official ever relies on the press as his sole external source of information. Rather, he develops a whole informal network of outside sources which he can use as listening posts to verify the things conveyed by his subordinates, or to give him new data. These sources include friends in other bureaus, members of his bureau's clientele, social acquaintances, politicians, official reports of other agencies, and even gossip.

Creation of overlapping areas of responsibility within a bureau

If A has three subordinates on the B level and he makes each of them partly responsible for a certain function, he introduces an element of competition among them that may improve the accuracy of their reports to him. Each knows that any distortions in his own reports may be exposed by the others. Even if A were unable to tell which of three conflicting reports was wrong, their disagreement would rouse his suspicions and perhaps lead him to in-

vestigate all reports more fully. . . . [A]ll officials dislike investigations of their own departments. Thus the threat of investigation forms part of the overall pressure upon each subordinate not to distort information.[8]

It is clear that the three B-level subordinates have much to gain from collusion. If they can read each other's reports beforehand and reconcile any differences before exposing them to A, they can avoid the possibility of investigation and retain their freedom to distort information. Since this freedom will be limited by the need to reach agreement on their reports to A, the accuracy of A's information may improve somewhat even if collusion exists. Nevertheless, such collusion will destroy most of the advantages A hopes to gain from establishing redundant channels; therefore, he must insure that no collusion exists if he wants this device to work. He can do this through the following available mechanisms:

— Use many other overlapping channels both inside and outside the bureau, and be sure that everyone knows it.
— Use physically separated channels. However informal communications and telephones usually make physical separation ineffective.
— Reduce the penalty for conflicting reports by encouraging a variety of viewpoints

[8] However, subordinates know that their superiors fear investigation by outsiders; hence they can sometimes get away with a great deal because they know their superiors will not want to reveal misbehavior in their own organization to possible outside observers.

and minimizing the threat of investigation. Leaders who really do not like "yes-men" usually do not get them.

—Structure the interests of the subordinates involved so they are in direct conflict. This may be the only device available if there are no alternative channels for receiving information (as in some covert activities or specialized fields of research).

Creation of overlapping areas of responsibility in different bureaus

Creating overlapping areas of responsibility in different bureaus has the same objective as the method discussed in the last section. However, it is better designed to prevent collusion because men in different bureaus are generally in different promotional hierarchies too. Colleagues within a single promotional hierarchy usually avoid making enemies of each other through excessive conflict. Each knows that he might some day be in a position where the other's decisions could seriously affect his own welfare. But men in different bureaus are under no such restraints; each is more likely to vigorously defend the interests of his own bureau against possible inroads by the others. Moreover, it is harder for men in different bureaus to communicate with each other informally than it is for men in the same bureau.

Counter-biases: their benefits and costs

A second major antidistortion technique that most officials apply almost automatically is the use of counter-biases. The recipients of information

at each level in the hierarchy are well aware that the data they get is distorted. Every general was once a lieutenant and remembers the type of distortion he used when he forwarded information to his own superiors. Therefore, he develops a counter-biased attitude toward most reports received from his subordinates. He adjusts these reports to counteract the distortions contained therein. Insofar as he is correctly able to estimate these distortions, he can restore the information to its original form. If such counter-biases are used at every level of the hierarchy, then much of the cumulative distortion effect described in Tullock's analysis will be eliminated. The principal remaining distortion will be that caused by errors made by each superior in estimating the nature of his subordinates' biases.

Experiments conducted in small groups tend to show that people do use counter-bias strategies to offset distorted information.[9] However, they do so only when they have some knowledge of the type of distortion originally used, and when it is in their own interest to reduce this distortion. Both these qualifying conditions have important implications for bureau communication systems.

If an official does not know what type of distortion has been incorporated into information he has received, he cannot accurately restore the data to its pure form. The only counter-bias strategy he can then use is to reduce his reliance upon such information in making decisions. In essence, he responds to it in the same way that he

[9] Richard M. Cyert and James G. March, *A Behavioral Theory of the Firm* (Englewood Cliffs, New Jersey: Prentice-Hall, 1963), pp. 67–82.

responds to most highly uncertain information.

Distortion is related to uncertainty in still another way: the more inherently uncertain any information is, the more scope there is for distortion in reporting it. Inherent uncertainty means that the range of values variables may assume cannot be reduced below a certain significant size. The greater the uncertainty, the wider this range, and the more latitude officials have in emphasizing one part of it without being proved wrong. They tend to designate one part as most probable not because it really is, but because the occurrence of that value would benefit them more than other possible outcomes.[10] This amounts to uncertainty absorption based upon self-interest or advocacy rather than objective estimates of real probabilities.

Officials using counter-bias strategies are well aware of this propensity for their subordinates to resolve uncertainty questions in their own favor. The problem for a counter-biaser is to recognize whether the estimates of his subordinates are really based on relatively certain information, or whether they embody false resolutions of uncertainty. Again, counter-biasers tend to shift their decisions away from dependence on uncertain data. These shifts may be of the following specific types:

—Away from information about the future toward information about the present or past.

—Away from qualitative and immeasurable factors toward quantitative and measurable factors.

—Away from those quantitative factors that cannot easily be verified toward those that can.

Thus the use of counter-biasing to counteract distortion has certain costs in terms of the quality of the resultant decisionmaking. The uncertainties involved force the counter-biasing officials to make distorted decisions in the very process of attempting to counteract distortion.

Such reliance upon counter-biasing can be reduced in organizations where stable personal relationships have sprung up between officials. Men who work closely together eventually learn the types of distortions they can expect from each other. Officials can then accurately judge the nature of each other's distortions instead of reducing their reliance upon distortion-prone information. Insofar as such information contains inherent uncertainty, they may still disregard it in making decisions. However, this tendency will then be a reaction to uncertainty itself, not to distortion.

This conclusion implies that relatively stable organizations develop better internal communications systems than those that are constantly changing personnel. Therefore, bureaus undergoing rapid growth tend to exhibit more distortion of information, and more excessive avoidance of uncertainty due to counter-biasing strategies than those that are growing more slowly or not growing at all. In communications, unfamiliarity with

---

[10] See J. G. March and H. A. Simon, *Organizations* (New York: John Wiley & Sons, 1958), pp. 164–166.

one's communicants is a form of cost.[11]

Another major qualification must be attached to the use of counter-biasing. Even if an official knows he is receiving distorted information from his subordinates, he may believe it is in his own interest to retain that distortion in his decisionmaking. He may even find it desirable to add to this distortion in forwarding the information to his own superiors.

Such cumulative distortion is likely whenever advocates, climbers, zealots, or even conservers are dealing with certain kinds of information. These officials all have a tendency to exaggerate the capabilities of their own sections of a bureau, as well as any information favorable to themselves or their sections. Conversely, they try to minimize any unfavorable information, especially if it might reduce the resources available to that section. Consider the case of the combat capabilities of certain aircraft used several years ago. These capabilities involved, among other things, radar bombing scores. Naturally, each bombardier was motivated to get as good scores as possible, and some even cheated to do so. Squadron commanders were motivated by competition to report the scores of their squadrons as favorably as they could; hence they did not inform their superiors that many of their most impressive scores were run on sunny days with no strong winds and lots of optical assistance. Similarly, the wing commander knew that he was competing for money with other types of weapons (such as submarines); hence he summarized the scores reported to him as optimistically as possible before forwarding the summary to his superiors, minimizing such qualifying facts as the percentage of air aborts. Cumulative distortion resulted, and the top men in the hierarchy received a report of capabilities grossly exaggerating the real situation. Such exaggeration need not result from any overt falsehoods, but simply from selective suppression of qualifying information. Moreover, the officials involved are quite aware that their subordinates are feeding them biased data, but they are all strongly motivated to increase or at least accept that distortion rather than to eliminate it through counter-biasing.[12]

Thus the fact that counter-biasing could counteract much of the distortion in bureau hierarchies does not mean that it will do so. In fact, cumulative distortion will tend to be increased by the structure of incentives facing officials regarding certain types of information. It is extremely difficult for top officials to check up on such distortions through redundancy whenever they involve highly technical matters. Only if the bureau serves a clientele capable of judging the quality of its performance will top officials have any alternative information channels with which to verify the performance reports of their own subordinates. In the case of the military services, this is very unlikely.

---

[11] See W. M. Jones, *On Decisionmaking in Large Organizations*, p. 20; and Thomas K. Glennan, Jr., "On the High Cost of Development" (unpublished mimeographed draft, 1964), pp. 8–13.

[12] In some cases, top-level officials deliberately remain officially ignorant of cheating and distortions going on below them so that they can pass on more glowing reports to their own superiors.

COMMUNICATION IN CRISIS
WILBUR SCHRAMM

"Communication in Crisis" . . . may be a misleading title, because it appears to reify communication. Communication, of course, has no life of its own. It is something people do. It is a—perhaps *the*—fundamental process of society. The chief reason for studying it is to find out more about people and their societies. [Our primary concern] is . . . about *people,* rather than communication, in crisis.

Yet because communication is one of the most common behaviors of man, and because in a crisis those who are responsible for information are deeply and powerfully involved, it is often possible in a time of crisis to see the social institutions and uses of communication in sharp outline and clear perspective. This is how one studies communication, not as a thing in itself, but rather as a window on man and society, which in turn throws light on the acts and organizations of communicating.

We are presently concerned about the reaction of the American people to the critical and shocking events beginning with the assassination of

President John F. Kennedy, and, in particular, how the flow of information through society helped shape that reaction.

THE CRISIS

The uniqueness of the happenings of November 22, 1963, and the days following has been often remarked. Yet it remains to say just what makes them unique. It was, of course, not the first assassination of an American President. Many people still alive remember the shock of McKinley's assassination in 1901, and a few must recall Garfield's twenty years earlier. A very few may still remember Lincoln's in 1865. Nor was the reaction to Mr. Kennedy's murder the first national outpouring of sorrow over the death of a chief executive within memory of a large proportion of Americans. The memory of Franklin D. Roosevelt's death, in 1945, is still fresh in the minds of most Americans over 25, and, as newspaper accounts and the few available studies show, many of the reactions at that time were much like those of November 1963.[1]

[1] H. Orlansky, "Reactions to the Death of President Roosevelt," *Journal of Social Psychology,* Vol. 26 (1947), pp. 236–266; D. E. Johannsen, "Reactions to the Death of President Roosevelt," *Journal of Abnormal and Social Psychology,* Vol. 41 (1946), pp. 218–222.

The unique quality of the events we are talking about arose from their surrounding circumstances. For one thing, the man struck down was an extraordinarily young and vital President, who, together with his beautiful wife and attractive children, had become well known in an unusually personal and intimate way through the mass media. Franklin Roosevelt had been struck down in the fullness of years and accomplishment. His loss, to a greater degree than John Kennedy's, must have been that of a father surrogate. Kennedy must have seemed less a father figure than a leader figure, and his loss focused attention, unconfused by the venerability of age or the psychological complications of father imagery, on what a *leader* means to Americans.

In the course of a nationwide survey during the week following the assassination, over 1,300 respondents were asked what other experiences they were reminded of by their feelings when they heard the news about President Kennedy. The majority said they "could not recall any other times in their lives" when they had the same sort of feelings. Of those who could think of similar feelings, most mentioned the death of someone near and dear to them, about 8 per cent mentioned Pearl Harbor, and about one-fourth named the death of Franklin Roosevelt.

The events in Dallas clearly had some of the impact of both Pearl Harbor and the death of Roosevelt, and yet the fact that so few people mentioned the resemblance shows that there were basic differences. Like Pearl Harbor, Dallas came suddenly, shockingly, unexpectedly; and it too bore a threat to national security and a blow to national pride, although less than Pearl Harbor. But Dallas was personified and focused on an individual in a way that Pearl Harbor was not. It was something we had done to ourselves rather than something done to us by a foreign enemy, and the disturbed ex-Marine and the impulsive nightclub owner offered no such broad target for hatred as the foreign aggressor who dropped bombs on Hawaii. There were no immediate channels for working off one's grief and anger on November 22. After Pearl Harbor one could seek one's place, civilian or military, in the war effort; there was much to be done, and in general everyone knew what it was. But after November 22—well, one could think it over by oneself, or say a prayer, or try to talk out one's feelings, or watch television. This is doubtless a reason for the rather compulsive attention to television: not only was it therapeutic, it also provided something to do when no one knew just what to do.

News of the death of President Roosevelt, like news of the death of President Kennedy, caused deep grief, mass anxiety, and widespread rumors. In 1945 it was widely reported that Fiorello LaGuardia and Jack Benny had also died; in 1963 it was reported widely that Lyndon Johnson had suffered another heart attack and that John McCormack had been slain.[2] But the death of Roosevelt had not been as completely unexpected as that of Kennedy. FDR's loss of weight, his weariness and grayness, had not been entirely hidden from the public. John Kennedy, on the other hand, was the epitome of youth, health, and vigor. When people talked about his future,

_____

[2] *Ibid.*

they were more likely to wonder what he would do when he retired from the presidency in his early fifties than to wonder whether he would survive that long. John Kennedy was a life and immortality symbol; the destruction of that symbol by violence was all the more shocking. Violence was missing from the story of Roosevelt's demise; as it must to all men, death came to him. But John Kennedy was jerked away from health, from a young family, from leadership, by a senseless act of violence.

It is of considerable importance that these events should have occurred in the full bloom of the Age of Television. President Kennedy's loss was the first loss of a national leader reported in any such detail on the picture tubes of a nation. President Harding's death, in 1923, came at the very beginning of the Age of Radio; both information and transportation were so slow that the impact was diffused. Roosevelt's death came when radio was well developed, but amidst the great distractions of war news and national preoccupation with wartime duties and casualty lists. The Kennedy story, however, was carried into more than 90 per cent of American homes by television so quickly that over half of all Americans apparently heard the news before the President was pronounced dead, only 30 minutes after the shooting, and so fully that millions of Americans actually saw Oswald killed and heard the shot as soon as it echoed through the basement of the Dallas courthouse. Immediacy was one striking quality of the information flow during those days of crisis; another was the pervasiveness of it. For all practical purposes there was no other news story in America during those four days, and all the

mass media concentrated on telling it. There were times during those days when *a majority of all Americans* were apparently looking at the same events and hearing the same words from their television sets—participating together, at least to that extent, in a great national event. Nothing like this on such a scale had ever occurred before. And if anything of significance connected with these events was not seen or heard at the instant it occurred, it was sure to be seen or heard or read shortly thereafter by almost everyone who could see, hear, or read. Never before, it is safe to say, has such a large proportion of the American people been able to feel so instantly and closely, for three and a half days, a part of events and deeds of great national significance.

These events were unique also because they represented the first such loss of a national leader that social scientists were ready to study. There was little or no social science in Lincoln's time, and the accounts by Sandburg and others can only suggest the opportunities that were missed to study social dynamics on that occasion. A few studies were made of reactions to Roosevelt's death, but the scholars who made them lamented that more data could not be gathered at the time. In 1963, however, social scientists were better able to seize opportunities. A series of studies of disasters had been made.[3] These had established the pattern of being able to go into the field on short notice. Survey research centers had interviewers available, and were

[3] For a summary, see A. H. Barton *et al.*, *Social Organization Under Stress: A Sociological Review of Disaster Studies* (Washington, D.C.: National Academy of Sciences—National Research Council, 1963).

prepared to draw samples and construct questionnaires quickly. Communication research had been considerably developed at enclaves of various kinds within a number of universities. When scholars recovered from the shock of the first news on November 22, many of them realized that this was a chapter in national history that should be studied, and they set plans in motion to collect information while it was still fresh. This was not a ghoulish act; rather it was an effort to contribute to the understanding of great national events, and through them to the better understanding of a national society.

A surprising amount of research was planned and conducted in the week following November 22. A national sample survey and at least 15 local studies were in the field within that time. Other studies were made later. This book represents by no means all of this research, although the editors have tried to represent the most interesting parts of it. Undoubtedly no unexpected event in our history has ever been so fully studied at the time it happened.

These studies confirm that the Kennedy story provided a stimulus more like the Roosevelt than the Pearl Harbor story, but with added overtones of violence and irony, and with full and vivid television coverage. Television, more than any of the other media, during the preceding years must have made Americans feel that they knew the Kennedys very well. To the American people the event was clearly a signal for grief and national mourning for a man who was as close at hand as the picture tube but still not close enough for people to do the usual

things they do about the death of a loved person. In this respect, too, television found itself playing an unusual part in the lives of its viewers.

There is relatively little previous scholarship about such an event. We have mentioned the series of studies on disaster. There are also studies of persons under stress.[4] There has been some attention to the behavior of personal bereavement and to the clinical nature of grief.[5] But these are only tangentially related to what happened on November 22, 1963, and the days following. That remains in most respects a unique event, in our scholarship as in our history, and the papers on this topic are therefore plowing new fields.

THE PART COMMUNICATION PLAYS IN CRISIS

When a crisis interrupts the slow, ongoing rhythms of communication—scanning the environment, disposing of the day-to-day needs and problems of the system, filing away and sharing the increment of experience—the rate of information flow is enormously increased. A message signals the emergency. Information rushes to and from the point of crisis, which becomes a new focus of attention as the system strives to adjust to the problem.

This is the case regardless of the

[4] For example, see Irving L. Janis, *Air War and Emotional Stress* (New York: McGraw-Hill, 1951).

[5] For example, E. Lindemann, "Symptomatology and Management of Acute Grief," *American Journal of Psychiatry*, Vol. 101 (1948), pp. 141–148, and G. L. Engel, "Is Grief a Disease?" *Psychosomatic Medicine*, Vol. 23 (1961), pp. 18–23.

size of system. A message that unusual heat is being felt on a finger will alert a human system to move the finger, check the situation visually if possible, take steps to repair the damage, and so forth. A message that one member of a group is deviating will interrupt the usual humdrum communication of the group for a great flow of persuasion to the deviant until he is restored to loyal membership or the cause is seen to be hopeless. So in Dallas on November 22 the reporters, broadcasters, photographers, and their equipment were operating routinely until 12:30. They were providing routine coverage of a chief executive. Then came the bulletin that roused the men and facilities of communication to such efforts that it was many days before information from Dallas and the coverage of the American chief executive could again be called routine.

The National Research Council's studies of disaster identified five stages in society's response to crisis. These are (1) the pre-disaster period, (2) the period of detection and communication of a specific threat, (3) the period of immediate, relatively unorganized response, (4) the period of organized social response, and (5) the long-run post-disaster period when the society is restored to equilibrium and the "permanent" effects of the disaster have been incorporated into it.[6] Each of these periods has its own kind of communication to meet its special needs. The pattern, however, fits great disasters and accidents better than it fits the events that concern us here. There is no warning of an assassination, as

there is of a tornado, and thus no period in which people can prepare, physically or psychologically, to meet the threat. There is no widespread need for physical help or relief, as in most disasters. Indeed, one of the characteristics of the events of November 22–25 was that there were no organized activities for most people to take part in; the widespread response to the suggestion that the slain policeman's wife, and later Mrs. Oswald, needed money, may have been an indication that organized social actions in time of crisis are themselves therapeutic. Another difference between the Kennedy assassination and most of the crises studied for the National Research Council was that in November of 1963 there was no widespread destruction of the sort on which the analysts of disaster-research base hypotheses relating the amount of communications to the amount of destruction seen. Except for the three dead men in Dallas, the casualties of the events we are considering were psychological and political.

Systems theory would describe the response to crisis as a sudden imbalance in the system, followed by emergency steps to restore balance, and then a gradual restoration of normal functioning around whatever new balance is achieved.[7] This comes closer to describing what seems to have happened in the case of the Kennedy assassination. We can identify three periods. First came the time when the

[6] See Barton *et al.*, *Social Organization Under Stress*, pp. 14–15.

[7] For example, L. Bertalanffy, "General Systems Theory: A Critical Review," *Yearbook of the Society for General Systems Research*, Vol. 7 (1962), pp. 1–22, and Kenneth E. Boulding, *The Image* (Ann Arbor: University of Michigan Press, 1956).

news had to be told. Then followed a period when society staggered under the blow but struggled to restore equilibrium—the shocked response of ordinary men and women, the shocked but disciplined response of officials striving to maintain law, order, and government. And finally came a period of social reintegration: the government closed ranks around a new chief, and the people overcame their shock, expiated their grief, and returned to old responsibilities in a new situation.

Each of these periods, as we have suggested, made its own special demands for communication. At 12:30 on November 22 the machinery of news-gathering was suddenly jarred out of its routine. The first staccato bulletin from Dallas was followed by a veritable ocean of telephoned news, wire copy, radio, television, and film, until all sides of the monstrous events had been filled in, and the chief actors had moved or been moved elsewhere.

This roused two great waves of communication in response. About one of these we know relatively little, and probably shall continue to know little until the autobiographies and the "now it can be told" articles begin to appear. This was the great and urgent flow of administrative communication, beginning in front of the Texas School Book Depository and the Parkland Hospital, and speedily involving the local and national police agencies, the White House, and Congress as officialdom took the actions required to protect the new President, bring the murderers to justice, and arrange a farewell to the leader and an orderly transition of leadership. The Warren report has told us a little of what went

on during that time, and it is possible to piece together other bits. For example, there was for a time a question whether the killing of the President was an isolated act or was part of a conspiracy that might strike other leaders in an effort to take over the government. Unlikely as it may seem, still this was a possibility that had to be recognized and guarded against.

About the other wave of response to the crisis news, however, we know a great deal. This was the great ground swell of grief aroused in the American people and to some extent in people of other countries. There were incredulous questions, as we know; there was anger, but less of it than one might have expected; there was a certain amount of anxiety and withdrawal, and a considerable feeling of need to "talk it over." There was apparently a compulsive need to glue oneself to television and thus vicariously take part in the events and the farewells. About this response of nonofficial America we know a great deal, and what we know is documented by the articles in this volume.

After the news of the crisis and the shocked official and unofficial responses, there was the longer period of reintegration, when society closed ranks again, resolved most of its doubts and questions, worked out its grief, and returned more or less to normal. Much of this, but by no means all, was accomplished by the end of the day when John Kennedy was laid to rest in Arlington. Some of the scars lingered. The enormous sale of the memorial books and pictures, and of the Warren Commission report nearly a year later, testifies to how long the memories and the questions have lingered.

Three periods, three different demands on communication. Throughout all three periods, but most urgently at first and diminishing with time, was the demand for facts, for swift and full answers to the questions the nation was asking: Exactly what had happened in Dallas? How had it happened? Who had done it? Was he caught? Did they know he had done it? Was the Vice-President all right? Had he been sworn in? And so forth. That was the first demand—for facts. The second was for interpretation. This demand increased after the first shock, and it was still high enough to sell upwards of a million copies of the Warren report. How could it have happened? Why did he do it? Can we be sure of his guilt? What will this event mean for us all? These were the kinds of questions for which American society began to demand answers as soon as the first harsh news was absorbed. The demand for this kind of information was greatest in the third period, the period of reintegration; the demand for facts and bulletins was greatest in the first period, when the events were just becoming known. There was still another demand, which was perhaps highest in the second response period. This was the need to shake off the shock of the news, to talk or be talked to, to draw strength and reassurance from the groups and individuals one values, and to do something, even if it were no more than watching the television, to express one's grief. In other words, communication was called on for a kind of therapy, as it had been also for facts and meanings.

In all these uses of communication, mass and interpersonal uses were intertwined. The first news came by mass media, but half the people heard it first by word of mouth. Therapeutic communication was as likely to come from "talking it over" with one's friends or family, as from watching the President's funeral on television. Interpretive communication was more likely to come from the media, but there were many amateur interpreters, and some surrendered their amateur status and began to lecture on the subject. Nevertheless, one of the things that distinguished the kind of communication in this crisis, as we have tried to point out, was the extraordinary amount of mass media coverage. The fact that the transition was so orderly and reintegration was accomplished so quickly must be credited in no small degree to the efficiency and amount of media attention. The very fact that so little, apparently, was kept from the people of this country, that the channels of information were so constantly open, that representatives of the public were on the scene to report by press and broadcast, must have helped greatly to reduce the anxiety that would have been fed by a more secretive policy or less full coverage. The fact that most of the people of a nation felt that they could join together, even through television, in memorial services to a fallen leader must have helped greatly to expiate the grief and speed social reintegration. For these reasons, and because it is easier to assemble hard facts on the content and performance of mass media than on the content and uses of interpersonal communication, we shall emphasize the media in the remainder of this paper.

WHAT THE MEDIA DID

The networks abandoned entertainment programs and commercials, and devoted themselves to the big story from Friday noon through Monday evening. Many of the smaller and independent stations did not abandon their usual programming after the first day; they had neither the program resources nor the financial security to do so.[8] But the networks and network stations concentrated on the great story and its background. The newspapers covered it in extenso, and the wire services moved hundreds of thousands of words on it. From Friday noon until Monday evening, this was the story.

There has been a great deal of study of the content of mass media, but relatively little study of what happens between a news event and its appearance in the media. This is what fascinates us about the handling of a great story like the events in Dallas. How was it covered? How were the decisions made about what people to talk to, what questions to ask, what pictures to take? What concepts of public interest governed the choice of details? What standards of evidence determined when a report should be incorporated into the news? What is the difference between news coverage policies for press and for broadcast? Matters like these obviously determine what kind of lens the news media use to show us the world, but we know less

than we should like to about them.[9] It is therefore interesting and revealing to read the accounts by professionals in this volume describing how they covered the Kennedy story.

Anyone who believes that the coverage of a crisis is a routine and straightforward job should ponder the events in Dallas. Despite the size of the news corps accompanying the President, there were simply not enough professionals at the right places to cover the confused story for the number of bureaus, services, and networks represented. Those who could send in more men did so. In the broadcasting networks, as Lower says, every member of the news department and many members of other departments worked constantly for the better part of four days. Wicker reported something that newspaper men ten years ago might not have admitted, that they often found television helpful: it gave them another pair of eyes where they could not be in person.

During the first hours the problem was to bring order out of confusion. Conflicting reports and wild rumors circulated. The new President was going to be sworn in when he returned to Washington—or while he

[9] There have been a few research studies in this area. Examples are M. Charnley's not very reassuring "A Study of Newspaper Accuracy," *Journalism Quarterly*, Vol. 12 (1935), pp. 349–401; a study by G. E. Lang and K. Lang of the MacArthur parade in Chicago, "The Unique Perspective of Television: A Pilot Study," *American Sociological Review*, Vol. 18 (1953), pp. 3–12, which demonstrates that television can convey an impression of an event that is quite different from what is seen by those present; and W. Breed's "The Newspaperman, News, and Society" (Ph.D. dissertation, Columbia University, 1952), which studies how policy is made and communicated in the city room. These are samples from a scant literature.

was still in Dallas. (Actually it was on the plane before it left the Dallas airport.) The gun was a Mauser; it was an Italian make; it was several other kinds. *Two* heads had been seen at the window from which the assassin's bullets were reported to have come. Some of the shots were thought to have come from an overpass rather than the building. Oswald had been seen with Ruby. Oswald had been heard to say this and that. These and potentially more serious reports (for example, about the assassin's relation to foreign countries and to political groups in this country) were spoken as gospel truth and offered to reporters.

Consequently, a reporter on the Dallas story was from the very first up against one of the classical problems of journalism: What constitutes evidence? When does a report have enough support to justify passing it along? The newspapers and wire services passed on some rumors with sources duly noted—a "buyer beware" technique that never has much to say for it, and still less in a delicate situation like that surrounding Dallas. The television reporters found, Love says, that "though rumors can be reported as rumors in a newspaper, to do so on television is much more difficult." In a sense television journalism grew up in Dallas, for never before had it faced such a story with so much of the responsibility for telling it. As a result of this experience journalists will come to understand better the differences between television and newspaper coverage of news. One thing that became clear, to quote Love again, is that "all the news that's fit to print is not necessarily fit to be seen." For example, there was the

question of whether the amateur movie containing pictures of the President actually being struck by the bullets should be shown on television. Apparently the networks decided against it, although *Life* later published a sequence of still pictures from the same film. Love said the picture would have been used if available on November 22, but later it would have seemed "too horrible" on television.

If the first problem was simply to get reporters where the news was breaking, and the second was to sort out the confused welter of evidence, half-truths, and rumors, a third was to provide enough background, enough news in depth, so that people could understand and evaluate what was happening. Here again Dallas suggested one of the fundamental differences between television and print journalism. Pettit expressed it this way: "Live television is peculiarly ill-equipped for investigative reporting. It shows only what is there". Therefore television was at its best in transporting the viewer to the scenes of news—the memorial events in Washington, the return of the new President to the capital, the news conferences, the unforgettable scenes of the dead President's wife and children, and the terrible scenes in the Dallas police headquarters. To fill in between events like these, the networks depended for a while on street interviews until they could prepare documentaries and memorial programs. With the newspapers, however, it was quite different. To see how at least one paper viewed its investigative responsibilities, one has only to read Harrison Salisbury's description. . . . He describes the working approach of the *New York Times* to an event of this type. The newspaper's first responsibility is to provide an "intimate, detailed, accurate chronology of events," an account that would "enable the reader to pick his way fairly well through fact, fiction, and rumor". But the *Times* did not propose to stop with that. It dug into the story with all the men it could assign, and, as a matter of fact, investigated many of the questions later given to the Warren Commission. The list of studies programmed by the *Times* will give many readers a new concept of how some newspapers view their public responsibilities. The *Times* actually found itself going over the same ground as the FBI and the Warren Commission, and kept up its private plowing of this ground until early in 1964.

In Dallas, then, reporters were covering a story that was a mystery from the first minute, and that was doomed to remain in part a mystery forever because of the shooting of the chief suspect. They were operating amidst great confusion and under the shadow of high emotion. Furthermore, they remained competitive on most of the coverage. This situation gave rise to some of the darker hours, as well as some of the most remarkable accomplishments, of news coverage in Dallas.

More than anything else, the newsmen have been criticized for what happened in the Dallas police headquarters. The worst that can be said about the news representatives in this respect is that they *share* responsibilities with Dallas police and officials for the confusion, for the statements in advance of trial about Oswald's guilt, and for the final public showing of Os-

wald that exposed him to Ruby's gun. Apparently nothing was done by the Dallas officials to systematize their contacts with newsmen or cameramen. There was no place through which news could be funneled. News conferences were held on the run, and police officers appeared to have no compunction about giving a frank interview whenever asked. Officials said things in these interviews that would surely have been ruled prejudicial if the case had ever come to trial. Some of this conduct on the part of the Dallas officers is explained by a document reprinted in the report of the Warren Commission. This is a general order of the Dallas Police Department that puts on the policemen "a responsibility to lend active assistance" to the press, and forbids an officer to "improperly attempt to interfere with the news media representative. . . . Such activity . . . is regarded by the press as an infringement of rights and the Department shares this view." So far as this goes it is all right, but the directive might well have defined proper "active assistance" and improper "interference." The lack of any well-understood limit of this kind set the stage for the drama of confusion played out on the third floor of the police headquarters, where officers sought to interrogate Oswald, as Oscar MacKenzie says drily in *The New Statesman*, "in the intervals between public appearances." [10]

Margaret Mead once wrote of the disastrous consequences that occurred when young people of two cultures were brought together during wartime, those of one culture having

[10] Oscar MacKenzie, "Attention Must Be Paid," *New Statesman*, Vol. 68 (1964), pp. 475–476.

learned that it is the girl's responsibility to say no, the others that it is the boy's responsibility.[11] Something like that was happening at Dallas. Newsmen were taught to be aggressive and to go as far as they could in covering a story, expecting officials to draw the limits necessary to protect the persons and rights of accused criminals. The Dallas police, one can imagine from the general order, had been taught to be permissive with newsmen and perhaps to expect them to exercise due restraint in criminal cases. Needless to say, there were special reasons on those days for newsmen to be especially aggressive and for Dallas officials to be especially permissive. But the cultural misunderstanding that occurred demonstrated the need for a clearer understanding of limits and responsibilities in this area, perhaps not a written code of conduct but at least a set of agreed-upon principles. As William L. Rivers says in his paper . . . , what happened in the Dallas police headquarters calls for serious discussion of the "area of uncertainty" about what are a reporter's rights, privileges, and duties in covering a criminal case, and especially a very important criminal case like this one. The Kennedy story was not the first one to bring these problems to light, but it throws a pitiless glare on them.[12]

HOW WAS THE NEWS CIRCULATED?

There are some remarkable figures in the Nielsen report on television viewing for November 22–25.[13] During these days the average home in the Nielsen sample had a television receiver tuned to the Kennedy report for a total of 31.6 hours. During that time, Nielsen estimates, approximately 166 million Americans in over 51 million homes were tuned at some time to the Kennedy program, and in one-sixth of those homes people had their television on the big story for more than 11 hours per day! These figures are supported by the NORC survey, for which people estimated that they spent, on the average, 8 hours Friday, 10 Saturday, 8 Sunday, and 8 Monday watching television or listening to the radio.[14]

Undoubtedly no event like this, where so many Americans have concentrated vision and hearing on the same story at the same time for so long a period, has ever occurred before. It is difficult from existing records to estimate the amount of listening to and viewing of the Roosevelt story, but at that time radio and newspapers carried the burden of news diffusion and there was no such concentration on

[11] Margaret Mead, "Some Cultural Approaches to Communication Problems," in Lyman Bryson (ed.), *The Communication of Ideas* (New York: Institute for Religious and Social Studies, distributed by Harper, 1948).

[12] Public reaction was in general quite favorable to the coverage of the story, particularly to its speed and ampleness, and to the three and a half days of television. The chief criticism was professional rather than general, and referred to the sort of things I have been talking about. Some

idea of the public criticism can be gained from the reports in this volume by Mindak and Hursh and by Anderson and Moran.

[13] A. C. Nielsen Co., "TV Responses to the Death of the President" (New York: A. C. Nielsen, 1963).

[14] However, Nielsen found Monday—the day of the funeral—the day of heaviest television viewing.

one story as there was in November of 1963.[15] A very rough estimate suggests that for an average family the television viewing of the Kennedy story was greater than the radio listening to the Roosevelt story by a factor of perhaps 5 to 8 times.

traveled with almost unbelievable swiftness. Two-thirds of the people seem to have heard it within half an hour, even before the President's death was announced. Table V-7 gives comparable figures for four of the studies made at the time.

TABLE V-7

Sample[a]	Proportion of people who heard news within			
	15 min.	30 min.	45 min.	60 min.
National.		68%		
Dallas 67%		84	89%	93%
San Jose, Calif.. 42		62	81	90
Iowa City, Iowa		70		91

a The national sample is reported on in this volume by Sheatsley and Feldman; the San Jose sample by Greenberg; and the Iowa City sample by Spitzer and Spitzer. The report on diffusion in Dallas is in R. J. Hill and C. M. Bonjean, "News Diffusion: A Test of the Regularity Hypothesis," *Journalism Quarterly* (1964), *41* 336–42.

One result of the enormous flow of information on the events in Dallas, and the extraordinary public attention to this information, was that there was apparently in this case no hard core of know-nothings. It is a rule of thumb in survey research that 10 to 20 per cent of a national sample will probably be unaware of almost any news event. But 99.8 per cent of the NORC national sample reported having heard the news by 6 P.M. on Friday —five and a half hours after the President was shot. Furthermore, the news

There are no entirely comparable figures from earlier events in this class. A sample of students attending one college at the time of Roosevelt's death showed that 83 per cent of them heard the news within 30 minutes and 93 per cent within an hour, but these young people were living in close contact in dormitories.[16] Eleven hours elapsed before 90 per cent of a university faculty community heard of the death of Senator Taft, and 14 hours before 90 per cent of the eventual knowers in a housing project heard it.[17] Samples of the general public on previous occasions have usually returned much lower figures than those obtained in

[15] A telegraphic poll taken after Roosevelt's funeral indicated that about 88 per cent of American adults had listened to the radio at *some* time during the three days following the President's death. This National Opinion Research Center poll is cited by Paul B. Sheatsley and Jacob J. Feldman, "A National Survey on Public Reactions and Behavior," in Bradley S. Greenberg and Edwin B. Parker (eds.), *The Kennedy Assassination and the American Public* (Stanford: Stanford University Press, 1965), p. 159.

[16] D. C. Miller, "A Research Note on Mass Communications," *American Sociological Review*, Vol. 10 (1945), pp. 691–694.

[17] O. M. Larsen and R. J. Hill, "Mass Media and Interpersonal Communication in the Diffusion of a News Event," *American Sociological Review*, Vol. 19 (1954), pp. 426–433.

TABLE V-8

Sample	TV	First source of news		
		Radio	*Personal*	*Newspaper*
National.	47% (TV + radio)		49%	4%
Dallas.	26	17%	57	
San Jose	20	28	50	
Iowa City	19	25	55	

1963, although it must be noted that these earlier stories have not had the news value of the Kennedy story. For example, 26 per cent of the persons in two samples in different parts of the country reported that they had heard of Eisenhower's stroke within an hour of the time the news became available, 43 per cent knew of the first Explorer satellite within an hour, and only 6 per cent had heard of the voting of statehood for Alaska within an hour.[18]

other person, either face to face or by telephone. Table V-8 gives comparative figures from the same four studies just reported upon. Here again we have no strictly comparable figures from the past. The telegraphic survey at the time of Roosevelt's death indicated that 47 per cent of people had learned the news from radio or the press, 53 per cent from interpersonal sources. Of the college students in dormitories studied by Miller, 88 per

TABLE V-9

Event[a]	TV	First source of news		
		Radio	*Newspaper*	*Personal*
Launching of Explorer I, 1958	41%	23%	18%	18%
Eisenhower's stroke, 1957.	38	32	12	18
Alaska statehood, 1958	29	27	38	6
Eisenhower decides to seek second term, 1956	14	39	27	20
Taft's death, 1953.	15	49	11	26

[a] The source of the first three of these events is Deutschmann and Danielson. The source for the fourth is W. Danielson, "Eisenhower's February Decision: A Study of News Impact," *Journalism Quarterly* (1956), *33*, 433–41. The source for the fifth is Larsen and Hill.

How was the news heard? The studies are in general agreement: a little less than half heard by television or radio; a little over half heard from an-

[18] P. Deutschmann and W. Danielson, "Diffusion of Knowledge of the Major News Story," *Journalism Quarterly*, Vol. 37 (1960), pp. 345–355.

cent reported they had heard the news from another student.

Table V-9 gives figures for lesser stories. These figures suggest a pattern as to how fast and by what means a news story reaches the public. The two chief variables would seem to be news value and the time of day when the story breaks. Greenberg was able to show that when a story has narrow interest so that it receives little or no mass media treatment, it is likely that more people who hear about it will hear from other persons.[19] When news value is perceived to be sufficient that the mass media generally carry the story, then, other things being equal, the greater the news value, the more the story is passed on by word of mouth and therefore the higher the proportion of persons who hear it from interpersonal sources. Thus, if the neighbor's child has measles, that news is likely to be heard, if at all, by word of mouth. If Alaska is voted statehood, that news may be passed around a great deal by word of mouth in Alaska but will be heard mostly by mass media in the rest of the country. Stories like the death of Taft, the launching of the first American satellite, President Eisenhower's stroke, and his decision to seek a second term are of generally higher news value and therefore more likely to be passed on by word of mouth. We find that about three times as many people heard about these stories from interpersonal sources as heard from such sources about the vote on Alaska, but still about four out of five persons heard these news stories first from the mass media. But when we have a story of the highest news value, like the assassination of a President, we find that as many as half the population hear the news from other persons rather than the media. Thus Greenberg found a J-curve when he plotted the proportion of people aware of

various news events against the proportion who heard of them from interpersonal sources:

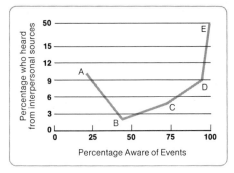

But the time of day makes some difference too. If an important story breaks during hours when many people are at work, then radio and interpersonal channels will handle most of the diffusion for them. If it breaks in the evening, then television will carry more of the diffusion for them. The Kennedy story broke just after noon for the eastern half of the country, just before noon for the western. Exactly half of the NORC sample reported they had heard the news at home, 29 per cent had heard at work, and 21 per cent had heard while shopping, having lunch, or doing something else neither at home nor at work. For the people at home, television and telephone calls were important; for the people at work, radio and interpersonal messages; for the others, a variety of media and interpersonal channels. But both the paramount interest of the news and the fact that it broke in midday contributed to an enormous amount of passing it on and talking about it. Members of the Iowa City sample reported having told the news on the average to between five and six

[19] Bradley S. Greenberg, "Person-to-Person Communication in the Diffusion of News Events," *Journalism Quarterly*, Vol. 41 (1964), pp. 489–494.

people each. The later news of Oswald's slaying was passed on to an average of three persons. This does not mean, of course, that each of these messages went to someone who had not heard the news; in many cases the conversation must have started, "Have you heard . . . ?" Thirty-seven per cent of the national sample reported that they phoned or visited someone else after they heard the news and, coincidentally, 38 per cent reported that someone visited them. Banta reports that 35 per cent of his Denver sample heard the news from a casual acquaintance, 11 per cent from a complete stranger! [20] Clearly the Kennedy story generated an enormous and uncommon amount of interpersonal news-carrying.

But when the news had once been heard, interpersonally or otherwise, then there was a rush to radio or television. Five out of six who could drop what they were doing turned to one of the broadcast media for confirmation or further details.

Thus we can say that the mass media in the crisis following the Kennedy assassination delivered the news with almost unparalleled speed and thoroughness, and stimulated interpersonal channels to carry it further. We can also note that the media filled an important role in providing confirmation, further details, and doubtless sometimes correction; apparently the public trusted what it heard on broadcasts or read in the newspapers. But the media must have been filling more functions than these; otherwise, how should we explain the enormous al-

location of time to television in the four days of the crisis? To understand better what use was being made of communication in those long hours of viewing between Friday noon and Monday night, let us look more closely at the general reaction of the public to the events.

THE PUBLIC REACTION AND THE FUNCTION OF COMMUNICATION

Beyond passing the news on, and rushing to TV or radio, how did people react? Obviously there was a very deep, a very widespread emotional response. Less than half the people in the national sample could continue their usual activities. Some felt the need to be with persons they knew or loved; they hurried home or telephoned or visited friends or relatives. Others wanted to be by themselves; the more they admired the President, the more they felt this need.[21] Television, under differing circumstances, might meet either of these needs; it could be either a solitary or a group activity.

Miller and Zimmerman describe the strange atmosphere in New York City on the afternoon of the slaying. It was a sort of "frantic quiet." The usual tumult and noise of New York were missing. Fewer people than usual were hurrying somewhere. There was an uncommon willingness to stop and talk. People gathered around newsstands or radios, surrounded people

---

[20] T. J. Banta, "The Kennedy Assassination: Early Thoughts and Emotions," *Public Opinion Quarterly*, Vol. 28 (1964), pp. 216–224.

[21] According to Sheatsley and Feldman, "A National Survey . . . ," p. 154, 51 per cent of Negroes said that they had wanted to be by themselves, but only 28 percent of Southern whites so reported.

with portable transistor sets. There was no hesitation about discussing one's feelings with anyone who wished to talk.

The most general pattern of personal response was at first shock and disbelief. Some merely sought to check the news; some wilfully denied it. As Orlansky reported newsdealers saying of their customers after Roosevelt's death, "They don't wanna believe it," so Greenstein reported respondents saying after Kennedy's, "It can't happen here!" [22]

That first shocked response was succeeded by a developing awareness of the loss, along with feelings of sorrow, sadness, shame, and anger. These feelings rolled over the nation in an immense tide. The most common reactions were to be sorry for Mrs. Kennedy and the children, sorry that a vital young man should be killed at the height of his powers, ashamed that such a thing could happen in our country, sad at the loss of someone well-known and dear, and angry that someone could have done such a deed. These responses were very generally reported. Less often reported, but still mentioned by nearly half the national sample, was worry over how the President's death would affect the political situation. For some Americans these feelings were followed by physical symptoms such as weeping, tenseness, sleeplessness, fatigue, or loss of appetite. This was the second stage.

There followed a gradual recovery and return to a normal emotional state. Mindak and Hursh report that their sample in Minneapolis was "normal" again by Monday. Both the national sample and the Dallas sample reported that the majority of physical symptoms had departed after four days.[23] By that time also, anger and anxiety were less, the worst of the grief was over, and there were indications of rededication on the part of some people. Hurn and Messer report that about a third of their Chicago sample felt they should personally rededicate themselves by becoming more tolerant, and Sears demonstrated that people became less partisan immediately after the events in Dallas. In general, there was a social reintegration covering over the scars of the sad weekend. That was the third stage.

Several things can be pointed out about this personal and public response. For one thing it was primarily grief rather than anxiety. The physical symptoms we have listed are typical of grief and bereavement. Anxiety has a different set of symptoms.[24] Bradburn and Feldman were able to document this by comparing two groups of respondents, who were interviewed in October and again after the assassination. One of these was a Negro sample in Detroit, the other a mostly white sample in a suburb of Washington. Between the first interview and the second, grief symptoms rose markedly in both samples, but anxiety symptoms rose only in the Negro sample, where people must have felt more personally threatened by events. And the pattern of reaction in general was typical of

[22] Orlansky, "Reactions to the Death of President Roosevelt," pp. 240 ff.

[23] Sheatsley and Feldman, "A National Survey . . . ," p. 160; Charles M. Bonjean, Richard J. Hill, and Harry W. Martin, "Reactions to the Assassination in Dallas," in Greenberg and Parker (eds.), *The Kennedy Assassination*, p. 185.

[24] Engel, "Is Grief a Disease?" pp. 18 ff.

mourning—shock and intense sorrow, which was poured out or worked out, permitting the individual to return after a fairly short time to normal patterns of behavior, often with a sense of rededication or moral obligation.

Another observation during those days was the relative scarcity of political anxiety and reactions built around fear of a political conspiracy. Concern over who the assassin was and whether he would be apprehended was evident from the first, and about four out of five named an immediate suspect. About one out of four at once suspected a Communist, a Castroite, or a leftist of some other kind; about half that many thought of a segregationist or another right-wing person. But as time passed these suspicions became markedly less; and in particular there was relatively little anxiety lest a foreign group or a conspiring political group be active in the situation (see Miller and Zimmerman, Coleman and Hollander). If Americans had been fearful about the succession of a new President, most of them soon lost these fears. If many of them had first rejected the idea that "one man could do what Oswald did," most of them apparently became sufficiently satisfied with the explanation so that the alternatives did not worry or arouse them.

In the third place, it is worth noting, as do Verba and Hurn and Messer, that this crisis was integrative rather than disintegrative for the United States. Unlike most of the world's crises in which a change of chief executive is occasioned by violence, the events of November 22–25 brought Americans together rather than driving them apart. They closed ranks around the new President. Partisanship on a national political level was abandoned during a month of mourning, and, as Sears was able to show, partisanship was reduced on a private and personal level also. If the reaction of the Chicago sample was typical, many Americans were thinking in December of 1963 about their obligation to practice brotherhood, tolerance, and other integrative behavior.

Now why should responses to President Kennedy's assassination and related events have taken these forms? Why should they have been so largely grief rather than anxiety, so relatively lacking in fear of a political conspiracy, and so largely integrative rather than divisive? Why should it have been Europe rather than the United States that kept alive, during the subsequent year, the suspicions of threatening conspiracy? Why was the period of recovery so relatively short, although the grief was manifestly so deep?

There are no simple answers to questions like these. One answer lies in the American people's faith in their national institutions, including the succession to the Presidency and the rule of law. Another is the firm and responsible actions of the new Chief Executive and his government. One out of many others is, as Coleman and Hollander say, that the events following the assassination remind us of "the different courses public opinion can take and of our meager knowledge of the dynamics."

But an important part of the answer to such questions must lie in the performance and use of mass communication during the four days. It was extremely important to a shocked public to have such a large and continuing flow of information on the matter that concerned them. Incomplete and grudging information at a time of crisis breeds suspicion and rumor. Able press representatives have always known this. Thus when President Eisenhower had his heart attack, James Hagerty had the President's doctor explain the illness and the prognosis to newsmen and to the television audience; as a result fears and doubts were allayed, people took the illness in stride, and ground was laid for public confidence in the President's ability to carry on his duties and ultimately to serve a second term. The flow of news from Dallas also did something like this. As much as we may regret some of the things that happened in the Dallas police headquarters, still if it were not for the aggressive news coverage by the media and the frankness of officials we should probably have had greater anxiety and a slower integration.

The swift, full coverage undoubtedly grounded many rumors before they could circulate. By speaking so fully and frankly of Oswald and the events in which he was involved, the media helped to reduce fears of a conspiracy and prepare people to believe the theory that a lone, disturbed man had done it. Demonstrating that the Presidential succession was working smoothly, that the government was going forward in firm hands, helped reduce fears and recriminations. For a student of communication, one of the most important deductions from the events of late November 1963 is that Americans trust their free press and their free broadcasting system. In this case it must be said that these did not fail the American people in any im-

portant way. The people got the full news, they got it fast, and they got it, with a very few exceptions, accurately.

The function of the news coverage of the Kennedy crisis is thus fairly clear. We understand less well what was happening during those long hours when so many tens of millions watched the television set. Many people have remarked about the compulsive quality of this viewing. Greenstein documents some of it in his transcriptions of discussion groups:

Subject$_1$. I don't know why we sit here and watch it.
S$_2$. I stayed right up until the network went off.
S$_3$. I don't know. It's just something like this creates . . . kind of like a vacuum in your head of all the things you're used to and you just have to fill it up.
S$_4$. I kept waiting for something that would make me feel more hopeful or feel better about it. It never came, of course, but you're tied to the TV set in hopes that it would.
S$_5$. After the TV went off last night, I thought about . . . why I had spent the whole day and it struck me that I was waiting for somebody to explain why this happened.

These viewers didn't know why they had viewed so long but realized they were doing it to fill a gap, looking for explanation, reassurance, perhaps for something they could not readily articulate. The explanation they were seeking must have been more than a surface one. They were probably seeking, whether they knew it or not, a kind of philosophical explanation for the irony of the loss of a young, admired, and beloved leader, a reconciliation of this event with their ideals of justice and fairness, and an opportunity to get rid of their weight of grief. And as we have said before, they were probably watching because they did not know just what else under the circumstances to do.

This is speculation, of course. Certain things we can say in a less speculative vein about the long listening to television. We can note what was coming to them through the picture tube. In addition to the flow of spot news, they were watching and hearing national leaders, being reminded of national history and the rituals and laws of the national government, reviewing the career of the dead President, seeing the norms and mores of American life exemplified for them by people they admired. In other words they were being *reassured* that the nation, and in particular the presidency, was continuing as they wanted it to, and they were being reminded of a *pattern of conduct* expected of them as Americans.

In the second place they were being shown symbols and events—the flag-draped casket, the young widow and the children, the terrible slow drumbeat of the funeral march—that gave them an opportunity to experience a real catharsis of grief if they wanted to. Aristotle used the word catharsis to describe the aesthetic effect of Greek drama in purging impure and excessive emotions. It has become a bit old-fashioned to talk about catharsis in this sense, and yet this is what introspection tells us must have been happening before many of those television sets. The viewers were purging themselves of their burden of grief and anger by going through acts of mourning, much as they might have

done for a family bereavement. They were weeping, secretly or openly, over the sights of the national tragedy. They were participating as much as they could in memorial events. They were going to a funeral.

And they were doing these things *together!* The enormous, the unequaled focus of attention that occurred around the television sets of America during the crisis, and especially on the day of the funeral, when audience measurements in New York found more than 90 per cent of sets tuned at one time to the funeral procession—this concentration of attention deserves more thought than it has been given. How many of the viewers actually felt that they were sitting in a congregation of 150 million Americans, we do not know. Many of them apparently had a sense of participating in a national act. This focus of attention, as Coleman and Hollander have pointed out, contained the potential for great national action. If a suitable object for great national anger had emerged from the news of the crisis, it is conceivable that a mass uprising might have occurred. But the very fullness of the news won confidence in it, and developments cut the ground out from under any belief that a nationally dangerous conspiracy was involved. Instead, the focus on the presidency reasserted America's deep commitment to that institution and to the rule of law and order.

The experiences of 150 million Americans before their television sets during the dark weekend, then, were a sharing of common information, a reassertion of national norms, and a national act of mourning, which must have been for many viewers a catharsis of grief. When the experience is seen in this way, it is somewhat easier to understand why the experience was so largely grief rather than anxiety, why Americans closed the book on an anxiety over conspiracy more quickly than Europeans did, and why the recovery after the weekend of grief came so comparatively soon, came with elements of rededication and reintegration rather than divisiveness and disquiet. To sum up, it appears that the essential elements in this response were the enormous flow of news and the enormous focus of attention on television sets that at times could have been described as a truly national act involving most of a major nation's citizens.

There has been a great deal of theorizing about the difference between the conditions under which the mass media have a significant effect directly on the public, and the conditions under which their effect has to be mediated by opinion leaders or other interpersonal carriers. Undoubtedly the interpersonal channels of information and influence were working from November 22 through November 25 as at other times, and we have already noted that the news of the two murders was passed along from person to person with phenomenal speed. But the,

general rush to radio or television as soon as the news was heard, and the enormous concentration on the mass media, especially television, during the next three days, lead us to think that a two-step flow was not the major factor in the effects we have been describing. Many Americans, of course, watched television in family groups during those days, but the significant fact is that such large numbers were watching: they were not told secondhand; they came themselves with their sadness, their questioning, to witness the dramatic events on the picture tube. Television during those four days was a communication event somewhat like the Kennedy-Nixon debates, in that both events brought very large numbers of people into direct contact with the developments and persons to which they expected to react. And like the changes in estimation of the candidates and voting intention that took place after the first debate, so the individual catharsis, the laying of doubts to rest, and the reinforcement of American norms that took place in audiences after the President's assassination appear to be examples of the powerful direct effects of which the mass media, under favorable conditions, are capable.

FOR FURTHER READING

CHERRY, Colin, *On Human Communication: A Review, A Survey and A Criticism* (New York: Wiley Science Editions, 1961).

DANCE, Frank E. X. (Ed.), *Human Communication Theory* (New York: Holt, Rinehart and Winston, 1967).

DEUTSCH, Karl W., *The Nerves of Government* (New York: Free Press of Glencoe, 1963).

DEXTER, Lewis A. and David Manning White (Eds.), *People, Society and Mass Communications* (New York: Free Press of Glencoe, 1964).

FAGEN, Richard R., *Politics and Communication* (Boston: Little, Brown, 1966).

JACOB, Phillip E. and James V. Toscano (Eds.), *The Integration of Political Communities* (Philadelphia and New York: J. B. Lippincott, 1964).

KELMAN, Herbert C. (Ed.), *International Behavior* (New York: Holt, Rinehart and Winston, 1965).

LUCE, R. Duncan, "The Theory of Selective Information and Some of its Behavioral Applications" in R. D. Luce (Ed.). *Developments in Mathematical Psychology* (Glencoe: Free Press, 1960).

PYE, Lucian W. (Ed.), *Communications and Political Development* (Princeton: Princeton University Press, 1963).

SHANNON, Claude E., "Information Theory," *Encyclopedia Britannica,* Vol. 12 (1969), pp. 246B–249.

SHANNON, Claude E. and Warren Weaver, *The Mathematical Theory of Communication* (Urbana: University of Illinois Press, 1949).

SMITH, Alfred G. (Ed.), *Communication and Culture* (New York: Holt, Rinehart and Winston, 1966).

WIENER, Norbert, *Cybernetics,* 2nd ed. (Cambridge: Massachusetts Institute of Technology Press, and New York: Wiley, 1961).

PART SIX: POWER

Warren Weaver has told us that the effectiveness of communications is one of the three main problems of information theory. "The problems of influence or effectiveness are concerned with the success with which the meaning conveyed to the receiver leads to the desired conduct on his part." [1] Robert A. Dahl, discussing the concept of power [2] tells us, "A influences B to the extent that he gets B to do something that B would not otherwise do." [3] Not only are the words used similarly, but communication theory is logically dependent on the analysis of power. Unless it can be shown that the receiver's conduct has been influenced, we have no way of *proving* that a message has been received.

We should not, of course, be under any illusion that a concern with power is a novel preoccupation. The study of power has a long and distinguished history. All the giants among the political theorists of the past—Plato, Aristotle, Hobbes, Montesquieu, Rousseau, Hegel, Marx, and Mill—have analyzed the location of political power and the justification for its use. Since the turn of the century the most general questions raised in this continuing dialogue are to be found in the varying interpretations of the elitists (such as Mosca, Pareto, and Schumpeter) and the pluralists (such as Cole, Lindsay, and Laski). Most of the elitists came from the continent; most of the pluralists from England.

The analysis of power by American political scientists in the middle decades of the twentieth century has been affected by this conflict between elitists and pluralists. This is perhaps most true of those who have written generally about the distribution of power throughout a political system. In the writings of Robert MacIver, Charles Merriam, and Harold Lasswell [4] one senses a tension caused by adhering to the democratic values of the pluralists while trying to incorporate some of the insights of the elitists.[5] The conflict has also colored interpretations of

---

[1] "The Mathematics of Communication," *Scientific American*, July, 1949, p. 11.

[2] There are at least four words—power, influence, authority, and control—which have similar connotations. We use these as synonyms. The reader should be warned, however, that scholars who analyze these matters often give these words different denotations. Each author should be read carefully enough to be certain how *he* is using each of these words.

[3] *Modern Political Analysis* (Englewood Cliffs, N.J.: Prentice-Hall, 1963), p. 40.

[4] The leading works here are Robert MacIver, *The Modern State* (Oxford: The Clarendon Press, 1926) and *The Web of Government* (New York: Macmillan, 1946); Charles Merriam, *Political Power* (New York: Whittlesey House, 1934) and *Systematic Politics* (Chicago: University of Chicago Press, 1945); Harold Lasswell, *Politics: Who Gets What When How* (New York: Whittlesey House, 1936); and Harold Lasswell and Abraham Kaplan, *Power and Society* (New Haven: Yale University Press, 1950). MacIver, the Scot, is closer in outlook to the pluralists.

[5] A fine summary of the power interpretations of American political scientists at mid-century may be found in the first chapter of V. O. Key, *Parties, Politics and Pressure Groups*, 5th ed. (New York: T. Y. Crowell, 1968).

community politics. Sociologists such as Robert and Helen Lynd [6] and Floyd Hunter find community power structures dominated by elites while political scientists, led by Robert A. Dahl and his students Raymond Wolfinger, Nelson Polsby, and Aaron Wildavsky, tell us that many actors in a system possess fragments of power. Students of international politics have been less preoccupied with this debate. Their concern, exemplified in texts such as Harold and Margaret Sprout's *The Foundations of National Power,* Frederick L. Schuman's *International Politics,* and Hans Morgenthau's *Politics Among Nations,* has been with identifying those factors which enabled a nation to exercise power in the international arena.

All three of these intellectual foci—political theory, community politics, and international politics—have been important in the developing thinking of American students of political power, but they will not concern us further here. For one thing, all these approaches were at the macrolevel. For another, since 1950 there have been several attempts to conceptualize and operationalize power which have direct applications at the microlevel. It is this line of analysis which is closest to our interests.

Some stimulus for this work came from the noted gestalt psychologist, Kurt Lewin. In 1951, Lewin suggested defining the power of b over a "as the quotient of the maximum force which b can induce on $a,$ and the maximum resistance which a can offer." [7] More important to political science, however, was the work of three men, Herbert Simon, James March, and Robert Dahl. All three were given to crisp, clear thinking, and all three published important papers on the measurement of power between 1953 and 1957. [8] Professor Simon saw there was a close relation between the concepts of causation and power. Once he had stated the power relationship "as a problem of giving operational meaning to the asymmetry of the relation between independent and dependent variables, it became clear that it was identical with the general problem of defining a *causal relation* between two variables. That is to say, for the assertion, 'A has power over B,' we can substitute the assertion, 'A's behavior causes B's behavior.' If we can

[6] For the current student generation, the Lynds might be best introduced as the parents of the New Left spokesman Staughton Lynd. However, Robert and Helen Lynd were distinguished sociologists in their own right, and are well known for *Middletown* and *Middletown in Transition* (New York: Harcourt, Brace & World, 1929, 1937).

[7] *Field Theory in Social Science* (New York: Harper & Row, 1951), quoted in James G. March, "The Power of Power" in David Easton, (Ed.), *Varieties of Political Theory* (Englewood Cliffs, N.J.: Prentice-Hall, 1966), p. 41.

[8] Herbert A. Simon, "Notes on the Observation and Measurement of Political Power" *Journal of Politics,* November, 1953, pp. 500–516; James G. March, "An Introduction to the Theory and Measurement of Influence, *American Political Science Review,* June, 1955, pp. 431–451; James G. March, "Measurements Concepts in the Theory of Influence" *Journal of Politics,* May, 1957, pp. 202–226; and Robert A. Dahl, "The Concept of Power" *Behavioral Science,* July, 1957, pp. 201–215. Trying to trace the lines of influence between Professors Simon, March, and Dahl is an exercise which gives one a sense of the elusiveness of this concept. Consider the following. Simon took his degree at Chicago where he was taught by Merriam and Lasswell; Dahl took his degree and taught at Yale where Lasswell was a senior colleague; March took his degree at Yale where Lasswell and Dahl were teaching and then began his career at Carnegie Tech where Simon was a senior colleague. Simon and March were at work on joint intellectual enterprises during this period as were March and Dahl. Who influenced whom?

define the causal relation, we can define influence, power, or authority, and *vice versa*." [9] Professor March continued the effort to define the nature of this relationship by restating the results of psychological experiments on influence in terms of set theory and probability. Professor Dahl, whose paper is the first one in this section, summarized the argument by providing a vocabulary—*base* of power, *means* of exercising power, *scope* of power, and *amount* of power—which has been used by many authorities on the subject since that time.

These four papers of the mid-fifties have been followed by much further work pursuing these lines of analysis. [10] At the present writing, it is of course impossible to say what the results will ultimately prove to be. There are those who now believe that power is a disappointing concept. Thus, James March has warned:

> Given the obviousness of power, we rarely reexamine the basic model by which social choice is viewed as being a combination of individual choices, the combination being dependent on the power of the various individuals. Since we have a persistent problem discovering a measurement procedure that consistently yields results which are consistent with the model, we assert a measurement problem and a problem of the concept of power. We clarify and reclarify the concept, and we define and redefine the measures. . . . Although I have some sympathy with these efforts, I think our perseverance may be extreme. . . . I think we too often ask *how* to measure power when we should ask *whether* to measure power. [11]

Not every one would agree that unsatisfactory results from intellectual effort extending only over a decade and a half are sufficient grounds for abandoning the effort, particularly when the concept of power is central to so much else. But it is clear that the task will not be easy, and, as is frequently the case, serious discussion of a "single" concept has shown that we had a category that subsumed several related concepts. Robert A. Dahl, commenting on the work that has been done, says:

> The simple models of power and authority in political systems that we have been employing for centuries have broken down. . . . In the last decade or so a number of writers—Lasswell, Kaplan, Simon, March, Riker, Oppenheim, Cartwright, and a number of others, including myself—have tried to explicate power-terms in a systematic way. Each has indicated explicitly or implicitly certain properties that should be used to determine the existence

---

[9] Herbert A. Simon, *Models of Men* (New York: Wiley, 1957), p. 5. In contrast to Simon's emphasis on asymmetry, the articles on various aspects of power in this section almost all note a good deal of give-and-take. Here again we see a difference between a concept with nice theoretical properties, and one which is useful for observation because of its nice fit with real-world data.

[10] For a good summary of much of this work, particularly that in psychology, see Dorwin Cartwright, "Influence, Leadership, Control" in James G. March (Ed.), *Handbook of Organizations,* chapter 1. For an able critique of theoretical difficulties in attempts to give a general definition of power, see William H. Riker, "Some Ambiguities in the Notion of Power" *American Political Science Review,* June, 1964, pp. 341–349.

[11] "The Power of Power," p. 69.

and direction of power. . . . At least seven different properties of a power-relationship can be isolated from these writings; with respect to these seven properties—symmetry and causality, for example—different writers have laid down different requirements. If you make a table of these seven properties and the alternative requirements that have been suggested, it turns out that there are some 856 theoretically possible ways of specifying the essential characteristics of power terms. . . .[12]

It is now quite clear, as Professor Dahl remarks in the same 1964 article, that power is a "family name for a big, sprawling, scattered collection of often very dissimilar relations." But it is equally clear that the concepts baptized *base, means, scope,* and *amount* in Dahl's paper are important members of that family. His "The Concept of Power" is consequently an excellent point of departure for an excursion through the current work on power.

There have been many fine studies of the *bases* of power. As Dahl pointed out, "The base of an actor's power consists of all the resources . . . that he can exploit to effect the behavior of another. Much of the best writing on power . . . consists of an examination of the possible bases of power." [13] One of the best of these earlier studies is to be found in a book by Herbert Simon and two colleagues. Donald W. Smithburg, and Victor A. Thompson, *Public Administration.* Professor Simon's concept of an influence base, the conditions which make it possible for a person to exercise influence, is quite close to Dahl's usage. (Both, as a matter of fact, are following Lasswell and Kaplan on this.) And Simon's most important contributions to political science [14] have come in the area of public administration and organizational theory. So "The Bases of Power in Bureaucracy" is useful in gaining an understanding of the bases of power as well as providing an example of Simon's thinking.

The examples provided by Simon, Smithburg, and Thompson are drawn from the world of bureaucracy, but their analytical categories—authority of confidence, authority of identification, authority of sanctions, and authority of legitimacy—are broad enough to give us a general answer to the question of why men obey. They show that there are many limits to the power base which seems most obvious at *first* thought, the authority of sanctions. Use of sanctions has a tendency to split an organization into rival groups. Sanctions are organizationally shared and hence cannot be easily employed by single hierarchical superiors. The "ultimate right" to hire and fire is constrained by civil service and a tight labor market. The implication of this, of course, is that those who would exercise effective influence must employ other bases of power. And Simon, Smithburg, and

---

[12] "Power, Pluralism and Democracy: A Modest Proposal," a paper prepared for delivery at the 1964 Annual Meeting of The American Political Science Association, Chicago, Illinois, September 9–12, 1964.

[13] Robert A. Dahl, "The Concept of Power," p. 203.

[14] Although Herbert Simon began his career as a political scientist, he has made seminal contributions in a wide range of disciplines. His *Models of Man* brought together scholarly papers originally published in *Studies in Econometric Method, Journal of the American Statistical Association, Journal of Philosophy, Journal of Politics, Public Opinion Quarterly, American Sociological Review, Psychological Review, British Journal of Statistical Psychology, Biometrika, Review of Economic Studies, Econometrica, Quarterly Journal of Economics,* and *Psychometrica!*

Thompson close with a suggestion of the changing importance of the four bases of authority. "Especially is the hierarchical procedure weakened as the social division of labor turns more and more people into indispensible and recondite specialists. With the growing importance of the professional and technical specialist, there is a corresponding tendency for the working rules of organization . . . to place more and more emphasis on functional status, and less and less upon hierarchy." [15] In a computer based organization, in other words, expertise on how to get data in and out of the computer may be a more significant base of influence than a vice presidency.

The most significant addition to Robert Dahl's list of power-terms has been John C. Harsanyi's concept, *opportunity costs*.[16] If A wishes B to do something, he may be able to bring that about if he is willing to make whatever effort is necessary in the circumstances. But making the effort requires A to invest some time, or share some expertise, or include one budget item while leaving out another, or give B some preferment. If A is both fortunate and skillful, he may be able to carry off the influence attempt in such a way as to enhance both B's reputation and his own. But the usual case is that A must be prepared to use up some of his power resources in the influence-attempt, and at least contemplate the use of sanctions if B refuses to do what A wishes. From A's point of view, these are very real costs. As Professor Harsanyi puts the matter, "One of the main purposes for which social scientists use the concept of A's power over B is for the description of the policy possibilities open to A. . . . a realistic description of A's policy possibilities must include not only A's ability or inability to get B to perform a certain action X, but also the *costs* that A has to bear in order to achieve this result." [17]

John Harsanyi does not cite Richard Neustadt as a source of this idea, but Professor Neustadt's *Presidential Power* provides an illuminating discussion of the *costs* of exercising power as well as the *means* of doing so. The costs of any exercise of presidential power stem from the situation in which the President finds himself. Those whom he would influence have responsibilities to others than the President. This is obvious when dealing with Congressmen elected by a different constituency, but it also applies to the President's nominal subordinates. They have reputations which will be damaged if they are out front on an enterprise that turns out badly. They are conscious of norms of their professions or their colleagues which suggest, for example, that certain things just aren't done. If the President is to enlist other prominent, influential men in support of his enterprises, he must be prepared to give them something they want as well. Consequently "The Power to Persuade" is well seasoned with the language of opportunity costs. "When a President seeks something from executive officials," Professor Neustadt tells us, "his persuasiveness is subject to the same sorts of limitations as in the case of congressmen, or governors, or national committeemen, or

[15] Herbert Simon, Donald W. Smithburg, and Victor A. Thompson, *Public Administration* (New York: Knopf, 1950), pp. 200–201.

[16] "The Measurement of Social Power, Opportunity Costs, and the Theory of Two Person Bargaining Games" *Behavioral Science*, January, 1962, pp. 67–80. In this article, Harsanyi also calls attention to the possibility of formulating power as a "production function" as well as in the probabilistic terms used by March and Dahl.

[17] Harsanyi, "The Measurement of Social Power, Opportunity Costs," p. 69.

private citizens, or foreign governments. . . . here as elsewhere influence derives from bargaining advantages; power is give-and-take." And again, "Truman could not do without their help, but he could not have had it without unremitting effort on his part. . . . Truman paid the price required for their services." [18]

If Richard Neustadt is a good source on opportunity costs, he is also most informative about the means of exercising power. This is the central focus of his book. "We deal here with the President himself and with his influence on governmental action. . . . What can *this* man accomplish to improve the prospect that he will have influence when he wants it." [19] Neustadt's answer to this question is that the sanctions available in this situation are grossly inadequate, and that the President must know how to *augment* other power resources. This process of building up power may be seen in two perspectives. When a President needs support for an important project at a given point in time, he must "buy" the prestige and influence of others by being prepared to pay the opportunity costs. Professor Neustadt illustrates this type of augmentation in the case of the Marshall Plan. But a President can also "stockpile" power over time in the sense that say, a good appointment, creates confidence in both the President and his appointee. This longitudinal perspective leads Neustadt to the conclusion that "adequate or not, a President's own choices are the only means *in his own hands* of guarding his own prospects for effective influence." [20]

Generally speaking, the *scope* of power refers to the responses of the person who is subject to influence. The scope of A's power is what he can get B to do. In a political application of this concept, it is sometimes helpful to think of A's scope of power as the set of policies over which he exercises influence.[21] If the scope of power was regarded as a function of legislator's committee assignments, one Congressman might influence armed forces appropriations, a second agricultural policy, and a third might exercise power with respect to public housing. Functional specialization in a complex modern society tends to restrict the scope of power. Wallace S. Sayre and Herbert Kaufman point out the narrow range of decision-maker's authority in "The Diffusion of Power in New York City." Sayre and Kaufman's conclusions are based generally on their knowledge of public administration, a field in which both men are noted authorities, and specifically on the many insights in a comprehensive study entitled *Governing New York City*.

In their conceptualization, Professors Sayre and Kaufman distinguish between core groups, those whose formal powers give them formal authority over the policies in question, and satellite groups, those which seek to influence decisions about the policies in question. As the other writers on power, they tend to play down formal authority. They note that decisions result from a complex interplay between the core groups and the satellite groups, and call attention to several factors that limit the scope of power of any one group. First, officials who are members of the core group concerned with one set of policies are usually

---

[18] Richard Neustadt, *Presidential Power* (New York: Wiley, 1960), pp. 39, 52.

[19] Neustadt, *Presidential Power*, pp. 1–2.

[20] Neustadt, *Presidential Power*, p. 57.

[21] To spell out what is implicit here, the power would apply to the set of all possible respondents. The distinction between a specific respondent, B, and the set of all possible respondents is comparable to the distinction in role theory between a specific other and a generalized other.

members of satellite groups with respect to other policies. Second, all core groups are engaged in constant bargaining with the other satellite groups in the particular policy area. Third, the decision centers tend to be autonomous. "Although the leaders may belong to many groups," Sayre and Kaufman point out, "they behave, when particular decisions are at issue, with a remarkable lack of ambivalence. . . . Most participants are galvanized to action by only a relatively narrow range of issues and ignore most others no matter where they occur; as a result, most of the actors in any center share very special interests in the problem at hand, and the casual outsider or the intermittent satellite group has much less effect on the decisions made there than do the strongly motivated 'regulars.' " [22]

New York City politics is thus characterized by many contending groups, each of whose power has a rather narrow scope. This variety of politics has a number of consequences which Professors Sayre and Kaufman review. At least two of these can be stated in power-terms. The large number of decision centers gives each group ample opportunity to concentrate on matters of importance to it. If it is conscious of its own priorities, a group therefore has some ability to determine the scope of its own power. Second, the scope of power is clearly related to both the means and opportunity costs of exercising that power. When the scope of each power group is narrow, the consent (or at least the acquiescence) of many power groups becomes necessary. In this setting, the means are likely to involve protracted efforts and the opportunity costs are usually high.

J. David Singer, as we noted in the Introduction, is one of those political scientists who has been most sensitive to the level-of-analysis problem and to the possibility of applying microlevel concepts to system level inquiries. In "Inter-Nation Influence: A Formal Model," he modifies the concept of power as necessary to apply it in the specific context of international relations. He broadens the definition of influence to include reinforcement (in which A acts to influence B to continue a satisfactory pattern of behavior) as well as modification of behavior. He also broadens the concept of power to include reciprocal influence, noting that inter-nation influence is rarely asymmetrical. Among the several bases of power, Professor Singer concentrates on coercion by threat because it "is, by process of elimination, [the] one influence technique upon which we must continue to rely until we have markedly modified the international system." [23] He calls attention to the subjective nature of the data relating to inter-nation influence attempts. Both influencer and influencee react to their perceptions of the other. The influencer, Professor Singer tells us, must consider his predictions and preferences; the influencee, he says (in different but logically equivalent language), must calculate probabilities and utilities.

Having set up possible combinations of these variables to call our attention to theoretically important influence situations, David Singer then considers the operational problems of getting a real world test of his model. Much work needs to be done before this is possible. "The central problem in . . . these 'real world' types of study is that of developing, pre-testing, and applying measures or indices of an operational and unambiguous nature. Until we have devised a means for recognizing and recording perceived, predicted, preferred, and actual

---

[22] *Governing New York City* (New York: Russell Sage Foundation, 1960), pp. 714–715.

[23] "Inter-Nation Influence: A Former Model," *American Political Science Review*, June, 1963, p. 429.

outcomes, such experimental research is impossible." [24] This being the case, and with appropriate caveats about the application of microlevel findings to macro-level phenomena, Professor Singer suggests a number of inferences about the uses and effects of threats in international politics drawn from microlevel studies.

Thus we come full circle. The line of analysis represented by the Simon, March, and Dahl papers did not begin because of a fascination with microlevel processes, or a wish to avoid system-level statements. It came about purely and simply because of a desire to explicate the nature of a particular concept—power. But these papers stimulated further attempts at conceptualization, and suggested some possible experiments. One result of that further work is when a careful observer wishes to make statements about the exercise of power in a complex political system, it turns out that some of the most reliable data available to him are those which have come from microlevel studies.

[24] Singer, "Inter-Nation Influence . . . ," p. 428.

THE CONCEPT OF POWER

ROBERT A. DAHL

That some people have more power than others is one of the most palpable facts of human existence. Because of this, the concept of power is as ancient and ubiquitous as any that social theory can boast. If these assertions needed any documentation, one could set up an endless parade of great names from Plato and Aristotle through Machiavelli and Hobbes to Pareto and Weber to demonstrate that a large number of seminal social theorists have devoted a good deal of attention to power and the phenomena associated with it. Doubtless it would be easy to show, too, how the word and its synonyms are everywhere embedded in the language of civilized peoples, often in subtly different ways: power, influence, control, pouvoir, puissance, Macht, Herrschaft, Gewalt, imperium, potestas, auctoritas, potentia, etc.

I shall spare the reader the fruits and myself the labor of such a demonstration. Reflecting on the appeal to authority that might be made does, however, arouse two suspicions: First (following the axiom that where there is smoke there is fire), if so many people at so many different times have felt the need to attach the label power, or something like it, to some Thing they

believe they have observed, one is tempted to suppose that the Thing must exist; and not only exist, but exist in a form capable of being studied more or less systematically. The second and more cynical suspicion is that a Thing to which people attach many labels with subtly or grossly different meanings in many different cultures and times is probably not a Thing at all but many Things; there are students of the subject, although I do not recall any who have had the temerity to say so in print, who think that because of this the whole study of "power" is a bottomless swamp.

Paradoxical as it may sound, it is probably too early to know whether these critics are right. For, curiously enough, the systematic study of power is very recent, precisely because it is only lately that serious attempts have been made to formulate the concept rigorously enough for systematic study.[1] If we take as our criterion for

CREDIT: Reprinted, somewhat abridged, by permission of author and publisher from *Behavioral Science*, July, 1957, pp. 201–209, 214.

[1] By demonstrating the importance of concepts such as power and influence, particularly in political analysis, and by insisting upon rigorous conceptual clarity. Harold Lasswell has had a seminal influence. . . . For the approach of the present article I owe a particularly heavy debt to March, with whom I had countless profitable discussions during a year we both spent as fellows at the Center for Advanced Study in the Behavioral Sciences. I have drawn freely not only on our joint work but on his own published and unpublished writings on the subject. The comments of Jacob Marschak on this paper have

the efficiency of a scientific concept its usability in a theoretical system that possesses a high degree of systematic and empirical import, then we simply cannot say whether rigorous definitions of the concept of power are likely to be useful in theoretical systems with a relatively large pay-off in the hard coin of scientific understanding. The evidence is not yet in.

I think it can be shown, however, that to define the concept "power" in a way that seems to catch the central intuitively understood meaning of the work must inevitably result in a formal definition that is not easy to apply in concrete research problems; and therefore, operational equivalents of the formal definition, designed to meet the needs of a particular research problem, are likely to diverge from one another in important ways. Thus we are not likely to produce—certainly not for some considerable time to come—anything like a single, consistent, coherent "Theory of Power." We are much more likely to produce a variety of theories of limited scope, each of which employs some definition of power that is useful in the context of the particular piece of research or theory but different in important respects from the definitions of other studies. Thus we may never get through the swamp. But it looks as

also been most helpful. There are, of course, approaches radically different from the one employed here and in the works mentioned above. John R. P. French, Jr., has developed a model that assumes "a unidimensional continuum of opinion which can be measured with a ratio scale," and he defines "the power of *A* over *B* (with respect to a given opinion) [to be] equal to the maximum force which *A* can induce on *B* minus the maximum resisting force which *B* can mobilize in the opposite direction." Game theory provides still another approach.

if we might someday get around it.

With this in mind, I propose first to essay a formal definition of power that will, I hope, catch something of one's intuitive notions as to what the Thing is. By "formal" I mean that the definition will presuppose the existence of observations of a kind that may not always or even frequently be possible. Second, I should like to indicate how operational definitions have been or might be modelled on the formal one for some specific purposes, and the actual or possible results of these operational definitions.

I should like to be permitted one liberty. There is a long and honorable history attached to such words as power, influence, control, and authority. For a great many purposes, it is highly important that a distinction should be made among them; thus to Max Weber, *"Herrschaft ist . . . ein Sonderfall von Macht,"* Authority is a special case of the first, and Legitimate Authority a subtype of cardinal significance. In this essay I am seeking to explicate the primitive notion that seems to lie behind *all* of these concepts. Some of my readers would doubtless prefer the term "influence," while others may insist that I am talking about control. I should like to be permitted to use these terms interchangeably when it is convenient to do so, without denying or seeming to deny that for many other purposes distinctions are necessary and useful. Unfortunately, in the English language power is an awkward word, for unlike "influence" and "control" it has no convenient verb form, nor can the subject and object of the relation be supplied with noun forms without resort to barbaric neologisms.

POWER AS A RELATION AMONG PEOPLE

What is the intuitive idea we are trying to capture? Suppose I stand on a street corner and say to myself, "I command all automobile drivers on this street to drive on the right side of the road"; suppose further that all the drivers actually do as I "command" them to do; still, most people will regard me as mentally ill if I insist that I have enough power over automobile drivers to compel them to use the right side of the road. On the other hand, suppose a policeman is standing in the middle of an intersection at which most traffic ordinarily moves ahead; he orders all traffic to turn right or left; the traffic moves as he orders it to do. Then it accords with what I conceive to be the bedrock idea of power to say that the policeman acting in this particular role evidently has the power to make automobile drivers turn right or left rather than go ahead. My intuitive idea of power, then, is something like this: *A* has power over *B* to the extent that he can get *B* to do something that *B* would not otherwise do.

If Hume and his intellectual successors had never existed, the distinction between the two events above might be firmer than it is. But anyone who sees in the two cases the need to distinguish mere "association" from "cause" will realize that the attempt to define power could push us into some messy epistemological problems that do not seem to have any generally accepted solutions at the moment. I shall therefore quite deliberately steer clear of the possible identity of "power" with "cause," and the host of problems this identity might give rise to.

Let us proceed in a different way. First, let us agree that power is a relation, and that it is a relation among people. Although in common speech the term encompasses relations among people and other animate or inanimate objects, we shall have our hands full if we confine the relationship to human beings. All of the social theory I mentioned earlier is interesting only when it deals with this limited kind of relationship. Let us call the objects in the relationship of power, actors. Actors may be individuals, groups, roles, offices, governments, nation-states, or other human aggregates.

To specify the actors in a power relation—*A* has power over *B*—is not very interesting, informative, or even accurate. Although the statement that the President has (some) power over Congress is not empty, neither is it very useful. A much more complete statement would include references to (*a*) the source, domain, or *base* of the President's power over Congress; (*b*) the *means* or instruments used by the President to exert power over Congress; (*c*) the *amount* or extent of his power over Congress; and (*d*) the range or *scope* of his power over Congress. The base of an actor's power consists of all the resources—opportunities, acts, objects, etc.—that he can exploit in order to effect the behavior of another. Much of the best writing on power— Bertrand Russell is a good example— consists of an examination of the possible bases of power. A study of the war potential of nations is also a study of the bases of power. Some of the possible bases of a President's power over a

Senator are his patronage, his constitutional veto, the possibility of calling White House conferences, his influence with the national electorate, his charisma, his charm, and the like.

In a sense, the base is inert, passive. It must be exploited in some fashion if the behavior of others is to be altered. The *means* or instruments of such exploitation are numerous; often they involve threats or promises to employ the base in some way and they may involve actual use of the base. In the case of the President, the means would include the *promise* of patronage, the *threat* of veto, the *holding* of a conference, the *threat* of appeal to the electorate, the *exercise* of charm and charisma, etc.

Thus the means is a mediating activity by A between A's base and B's response. The *scope* consists of B's responses. The scope of the President's power might therefore include such Congressional actions as passing or killing a bill, failing to override a veto, holding hearings, etc.

The *amount* of an actor's power can be represented by a probability statement: e.g., "the chances are 9 out of 10 that if the President promises a judgeship to five key Senators, the Senate will not override his veto," etc. Clearly the amount can only be specified in conjunction with the means and scope.

Suppose now we should wish to make a relatively complete and concise statement about the power of individual A over individual a (whom I shall call the respondent) with respect to some given scope of responses. In order to introduce the basic ideas involved, let us restrict ourselves to the 2 by 2 case, where the actor A does or does not perform some act and the respondent a does or does not "respond." Let us employ the following symbols:

$(A, w) = A$ does w. For example, the President makes a nationwide television appeal for tax increases.

$(A, \overline{w}) = A$ does not do w.

$(a, x) = a$, the respondent, does x. For example, the Senate votes to increase taxes.

$(a, \overline{x}) = a$ does not do x.

$P(u|v) = $ Probability that u happens when v happens.

Then a relatively complete and concise statement would be symbolized:

$$P(a, x | A, w) = p_1$$
$$P(a, x | A, \overline{w}) = p_2$$

Suppose now, that $p_1 = 0.4$ and $p_2 = 0.1$. Then one interpretation might be: "The probability that the Senate will vote to increase taxes if the President makes a nationwide television appeal for a tax increase is 0.4. The probability that the Senate will vote to increase taxes if the President does not make such an appeal is 0.1."

PROPERTIES OF THE POWER RELATION

Now let us specify some properties of the power relation.

1. A necessary condition for the power relation is that there exists a time lag, however small, from the actions of the actor who is said to exert power to the responses of the respon-

dent. This requirement merely accords with one's intuitive belief that A can hardly be said to have power over a unless A's power attempts precede a's responses. The condition, obvious as it is, is critically important in the actual study of power relations. Who runs the XYZ Corporation? Whenever the president announces a new policy, he immediately secures the compliance of the top officials. But upon investigation it turns out that every new policy he announces has first been put to him by the head of the sales department. Or again, suppose we had a full record of the times at which each one of the top Soviet leaders revealed his positions on various issues; we could then deduce a great deal about who is running the show and who is not. A good bit of the mystery surrounding the role of White House figures like Sherman Adams and Harry Hopkins would also be clarified by a record of this kind.

2. A second necessary condition is, like the first, obvious and nonetheless important in research: there is no "action at a distance." Unless there is some "connection" between A and a, then no power relation can be said to exist. I shall leave the concept of "connection" undefined, for I wish only to call attention to the practical significance of this second condition. In looking for a flow of influence, control, or power from A to a, one must always find out whether there is a connection, or an opportunity for a connection, and if there is not, then one need proceed no further. The condition, obvious as it is, thus has considerable practical importance for it enables one to screen out many possible relations quite early in an inquiry.

3. In examining the intuitive view of the power relation, I suggested that it seemed to involve a successful attempt by A to get a to do something he would not otherwise do. This hints at a way of stating a third necessary condition for the power relation. Suppose the chances are about one out of a hundred that one of my students, Jones, will read *The Great Transformation* during the holidays even if I do not mention the book to him. Suppose that if I mention the book to him and ask him to read it, the chances that he will do so are still only one out of a hundred. Then it accords with my intuitive notions of power to say that evidently I have no power over Jones with respect to his reading *The Great Transformation* during the holidays —at least not if I restrict the basis of my action to mentioning the book and asking him (politely) to read it. Guessing this to be the case, I tell Jones that if he does not read the book over the holidays I shall fail him in my course. Suppose now that the chances he will read the book are about 99 out of 100. Assume further that nothing else in Jones's environment has changed, at least nothing relevant to his reading or not reading the book. Then it fully accords with my intuitive notions of power to say that I have some power over Jones's holiday reading habits. The basis of my power is the right to fail him in his course with me, and the means I employ is to invoke this threat.

Let me now set down symbolically what I have just said. Let

$(D, w) =$ my threat to fail Jones if he does not read *The Great Transformation* during the holidays.

$(D, \overline{w}) =$ no action on my part.

$(J, x) =$ Jones reads *The Great Transformation* during the holidays.

Further, let

$p_1 = P(J, x | D, w)$ the probability that Jones will read *The Great Transformation* if I threaten to fail him.

$p_2 = P(J, x | D, \overline{w})$ the probability that Jones will read the book if I do not threaten to fail him.

Now, let us define the *amount of power*. To avoid the confusion that might arise from the letter p, let us use the symbol M (from *Macht*) to designate the amount of power. Then, in accordance with the ideas set out in the illustration above, we define A's power over a, with respect to the response x, by means of w, as M, or, more fully:

$$M\left(\frac{A}{a} : w, x\right) = P(a, x | A, w)$$
$$- P(a, x | A, \overline{w}) = p_1 - p_2$$

Thus in the case of myself and Jones, M, my power over Jones, with respect to reading a book during the holidays, is 0.98.

We can now specify some additional properties of the power relation in terms of M:

a. If $p_1 = p_2$, then $M = 0$ and no power relation exists. The absence of power is thus equivalent to statistical independence.

b. M is at a maximum when $p_1 = 1$ and $p_2 = 0$. This is roughly equivalent to saying that A unfailingly gets B to do something B would never do otherwise.

c. M is at a minimum when $p_1 = 0$ and $p_2 = 1$. If negative values of M are to be included in the power relation at all—and some readers might object to the idea—then we shall have a concept of "negative power." This is not as foolish as it may seem, although one must admit that negative control of this kind is not ordinarily conceived of as power. If, whenever I ask my son to stay home on Saturday morning to mow the lawn, my request has the inevitable effect of inducing him to go swimming, when he would otherwise have stayed home, I do have a curious kind of negative power over him. The Legion of Decency sometimes seems to have this kind of power over moviegoers. Stalin was often said to wield negative power over the actions on appropriations for foreign aid by the American Congress. A study of the Senate that will be discussed later suggested that at least one Senator had this kind of effect on the Senate on some kinds of issues.

Note that the concept of negative power, and M as a measure, are both independent of the *intent* of A. The measure does, to be sure, require one to assign a positive and negative *direction* to the responses of the respondent; what one chooses as a criterion of direction will depend upon his research purposes and doubtless these will often include some idea as to the intent of the actors in a power relation. To take a specific case, p_1 *could* mean "the probability that Congress will defeat a bill if it is contained in the President's legislative program," and p_2 could mean "the probability that Congress will defeat such a bill if it is not contained in the President's legislative program." By assigning direction in this way, positive values of M would be associated with what ordinarily would be interpreted as meaning a "negative" influence of the President over Congress. The point of the example is to show that while the measure does require that direction be specified, the intent of A is not the only criterion for assigning direction.

POWER COMPARABILITY

The main problem, however, is not to determine the existence of power but to make comparisons. Doubtless we are all agreed that Stalin was more powerful than Roosevelt in a great many ways, that McCarthy was less powerful after his censure by the Senate than before, etc. But what, precisely, do we mean? Evidently we need to define the concepts "more power than," "less-power than," and "equal power."

Suppose we wish to compare the power of two different individuals. We have at least five factors that might be included in a comparison: (1) differences in the basis of their power, (2) differences in means of employing the basis, (3) differences in the scope of their power, i.e., in type of response evoked, (4) differences in the number of comparable respondents, and (5) differences in the change in probabilities, or M.

The first two of these may be conveniently thought of as differences in properties of the actors exercising power, and the last three may be thought of as differences in the responses of the respondents. Now it is clear that the pay-off lies in the last three—the responses. When we examine the first two in order to compare the power of individuals, rulers, or states, we do so on the supposition that differences in bases and means of actors are very likely to produce differences in the responses of those they seek to control.

As I have already indicated, much of the most important and useful research and analysis on the subject of power concerns the first two items, the properties of the actors exercising power, and there is good reason to suppose that studies of this kind will be as indispensable in the future as they have been in the past. But since we are concerned at the moment with a formal explication of the concept of power, and not with an investigation of research problems, (some of these will be taken up later on) it is important to make clear that analysis of the first two items does not, strictly speaking, provide us with a comparison of the power of two or more actors, except insofar as it permits us to make inferences about the last three items. If we could make these inferences more directly, we should not be particularly interested in the first two items at least not for purposes of making comparisons of power. On the other hand, given information about the responses, we may be interested in comparing the efficiency of different bases or means; in this case, evidently, we can make a comparison only by holding one or both of the first two factors constant, so to speak. In general, the properties of the power wielder that we bring into the problem are determined by the goals of one's specific research. For example, one might be interested in the relative power of different state governors to secure favorable legislative action on their proposals by means of patronage; or alternatively, one might be interested in the relative effectiveness of the threat of veto employed by different governors.

In whatever fashion one chooses to define the relevant properties of the actors whose power he wishes to compare, strictly speaking one must compare them with respect to the responses they are capable of evoking. Ideally, it would be desirable to have a single measure combining differences in scope, number of comparable respondents controlled, and change in probabilities. But there seems to exist no intuitively satisfying method for doing so. With an average probability approaching one, I can induce each of 10 students to come to class for an examination on a Friday afternoon when they would otherwise prefer to make off for New York or Northampton. With its existing resources and techniques, the New Haven Police Department can prevent about half the students who park along the streets near my office from staying beyond the legal time limit. Which of us has the more power? The question is, I believe, incapable of being answered unless we are ready to treat my relationships with my students as in some sense comparable with the relations of the Police Department to another group of students. Otherwise any answer would be arbitrary, because there is no valid way of combining the three variables—scope, number of respondents, and change in probabilities—into a single scale.

Let us suppose, for a moment, that with respect to two of the three variables the responses associated with the actions of two (or more) actors we wish to compare are identical. Then it is reasonable to define the power of A as greater than the power of B if, with respect to the remaining variable, the responses associated with A's acts are greater than the responses associated with B's acts. It will be readily seen, however, that we may have jumped from the frying pan into the fire, for the term "greater than" is still to be defined. Let us take up our variables one by one.

To begin with, we may suppose that the probability of evoking the response being the same for two actors and the numbers of comparable persons in whom they can evoke the response also being the same, then if the scope of responses evoked by A is greater than that evoked by B, A's power is greater than B's. But how can we decide whether one scope is larger than another? Suppose that I could induce my son to bathe every evening and to brush his teeth before going to bed and that my neighbor could induce his son to serve him breakfast in bed every morning. Are the two responses I can control to be counted as greater than the one response my neighbor can control? Evidently what we are willing to regard as a "greater" or "lesser" scope of responses will be dictated by the particular piece of research at hand; it seems fruitless to attempt to devise any single scale. At one extreme we may wish to say that A's scope is greater than B's only if A's scope contains in it every response in B's and at least one more; this would appear to be the narrowest definition. At the other extreme, we may be prepared to treat a broad category of responses as comparable, and A's scope is then said to be greater than B's if the number of comparable responses in his scope is larger than the number in B's. There are other possible definitions. The important point is that the particular definition one chooses will evidently have to merge from considerations of the substance and objectives of a specific piece of research, and not from general theoretical considerations.

Much the same argument applies to the second variable. It is clear, I think, that we cannot compare A's power with respect to the respondents $a_1, a_2 \ldots a_n$ and B's power with respect to the respondents $b_1, b_2 \ldots b_n$ unless we are prepared to regard the two sets of individuals as comparable. This is a disagreeable requirement, but obviously a sensible one. If I can induce 49 undergraduates to support or oppose federal aid to education, you will scarcely regard this as equivalent to the power I would have if I could induce 49 Senators to support or oppose federal aid. Again, whether or not we wish to treat Senators as comparable to students, rich men as comparable to poor men, soldiers as comparable to civilians, enlisted men as comparable to officers, military officers as comparable to civil servants, etc., is a matter that can be determined only in view of the nature and aims of the research at hand.

The third variable is the only one of the three without this inherent limitation. If scope and numbers are identical, then there can be no doubt, I think, that it fully accords with our intuitive and common-sense notions of the meaning of power to say that the actor with the highest probability of securing the response is the more powerful. Take the set of Democratic Senators in the United States Senate. Suppose that the chance that at least two-thirds of them will support the President's proposals on federal aid to education is 0.6. It is fair to say that no matter what I may do in behalf of federal aid to education, if there are no other changes in the situation except those brought about by my efforts the probability that two-thirds of them will support federal aid will remain virtually at 0.6. If, on the other hand, Senator Johnson, as majority leader, lends his full support and all his skill of maneuver to the measure the probability may rise, let us say, to 0.8. We may then conclude (what we already virtually know is the case, of course) that Senator Johnson has more power over Democratic Senators with respect to federal aid to education than I have.

Earlier in defining the amount cf power by the measure, M, I had already anticipated this conclusion. What I have just said is precisely equivalent to saying that the power of A with respect to some set of respondents and responses is greater than the power of B with respect to an equivalent set if and only if the measure M associated with A is greater than the measure M associated with B. To recapitulate:

$$M\left(\frac{A}{a}:w, x\right) = p_1 - p_2, \text{ where}$$

$$p_1 = P(a, x \mid A, w)$$

the probability that a will do x, given action w by A

$$p_2 = P(a, x | A, \overline{w})$$

the probability that a will do x, given no action w by A.

$$M\left(\frac{B}{b} : y, z\right) = p_1{}^* - p_2{}^*, \text{ where}$$

$$p_1{}^* = P(b, z / B, y)$$
$$p_2{}^* = P(b, z / B, \overline{y}).$$

Now if these two situations are *power comparable* (a notion we shall examine in a moment) then A's power is greater than B's if and only if

$$M\left(\frac{A}{a} : w, x\right) > M\left(\frac{B}{b} : y, z\right).$$

In principle, then, whenever there are two actors, A and B, provided only that they are power comparable, they can be ranked according to the amount of power they possess, or M. But if it is possible to rank A and B, it is possible to rank any number of pairs. And it is obvious from the nature of M that this ranking must be transitive, i.e.,

$$\text{if } \ M\left(\frac{A}{a} : w, x\right) > M\left(\frac{B}{b} : y, z\right), \text{and}$$

$$M\left(\frac{B}{b} : y, z\right) > M\left(\frac{C}{c} : u, v\right), \text{ then}$$

$$M\left(\frac{A}{a} : w, x\right) > M\left(\frac{C}{c} : u, v\right)$$

In principle, then, where any number of actors are in some relation to any number of equivalent subjects, and these relations are regarded as power comparable, then all the actors can be unambiguously ranked according to their power with respect to these subjects.

There is, as everyone knows, many a slip 'twixt principle and practice. How can one convert the theoretical measure, M, into a measure usable in practical research? Specifically, suppose one wishes to examine the power relations among some group of people —a city council, legislature, community, faculty, trade union. One wants to rank the individuals in the group according to their power. How can one do so?

The first problem to be faced is whether given the aims, substance, and possible theoretical import of his study, one does in fact have *power comparability*. One of the most important existing studies of the power structure of a community has been criticized because of what appears to be a failure to observe this requirement. A number of leaders in a large Southern city were asked, "If a project were before the community that required *decision* by a group of leaders—leaders that nearly everyone would accept—which *ten* on the list of forty would you choose?" On the basis of the answers, individuals were ranked in such a way that a "pyramidal" power structure was inferred to exist in the city, i.e., one consisting of a small number of top leaders who made the key decisions, which were then executed by a larger middle-group of subordinate leaders. The significance of this conclusion is considerably weakened, however, if we consider whether the question did in fact discriminate among different kinds of responses. Specifically, suppose the leaders had been asked to distinguish between decisions over local taxes, decisions on schools, and efforts to bring a new industry to the community: would there be significant differences in the rankings according to these three different kinds of issues? Because the study does not provide an answer to this question, we do not know how to interpret the significance of the "pyramidal" power structure that assertedly exists. Are we to conclude that in "Regional City" there is a small determinate group of leaders whose power significantly exceeds that of all other members of the community on all or nearly all key issues that arise? Or are we to conclude, at the other extreme, that some leaders are relatively powerful on some issues and not on others, and that no leaders are relatively powerful on all issues? We have no way of choosing between these two interpretations or indeed among many others that might be formulated.

Let us define A and B as formally power comparable (in the sense that the relative magnitudes of the measure M are held to order the power of A and B correctly) if and only if the actors, the means, the respondents and the responses or scopes are comparable. That is,

must be taken as an undefined term. That is, power comparability will have to be interpreted in the light of the specific requirements of research and theory, in the same way that the decision as to whether to regard any two objects—animals, plants, atoms, or whatnot—as comparable depends upon general considerations of classification and theoretical import. To this extent, and to this extent only, the decision is "arbitrary"; but it is not more "arbitrary" than other decisions that establish the criteria for a class of objects.

To political scientists it might seem farfetched to compare the power of a British prime minister over tax legislation in the House of Commons with the power of the President of the United States over foreign policy decisions in the Senate. It would seem farfetched because the theoretical advantages of such a comparison are not at all clear. On the other hand, it would not seem quite so farfetched to compare the two institutional positions with respect to the "same" kind of policy—say tax legislation or foreign policy; indeed, political scientists do

the actor	A	is comparable	to the actor	$B;$
A's respondent,	$a,$	" "	" B's respondent,	$b;$
A's means,	w "	"	" B's means,	$y;$ and
a's response,	x "	"	" b's response,	$z.$

But this is not a very helpful definition. For the important question is whether we can specify some properties that will insure comparability among actors, respondents, means, and scopes. The answer, alas, is no. So far as an explication of the term "power" is concerned, power comparability

make comparisons of this kind. Yet the decision to regard tax legislation in the House of Commons as comparable in some sense to tax legislation in the Senate is "arbitrary." Even the decision to treat as comparable two revenue measures passed at different times in the United States Senate is "arbitrary." What saves a comparison from being genuinely arbitrary is, in the end, its scientific utility. Some kinds of comparisons will seem more artificial than others; some will be theoretically more interesting and more productive than others. But these are criteria derived from theoretical and empirical considerations independent of the fundamental meaning of the term power.

On what grounds, then, can one criticize the study mentioned a moment ago? Because the use of undiscriminating questions produced results of very limited theoretical significance. By choosing a relatively weak criterion of power comparability, the author inevitably robbed his inquiry of much of its potential richness. Considerations of comparability are, therefore, critical. But the criteria employed depend upon the problem at hand and the general state of relevant theory. The only way to avoid an arbitrary and useless definition of "power comparability" is to consider carefully the goals and substance of a particular piece of research in view of the theoretical constructs one has in mind. Thus in the case of the Senate, it may be satisfactory for one piece of research to define all Senate roll-call votes on all issues as comparable; for another, only votes on foreign policy issues will be comparable; and for still another, only votes on foreign policy issues involving large appropriations; etc. In a word, the researcher himself must define what he means by comparability and he must do so in view of the purpose of the ranking he is seeking to arrive at, the information available, and the relevant theoretical constructs governing the research. . . .

CONCLUSIONS: A DIALOGUE BETWEEN A "CONCEPTUAL" THEORETICIAN AND AN "OPERATIONALIST"

The conclusions can perhaps best be stated in the form of a dialogue between a "conceptual" theoretician and a strict "operationalist." I shall call them C and O.

C. The power of an actor, A, would seem to be adequately defined by the measure M which is the difference in the probability of an event, given certain action by A, and the probability of the event given no such action by A. Because the power of any actor may be estimated in this way, at least in principle, then different actors can be ranked according to power, provided only that there exists a set of comparable subjects for the actors who are to be ranked.

O. What you say may be true in principle, but that phrase "in principle" covers up a host of practical difficulties. In fact, of course, the necessary data may not exist.

C. That is, of course, quite possible. When I say "in principle" I mean only that no data are demanded by the definition that we cannot imagine securing with combinations of known techniques of observation and measurement. The observations may be exceedingly difficult but they are not inherently impossible: they don't defy the laws of nature as we understand them.

O. True. But the probability that we can actually make these observations on, say, the U.S. Senate is so low as to be negligible, at least if we want relatively large numbers of decisions. It seems to me that from a strict operational point of view, your concept of power is not a single concept, as you have implied; operationally, power would appear to be many different concepts, depending on the kinds of data available. The way in which the researcher must adapt to the almost inevitable limitations of his data means that we shall have to make do with a great many different and not strictly comparable concepts of power.

C. I agree with all you have said. In practice, the concept of power will have to be defined by operational criteria that will undoubtedly modify its pure meaning.

O. In that case, it seems wiser to dispense with the concept entirely. Why pretend that power, in the social sense, is a concept that is conceptually clear-cut and capable of relatively un-ambiguous operational definitions— like mass, say, in physics? Indeed, why not abandon the concept of power altogether, and admit that all we have or can have is a great variety of operational concepts, no one of which is strictly comparable with another? Perhaps we should label them: Power 1, Power 2, etc.; or better, let's abandon single, simple, misleading words like "power" and "influence", except when these are clearly understood to be a part of a special operational definition explicitly defined in the particular piece of research.

C. I'm afraid that I must disagree with your conclusion. You have not shown that the concept of power as defined by the measure *M* is inherently defective or that it is never capable of being used. It is true, of course, that we cannot always make the observations we need in order to measure power; perhaps we can do so only infrequently. But the concept provides us with a standard against which to compare the operational alternatives we actually employ. In this way it helps us to specify the defects of the operational definitions as measures of power. To be sure, we may have to use defective measures; but at least we shall know that they are defective and in what ways. More than that, to explicate the concept of power and to pin-point the deficiencies of the operational concepts actually employed may often help us to invent alternative concepts and research methods that produce a much closer approximation in practice to the theoretical concept itself.

WHY MEN OBEY
HERBERT A. SIMON, DONALD W. SMITHBURG, AND VICTOR A. THOMPSON

Late in the evening we stand at the roadside by an intersection with a stop sign and watch the few straggling cars as they come up to the sign at long intervals. Each carefully pulls to a halt, although it is obvious to the driver that there is not another car (nor a policeman) within many miles. Why do they stop? A clerk processes a great many applications as he has been told to process them and does so without questioning either the techniques used—although they may appear silly to him—or the end sought. Why does he obey?

In another situation, an employee is given clear and specific instructions to do something, and yet he "forgets" to do it or even refuses to do it. Why the variance? Why is it easy to get some persons to obey almost any order, while others will belligerently refuse to obey even the simplest sort of command? Why is the order given by someone who is recognized as a "boss" accepted, but the same order resented and sabotaged if it is given by another person? This is the sort of question we

CREDIT: From *Public Administration* by Herbert A. Simon, Donald W. Smithburg and Victor A. Thompson. Copyright © 1950 by Herbert A. Simon, Donald W. Smithburg and Victor A. Thompson. Reprinted by permission of Alfred A. Knopf, Inc. [*Footnotes renumbered.*]

must answer in the following pages. . . .

Because the person who accepts proposals may do so for a variety of motives, there will be seen in any organization a number of different types of authority relationship, corresponding to these different motives for acceptance. In the following sections these various kinds of authority will be described as: authority of confidence, authority of identification, authority of sanctions, and authority of legitimacy.

THE AUTHORITY OF CONFIDENCE

People accept the proposals of persons in whom they have great confidence. In any organization there are some individuals who, because of past performance, general reputation, or other factors, have great influence or authority. Their proposals will often be accepted without analysis as to their wisdom. Even when the suggestions of such a person are not accepted, they will be rejected reluctantly and only because a stronger authority contradicts them.

The authority of confidence may be limited to a special area of competence in which a person has acquired a reputation. Thus an executive may sign a requisition for office equipment prepared by his secretary without analyzing it or even reading it because he has confidence in his secretary's ability to make a good decision in that field. In such a case, the secretary is exercising authority over her employer. In any complex organization, an upper level executive, by the very nature of his position, must either accept suggestions from below on the basis of confidence, accept them blindly on no basis whatsoever, or refuse to accept them on the basis of his own prejudices and feeling. The idea that the President of the United States or the mayor of a great city can evaluate intelligently the combined suggestions of a whole complex organization is ridiculous.

In many situations, confidence in the decisions of persons who are not even members of the organization gives authority to these decisions. To take a recent and world-shaking example, the late President Roosevelt is supposed to have based his decision to spend two billion dollars for development of the atomic bomb on the recommendation of Albert Einstein. The President had no basis for independently checking that recommendation. True, he could have, and probably did, get the opinion of other physicists. But if so he was still making the decision upon the basis of his confidence in the physicists he consulted. He could not even have understood their arguments for this course of action without himself undergoing the rigorous training of mathematical physics.

We have already noted that authority based upon confidence is a fa-miliar phenomenon of everyday life, quite apart from organizations. In society in general, it is probably the principal type of authority that operates. In general, people have confidence that physicians can cure their ills; that carpenters can build their houses; that mechanics can fix their cars; that lawyers can give them sound legal advice. These specialists are usually obeyed within their supposed fields of competence. People who seek and accept their advice do so almost entirely on the basis of confidence in the ability and intention of the specialists to suggest the correct behavior.[1]

Functional status

The willingness to accept authority on the basis of confidence, both within and outside organizations, goes even one step further. Not only is the layman generally unable to judge the quality of the advice he is getting from the specialist, but he often is in no position to judge the competence of the specialist, except on the basis of certain superficial and formal criteria that give the specialist his *status*.

As we shall see in the course of this chapter, there are at least two kinds of status, which may be called *functional status* and *hierarchical status*. It is with functional status that we are concerned at the moment. A person has functional status in a particular area of knowledge when his decisions and recommendations in that

[1] For further development of this point see Talcott Parsons, "The Professions and Social Structure," in his *Essays in Sociological Theory Pure and Applied* (Glencoe, Illinois: The Free Press, 1949), especially p. 189.

area are accepted as more or less authoritative.

In the established professions, status is generally conferred on the basis of standards developed by the profession itself. The M.D. degree is conferred on the young doctor by the medical profession (acting through an "accredited" medical school). Law and engineering degrees and the certificate of the public accountant are awarded in much the same way. In other cases, job experience in a particular field confers functional status in that field. A person with long experience in a professional position in the Interstate Commerce Commission may acquire status as a transportation economist.

The reader can undoubtedly supply other examples of the acquisition of functional status. It is noteworthy that in most cases the specialists themselves, as a more or less organized professional group, play an important role in determining who has status in their field of specialization. Since there are formal "legitimate" ways of acquiring status, the authority derived therefrom is a composite of authority of confidence and authority of legitimacy.

Relation of the authority of confidence to hierarchy

It should not be supposed that the authority of confidence always operates *across* hierarchical lines. Confidence can be a powerful support for hierarchical as well as for nonhierarchical authority. A subordinate will much more readily obey a command of a superior if he has confidence in the intelligence and judgment of that superior or if he believes that the superior has knowledge of the situation not available to himself.

In particular, where a problem requiring decision affects the work of several units in an organization, the superior who has hierarchical authority in the formal organization plan over all the units involved is often accepted as the person best located— because he has the "whole picture"— to make the decision. Hence, the coordinating functions that are commonly performed by those in hierarchical authority are based, in part at least, upon the authority of confidence —upon the belief of subordinates that the superior is the best informed about the situation as a whole.[2]

Persons at the higher levels of the administrative hierarchy often devote more time than do their subordinates to the organization's external relations—to its relations with other organizations, with the legislative body, with pressure groups, and the like. In the case of decisions having "political" or "public relations" implications, the authority of the hierarchical superior may be accepted by his subordinates because of their confidence that he is more expert or better informed than they regarding the political "angles" of the decision.

One of the techniques of superiors in building morale is that of instilling

---

[2] Of course, in many instances the subordinates prefer to negotiate directly with each other— pooling the specialized knowledge of the various units involved. In such cases, the hierarchical superior may or may not participate in the decision; or he may be asked merely to ratify a decision his subordinates have agreed upon among themselves. In this case, the authority may be exercised by the subordinates as a group over their superior, who places confidence in the decision they have worked out together.

confidence so that employees will go along with orders willingly, rather than simply because they feel they ought to or because they are afraid not to. The annals of military history are full of the exploits of troops who pushed forward into extremely difficult situations because they had confidence in the ability and wisdom of their commanding officer. General Patton is an example of an officer who instilled a high degree of confidence and whose authority was accepted with enthusiasm, even though he inspired little affection and made unusually frequent use of formal sanctions.

Charismatic leadership

There are numerous examples in history of leaders—sometimes, but not always, in the formal hierarchy—who inspire such a high level of confidence in their followers that they "can do no wrong." In such cases, the leader usually also becomes a symbol of group identification, and the authority of confidence is reinforced by the authority of identification. In fact, the process is circular, because a group that identifies with a leader becomes less critical of his judgment and more and more confident in the wisdom of his leadership.

Such individuals have been labelled by the German sociologist Max Weber, "charismatic leaders," and the authority they exercise over their followers "charisma." Unfortunately, the discussion of charismatic leadership by Weber and others has had vague mystical overtones, and a satisfactory social-psychological theory of charisma has nowhere been fully developed. As suggested above, charisma is perhaps best understood as some combination of the authority of confidence with the authority of identification.[3]

THE AUTHORITY OF IDENTIFICATION

The role of group loyalties in influencing behavior [need not be discussed at this point]. . . . Here we will show the relation between identification and the acceptance of authority.

This relation is twofold. In the first place . . . most individuals have a very wide area of acceptance for decisions agreed upon by a group with which they are strongly identified. It is often more realistic to speak of acceptance of authority *by an identification group* than acceptance *by an individual*. Since the existence of such a group creates new values for its members—in particular, the survival of the group itself—in addition to the values to which they are attached as individuals, the area of acceptance of group members is quite different from the area of acceptance of unattached individuals.

In the second place, proposals advanced by members of the group will often be more acceptable than the

[3] H. H. Gerth and C. Wright Mills, *From Max Weber: Essays in Sociology* (New York: Oxford University Press, 1946), pp. 245–52. The "founder" of a movement or an organization is often a charismatic leader—for example, George Washington, Gifford Pinchot (the U. S. Forest Service). The feeling of a group that it is surrounded by external dangers undoubtedly encourages group identification and confidence in leaders (as a means of reducing fear). Hence charismatic leadership is characteristic of crisis situations—as evidence, F. D. Roosevelt, John L. Lewis, Abraham Lincoln, and so forth.

same proposals when advanced by "outsiders." This fact is a basic one in pressure techniques. To get an "insider" to sponsor your proposal is to enhance considerably the chance that it will be accepted. Professional people are often far more susceptible to suggestions from their own profession than those from other people, even though the suggestions concern matters entirely outside their professional competence. A fraternity brother is likely to accept the suggestion of a fellow fraternity brother; an attorney may be disposed to look favorably on recommendations of other attorneys; a Foreign Service Officer to respect the judgment of other Foreign Service Officers. In addition, common identification makes access to the persons making a decision easier. A person going to Washington may well find it difficult to locate a person who can make or influence a decision. Access is much easier if he can find a friend who "knows the ropes."

For this reason, a person who belongs to two identification groups often becomes an important channel of communications and influence between these groups. The importance of this dual identification has already been shown . . . with regard to the dual identification of executives with the work group of their subordinates on the one hand and with their co-equals and their common superior, on the other.

THE AUTHORITY OF SANCTIONS

The most generally recognized weapon of the superior is the sanction —the ability of the superior to attach pleasant or unpleasant consequences to the actions of the subordinate. What is not so often recognized is that this aspect of authority, like those mentioned above, is not a sole prerogative of the hierarchical superior. It is possessed by subordinates and by persons outside the organization as well.[4]

Non-hierarchical sanctions

One of the most obvious sanctions possessed by hierarchical inferiors is the strike. Most often the technique of the strike is forbidden or not utilized by government employees, but mass sanctions along the same lines exist nonetheless. Widespread resentment against an order from above can lead to organized or even unorganized slowdowns. It can lead to widespread "misinterpretation" of orders and the like. [For instance,] the techniques of obstruction available to a disgruntled work group against fellow employers and superiors alike [are many]. . . . The point we want to make here is that workers do have sanctions against superiors as well as vice versa.

Similarly, groups outside the work unit or even agency very often have the powers of sanction. For example, a personnel office may refuse to

---

[4] The term "sanctions" is used broadly here to include both rewards (positive sanctions) and punishments (negative sanctions). The distinction between reward and punishment is a difficult one to make. The failure to receive an anticipated reward is an undesirable experience. For example, is promotion a reward or a punishment? Failure to promote is a typical sanction and is an undesirable experience. If a person expects or hopes for a reward, the power to withhold the reward is the power to apply negative sanctions. Whether a person is motivated by desire for the reward or desire to avoid the negative sanction (i.e., to not receive the reward) is partly a verbal conundrum.

"clear" a desired promotion. To get the promotion may necessitate an appeal to the over-burdened agency head, or even negotiations with some outside agency like the Civil Service Commission. Accomplishing the task might require getting superiors lined up in support; argument, perhaps heated, before the common superior; a decision which is really a division; ruffled feelings and perhaps strained working relations in the future; a test of strength or influence with a common superior which, if lost, may involve a change in the organization power situation; frustration for the losers and their superiors; and so forth. Hence, to the extent that an appeal from the personnel office's ruling is burdensome and unpleasant that office possesses a powerful sanction.

In one sense, any suggestion carries a sanction. People generally dislike to say "no," to turn someone down, their reactions varying all the way from a pathological inability to say "no" to an almost inhuman disregard of other people's feelings. Thus to say "no" to a proposal involves at least the unpleasantness of disappointing someone. Capitalizing on this sentiment, anyone can acquire more authority by learning to make his proposals in such a way as to secure the maximum benefit from this "sanction."

Sanctions and hierarchy

The relationship of the authority of sanctions with the organizational hierarchy can be viewed from a more general standpoint. When a person joins an organization he is accepting a system of relationships that restricts his individuality or his freedom of ac-

tion. He is willing to do so because he feels that, in spite of the organizational restraints, being a member of the organization is preferable to other alternatives available to him.[5] To continue as a member of the organization, he must continue, to some extent, to abide by the complex of procedures which constitutes the organization. Although, increasingly, the power to discharge an employee is not lodged in any specific superior (because of merit systems, central personnel offices, labor unions, etc.), nevertheless, this power resides somewhere in the organization, being, in fact, one of its working procedures. The sanctions discussed in this section are increasingly *organization* sanctions, brought into play through the working procedures of the organization, and not the special prerogatives or powers of *individual superiors*. However, at this stage of our development, individual superiors usually have a greater influence on the process than recalcitrant inferiors, and thus hierarchical authority is somewhat strengthened by organizational sanctions.

The rule of anticipated reactions

In essence, a sanction is a whip on the wall—its mere existence tends to induce compliance, although its actual use may be infrequent. For the most part the authority of sanction rests on the behavior responses that are induced by *the possibility* that a sanction may be applied. An organization member is seldom presented with an

[5] On this point, see Herbert A. Simon, *Administrative Behavior* (New York: Macmillan, 1947), chapter 6; and Chester I. Barnard, *The Functions of the Executive* (Cambridge, Harvard University Press, 1938), chapter 11.

ultimatum "to do so and so or suffer the consequences." Rather, he anticipates the consequences of continual insubordination or failure to please the person or persons who have the ability to apply sanctions to him, and this anticipation acts as a constant motivation without expressed threats from any person. If actual punishment is necessary, the sanction has failed—anticipation of possible punishment has not prevented the undesired behavior.

Reaction to sanctions

As a device of authority, negative sanctions (punishments) are of limited usefulness. People, even government servants, resent being "pushed around," and a threat to impose a sanction often imperils a proposal rather than the contrary. A proposal backed by the overt threat of punishment often has many consequences other than the desired one of acceptance. It can be destructive of organization because it is divisive—it divides the organization into hostile camps. It also tends to lower morale, which means that it lessens the unsolicited contributions of organization members.

Such positive rewards as raises in pay, or promotion are likely to be of only moderate effectiveness except for the highly mobile employee . . . for whom these types of rewards correspond to strong internalized values. In many situations, positive inducements based upon the internalized values of the employee—acceptance of the organization goals as his own, desire for approval of the work group, a desire to participate in the planning process—can secure an enthusiasm in the con-

tributors that will make the need for negative sanctions fade into the background.

Other limits on sanctions

The power of sanction is restricted even beyond the desire of those who possess sanctions to limit its use. Most executives in government operate within the framework of a civil service system that severely limits the traditional executive sanction—namely, the right to hire and fire. In one of the nation's largest cities, for example, the Police Commissioner has the right to fire police captains only after a trial before the Civil Service Commission and then an appeal to the courts. For all practical purposes, and except in the most extreme situations, he does not really possess this sanction. The same general limitation exists at the national and at many state levels.

But the right to hire and fire may be restricted in many other ways. In a period of a tight labor market, the use of this sanction is quite limited because of the inability of the employer to get workers to take the place of those whom he discharges. Nor does this apply only to discharges. The power of reprimand is also more limited, since the worker can more freely exercise his right to resign.

Very often, organizational peculiarities may prevent the use of particular sanctions. A person may be obligated to carry out a set of tasks but be forced to depend for the execution of those tasks on persons in other units to whom he can apply no effective sanctions. In such a case, dependence must be on other sources of authority than sanction. As organizations grow more complex this problem becomes greater, and probably reaches its peak in the Federal government.

In public administration, sanctions may be limited by the political connections of the employee. This kind of limitation is probably less important in jurisdictions having civil service systems than in others, but it is a factor at all levels of government. Many supervisors will put up with behavior from a cousin of a powerful Congressman which they would not tolerate in other circumstances.

Because the notion of authority is in the minds of most people so closely tied in with the idea of negative sanctions—the fearsome things the boss can do—it is important to emphasize: (1) sanctions do not operate strictly on hierarchical lines: subordinates and "coordinates" have sanctions as well as do superiors; (2) agencies can, and often do, accomplish their tasks when the superiors do not possess all the usual formal sanctions; (3) sanctions are very often not the most effective means of enforcing authority.

THE AUTHORITY OF LEGITIMACY

There is another reason why employees accept the proposals of other organization members—a reason less rationalistic but probably more important than the desire to avoid the organization sanctions discussed above. People accept "legitimate" authority because they feel that they *ought* to go along with the "rules of the game."

Legitimacy

. . . [T]hroughout their development to maturity and after, people are educated in the beliefs, values, or mores of society. They learn what they ought to do and what they ought not to do. One of the values with which they are indoctrinated is that a person should play according to the rules of the game. This ethic is acquired very early. When a child enters a ball game in the sand lot he does not expect the game to be altered at various points to suit his convenience. Rather he expects to adjust his behavior to the rules of the game. Although there may be disputes as to what the rule is on some point, once this is established, the proposition that he should abide by the rule is unquestioned.

Likewise, when people enter organizations most of them feel that they ought to abide by the rules of the game—the working procedures of the organization. These working procedures define how the work will be done; how working problems will be solved when they arise; how conflicts will be settled. They prescribe that on such and such matters the individual will accept the suggestions of this or that person or organization; secure the advice of such and such unit; clear his work with so and so; work on matters that come to him in such and such a way; etc.

The working procedures of an organization prescribe that the individual member will accept the proposals of other members in matters assigned to them. This acceptance is one of the rules of the game which he feels he should abide by. Thus, individuals in organizations also accept the authority of other persons because they think they *ought* to accept it.

Let us consider, a concrete though hypothetical example. After graduation from college a student decides to embark on a career as a personnel officer in the Federal civil service. As a condition of entry to the service he takes a civil service examination. He passes the examination and is admitted to the service and given a position as Junior Classification Officer in the central personnel office of the United States Department of Agriculture. Upon entering he is assigned a desk, and the procedures and methods of classification followed in that office are explained to him. He is given a manual of instructions which tells him how he is to behave in certain circumstances. His relationships with other persons in the organization are explained to him—who is his "boss," the section of the agency that falls under his purview for classification, and so forth. He would be expected, and he would expect, to govern his behavior along the general lines of the instructions given him. He wouldn't normally decide that the classification methods used were unsatisfactory; or that he should report to someone who was not his boss. He would follow the rules of the game; the established procedures of the organization to which he is attached.

Legitimacy and hierarchy

The working relationships in an organization designated by the term "hierarchy" constitute a particular organization procedure for handling the authority of legitimacy. Acceptance of the working procedures of an organization by a member includes acceptance of the obligation to go along with the proposals of an hierarchical superior, at least within a limit of toleration—the "area of acceptance."

Thus, whether the other reasons for obedience are operating or not (confidence, identification, or sanctions), organization members will feel that they ought to obey their superiors. Legitimacy is one of the most important sources of the authority of the hierarchical superior.

The feeling that hierarchical authority is legitimate is immensely strengthened by previous social conditioning. Hierarchical behavior is an institutionalized behavior that all organization members bring to the organization with them. Like the players in the Oberammergau Passion Play who begin to learn their roles in early childhood, "inferiors" obey "superiors" because they have been taught to do so from infancy, beginning with the parent-child relationship and running through almost constant experience with social and organizational hierarchies until death brings graduation from this particular social schooling. Hierarchical behavior involves an inferior-superior role-taking of persons well versed in their roles. "Inferiors" feel that they ought to obey "superiors"; "superiors" feel that they ought to be obeyed.

Our society is extremely hierarchical. Success is generally interpreted in terms of hierarchical preferment. Social position and financial rewards are closely related to hierarchical preferment, as also are education and even perhaps romantic attainment. Advancement up a hierarchy is generally considered a sign of moral worth, of good character, of good stewardship, of social responsibility, and of the possession of superior intellectual qualities.

Hierarchy receives a tremendous

emphasis in nearly all organizations. This is so because hierarchy is a procedure that requires no training, no indoctrination, no special inducements. It rests almost entirely on "pre-entry" training—a training so thorough that few other organization procedures can ever compete with it. Furthermore, hierarchy is a great simplification. It is much simpler to say to a new organization member, "X is your boss," than to say, "in this situation, do this; in that situation, do that."

LIMITS ON HIERARCHY AS SOURCE OF LEGITIMATE AUTHORITY

Although our society does a good "pre-entry" job of training for the procedure of hierarchy, it probably does not do so good a job as other societies or other times. Since the behaviors involved in the phenomenon of hierarchy are behaviors that reflect prevailing social mores, as those mores change so do the behaviors. Western man of the nineteenth century probably received a far better training for this organizational procedure than does modern Western man. It is clear that the days when an executive could do almost anything he wanted to do with his organization are past. As the individual, through education and a wide variety of extra-organizational experiences, acquires an increasing sense of personal dignity, he probably becomes less and less amenable to the particular type of authority associated with the hierarchical procedure.

Furthermore, it seems probable that certain aspects of our modern civilization are changing people's expectations with regard to organizational behavior and treatment generally. Especially is the hierarchical procedure weakened as the social division of labor turns more and more people into indispensable and recondite specialists. With the growing importance of the professional and technical specialist, there is a corresponding tendency for the working rules of organization—the rules that define the authority of legitimacy—to place more and more emphasis upon functional status, and less and less upon hierarchy. Employees are becoming more and more accustomed to accepting the proposals of functional specialists—and to feeling that they ought to accept these proposals. As a consequence the authority of legitimacy is much less an exclusive possession of the formal hierarchy than it was even a generation ago.

A PRESIDENT'S POWER TO PERSUADE
RICHARD E. NEUSTADT

The limits on command suggest the structure of our government. The constitutional convention of 1787 is supposed to have created a government of "separated powers." It did nothing of the sort. Rather, it created a government of separated institutions *sharing* powers.[1] "I am part of the legislative process," Eisenhower often said in 1959 as a reminder of his veto.[2] Congress, the dispenser of authority and funds, is no less part of the administrative process. Federalism adds another set of separated institutions. The Bill of Rights adds others. Many public purposes can only be achieved by voluntary acts of private institutions; the press, for one, in Douglass Cater's phrase, is a "fourth branch of government."[3] And with the coming of alliances abroad, the separate institutions of a London, or a Bonn, share in the making of American public policy.

What the Constitution separates our political parties do not combine. The parties are themselves composed of separated organizations sharing public authority. The authority consists of nominating powers. Our national parties are confederations of state and local party institutions, with a headquarters that represents the White House, more or less, if the party has a President in office. These confederacies manage presidential nominations. All other public offices depend upon electorates confined within the states.[4] All other nominations are controlled within the states. The President and congressmen who bear one party's label are divided by dependence upon different sets of voters. The differences are sharpest at the stage of nomination. The White House has too small a share in nominating congressmen, and Congress l:as too little weight in nominating Presidents for party to erase their constitutional separation. Party links are stronger than is frequently supposed,

CREDIT: Reprinted by permission of author and publisher from *Presidential Power* by Richard E. Neustadt, pp. 33–57. Copyright © 1960 by John Wiley & Sons, Inc.

[1] The reader will want to keep in mind the distinction between two senses in which the word *power* is employed. When I have used the word (or its plural) to refer to formal constitutional, statutory, or customary authority, it is either qualified by the adjective "formal" or placed in quotation marks as "power(s)." Where I have used it in the sense of effective influence upon the conduct of others, it appears without quotation marks (and always in the singular). Where clarity and convenience permit, *authority* is substituted for "power" in the first sense and *influence* for power in the second sense.

[2] See, for example, his press conference of July 22, 1959, as reported in the *New York Times* for July 23, 1959.

[3] See Douglass Cater, *The Fourth Branch of Government* (Boston: Houghton-Mifflin, 1959).

[4] With the exception of the Vice-Presidency, of course.

but nominating processes assure the separation.[5]

The separateness of institutions and the sharing of authority prescribe the terms on which a President persuades. When one man shares authority with another, but does not gain or lose his job upon the other's whim, his willingness to act upon the urging of the other turns on whether he conceives the action right for him. The essence of a President's persuasive task is to convince such men that what the White House wants of them is what they ought to do for their sake and on their authority.

Persuasive power, thus defined, amounts to more than charm or reasoned argument. These have their uses for a President, but these are not the whole of his resources. For the men he would induce to do what he wants done on their own responsibility will need or fear some acts by him on his responsibility. If they share his authority, he has some share in theirs. Presidential "powers" may be inconclusive when a President commands; but always remain relevant as he persuades. The status and authority inherent in his office reinforce his logic and his charm.

Status adds something to persuasiveness; authority adds still more. When Truman urged wage changes on his Secretary of Commerce while the latter was administering the steel mills, he and Secretary Sawyer were not just two men reasoning with one another. Had they been so, Sawyer probably would never have agreed to

[5] See David B. Truman's illuminating study of party relationships in the 81st Congress, *The Congressional Party* (New York: Wiley, 1959), especially chaps. 4, 6, and 8.

act. Truman's status gave him special claims to Sawyer's loyalty, or at least attention. In Walter Bagehot's charming phrase "no man can *argue* on his knees." Although there is no kneeling in this country, few men—and exceedingly few Cabinet officers—are immune to the impulse to say "yes" to the President of the United States. It grows harder to say "no" when they are seated in his oval office at the White House, or in his study on the second floor, where almost tangibly he partakes of the aura of his physical surroundings. In Sawyer's case, moreover, the President possessed formal authority to intervene in many matters of concern to the Secretary of Commerce. These matters ranged from jurisdictional disputes among the defense agencies to legislation pending before Congress and, ultimately, to the tenure of the Secretary, himself. There is nothing in the record to suggest that Truman voiced specific threats when they negotiated over wage increases. But given his *formal* powers and their relevance to Sawyer's other interests, it is safe to assume that Truman's very advocacy of wage action conveyed an implicit threat.

A President's authority and status give him great advantages in dealing with the men he would persuade. Each "power" is a vantage point for him in the degree that other men have use for his authority. From the veto to appointments, from publicity to budgeting, and so down a long list, the White House now controls the most encompassing array of vantage points in the American political system. With hardly an exception, the men who share in governing this country are aware that at some time, in some degree, the doing of *their* jobs, the furthering of *their* ambitions, may depend upon the President of the United States. Their need for presidential action, or their fear of it, is bound to be recurrent if not actually continuous. Their need or fear is his advantage.

A President's advantages are greater than mere listing of his "powers" might suggest. The men with whom he deals must deal with him until the last day of his term. Because they have continuing relationships with him, his future, while it lasts, supports his present influence. Even though there is no need or fear of him today, what he could do tomorrow may supply today's advantage. Continuing relationships may convert any "power," any aspect of his status, into vantage points in almost any case. When he induces other men to do what he wants done, a President can trade on their dependence now *and* later.

The President's advantages are checked by the advantages of others. Continuing relationships will pull in both directions. These are relationships of mutual dependence. A President depends upon the men he would persuade; he has to reckon with his need or fear of them. They too will possess status, or authority, or both, else they would be of little use to him. Their vantage points confront his own; their power tempers his.

Persuasion is a two-way street. Sawyer, it will be recalled, did not respond at once to Truman's plan for wage increases at the steel mills. On the contrary, the Secretary hesitated and delayed and only acquiesced when he was satisfied that publicly he would not bear the onus of decision. Sawyer

had some points of vantage all his own from which to resist presidential pressure. If he had to reckon with coercive implications in the President's "situations of strength," so had Truman to be mindful of the implications underlying Sawyer's place as a department head, as steel administrator, and as a Cabinet spokesman for business. Loyalty is reciprocal. Having taken on a dirty job in the steel crisis, Sawyer had strong claims to loyal support. Besides, he had authority to do some things that the White House could ill afford. Emulating Wilson, he might have resigned in a huff (the removal power also works two ways). Or emulating Ellis Arnall, he might have declined to sign necessary orders. Or, he might have let it be known publicly that he deplored what he was told to do and protested its doing. By following any of these courses Sawyer almost surely would have strengthened the position of management, weakened the position of the White House, and embittered the union. But the whole purpose of a wage increase was to enhance White House persuasiveness in urging settlement upon union and companies alike. Although Sawyer's status and authority did not give him the power to prevent an increase outright, they gave him capability to undermine its purpose. If his authority over wage rates had been vested by a statute, not by revocable presidential order, his power of prevention might have been complete. So Harold Ickes demonstrated in the famous case of helium sales to Germany before the Second World War.[6]

[6] As Secretary of the Interior in 1939, Harold Ickes refused to approve the sale of helium to Germany despite the insistence of the State De-

The power to persuade is the power to bargain. Status and authority yield bargaining advantages. But in a government of "separated institutions sharing powers," they yield them to all sides. With the array of vantage points at his disposal, a President may be far more persuasive than his logic or his charm could make him. But outcomes are not guaranteed by his advantages. There remain the counter pressures those whom he would influence can bring to bear on him from vantage points at their disposal. Command has limited utility; persuasion becomes give-and-take. It is well that the White House holds the vantage points it does. In such a business any President may need them all—and more.

II

This view of power as akin to bargaining is one we commonly accept in the sphere of congressional relations. Every textbook states and every legis-

partment and the urging of President Roosevelt. Without the Secretary's approval, such sales were forbidden by statute. See *The Secret Diaries of Harold L. Ickes* (New York: Simon and Schuster, 1954), Vol. 2, especially pp. 391–393, 396–399. See also Michael J. Reagan, "The Helium Controversy," in Harold Stein (ed.), *American Civil-Military Decisions: A Book of Case Studies* (University, Alabama: University of Alabama Press, 1963).

In this instance the statutory authority ran to the Secretary as a matter of *his* discretion. A President is unlikely to fire Cabinet officers for the conscientious exercise of such authority. If the President did so, their successors might well be embarrassed both publicly and at the Capitol were they to reverse decisions previously taken. As for a President's authority to set aside discretionary determinations of this sort, it rests, if it exists at all, on shaky legal ground not likely to be trod save in the gravest of situations.

lative session demonstrates that save in times like the extraordinary Hundred Days of 1933—times virtually ruled out by definition at mid-century—a President will often be unable to obtain congressional action on his terms or even to halt action he opposes. The reverse is equally accepted: Congress often is frustrated by the President. Their formal powers are so intertwined that neither will accomplish very much, for very long, without the acquiescence of the other. By the same token, though, what one demands the other can resist. The stage is set for that great game, much like collective bargaining, in which each seeks to profit from the other's needs and fears. It is a game played catch-as-catch-can, case by case. And everybody knows the game, observers and participants alike.

The concept of real power as a give-and-take is equally familiar when applied to presidential influence outside the formal structure of the Federal government. The Little Rock affair may be extreme, but Eisenhower's dealings with the Governor—and with the citizens—become a case in point. Less extreme but no less pertinent is the steel seizure case with respect to union leaders, and to workers, and to company executives as well. When he deals with such people a President draws bargaining advantage from his status or authority. By virtue of their public places or their private rights they have some capability to reply in kind.

In spheres of party politics the same thing follows, necessarily, from the confederal nature of our party organizations. Even in the case of national nominations a President's advantages are checked by those of others. In 1944 it is by no means clear that Roosevelt got his first choice as his running mate. In 1948 Truman, then the President, faced serious revolts against his nomination. In 1952 his intervention from the White House helped assure the choice of Adlai Stevenson, but it is far from clear that Truman could have done as much for any other candidate acceptable to him.[7] In 1956 when Eisenhower was President, the record leaves obscure just who backed Harold Stassen's effort to block Richard Nixon's renomination as Vice-President. But evidently everything did not go quite as Eisenhower wanted, whatever his intentions may have been.[8] The outcomes in these in-

stances bear all the marks of limits on command and of power checked by power that characterize congressional relations. Both in and out of politics these checks and limits seem to be quite widely understood.

Influence becomes still more a matter of give-and-take when Presidents attempt to deal with allied governments. A classic illustration is the long unhappy wrangle over Suez policy in 1956. In dealing with the British and the French before their military intervention, Eisenhower had his share of bargaining advantages but no effective power of command. His allies had their share of counter pressures, and they finally tried the most extreme of all: action despite him. His pressure then was instrumental in reversing them. But had the British government been on safe ground *at home,* Eisenhower's wishes might have made as little difference after intervention as before. Behind the decorum of diplomacy—which was not very decorous in the Suez affair—relationships among allies are not unlike relationships among state delegations at a national convention. Power is persuasion and persuasion becomes bargaining.

[7] Truman's *Memoirs* indicate that having tried and failed to make Stevenson an avowed candidate in the spring of 1952, the President decided to support the candidacy of Vice President Barkley. But Barkley withdrew early in the convention for lack of key northern support. Though Truman is silent on the matter, Barkley's active candidacy nearly was revived during the balloting, but the forces then aligning to revive it were led by opponents of Truman's Fair Deal, principally Southerners. As a practical matter, the President could not have lent his weight to *their* endeavors and could back no one but Stevenson to counter them. The latter's strength could not be shifted, then, to Harriman or Kefauver. Instead the other Northerners had to be withdrawn. Truman helped withdraw them. But he had no other option. See *Memoirs* by Harry S. Truman, Vol. 2, *Years of Trial and Hope* (Garden City: Doubleday, 1956), pp. 495–496.

[8] The reference is to Stassen's public statement of July 23, 1956, calling for Nixon's replacement on the Republican ticket by Governor Herter of Massachusetts, the later Secretary of State. Stassen's statement was issued after a conference with the President. Eisenhower's public statements on the vice-presidential nomination, both before and after Stassen's call, permit of alternative inferences: either that the President would have preferred another candidate, provided this could be arranged without a showing of White House dictation, or that he wanted Nixon on condition

that the latter could show popular appeal. In the event, neither result was achieved. Eisenhower's own remarks lent strength to rapid party moves which smothered Stassen's effort. Nixon's nomination thus was guaranteed too quickly to appear the consequence of popular demand. For the public record on this matter see reported statements by Eisenhower, Nixon, Stassen, Herter, and Leonard Hall (the National Republican Chairman) in the *New York Times* for March 1, 8, 15, 16; April 27; July 15, 16, 25–31; August 3, 4, 17, 23, 1956. See also the account from private sources by Earl Mazo in *Richard Nixon: A Personal and Political Portrait* (New York: Harper, 1959), pp. 158–187.

The concept is familiar to everyone who watches foreign policy.

In only one sphere is the concept unfamiliar: the sphere of executive relations. Perhaps because of civics textbooks and teaching in our schools, Americans instinctively resist the view that power in this sphere resembles power in all others. Even Washington reporters, White House aides, and congressmen are not immune to the illusion that administrative agencies comprise a single structure, "the" Executive Branch, where presidential word is law, or ought to be. Yet . . . when a President seeks something from executive officials his persuasiveness is subject to the same sorts of limitations as in the case of congressmen, or governors, or national committeemen, or private citizens, or foreign governments. There are no generic differences, no differences in kind and only sometimes in degree. The incidents preceding the dismissal of MacArthur and the incidents surrounding seizure of the steel mills make it plain that here as elsewhere influence derives from bargaining advantages; power is a give-and-take.

Like our governmental structure as a whole, the executive establishment consists of separated institutions sharing powers. The President heads one of these; Cabinet officers, agency administrators, and military commanders head others. Below the departmental level, virtually independent bureau chiefs head many more. Under mid-century conditions, Federal operations spill across dividing lines on organization charts; almost every policy entangles many agencies; almost every program calls for inter-agency collaboration. Everything somehow involves the President. But operating agencies owe their existence least of all to one another—and only in some part to him. Each has a separate statutory base; each has its statutes to administer; each deals with a different set of subcommittees at the Capitol. Each has its own peculiar set of clients, friends, and enemies outside the formal government. Each has a different set of specialized careerists inside its own bailiwick. Our Constitution gives the President the "take-care" clause and the appointive power. Our statutes give him central budgeting and a degree of personnel control. All agency administrators are responsible to him. But they *also* are responsible to Congress, to their clients, to their staffs, and to themselves. In short, they have five masters. Only after all of those do they owe any loyalty to each other.

"The members of the Cabinet," Charles G. Dawes used to remark, "are a President's natural enemies." Dawes had been Harding's Budget Director, Coolidge's Vice-President, and Hoover's Ambassador to London; he also had been General Pershing's chief assistant for supply in the First World War. The words are highly colored, but Dawes knew whereof he spoke. The men who have to serve so many masters cannot help but be somewhat the "enemy" of any one of them. By the same token, any master wanting service is in some degree the "enemy" of such a servant. A President is likely to want loyal support but not to relish trouble on his doorstep. Yet the more his Cabinet members cleave to him, the more they may need help from him in fending off the wrath of rival masters. Help, though, is synonymous with trouble. Many a Cabinet officer, with loyalty ill-rewarded by his lights and help withheld, has come to view the White House as innately hostile to department heads. Dawes's dictum can be turned around.

A senior presidential aide remarked to me in Eisenhower's time: "If some of these Cabinet members would just take time out to stop and ask themselves 'What would I want if I were President?', they wouldn't give him all the trouble he's been having." But even if they asked themselves the question, such officials often could not act upon the answer. Their personal attachment to the President is all too often overwhelmed by duty to their other masters.

Executive officials are not equally advantaged in their dealings with a President. Nor are the same officials equally advantaged all the time. Not every officeholder can resist like a MacArthur, or like Arnall, Sawyer, Wilson, in a rough descending order of effective counter pressure. The vantage points conferred upon officials by their own authority and status vary enormously. The variance is heightened by particulars of time and circumstance. In mid-October 1950, Truman, at a press conference, remarked of the man he had considered firing in August and would fire the next April for intolerable insubordination:

Let me tell you something that will be good for your souls. It's a pity that you . . . can't understand the ideas of two intellectually honest men when they meet. General MacArthur . . . is a member of the Government of the United States. He is loyal to that Government. He is loyal to the President. He is loyal to the President in his foreign policy. . . . There is no disagreement between General MacArthur and myself. . . .[9]

MacArthur's status in and out of government was never higher than when Truman spoke those words. The words, once spoken, added to the General's credibility thereafter when he sought to use the press in his campaign against the President. And what had happened between August and October? Near-victory had happened, together with that premature conference on *post*-war plans, the meeting at Wake Island.

If the bargaining advantages of a MacArthur fluctuate with changing circumstances, this is bound to be so with subordinates who have at their disposal fewer "powers," lesser status, to fall back on. And when officials have no "powers" in their own right, or depend upon the President for status, their counter pressure may be limited indeed. White House aides, who fit both categories, are among the most responsive men of all, and for good reason. As a Director of the Budget once remarked to me, "Thank God I'm here and not across the street. If the President doesn't call me, I've got plenty I can do right here and plenty coming up to me, by rights, to justify my calling him. But those poor fellows over there, if the boss doesn't call them, doesn't ask them to do something, what *can* they do but sit?" Authority and status so conditional are frail reliances in resisting a President's own wants. Within the White House pre-

[9] Stenographic transcript of presidential press conference, October 19, 1950, on file in the Truman Library at Independence, Missouri.

cincts, lifted eyebrows may suffice to set an aide in motion; command, coercion, even charm aside. But even in the White House a President does not monopolize effective power. Even there persuasion is akin to bargaining. A former Roosevelt aide once wrote of Cabinet officers:

Half of a President's suggestions, which theoretically carry the weight of orders, can be safely forgotten by a Cabinet member. And if the President asks about a suggestion a second time, he can be told that it is being investigated. If he asks a third time, a wise Cabinet officer will give him at least part of what he suggests. But only occasionally, except about the most important matters, do Presidents ever get around to asking three times.[10]

The rule applies to staff as well as to the Cabinet, and certainly has been applied *by* staff in Truman's time and Eisenhower's.

Some aides will have more vantage points than a selective memory. Sherman Adams, for example, as The Assistant to the President under Eisenhower, scarcely deserved the appelation "White House aide" in the meaning of the term before his time or as applied to other members of the Eisenhower entourage. Although Adams was by no means "chief of staff" in any sense so sweeping—or so simple—as press commentaries often took for granted, he apparently became no more dependent on the President than Eisenhower on him. "I need him," said the President when Adams turned out to have been remarkably imprudent in the Goldfine case, and delegated to him even the decision on

his own departure.[11] This instance is extreme, but the tendency it illustrates is common enough. Any aide who demonstrates to others that he has the President's consistent confidence and a consistent part in presidential business will acquire so much business on his own account that he becomes in some sense independent of his chief. Nothing in the Constitution keeps a well-placed aide from converting status into power of his own, usable in some degree even against the President— an outcome not unknown in Truman's regime or, by all accounts, in Eisenhower's.

The more an officeholder's status and his "powers" stem from sources independent of the President, the stronger will be his potential pressure *on* the President. Department heads in general have more bargaining power than do most members of the White House staff; but bureau chiefs may have still more, and specialists at upper levels of established career services may have almost unlimited reserves of the enormous power which consists of sitting still. As Franklin Roosevelt once remarked:

The Treasury is so large and far-flung and ingrained in its practices that I find it is

[10] Jonathan Daniels, *Frontier on the Potomac* (New York: Macmillan, 1946), pp. 31–32.

[11] Transcript of presidential press conference, June 18, 1958, in *Public Papers of the Presidents: Dwight D. Eisenhower, 1958* (Washington: The National Archives, 1959), p. 479. In the summer of 1958, a congressional investigation into the affairs of a New England textile manufacturer, Bernard Goldfine, revealed that Sherman Adams had accepted various gifts and favors from him (the most notoriety attached to a vicuña coat). Adams also had made inquiries about the status of a Federal Communications Commission proceeding in which Goldfine was involved. In September 1958, Adams was allowed to resign. The episode was highly publicized and much discussed in that year's congressional campaigns.

almost impossible to get the action and re-sults I want—even with Henry [Mor-genthau] there. But the Treasury is not to be compared with the State Department. You should go through the experience of trying to get any changes in the thinking, policy, and action of the career diplomats and then you'd know what a real problem was. But the Treasury and the State De-partment put together are nothing com-pared with the Na-a-vy. The admirals are really something to cope with—and I should know. To change anything in the Na-a-vy is like punching a feather bed. You punch it with your right and you punch it with your left until you are finally exhausted, and then you find the damn bed just as it was before you started punching.[12]

In the right circumstances, of course, a President can have his way with any of these people. [There may be] in-stances where circumstances were "right" and a presidential order was promptly carried out. But one need only note the favorable factors giving those orders their self-executing qual-ity to recognize that as between a Pres-ident and his "subordinates," no less than others on whom he depends, real power is reciprocal and varies mark-edly with organization, subject matter, personality, and situation. The mere fact that persuasion is directed at exec-utive officials signifies no necessary easing of his way. Any new congress-man of the Administration's party, es-pecially if narrowly elected, may turn out more amenable (though less use-ful) to the President than any seasoned bureau chief "downtown." *The prob-abilities of power do not derive from the literary theory of the Constitution.*

[12] As reported in Marriner S. Eccles, *Beckoning Frontiers* (New York: Alfred A. Knopf, 1951), p. 336.

III

There is a widely held belief in the United States that were it not for folly or for knavery, a reasonable President would need no power other than the logic of his argument. No less a per-sonage than Eisenhower has sub-scribed to that belief in many a cam-paign speech and press-conference remark. But faulty reasoning and bad intentions do not cause all quarrels with Presidents. The best of reasoning and of intent cannot compose them all. For in the first place, what the Presi-dent wants will rarely seem a trifle to the men he wants it from. And in the second place, they will be bound to judge it by the standard of their own responsibilities, not his. However logi-cal his argument according to his lights, their judgment may not bring them to his view.

The men who share in governing this country frequently appear to act as though they were in business for them-selves. So, in a real though not entire sense, they are and have to be. When Truman and MacArthur fell to quar-reling, for example, the stakes were no less than the substance of American foreign policy, the risks of greater war or military stalemate, the prerogatives of Presidents and field commanders, the pride of a pro-consul and his place in history. Intertwined, inevitably, were other stakes, as well: political stakes for men and factions of both parties; power stakes for interest groups with which they were or wished to be affiliated. And every stake was raised by the apparent discontent in the American public mood. There is no reason to suppose that in such circumstances men of large but differing responsibilities will see all things through the same glasses. On the contrary, it is to be expected that their views of what ought to be done and what they then should do will vary with the differing perspectives their particular responsibilities evoke. Since their duties are not vested in a "team" or a "collegium" but in themselves, as individuals, one must expect that they will see things *for* themselves. Moreover, when they are responsible to many masters and when an event or policy turns loyalty against loyalty— a day by day occurrence in the nature of the case—one must assume that those who have the duties to perform will choose the terms of reconciliation. This is the essence of their personal responsibility. When their own duties pull in opposite directions, who else but they can choose what they will do?

When Truman dismissed MacArthur, the latter lost three posts: the American command in the Far East, the Allied command for the occupation of Japan, and the United Nations command in Korea. He also lost his status as the senior officer on active duty in the United States armed forces. So long as he held those positions and that status, though, he had a duty to his troops, to his profession, to himself (the last is hard for any man to disentangle from the rest). As a public figure and a focus for men's hopes he had a duty to constituents at home, and in Korea and Japan. He owed a duty also to those other constituents, the UN governments contributing to his field forces. As a patriot he had a duty to his country. As an accountable official and an expert guide he stood at the call of Congress. As a military officer he had, besides, a duty to the President, his constitutional commander. Some of these duties may have manifested themselves in terms more tangible or more direct than others. But it would be nonsense to argue that the last *negated* all the rest, however much it might be claimed to override them. And it makes no more sense to think that anybody but MacArthur was effectively empowered to decide how he, himself, would reconcile the competing demands his duties made upon him.

Similar observations could be made about [other] executive officials. . . . Price Director [Ellis] Arnall, . . . refused in advance to sign a major price increase for steel if Mobilization Director Wilson or the White House should concede one before management had settled with the union. When Arnall did this, he took his stand, in substance, on his oath of office. He would do what he had sworn to do in *his* best judgment, so long as he was there to do it. This posture may have been assumed for purposes of bargaining and might have been abandoned had his challenge been accepted by the President. But no one could be sure and no one, certainly, could question Arnall's right to make the judgment for himself. As head of an agency and as a politician, with a program to defend and a future to advance, *he* had to decide what he had to do on matters that, from his perspective, were exceedingly important. Neither in policy nor in personal terms, nor in terms of agency survival, were the issues of a sort to be considered secondary by an Arnall, however much they might have seemed so to a Wilson (or a Truman). Nor were the merits likely to appear the same to a price stabilizer and to men with broader duties. Reasonable men, it is so often said, *ought* to be able to agree on the requirements of given situations. But when the outlook varies with the placement of each man, and the response required in his place is for each to decide, their reasoning may lead to disagreement quite as well—and quite as reasonably. Vanity, or vice, may weaken reason, to be sure, but it is idle to assign these as the cause of Arnall's threat or MacArthur's defiance. Secretary Sawyer's hesitations, cited earlier, are in the same category. One need not denigrate such men to explain their conduct. For the responsibilities they felt, the "facts" they saw, simply were not the same as those of their superiors; yet they, not the superiors, had to decide what they would do.

Outside the Executive Branch the situation is the same, except that loyalty to the President may often matter *less*. There is no need to spell out the comparison with Governors of Arkansas, steel company executives, trade union leaders, and the like. And when one comes to congressmen who can do nothing for themselves (or their constituents) save as they are elected, term by term, in districts and through party structures *differing* from those on which a President depends, the case is very clear. An able Eisenhower aide with long congressional experience remarked to me in 1958: "The people on the Hill don't do what they might *like* to do, they do what they think they *have* to do in their own interest as *they*

see it. . . ." This states the case precisely.

The essence of a President's persuasive task with congressmen and everybody else, *is to induce them to believe that what he wants of them is what their own appraisal of their own responsibilities requires them to do in their interest, not his.* Because men may differ in their views on public policy, because differences in outlook stem from differences in duty—duty to one's office, one's constituents, oneself—that task is bound to be more like collective bargaining than like a reasoned argument among philosopher kings. Overtly or implicitly, hard bargaining has characterized all illustrations offered up to now. This is the reason why: persuasion deals in the coin of self-interest with men who have some freedom to reject what they find counterfeit.

IV

A President draws influence from bargaining advantages. But does he always need them? [There may be] episodes . . . where views on public policy diverge with special sharpness. Suppose such sharp divergences are lacking, suppose most players of the governmental game see policy objectives much alike, then can he not rely on logic (or on charm) to get him what he wants? The answer is that even then most outcomes turn on bargaining. The reason for this answer is a simple one: most men who share in governing have interests of their own beyond the realm of policy *objectives*. The sponsorship of policy, the form it takes, the conduct of it, and the credit for it separate their interest from the President's despite agreement on the end in view. In political government, the means can matter quite as much as ends; they often matter more. And there are always differences of interest in the means.

Let me introduce a case externally the opposite of my previous examples: the European Recovery Program of 1948, the so-called Marshall Plan. This is perhaps the greatest exercise in policy *agreement* since the cold war began. When the then Secretary of State, George Catlett Marshall, spoke at the Harvard commencement in June of 1947, he launched one of the most creative, most imaginative ventures in the history of American foreign relations. What makes this policy most notable for present purposes, however, is that it became effective upon action by the 80th Congress, at the behest of Harry Truman, in the election year of 1948.[13]

Eight months before Marshall spoke at Harvard, the Democrats had lost control of both Houses of Congress for the first time in fourteen years.

Truman, whom the Secretary represented, had just finished his second troubled year as President-by-succession. Truman was regarded with so little warmth in his own party that in 1946 he had been urged *not* to participate in the congressional campaign. At the opening of Congress in January 1947, Senator Robert A. Taft, "Mr. Republican," had somewhat the attitude of a President-elect. This was a vision widely shared in Washington, with Truman relegated, thereby, to the role of caretaker-on-term. Moreover, within just two weeks of Marshall's commencement address, Truman was to veto two prized accomplishments of Taft's congressional majority: the Taft-Hartley Act and tax reduction.[14] Yet scarcely ten months later the Marshall Plan was under way on terms to satisfy its sponsors, its authorization completed, its first-year funds in sight, its administering agency in being: all managed by as thorough a display of executive-congressional cooperation as any we have seen since the Second World War. For any President at any time this would have been a great accomplishment. In years before mid-century it would have been enough to make the future reputation of his term. And for a Truman, at this time, enactment of

[13] In drawing together these observations on the Marshall Plan, I have relied on the record of personal participation by Joseph M. Jones, *The Fifteen Weeks* (New York: Viking, 1955), especially pp. 89–256; on the recent study by Harry Bayard Price, *The Marshall Plan and Its Meaning* (Ithaca: Cornell University Press, 1955), especially pp. 1–86; on the Truman *Memoirs*, Vol. 2, chapters 7–9; on Arthur H. Vandenberg, Jr. (ed.), *The Private Papers of Senator Vandenberg* (Boston: Houghton, Mifflin, 1952), especially pp. 373 ff.; and on notes of my own made at the time. This is an instance of policy development not covered, to my knowledge, by any of the university programs engaged in the production of case studies.

[14] Secretary Marshall's speech, formally suggesting what became known as the Marshall Plan, was made at Harvard on June 5, 1947. On June 20 the President vetoed the Taft-Hartley Act; his veto was overridden three days later. On June 16 he vetoed the first of two tax reduction bills (HR 1) passed at the first session of the 80th Congress; the second of these (HR 3950), a replacement for the other, he also disapproved on July 18. In both instances his veto was narrowly sustained.

the Marshall Plan appears almost miraculous.

How was the miracle accomplished? How did a President so situated bring it off? In answer, the first thing to note is that he did not do it by himself. Truman had help of a sort no less extraordinary than the outcome. Although each stands for something more complex, the names of Marshall, Vandenberg, Patterson, Bevin, Stalin, tell the story of that help.

In 1947, two years after V-J Day, General Marshall was something more than Secretary of State. He was a man venerated by the President as "the greatest living American," literally an embodiment of Truman's ideals. He was honored at the Pentagon as an architect of victory. He was thoroughly respected by the Secretary of the Navy, James V. Forrestal, who that year became the first Secretary of Defense. On Capitol Hill Marshall had an enormous fund of respect stemming from his war record as Army Chief of Staff, and in the country generally no officer had come out of the war with a higher reputation for judgment, intellect, and probity. Besides, as Secretary of State, he had behind him the first generation of matured foreign service officers produced by the reforms of the 1920's, and mingled with them, in the departmental service, were some of the ablest of the men drawn by the war from private life to Washington. In terms both of staff talent and staff's use, Marshall's years began a State Department "golden age" which lasted until the era of McCarthy. Moreover, as his Under Secretary, Marshall had, successively, Dean Acheson and Robert Lovett, men who commanded the respect of the professionals and the re-

gard of congressmen. (Acheson had been brilliantly successful at congressional relations as Assistant Secretary in the war and postwar years.) Finally, as a special undersecretary Marshall had Will Clayton, a man highly regarded, for good reason, at both ends of Pennsylvania Avenue.

Taken together, these are exceptional resources for a Secretary of State. In the circumstances, they were quite as necessary as they obviously are relevant. The Marshall Plan was launched by a "lame duck" Administration "schedule" to leave office in eighteen months. Marshall's program faced a congressional leadership traditionally isolationist and currently intent upon economy. European aid was viewed with envy by a Pentagon distressed and virtually disarmed through budget cuts, and by domestic agencies intent on enlarged welfare programs. It was not viewed with liking by a Treasury intent on budget surpluses. The plan had need of every asset that could be extracted from the personal position of its nominal author and from the skills of his assistants.

Without the equally remarkable position of the senior Senator from Michigan, Arthur H. Vandenberg, it is hard to see how Marshall's assets could have been enough. Vandenberg was chairman of the Senate Foreign Relations Committee. Actually, he was much more than that. Twenty years a senator, he was the senior member of his party in the Chamber. Assiduously cultivated by F.D.R. and Truman, he was a chief Republican proponent of "bipartisanship" in foreign policy, and consciously conceived himself its living symbol to his party, to the country, and abroad. Moreover, by informal but entirely operative agreement with his colleague Taft, Vandenberg held the acknowledged lead among Senate Republicans in the whole field of international affairs. This acknowledgement meant more in 1947 than it might have meant at any other time. With confidence in the advent of a Republican administration two years hence, most of the gentlemen were in a mood to be responsive and responsible. The war was over, Roosevelt dead, Truman a caretaker, theirs the trust. That the Senator from Michigan saw matters in this light, his diaries make clear.[15] And this was not the outlook from the Senate side alone; the attitudes of House Republicans associated with the Herter Committee and its tours abroad suggest the same mood of responsibility. Vandenberg was not the only source of help on Capitol Hill. But relatively speaking, his position there was as exceptional as Marshall's was downtown.

Help of another sort was furnished by a group of dedicated private citizens who organized one of the most effective instruments for public information seen since the Second World War: the Committee for the Marshall Plan, headed by the eminent Republicans whom F.D.R., in 1940, had brought to the Department of War: Henry L. Stimson as honorary chairman and Robert P. Patterson as active spokesmen. The remarkable array of bankers, lawyers, trade unionists, and editors, who had drawn together in defense of "internationalism" before Pearl Harbor and had joined their talents in the war itself, combined again

to spark the work of this committee. Their efforts generated a great deal of vocal public support to buttress Marshall's arguments, and Vandenberg's, in Congress.

But before public support could be rallied, there had to be a purpose tangible enough, concrete enough, to provide a rallying ground. At Harvard, Marshall had voiced an idea in general terms. That this was turned into a hard program susceptible of presentation and support is due, in major part, to Ernest Bevin, the British Foreign Secretary. He well deserves the credit he has sometimes been assigned as, in effect, co-author of the Marshall Plan. For Bevin seized on Marshall's Harvard speech and organized a European response with promptness and concreteness beyond the State Department's expectations. What had been virtually a trial balloon to test reactions on both sides of the Atlantic was hailed in London as an invitation to the Europeans to send Washington a bill of particulars. This they promptly organized to do, and the American Administration then organized in turn for its reception without further argument internally about the pros and cons of issuing the "invitation" in the first place. But for Bevin there might have been trouble from the Secretary of the Treasury and others besides.[16]

---

[15] *Private Papers of Senator Vandenberg*, pp. 378–379 and 446.

[16] The initial reluctance of Secretary of the Treasury, John Snyder, to support large-scale spending overseas became a matter of public knowledge on June 25, 1947. At a press conference on that day he interpreted Marshall's Harvard speech as a call on Europeans to help themselves, by themselves. At another press conference the same day, Marshall for his own part had indicated that the U.S. would consider helping programs on which Europeans agreed. The next day Truman held a

If Bevin's help was useful at that early stage, Stalin's was vital from first to last. In a mood of self-deprecation Truman once remarked that without Moscow's "crazy" moves "we never would have had our foreign policy . . . we never could have got a thing from Congress." [17] George Kennan, among others, has deplored the anti-Soviet overtone of the case made for the Marshall Plan in Congress and the country, but there is no doubt that this clinched the argument for many segments of American opinion. There also is no doubt that Moscow made the crucial contributions to the case.

By 1947 events, far more than governmental prescience or open action, had given a variety of publics an impression of inimical Soviet intentions (and of Europe's weakness), and a growing urge to "do something about it." Three months before Marshall spoke at Harvard, Greek-Turkish aid and promulgation of the Truman Doctrine had seemed rather to crystallize than to create a public mood and a congressional response. The Marshall planners, be it said, were poorly placed

to capitalize on that mood, nor had the Secretary wished to do so. Their object, indeed, was to cut across it, striking at the cause of European weakness rather than at Soviet aggressiveness, *per se*. A strong economy in Western Europe called, ideally, for restorative measures of continental scope. American assistance proffered in an anti-Soviet context would have been contradictory in theory and unacceptable in fact to several of the governments that Washington was anxious to assist. As Marshall, himself, saw it, the logic of his purpose forbade him to play his strongest congressional card. The Russians then proceeded to play it for him. When the Europeans met in Paris, Molotov walked out. After the Czechs had shown continued interest in American aid, a communist coup overthrew their government while Soviet forces stood along their borders within easy reach of Prague. Molotov transformed the Marshall Plan's initial presentation; Czechoslovakia assured its final passage, which followed by a month the take-over in Prague.

Such was the help accorded Truman in obtaining action on the Marshall Plan. Considering his politically straightened circumstances he scarcely could have done with less. Conceivably, some part of Moscow's contribution might have been dispensable, but not Marshall's, or Vandenberg's, or Bevin's, or Patterson's, or that of the great many other men whose work is represented by their names in my account. Their aid was not extended to the President for his own sake. He was not favored in this fashion just because they liked him personally, or were spellbound by his intellect or charm. They might have been as helpful had

press conference and was asked the inevitable question. He replied, "General Marshall and I are in complete agreement." When pressed further, Truman remarked sharply, "The Secretary of the Treasury and the Secretary of State and the President are in complete agreement." Thus the President cut Snyder off, but had had programming gathered less momentum overseas, no doubt he would have been heard from again as time passed and opportunity offered.

The foregoing quotations are from the stenographic transcript of the presidential press conference June 26, 1947, on file in the Truman Library at Independence, Missouri.

[17] A remark made in December, 1955, three years after he left office, but not unrepresentative of views he expressed, on occasion, while he was President.

all held him in disdain, which some of them certainly did. The Londoners who seized the ball, Vandenberg and Taft and the congressional majority, Marshall and his planners, the officials of other agencies who actively supported them or "went along," the host of influential private citizens who rallied to the cause—all these played the parts they did because they thought they had to, in their interest, given their responsibilities, not Truman's. Yet they hardly would have found it in their interest to collaborate with one another, or with him, had he not furnished them precisely what *they* needed from the White House. Truman could not do without their help, but he could not have had it without unremitting effort on his part.

The crucial thing to note about this case is that despite compatibility of views on public policy, Truman got no help he did not pay for (except Stalin's). Bevin scarcely could have seized on Marshall's words had Marshall not been plainly backed by Truman. Marshall's interest would not have comported with the exploitation of his prestige by a President who undercut him openly, or subtly, or even inadvertently, at any point. Vandenberg, presumably, could not have backed proposals by a White House which begrudged him deference and access gratifying to his fellow-partisans (and satisfying to himself). Prominent Republicans in private life would not have found it easy to promote a cause identified with Truman's claims on 1948—and neither would the prominent New Dealers then engaged in searching for a substitute.

Truman paid the price required for their services. So far as the record

shows, the White House did not falter once in firm support for Marshall and the Marshall Plan. Truman backed his Secretary's gamble on an invitation to all Europe. He made the plan his own in a well-timed address to the Canadians. He lost no opportunity to widen the involvements of his own official family in the cause. Averell Harriman the Secretary of Commerce, Julius Krug the Secretary of the Interior, Edwin Nourse the Economic Council Chairman, James Webb the Director of the Budget—all were made responsible for studies and reports contributing directly to the legislative presentation. Thus these men were committed in advance. Besides, the President continually emphasized to everyone in reach that he did not have doubts, did not desire complications and would foreclose all he could. Reportedly, his emphasis was felt at the Treasury, with good effect. And Truman was at special pains to smooth the way for Vandenberg. The Senator insisted on "no politics" from the Administration side; there was none. He thought a survey of American resources and capacity essential; he got it in the Krug and Harriman reports. Vandenberg expected advance consultation; he received it, step by step, in frequent meetings with the President and weekly conferences with Marshall. He asked for an effective liaison between Congress and agencies concerned; Lovett and others gave him what he wanted. When the Senator decided on the need to change financing and administrative features of the legislation, Truman disregarded Budget Bureau grumbling and acquiesced with grace. When, finally, Vandenberg desired a Republican to head the new administering agency, his candidate, Paul Hoffman, was appointed despite the President's own preference for another. In all of these ways Truman employed the sparse advantages his "powers" and his status then accorded him to gain the sort of help he had to have.

Truman helped himself in still another way. Traditionally and practically no one was placed as well as he to call public attention to the task of *Congress* (and its Republican leadership). Throughout the fall and winter of 1947 and on into the spring of 1948, he made repeated use of presidential "powers" to remind the country that congressional action was required. Messages, speeches, and an extra session were employed to make the point. Here, too, he drew advantage from his place. However, in his circumstances, Truman's public advocacy might have hurt, not helped, had his words seemed directed toward the forthcoming election. Truman gained advantage for his program only as his own endorsement of it stayed on the right side of that fine line between the "caretaker" in office and the would-be candidate. In public statements dealing with the Marshall Plan he seems to have risked blurring this distinction only once, when he called Congress into session in November 1947 asking both for interim aid to Europe *and* for peacetime price controls. The second request linked the then inflation with the current Congress (and with Taft), becoming a first step toward one of Truman's major themes in 1948. By calling for both measures at the extra session he could have been accused—and was— of mixing home-front politics with foreign aid. In the event no harm was

done the European program (or his politics). But in advance a number of his own advisers feared that such a double call would jeopardize the Marshall Plan. Their fears are testimony to the narrowness of his advantage in employing his own "powers" for its benefit.[18]

It is symptomatic of Truman's situation that "bipartisan" accommodation by the White House then was thought to mean congressional consultation and conciliation on a scale unmatched in Eisenhower's time. Yet Eisenhower did about as well with opposition Congresses as Truman did, in terms of requests granted for defense and foreign aid. It may be said that Truman asked for more extraordinary measures. But it also may be said that Eisenhower never lacked for the prestige his predecessor had to borrow. It often was remarked, in Truman's time, that he seemed a "split-personality," so sharply did his conduct differentiate domestic politics from national security. But personality aside, how else could *he,* in his first term, gain ground for an evolving foreign policy? The plain fact is that Truman had to play bipartisanship as he did or lose the game.

V

Had Truman lacked the personal advantages his "powers" and his status gave him, or if he had been maladroit

[18] This might also be taken as testimony to the political timidity of officials in the State Department and the Budget Bureau where that fear seems to have been strongest. However, conversations at the time with White House aides incline

in using them, there probably would not have been a massive European aid program in 1948. Something of the sort, perhaps quite different in its emphasis, would almost certainly have come to pass before the end of 1949. *Some* American response to European weakness and to Soviet expansion was as certain as such things can be. But in 1948 temptations to await a Taft Plan or a Dewey Plan might well have caused at least a year's postponement of response had the "outgoing" Administration bungled its congressional, or public, or allied, or executive relations. Quite aside from the specific virtues of their plan, Truman and his helpers gained that year, at least, in timing the American response. As European time was measured then, this was a precious gain. The President's own share in this accomplishment was vital. He made his contribution by exploiting his advantages. Truman, in effect, lent Marshall and the rest the perquisites and status of his office. In return they lent him their prestige and their own influence. The transfer multiplied *his* influence despite his limited authority in form and lack of strength politically. Without the wherewithal to make this bargain, Truman could not have contributed to European aid.

Bargaining advantages convey no guarantees. Influence remains a two-way street. In the fortunate instance of the Marshall Plan, what Truman needed was actually in the hands of

men who were prepared to "trade" with him. He personally could deliver what they wanted in return. Marshall, Vandenberg, Harriman, *et. al.,* possessed the prestige, energy, associations, staffs, essential to the legislative effort. Truman himself had a sufficient hold on presidential messages and speeches, on budget policy, on high-level appointments, and on his own time and temper to carry through all aspects of his necessary part. But it takes two to make a bargain. It takes those who have prestige to lend it on whatever terms. Suppose that Marshall had declined the Secretaryship of State in January 1947; Truman might not have found a substitute so well-equipped to furnish what he needed in the months ahead. Or suppose that Vandenberg had fallen victim to a cancer two years before he actually did; Senator Wiley of Wisconsin would not have seemed to Taft a man with whom the world need be divided. Or suppose that the Secretary of the Treasury had been possessed of stature, force, and charm commensurate with that of his successor in Eisenhower's time, the redoubtable George M. Humphrey. And what if Truman then had seemed to the Republicans what he turned out to be in 1948, a formidable candidate for President? It is unlikely that a single one of these "supposes" would have changed the final outcome; two or three, however, might have altered it entirely. Truman was not guaranteed more power than his "powers" just because he had continuing relationships with Cabinet secretaries and with senior senators. Here, as everywhere, the outcome was conditional on who they were and what he was and how each viewed

me to believe that there, too, interjection of the price issue was thought a gamble and a risk. For further comment see my "Congress and the Fair Deal: A Legislative Balance Sheet," *Public Policy* (Cambridge: Harvard University Press, 1954), Vol. 5, pp. 362–364.

events, and on their actual performance in response.

Granting that persuasion has no guarantee attached, how can a President reduce the risks of failing to persuade? How can he maximize his prospects for effectiveness by minimizing chances that his power will elude him? The Marshall Plan suggests an answer: he guards his power prospects in the course of making choices. Marshall himself, and Forrestal, and Harriman, and others of the sort held office on the President's appointment. Vandenberg had vast symbolic value partly because F.D.R. and Truman had done everything they could, since 1944, to build him up. The Treasury Department and the Budget Bureau—which together might have jeopardized the plans these others made—were headed by officials whose prestige depended wholly on their jobs. What Truman needed from those "givers" he received, in part, because of his past choice of men and measures. What they received in turn were actions taken or withheld by him, himself. The things they needed from him mostly involved his own conduct where his current choices ruled. The President's own actions in the past had cleared the way for current bargaining. His actions in the present were his trading stock. Behind each action lay a personal choice, and these together comprised *his* control over the give-and-take that gained him what he wanted. In the degree that Truman, personally, affected the advantages he drew from his relationships with other men in government, *his power was protected by his choices.*

By "choice" I mean no more than what is commonly referred to as "deci-sion": a President's own act of doing or not doing. Decision is so often indecisive and indecision is so frequently conclusive, that choice becomes the preferable term. "Choice" has its share of undesired connotations. In common usage it implies a black-and-white alternative. Presidential choices are rarely of that character. It also may imply that the alternatives are set before the choice-maker by someone else. A President is often left to figure out his options for himself. Neither implication holds in any of the references to "choice" throughout this book.

If Presidents could count upon past choices to enhance their current influence, as Truman's choice of men had done for him, persuasion would pose fewer difficulties than it does. But Presidents can count on no such thing. Depending on the circumstances, prior choices can be as embarrassing as they were helpful in the instance of the Marshall Plan. [There are] some sharp examples of embarrassment. Among others: Eisenhower's influence with Faubus was diminished by his earlier statements to the press and by his unconditional agreement to converse in friendly style at Newport. Truman's hold upon MacArthur was weakened by his deference toward him in the past.

Assuming that past choices have protected influence, not harmed it, present choices still may be inadequate. If Presidents could count on their own conduct to provide them *enough* bargaining advantages, as Truman's conduct did where Vandenberg and Marshall were concerned, effective bargaining might be much easier to manage than it often is. In the steel crisis, for instance, Truman's own persuasiveness with companies and union, both, was burdened by the conduct of an independent Wage Board and of government attorneys in the courts, to say nothing of Wilson, Arnall, Sawyer, and the like. Yet in practice, if not theory, many of *their* crucial choices never were the President's to make. Decisions that are legally in other's hands, or delegated past recall, have an unhappy way of proving just the trading stock most needed when the White House wants to trade. One reason why Truman was consistently more influential in the instance of the Marshall Plan than in the steel case, or the MacArthur case, is that the Marshall Plan directly involved Congress. In congressional relations there are some things that no one but the President can do. His chance to choose is higher when a message must be sent, or a nomination submitted, or a bill signed into law, than when the sphere of action is confined to the Executive, where all decisive tasks may have been delegated past recall.

But adequate or not, a President's own choices are the only means *in his own hands* of guarding his own prospects for effective influence. He can draw power from continuing relationships in the degree that he can capitalize upon the needs of others for the Presidency's status and authority. He helps himself to do so, though, by nothing save ability to recognize the pre-conditions and the chance advantages and to proceed accordingly in the course of choice-making that comes his way. To ask how he can guard prospective influence is thus to raise a further question: what helps him guard his power stakes in his own acts of choice?

THE DIFFUSION
OF POWER IN
NEW YORK CITY
WALLACE S. SAYRE AND
HERBERT KAUFMAN

A full view and a fair judgment of New York City's many-faceted political and governmental system has been a matter of national as well as local debate for at least a century and a half. Historians and journalists, statesmen and politicians, social scientists and other analysts, writers in verse and prose have all been fascinated by the power, the variety, the size, and the significance of the city, its politics, and its government. But they have not achieved consensus. The city in the nation, the city in the state, the city in its metropolitan region, the city as a city, the quality of its political and governmental life—all these remain, and will continue, as matters of debate and discussion, of interest and concern— for the nation as well as for the city.

The most striking characteristic of the city's politics and government is one of scale. No other American city approaches the magnitude, scope, variety, and complexity of the city's governmental tasks and accomplishments. Nor does any other city repre-

sent so important a political prize, in its electorate and its government, in the national party contest. Nor can any other city match the drama, the color, and the special style of the city's own politics. In all these respects the city is imperial, if not unique, among American cities.

The city's politics and government have been more widely known for their defects than for their claims to excellence. This notoriety rather than fame for the city has been the product of many causes. There has been the city's high visibility as the nation's largest urban center. There have been the effective processes of exposure built into the city's political system. There have been the highly articulate voices of dissent and criticism always present in the city. There have been, too, the scale and theatrical qualities of the defects in the city's political system. And the citizens of the city have themselves been more given to eloquence in their indignation at "failures" than in their pride over "successes." Notoriety is, in this sense, perhaps itself a valid claim to fame for the city: the city's political and governmental system has never produced contentment, acquiescence, or a sense

CREDIT: Reprinted by permission of the authors and publisher from *Governing New York City*, pp. 709–725. Copyright © 1960 by Russell Sage Foundation.

of lasting defeat among its critics. The voice of the critic has often had the most attentive audience.

The city's political system is, in fact, vigorously and incessantly competitive. The stakes of the city's politics are large, the contestants are numerous and determined, the rules of the competition are known to and enforced against each other by the competitors themselves, and the city's electorate is so uncommitted to any particular contestant as to heighten the competition for the electorate's support or consent. No single ruling élite dominates the political and governmental system of New York City.

CHARACTERISTICS OF THE CITY'S SYSTEM

A multiplicity of decision centers

The decisions that distribute the prizes of politics in New York City issue from a large number of sources.

Each source consists of two parts: a "core group" at the center, invested by the rules with the formal authority to legitimize decisions (that is, to promulgate them in the prescribed forms and according to the specified procedures that make them binding under the rules) and a constellation of "satellite groups," seeking to influence the authoritative issuances of the core group. The five large categories of participants in the city's political contest . . .—the party leaders, the elected and appointed public officials, the organized bureaucracies, the numerous nongovernmental associations (including the mass media of communication), the officials and agencies of

other governments—play their parts upon the many stages the city provides. The most visible of these stages are those provided by the formal decision centers in each of which a core group and its satellite groups occupy the middle of the stage. Every center (every core group and its satellite groups), whatever its stage, must also continuously acknowledge the supervising presence of the city's electorate, possessing the propensity and the capacity to intervene decisively in the contest on the side of one contestant or the other.

Party leaders are core groups for nominations. They function as satellites, however, in many decisions about appointments, and in connection with substantive program and policy decisions in their role as brokers for other claimants. The city's electorate is the core group for electoral decisions, where it has a virtual monopoly. Other participants in the contest for the stakes of politics may exert considerable influence on the electorate, but only in the same fashion as satellite groups in other special areas influence each appropriate core group.

In all other decision centers the core groups are composed of officials. Most prominent among these core groups are the officials presiding over the decision centers of the general organs of government—the Mayor, the Board of Estimate, the Council, and the legislators and executives at the higher levels of government. Their decisions spread across the entire spectrum of the city's governmental functions and activities; consequently, all the other participants in the political process are, at one time or another and in varying combinations, satellite groups to these central core groups, trying to influence their actions. Each of their decisions, it is true, evokes active responses only from those participants particularly interested in the affected sphere of governmental activity, but most of their decisions prove to be of interest to some participants in all the five major categories (though rarely to all participants in all categories). In the course of time, most groups taking part in the city's politics apply leverage to the core groups in the general governmental institutions in efforts to secure favorable decisions. The courts are also general organs, and therefore the judges as the core group in that arena are of interest to most contestants at one time or another, but the modes of influence exerted on them are somewhat more restricted and institutionalized than those exerted on the core groups of other general organs.

Functionally specialized officials constitute the core groups for decisions in particular functional areas of governmental action, whether these are in line agencies (such as the Board of Education, the Department of Welfare, the Police Department, the Fire Department, the Department of Health), in special authorities (Transit, Housing, Triborough Bridge and Tunnel, or the Port of New York Authority), or in overhead agencies (the Budget Bureau, the Personnel Department, the Law Department, the City Planning Department, for example). Each of these decision centers is surrounded by satellite groups especially concerned with its decisions— the leaders of the interests served, the interests regulated, professional societies and associations, organized bu-

reaucracies, labor unions, suppliers of revenues and materials, and others. Usually, the groups concerned chiefly with particular functions are uninterested in decisions in other, unrelated functional areas, so that most of the decisions (about appointments as well as programs and policies) in each decision center are worked out by an interplay among the specialized core and its satellite groups.

Most officials have a dual role. They appear not merely in core groups but also as satellites of other officials. From the point of view of the general organs, for instance, the agency heads are claimants endeavoring to influence decisions in the city's central governmental institutions. From the point of view of a department head, the general organs are satellites making demands. Although the general organs' influence on agency leaders is especially strong, it is not by any measure complete domination; the agency leaders commonly preserve a region of autonomy free from invasion by the central organs as well as from other groups and institutions. Department heads also often see their own official colleagues (particularly the heads of overhead agencies), as well as the leaders of the organized bureaucracies, acting as satellite groups, as wielders of influence, and as competitors. Their counterparts in other governments tend to appear in the same light. Other officials (themselves core groups in their own respective areas) are thus likely to appear among the satellites of any particular official core group.

The leaders of the city's organized bureaucracies are, strictly speaking, never members of a core group but always a satellite group seeking to exert influence over one or more core groups. Their role is not without ambiguity in this respect, however, for many bureaucrats also occupy significant decision-making posts in the city government. As members or leaders in their organized bureaucratic groups, these bureaucrats thus occasionally play a dual part; as leaders or members of satellite groups they engage in efforts to influence the actions of a core group in which they are also members. But these are not yet typical situations. In most instances, the leaders of the organized bureaucracies are satellite groups.

The leaders of the city's nongovernmental groups never formally constitute core groups, but appear instead as satellites. Functionally specialized groups, being close to the agency officials whose decisions affect them, are not far from the center of the particular arena in which they operate. But, except when they are coopted into what amounts to a part of officialdom, they cannot do what the core groups do: issue authoritative, official, binding decisions. As satellites, some of the civic groups, and the communication media, are active and frequently highly influential in a broad range of functional spheres. In any specific functional area of governmental activity, however, it is the specialized, well-organized, persistent, professionally staffed nongovernmental organizations that continuously affect the pattern of decisions. Core groups of officials tend to estimate the reactions of other nongovernmental groups that might be galvanized to action by specific decisions, and the officials respond to the representations of such groups when these groups are suffi-

ciently provoked to exert pressure. But the impact of these organizations is more intermittent and uncertain than that of those with sustained and specialized programs of influence. Yet even the specialized are compelled by the nature of the rules to accept roles as satellites.

Decisions as accommodations

No single group of participants in the city's political contest is self-sufficient in its power to make decisions or require decisions of others. Every decision of importance is consequently the product of mutual accommodation. Building temporary or lasting alliances, working out immediate or enduring settlements between allies or competitors, and bargaining for an improved position in the decision centers are the continuing preoccupations of all leaders—whether party leaders, public officials, leaders of organized bureaucracies, or leaders of nongovernmental groups.

Each core group is constantly bargaining and reaching understandings of varying comprehensiveness and stability with some of its satellite groups, seeking a coalition of forces which will enable it to issue decisions that will stand against the opposition of those outside the coalition. The satellite groups, in turn, are just as constantly bargaining with each other for alliances on specific decisions or more permanent agreements. These accommodations between core and satellite group and among satellite groups represent an infinite variety of bargains, some leaving the core group with considerable freedom of movement, others tying it into close partnership with other members of an alliance, and still others imprisoning it within a powerful coalition of satellite groups. Since almost all core groups confront a competing and often numerous field of satellite groups, bargaining is perpetual.

Bargaining and accommodation are equally characteristic of the relations between one core group plus its satellites and other core groups with their satellites. These accommodations are necessary since some core groups have supervisory authority over others, some have competing jurisdictional claims, and almost all are competitors for the scarce dollars available through the budget.

Indeed, core groups themselves do not exhibit solid internal unity; each is in many respects a microcosm of the entire system. The central organs of government, for example, are in reality mosaics: The Board of Estimate with its powerful borough representatives, the office of Mayor with its many commissioners and assistants chosen by expediency rather than preference, the Council composed of councilmen representing small districts and operating through many committees—all three are assemblages of many parts. The state legislature, the Governor, and the other elected and appointed state executives are similarly divided when they become involved in the city's government and politics. Even more so are the central institutions of the federal government dealing with the city.

In much the same way, the city's administrative agencies are not monoliths but aggregates of components enjoying varying degrees of autonomy. Each department head must learn to deal with his deputies and assistants, his bureau chiefs, sometimes his orga-

nized bureaucracies. The organized bureaucracies are likewise splintered along functional, religious, professional, trade union, rank, and other lines. Party leaders may be described as a class but, in fact, they constitute a large number of rather independent participants in city government, rivaling each other, bargaining with each other, working out more or less unstable agreements with each other. The electorate itself, the sometimes remote and nebulous presence that shapes and colors the entire contest for the stakes of politics, is composed of a multitude of subdivisions—the various geographical constituencies, the regular voters and those who appear only for spectacular electoral battles, the party-line voters and the selective nonvoters, the ticket-splitters, the ethnic and religious voters, the ideological voters of all persuasions, as well as the social and economic class voters.

The process of bargaining, in short, reaches into the core of each decision center and is not confined to relations between core groups, or between core groups and their satellites, or between satellites. If there is any single feature of the system of government and politics in New York City that may be called ubiquitous and invariant, it would seem to be the prevalence of mutual accommodation. Every program and policy represents a compromise among the interested participants.

Partial self-containment of decision centers

The decisions that flow from each constellation of groups active in each of the city's decision centers are ordinarily formulated and carried out without much calculated consideration of the decisions emanating from the other centers. They are usually made in terms of the special perspectives and values of the groups with particular interests in the governmental functions or activities affecting them. Only occasionally are they formulated in a broader frame of reference.

This fragmentation of governmental decision-making in the city is partially offset by features of the system tending to introduce more or less common premises of decision into the centers. A major "balance wheel" has been noted by David B. Truman: the overlapping memberships of many groups in society. The same individuals turn up in many contexts and in many guises, carrying to each the viewpoints and information acquired in the others. A second balance wheel is the frequency with which the core groups of one center operate as satellite groups in other centers; no center is completely isolated from the others. Overhead agencies serve as a third unifying element, for they cut across the whole range of governmental functions and activities, introducing, within the limits of their own specialties, a common set of assumptions and goals into many of the decisions of other centers. A fourth unifying factor is represented by the civic groups and the press, which exert their influence on a wide variety of decision centers without regard to the subject-matter specialties of the centers. They are not equally effective everywhere, and they are seldom so effective in any given center as the more specialized participants in it, but they help to relate what happens in every center to what goes on in others. Finally, the central institutions of government (including the

courts) operate under relatively few functional restrictions and therefore make decisions with respect to all phases of the city's government and politics. Collectively, their perspectives are broad, their interests are inclusive, their desire to rationalize and balance the actions in all decision centers are strong, and their formal authority to impose a common basis for decisions is superior to that of other groups. These five factors help to keep the system from flying apart.

Yet the autonomous nature of the core group and its satellite groups in each decision center is striking. Although the leaders may belong to many groups, they behave, when particular decisions are at issue, with a remarkable lack of ambivalence. The interests immediately at stake provide the criteria of action, and they often seem unambiguous; at any given moment, group leaders and members act as though they had only one interest, one membership, at that moment. Most participants are galvanized to action by only a relatively narrow range of issues and ignore most others no matter where they occur; as a result, most of the actors in any center share very special interests in the problems at hand, and the casual outsider or the intermittent satellite group has much less effect on the decisions made there than do the strongly motivated "regulars." As modes of integrating the decisions of the city's whole governmental system, the balance wheels have therefore not been spectacularly successful.

What is perhaps most surprising is the failure of the central organs of government to provide a high level of integration for the city's system. The Council has been weak, the Board of Estimate inert, the Mayor handicapped. The government at Albany cannot do the job of pulling the decision centers of the city together, even if it were so inclined. This would mean running the city, a task the state is unable and unwilling to assume, a task that would not win it the thanks of the city's residents or of other residents of the state. Moreover, the state government has not been inclined to strengthen the central institutions of the city, but has enacted legislation and created agencies that intensify the independence of many local officials. State administrative supervision of city agencies has encouraged many city officers and employees to develop close links with their functional counterparts in the state capital, and to rely on these to buttress their resistance to leadership from the city's central institutions. The nature of the judicial process renders the courts incapable of performing an integrative function. Thus, despite the opportunities for integration presented by the formal powers of the city's central institutions, they have generally either officially ratified the agreements reached by the active participants in each decision center, which are offered to them as the consensus of experts and interested groups, or, on an *ad hoc* basis, have chosen one or another alternative suggested when the experts and interested groups have been divided on an issue. It is in the latter role that the city's central institutions have had their greatest significance. Seldom have they imposed, on their own initiative, a common set of objectives on all the centers of decision. The central institutions are important participants in all the decision-making in the contest for the stakes of politics in

the city, but they are rarely the prime movers or the overriding forces.

As a result, most individual decisions are shaped by a small percentage of the city's population—indeed, by a small percentage of those who engage actively in its politics—because only the participants directly concerned have the time, energy, skill, and motivation to do much about them. The city government is most accurately visualized as a series of semiautonomous little worlds, each of which brings forth official programs and policies through the interaction of its own inhabitants. There are commentators who assert that Tammany, or Wall Street, or the Cathedral, or the labor czars, or the bureaucracy, or even the underworld rules New York. Some of these, it is true, are especially influential in shaping some decisions in some specialized areas. Taking the system over-all, however, none, nor all combined, can be said to be in command; large segments of the city's government do not attract their attention at all. New York's huge and diverse system of government and politics is a loose-knit and multicentered network in which decisions are reached by ceaseless bargaining and fluctuating alliances among the major categories of participants in each center, and in which the centers are partially but strikingly isolated from one another.

THE PERILS OF A MULTICENTERED SYSTEM

Tendencies toward stasis

One consequence of this ordering of the city's political relationships is that every proposal for change must run a gantlet that is often fatal. The system is more favorable to defenders of the *status quo* than to innovators. It is inherently conservative. The reasons for this are threefold.

No Change Without Cost. In the first place, every modification of the existing state of affairs—of the rules, of personnel, of governmental or administrative structure or procedure, or of public policies and programs—entails the fear of cost for some participants as well as hope of gain for the proponents. Any proposed increase in dollar costs, for example, stirs up the revenue-providing nongovernmental groups and their allies among the core groups. Proposals to change regulatory policies arouse quick opposition from the regulated groups and their core group allies if the proposal is to tighten regulation; from the protected groups and their official allies if the proposal is to relax regulation. Curtailed service angers those served and alarms the core groups of officials, as well as the bureaucracies, whose status, jurisdiction, and jobs are threatened, while expanded service alerts those who must pay the dollar costs as well as those who are competing for dollars to be expended for other purposes. Proposals for public works represent threats of displacement for some groups, risks in property values and neighborhood amenities for others. Proposals to reorganize agencies or other governmental and political institutions change adversely the lines of access to decision centers for some groups, affect adversely the career ladders of others, reduce the status and prestige of some others. In most instances, the costs of change are more intensely perceived by participants close to the center of decisions than are the benefits of innovation.

Those who perceive the costs of change in the city's going system have strategies and weapons with which to resist. They ordinarily have prizes to withhold, inducements to offer, sanctions to impose. The core groups of party leaders, for example, have nominations to confer or deny; they have, in addition, experience and skill in the exercise of influence in campaigns, elections, and appointments to office. The core groups of officials have their formal authority of decision with which to bargain with other groups. The organized bureaucracies can resist change by dragging their feet, the issuance of threats to strike or to "demonstrate," or appeals to allies or to the general public. Nongovernmental groups can use their special knowledge and skills, mobilize their members, resort to publicity in criticism of a proposed change. Almost all the participants have allies at other levels of government to whom they may turn for help in their opposition to a proposal. And most participants can threaten to withdraw from existing alliances as a sanction against change. The prospects for any advocate of change are intense opposition: lengthy, costly, wearing maneuvering and negotiation, and uncertainty about results until the last battle is won. If the *anticipation* of such a struggle, with all its costs in money, time, energy, and the possible disruption of longstanding friendships and alliances, is not enough to discourage campaigns in support of many proposed innovations, the strain and the drain of the *actual* fight may well exhaust the supporters and induce them to abandon their causes before they have come near their goals.

Official Hesitancy. In the second place, public officers and employees, whose action is required to make official the decisions reached by the participants in the specialized centers in which they operate, are ordinarily reluctant to move vigorously when there is extensive opposition within the constellation of interested individuals and groups. For they, as the formal authors of changes, are most likely to bear the brunt of enmities and retaliations provoked by adverse consequences of departure from established practice. They are the visible and vulnerable targets of blame for failures, though they must often share with others any credit for achievements. If they yield to demands of economy groups to curtail services or expenditures, the groups that are hurt direct their retribution against the officials in the decision centers and not against the originators of the reductions (who may have virtually compelled the decisions) or the less salient officials in other decision centers who may have cooperated with the economy groups (the Comptroller, for example, or the Director of the Budget). On the other hand, if officials yield to service-demanding groups or other groups (such as the bureaucracies) urging increased service and expenditures that are followed by fiscal crisis and rises in taxation, they may feel the wrath of those affected. If fluorine is added to the city's drinking water at the behest of health and dental groups and their allies in the Health Department, and if there should be later charges of fluorine poisoning attributed to engineering difficulties connected with keeping the fluorine content of the water within safe tolerances, it is the elected members of the Board of Estimate and the water supply engineers who will pay the penalty; hence their unwillingness to go ahead with this program despite the impressive array of advocates behind it. Indeed, officials are understandably wary even when there is a general consensus on the desirability of a particular novelty, for they must try to take into account consequences unanticipated by the assenters. They are doubly cautious when an important and highly vocal segment of their constituency stresses the dangers and costs. So the world of officialdom is often prudent when confronted by recommendations for innovation.

Incentives to Delay. When the specialists and other groups immediately interested in decisions disagree sharply among themselves about the wisdom or soundness of a proposed measure, or when the participants in one decision center line up in opposition to an action taken or projected in another decision center, the controversy is likely to find its way to the general organs of government, usually to the Mayor and the Board of Estimate, but frequently to the Governor and the state legislature. These governmental leaders then find they must choose between courses of action on which the experts and other informed interests are themselves divided. They must weigh the possible consequences of the choices they face—the possibilities of serious errors of judgment, of alienation of substantial blocs of voters, or repercussions on contributions to their parties and their campaigns. The course of prudence for them, therefore, is to temporize in the hope that the disagreements will work themselves out, or that they will have time enough to inform themselves more fully about the situations, or that the circumstances giving rise to the clashes will pass and obviate the need for their action, or that one side or the other will lose heart and abandon its fight. Sometimes they simply defer decision; this is the characteristic strategy of the Board of Estimate. Sometimes they set up study commissions to investigate and bring in recommendations. Rarely do they leap eagerly into the fray.

If some of the participants resort to litigation as part of their strategy, they may find the judges less hesitant to decide (because of the insulation of the courts, designed to encourage judicial independence). They also discover that legal proceedings are often protracted, costly, and time-consuming. This lends to litigation a special attraction and utility for the opponents of change.

The Tortuous Path. Changes of any magnitude thus encounter a long, rocky, twisting path from conception to realization. They are likely to be blocked almost at the start unless their authors revise and modify them to appease strong opponents, and to win the active and enthusiastic support of their allies. At the outset, the authors are likely to be the only zealous advocates in any decision center, and their proposals will face a group of equally zealous critics and a large number of relatively indifferent (that is, unaffected) observers. To overcome the objections and to stimulate the indifferent, plans must be adjusted— altered here, modified there, strengthened in another place. After all the

bargaining and concessions, a plan may well have lost much of its substance, much of its novelty. If plans are radical, they seldom survive; if they survive, they seldom work major changes in the going system.

There is nothing intrinsically desirable about change. But it becomes a problem of major importance to the well-being of the city if the governmental system has such a built-in resistance to change, such a tendency to suppress innovation, that it cannot keep up with the problems that confront it in a constantly and rapidly changing world. A city in stasis faces the potential fate of many of the great urban centers of the past, whose glories are all in archives and museums, whose significance is solely historical.

Neglect of communitywide perspectives

Another risk inherent in the multi-centered system of New York City's government and politics is the subordination of widely shared community values to the special interests of the separate and numerous "islands of power" within it. The tendencies of each core group and its attendant satellite groups to arrive at decisions maximizing their own special interests, including the comfort and convenience of officials and bureaucrats, are sometimes described as characteristic products of the system.

The fact is clear that only a few central institutions in the city produce decisions made on the basis of premises relevant to the entire community. Moreover, these central institutions often actually possess no more than the role of satellite groups with respect to the core groups in each decision center; although they may have theoretical, formal superiority over all the other groups, the central institutions often function, in fact, merely as additional participants in the decision-making processes rather than as masters of the system. They most often appear vulnerable to, and anxious about, the capacity of "lesser" contestants to extract concessions from them. If communitywide perspectives are introduced into the governmental decision-making system, this is usually an incidental by-product of the interaction of special interests.

Weakening of popular control

Since each decision center in the city's government and politics has attained a high degree of self-containment, the problem of exerting popular control over them has been complicated. For one thing, it is difficult to assign responsibility for unpopular policies. For another, and more importantly, the capacity of these many separate centers to maintain their essential autonomy, to outwait efforts to supervise them from outside each center itself, or to adulterate the effects of such efforts, sometimes seems so great that popular control over these "freewheeling" islands takes on a largely ritualistic character. In many ways, the electoral mechanisms of popular control are predicated on the assumption that the officials voted into office are in full command of policy and program, and that the other components of governmental machinery are little more than executors of their collective will. The preferences of the general populace, registered through the medium of elections, thus have an opportunity to impress themselves on what the gov-

ernment—all the public officers and employees—actually do. To the extent that what these public officials and bureaucrats do is actually decided in a host of relatively independent centers of decision, much of the force of the assumptions about the electoral mandate is dissipated. In New York City elected officials have not achieved full command of policy and program.

Frustration of leadership

Leadership is a difficult concept to define, but any definition would surely include among its elements, first, the coordination of the system (that is, relating the activities of the various parts so that the operations of the whole are beset by a minimum of confusion, conflict, and contradiction, and contribute significantly to the end-product) and, second, the main responsibility for innovation (so that the system does not become obsolete or lose its efficiency and appropriateness for its time and circumstances). Neither of these elements appears to be promoted by the multicentered system of politics and government in New York, and they may, in fact, be positively discouraged.

With little effective attention being paid to the over-all structure and functioning of the system, its design and its output often appear to have an almost chance quality. In its entirety, it often displays a lack of rational ordering, of a sustained sense of direction. Someone once defined a camel as a horse designed by a committee. One might apply similar contumely to the appearance of the New York City governmental system, and add that the same complaint is in many ways appropriate to its behavior as well as its organization.

ACHIEVEMENTS OF THE SYSTEM

Openness, responsiveness, and tolerance

Because the city's system is multi-centered, then, it harbors traits that may be serious risks to its own continued existence. But it also has qualities richly rewarding to all the inhabitants of the city and particularly to the active participants in the contest for the stakes of politics.

One of these qualities is its openness. No part of the city's large and varied population is alienated from participation in the system. The channels of access to the points of decision are numerous, and most of them are open to any group alert to the opportunities offered and persistent in pursuit of its objectives. All the diverse elements in the city, in competition with each other, can and do partake of the stakes of politics; if none gets all it wants, neither is any excluded.

Consequently, no group is helpless to defend itself, powerless to prevent others from riding roughshod over it, or unable to assert its claims and protect its rights. The great number of *de facto* vetoes built into the system intensifies the tendencies toward immobilization that constitute one of the hazards of the system, but these vetoes also enable every group to obstruct governmental decisions that fail to take its interests into account, to restrain governmental actions that ignore its rights or its aspirations, and to employ its possession of veto power

as a basis from which to bargain for recognition and concessions. Furthermore, the abundance of decision centers enables each group to concentrate on selected arenas of special importance to it instead of being cast into a broader environment in which it might have far more difficulty making its voice heard. Some inhabitants of the city have been slower than others to make use of the weapons the political system places within their grasp, but most—even immigrants from lands with altogether different traditions—have learned quickly, and there are not many who accept passively whatever the system deals out. They have learned that governmental decisions of every kind in the city are responsive to the demands upon the decision centers.

The city's system is, at the very least, tolerant of differences of every kind, and usually is even more than that: it engenders official respect for differences. That is not to say the forces working everywhere for orthodoxy and conformity are not at work in New York, or that the city is free from racial, religious, and ethnic prejudices. It does not mean that dissenters and minorities of all kinds are welcomed, or that their claims are immediately and warmly acknowledged and fulfilled. It does mean, however, that they are not suppressed, and that in official and party circles they will generally receive respectful attention. It does mean that personal antagonisms to groups or creeds will generally be stifled by officials. It does mean that candidates and party leaders will not only recognize, but will court the favor of, groups of every kind. And it does mean that third parties and insurgent factions in the major parties cannot be prevented (in spite of the roadblocks often thrown in their paths) from challenging the dominant political parties and factions. There are too many points of entry, too many opportunities for retaliation, too many methods of self-protection and self-assertion, for bigotry or intolerance or fear of heterodoxy to become major elements of official decisions or behavior.

If these attributes are measures of the democratic qualities of a governmental system, then New York City's system must be rated highly democratic. It may run the serious risks noted above, and it may pay a cost in terms of engineering concepts of efficiency, but the system can justly claim to possess openness, responsiveness, and tolerance as essential characteristics of its democracy.

Growth, progress, and flexibility

The city's system may also claim to have functioned remarkably well in other ways and to have been unexpectedly creative and adaptive in its six decades.

The quantity and quality of governmental services are high. The difficulties of providing these services to eight million people are immense, but the city government, almost as a matter of routine, has mastered most problems of size and complexity that confront it, and performs without fanfare tasks that would overwhelm the leaders and institutions of communities less accustomed to dealing with the dilemmas of policy and the difficulties of administration presented by the magnitude and intricacy of the city's operations. Every day, the government of the city competently discharges a

staggering burden of responsibility.

To be able to do so has required considerable governmental inventiveness and daring. Some of the innovations to which New Yorkers may point with pride as examples of the adaptiveness of their institutions include, among others, the "consolidation" or creation of the Greater City in 1898; the invention of that unique and controversial institution, the Board of Estimate; the early establishment of a Tenement House Department; the beginning of a subway system in 1905 and its expansion, eventual unification, and city operation; the pioneer zoning code of 1916; the steady expansion and maintenance of an unexcelled water supply system; the Health Department's pioneering district health plan in 1915 and its subsequent growth; the establishment of a Department of Hospitals in 1929; the first City Housing Authority in 1934; the transformation of the city's park system since 1934; the charter of 1938, with its creation of a City Planning Commission, the office of Deputy Mayor, and the experiment with proportional representation in the election of councilmen; the creation of a Traffic Department in 1949, an Air Pollution Control Department in 1953, and the office of City Administrator in 1954. The city government, in short, has not been static over the years.

One reason for these innovations is that many forces outside the system impose changes in its operation. The increase in the city's population—especially during the period of mass immigration—and its shifting distribution among the boroughs, for instance, has forced constant adjustments in the pattern of public services and has continually altered the political strength and complexion of various sections. The changing composition of the population—in ethnic, national, and religious characteristics, in income distribution, in occupational categories, in age—has had similar effects. Changes in the city's economy, with some activities rising (such as corporate management) and others declining (such as heavy manufacturing), lead to differing demands upon the system. Economic cycles of inflation and depression generate fiscal pressures, leading often to new coalitions, new types of decisions, new organizations and structures (of which the special authorities are perhaps a prime illustration). Science and technology also have great impacts on the system, introducing new tasks and problems (as in the case of the automobile and the airplane), providing new goals and methods (as in public health), offering new challenges (as does the St. Lawrence Seaway), and creating new demands for change from nongovernmental groups. Obsolescence or deterioration of the city's physical plant (the spread of slums, the growth of depressed business districts, the aging of the port facilities, for example) constitute problems crying for solution, and move previously quiescent groups to political action that brings new pressures, new centers of influence. Financial assistance and inducements offered by the state and by the federal government are often additional incentives to strike out in new directions.

So, too, are the changing aspirations and expectations of the city's general public, reflected especially in the mass media of communication and in the rise of new nongovernmental groups. This is particularly true of those participants in the system whose interests and expectations are not sufficiently satisfied by their roles in it. Leaders of minority ethnic and racial groups, for example, demand changes that will more nearly meet the expectations of their constituents for representation in party and public office and for governmental solutions to some of their social and economic problems. Leaders in the professions often advocate changes that will in their view represent progress toward higher professional standards. Leaders of "civic" and "reform" groups are almost by definition cast in the role of dissenters, critics, and advocates of change in the system, although their energies are usually centered upon limited aspects of the system. As agents of change, they are mainly effective in changing the formal rules of the system (particularly in efforts to make the actions of the participants more ethical and more visible, and the actors more responsible and accountable for their methods and decisions) and in enforcing these rules by exposure and criticism of violation. A great variety of groups—some long-lived, some quite transitory—from time to time succeed in breaking into the system at some point, carrying demands for change which are regarded by the established participants in a particular decision center as "visionary" or "ideological" or "impractical," but these "crusades" are now and then successful. The communication media are not only valued allies of almost all of these groups demanding change, but the press itself is both a reporter and a critic of the system. As a participant-critic in the city's multicentered system, the press is one of the most constant advocates of change, although in no sense does it speak with a single or consistent voice.

Another source of change within the system is those highly visible and usually dramatic public figures who build their careers as apostles of innovation. These leaders perceive the opportunities and the rewards (personal and impersonal) in being skilled and persistent "mavericks" within the system—as rule-changers, as builders of new centers of decisions and of new coalitions of participants, and as creators of new sets of incentives. And the system has also exhibited an unusual capacity to produce outstanding elected and appointed officials as effective leaders in the city's politics and government. The list of the twelve mayors of the city—a list that includes such names as Low, McClellan, Gaynor, Mitchel, La Guardia, Wagner —cannot be matched in quality, it has been asserted, by any other city. Other outstanding leaders cited as products of the city's political system include Theodore Roosevelt, Al Smith, Robert F. Wagner, Sr., each having begun his political and governmental career as a state legislator elected from the city. The administrators of the city's departments and agencies, it is also claimed, compare favorably and are usually superior in quality, capacity, and performance to those of other cities and of the state governments.

As still another source of change within the system itself, there is the fact that every change tends to produce further change in a kind of slow-motion chain-reaction. Recognition of one set of claimants to nomination, for instance, encourages other claimants to increase their efforts. A subway system rearranges the distribution of population, requiring adjustments in many public policies and in many agency decisions. An expanded highway system generates new traffic; traffic congestion requires the establishment of a new city department; and increased reliance upon automobiles brings crises in subway transit and commuter railways. These kinds of changes, springing from many separate and only loosely coordinated decision centers, are more numerous than they might be if they were directed from a single center; thus the existence of a multicentered system often is in itself a contributor to the process of change.

The exposé or highly publicized scandal is also a cause of change. In these situations, leaders of one of the core groups (or an ally, or the two together) are discovered to have violated the formal rules, or at least some of the informal rules. The discovery of the violation is usually made by one of the participants in the system—sometimes by officials of another level of government, at other times by a satellite group, on other occasions by a supervising or a competitive core group, often by the press, not infrequently by a nongovernmental group with a general interest in the whole system (rather than in a single area of decision). The scandal often leads to change, especially if it produces a new coalition of participants advocating specific reforms. The rules may thus be changed, new agencies established or old ones reorganized, new core groups (with their accompanying satellite groups) created.

These exposés have happened often enough to give wide circulation to the notion that the government and politics of New York City hold high rank, if not the highest place, among American cities in the art and practice of official corruption. Actually, this impression is largely the result of the tendency of the city's system to ferret out and give great and dramatic publicity to violations of the rules. The system might properly claim first rank among American cities in the art and practice of exposing corruption. The very fragmentation of the city's system places such high obstacles in the way of the conspiracy and secrecy essential to exploitation, and there are so many participants whose specialization is exposure (the press, insurgent and dissenting participants of many kinds, and the civic groups that often assume the mantle of surrogate for the public conscience) that corruption is difficult to perpetrate, let alone to conceal. Nevertheless the myth of wholesale public corruption continues, in part because it has a perennial usefulness to some of those who participate in the political process (the minority groups, civic groups, economy groups, the press, and, on a short-term basis, the insurgent party groups); in part because New Yorkers, like Texans, take a perverse pride in, and often add to, the exaggerations that award a kind of ironic distinction to themselves and their city; and in part because the myth has become a familiar part of the city's political process itself. Its disappearance would compel alterations in the premises and bargaining vocabulary of the participants that they are unlikely to welcome. The myth gives added impetus to the search for corruption and gains in acceptance whenever the search is successful.

INTER-NATION INFLUENCE: A FORMAL MODEL
J. DAVID SINGER

Students of international politics often state that power is to us what money is to the economist: the medium via which transactions are observed and measured. Further, there seems to be a solid consensus that power is a useful concept only in its relative sense; such objective measures as military manpower, technological level, and gross national product are viewed as helpful, but incomplete, indices. The concept does not come to life except as it is observed in action, and that action can be found only when national power is brought into play by nations engaged in the process of influencing one another. Until that occurs, we have no operational indices of power, defined here as the *capacity to influence*. In this paper, then, my purpose is to seek a clarification of the concept of power by the presentation of a formal, analytic model of bilateral inter-nation influence.

Two caveats, however. First, I am using the word "model" in its most modest sense; I mean somewhat more than a conceptual framework, but con-

siderably less than a theory. If, by theory, we refer to a body of internally consistent empirical generalizations of descriptive, predictive, and explanatory power, it is much less than a theory. And since it is not a theory, there is no need to label it "normative" or "descriptive"; it is merely analytical, with normative or prescriptive implications.

Second, it represents in no sense the result of a systematic search of the historical past from which we might draw empirical generalizations. Nor is it a systematic survey of those other analogous worlds from which such generalizations might be drawn: the experimental or empirical literature of psychology, sociology, or anthropology.[1] Recourse to all of these worlds would be valuable, but would go beyond the task I have set myself here.

[1] The worlds of the diplomatic past and the experimental present may both be called analogous to that of the diplomatic present in that neither is an exact replication, yet each has a number of important similarities to it. In some respects, one might even find that the small group experiment provides a closer replication of the present international system than does the international system of the 18th or 19th centuries. See J. David Singer, "The Relevance of the Behavioral Sciences to the Study of International Relations," *Behavioral Science*, Vol. 6 (October 1961), pp. 324–35.

CREDIT: Reprinted by permission of author and publisher from *The American Political Science Review*, June, 1963, pp. 420–430. [*Figures renumbered.*]

Moreover, such empirical investigations are best not undertaken until we have a clear picture of the sorts of data we seek. To do so in the absence of such a picture might produce some interesting anecdotes, and an occasionally valuable insight, but it would open no direct path toward a body of empirically "verified" and logically consistent propositions of such explanatory power or predictive reliability as to be useful for either theory building or policy purposes. Until these prior model-building steps have been taken, any comprehensive search of the historical literature would be little more than a fishing expedition, or a ransacking of the past in search of support for *a priori* convictions.

In attempting this preliminary examination of inter-nation influence, I will begin with a search for clarification of the central concepts and variables; then suggest a systematic linking of them; follow this with a search for some general rules about the role of reward and punishment and promise and threat; and conclude with a discussion of the particular limits and uses of threat.

i. Some general properties of influence

In trying to clarify what we mean by influence, and to articulate its dominant properties, the first point to be noted is that all influence attempts are *future-oriented*. The past and present behavior of the potential influenc*ee* (whom we will label B) may be of interest to A (the influenc*er*) and will certainly affect A's predictions of B's future behavior, but there is nothing A can do about controlling such actions.

He[2] may *interpret* the past and present behavior of B in a variety of ways, but obviously he can no longer *influence* it.

The second general observation is that influence may or may not imply a modification of B's behavior. While the tendency (there are exceptions) in both political science and social psychology is to define an influence attempt as one in which A seeks to *modify* the behavior of B, or to identify A's influence over B in terms of "the extent to which he can get B to do something that B would not otherwise do," there are several objections to this restricted meaning.[3] One is that it excludes that very common form of influence which we might call perpetu-

[2] Throughout this paper, we will often use the singular personal pronoun to denote a nation, but it will always be understood that the nation is not a person and is not capable of perceiving, predicting, and preferring in the literal psychological sense. Thus all designations will, unless otherwise specified, refer to those who act for and on behalf of, the nation: the foreign policy decision-makers. We are not, however, accepting the proposition of the "methodological individualists," who deny the empirical existence or conceptual legitimacy of the group or nation. Their point of view is articulated in Floyd H. Allport, *Social Psychology* (Boston: Houghton Mifflin Co., 1924), while two persuasive refutations are Ernest Nagel, *The Structure of Science* (New York: Harcourt, Brace and World, 1961) and Charles K. Warringer, "Groups are Real: A Reaffirmation," *American Sociological Review*, Vol. 21 (October 1956), pp. 549–554.

On the choice of the nation-as-actor, see Arnold Wolfers, "The Actors in International Politics," in W. T. R. Fox (ed.), *Theoretical Aspects of International Relations* (Notre Dame: University of Notre Dame Press, 1959) and J. David Singer, "The Level of Analysis Problem in International Relations," *World Politics*, Vol. 14 (October 1961), pp. 77–92.

[3] This definition is tentatively employed in Robert A. Dahl, "The Concept of Power," *Behavioral Science*, Vol. 2 (July 1957) pp. 201–15; Dahl tends to use "power" and "influence" interchangeably.

ation or "reinforcement." [4] That is, it overlooks the many cases of inter-personal and inter-group influence in which B is behaving, or is predicted to behave, in essentially the manner desired by A, but in which A nevertheless attempts to insure the continuation of such behavior, or the fulfillment of the prediction, by various influence techniques.

The second (and more elusive) objection is that it implies no difficulty in A's prediction of what B will do in the absence of the influence attempt. If A could, with a very high degree of confidence, predict how B will act if *no* attempt to modify or reinforce is made, then reinforcement measures would be unnecessary and influence would only be attempted when changes (from predicted to preferred) are sought. For a multitude of reasons, ranging from the complexity of the international system to the theoretical poverty of the disciplines which study that system, such predictability is a long way off. Consequently, A will tend to seek insurance against the possibility of an error in his prediction as long as he is modest in evaluating his predictive abilities.

This leads in turn to a third difficulty, if not objection, which is the probabilistic nature of all predictions. Even if the "state of the art" in international relations were well advanced, there would still be no *certainty*

The emphasis on change or modification is also retained by John R. P. French and Bertram Raven, "The Bases of Social Power," in Dorwin Cartwright (ed.), *Studies in Social Power* (Ann Arbor: Institute for Social Research, 1959), pp. 150–67.

[4] We will use this word in its generic sense, rather than in the various specialized ways found in such psychological theories as conditioning, learning, and S-R.

(probability $= 1.0$) on the part of A that B will behave in the predicted fashion. Consequently, there will always be some incentive to attempt to influence.

Having made the case for both the modification and the reinforcement types as legitimately belonging in the influence attempt category, however, it would be misleading to suggest that they are of equal significance in inter-nation relations. The fact is that if A's decision makers are *reasonably confident* that nation B either *will* behave in a fashion *desirable* to A or *not* behave in an *un*desirable fashion, the incentive to attempt to influence B will diminish, and A may conserve its limited skills and resources for application elsewhere. As the forces at work in A's foreign policy processes move A's decision makers in a pessimistic direction, there will be an increasing application of A's available resources to the influencing of B, until the point is reached where A predicts that *no* influence attempt would be successful.

A third preliminary observation is that inter-nation influence is far from a one-way affair. In the first place, while A is planning or attempting to influence B, B is itself exercising some impact on A's behavior. The very classification of B by A as a potential influencee immediately leads to some degree of influence by B upon A, even when B makes no conscious influence attempt. And in the second place, the international system is neither a dyad (duopoly) nor a multitude of dyads. For analytical purposes, it is often convenient to scrutinize only two nations at a time, but we cannot forget that all are influencing all, directly or indirectly, merely by sharing the same spatial, temporal, and socio-political environment. Thus, the system is characterized not only by reciprocity but by multiple reciprocity. For the sake of simplicity, however, we will restrict the analysis which follows to direct bilateral relationships between nations of more or less equal power, in which influence or influence attempts are a conscious effort of the national decision makers.[5]

Finally, we might distinguish between an influence *attempt* and the *outcome* of such an attempt. Not only are they not the same phenomena, but they are described and measured in terms of different variables. An influence attempt is described primarily in terms of: (a) A's *prediction* as to how B will behave in a given situation in the absence of the influence attempt; (b) A's *preference* regarding B's behavior; and (c) the techniques and resources A utilizes to make (a) and (b) coincide as nearly as possible. The outcome of such an attempt will be a function not only of (c) above, but also (d) the accuracy of A's prior prediction; (e) B's own value, utility, or preference system; (f) B's estimate of the probabilities of various contemplated outcomes; (g) B's resistance (or counter-influence) techniques and resources;

---

[5] "Power" may be measured in a multitude of ways: relative or absolute, perceived or objective, potential or present; and many criteria may be used in making such measurements. Furthermore, the distinction between "fate control" and "behavior control" made by John W. Thibaut and Harold H. Kelley in *The Social Psychology of Groups* (New York: John Wiley & Sons, 1959) is quite relevant here. Thus, the United States certainly has the power to decide the ultimate *fate* of Cuba, for example, but lacks the power to exercise effective and continuing control over Cuba's day-to-day *behavior*.

and (h) the effects of the international environment.

ii. The international system as an influence environment

Before turning to more refined characteristics of influence, let us place its general properties, as noted above, in their larger setting within the international system.

The fact that nations invest a great deal of their energies in attempts to influence one another is perfectly obvious, but *why* this should be so is somewhat less apparent. One of the most frequently recurring themes among the peace-makers is that all would be well if nations would only "live and let live." The naïveté of this prescription becomes evident, however, when we recall that such a doctrine can only be effective if one of the following conditions is present: (a) each nation is so completely isolated from all the others that the activities of one have almost no impact on the others; or (b) each is so completely self-sufficient that it has no dependence upon the goals or behavior of the others in order to meet its own "real" and perceived needs. Neither of these conditions characterizes the international system, and it is doubtful whether they ever did. Not only do nations rely heavily upon one another for the commodities (tangible and otherwise) which are sought after, but it is extremely difficult for any nation to trade with or steal from another without this inter-action having some impact on some third party.

But this is only part of the story, and it is the part which is equally applicable to relations among many other forms of social organization. The international system has another characteristic which distinguishes it from other social systems: each actor has the legal, traditional, and physical capacity to severely damage or destroy many of the others with a considerable degree of impunity. In inter-personal, inter-family or other inter-group relations, regardless of the culture, normative restraints and superior third-party governors are sufficient to make murder, plunder and mayhem the exception rather than the rule. But in inter-nation relations the gross inadequacy of both the ethical and the political restraints make violence not only accepted but anticipated. As a consequence, the scarcest commodity in the international system is security—the freedom to pursue those activities which are deemed essential to national welfare and to survival itself.

To be more specific then, we might assert that under the survival rubric the highest priority is given to autonomy—nations are constantly behaving in a fashion intended to maximize their present and future freedom of action and to minimize any present or future restraints upon that freedom. In such a system, no single nation can afford to "live and let live" as long as the well established and widely recognized anarchic norms are adhered to, acted upon, and anticipated by, most of the others. Any social system must contain some inevitable competition and conflict, but in the international system they are handled in a more primitive fashion. Moreover, there seems to be only the barest correlation between the way a nation pursues its interests and the nature of its leadership or its socio-political institutions. To suggest otherwise would be,

to quote an excellent analysis of the problem, to commit the "second-image fallacy." [6] Rather, we might more accurately conclude that the international system itself is the key element in explaining why and how nations attempt to influence the behavior of one another.

iii. Perceived behavior as a determinant in influence attempts

Though the international system is definitely one in which influence and counter-influence attempts are a dominant characteristic, our interest is in analyzing the factors which tend to produce any given such attempt. The first prerequisite for an influence attempt is the perception on the part of A's decision-makers that A and B are, or will be, in a relationship of significant interdependence, and that B's future behavior consequently could well be such as to exercise either a harmful or beneficial impact on A.

Not too long ago, most nations were in such a relationship with only a handful of other nations. Even in today's highly interdependent world, one still finds, for example, little interaction between Paraguay and Burma or Egypt and Iceland. Moreover, no nation has the resources to engage in serious efforts to influence a great many of the others at any given time; we select our influence targets because of the perceived importance of our relationship to, and dependence upon, them. In addition, there is a particular

[6] See Kenneth N. Waltz, *Man, the State, and War* (New York: Columbia University Press, 1959) and the review article based on it: J. David Singer, "International Conflict: Three Levels of Analysis," *World Politics,* Vol. 12 (April 1960), pp. 453–61.

tendency to concentrate such efforts upon those nations with which we are already in a highly competitive and conflictful relationship, devoting far fewer resources to those with whom our relations are either friendly or negligible.

Not only do our perceptions of interdependence and conflict-cooperation strongly determine whom we will attempt to influence, but, as subsequent sections will suggest, they affect the types of influence attempt we will make and the likelihood of success or failure in that attempt.

iv. Predicted behavior as a determinant in influence attempts

The second determinant is that of the *predictions* which A's decision-makers reach regarding the nature of B's future behavior: what is B likely to do, in the absence of any conscious influence attempt by A? This expectation may be of two rather distinct types. One deals with the affirmative *commission* of an act, and the other deals with the more passive *non-commission* or *omission* of an act. In the first case, illustrations range from the American expectation that, in the absence of any conscious influence attempt by ourselves, India might endorse a troika arrangement for arms control supervision, to the fear that the Soviet Union might employ military force in an effort to drive us out of Berlin. In the second case, we think of such examples of non-commission or failure to act as Germany *not* meeting its ground force commitment to NATO, or mainland China *not* participating in a disarmament conference to which it had been invited. Though one can often describe expected acts of omission as ones of commission (*i.e.,* Germany *refusing* to draft more soldiers or China *rejecting* the conference bid), and with somewhat greater conceptual straining even describe acts of commission in the semantics of omission (India *not rejecting* the troika, or Soviet *not refraining from* force) one or the other of these two emphases is almost always more obvious and salient to the influencer, as discussed in the next section.

v. Preferred behavior as a determinant in influence attempts

Finally, and perhaps most important, there is A's *preference* regarding B's future behavior. Without preferences, the perception of B's present behavior and predictions regarding his future behavior have only limited importance to A and would exercise only a minor impact on A's tendency to invest in an influence attempt. Here we might illustrate by reference to the contingent predictions suggested above. The United States prefers that India *not* accept the troika plan, and that the Soviets *not* use force in Berlin; we care much less what administrative arrangements New Delhi *does* accept, or what other techniques the Kremlin *does* apply in Berlin. Our main concern is that they *not* do the specified, but partially likely, act from among a number of possible acts. For us, removing or reducing the likelihood of what they *might* do is much more salient than which one of a host of alternative acts they select in its place. Conversely, the concern of our decision-makers (as the potential influences) over what the Germans do *not* do with their limited manpower, or what the Chinese do *not* do regarding a disarmament conference is much less than our concern that they *do* engage in the act which we prefer. The salience of what they *do* do is higher for us than the salience of what they do *not* do, because of the nature of our preferences.

To illustrate this crucial distinction further, let us suppose that A predicts that B is about to supply weapons to an insurgent group opposing the government of an ally of A's; A's concern is not so much what else B does with these weapons as with seeing that B does *not* supply them as predicted. B might, at this juncture, scrap them, sell them to a neutral nation outside the immediate conflict area, or give them to an ally, and A would have a much less intense concern over which of these alternatives B selected. In another—and very real—case, A might want desperately to prevent its major adversary B from supplying nuclear weapons to an ally of B with whom A has had a number of disastrous military encounters in the past. Whether B gives these nuclear weapons to another ally, converts them for peaceful uses, or retains them in its own arsenal is of much less moment than that they *not* be supplied to the feared recipient. In both these cases, avoiding or preventing a specific outcome is of considerably greater salience to the influencer than is the remaining range of alternatives open to B.

vi. Perception, prediction, and preference: their composite effect

So far, we have discussed individually the way in which A's perceptions, predictions, and preferences will tend to move him toward an influence attempt *vis-à-vis* B. What are the implications of combining these three sets of variables? More particularly, what are the possible combinations, and what is the effect of each upon: (a) the motivation of A to undertake an influence attempt, (b) the relative amount of effort required for success, and (c) the techniques and instruments A will employ?

As the following chart will indicate, there are eight possible combinations of influence situations, four dealing with cases in which A prefers that B *do* a certain act (*X*) and four in which A prefers that B *not* do a particular act, but do almost anything else (non-*X* or *O*) instead. The first four might be called *persuasion* cases, and the latter four *dissuasion*. Since each of these eight cases would seem to pose a different type of influence problem for A and call for varying combinations of techniques, let us list and label them as in Figure VI-1.

FIGURE VI-1   Types of Influence Situations

	Persuasion situations: A prefers X				*Dissuasion situations:* A prefers O			
	1	*2*	*3*	*4*	*5*	*6*	*7*	*8*
Preferred Future Behavior	X	X	X	X	O	O	O	O
Predicted Future Behavior	X	X	O	O	O	O	X	X
Perceived Present Behavior	X	O	X	O	O	X	O	X

In cases 1 through 4, A prefers that B do act *X,* and in cases 5 through 8, A prefers that B *not* do act *X,* but do *O* (anything else but act *X*). Cases 1 and 5 are relatively simple and normally would call for no impressive influence attempt: B not only is already acting or not acting as A prefers, but the prediction is that such behavior will continue into the relevant future. Cases 2 and 6 are, however, slightly more interesting: again B's predicted behavior is seen as congruent to that which A prefers in the future, but A observes that for the moment B's behavior is different from the preferred or predicted. And in cases 3 and 7, B's present behavior *is* what A prefers, but the prediction is that it will *not* remain so without any effort on A's part. Finally, in cases 4 and 8 we have the most difficult situation for A: he perceives B not only as not behaving as preferred, but as unlikely to do so in the future, without some effort on the part of A. These, then, are the eight typical situations confronting a potential influencer, ranged more or less in order of increasing difficulty.

vii. The influencee's decisional calculus

Having examined the varieties of influence situations, we should notice one other consideration prior to evaluating the range of techniques available to the influencer in these situations. This is the influencee's decisional calculus: the abstract dimensions upon which he (*i.e.,* those individuals who, alone or together, act on behalf of the target nation) weighs a range of conceivable outcomes in any influence situation. For every outcome which any

decision-maker can conceive of as possible, there are at least two such dimensions. The degree to which he likes or dislikes the prospect is called the *utility* or *disutility,* and the likelihood which he assigns to its ever occurring is called the *probability.* Both of these are, of course, subjective variables: preferences and predictions of the influencee (B).

In the abstract, the combined judgments which the influencee makes along both of these dimensions will determine his contingent expectations and thus his response to the influence attempt. Before combining them, let us examine each in somewhat more detail. As to the subjective utility dimension, we proceed from the assumption that an individual or a group does— implicitly or explicitly—have a set of benchmarks by which it is able to arrange conceivable outcomes (be they threatening, rewarding, or more typically, both) in some order of preference. These benchmarks usually derive from value systems and goal structures and, though they are by no means uniform from nation to nation, those relevant to foreign policy behavior tend to have a great deal in common. For example, outcomes that appear to restrict short-range freedom of action will almost invariably be placed very low in any such utility scale; they will be assigned a high *dis-*utility score. Conversely, those which seem likely to minimize the power of some other competing nation (A, C, or D), and hence reduce that competitor's capacity to restrict one's own (B's) freedom, are normally rated high on utility. If we go much beyond these basic drives of nations, however, we get into the peculiar webs of their secondary goals and their varying formal and informal ideologies.

We may pause, though, to point out that national preferences are by no means fixed and permanent. Not only do successive parties and factions in a particular nation bring differing preference structures into office, but even the same sub-group or individuals undergo value changes while in power. Consequently, we must not overlook the usefulness to A of seeking to induce attitudinal (especially value and preference) changes in B's elites as an alternative means of influencing B's existing preferences, or of seeking to change them now in order to make it easier to appeal to them later.

Nations do not, however, commit themselves to actions merely because one possible outcome of such actions seems to be extremely attractive or because it may avoid an extremely *unat*tractive outcome. No nation has the unlimited resources and skills which such behavior would require. They must compare these possible outcomes not only in terms of a *preference* ordering, but also in terms of their estimated *likelihood*. And just as there are important differences between nations in the matter of assigning utilities and disutilities, there are equally important (but more subtle) differences when it comes to assigning probabilities to future events. Some are more willing than others to play the "long shot," and pursue an objective whose probability of attainment may be quite low. On the other hand, there do seem to be strong similarities here, as in preference ordering. A perusal of recent diplomatic history strongly suggests that most nations are remarkably conservative in foreign policy; *i.e.,* they seldom commit resources and prestige to the pursuit of an outcome which seems improbable—no matter how attractive that outcome may be. Individuals, on the other hand, reveal far greater ranges of risk-taking propensities, with many getting a large measure of psychological satisfaction from the low-probability-of-success decision.[7]

The point which concerns us here, however, is that—despite idiosyncrasies on one or the other dimension—nations *combine* both sets of considerations in responding to an influence attempt or in any other choice situation. In graphic terms, we might depict this combining process as in Figure VI-2.

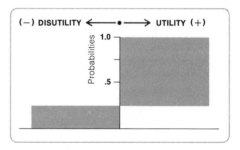

Figure VI-2. Influencee's Decisional Calculus

Suppose that A is attempting to influence B by the use of threatened punishment in order to deter B from pursuing a certain goal (*i.e.,* A is trying to induce *O*). If B attaches a high utility to the outcome which he is pursuing while the threat which A makes

[7] See Ward Edwards, "Utility and Subjective Probability: Their Interaction and Variance Preferences," *Journal of Conflict Resolution*, Vol. 6 (March 1962), pp. 42–51.

would—if carried out—constitute a loss whose disutility is of approximately the same magnitude, these two considerations will tend to cancel out and the important dimension becomes the probability of each outcome actually eventuating. If B estimates that the probability of A carrying out the threatened punishment is quite low (let us say .25) and that he therefore has a .75 probability of pursuing his goal *without* A executing the threat (perhaps its cost to A is seen as quite high) the resultant product would tend to make B adhere to his original intention. Though he realizes that there is *some* chance that A will act to punish him, the combined probability and disutility is so much less than the combined probability and utility of A's *not* acting, that B decides to take the gamble.

This is, of course, a rather abstract model, and it not only deviates from the kinds of articulate, as well as implicit, calculations which policy makers employ, but it oversimplifies the choice situation with which nations are ordinarily confronted. For example, B must normally weigh his utility-times-probability product against not only the disutility-times-probability of A's *threatened* punishment but against a range of greater or lesser punishments which A is capable of inflicting and against the probability of each of these occurring.[8] Furthermore this model assumes that choice situations and influence attempts, as well as their possible outcomes, occur at discrete and identi-

fiable moments in time. The assumption is extremely useful for analytical purposes, but it pays insufficient attention to the overlapping and highly unpredictable time scale along which such situations and alternate outcomes may occur. Finally, it ignores three important quantitative considerations. One of these is the relative weight which a given set of decision-makers might assign to each of the two dimensions; in their implicit fashion, nations do differ in the degree to which they emphasize either the probability or the preference element in their appraisal of an outcome. Moreover, these two dimensions are by no means psychologically independent; the more highly valued an outcome is, the greater the tendency to exaggerate the probability that it can be achieved (the wish is father to the thought), and conversely, when a probability looks very low, the tendency will be to downgrade the attractiveness of the associated outcome. Thirdly, there is the tendency toward polarity: as subjective probabilities move up or down from .5 they will be exaggerated in the direction of either the certainty (1.0) or the impossibility (0.0) end of the scale. Recognizing these limitations does not, however, invalidate this influencee's decisional model. It merely reminds us that it cannot be employed for either descriptive or predictive purposes in a purely mechanical way. But used in a careful, self-conscious fashion it can be helpful to both the study and the execution of the decision process. For the scholar, much of the confusion and mystery of that process could be clarified, and for the policy maker, regardless of the weights and values he attaches, it could identify the

---

[8] Among the outcomes to be considered are those which might impinge on the domestic setting upon one's allies or any Nth powers.

range of alternatives and indicate the implications of each. It might even lead to consideration of a larger number of alternatives and hence mitigate one of the greatest causes of diplomatic disaster—the prematurely restricted repertoire.

viii. Influence techniques

Up to this juncture, we have delineated some of the general characteristics of inter-nation influence, identified its three major dimensions alone and together, and articulated a sub-model of the influencee's decisional considerations. Now let us turn to the two broad classes of technique available to the influencer: threat and promise. Each may be used either to modify or to reinforce, although, as we shall see later, not with equal efficacy. Each has an appropriate role, but careful choice must be made in determining which is best suited to the various classes of influence situation.

By *threat* we mean the communication to the influencee (B) by the influencer (A) that if a certain preferred act (X) is not taken, or non-act (O) is not avoided by B, there is a given probability that A will act to punish B in a particular fashion. That punishment may take the form either of withholding a reward, denying a preference, or positively damaging that which B values.[9]

[9] One quite successful attempt has been made to draw an analytic distinction between punishment and denial, but it seems less relevant here. In *Deterrence by Denial and Punishment* (Princeton: Center of International Studies, 1959) and in *Deterrence and Defense* (Princeton: Princeton University Press, 1961) Glenn Snyder refers to retaliation as punishment, while denial refers to the costs inflicted upon B (the deterree who was not deterred) while trying to gain his military objective.

By *promise* we mean the communication to B that if he complies with A's preference, A will, with some given probability, act to reward B. Again, that reward may range from withholding a contemplated punishment to the enhancement of one or more of B's values and preferences.

Threat and punishment and promise and reward go together, but the distinction must be constantly kept in mind. Threat and promise refer to nothing but contingent, probable future events, while punishment and reward are concrete acts that already have taken, or are in the process of taking, place. Thus punishments and rewards may be threatened or promised respectively, and they may be contemplated by both A and B, but they have none of the empirical concreteness in a future situation that they have in past or present situations.

In inter-nation influence, reward and punishment for past or ongoing behavior may be said to serve primarily as a link between B's experiential present and his anticipated future. The outcomes which accompany particular actions in B's past and present serve as predictors of such associations in the future. Therefore, the use of rewards and punishments by A should be devoted, among other aims, to increasing the *credibility* of the promises and threats which he transmits to B. This is not to suggest that credibility-building is the only relevant use for reward and punishment in attempting to influence an opponent of approximately equal power. Present-oriented techniques might also serve the supplementary purposes of (a) hastening an influencee's *shift* from non-preferred to preferred behavior, or (b) reinforcing current preferred behavior if there is some indication that it might not continue.

Be that as it may, we have little evidence at this point to justify any confident generalizations regarding the applicability of the four types of influence technique to the eight classes of influence situations. Let me therefore pause briefly in order to hypothesize, before going on to suggest what next needs to be done to develop a coherent theory of inter-nation influence. Given the speculativeness of these hypotheses and the limitations of space, let me present them in the form of a chart which is merely an extension of Figure VI-1.

Then in rows 5 and 6 we ask whether punishment and reward (our present-oriented techniques) are relevant to each of these, while in 7 and 8 the question is whether the future-oriented techniques of threat and promise have any applicability. In situations 2 and 6 and 1 and 5, the ambiguous entry (P for "perhaps") is meant to suggest that A's confidence in his prediction regarding B's future behavior will be controlling. If, in the two ambiguous modification situations (2 and 6) A's subjective probability that B will change without any influence attempt is not satisfactorily high, A might consider punishment as an appropriate technique. Likewise,

FIGURE VI-3   Hypothesized Relevance of Influence Techniques

	Persuasion situations: *A prefers* **X**				*Dissuasion situations:* *A prefers* **O**			
	1	*2*	*3*	*4*	*5*	*6*	*7*	*8*
Preferred Future Behavior	X	X	X	X	O	O	O	O
Predicated Future Behavior	X	X	O	O	O	O	X	X
Perceived Present Behavior	X	O	X	O	O	X	O	X
Reinforce or Modify	R	M	R	M	R	M	R	M
Punish?	No	P	No	Yes	No	P	No	Yes
Reward?	Yes	No	Yes	No	Yes	No	Yes	No
Threaten?	P	Yes	Yes	Yes	P	Yes	Yes	Yes
Promise?	Yes	Yes	Yes	Yes	Yes	Yes	Yes	Yes

In Figure VI-3, we have added five rows to the original three. Row 4 emphasizes that cases 1, 3, 5, and 7 are reinforcement or behavior stabilization situations, in which A, regardless of his predictions, prefers that B's future behavior remain as it is in the present. Conversely, cases 2, 4, 6, and 8 are modification or behavior change situations, again disregarding A's prediction of B's future behavior.

in the two ambiguous reinforcement situations, A's lack of confidence in the prediction that B will continue his present behavior might well impel him to utilize threat as a form of insurance.

ix. Some experimental possibilities

Can the hypotheses in Figure VI-3 be confirmed or disconfirmed? Clearly, the preferable longrun method of proof would lie in direct testing within the international system, and though the bona-fide experiment is hardly a routine matter in this area, some modified form of it seems possible. I refer to the so-called *ex-post-facto* experiment, in which we determine some reasonable and fixed limits in time and space, and then devise the criteria by which our population of influence situations is selected. From that population we then sample in such a manner as to get a sufficient number of each of our eight classes of influence situation. Of course, the difficulty here is in setting up and refining the operational rules by which we identify each of these situations in the ongoing welter of diplomatic history so as to permit reliable classification by two or more independent coders. Once the experimental cases are selected, we then go on (again with operationally articulated criteria) to determine which influence techniques were used in each. Following that, we measure—with either a simple yes-no dichotomy or (at later stages in the study) a graduated scale—B's compliance with A's preference. By correlating our predicted influence attempt outcomes with those observed in the "experiment" we get a test of the hypotheses generated by the model.

If this particular project worked out satisfactorily, a more nearly "natural" experiment, involving *pre*diction rather than *post*diction, could be attempted. In this case, we would want to ascertain the applicability of our historical findings to the real world of the present, by classifying some sample of influence situations as they unfold, and then actually predicting the attempt outcomes before they are known.[10] The central problem in either of these "real world" types of study is that of developing, pre-testing, and applying measures or indices of an operational and unambiguous nature. Until we have devised a means for recognizing and recording perceived, predicted, preferred, and actual outcomes, such experimental research is impossible.

While the development of measures for the key variables in inter-nation relations goes forward—and it is doing so at much too slow a pace—another possibility remains. Systematic data-gathering with relatively operational classification and measurement criteria has been going on in sociology and social psychology for several decades. As a consequence, these disciplines have accumulated a respectable body of empirical generalizations regarding inter-group and inter-personal influence. These generalizations, moreover, have two possible linkages to a theory of inter-nation influence in particular and inter-nation relations in general. The more useful one is that of empirical inputs into the inter-personal and inter-group interactions which occur in the foreign policy decision process. There is no reason to expect that the findings in industrial, academic, community, or other social settings should be too disparate for application to the inter-personal and inter-group influence processes which obtain in governmental policy processes. Enough inference is

---

[10] Some suggestive versions of such a technique are advocated in Richard C. Snyder and James A. Robinson, *National and International Decision-Making* (New York: Institute for International Order, 1960), pp. 30–34.

called for, however, to preclude any automatic assumption that the results will be identical in, for example, business firms and foreign ministries.

Requiring a somewhat longer inferential leap would be the effort to analogize directly from our inter-personal and inter-group results to inter-nation influence situations. Though this sort of extrapolation is often more legitimate than the naive critic would have us believe, one must first demonstrate a high degree of isomorphism between the setting which produced our data and that to which the generalizations are to be applied. But whether one employs the indirect or direct application of these psychological and sociological findings, it should be clear that they cannot suffice for confirmation or disconfirmation of our hypotheses. The final test must be made with data from the real world of inter-nation relations.

x. The limits and uses of threat

Despite these caveats, it might nevertheless be useful to examine some of the propositions that emerge from the inter-personal and small group literature, in order to suggest their possible relevance. For these illustrative purposes, let me summarize and speculate upon some of the empirical findings regarding one of the four major influence techniques: threat. First, what do these inter-personal experiments suggest regarding the dysfunctional effects of this future-oriented influence technique?

The most obvious undesirable side effect of threat is that it may often do no more than "modify the form of anti-social behavior which is chosen." [11] In other words, by making one path of behavior which is undesirable to A seem unattractive to B, A may merely drive B into other behavior which, while more attractive to B than the action which has been associated with impending punishment, is equally undesirable to A. And for A to threaten B for so wide a range of anticipated acts could either exceed A's capabilities or create such a dilemma for B that he had no choice but to carry out the action and accept (or retaliate for) the consequences.

As to the effect of threat on B's capacity to respond rationally, a number of disturbing findings appear. First of all, threat often exercises a negative influence on B's capacity to recognize signals and communications accurately. Not only might B become less able to identify and respond to neutral messages, but he may also lose some of his ability to recognize subsequent threats. Thus, threats might well make it difficult or impossible for A to convey the very messages upon which his capacity to influence B must rest.[12] An equally dysfunctional result is that of "cognitive rigidity:" the inability of B to respond efficiently and adequately to changing stimuli, and a consequent breakdown in B's problem-solving capacity.[13] This experiment also sug-

[11] Alex Comfort, *Authority and Delinquency in the Modern State* (London: Routledge and Kegan Paul, 1950), p. 74.

[12] Charles D. Smock, "The Relationship Between Test Anxiety, Threat-Expectancy, and Recognition Thresholds for Words," *Journal of Personality*, Vol. 25 (1956), pp. 191–201.

[13] Sidney Pally, "Cognitive Rigidity as a Function of Threat," *Journal of Personality*, Vol. 23 (1955), pp. 346–55.

gests that the ultimatum is a particularly dangerous form of threat, inasmuch as the subjects dropped markedly in their capacity to respond appropriately when the experimenter reduced the time allowed for making that response.

Similar results were found when subjects were threatened with a physical shock. The threat of this highly undesirable possibility produced a high level of stress and markedly hampered their problem-solving capacity.[14] The stress induced by threat has also been reported as not only degrading an actor's predictability but his own confidence in that predictability as well.[15]

On the other hand, there is a tendency among some observers of international relations to exaggerate the dysfunctional effects of threat and to ignore the very real role it does and must play in the contemporary international system. These critics forget that most of the influence and social control situations from which they analogize take place in an ordered, hierarchical environment in which influence is normally based on legitimate authority, recognized roles, and accepted norms. To illustrate, one of the more thorough analyses of social power lists five major bases of such power: reward power, coercive power, legitimate power, referent power, and expert power.[16] Of these five, reward often requires more resources than are found in a highly competitive influence relationship between equals, legitimate power can only be exercised through the frail channels of international law or organization, referent power is generally absent between rivals, and expert power is seldom recognized by national decision-makers. Coercion via threat is, by process of elimination, one influence technique upon which we must continue to rely until we have markedly modified the international system.

A point worth noting in this connection has been demonstrated in a number of experiments on group performance under varying degrees of stress. The results "indicated that the performance of the group was best under mild stress." [17] If threat produces stress (as we assume), the absence of threat may often be as detrimental to successful influence attempts as too heavy a dose of it. The lesson seems to be to use enough threat to generate stress, but not so much as to produce high anxiety. If the upper threshold is crossed (and it varies from nation to nation and situation to situation) we are likely to generate the sort of undesirable effects which reduce B's rationality. The less rational B is, the less likely he is to consider the entire range of alternative actions open to him, and the less likely he is to analyze ade-

[14] Robert E. Murphy, "Effects of Threat of Shock, Distraction and Task Design on Performance," *Journal of Experimental Psychology*, Vol. 58 (1959), pp. 134–141.

[15] Alvin Landfield, "Self-predictive Orientation and the Movement Interpretation of Threat," *Journal of Abnormal and Social Psychology*, Vol. 51 (1955), pp. 434–38.

[16] John R. P. French and Bertram Raven, "The Bases of Social Power," in Dorwin Cartwright (ed.), *Studies in Social Power* (Ann Arbor: Institute for Social Research, 1959).

[17] John T. Lanzetta, "Group Behavior Under Stress," *Human Relations*, Vol. 8 (1955), pp. 29–52.

quately the implications of each such alternative. Anxiety induced by excessive threat may be said to contract B's repertoire of possible responses as well as his ability to predict the payoffs associated with each.

In the same vein, we have some experimental results which indicate the impact of threat upon group cohesiveness. While it is generally true that external threat exercises a unifying effect, there are some important exceptions, and when cohesiveness in B is reduced, some serious problems arise.[18] Admittedly, internal divisions may lead to a diminution in B's power *vis-à-vis* A, thus enhancing the credibility of threat even further. But on the other hand, a drop in B's relative power is not necessarily a precursor to compliance. Moreover—and this is a frequently overlooked consideration—the creation of divisions within B may make an intelligent response to A's influence attempt almost impossible. When B's top elites are in firm control of their nations, they are more capable of (a) making rational choices and (b) making the concessions necessary to A's successful influence attempt. Conversely, when they are preoccupied with critics, conspirators, and powerful "inevitable war" factions at home, they must resist influence attempts in order to stabilize their shaky power base.

Another point that seems to emerge in regard to the role of threat, (and to a lesser extent, promise) is that

B must be provided with two categories of information. One is the precise nature of the action which A prefers to see B take (*X*) or avoid (*O*); without this information B is unable to respond in a mutually advantageous fashion. The other is the availability of alternatives, and this is particularly relevant in the dissuasion situation.[19] For A to try to dissuade B from a given action (to induce *O*) when B must clearly do *X* or something similar to *X*, without helping B to ascertain which *O* acts are available to B and acceptable to A, is to call for a probable showdown. If B is completely thwarted, he has little choice but to resist.

Also worth considering, in terms of the limitations of threat, is the fact that A may well be able to modify B's decisional calculus in the appropriate fashion and still fail in his influence attempt. Even though, in the time period implied by the effort to modify or reinforce, B might find A's preferences the most attractive alternative behavior for himself, he may nevertheless refuse to comply. The explanation lies primarily in the context of longer-range considerations on B's part: precedent. B (or A, when in the B role) may be concerned that his compliance under threat will set a precedent. Each

---

[18] For example, Albert Pepitone and Robert Kleiner, "The Effects of Threat and Frustration on Group Cohesiveness," *Journal of Abnormal and Social Psychology*, Vol. 54 (1957), pp. 192–99.

[19] Daniel Katz, "The Functional Approach to the Study of Attitudes," *Public Opinion Quarterly* Vol. 24 (1960), pp. 163–204. Note that this does not preclude the use of influence by ambiguity; it calls for clarity regarding A's preferences but permits ambiguity regarding A's behavior if B does not comply. Highly suggestive in this regard is Thomas C. Schelling, "The Threat That Leaves Something to Chance," in *The Strategy of Conflict* (Cambridge, Harvard University Press, 1960).

time that B does the rational thing and complies with the preferences of A, he increases A's propensity to believe in the efficacy of threat, and to utilize it again and again. As a result, B has an additional reason to do the thing which is, in the specific and discrete influence situation, irrational. Moreover, B must combine his refusal to comply with a more-or-less immediate counter-influence effort, in order to compel A to re-allocate those resources which might otherwise be used to carry out his threat. In a simplified way, this is what an armaments race boils down to: threat and counter-threat, coupled with the drive toward ever-increasing military capabilities with which to resist these threats.

xi. Conclusion

Without laboring the need for an empirically based theory of internation influence, it should not be amiss to note that its lack is both a cause of intellectual embarrassment to political science and a menace to the human race. For the policy-maker to select intelligently from among a wide range of alternative decisions, he must be able to predict their outcomes with *some* degree of reliability. Such prediction requires far more than the "hunches" by which we operate today; having no sound criteria for behavior choices, the policy-maker will tend, as he has in the past, to adopt those policies which have the most powerful or persuasive advocates, regardless of the accuracy (or even the existence) of the "theory" upon which those policies are allegedly based. And as long as the nations continue to base their policies on so flimsy a foundation, our understanding will be incomplete, our predictions unreliable, and our policies deficient. I would not want to exaggerate the reliability of any theory we might build, nor minimize the difficulties of injecting it into the policy process, but neither we nor our adversaries of the moment can afford these present deficiencies. The probabilities of error are already much too high, and the disutilities could be disastrous.

FOR FURTHER READING

BANFIELD, Edward C., *Political Influence* (Glencoe: Free Press, 1961).

COLEMAN, James, "Foundations for a Theory of Collective Decisions," *American Journal of Sociology*, May, 1966, pp. 615–627.

CUTRIGHT, Dorwin, "Influence, Leadership, Control," in James G. March (Ed.). *Handbook of Organizations* (Chicago: Rand McNally, 1965), pp. 1–47.

DAHL, Robert A., *Who Governs?* (New Haven: Yale University Press, 1961).

GAMSON, William A., *Power and Discontent* (Homewood, Illinois: Dorsey Press, 1968).

HARSANYI, John C., "The Measurement of Social Power, Opportunity Costs, and the Theory of Two Person Bargaining Games," *Behavioral Science,* January, 1962, pp. 67–75.

LASSWELL, Harold D. and Abraham Kaplan, *Power and Society* (New Haven: Yale University Press, 1950).

MACRAE, Duncan and Hugh D. Price, "Scale Positions and 'Power' in the Senate," *Behavioral Science*, July, 1959, pp. 212–218.

MARCH, James G., "An Introduction to the Theory and Measurement of Influence," *American Political Science Review*, June, 1955, pp. 431–451.

OPPENHEIM, Felix E., *Dimensions of Freedom* (New York: St. Martin's Press, 1961).

RIKER, William H., "Some Ambiguities in the Notion of Power," *American Political Science Review*, June, 1964, pp. 341–349.

SCHELLING, Thomas C., *The Strategy of Conflict* (Cambridge: Harvard University Press, 1960).

SHAPLEY, L. S. and Martin Shubik, "A Method for Evaluating the Distribution of Power in a Committee System," *American Political Science Review*, September, 1954, pp. 787–792.

SIMON, Herbert, "Notes on the Observation and Measurement of Political Power," *Journal of Politics*, November, 1953, pp. 500–516.

WILDAVSKY, Aaron, "The Political Economy of Efficiency: Cost–Benefit Analysis, Systems Analysis and Program Budgeting," *Public Administration Review*, December, 1966, pp. 292–310.